HARRIET BEECHE

A KEY

TO

UNCLE TOM'S CABIN

PRESENTING THE ORIGINAL

FACTS AND DOCUMENTS
UPON WHICH THE STORY IS FOUNDED

TOGETHER WITH

CORROBORATIVE STATEMENTS VERIFYING
THE TRUTH OF THE WORK

Elibron Classics
www.elibron.com

Elibron Classics series.

© 2005 Adamant Media Corporation.

ISBN 1-4212-7027-7 (paperback)
ISBN 1-4212-7026-9 (hardcover)

This Elibron Classics Replica Edition is an unabridged facsimile
of the edition published in 1853 by John P. Jewett & Co.,
Boston.

A KEY

TO

UNCLE TOM'S CABIN;

PRESENTING THE ORIGINAL

FACTS AND DOCUMENTS

UPON WHICH THE STORY IS FOUNDED.

TOGETHER WITH

Corroborative Statements

VERIFYING

THE TRUTH OF THE WORK.

BY HARRIET BEECHER STOWE,
AUTHOR OF "UNCLE TOM'S CABIN."

BOSTON:
PUBLISHED BY JOHN P. JEWETT & CO.
CLEVELAND, OHIO:
JEWETT, PROCTOR & WORTHINGTON
LONDON: LOW AND COMPANY.
1853.

STEREOTYPED BY
HOBART & ROBBINS,
NEW ENGLAND TYPE AND STEREOTYPE FOUNDERY,
BOSTON.

PREFACE.

THE work which the writer here presents to the public is one which has been written with no pleasure, and with much pain.

In fictitious writing, it is possible to find refuge from the hard and the terrible, by inventing scenes and characters of a more pleasing nature. No such resource is open in a work of fact; and the subject of this work is one on which the truth, if told at all, must needs be very dreadful. There is no bright side to slavery, as such. Those scenes which are made bright by the generosity and kindness of masters and mistresses, would be brighter still if the element of slavery were withdrawn. There is nothing picturesque or beautiful, in the family attachment of old servants, which is not to be found in countries where these servants are legally free. The tenants on an English estate are often more fond and faithful than if they were slaves. Slavery, therefore, is not the element which forms the picturesque and beautiful of Southern life. What is peculiar to slavery, and distinguishes it from free servitude, is evil, and only evil, and that continually.

In preparing this work, it has grown much beyond the author's original design. It has so far overrun its limits that she has been obliged to omit one whole department; — that of the characteristics and developments of the colored race in various countries and circumstances. This is more properly the subject for a volume; and she hopes that such an one will soon be prepared by a friend to whom she has transferred her materials.

The author desires to express her thanks particularly to those legal gentlemen who have given her their assistance and support in the legal part of the discussion. She also desires to thank those, at the North and at the South, who have kindly furnished materials for her use. Many more have been supplied than could possibly be used. The book is actually selected out of a mountain of materials.

The great object of the author in writing has been to bring this subject of slavery, as a moral and religious question, before the minds of all those who profess to be followers of Christ, in this country. A minute history has been given of the action of the various denominations on this subject.

The writer has aimed, as far as possible, to say what is true, and only that, without regard to the effect which it may have upon any person or party. She hopes that what she has said will be examined without bitterness, — in that serious and earnest spirit which is appropriate for the examination of so very serious a subject. It would be vain for her to indulge the hope of being wholly free from error. In the wide field which she has been called to go over, there is a possibility of many mistakes. She can only say that she has used the most honest and earnest endeavors to learn the truth.

The book is commended to the candid attention and earnest prayers of all true Christians, throughout the world. May they unite their prayers that Christendom may be delivered from so great an evil as slavery !

PART I.

CHAPTER I.

At different times, doubt has been expressed whether the representations of "Uncle Tom's Cabin" are a fair representation of slavery as it at present exists. This work, more, perhaps, than any other work of fiction that ever was written, has been a collection and arrangement of real incidents,— of actions really performed, of words and expressions really uttered,— grouped together with reference to a general result, in the same manner that the mosaic artist groups his fragments of various stones into one general picture. His is a mosaic of gems,— this is a mosaic of facts.

Artistically considered, it might not be best to point out in which quarry and from which region each fragment of the mosaic picture had its origin; and it is equally unartistic to disentangle the glittering web of fiction, and show out of what real warp and woof it is woven, and with what real coloring dyed. But the book had a purpose entirely transcending the artistic one, and accordingly encounters, at the hands of the public, demands not usually made on fictitious works. It is *treated* as a reality, — sifted, tried and tested, as a reality; and therefore as a reality it may be proper that it should be defended.

The writer acknowledges that the book is a very inadequate representation of slavery; and it is so, necessarily, for this reason,— that slavery, in some of its workings, is too dreadful for the purposes of art. A work which should represent it strictly as it is would be a work which could not be read. And all works which ever mean to give pleasure must draw a veil somewhere, or they cannot succeed.

The author will now proceed along the course of the story, from the first page onward, and develop, as far as possible, the incidents by which different parts were suggested.

CHAPTER II.

MR. HALEY.

In the very first chapter of the book we encounter the character of the negro-trader, Mr. Haley. His name stands at the head of this chapter as the representative of all the different characters introduced in the work which exhibit the trader, the kidnapper, the negro-catcher, the negro-whipper; and all the other inevitable auxiliaries and indispensable appendages of what is often called the "divinely-instituted relation" of slavery. The author's first personal observation of this class of beings was somewhat as follows:

Several years ago, while one morning employed in the duties of the nursery, a colored•woman was announced. She was ushered into the nursery, and the author thought, on first survey, that a more surly, unpromising face she had never seen. The woman was thoroughly black, thick-set, firmly built, and with strongly-marked African features. Those who have been accustomed to•read the expressions of. the African face know what a peculiar effect is produced by a lowering, desponding expression upon its dark features. It is like the shadow of a thunder-cloud. Unlike her race generally, the woman did not smile when smiled upon, nor utter any pleasant remark in reply to such as were addressed to her. The youngest pet of the nursery, a boy about three years old, walked up, and laid his little hand on her knee, and seemed astonished not to meet the quick smile which the negro almost always has in reserve for the little child. The writer thought her very cross and disagreeable, and, after a few moments' silence, asked, with perhaps a little impatience, "Do you want anything of me to-day?"

"Here are some papers," said the woman, pushing them towards her; "perhaps you would read them."

The first paper opened was a letter from

a negro-trader in Kentucky, stating concisely that he had waited about as long as he could for her child; that he wanted to start for the South, and must get it off his hands; that, if she would send him two hundred dollars before the end of the week, she should have it; if not, that he would set it up at auction, at the court-house door, on Saturday. He added, also, that he might have got more than that for the child, but that he was willing to let her have it cheap.

"What sort of a man is this?" said the author to the woman, when she had done reading the letter.

"Dunno, ma'am; great Christian, I know,— member of the Methodist church, anyhow."

The expression of sullen irony with which this was said was a thing to be remembered.

"And how old is this child?" said the author to her.

The woman looked at the little boy who had been standing at her knee, with an expressive glance, and said, "She will be three years old this summer."

On further inquiry into the history of the woman, it appeared that she had been set free by the will of her owners; that the child was legally entitled to freedom, but had been seized on by the heirs of the estate. She was poor and friendless, without money to maintain a suit, and the heirs, of course, threw the child into the hands of the trader. The necessary sum, it may be added, was all raised in the small neighborhood which then surrounded the Lane Theological Seminary, and the child was redeemed.

If the public would like a specimen of the correspondence which passes between these worthies, who are the principal reliance of the community for supporting and extending the institution of slavery, the following may be interesting as a matter of literary curiosity. It was forwarded by Mr. M. J. Thomas, of Philadelphia, to the *National Era*, and stated by him to be "a copy taken verbatim from the original, found among the papers of the person to whom it was addressed, at the time of his arrest and conviction, for passing a variety of counterfeit bank-notes."

Poolsville, Montgomery Co., Md.,
March 24, 1831.

DEAR SIR : I arrived home in safety with Louisa, John having been rescued from me, out of a two-story window, at twelve o'clock at night. I offered a reward of fifty dollars, and have him here safe in jail. The persons who took him brought him to Fredericktown jail. I wish you to write to no person in this state but myself. Kephart and myself are determined to go the whole hog for any negro you can find, and you must give me the earliest information, as soon as you do find any. Enclosed you will receive a handbill, and I can make a good bargain, if you can find them. I will in all cases, as soon as a negro runs off, send you a handbill immediately, so that you may be on the look-out. Please tell the constable to go on with the sale of John's property; and, when the money is made, I will send on an order to you for it. Please attend to this for me ; likewise write to me, and inform me of any negro you think has run away, — no matter where you think he has come from, nor how far, — and I will try and find out his master. Let me know where you think he is from, with all particular marks, and if I don't find his master, *Joe's dead!*

Write to me about the crooked-fingered negro, and let me know which hand and which finger, color, &c.; likewise any mark the fellow has who says he got away from the negro-buyer, with his height and color, or any other you think has run off.

Give my respects to your partner, and be sure you write to no person but myself. If any person writes to you, you can inform me of it, and I will try to *buy* from them. I think we can make money, if we do business together ; for I have plenty of money, if you can find plenty of negroes. Let me know if Daniel is still where he was, and if you have heard anything of Francis since I left you. Accept for yourself my regard and esteem.

REUBEN B. CARLLEY.
JOHN C. SAUNDERS.

This letter strikingly illustrates the character of these fellow-patriots with whom the great men of our land have been acting in conjunction, in carrying out the beneficent provisions of the Fugitive Slave Law.

With regard to the *Kephart* named in this letter the community of Boston may have a special interest to know further particulars, as he was one of the dignitaries sent from the South to assist the good citizens of that place in the religious and patriotic enterprise of 1851, at the time that Shadrach was unfortunately rescued. It therefore may be well to introduce somewhat particularly JOHN KEPHART, as sketched by RICHARD H. DANA, Jr., one of the lawyers employed in the defence of the perpetrators of the rescue.

I shall never forget John Caphart. I have been eleven years at the bar, and in that time have seen many developments of vice and hardness, but I never met with anything so cold-blooded as the testimony of that man. John Caphart is a tall, sallow man, of about fifty, with jet-black hair, a restless, dark eye, and an anxious, care-worn look, which, had there been enough of moral element in the expression, might be called melancholy. His frame was strong, and in youth he had evidently been powerful, but he was not robust. Yet there was a calm, cruel look, a power of will and a quickness of muscular action, which still render him a terror in his vocation.

In the manner of giving in his testimony there was no bluster or outward show of insolence. His contempt for the humane feelings of the audience and community about him was too true to require any assumption of that kind. He neither paraded nor attempted to conceal the worst features of his calling. He treated it as a matter of business which he knew the community shuddered at, but the moral nature of which he was utterly indifferent to, beyond a certain secret pleasure in thus indirectly inflicting a little torture on his hearers.

I am not, however, altogether clear, to do John Caphart justice, that he is entirely conscience-proof. There was something in his anxious look which leaves one not without hope.

At the first trial we did not know of his pursuits, and he passed merely as a police-man of Norfolk, Virginia. But, at the second trial, some one in the room gave me a hint of the occupations many of these police-men take to, which led to my cross-examination.

From the Examination of John Caphart, in the "Rescue Trials," at Boston, in June and Nov., 1851, and October, 1852.

Question. Is it a part of your duty, as a police-man, to take up colored persons who are out after hours in the streets?

Answer. Yes, sir.

Q. What is done with them?

A. We put them in the lock-up, and in the morning they are brought into court and ordered to be punished, — those that are to be punished.

Q. What punishment do they get?

A. Not exceeding thirty-nine lashes.

Q. Who gives them these lashes?

A. Any of the officers. I do, sometimes.

Q. Are you paid *extra* for this? How much?

A. Fifty cents a head. It used to be sixty-two cents. Now it is fifty. Fifty cents for each one we arrest, and fifty more for each one we flog.

Q. Are these persons you flog men and boys only, or are they women and girls also?

A. Men, women, boys and girls, just as it happens.

[The government interfered, and tried to prevent any further examination; and said, among other things, that he only performed his duty as police-officer under the law. After a discussion, Judge Curtis allowed it to proceed.]

Q. Is your flogging confined to these cases? Do you not flog slaves at the request of their masters?

A. Sometimes I do. Certainly, when I am called upon.

Q. In these cases of private flogging, are the negroes sent to you? Have you a place for flogging?

A. No. I go round, as I am sent for.

Q. Is this part of your duty as an officer?

A. No, sir.

Q. In these cases of private flogging, do you inquire into the circumstances, to see what the fault has been, or if there is any?

A. That's none of my business. I do as I am requested. The master is responsible.

Q. In these cases, too, I suppose you flog women and girls, as well as men.

A. Women and men.

Q. Mr. Caphart, how long have you been engaged in this business?

A. Ever since 1836.

Q. How many negroes do you suppose you have flogged, in all, women and children included?

A. [Looking calmly round the room.] I don't know how many niggers you have got here in Massachusetts, but I should think I had flogged as many as you 've got in the state.

[The same man testified that he was often employed to pursue fugitive slaves. His reply to the question was, " I never refuse a good job in that line."]

Q. Don't they sometimes turn out bad jobs?

A. Never, if I can help it.

Q. Are they not sometimes discharged after you get them?

A. Not often. I don't know that they ever are, except those Portuguese the counsel read about.

[I had found, in a Virginia report, a case of some two hundred Portuguese negroes, whom this John Caphart had seized from a vessel, and endeavored to get condemned as slaves, but whom the court discharged.]

Hon. John P. Hale, associated with Mr. Dana, as counsel for the defence, in the Rescue Trials, said of him, in his closing argument:

Why, gentlemen, *he sells agony!* Torture is his stock-in-trade! He is a walking scourge! He hawks, peddles, retails, groans and tears about the streets of Norfolk!

See also the following correspondence between two traders, one in North Carolina, the other in New Orleans; with a word of comment, by Hon. William Jay, of New York:

Halifax, N. C., Nov. 16, 1839.

DEAR SIR: I have shipped in the brig Addison, — prices are below:

No. 1. Caroline Ennis,			$650 00
" 2. Silvy Holland,			625.00
" 3. Silvy Booth,			487.50.
" 4. Maria Pollock,			475.00
" 5. Emeline Pollock,			475.00
" 6. Delia Averit,			475.00

The two girls that cost $650 and $625 were bought before I shipped my first. I have a great many negroes offered to me, but I will not pay the prices they ask, for I know they will come down. I have no opposition in market. I will wait until I hear from you before I buy, and then I can judge what I must pay. Goodwin will send you the bill of lading for my negroes, as he shipped them with his own, Write often, as the times are critical, and it depends on the prices you get to govern me in buying. Yours, &c.,

G. W. BARNES.

Mr. THEOPHILUS FREEMAN, }
New Orleans. }

The above was a small but choice invoice of wives and mothers. Nine days before, namely, 7th Nov., Mr. Barnes advised Mr. Freeman of having shipped a lot of forty-three men and women. Mr. Freeman, informing one of his correspondents of the state of the market, writes (*Sunday*, 21st Sept., 1839), " I bought a boy yesterday, sixteen years old, and likely, *weighing* one hundred and ten pounds, at $700. I sold a likely girl, twelve years old, at $500. I bought a man yesterday, twenty years old, six feet high, at $820; one *to-day*, twenty-four years old, at $850, black and sleek as a mole."

The writer has drawn in this work only one class of the negro-traders. There are all varieties of them, up to the great wholesale purchasers, who keep their large trading-houses ; who are gentlemanly in manners and courteous in address ; who, in many respects, often perform actions of real generosity ; who consider slavery a very great evil, and hope the country will at some time be delivered from it, but who think that so long as clergyman and layman, saint and sinner, are all agreed in the propriety and necessity of slave-holding, it is better that the necessary trade in the article be conducted by men of humanity and decency, than by swearing, brutal men, of the Tom Loker school. These men are exceedingly sensitive with regard to what they consider the injustice of the world in excluding them from good society, simply because they undertake to supply a demand in the community which the bar, the press and the pulpit, all pronounce to be a proper one. In this respect, society certainly imitates the unreasonableness of the ancient Egyptians, who employed a certain class of men to prepare dead bodies for embalming, but flew at them with sticks and stones the moment the operation was over, on account of the sacrilegious liberty which they had taken. If there is an ill-used class of men in the world, it is certainly the slave-traders ; for, if there is no harm in the institution of slavery,—if it is a divinely-appointed and honorable one, like civil government and the family state, and like other species of property relation,— then there is no earthly reason why a man may not as innocently be a slave-trader as any other kind of trader.

CHAPTER III.

MR. AND MRS. SHELBY.

IT was the design of the writer, in delineating the domestic arrangements of Mr. and Mrs. Shelby, to show a picture of the fairest side of slave-life, where easy indulgence and good-natured forbearance are tem-

pered by just discipline and religious instruction, skilfully and judiciously imparted.

The writer did not come to her task without reading much upon both sides of the question, and making a particular effort to collect all the most favorable representations of slavery which she could obtain. And, as the reader may have a curiosity to examine some of the documents, the writer will present them quite at large. There is no kind of danger to the world in letting the very fairest side of slavery be seen ; in fact, the horrors and barbarities which are necessarily inherent in it are so terrible that one stands absolutely in need of all the comfort which can be gained from incidents like the subjoined, to save them from utter despair of human nature. The first account is from Mr. J. K. Paulding's Letters on Slavery ; and is a letter from a Virginia planter, whom we should judge, from his style, to be a very amiable, agreeable man, and who probably describes very fairly the state of things on his own domain.

DEAR SIR : As regards the first query, which relates to the "rights and duties of the slave," I do not know how extensive a view of this branch of the subject is contemplated. In its simplest aspect, as understood and acted on in Virginia, I should say that the slave is entitled to an abundance of good plain food ; to coarse but comfortable apparel ; to a warm but humble dwelling ; to protection when well, and to succor when sick ; and, in return, that it is his duty to render to his master all the service he can consistently with perfect health, and to behave submissively and honestly. Other remarks suggest themselves, but they will be more appropriately introduced under different heads.

2d. "The domestic relations of master and slave."—These relations are much misunderstood by many persons at the North, who regard the terms as synonymous with oppressor and oppressed. Nothing can be further from the fact. The condition of the negroes in this state has been greatly ameliorated. The proprietors were formerly fewer and richer than at present. Distant quarters were often kept up to support the aristocratic mansion. They were rarely visited by their owners ; and heartless overseers, frequently changed, were employed to manage them for a share of the crop. These men scourged the land, and sometimes the slaves. Their tenure was but for a year, and of course they made the most of their brief authority. Owing to the influence of our institutions, property has become subdivided, and most persons live on or near their estates. There are exceptions, to be sure, and particularly among wealthy gentlemen in the towns ; but these last are almost all enlightened and humane, and alike liberal to the soil and to the slave who cultivates it. I could point out some noble instances of patriotic and spirited improvement among them. But, to return to the resident proprietors : most of them have been raised on the estates ; from the older negroes they have received in infancy numberless acts of kindness ; the younger ones have not unfrequently been their playmates (not the most suitable, I admit), and much good-will is thus generated on both sides. In addition to this, most men feel attached to their property ; and this attachment is stronger in the case of persons than of things. I know it, and feel it. It is true, there are harsh masters ; but there are also bad husbands and bad fathers. They are all exceptions to the rule, not the rule itself. Shall we therefore condemn in the gross those relations, and the rights and authority they imply, from their occasional abuse ? I could mention many instances of strong attachment on the part of the slave, but will only adduce one or two, of which I have been the object. It became a question whether a faithful servant, bred up with me from boyhood, should give up his master or his wife and children, to whom he was affectionately attached, and most attentive and kind. The trial was a severe one, but he determined to break those tender ties and remain with me. I left it entirely to his discretion, though I would not, from considerations of interest, have taken for him quadruple the price I should probably have obtained. Fortunately, in the sequel, I was enabled to purchase his family, with the exception of a daughter, happily situated ; and nothing but death shall henceforth part them. Were it put to the test, I am convinced that many masters would receive this striking proof of devotion. A gentleman but a day or two since informed me of a similar, and even stronger case, afforded by one of his slaves. As the reward of assiduous and delicate attention to a venerated parent, in her last illness, I proposed to purchase and liberate a healthy and intelligent woman, about thirty years of age, the best nurse, and, in all respects, one of the best servants in the state, of which I was only part owner ; but she declined to leave the family, and has been since rather better than free. I shall be excused for stating a ludicrous case I heard of some time ago : — A favorite and indulged servant requested his master to sell him to another gentleman. His master refused to do so, but told him he was at perfect liberty to go to the North, if he were not already free enough. After a while he repeated the request ; and, on being urged to give an explanation of his singular conduct, told his master that he considered himself consumptive, and would soon die ; and he thought Mr. B—— was better able to bear the loss than his master. He was sent to a medicinal spring and recovered his health, if, indeed, he had ever lost it, of which his master had been unapprized. It may not be amiss to describe my deportment towards my servants, whom I endeavor to render happy while I make them profitable. I never turn a deaf ear, but listen patiently to their communications. I chat familiarly with those who have passed service, or have not begun to render it. With the others I observe a more prudent reserve, but I encourage all to approach me without awe. I hardly ever go to town without having commissions to execute for some of them ; and think they prefer to employ me, from a belief that, if their money should not quite hold out, I would add a little to it ; and I not unfrequently do, in order to get a better article. The relation between myself and my slaves is decidedly friendly. I keep up pretty exact discipline, mingled with kindness, and hardly ever lose property by thievish, or labor by run-

away slaves. I never lock the outer doors of my house. It is done, but done by the servants ; and I rarely bestow a thought on the matter. I leave home periodically for two months, and commit the dwelling-house, plate, and other valuables, to the servants, without even an enumeration of the articles.

3d. "The duration of the labor of the slave."— The day is usually considered long enough. Employment at night is not exacted by me, except to shell corn once a week for their own consumption, and on a few other extraordinary occasions. *The people,* as we generally call them, are required to leave their houses at daybreak, and to work until dark, with the intermission of half an hour to an hour at breakfast, and one to two hours at dinner, according to the season and sort of work. In this respect I suppose our negroes will bear a favorable comparison with any laborers whatever.

4th. "The liberty usually allowed the slave,— his holidays and amusements, and the way in which they usually spend their evenings and holidays." —They are prohibited from going off the estate without first obtaining leave ; though they often transgress, and with impunity, except in flagrant cases. Those who have wives on other plantations visit them on certain specified nights, and have an allowance of time for going and returning, proportioned to the distance. My negroes are permitted, and, indeed, encouraged, to raise as many ducks and chickens as they can ; to cultivate vegetables for their own use, and a patch of corn for sale ; to exercise their trades, when they possess one, which many do ; to catch muskrats and other animals for the fur or the flesh ; to raise bees, and, in fine, to earn an honest penny in any way which chance or their own ingenuity may offer. The modes specified are, however, those most commonly resorted to, and enable provident servants to make from five to thirty dollars apiece. The corn is of a different sort from that which I cultivate, and is all bought by me. A great many fowls are raised ; I have this year known ten dollars worth sold by one man at one time. One of the chief sources of profit is the fur of the muskrat ; for the purpose of catching which the marshes on the estate have been parcelled out and appropriated from time immemorial, and are held by a tenure little short of fee-simple.[1] The negroes are indebted to Nat Turner * and Tappan for a curtailment of some of their privileges. As a sincere friend to the blacks, I have much regretted the reckless interference of these persons, on account of the restrictions it has become, or been thought, necessary to impose. Since the exploit of the former hero, they have been forbidden to preach, except to their fellow-slaves, the property of the same owner ; to have public funerals, unless a white person officiates ; or to be taught to read and write. Their funerals formerly gave them great satisfaction, and it was customary here to furnish the relations of the deceased with bacon, spirit, flour, sugar and butter, with which a grand entertainment, in their way, was got up. We were once much amused by a hearty fellow requesting his mistress to let him have his funeral during his lifetime, when it would do him some good. The waggish request was granted ; and I venture to say there never was a

* The leader of the insurrection in lower Virginia, in which upwards of a hundred white persons, principally women and children, were massacred in cold blood.

funeral the subject of which enjoyed it so much. When permitted, some of our negroes preached with great fluency. I was present, a few years since, when an Episcopal minister addressed the people, by appointment. On the conclusion of an excellent sermon, a negro preacher rose and thanked the gentleman kindly for his discourse, but frankly told him the congregation "did not understand his *lingo*." He then proceeded himself, with great vehemence and volubility, coining words where they had not been made to his hand, or rather his tongue, and impressing his hearers, doubtless, with a decided opinion of his superiority over his white co-laborer in the field of grace. My brother and I, who own contiguous estates, have lately erected a chapel on the line between them, and have employed an acceptable minister of the Baptist persuasion, to which the negroes almost exclusively belong, to afford them religious instruction. Except as a preparatory step to emancipation, I consider it exceedingly impolitic, even as regards the slaves themselves, to permit them to read and write : " Where ignorance is bliss, 't is folly to be wise." And it is certainly impolitic as regards their masters, on the principle that " knowledge is power." My servants have not as long holidays as those of most other persons. I allow three days at Christmas, and a day at each of three other periods, besides a little time to work their patches ; or, if very busy, I sometimes prefer to work them myself. Most of the ancient pastimes have been lost in this neighborhood, and religion, mock or real, has succeeded them. The banjo, their national instrument, is known but in name, or in a few of the tunes which have survived. Some of the younger negroes sing and dance, but the evenings and holidays are usually occupied in working, in visiting, and in praying and singing hymns. The primitive customs and sports are, I believe, better preserved further south, where slaves were brought from Africa long after they ceased to come here.

6th. "The provision usually made for their food and clothing, — for those who are too young or too old to labor." — My men receive twelve quarts of Indian meal (the abundant and universal allowance in this state), seven salted herrings, and two pounds of smoked bacon or three pounds of pork, a week ; the other hands proportionally less. But, generally speaking, their food is issued daily, with the exception of meal, and consists of fish or bacon for breakfast, and meat, fresh or salted, with vegetables whenever we can provide them, for dinner ; or, for a month or two in the spring, fresh fish cooked with a little bacon. This mode is rather more expensive to me than that of weekly rations, but more comfortable to the servants. Superannuated or invalid slaves draw their provisions regularly once a week ; and the moment a child ceases to be nourished by its mother, it receives eight quarts of meal (more than it can consume), and one half-pound of lard. Besides the food furnished by me, nearly all the servants are able to make some addition from their private stores ; and there is among the adults hardly an instance of one so improvident as not to do it. He must be an unthrifty fellow, indeed, who cannot realize the wish of the famous Henry IV. in regard to the French peasantry, and enjoy his fowl on Sunday. I always keep on hand, for the use of the negroes, sugar, molasses, &c., which, though not regularly issued, are applied

for, on the slightest pretexts, and frequently no pretext at all, and are never refused, except in cases of misconduct. In regard to clothing : — the men and boys receive a winter coat and trousers of strong cloth, three shirts, a stout pair of shoes and socks, and a pair of summer pantaloons, every year ; a hat about every second year, and a great-coat and blanket every third year. Instead of great-coats and hats, the women have large capes to protect the bust in bad weather, and handkerchiefs for the head. The articles furnished are good and serviceable ; and, with their own acquisitions, make their appearance decent and respectable. On Sunday they are even fine. The aged and invalid are clad as regularly as the rest, but less substantially. Mothers receive a little raw cotton, in proportion to the number of children, with the privilege of having the yarn, when spun, woven at my expense. I provide them with blankets. Orphans are put with careful women, and treated with tenderness. I am attached to the little slaves, and encourage familiarity among them. Sometimes, when I ride near the quarters, they come running after me with the most whimsical requests, and are rendered happy by the distribution of some little donation. The clothing described is that which is given to the crop hands. Home-servants, a numerous class in Virginia, are of course clad in a different and very superior manner. I neglected to mention, in the proper place, that there are on each of my plantations a kitchen, an oven, and one or more cooks ; and that each hand is furnished with a tin bucket for his food, which is carried into the field by little negroes, who also supply the laborers with water.

7th. " Their treatment when sick."—My negroes go, or are carried, as soon as they are attacked, to a spacious and well-ventilated hospital, near the mansion-house. They are there received by an attentive nurse, who has an assortment of medicine, additional bed-clothing, and the command of as much light food as she may require, either from the table or the store-room of the proprietor. Wine, sago, rice, and other little comforts appertaining to such an establishment, are always kept on hand. The condition of the sick is much better than that of the poor whites or free colored people in the neighborhood.

8th. " Their rewards and punishments." — I occasionally bestow little gratuities for good conduct, and particularly after harvest ; and hardly ever refuse a favor asked by those who faithfully perform their duty. Vicious and idle servants are punished with stripes, moderately inflicted ; to which, in the case of theft, is added privation of meat, a severe punishment to those who are never suffered to be without it on any other account. From my limited observation, I think that servants to the North work much harder than our slaves. I was educated at a college in one of the free states, and, on my return to Virginia, was struck with the contrast. I was astonished at the number of idle domestics, and actually worried my mother, much to my contrition since, to reduce the establishment. I say to my contrition, because, after eighteen years' residence in the good Old Dominion, I find myself surrounded by a troop of servants about as numerous as that against which I formerly so loudly exclaimed. While on this subject it may not be amiss to state a case of manumission which occurred about three years since. My nearest neighbor, a man of immense wealth, owned a favorite servant, a fine fellow, with polished manners and excellent disposition, who reads and writes, and is thoroughly versed in the duties of a butler and housekeeper, in the performance of which he was trusted without limit. This man was, on the death of his master, emancipated with a legacy of six thousand dollars, besides about two thousand dollars more which he had been permitted to accumulate, and had deposited with his master, who had given him credit for it. The use that this man, apparently so well qualified for freedom, and who has had an opportunity of travelling and of judging for himself, makes of his money and his time, is somewhat remarkable. In consequence of his exemplary conduct, he has been permitted to reside in the state, and for very moderate wages occupies the same situation he did in the old establishment, and will probably continue to occupy it as long as he lives. He has no children of his own, but has put a little girl, a relation of his, to school. Except in this instance, and in the purchase of a few plain articles of furniture, his freedom and his money seem not much to have benefited him. A servant of mine, who is intimate with him, thinks he is not as happy as he was before his liberation. Several other servants were freed at the same time, with smaller legacies, but I do not know what has become of them.

I do not regard negro-slavery, however mitigated, as a Utopian system, and have not intended so to delineate it. But it exists, and the difficulty of removing it is felt and acknowledged by all, save the fanatics, who, like "fools, rush in where angels dare not tread." It is pleasing to know that its burdens are not too heavy to be borne. That the treatment of slaves in this state is humane, and even indulgent, may be inferred from the fact of their rapid increase and great longevity. I believe that, constituted as they are, morally and physically, they are as happy as any peasantry in the world; and I venture to affirm, as the result of my reading and inquiry, that in no country are the laborers so liberally and invariably supplied with bread and meat as are the negro slaves of the United States. However great the dearth of provisions, famine never reaches them.

P. S. — It might have been stated above that on this estate there are about one hundred and sixty blacks. With the exception of infants, there has been, in eighteen months, but one death that I remember, — that of a man fully sixty-five years of age. The bill for medical attendance, from the second day of last November, comprising upwards of a year, is less than forty dollars.

The following accounts are taken from "Ingraham's Travels in the South-west," a work which seems to have been written as much to show the beauties of slavery as anything else. Speaking of the state of things on some Southern plantations, he gives the following pictures, which are presented without note or comment:

The little candidates for "field honors" are useless articles on a plantation during the first five or six years of their existence. They are then to take their first lesson in the elementary part of their education. When they have learned their manual alphabet tolerably well, they are placed in the field to take a spell at cotton-picking. The first day in the field is their proudest day. The young negroes look forward to it with as much restlessness and impatience as school-boys to a vacation. Black children are not put to work so young as many children of poor parents in the North. It is often the case that the children of the domestic servants become pets in the house, and the playmates of the white children of the family. No scene can be livelier or more interesting to a Northerner, than that which the negro quarters of a well-regulated plantation present on a Sabbath morning, just before church-hours. In every cabin the men are shaving and dressing; the women, arrayed in their gay muslins, are arranging their frizzly hair, — in which they take no little pride, — or investigating the condition of their children; the old people, neatly clothed, are quietly conversing or ... king about the doors; and those of the younger portion who are not undergoing the infliction of the wash-tub are enjoying themselves in the shade of the trees, or around some little pond, with as much zest as though slavery and freedom were synonymous terms. When all are dressed, and the hour arrives for worship, they lock up their cabins, and the whole population of the little village proceeds to the chapel, where divine service is performed, sometimes by an officiating clergyman, and often by the planter himself, if a church-member. The whole plantation is also frequently formed into a Sabbath class, which is instructed by the planter, or some member of his family; and often, such is the anxiety of the master that they should perfectly understand what they are taught, — a hard matter in the present state of their intellect, — that no means calculated to advance their progress are left untried. I was not long since shown a manuscript catechism, drawn up with great care and judgment by a distinguished planter, on a plan admirably adapted to the comprehension of the negroes.

It is now popular to treat slaves with kindness; and those planters who are known to be inhumanly rigorous to their slaves are scarcely countenanced by the more intelligent and humane portion of the community. Such instances, however, are very rare; but there are unprincipled men everywhere, who will give vent to their ill feelings and bad passions, not with less good will upon the back of an indented apprentice, than upon that of a purchased slave. Private chapels are now introduced upon most of the plantations of the more wealthy, which are far from any church; Sabbath-schools are instituted for the black children, and Bible-classes for the parents, which are superintended by the planter, a chaplain, or some of the female members of the family.

Nor are planters indifferent to the comfort of their gray-headed slaves. I have been much affected at beholding many exhibitions of their kindly feeling towards them. They always address them in a mild and pleasant manner, as "Uncle," or "Aunty," — titles as peculiar to the old negro and negress as "boy" and "girl" to all under forty years of age. Some old Africans are allowed to spend their last years in their houses, without doing any kind of labor; these, if not too infirm, cultivate little patches of ground, on which they raise a few vegetables, — for vegetables grow nearly all the year round in this climate, — and make a little money to purchase a few extra comforts. They are also always receiving presents from their masters and mistresses, and the negroes on the estate, the latter of whom are extremely desirous of seeing the old people comfortable. A relation of the extra comforts which some planters allow their slaves would hardly obtain credit at the North. But you must recollect that Southern planters are men, and men of feeling, generous and high-minded, and possessing as much of the "milk of human kindness" as the sons of colder climes — although they may have been educated to regard that as right which a different education has led Northerners to consider wrong.

With regard to the character of Mrs. Shelby the writer must say a few words. While travelling in Kentucky, a few years since, some pious ladies expressed to her the same sentiments with regard to slavery which the reader has heard expressed by Mrs. Shelby.

There are many whose natural sense of justice cannot be made to tolerate the enormities of the system, even though they hear it defended by clergymen from the pulpit, and see it countenanced by all that is most honorable in rank and wealth.

A pious lady said to the author, with regard to instructing her slaves, "I am ashamed to teach them what is right; I know that they know as well as I do that it is wrong to hold them as slaves, and I am ashamed to look them in the face." Pointing to an intelligent mulatto woman who passed through the room, she continued, "Now, there's B——. She is as intelligent and capable as any white woman I ever knew, and as well able to have her liberty and take care of herself; and she knows it is n't right to keep her as we do, and I know it too; and yet I cannot get my husband to think as I do, or I should be glad to set them free."

A venerable friend of the writer, a lady born and educated a slave-holder, used to the writer the very words attributed to Mrs. Shelby: — "I never thought it was right to hold slaves. I always thought it was wrong when I was a girl, and I thought so still more when I came to join the church." An incident related by this friend of her examination for the church shows in a striking manner what a difference may often exist between theoretical and practical benevolence.

A certain class of theologians in America have advocated the doctrine of disinterested benevolence with such zeal as to make it an imperative article of belief that every individual ought to be willing to endure everlasting misery, if by doing so they could,

on the whole, produce a greater amount of general good in the universe; and the inquiry was sometimes made of candidates for church-membership whether they could bring themselves to this point, as a test of their sincerity. The clergyman who was to examine this lady was particularly interested in these speculations. When he came to inquire of her with regard to her views as to the obligations of Christianity, she informed him decidedly that she had brought her mind to the point of emancipating all her slaves, of whom she had a large number. The clergyman seemed rather to consider this as an excess of zeal, and recommended that she should take time to reflect upon it. He was, however, very urgent to know whether, if it should appear for the greatest good of the universe, she would be willing to be damned. Entirely unaccustomed to theological speculations, the good woman answered, with some vehemence, that "she was sure she was not;" adding, naturally enough, that if that had been her purpose she need not have come to join the church. The good lady, however, was admitted, and proved her devotion to the general good by the more tangible method of setting all her slaves at liberty, and carefully watching over their education and interests after they were liberated.

Mrs. Shelby is a fair type of the very best class of Southern women; and while the evils of the institution are felt and deplored, and while the world looks with just indignation on the national support and patronage which is given to it, and on the men who, knowing its nature, deliberately make efforts to perpetuate and extend it, it is but justice that it should bear in mind the virtues of such persons.

Many of them, surrounded by circumstances over which they can have no control, perplexed by domestic cares of which women in free states can have very little conception, loaded down by duties and responsibilities which wear upon the very springs of life, still go on bravely and patiently from day to day, doing all they can to alleviate what they cannot prevent, and, as far as the sphere of their own immediate power extends, rescuing those who are dependent upon them from the evils of the system.

We read of Him who shall at last come to judgment, that "His fan is in his hand, and he will thoroughly purge his floor, and gather his wheat into the garner." Out of the great abyss of national sin he will rescue every grain of good and honest purpose and intention. His eyes, which are as a flame of fire, penetrate at once those intricate mazes where human judgment is lost, and will save and honor at last the truly good and sincere, however they may have been involved with the evil; and such souls as have resisted the greatest temptations, and persisted in good under the most perplexing circumstances, are those of whom he has written, "And they shall be mine, saith the Lord of Hosts, in that day when I make up my jewels; and I will spare them as a man spareth his own son that serveth him."

CHAPTER IV.

GEORGE HARRIS.

THE character of George Harris has been represented as overdrawn, both as respects personal qualities and general intelligence. It has been said, too, that so many afflictive incidents happening to a slave are improbable, and present a distorted view of the institution.

In regard to person, it must be remembered that the half-breeds often inherit, to a great degree, the traits of their white ancestors. For this there is abundant evidence in the advertisements of the papers. Witness the following from the *Chattanooga* (Tenn.) *Gazette*, Oct. 5th, 1852:

$500 REWARD.

Runaway from the subscriber, on the 25th May, a VERY BRIGHT MULATTO BOY, about 21 or 22 years old, named WASH. Said boy, without close observation, might pass himself for a white man, as he is very bright — has sandy hair, blue eyes, and a fine set of teeth. He is an excellent bricklayer; but I have no idea that he will pursue his trade, for fear of detection. Although he is like a white man in appearance, he has the disposition of a negro, and delights in comic songs and witty expressions. He is an excellent house servant, very handy about a hotel, — tall, slender, and has rather a down look, especially when spoken to, and is sometimes inclined to be sulky. I have no doubt but he has been decoyed off by some scoundrel, and I will give the above reward for the apprehension of the boy and thief, if delivered at Chattanooga. Or, I will give $200 for the boy alone; or $100 if confined in any jail in the United States, so that I can get him.

GEORGE O. RAGLAND.
Chattanooga, June 15, 1852.

From the *Capitolian Vis-a-vis*, West Baton Rouge, Louisiana, Nov. 1, 1852:

$150 REWARD.

Runaway about the 15th of August last, *Joe,* a yellow man; small, about 5 feet 8 or 9 inches high, and about 20 years of age. *Has a Roman nose,* was raised in New Orleans, and *speaks French and English.* He was bought last winter of Mr. Digges, Banks Arcade, New Orleans.

In regard to general intelligence, the reader will recollect that the writer stated it as a fact which she learned while on a journey through Kentucky, that a young colored man invented a machine for cleaning hemp, like that alluded to in her story.

Advertisements, also, occasionally propose for sale artisans of different descriptions. Slaves are often employed as pilots for vessels, and highly valued for their skill and knowledge. The following are advertisements from recent newspapers.

From the *South Carolinian* (Columbia), Dec. 4th, 1852:

VALUABLE NEGROES AT AUCTION.

BY J. & L. T. LEVIN.

WILL be sold, on MONDAY, the 6th day of December, the following valuable NEGROES:

Andrew, 24 years of age, a bricklayer and plasterer, and thorough workman.

George, 22 years of age, one of the best barbers in the State.

James, 19 years of age, an excellent painter.

These boys were raised in Columbia, and are exceptions to most of boys, and are sold for no fault whatever.

The terms of sale are one-half cash, the balance on a credit of six months, with interest, for notes payable at bank, with two or more approved endorsers.

Purchasers to pay for necessary papers.

WILLIAM DOUGLASS.
November 27, 36.

From the same paper, of November 18th, 1852:

Will be sold at private sale, a LIKELY MAN, boat hand, and good pilot; is well acquainted with all the inlets between here and Savannah and Georgetown.

With regard to the incidents of George Harris' life, that he may not be supposed a purely exceptional case, we propose to offer some parallel facts from the lives of slaves of our personal acquaintance.

Lewis Clark is an acquaintance of the writer. Soon after his escape from slavery, he was received into the family of a sister-in-law of the author, and there educated. His conduct during this time was such as to win for him uncommon affection and respect, and the author has frequently heard him spoken of in the highest terms by all who knew him.

The gentleman in whose family he so long resided says of him, in a recent letter to the writer, "I would trust him, as the saying is, with untold gold."

Lewis is a quadroon, a fine-looking man, with European features, hair slightly wavy, and with an intelligent, agreeable expression of countenance.

The reader is now desired to compare the following incidents of his life, part of which he related personally to the author, with the incidents of the life of George Harris.

His mother was a handsome quadroon woman, the daughter of her master, and given by him in marriage to a free white man, a Scotchman, with the express understanding that she and her children were to be free. This engagement, if made sincerely at all, was never complied with. His mother had nine children, and, on the death of her husband, came back, with all these children, as slaves in her father's house.

A married daughter of the family, who was the dread of the whole household, on account of the violence of her temper, had taken from the family, upon her marriage, a young girl. By the violence of her abuse she soon reduced the child to a state of idiocy, and then came imperiously back to her father's establishment, declaring that the child was good for nothing, and that she would have another; and, as poor Lewis' evil star would have it, fixed her eye upon him.

To avoid one of her terrible outbreaks of temper, the family offered up this boy as a pacificatory sacrifice. The incident is thus described by Lewis, in a published narrative:

Every boy was ordered in, to pass before this female sorceress, that she might select a victim for her unprovoked malice, and on whom to pour the vials of her wrath for years. I was that unlucky fellow. Mr. Campbell, my grandfather, objected, because it would divide a family, and offered her Moses; * * * but objections and claims of every kind were swept away by the wild passion and shrill-toned voice of Mrs. B. Me she would have, and none else. Mr. Campbell went out to hunt, and drive away bad thoughts; the old lady became quiet, for she was sure none of her blood run in my veins, and, if there was any of her husband's there, it was no fault of hers. Slave-holding women are always revengeful toward the children of slaves that have any of the blood of their husbands in them. I was too young — only seven years of age — to understand what was going on. But my poor and affectionate mother understood and appreciated it all. When she left the kitchen of the mansion-house, where she was employed as cook, ?   me home to her

own little cottage, the tear of anguish was in her eye, and the image of sorrow upon every feature of her face. She knew the female Nero whose rod was now to be over me. That night sleep departed from her eyes. With the youngest child clasped firmly to her bosom, she spent the night in walking the floor, coming ever and anon to lift up the clothes and look at me and my poor brother, who lay sleeping together. *Sleeping*, I said. Brother slept, but not I. I saw my mother when she first came to me, and I could not sleep. The vision of that night — its deep, ineffaceable impression — is now before my mind with all the distinctness of yesterday. In the morning I was put into the carriage with Mrs. B. and her children, and my weary pilgrimage of suffering was fairly begun.

Mrs. Banton is a character that can only exist where the laws of the land clothe with absolute power the coarsest, most brutal and violent-tempered, equally with the most generous and humane.

If irresponsible power is a trial to the virtue of the most watchful and careful, how fast must it develop cruelty in those who are naturally violent and brutal!

This woman was united to a drunken husband, of a temper equally ferocious. A recital of all the physical torture which this pair contrived to inflict on a hapless child, some of which have left ineffaceable marks on his person, would be too trying to humanity, and we gladly draw a veil over it.

Some incidents, however, are presented in the following extracts:

A very trivial offence was sufficient to call forth a great burst of indignation from this woman of ungoverned passions. In my simplicity, I put my lips to the same vessel, and drank out of it, from which her children were accustomed to drink. She expressed her utter abhorrence of such an act by throwing my head violently back, and dashing into my face two dippers of water. The shower of water was followed by a heavier shower of *kicks*; but the words, bitter and cutting, that followed, were like a storm of hail upon my young heart. "She would teach me better manners than that; she would let me know I was to be brought up to her hand; she would have *one* slave that knew his place: if I wanted water, go to the spring, and not drink there in the house." This was new times for me; for some days I was completely benumbed with my sorrow.

    *   *   *   *

If there be one so lost to all feeling as even to say that the slaves do not suffer when *families* are separated, let such a one go to the ragged quilt which was my couch and pillow, and stand there night after night, for long, weary hours, and see the bitter tears streaming down the face of that more than orphan boy, while with half-suppressed sighs and sobs he calls again and again upon his absent mother.

"Say, wast thou conscious of the tears I shed ?
Hovered thy spirit o'er thy sorrowing son ?
Wretch even *then !* life's journey just begun."

He was employed till late at night in spinning flax or rocking the baby, and called at a very early hour in the morning; and if he did not start at the first summons, a cruel chastisement was sure to follow. He says:

Such horror has seized me, lest I might not hear the first shrill call, that I have often in dreams fancied I heard that unwelcome voice, and have leaped from my couch and walked through the house and out of it before I awoke. I have gone and called the other slaves, in my sleep, and asked them if they did not hear master call. Never, while I live, will the remembrance of those long, bitter nights of fear pass from my mind.

He adds to this words which should be deeply pondered by those who lay the flattering unction to their souls that the oppressed do not feel the sundering of family ties.

But all my severe labor, and bitter and cruel punishments, for these ten years of captivity with this worse than Arab family, all these were as nothing to the sufferings I experienced by being separated from my mother, brothers and sisters; the same things, with them near to sympathize with me, to hear my story of sorrow, would have been comparatively tolerable.

They were distant only about thirty miles; and yet, in ten long, lonely years of childhood, I was only permitted to see them three times.

My mother occasionally found an opportunity to send me some token of remembrance and affection, — a sugar-plum or an apple; but I scarcely ever ate them; they were laid up, and handled and wept over, till they wasted away in my hand.

My thoughts continually by day, and my dreams by night, were of mother and home; and the horror experienced in the morning, when I awoke and behold it was a dream, is beyond the power of language to describe.

Lewis had a beautiful sister by the name of Delia, who, on the death of her grandfather, was sold, with all the other children of his mother, for the purpose of dividing the estate. She was a pious girl, a member of the Baptist church. She fell into the hands of a brutal, drunken man, who wished to make her his mistress. Milton Clark, a brother of Lewis, in the narrative of his life describes the scene where he, with his mother, stood at the door while this girl was brutally whipped before it for wishing to conform to the principles of her Christian profession. As her resolution was unconquerable, she was placed in a coffle and sent down to the New Orleans market. Here she was sold to a Frenchman, named Coval. He took her to Mexico, emancipated and married

her. After residing some time in France and the West Indies with him, he died, leaving her a fortune of twenty or thirty thousand dollars. At her death she endeavored to leave this by will to purchase the freedom of her brothers; but, as a slave cannot take property, or even have it left in trust for him, they never received any of it.

The incidents of the recovery of Lewis' freedom are thus told:

I had long thought and dreamed of LIBERTY; I was now determined to make an effort to gain it. No tongue can tell the doubt, the perplexities, the anxiety, which a slave feels, when making up his mind upon this subject. If he makes an effort, and is not successful, he must be laughed at by his fellows, he will be beaten unmercifully by the master, and then watched and used the harder for it all his life.

And then, if he gets away, *who, what* will he find? He is ignorant of the world. All the white part of mankind, that he has ever seen, are enemies to him and all his kindred. How can he venture where none but white faces shall greet him? The master tells him that abolitionists *decoy* slaves off into the free states to catch them and sell them to Louisiana or Mississippi; and, if he goes to Canada, the British will put him in a *mine under ground, with both eyes put out, for life.* How does he know what or whom to believe? A horror of great darkness comes upon him, as he thinks over what may befall him. Long, very long time did I think of escaping, before I made the effort.

At length, the report was started that I was to be sold for Louisiana. Then I thought it was time to act. My mind was made up.

*　　*　　*　　*　　*

What my feelings were when I reached the free shore can be better imagined than described. I trembled all over with deep emotion, and I could feel my hair rise up on my head. I was on what was called a *free* soil, among a people who had no slaves. I saw white men at work, and no slave smarting beneath the lash. Everything was indeed *new* and wonderful. Not knowing where to find a friend, and being ignorant of the country, unwilling to inquire, lest I should betray my ignorance, it was a whole week before I reached Cincinnati. At one place where I put up, I had a great many more questions put to me than I wished to answer. At another place, I was very much annoyed by the officiousness of the landlord, who made it a point to supply every guest with newspapers. I took the copy handed me, and turned it over, in a somewhat awkward manner, I suppose. He came to me to point out a veto, or some other very important news. I thought it best to decline his assistance, and gave up the paper, saying my eyes were not in a fit condition to read much.

At another place, the neighbors, on learning that a Kentuckian was at the tavern, came, in great earnestness, to find out what my business was. Kentuckians sometimes came there to kidnap their citizens. They were in the habit of watching them close. I at length satisfied them by assuring them that I was not, nor my father before me, any slave-holder at all ; but, lest their suspicions should be excited in another direction, I added my grandfather was a slave-holder.

*   *   *   *   *

At daylight we were in Canada. When I stepped ashore here, I said, sure enough, I AM FREE. Good heavens ! what a sensation, when it first visits the bosom of a full-grown man ; one *born* to bondage ; one who had been taught, from early infancy, that this was his inevitable lot for life ! Not till *then* did I dare to cherish, for a moment, the feeling that *one* of the limbs of my body was my own. The slaves often say, when cut in the hand or foot, "Plague on the old foot" or " the old hand ! `It is master's, — let him take care of it. Nigger don't care if he never get well." My hands, my feet, were now my own.

It will be recollected that George, in conversing with Eliza, gives an account of a scene in which he was violently beaten by his master's young son. This incident was suggested by the following letter from John M. Nelson to Mr. Theodore Weld, given in *Slavery as It Is*, p. 51.

Mr. Nelson removed from Virginia to Highland County, Ohio, many years since, where he is extensively known and respected. The letter is dated January 3d, 1839.

I was born and raised in Augusta County, Virginia ; my father was an elder in the Presbyterian church, and was " owner " of about twenty slaves ; he was what was generally termed a " good master." His slaves were generally tolerably well fed and clothed, and not over-worked ; they were sometimes permitted to attend church, and called in to family worship ; few of them, however, availed themselves of these privileges. On *some occasions* I have seen him whip them severely, particularly for the crime of trying to obtain their liberty, or for what was called " running away." For *this* they were scourged more severely than for anything else. After they have been retaken I have seen them stripped naked and suspended by the hands, sometimes to a tree, sometimes to a post, until their toes barely touched the ground, and whipped with a cowhide until the blood dripped from their backs. A boy named Jack, particularly, I have seen served in this way more than once. When I was quite a child, I recollect it grieved me very much to see one *tied up* to be whipped, and I used to intercede with tears in their behalf, and mingle my cries with theirs, and feel almost willing to take part of the punishment ; I have been severely rebuked by my father for this kind of sympathy. Yet, such is the hardening nature of such scenes, that from this kind of commiseration for the suffering slave I became so blunted that I could not only witness their stripes with composure, but *myself* inflict them, and that without remorse. One case I have often looked back to with sorrow and contrition, particularly since I have been convinced that " negroes are men." When I was perhaps fourteen or fifteen years of age, I undertook to correct a young fellow named Ned, for some supposed offence, — I think it was leaving a bridle out of its proper place ; he, being larger

and stronger than myself, took hold of my arms and held me, in order to prevent my striking him. This I considered the height of insolence, and cried for help, when my father and mother both came running to my rescue. My father stripped and tied him, and took him into the orchard, where switches were plenty, and directed me to whip him ; when one switch wore out, he supplied me with others. After I had whipped him a while, he fell on his knees to implore forgiveness, and I kicked him in the face ; my father said, " Don't kick him, but whip him ;" this I did until his back was literally covered with *welts*. I know I have repented, and trust I have obtained pardon for these things.

My father owned a woman (we used to call aunt Grace) ; she was purchased in Old Virginia. She has told me that her old master, in his *will*, gave her her freedom, but at his death his sons had sold her to my father : when he bought her she manifested some unwillingness to go with him, when she was put in irons and taken by force. This was before I was born ; but I remember to have seen the irons, and was told that was what they had been used for. Aunt Grace is still living, and must be between seventy and eighty years of age ; she has, for the last forty years, been an exemplary Christian. When I was a youth I took some pains to learn her to read ; this is now a great consolation to her. Since age and infirmity have rendered her of little value to her " owners," she is permitted to read as much as she pleases ; this she can do, with the aid of glasses, in the old family Bible, which is almost the only book she has ever looked into. This, with some little mending for the black children, is all she does ; she is still held as a slave. I well remember what *a heart-rending scene* there was in the family when *my father sold her husband ;* this was, I suppose, thirty-five years ago. And yet my father was considered one of the best of masters. I know of few who were better, but of *many* who were worse.

With regard to the intelligence of George, and his teaching himself to read and write, there is a most interesting and affecting parallel to it in the " Life of Frederick Douglass," — a book which can be recommended to any one who has a curiosity to trace the workings of an intelligent and active mind through all the squalid misery, degradation and oppression, of slavery. A few incidents will be given.

Like Clark, Douglass was the son of a white man. He was a plantation slave in a proud old family. His situation, probably, may be considered as an average one ; that is to say, he led a life of dirt, degradation, discomfort of various kinds, made tolerable as a matter of daily habit, and considered as enviable in comparison with the lot of those who suffer worse abuse. An incident which Douglass relates of his mother is touching. He states that it is customary at an early age to separate mothers from their children, for the purpose of blunting and deadening natural affection. When he was three years old his mother was sent to work on a plantation eight or ten miles distant, and after that he never saw her except in the night. After her day's toil she would occasionally walk over to her child, lie down with him in her arms, hush him to sleep in her bosom, then rise up and walk back again to be ready for her field work by daylight. Now, we ask the highest-born lady in England or America, who is a mother, whether this does not show that this poor field-laborer had in her bosom, beneath her dirt and rags, a true mother's heart?

The last and bitterest indignity which has been heaped on the head of the unhappy slaves has been the denial to them of those holy affections which God gives alike to all. We are told, in fine phrase, by languid ladies of fashion, that "it is not to be supposed that those creatures have the same feelings that we have," when, perhaps, the very speaker could not endure one tithe of the fatigue and suffering which the slave-mother often bears for her child. Every mother who has a mother's heart within her, ought to know that this is blasphemy against nature, and, standing between the cradle of her living and the grave of her dead child, should indignantly reject such a slander on all motherhood.

Douglass thus relates the account of his learning to read, after he had been removed to the situation of house-servant in Baltimore.

It seems that his mistress, newly married and unaccustomed to the management of slaves, was very kind to him, and, among other acts of kindness, commenced teaching him to read. His master, discovering what was going on, he says,

At once forbade Mrs. Auld to instruct me further, telling her, among other things, that it was unlawful, as well as unsafe, to teach a slave to read. To use his own words, further, he said, "If you give a nigger an inch, he will take an ell. A nigger should know nothing but to obey his master — to do as he is told to do. Learning would spoil the best nigger in the world. Now," said he, "if you teach that nigger (speaking of myself) how to read, there would be no keeping him. It would forever unfit him to be a slave. He would at once become unmanageable, and of no value to his master. As to himself, it could do him no good, but a great deal of harm. It would make him discontented and unhappy." These words sank deep into my heart, stirred up sentiments within that lay slumbering, and called into existence an entirely new train of thought. It was a new and special revelation, explaining dark and mysterious things, with which my youth-

ful understanding had struggled, but struggled in vain. I now understood what had been to me a most perplexing difficulty — to wit, the white man's power to enslave the black man. It was a grand achievement, and I prized it highly. From that moment, I understood the pathway from slavery to freedom.

After this, his mistress was as watchful to prevent his learning to read as she had before been to instruct him. His course after this he thus describes:

From this time I was most narrowly watched. If I was in a separate room any considerable length of time, I was sure to be suspected of having a book, and was at once called to give an account of myself. All this, however, was too late. The first step had been taken. Mistress, in teaching me the alphabet, had given me the inch, and no precaution could prevent me from taking the ell. The plan which I adopted, and the one by which I was most successful, was that of making friends of all the little white boys whom I met in the street. As many of these as I could I converted into teachers. With their kindly aid, obtained at different times and in different places, I finally succeeded in learning to read. When I was sent of errands I always took my book with me, and by going one part of my errand quickly, I found time to get a lesson before my return. I used also to carry bread with me, enough of which was always in the house, and to which I was always welcome; for I was much better off in this regard than many of the poor white children in our neighborhood. This bread I used to bestow upon the hungry little urchins, who, in return, would give me that more valuable bread of knowledge. I am strongly tempted to give the names of two or three of those little boys, as a testimonial of the gratitude and affection I bear them; but prudence forbids; — not that it would injure me, but it might embarrass them; for it is almost an unpardonable offence to teach slaves to read in this Christian country. It is enough to say of the dear little fellows, that they lived on Philpot-street, very near Durgin and Bailey's ship-yard. I used to talk this matter of slavery over with them. I would sometimes say to them I wished I could be as free as they would be when they got to be men. "You will be free as soon as you are twenty-one, but I am a slave for life!" Have not I as good a right to be free as you have?" These words used to trouble them; they would express for me the liveliest sympathy, and console me with the hope that something would occur by which I might be free.

I was now about twelve years old, and the thought of being a slave for life began to bear heavily upon my heart. Just about this time I got hold of a book entitled "The Columbian Orator." Every opportunity I got I used to read this book. Among much of other interesting matter, I found in it a dialogue between a master and his slave. The slave was represented as having run away from his master three times. The dialogue represented the conversation which took place between them when the slave was retaken the third time. In this dialogue, the whole argument in behalf of slavery was brought forward by the master, all of which was disposed of by the slave. The slave was made to say some very smart as well as impressive things in reply to his master,

2

— things which had the desired though unexpected effect; for the conversation resulted in the voluntary emancipation of the slave on the part of the master.

In the same book I met with one of Sheridan's mighty speeches on and in behalf of Catholic emancipation. These were choice documents to me. I read them over and over again, with unabated interest. They gave tongue to interesting thoughts of my own soul, which had frequently flashed through my mind, and died away for want of utterance. The moral which I gained from the dialogue was the power of truth over the conscience of even a slave-holder. What I got from Sheridan was a bold denunciation of slavery, and a powerful vindication of human rights. The reading of these documents enabled me to utter my thoughts, and to meet the arguments brought forward to sustain slavery; but, while they relieved me of one difficulty, they brought on another even more painful than the one of which I was relieved. The more I read, the more I was led to abhor and detest my enslavers. I could regard them in no other light than a band of successful robbers, who had left their homes, and gone to Africa, and stolen us from our homes, and in a strange land reduced us to slavery. I loathed them as being the meanest as well as the most wicked of men. As I read and contemplated the subject, behold! that very discontentment which Master Hugh had predicted would follow my learning to read had already come, to torment and sting my soul to unutterable anguish. As I writhed under it, I would at times feel that learning to read had been a curse rather than a blessing. It had given me a view of my wretched condition without the remedy. It opened my eyes to the horrible pit, but to no ladder upon which to get out. In moments of agony I envied my fellow-slaves for their stupidity. I have often wished myself a beast. I preferred the condition of the meanest reptile to my own. Anything, no matter what, to get rid of thinking! It was this everlasting thinking of my condition that tormented me. There was no getting rid of it. It was pressed upon me by every object within sight or hearing, animate or inanimate. The silver trump of freedom had roused my soul to eternal wakefulness. Freedom now appeared, to disappear no more forever. It was heard in every sound, and seen in every thing. It was ever present to torment me with a sense of my wretched condition. I saw nothing without seeing it, I heard nothing without hearing it, and felt nothing without feeling it. It looked from every star, it smiled in every calm, breathed in every wind, and moved in every storm.

I often found myself regretting my own existence, and wishing myself dead; and but for the hope of being free, I have no doubt but that I should have killed myself, or done something for which I should have been killed. While in this state of mind I was eager to hear any one speak of slavery. I was a ready listener. Every little while I could hear something about the abolitionists. It was some time before I found what the word meant. It was always used in such connections as to make it an interesting word to me. If a slave ran away and succeeded in getting clear, or if a slave killed his master, set fire to a barn, or did anything very wrong in the mind of a slave-holder, it was spoken of as the fruit of *abolition*. Hearing the word in this connection very often. I

set about learning what it meant. The dictionary afforded me little or no help. I found it was "the act of abolishing;" but then I did not know what was to be abolished. Here I was perplexed. I did not dare to ask any one about its meaning, for I was satisfied that it was something they wanted me to know very little about. After a patient waiting, I got one of our city papers, containing an account of the number of petitions from the North praying for the abolition of slavery in the District of Columbia, and of the slave-trade between the states. From this time I understood the words *abolition* and *abolitionist*, and always drew near when that word was spoken, expecting to hear something of importance to myself and fellow-slaves. The light broke in upon me by degrees. I went one day down on the wharf of Mr. Waters; and, seeing two Irishmen unloading a scow of stone, I went, unasked, and helped them. When we had finished, one of them came to me and asked me if I were a slave. I told him I was. He asked, "Are ye a slave for life?" I told him that I was. The good Irishman seemed to be deeply affected by the statement. He said to the other that it was a pity so fine a little fellow as myself should be a slave for life. He said it was a shame to hold me. They both advised me to run away to the North; that I should find friends there, and that I should be free. I pretended not to be interested in what they said, and treated them as if I did not understand them; for I feared they might be treacherous. White men have been known to encourage slaves to escape, and then, to get the reward, catch them and return them to their masters. I was afraid that these seemingly good men might. use me so; but I nevertheless remembered their advice. and from that time I resolved to run away. I looked forward to a time at which it would be safe for me to escape. I was too young to think of doing so immediately; besides, I wished to learn how to write, as I might have occasion to write my own pass. I consoled myself with the hope that I should one day find a good chance. Meanwhile I would learn to write.

The idea as to how I might learn to write was suggested to me by being in Durgin and Bailey's ship-yard, and frequently seeing the ship carpenters, after hewing and getting a piece of timber ready for use, write on the timber the name of that part of the ship for which it was intended. When a piece of timber was intended for the larboard side it would be marked thus — "L." When a piece was for the starboard side it would be marked thus — "S." A piece for the starboard side forward would be marked thus — "L. F." When a piece was for starboard side forward it would be marked thus — "S. F." For larboard aft it would be marked thus — "L. A." For starboard aft it would be marked thus — "S. A." I soon learned the names of these letters, and for what they were intended when placed upon a piece of timber in the ship-yard. I immediately commenced copying them, and in a short time was able to make the four letters named. After that, when I met with any boy who I knew could write, I would tell him I could write as well as he. The next word would be, "I don't believe you. Let me see you try it." I would then make the letters which I had been so fortunate as to learn, and ask him to beat that. In this way I got a good many lessons in writing, which it is quite possible I should never have gotten in any other way. During this time my copy-book was the board fence, brick wall and pavement; my pen and ink was a lump of chalk. With these I learned mainly how to write. I then commenced and continued copying the Italics in Webster's Spelling-book, until I could make them all without looking on the book. By this time my little Master Thomas had gone to school and learned how to write, and had written over a number of copy-books. These had been brought home, and shown to some of our near neighbors, and then laid aside. My mistress used to go to class-meeting at the Wilk-street meeting-house every Monday afternoon, and leave me to take care of the house. When left thus I used to spend the time in writing in the spaces left in Master Thomas' copy-book, copying what he had written. I continued to do this until I could write a hand very similar to that of Master Thomas. Thus, after a long, tedious effort for years, I finally succeeded in learning how to write.

These few quoted incidents will show that the case of George Harris is by no means so uncommon as might be supposed.

Let the reader peruse the account which George Harris gives of the sale of his mother and her children, and then read the following account given by the venerable Josiah Henson, now pastor of the missionary settlement at Dawn, in Canada.

After the death of his master, he says, the slaves of the plantation were all put up at auction and sold to the highest bidder.

My brothers and sisters were bid off one by one, while my mother, holding my hand, looked on in an agony of grief, the cause of which I but ill understood at first, but which dawned on my mind with dreadful clearness as the sale proceeded. My mother was then separated from me, and put up in her turn. She was bought by a man named Isaac R., residing in Montgomery County [Maryland], and then I was offered to the assembled purchasers. My mother, half distracted with the parting forever from all her children, pushed through the crowd, while the bidding for me was going on, to the spot where R. was standing. She fell at his feet, and clung to his knees, entreating him, in tones that a mother only could command, to buy her baby as well as herself, and spare to her one of her little ones at least. Will it, can it be believed, that this man, thus appealed to, was capable not merely of turning a deaf ear to her supplication, but of disengaging himself from her with such violent blows and kicks as to reduce her to the necessity of creeping out of his reach, and mingling the groan of bodily suffering with the sob of a breaking heart?

Now, all these incidents that have been given are real incidents of slavery, related by those who know slavery by the best of all tests — experience; and they are given by men who have earned a character in freedom which makes their word as good as the word of any man living.

The case of Lewis Clark might be called a harder one than common. The case of

Douglass is probably a very fair average specimen.

The writer has conversed, in her time, with a very considerable number of liberated slaves, many of whom stated that their own individual lot had been comparatively a mild one; but she never talked with one who did not let fall, first or last, some incident which he had observed, some scene which he had witnessed, which went to show some most horrible abuse of the system; and, what was most affecting about it, the narrator often evidently considered it so much a matter of course as to mention it incidentally, without any particular emotion.

It is supposed by many that the great outcry among those who are opposed to slavery comes from a morbid reading of unauthenticated accounts gotten up in abolition papers, &c. This idea is a very mistaken one. The accounts which tell against the slave-system are derived from the continual living testimony of the poor slave himself; often from that of the fugitives from slavery who are continually passing through our Northern cities.

As a specimen of some of the incidents thus developed, is given the following fact of recent occurrence, related to the author by a lady in Boston. This lady, who was much in the habit of visiting the poor, was sent for, a month or two since, to see a mulatto woman who had just arrived at a colored boarding-house near by, and who appeared to be in much dejection of mind. A little conversation showed her to be a fugitive. Her history was as follows: She, with her brother, were, as is often the case, both the children and slaves of their master. At his death they were left to his legitimate daughter as her servants, and treated with as much consideration as very common kind of people might be expected to show to those who were entirely and in every respect at their disposal.

The wife of her brother ran away to Canada; and as there was some talk of selling her and her child, in consequence of some embarrassment in the family affairs, her brother, a fine-spirited young man, determined to effect her escape, also, to a land of liberty. He concealed her for some time in the back part of an obscure dwelling in the city, till he could find an opportunity to send her off. While she was in this retreat, he was indefatigable in his attentions to her, frequently bringing her fruit and flowers, and doing everything he could to beguile the weariness of her imprisonment.

At length, the steward of a vessel, whom he had obliged, offered to conceal him on board the ship, and give him a chance to escape. The noble-hearted fellow, though tempted by an offer which would enable him immediately to join his wife, to whom he was tenderly attached, preferred to give this offer to his sister, and during the absence of the captain of the vessel she and her child were brought on board and secreted.

The captain, when he returned and discovered what had been done, was very angry, as the thing, if detected, would have involved him in very serious difficulties. He declared, at first, that he would send the woman up into town to jail; but, by her entreaties and those of the steward, was induced to wait till evening, and send word to her brother to come and take her back. After dark the brother came on board, and, instead of taking his sister away, began to appeal to the humanity of the captain in the most moving terms. He told his sister's history and his own, and pleaded eloquently his desire for her liberty. The captain had determined to be obdurate, but, alas! he was only a man. Perhaps he had himself a wife and child,— perhaps he felt that, were he 'in the young man's case, he would do just so for his sister. Be it as it may, he was at last overcome. He said to the young man, " I must send you away from my ship; I 'll put off a boat and see you got into it, and you must row off, and never let me see your faces again; and if, after all, you should come back and get on board, it will be your fault, and not mine."

So, in the rain and darkness, the young man and his sister and child were lowered over the side of the vessel, and rowed away. After a while the ship weighed anchor, but before she reached Boston it was discovered that the woman and child were on board.

The lady to whom this story was related was requested to write a letter, in certain terms, to a person in the city whence the fugitive had come, to let the brother know of her safe arrival.

The fugitive was furnished with work, by which she could support herself and child, and the lady carefully attended to her wants for a few weeks.

One morning she came in, with a good deal of agitation, exclaiming, " O, ma'am, he 's come! George is come!" And in a few minutes the young man was introduced. The lady who gave this relation belongs to the first circles of Boston society; she says that she never was more impressed by the personal manners of any gentleman than by those of this fugitive brother. So much did he have the air of a perfect, finished gentleman, that she felt she could not question him with regard to his escape with the familiarity with which persons of his condition are commonly approached; and it was not till he requested her to write a letter for him, because he could not write himself, that she could realize that this fine specimen of manhood had been all his life a slave.

The remainder of the history is no less romantic. The lady had a friend in Montreal, whither George's wife had gone; and, after furnishing money to pay their expenses, she presented them with a letter to this gentleman, requesting the latter to assist the young man in finding his wife. When they landed at Montreal, George stepped on shore and presented this letter to the first man he met, asking him if he knew to whom it was directed. The gentleman proved to be the very person to whom the letter was addressed. He knew George's wife, brought him to her without delay, so that, by return mail, the lady had the satisfaction of learning the happy termination of the adventure.

This is but a specimen of histories which are continually transpiring; so that those who speak of slavery can say, " We speak that which we do know, and testify that we have seen."

But we shall be told the slaves are all a lying race, and that these are lies which they tell us. There are some things, however, about these slaves, which cannot lie. Those deep lines of patient sorrow upon the face; that attitude of crouching and humble subjection; that sad, habitual expression of hope deferred, in the eye,— would tell their story, if the slave never spoke.

It is not long since the writer has seen faces such as might haunt one's dreams for weeks.

Suppose a poor, worn-out mother, sickly, feeble and old,— her hands worn to the bone with hard, unpaid toil,—whose nine children have been sold to the slave-trader, and whose tenth soon is to be sold, unless by her labor as washer-woman she can raise nine hundred dollars! Such are the kind of cases constantly coming to one's knowledge, such are the witnesses which will not let us sleep.

Doubt has been expressed whether such

a thing as an advertisement for a man, "*dead or alive,*" like the advertisement for George Harris, was ever published in the Southern States. The scene of the story in which that occurs is supposed to be laid a few years back, at the time when the black laws of Ohio were passed. That at this time such advertisements were common in the newspapers, there is abundant evidence. That they are less common now, is a matter of hope and gratulation.

In the year 1839, Mr. Theodore D. Weld made a systematic attempt to collect and arrange the statistics of slavery. A mass of facts and statistics was gathered, which were authenticated with the most unquestionable accuracy. Some of the "*one thousand witnesses,*" whom he brings upon the stand, were ministers, lawyers, merchants, and men of various other callings, who were either natives of the slave states, or had been residents there for many years of their life. Many of these were slave-holders. Others of the witnesses were, or had been, slave-drivers, or officers of coasting-vessels engaged in the slave-trade. Another part of his evidence was gathered from public speeches in Congress, in the state legislatures, and elsewhere. But the majority of it was taken from recent newspapers.

The papers from which these facts were copied were preserved and put on file in a public place, where they remained for some years, for the information of the curious. After Mr. Weld's book was completed, a copy of it was sent, through the mail, to every editor from whose paper such advertisements had been taken, and to every individual of whom any facts had been narrated, with the passages which concerned them marked.

It is quite possible that this may have had some influence in rendering such advertisements less common. Men of sense often go on doing a thing which is very absurd, or even inhuman, simply because it has always been done before them, and they follow general custom, without much reflection. When 'their attention, however, is called to it by a stranger who sees the thing from another point of view, they become immediately sensible of the impropriety of the practice, and discontinue it. The reader will, however, be pained to notice, when he comes to the legal part of the book, that even in some of the largest cities of our slave states this barbarity had not been entirely discontinued, in the year 1850.

The list of advertisements in Mr. Weld's book is here inserted, not to weary the reader with its painful details, but that, by running his eye over the dates of the papers quoted, and the places of their publication, he may form a fair estimate of the extent to which this atrocity was *publicly* practised :

The *Wilmington* (North Carolina) *Advertiser* of July 13, 1838, contains the following advertisement :

"$100 will be paid to any person who may apprehend and safely confine in any jail in this state a certain negro man, named ALFRED. And the same reward will be paid, if satisfactory evidence is given of *his having been* KILLED. He has one or more scars on one of his hands, caused by his having been shot. THE CITIZENS OF ONSLOW. "*Richlands, Onslow Co., May* 16, 1838."

In the same column with the above, and directly under it, is the following :

"RANAWAY, my negro man RICHARD. A reward of $25 will be paid for his apprehension, DEAD or ALIVE. Satisfactory proof will only be required of his being KILLED. He has with him, in all probability, his wife, ELIZA, who ran away from Col. Thompson, now a resident of Alabama, about the time he commenced his journey to that state. DURANT H. RHODES."

In the *Macon* (Georgia) *Telegraph*, May 28, is the following :

"About the 1st of March last the negro man RANSOM left me without the least provocation whatever ; I will give a reward of twenty dollars for said negro, if taken, DEAD OR ALIVE, — and if killed in any attempt, an advance of five dollars will be paid. BRYANT JOHNSON. "*Crawford Co., Georgia.*"

See the *Newbern* (N. C.) *Spectator*, Jan. 5, 1838, for the following :

"RANAWAY from the subscriber, a negro man named SAMPSON. Fifty dollars reward will be given for the delivery of him to me, or his confinement in any jail, so that I get him ; and should he resist in being taken, so that violence is necessary to arrest him, I will not hold any person liable for damages should the slave be KILLED. ENOCH FOY. "*Jones Co., N. C.*"

From the *Charleston* (S. C.) *Courier*, Feb. 20, 1836 :

"$300 REWARD. — Ranaway from the subscriber, in November last, his two negro men, named Billy and Pompey. "Billy is 25 years old, and is known as the patroon of my boat for many years ; in all probability he may resist ; in that event 50 dollars will be paid for his HEAD."

CHAPTER V.

ELIZA.

THE writer stated in her book that Eliza was a portrait drawn from life. The incident which brought the original to her notice may be simply narrated.

While the writer was travelling in Kentucky, many years ago, she attended church in a small country town. While there, her attention was called to a beautiful quadroon girl, who sat in one of the slips of the church, and appeared to have charge of some young children. The description of Eliza may suffice for a description of her. When the author returned from church, she inquired about the girl, and was told that she was as good and amiable as she was beautiful; that she was a pious girl, and a member of the church; and, finally, that she was *owned* by Mr. So-and-so. The idea that this girl was a slave struck a chill to her heart, and she said, earnestly, " O, I hope they treat her kindly."

" O, certainly," was the reply; "they think as much of her as of their own children."

" I hope they will never sell her," said a person in the company.

" Certainly they will not; a Southern gentleman, not long ago, offered her master a thousand dollars for her; but he told him that she was too good to be his wife, and he certainly should not have her for a mistress."

This is all that the writer knows of that girl.

With regard to the incident of Eliza's crossing the river on the ice, — as the possibility of the thing has been disputed, — the writer gives the following circumstance in confirmation.

Last spring, while the author was in New York, a Presbyterian clergyman, of Ohio, came to her, and said, " I understand this dispute that fact about the woman's crossing the river. Now, I know all about that, for I got the story from the very man that helped her up the bank. I know it is true, for she is now living in Canada."

It has been objected that the representation of the scene in which the plan for kidnapping Eliza, concocted by Haley, Marks and Loker, at the tavern, is a gross caricature on the state of things in Ohio.

What knowledge the author has had of the facilities which some justices of the peace, under the old fugitive law of Ohio, were in the habit of giving to kidnapping, may be inferred by comparing the statement in her book with some in her personal knowledge.

" Ye see," said Marks to Haley, stirring his punch as he did so, " ye see, we has justices convenient at all p'ints along shore, that does up any little jobs in our line quite reasonable. Tom, he does the knockin' down, and that ar; and I come in all dressed up, — shining boots, — everything first chop, — when the swearin' 's to be done. Yo" oughter see me, now !" said Marks, in a glow of professional pride, " how I can tone it off. One day I 'm Mr. Twickem, from New Orleans; 'nother day, I 'm just come from my plantation on Pearl river, where I works seven hundred niggers; then, again, I come out a distant relation to Henry Clay, or some old cock in Kentuck. Talents is different, you know. Now, Tom 's a roarer when there 's any thumping or fighting to be done; but at lying he an't good, Tom an't; ye see it don't come natural to him; but, Lord ! if thar 's a feller in the country that can swear to anything and everything, and put in all the circumstances and flourishes with a longer face, and carry 't through better 'n I can, why, I 'd like to see him, that 's all ! I b'lieve, my heart, I could get along, and make through, even if justices were more particular than they is. Sometimes I rather wish they was more particular; 't would be a heap more relishin' if they was, — more fun, yer know."

In the year 1839, the writer received into her family, as a servant, a girl from Kentucky. She had been the slave of one of the lowest and most brutal families, with whom she had been brought up, in a log-cabin, in a state of half-barbarism. In proceeding to give her religious instruction, the author heard, for the first time in her life, an inquiry which she had not supposed possible to be made in America : — " Who is Jesus Christ, now, anyhow ? "

When the author told her the history of the love and life and death of Christ, the girl seemed wholly overcome; tears streamed down her cheeks; and she exclaimed, piteously, " Why did n't nobody never tell me this before ? "

" But," said the writer to her, " have n't you ever seen the Bible ? "

" Yes, I have seen missus a-readin' on 't sometimes; but, law sakes ! she 's just a-readin' on 't 'cause she could; don't s'pose it did her no good, no way."

She said she had been to one or two camp-meetings in her life, but " did n't notice very particular."

At all events, the story certainly made great impression on her, and had such an effect in improving her conduct, that the writer had great hopes of her.

On inquiring into her history, it was discovered that, by the laws of Ohio, she was legally entitled to her freedom, from the fact of her having been brought into the state, and left there, temporarily, by the consent of her mistress. These facts being properly authenticated before the proper authorities, papers attesting her freedom were drawn up, and it was now supposed that all danger of pursuit was over. After she had remained in the family for some months, word was sent, from various sources, to Professor Stowe, that the girl's young master was over, looking for her, and that, if care were not taken, she would be conveyed back into slavery.

Professor Stowe called on the magistrate who had authenticated her papers, and inquired whether they were not sufficient to protect her. The reply was, " Certainly they are, in law, if she could have a fair hearing ; but they will come to your house in the night, with an officer and a warrant ; they will take her before Justice D——, and swear to her. He's the man that does all this kind of business, and he'll deliver her up, and there'll be an end to it.",

Mr. Stowe then inquired what could be done ; and was recommended to carry her to some place of security till the inquiry for her was over. Accordingly, that night, a brother of the author, with Professor Stowe, performed for the fugitive that office which the senator is represented as performing for Eliza. They drove about ten miles on a solitary road, crossed the creek at a very dangerous fording, and presented themselves, at midnight, at the house of John Van Zandt, a noble-minded Kentuckian, who had performed the good deed which the author, in her story, ascribes to Van Tromp.

After some rapping at the door, the worthy owner of the mansion appeared, candle in hand, as has been narrated.

" Are you the man that would save a poor colored girl from kidnappers ?" was the first question.

" Guess I am," was the prompt response ; " where is she ? "

" Why, she's here."

" But how did you come ? "

" I crossed the creek."

" Why, the Lord helped you ! " said he ; " I shouldn't dare cross it myself in the night. A man and his wife, and five children, were drowned there, a little while ago."

The reader may be interested to know that the poor girl never was re-taken ; that she married well in Cincinnati, is a very respectable woman, and the mother of a large family of children.

CHAPTER VI.

UNCLE TOM.

THE character of Uncle Tom has been objected to as improbable ; and yet the writer has received more confirmations of that character, and from a greater variety of sources, than of any other in the book.

Many people have said to her, " I knew an Uncle Tom in such and such a Southern State." All the histories of this kind which have thus been related to her would of themselves, if collected, make a small volume. The author will relate a few of them.

While visiting in an obscure town in Maine, in the family of a friend, the conversation happened to turn upon this subject, and the gentleman with whose family she was staying related the following. He said that, when on a visit to his brother, in New Orleans, some years before, he found in his possession a most valuable negro man, of such remarkable probity and honesty that his brother literally trusted him with all he had. He had frequently seen him take out a handful of bills, without looking at them, and hand them to this servant, bidding him go and provide what was necessary for the family, and bring him the change. He remonstrated with his brother on this imprudence ; but the latter replied that he had had such proof of this servant's impregnable conscientiousness that he felt it safe to trust him to any extent.

The history of the servant was this. He had belonged to a man in Baltimore, who, having a general prejudice against all the religious exercises of slaves, did all that he could to prevent his having any time for devotional duties, and strictly forbade him to read the Bible and pray, either by himself, or with the other servants ; and because, like a certain man of old, named Daniel, he constantly disobeyed this unchristian edict, his master inflicted upon him that punishment which a master always has in his power to inflict,— he sold him into perpetual exile from his wife and children, down to New Orleans.

The gentleman who gave the writer this information says that, although not himself a religious man at the time, he was so struck with the man's piety that he said to his brother, " I hope you will never do anything to deprive this man of his religious privileges, for I think a judgment will come upon you if you do." To this his brother replied that he should be very foolish to do it, since he had made up his mind that the man's religion was the root of his extraordinary excellences.

Some time since, there was sent to the writer from the South, through the mail, a little book, entitled, "Sketches of Old Virginia Family Servants," with a preface by Bishop Meade. The book contains an account of the following servants: African Bella, Old Milly, Blind Lucy, Aunt Betty, Springfield Bob, Mammy Chris, Diana Washington, Aunt Margaret, Rachel Parker, Nelly Jackson, My Own Mammy, Aunt Beck.

The following extract from Bishop Meade's preface may not be uninteresting.

The following sketches were placed in my hands with a request that I would examine them with a view to publication.

After reading them I could not but think that they would be both pleasing and edifying.

Very many such examples of fidelity and piety might be added from the old Virginia families. These will suffice as specimens, and will serve to show how interesting the relation between master and servant often is.

Many will doubtless be surprised to find that there was so much intelligence, as well as piety, in some of the old servants of Virginia, and that they had learned to read the Sacred Scriptures, so as to be useful in this way among their fellow-servants. It is, and always has been true, in regard to the servants of the Southern States, that although public schools may have been prohibited, yet no interference has been attempted, where the owners have chosen to teach their servants, or permit them to learn in a private way, how to read God's word. Accordingly, there always have been some who were thus taught. In the more southern states the number of these has most abounded. Of this fact I became well assured, about thirty years since, when visiting the Atlantic states, with a view to the formation of auxiliary colonization societies, and the selection of the first colonists for Africa. In the city of Charleston, South Carolina, I found more intelligence and character among the free colored population than anywhere else. The same was true of some of those in bondage. A respectable number might be seen in certain parts of the Episcopal churches which I attended using their prayer-books, and joining in the responses of the church. Many purposes of convenience and hospitality were subserved by this encouragement of cultivation in some of the servants, on the part of the owners.

When travelling many years since with a sick wife, and two female relatives, from Charleston to Virginia, at a period of the year when many of the families from the country resort to the town for health, we were kindly urged to call at the seat of one of the first families in South Carolina, and a letter from the mistress, then in the city, was given us, to her servant, who had charge of the house in the absence of the family. On reaching there and delivering the letter to a most respectable-looking female servant, who immediately read it, we were kindly welcomed, and entertained, during a part of two days, as sumptuously as though the owner had been present. We understood that it was no uncommon thing in South Carolina for travellers to be thus entertained by the servants in the absence of the owners, on receiving letters from the same.

Instances of confidential and affectionate relationship between servants and their masters and mistresses, such as are set forth in the following Sketches, are still to be found in all the slave-holding states. I mention one, which has come under my own observation. The late Judge Upshur, of Virginia, had a faithful house-servant (by his will now set free), with whom he used to correspond on matters of business, when he was absent on his circuit. I was dining at his house, some years since, with a number of persons, himself being absent, when the conversation turned on the subject of the presidential election, then going on through the United States, and about which there was an intense interest; when his servant informed us that he had that day received a letter from his master, then on the western shore, in which he stated that the friends of General Harrison might be relieved from all uneasiness, as the returns already received made his election quite certain.

Of course it is not to be supposed that we design to convey the impression that such instances are numerous, the nature of the relationship forbidding it; but we do mean emphatically to affirm that there is far more of kindly and Christian intercourse than many at a distance are apt to believe. That there is a great and sad want of Christian instruction, notwithstanding the more recent efforts put forth to impart it, we most sorrowfully acknowledge.

Bishop Meade adds that these sketches are published with the hope that they might have the effect of turning the attention of ministers and heads of families more seriously to the duty of caring for the souls of their servants.

With regard to the servant of Judge Upshur, spoken of in this communication of Bishop Meade, his master has left, in his last will, the following remarkable tribute to his worth and excellence of character:

I emancipate and set free my servant, David Rice, and direct my executors to give him one hundred dollars. I recommend him in the strongest manner to the respect, esteem and confidence, of any community in which he may happen to live. He has been my slave for twenty-four years, during all which time he has been trusted to every extent, and in every respect; my confidence in him has been unbounded; his relation to myself and family has always been such as to afford him daily opportunities to deceive and injure us, yet he has never been detected in any serious fault, nor even in an unintentional breach of the decorum of his station. His intelligence is of a high order, his integrity above all suspicion, and his sense of right and propriety correct, and even refined. I feel that he is justly entitled to carry this certificate from me in the new relations which he must now form; it is due to his long and most faithful services, and to the sincere and steady friendship which I bear to him In the uninter-

-upted confidential intercourse of twenty-four years, I have never given him, nor had occasion to give him, one unpleasant word. I know no man who has fewer faults or more excellences than he.

In the free states there have been a few instances of such extraordinary piety among negroes, that their biography and sayings have been collected in religious tracts, and published for the instruction of the community.

One of these was, before his conversion, a convict in a state-prison in New York, and there received what was, perhaps, the first religious instruction that had ever been imparted to him. He became so eminent an example of humility, faith, and, above all, fervent love, that his presence in the neighborhood was esteemed a blessing to the church. A lady has described to the writer the manner in which he would stand up and exhort in the church-meetings. for prayer, when, with streaming eyes and the deepest abasement, humbly addressing them as his masters and misses, he would nevertheless pour forth religious exhortations which were edifying to the most cultivated and refined.

In the town of Brunswick, Maine, where the writer lived when writing " Uncle Tom's Cabin," may now be seen the grave of an aged colored woman, named Phebe, who was so eminent for her piety and loveliness of character, that the writer has never heard her name mentioned except with that degree of awe and respect which one would imagine due to a saint. The small cottage where she resided is still visited and looked upon as a sort of shrine, as the spot where old Phebe lived and prayed. Her prayers and pious exhortations were supposed to have been the cause of the conversion of many young people in the place. Notwithstanding that the unchristian feeling of caste prevails as strongly in Maine as anywhere else in New England, and the negro, commonly speaking, is an object of aversion and contempt, yet, so great was the influence of her piety and loveliness of character, that she was uniformly treated with the utmost respect and attention by all classes of people. The most cultivated and intelligent ladies of the place esteemed it a privilege to visit her cottage ; and when she was old and helpless, her wants were most tenderly provided for. When the news of her death was spread abroad in the place, it excited a general and very tender sensation of regret. " We have lost Phebe's prayers," was the remark frequently made afterwards by members of the church, as they met one

another. At her funeral the ex-governor of the state and the professors of the college officiated as pall-bearers, and a sermon was preached in which the many excellences of her Christian character were held up as an example to the community, A small religious tract, containing an account of her life, was published by the American Tract Society, prepared by a lady of Brunswick. The writer recollects that on reading the tract, when she first went to Brunswick, a doubt arose in her mind whether it was not somewhat exaggerated. Some time afterwards she overheard some young persons conversing together about the tract, and saying that they did not think it gave exactly the right idea of Phebe. " Why, is it too highly colored ? " was the inquiry of the author. " O, no, no, indeed," was the earnest response ; " it does n't begin to give an idea of how good she was."

Such instances as these serve to illustrate the words of the apostle, " God hath chosen the foolish things of the world to confound the wise ; and God hath chosen the weak things of the world to confound the things which are mighty."

John Bunyan says that although the valley of humiliation be unattractive in the eyes of the men of this world, yet the very sweetest flowers grow there. So it is with the condition of the lowly and poor in this world. God has often, indeed always, shown a particular regard for it, in selecting from that class the recipients of his grace. It is to be remembered that Jesus Christ, when he came to found the Christian dispensation, did not choose his apostles from the chief priests and the scribes, learned in the law, and high in the church ; nor did he choose them from philosophers and poets, whose educated and comprehensive minds might be supposed best able to appreciate his great designs ; but he chose twelve plain, poor fishermen, who were ignorant, and felt that they were ignorant, and who, therefore, were willing to give themselves up with all simplicity to his guidance. What God asks of the soul more than anything else is faith and simplicity, the affection and reliance of the little child. Even these twelve fancied too much that they were wise, and Jesus was obliged to set a little child in the midst of them, as a more perfect teacher.

The negro race is confessedly more simple, docile, child-like and affectionate, than other races ; and hence the divine graces of love and faith, when in-breathed by the Holy Spirit, find in their natural temperament a more congenial atmosphere.

A last instance parallel with that of Uncle Tom is to be found in the published memoirs of the venerable Josiah Henson, now, as we have said, a clergyman in Canada. He was "raised" in the State of Maryland. His first recollections were of seeing his father muti- lated and covered with blood, suffering the penalty of the law for the crime of raising his hand against a white man,— that white man being the overseer, who had attempted a brutal assault upon his mother. This punish- ment made his father surly and dangerous, and he was subsequently sold south, and thus parted forever from his wife and children. Henson grew up in a state of heathenism, without any religious instruction, till, in a camp-meeting, he first heard of Jesus Christ, and was electrified by the great and thrill- ing news that He had tasted death for every man, the bond as well as the free. This story produced an immediate conversion, such as we read of in the Acts of the Apostles, where the Ethiopian eunuch, from one inter- view, hearing the story of the cross, at once believes and is baptized. Henson forthwith not only became a Christian, but began to declare the news to those about him; and, being a man of great natural force of mind and strength of character, his earnest endeav- ors to enlighten his fellow-heathen were so successful that he was gradually led to assume the station of a negro preacher; and though he could not read a word of the Bible or hymn-book, his labors in this line were much prospered. He became immediately a very valuable slave to his master, and was in- trusted by the latter with the oversight of his whole estate, which he managed with great judgment and prudence. His master appears to have been a very ordinary man in every respect,— to have been entirely in- capable of estimating him in any other light then as exceedingly valuable property, and to have had no other feeling excited by his extraordinary faithfulness than the desire to make the most of him. When his affairs became embarrassed, he formed the design of removing all his negroes into Kentucky, and intrusted the operation entirely to his over- seer. Henson was to take them alone, with- out any other attendant, from Maryland to Kentucky, a distance of some thousands of miles, giving only his promise as a Christian that he would faithfully perform this under- taking. On the way thither they passed through a portion of Ohio, and there Hen- son was informed that he could now secure his own freedom and that of all his fellows, and he was strongly urged to do it. He was exceedingly tempted and tried, but his Christian principle was invulnerable. No inducements could lead him to feel that it was right for a Christian to violate a pledge solemnly given, and his influence over the whole band was so great that he took them all with him into Kentucky. Those casuists among us who lately seem to think and teach that it is right for us to violate the plain commands of God whenever some great national good can be secured by it, would do well to contemplate the inflexible prin- ciple of this poor slave, who, without being able to read a letter of the Bible, was yet enabled to perform this most sublime act of self-renunciation in obedience to its com- mands. Subsequently to this, his master, in a relenting moment, was induced by a friend to sell him his freedom for four hun- dred dollars; but, when the excitement of the importunity had passed off, he regretted that he had suffered so valuable a piece of prop- erty to leave his hands for so slight a remu- neration. By an unworthy artifice, therefore, he got possession of his servant's free papers, and condemned him still to hopeless slavery. Subsequently, his affairs becoming still more involved, he sent his son down the river with a flat-boat loaded with cattle and produce for the New Orleans market, directing him to take Henson along, and sell him after they had sold the cattle and the boat. All the depths of the negro's soul were torn up and thrown into convulsion by this horrible piece of ingratitude, cruelty and injustice; and, while outwardly calm, he was struggling with most bitter temptations from within, which, as he could not read the Bible, he could repel only by a recollection of its sacred truths, and by earnest prayer. As he neared the New Orleans market, he says that these convulsions of soul increased, especially when he met some of his old companions from Kentucky, whose despairing countenances and emaciated forms told of hard work and insufficient food, and confirmed all his worst fears of the lower country. In the trans- ports of his despair, the temptation was more urgently presented to him to murder his young master and the other hand on the flat- boat in their sleep, to seize upon the boat, and make his escape. He thus relates the scene where he was almost brought to the perpetration of this deed:

One dark, rainy night, within a few days of New Orleans, my hour seemed to have come I was alone on the deck; Mr. Amos and the hands were all asleep below, and I crept down noise- lessly, got hold of an axe, entered the cabin, and looking by the aid of the dim light there for my victims, my eye fell upon Master Amos, who was nearest to me; my hand slid along the axe-handle, I raised it to strike the fatal blow, — when suddenly the thought came to me, "What! commit *murder!* and you a Christian?" I had not called it murder before. It was self-defence, — it was preventing others from murdering me, — it was justifiable, it was even praiseworthy. But now, all at once, the truth burst upon me that it was a crime. I was going to kill a young man, who had done nothing to injure me, but obey commands which he could not resist; I was about to lose the fruit of all my efforts at self-improvement, the character I had acquired, and the peace of mind which had never deserted me. All this came upon me instantly, and with a distinctness which made me almost think I heard it whispered in my ear; and I believe I even turned my head to listen. I shrunk back, laid down the axe, crept up on deck again, and thanked God, as I have done every day since, that I had not committed murder.

My feelings were still agitated, but they were changed. I was filled with shame and remorse for the design I had entertained, and with the fear that my companions would detect it in my face, or that a careless word would betray my guilty thoughts. I remained on deck all night, instead of rousing one of the men to relieve me; and nothing brought composure to my mind, but the solemn resolution I then made to resign myself to the will of God, and take with thankfulness, if I could, but with submission, at all events, whatever he might decide should be my lot. I reflected that if my life were reduced to a brief term I should have less to suffer, and that it was better to die with a Christian's hope, and a quiet conscience, than to live with the incessant recollection of a crime that would destroy the value of life, and under the weight of a secret that would crush out the satisfaction that might be expected from freedom, and every other blessing.

Subsequently to this, his young master was taken violently down with the river fever, and became as helpless as a child. He passionately entreated Henson not to desert him, but to attend to the selling of the boat and produce, and put him on board the steamboat, and not to leave him, dead or alive, till he had carried him back to his father.

The young master was borne in the arms of his faithful servant to the steamboat, and there nursed by him with unremitting attention during the journey up the river; nor did he leave him till he had placed him in his father's arms.

Our love for human nature would lead us to add, with sorrow, that all this disinterestedness and kindness was rewarded only by empty praises, such as would be bestowed upon a very fine dog; and Henson indignantly resolved no longer to submit to the injustice. With a degree of prudence, courage and address, which can scarcely find a parallel in any history, he managed, with his wife and two children, to escape into Can-

ada. Here he learned to read, and, by his superior talent and capacity for management, laid the foundation for the fugitive settlement of Dawn, which is understood to be one of the most flourishing in Canada.

It would be well for the most cultivated of us to ask, whether our ten talents in the way of religious knowledge have enabled us to bring forth as much fruit to the glory of God, to withstand temptation as patiently, to return good for evil as disinterestedly, as this poor, ignorant slave. A writer in England has sneeringly remarked that such a man as Uncle Tom might be imported as a missionary to teach the most cultivated in England or America the true nature of religion. These instances show that what has been said with a sneer is in truth a sober verity; and it should never be forgotten that out of this race whom man despiseth have often been chosen of God true messengers of his grace, and temples for the indwelling of his Spirit.

"*For thus saith the high and lofty One that inhabiteth eternity, whose name is Holy, I dwell in the high and holy place, with him also that is of a contrite and humble spirit, to revive the spirit of the humble, and to revive the heart of the contrite ones.*"

The vision attributed to Uncle Tom introduces quite a curious chapter of psychology with regard to the negro race, and indicates a peculiarity which goes far to show how very different they are from the white race. They are possessed of a nervous organization peculiarly susceptible and impressible. Their sensations and impressions are very vivid, and their fancy and imagination lively. In this respect the race has an oriental character, and betrays its tropical origin. Like the Hebrews of old and the oriental nations of the present, they give vent to their emotions with the utmost vivacity of expression, and their whole bodily system sympathizes with the movements of their minds. When in distress, they actually lift up their voices to weep, and "cry with an exceeding bitter cry." When alarmed, they are often paralyzed, and rendered entirely helpless. Their religious exercises are all colored by this sensitive and exceedingly vivacious temperament. Like oriental nations, they incline much to outward expressions, violent gesticulations, and agitating movements of the body. Sometimes, in their religious meetings, they will spring from the floor many times in succession, with a violence and rapidity which is perfectly astonishing.

They will laugh, weep, embrace each other convulsively, and sometimes become entirely paralyzed and cataleptic. A clergyman from the North once remonstrated with a Southern clergyman for permitting such extravagances among his flock. The reply of the Southern minister was, in effect, this: "Sir, I am satisfied that the races are so essentially different that they cannot be regulated by the same rules. I, at first, felt as you do; and, though I saw that genuine conversions did take place, with all this outward manifestation, I was still so much annoyed by it as to forbid it among my negroes, till I was satisfied that the repression of it was a serious hindrance to real religious feeling; and then I became certain that all men cannot be regulated in their religious exercises by one model. I am assured that conversions produced with these accessories are quite as apt to be genuine, and to be as influential over the heart and life, as those produced in any other way." The fact is, that the Anglo-Saxon race — cool, logical and practical — have yet to learn the doctrine of toleration for the peculiarities of other races; and perhaps it was with a foresight of their peculiar character, and dominant position in the earth, that God gave the Bible to them in the fervent language and with the glowing imagery of the more susceptible and passionate oriental races.

Mesmerists have found that the negroes are singularly susceptible to all that class of influences which produce catalepsy, mesmeric sleep, and partial clairvoyant phenomena.

The African race, in their own climate, are believers in spells, in "fetish and obi," in "the evil eye," and other singular influences, for which, probably, there is an origin in this peculiarity of constitution. The magicians in scriptural history were Africans; and the so-called magical arts are still practised in Egypt, and other parts of Africa, with a degree of skill and success which can only be accounted for by supposing peculiarities of nervous constitution quite different from those of the whites. Considering these distinctive traits of the race, it is no matter of surprise to find in their religious histories, when acted upon by the powerful stimulant of the Christian religion, very peculiar features. We are not surprised to find almost constantly, in the narrations of their religious histories, accounts of visions, of heavenly voices, of mysterious sympathies and transmissions of knowledge from heart to heart without the intervention of the senses, or what the Quakers call being "baptized into the spirit" of those who are distant.

Cases of this kind are constantly recurring in their histories. The young man whose story was related to the Boston lady, and introduced above in the chapter on George Harris, stated this incident concerning the recovery of his liberty: That, after the departure of his wife and sister, he, for a long time, and very earnestly, sought some opportunity of escape, but that every avenue appeared to be closed to him. At length, in despair, he retreated to his room, and threw himself upon his bed, resolving to give up the undertaking, when, just as he was sinking to sleep, he was roused by a voice saying in his ear, "Why do you sleep now? Rise up, if you ever mean to be free!" He sprang up, went immediately out, and, in the course of two hours, discovered the means of escape which he used.

A lady whose history is known to the writer resided for some time on a Southern plantation, and was in the habit of imparting religious instruction to the slaves. One day, a woman from a distant plantation called at her residence, and inquired for her. The lady asked, in surprise, "How did you know about me?" The old woman's reply was, that she had long been distressed about her soul; but that, several nights before, some one had appeared to her in a dream, told her to go to this plantation and inquire for the strange lady there, and that she would teach her the way to heaven.

Another specimen of the same kind was related to the writer by a slave-woman who had been through the whole painful experience of a slave's life. She was originally a young girl of pleasing exterior and gentle nature, carefully reared as a seamstress and nurse to the children of a family in Virginia, and attached, with all the warmth of her susceptible nature, to these children. Although one of the tenderest of mothers when the writer knew her, yet she assured the writer that she had never loved a child of her own as she loved the dear little young mistress who was her particular charge. Owing, probably, to some pecuniary difficulty in the family, this girl, whom we will call Louisa, was sold, to go on to a Southern plantation. She has often described the scene when she was forced into a carriage, and saw her dear young mistress leaning from the window, stretching her arms towards her, screaming, and calling her name, with all the vehemence of childish grief. She was carried in a coffle, and sold as cook on a Southern plantation. With the utmost earnestness of language she has described to the writer her utter loneliness, and the distress and despair of her heart, in this situation, parted forever from all she held dear on earth, without even the possibility of writing letters or sending messages, surrounded by those who felt no kind of interest in her, and forced to a toil for which her more delicate education had entirely unfitted her. Under these circumstances, she began to believe that it was for some dreadful sin she had thus been afflicted. The course of her mind after this may be best told in her own simple words:

"After that, I began to feel awful wicked, — O, so wicked, you've no idea! I felt so wicked that my sins seemed like a load on me, and I went so heavy all the day! I felt so wicked that I did n't feel worthy to pray in the house, and I used to go way off in the lot and pray. At last, one day, when I was praying, the Lord he came and spoke to me."

"The Lord spoke to you?" said the writer; "what do you mean, Louisa?"

With a face of the utmost earnestness, she answered, "Why, ma'am, the Lord Jesus he came and spoke to me, you know; and I never, till the last day of my life, shall forget what he said to me."

"What was it?" said the writer.

"He said, 'Fear not, my little one; thy sins are forgiven thee;'" and she added to this some verses, which the writer recognized as those of a Methodist hymn.

Being curious to examine more closely this phenomenon, the author said,

"You mean that you dreamed this, Louisa."

With an air of wounded feeling, and much earnestness, she answered,

"O no, Mrs. Stowe; that never was a dream; you'll never make me believe that."

The thought at once arose in the writer's mind, If the Lord Jesus is indeed everywhere present, and if he is as tender-hearted and compassionate as he was on earth,— and we know he is,— must he not sometimes long to speak to the poor, desolate slave, when he knows that no voice but His can carry comfort and healing to his soul?

This instance of Louisa is so exactly parallel to another case, which the author rec ed from an authentic source, that she is tempted to place the two side by side.

Among the slaves who were brought into the New England States, at the time when slavery was prevalent, was one woman, who, immediately on being told the history of the love of Jesus Christ, exclaimed, "He is the one; this is what I wanted."

This language causing surprise, her history was inquired into. It was briefly this: While living in her simple hut in Africa, the kidnappers one day rushed upon her family, and carried her husband and children off to the slave-ship, she escaping into the woods. On returning to her desolate home, she mourned with the bitterness of "Rachel weeping for her children." For many days her heart was oppressed with a heavy weight of sorrow; and, refusing all sustenance, she wandered up and down the desolate forest.

At last, she says, a strong impulse came over her to kneel down and pour out her sorrows into the ear of some unknown Being whom she fancied to be above her, in the sky.

She did so; and, to her surprise, found an inexpressible sensation of relief. After this, it was her custom daily to go out to this same spot, and supplicate this unknown Friend. Subsequently, she was herself taken, and brought over to America; and, when the story of Jesus and his love was related to her, she immediately felt in her soul that this Jesus was the very friend who had spoken comfort to her yearning spirit in the distant forest of Africa.

Compare now these experiences with the earnest and beautiful language of Paul: "He hath made of one blood all nations of men, for to dwell on all the face of the earth; and hath determined the times before appointed *and the bounds* of their habitation, *that* THEY SHOULD *seek the Lord, if haply they might* FEEL AFTER HIM AND FIND HIM, *though he be not far from every one of us.*"

Is not this truly "*feeling after God and finding Him*"? And may we not hope that the yearning, troubled, helpless heart of man, pressed by the insufferable anguish of this short life, or wearied by its utter vanity, never extends its ignorant, pleading hand to God in vain? Is not the veil which divides us from an almighty and most merciful Father much thinner than we, in the pride of our philosophy, are apt to imagine? and is it not the most worthy conception of Him to suppose that the more utterly helpless and ignorant the human being is that seeks His aid, the more tender and the more condescending will be His communication with that soul?

If a mother has among her children one whom sickness has made blind, or deaf, or dumb, incapable of acquiring knowledge through the usual channels of communication, does she not seek to reach its darkened mind by modes of communication tenderer and more intimate than those which she uses with the stronger and more favored ones? But can the love of any mother be compared with the infinite love of Jesus? Has He not described himself as that good Shepherd who leaves the whole flock of secure and well-instructed ones, to follow over the mountains of sin and ignorance the one lost sheep; and, when He hath found it, rejoicing more over that one than over the ninety and nine that went not astray? Has He not told us that each of these little ones has a guardian angel that doth always behold the face of his Father which is in heaven? And is it not comforting to us to think that His love and care will be in proportion to the ignorance and the wants of His chosen ones?

*　　*　　*　　*　　*　　*

Since the above was prepared for the press the author has received the following extract from a letter written by a gentleman in Missouri to the editor of the *Oberlin* (Ohio) *Evangelist:*

I really thought, while reading "Uncle Tom's Cabin," that the authoress, when describing the character of Tom, had in her mind's eye a slave whose acquaintance I made some years since, in the State of Mississippi, called "Uncle Jacob." I was staying a day or two with a planter, and in the evening, when out in the yard, I heard a well-known hymn and tune sung in one of the "quarters," and then the voice of prayer; and O, *such* a prayer! what fervor, what unction, — nay, the man "prayed right up;" and when I read of Uncle Tom, how "nothing could exceed the touching simplicity, the childlike earnestness, of his prayer, enriched with the language of Scripture, which seemed so entirely to have wrought itself into his being as to have become a part of himself," the recollections of that evening prayer were strangely vivid. On entering the house and referring to what I had heard, his master replied, "Ah, sir, if I covet anything in this world, it is Uncle Jacob's religion. If there is a good man on earth, he certainly is one." He said Uncle Jacob was a regulator on the plantation; that a *word*, or a *look* from him, addressed to younger slaves, had more efficacy than a *blow* from the overseer.

The next morning Uncle Jacob informed me he was from Kentucky, opposite Cincinnati; that his opportunities for attending religious worship had been frequent; that at about the age of forty he was sold south, was set to picking cotton; could not, when doing his best, pick the task assigned him; was whipped and whipped, he could not possibly tell how often; was of the opinion that the overseer came to the conclusion that

whipping could not bring one more pound out of him, for he set him to driving a team. At this and other work he could "make a *hand;*" had changed owners three or four times. He expressed himself as well pleased with his present situation as he expected to be in the South, but was yearning to return to his former associations in Kentucky.

CHAPTER VII.

MISS OPHELIA.

MISS OPHELIA stands as the representative of a numerous class of the very best of Northern people; to whom, perhaps, if our Lord should again address his churches a letter, as he did those of old time, he would use the same words as then: "I know thy works, and thy labor, and thy patience, and how thou canst not bear them which are evil; and thou hast tried them which are apostles and are not, and hast found them liars: and hast borne, and hast patience, and for my name's sake hast labored and hast not fainted. Nevertheless, I have somewhat against thee, because thou hast left thy first love."

There are in this class of people activity, zeal, unflinching conscientiousness, clear intellectual discriminations between truth and error, and great logical and doctrinal correctness; but there is a want of that spirit of love, without which, in the eye of Christ, the most perfect character is as deficient as a wax flower — wanting in life and perfume.

Yet this blessed principle is not dead in their hearts, but only sleepeth; and so great is the real and genuine goodness, that, when the true magnet of divine love is applied, they always answer to its touch.

So when the gentle Eva, who is an impersonation in childish form of the love of Christ, solves at once, by a blessed instinct, the problem which Ophelia has long been unable to solve by dint of utmost hammering and vehement effort, she at once, with a good and honest heart, perceives and acknowledges her mistake, and is willing to learn even of a little child.

Miss Ophelia, again, represents one great sin, of which, unconsciously, American Christians have allowed themselves to be guilty. Unconsciously it must be, for nowhere is conscience so predominant as among this class, and nowhere is there a more honest strife to bring every thought into captivity to the obedience of Christ.

One of the first and most declared objects of the gospel has been to break down all those irrational barriers and prejudices which separate the human brotherhood into diverse and contending clans. Paul says, "In Christ Jesus there is neither Jew nor Greek, barbarian, Scythian, bond nor free." The Jews at that time were separated from the Gentiles by an insuperable wall of prejudice. They could not eat and drink together, nor pray together. But the apostles most earnestly labored to show them the sin of this prejudice. St. Paul says to the Ephesians, speaking of this former division, " He is our peace, who hath made both one, and hath broken down the middle wall of partition between us."

It is very easy to see that although slavery has been abolished in the New England States, it has left behind it the most baneful feature of the system — that which makes American worse than Roman slavery — the prejudice of caste and color. In the New England States the negro has been treated as belonging to an inferior race of beings : — forced to sit apart by himself in the place of worship; his children excluded from the schools; himself excluded from the railroad-car and the omnibus, and the peculiarities of his race made the subject of bitter contempt and ridicule.

This course of conduct has been justified by saying that they are a degraded race. But how came they degraded ? Take any class of men, and shut them from the means of education, deprive them of hope and self-respect, close to them all avenues of honorable ambition, and you will make just such a race of them as the negroes have been among us.

So singular and so melancholy is the dominion of prejudice over the human mind, that professors of Christianity in our New England States have often, with very serious self-denial to themselves, sent the gospel to heathen as dark-complexioned as the Africans, when in their very neighborhood were persons of dark complexion, who, on that account, were forbidden to send their children to the schools, and discouraged from entering the churches. The effect of this has been directly to degrade and depress the race, and then this very degradation and depression has been pleaded as the reason for continuing this course.

Not long since the writer called upon a benevolent lady, and during the course of the call the conversation turned upon the incidents of a fire which had occurred the night before in the neighborhood. A deserted house had been burned to the ground.

The lady said it was supposed it had been set on fire. "What could be any one's motive for setting it on fire?" said the writer.

"Well," replied the lady, "it was supposed that a colored family was about to move into it, and it was thought that the neighborhood would n't consent to that. So it was supposed that was the reason."

This was said with an air of innocence and much unconcern.

The writer inquired, " Was it a family of bad character ?"

" No, not particularly, that I know of," said the lady; " but then they are negroes, you know."

Now, this lady is a very pious lady. She probably would deny herself to send the gospel to the heathen, and if she had ever thought of considering this family a heathen family, would have felt the deepest interest in their welfare; because on the subject of duty to the heathen she had been frequently instructed from the pulpit, and had all her religious and conscientious sensibilities awake. Probably she had never listened from the pulpit to a sermon which should exhibit the great truth, that " in Christ Jesus there is neither Jew nor Greek, barbarian, Scythian, bond nor free."

Supposing our Lord was now on earth, as he was once, what course is it probable that he would pursue with regard to this unchristian prejudice of color ?

There was a class of men in those days as much despised by the Jews as the negroes are by us; and it was a complaint made of Christ that he was a friend of publicans and sinners. And if Christ should enter, on some communion season, into a place of worship, and see the colored man sitting afar off by himself, would it not be just in his spirit to go there and sit with him, rather than to take the seats of his richer and more prosperous brethren ?

It is, however, but just to our Northern Christians to say that this sin has been committed ignorantly and in unbelief, and that within a few years signs of a much better spirit have begun to manifest themselves. In some places, recently, the doors of school-houses have been thrown open to the children, and many a good Miss Ophelia has opened her eyes in astonishment to find that, while she has been devouring the *Missionary Herald*, and going without butter on her bread and sugar in her tea to send the gospel to the Sandwich Islands, there is a very thriving colony of heathen in her own neighborhood at home; and, true to her own good and honest heart, she has resolved, *not* to give up her prayers and efforts for the heathen abroad, but to add thereunto labors for the heathen at home.

Our safety and hope in this matter is this: that there are multitudes in all our churches who do most truly and sincerely love Christ above all things, and who, just so soon as a little reflection shall have made them sensible of their duty in this respect, will most earnestly perform it.

It is true that, if they do so, they may be called Abolitionists; but the true Miss Ophelia is not afraid of a hard name in a good cause, and has rather learned to consider "the reproach of Christ a greater treasure than the riches of Egypt."

That there is much already for Christians to do in enlightening the moral sense of the community on this subject, will appear if we consider that even so well-educated and gentlemanly a man as Frederick Douglass was recently obliged to pass the night on the deck of a steamer, when in delicate health, because this senseless prejudice deprived him of a place in the cabin; and that that very laborious and useful minister, Dr. Pennington, of New York, has, during the last season, been often obliged seriously to endanger his health, by walking to his pastoral labors, over his very extended parish, under a burning sun, because he could not be allowed the common privilege of the omnibus, which conveys every class of white men, from the most refined to the lowest and most disgusting.

Let us consider now the number of professors of the religion of Christ in New York, and consider also that, by the very fact of their profession, they consider Dr. Pennington the brother of their Lord, and a member with them of the body of Christ.

Now, these Christians are influential, rich and powerful; they can control public sentiment on any subject that they think of any particular importance, and they profess, by their religion, that "if one member suffers, all the members suffer with it."

It is a serious question, whether such a marked indignity offered to Christ and his ministry, in the person of a colored brother, without any remonstrance on their part, will not lead to a general feeling that all that the Bible says about the union of Christians is a mere hollow sound, and means nothing.

Those who are anxious to do something directly to improve the condition of the slave, can do it in no way so directly as by elevat-ing the condition of the free colored people around them, and taking every pains to give them equal rights and privileges.

This unchristian prejudice has doubtless stood in the way of the emancipation of hundreds of slaves. The slave-holder, feeling and acknowledging the evils of slavery, has come to the North, and seen evidences of this unkindly and unchristian state of feeling towards the slave, and has thus reflected within himself:

"If I keep my slave at the South, he is, it is true, under the dominion of a very severe law; but then he enjoys the advantage of my friendship and assistance, and derives, through his connection with me and my family, some kind of a position in the community. As my servant he is allowed a seat in the car and a place at the table. But if I emancipate and send him North, he will encounter substantially all the disadvantages of slavery, with no master to protect him."

This mode of reasoning has proved an apology to many a man for keeping his slaves in a position which he confesses to be a bad one; and it will be at once perceived that, should the position of the negro be conspicuously reversed in our northern states, the effect upon the emancipation of the slave would be very great. They, then, who keep up this prejudice, may be said to be, in a certain sense, slave-holders.

It is not meant by this that all distinctions of society should be broken over, and that people should be obliged to choose their intimate associates from a class unfitted by education and habits to sympathize with them.

The negro should not be lifted out of his sphere of life because he is a negro, but he should be treated with Christian courtesy in his sphere. In the railroad car, in the omnibus and steamboat, all ranks and degrees of white persons move with unquestioned freedom side by side; and Christianity requires that the negro have the same privilege.

That the dirtiest and most uneducated foreigner or American, with breath redolent of whiskey and clothes foul and disordered, should have an unquestioned right to take a seat next to any person in a railroad car or steamboat, and that the respectable, decent and gentlemanly negro should be excluded simply because he is a negro, cannot be considered otherwise than as an irrational and unchristian thing: and any Christian who allows such things done in his presence without remonstrance, and the use of his Christian influence, will certainly be made deeply sensible of his error when he comes at last to direct and personal interview with his Lord.

There is no hope for this matter, if the love of Christ is not strong enough, and if it cannot be said, with regard to the two races, "He is our peace who hath made both one, and hath broken down the middle wall of partition between us."

The time is coming rapidly when the upper classes in society must learn that their education, wealth and refinement, are not their own; that they have no right to use them for their own selfish benefit; but that they should hold them rather, as Fenelon expresses it, as "a ministry," a stewardship, which they hold in trust for the benefit of their poorer brethren.

In some of the very highest circles in England and America we begin to see illustrious examples of the commencement of such a condition of things.

One of the merchant princes of Boston, whose funeral has lately been celebrated in our city, afforded in his life a beautiful example of this truth. His wealth was the wealth of thousands. He was the steward of the widow and the orphan. His funds were a savings bank, wherein were laid up the resources of the poor; and the mourners at his funeral were the scholars of the schools which he had founded, the officers of literary institutions which his munificence had endowed, the widows and orphans whom he had counselled and supported, and the men, in all ranks and conditions of life, who had been made by his benevolence to feel that his wealth was their wealth. May God raise up many men in Boston to enter into the spirit and labors of Amos Lawrence!

This is the *true* socialism, which comes from the spirit of Christ, and, without breaking down existing orders of society, *by love* makes the property and possessions of the higher class the property of the lower.

Men are always seeking to begin their reforms with the *outward* and *physical.* Christ begins his reforms in the heart. Men would break up all ranks of society, and throw all property into a common stock; but Christ would inspire the higher class with that Divine Spirit by which all the wealth and means and advantages of their position are used for the good of the lower.

We see, also, in the highest aristocracy of England, instances of the same tendency.

Among her oldest nobility there begin to arise lecturers to mechanics and patrons of ragged schools; and it is said that even on the throne of England is a woman who weekly instructs her class of Sunday-school scholars from the children in the vicinity of her country residence.

In this way, and not by an outward and physical division of property, shall all things be had in common. And when the white race shall regard their superiority over the colored one only as a talent intrusted for the advantage of their weaker brother, *then* will the prejudice of caste melt away in the light of Christianity.

CHAPTER VIII.

MARIE ST. CLARE.

MARIE ST. CLARE is the type of a class of women not peculiar to any latitude, nor any condition of society. She may be found in England or in America. In the northern free states we have many Marie St. Clares, more or less fully developed.

When found in a northern latitude, she is forever in trouble about her domestic relations. Her servants never do anything right. Strange to tell, they are not perfect, and she thinks it a very great shame. She is fully convinced that she ought to have every moral and Christian virtue in her kitchen for a little less than the ordinary wages; and when her cook leaves her, because she finds she can get better wages and less work in a neighboring family, she thinks it shockingly selfish, unprincipled conduct. She is of opinion that servants ought to be perfectly disinterested; that they ought to be willing to take up with the worst rooms in the house, with very moderate wages, and very indifferent food, when they can get much better elsewhere, purely for the sake of pleasing her. She likes to get hold of foreign servants, who have not yet learned our ways, who are used to working for low wages, and who will be satisfied with almost anything; but she is often heard to lament that they soon get spoiled, and want as many privileges as anybody else,— which is perfectly shocking. Marie often wishes that she could be a slave-holder, or could live somewhere where the lower class are kept down, and made to know their place. She is always hunting for cheap seamstresses, and will tell you, in an under-tone, that she has discovered a woman who will make linen shirts beautifully, stitch the collars and wristbands twice, all for thirty-seven cents.

when many seamstresses get a dollar for it; says she does it because she's poor, and has no friends; thinks you had better be careful in your conversation, and not let her know what prices are, or else she will get spoiled, and go to raising her price,—these sewing-women are so selfish. When Marie St. Clare has the misfortune to live in a free state, there is no end to her troubles. Her cook is always going off for better wages and more comfortable quarters; her chamber-maid, strangely enough, won't agree to be chambermaid and seamstress both for half wages, and so she deserts. Marie's kitchen-cabinet, therefore, is always in a state of revolution; and she often declares, with affecting earnestness, that servants are the torment of her life. If her husband endeavor to remonstrate, or suggest another mode of treatment, he is a hard-hearted, unfeeling man; "he does n't love her, and she always knew he did n't;" and so he is disposed of.

But, when Marie comes under a system of laws which gives her absolute control over her dependants,—which enables her to separate them, at her pleasure, from their dearest family connections, or to inflict upon them the most disgraceful and violent punishments, without even the restraint which seeing the execution might possibly produce, —then it is that the character arrives at full maturity. Human nature is no worse at the South than at the North; but law at the South distinctly provides for and protects the worst abuses to which that nature is liable.

It is often supposed that domestic servitude in slave states is a kind of paradise; that house-servants are invariably pets; that young mistresses are always fond of their "mammies," and young masters always handsome, good-natured and indulgent.

Let any one in Old England or New England look about among their immediate acquaintances, and ask how many there are who would use absolute despotic power amiably in a family, especially over a class degraded by servitude, ignorant, indolent, deceitful, provoking, as slaves almost necessarily are, and always must be.

Let them look into their own hearts, and ask themselves if they would dare to be trusted with such a power. Do they not find in themselves temptations to be unjust to those who are inferiors and dependants? Do they not find themselves tempted to be irritable and provoked, when the service of their families is negligently performed?

And, if they had the power to inflict cruel punishments, or to have them inflicted by sending the servant out to some place of correction, would they not be tempted to use that liberty?

With regard to those degrading punishments to which females are subjected, by being sent to professional whippers, or by having such functionaries sent for to the house,—as John Caphart testifies that he has often been, in Baltimore,—what can be said of their influence both on the superior and on the inferior class? It is very painful indeed to contemplate this subject. The mind instinctively shrinks from it; but still it is a very serious question whether it be not our duty to encounter this pain, that our sympathies may be quickened into more active exercise. For this reason, we give here the testimony of a gentleman whose accuracy will not be doubted, and who subjected himself to the pain of being an eye-witness to a scene of this kind in the calaboose in New Orleans. As the reader will perceive from the account, it was a scene of such every-day occurrence as not to excite any particular remark, or any expression of sympathy from those of the same condition and color with the sufferer.

When our missionaries first went to India, it was esteemed a duty among Christian nations to make themselves acquainted with the cruelties and atrocities of idolatrous worship, as a means of quickening our zeal to send them the gospel.

If it be said that we in the free states have no such interest in slavery, as we do not support it, and have no power to prevent it, it is replied that slavery does exist in the District of Columbia, which belongs to the whole United States; and that the free states are, before God, guilty of the crime of continuing it there, unless they will honestly do what in them lies for its extermination.

The subjoined account was written by the benevolent Dr. Howe, whose labors in behalf of the blind have rendered his name dear to humanity, and was sent in a letter to the Hon. Charles Sumner. If any one think it too painful to be perused, let him ask himself if God will hold those guiltless who suffer a system to continue, the details of which they cannot even read. That this describes a common scene in the calaboose, we shall by and by produce other witnesses to show.

I have passed ten days in New Orleans, not unprofitably, I trust, in examining the public institutions, — the schools, asylums, hospitals, prisons, &c. With the exception of the first, there is little hope of amelioration. I know not how much merit there may be in their system; but I do know that, in the administration of the penal code, there are abominations which should bring down the fate of Sodom upon the city. If Howard or Mrs. Fry ever discovered so ill-administered a den of thieves as the New Orleans prison, they never described it. In the negro's apartment I saw much which made me blush that I was a white man, and which, for a moment, stirred up an evil spirit in my animal nature. Entering a large paved court-yard, around which ran galleries filled with slaves of all ages, sexes and colors, I heard the snap of a whip, every stroke of which sounded like the sharp crack of a pistol. I turned my head, and beheld a sight which absolutely chilled me to the marrow of my bones, and gave me, for the first time in my life, the sensation of my hair stiffening at the roots. There lay a black girl flat upon her face, on a board, her two thumbs tied, and fastened to one end, her feet tied, and drawn tightly to the other end, while a strap passed over the small of her back, and, fastened around the board, compressed her closely to it. Below the strap she was entirely naked. By her side, and six feet off, stood a huge negro, with a long whip, which he applied with dreadful power and wonderful precision. Every stroke brought away a strip of skin, which clung to the lash, or fell quivering on the pavement, while the blood followed after it. The poor creature writhed and shrieked, and, in a voice which showed alike her fear of death and her dreadful agony, screamed to her master, who stood at her head, " O, spare my life! don't cut my soul out!" But still fell the horrid lash; still strip after strip peeled off from the skin; gash after gash was cut in her living flesh, until it became a livid and bloody mass of raw and quivering muscle. It was with the greatest difficulty I refrained from springing upon the torturer, and arresting his lash; but, alas! what could I do, but turn aside to hide my tears for the sufferer, and my blushes for humanity! This was in a public and regularly-organized prison; the punishment was one recognized and authorized by the law. But think you the poor wretch had committed a heinous offence, and had been convicted thereof, and sentenced to the lash! Not at all. She was brought by her master to be whipped by the common executioner, without trial, judge or jury, just at his beck or nod, for some real or supposed offence, or to gratify his own whim or malice. And he may bring her day after day, without cause assigned, and inflict any number of lashes he pleases, short of twenty-five, provided only he pays the fee. Or, if he choose, he may have a private whipping-board on his own premises, and brutalize himself there. A shocking part of this horrid punishment was its publicity, as I have said; it was in a court-yard surrounded by galleries, which were filled with colored persons of all sexes, — runaway slaves, committed for some crime, or slaves up for sale. You would naturally suppose they crowded forward, and gazed, horror-stricken, at the brutal spectacle below; but they did not; many of them hardly noticed it, and many were entirely indifferent to it. They went on in their childish pursuits, and some were laughing outright in the distant parts of the galleries; so low can man, created in God's image, be sunk in brutality.

CHAPTER IX.

ST. CLARE.

IT is with pleasure that we turn from the dark picture just presented, to the character of the generous and noble-hearted St. Clare, wherein the fairest picture of our Southern brother is presented.

It has been the writer's object to separate carefully, as far as possible, the system from the men. It is her sincere belief that, while the irresponsible power of slavery is such that no human being ought ever to possess it, probably that power was never exercised more leniently than in many cases in the Southern States. She has been astonished to see how, under all the disadvantages which attend the early possession of arbitrary power, all the temptations which every reflecting mind must see will arise from the possession of this power in various forms, there are often developed such fine and interesting traits of character. To say that these cases are common, alas! is not in our power. Men know human nature too well to believe us, if we should. But the more dreadful the evil to be assailed, the more careful should we be to be just in our apprehensions, and to balance the horror which certain abuses must necessarily excite, by a consideration of those excellent and redeeming traits which are often found in individuals connected with the system.

The twin brothers, Alfred and Augustine St. Clare, represent two classes of men which are to be found in all countries. They are the radically aristocratic and democratic men. The aristocrat by position is not always the aristocrat by nature, and *vice versa;* but the aristocrat by nature, whether he be in a higher or lower position in society, is he who, though he may be just, generous and humane, to those whom he considers his equals, is entirely insensible to the wants, and sufferings, and common humanity, of those whom he considers the lower orders. The sufferings of a countess would make him weep; the sufferings of a seamstress are quite another matter.

On the other hand, the democrat is often found in the highest position of life. To this man, superiority to his brother is a thing which he can never boldly and nakedly assert without a secret pain. In the lowest and humblest walk of life, he acknowledges the sacredness of a common humanity; and however degraded by the opinions and institutions of society any particular class may be, there is an instinctive feeling in his soul which teaches him that they are *men* of like passions with himself. Such men have a penetration which at once sees through all the false shows of outward custom which make one man so dissimilar to another, to those great generic capabilities, sorrows, wants and weaknesses, wherein all men and women are alike; and there is no such thing as making them realize that one order of human beings have any prescriptive right over another order, or that the tears and sufferings of one are not just as good as those of another order.

That such men are to be found at the South in the relation of slave-masters, that when so found they cannot and will not be deluded by any of the shams and sophistry wherewith slavery has been defended, that they look upon it as a relic of a barbarous age, and utterly scorn and contemn all its apologists, we can abundantly show. Many of the most illustrious Southern men of the Revolution were of this class, and many men of distinguished position of later day have entertained the same sentiments.

Witness the following letter of Patrick Henry, the sentiments of which are so much an echo of those of St. Clare that the reader might suppose one to be a copy of the other:

LETTER OF PATRICK HENRY.

Hanover, January 18*th,* 1773.

DEAR SIR: I take this opportunity to acknowledge the receipt of Anthony Benezet's book against the slave-trade; I thank you for it. Is it not a little surprising that the professors of Christianity, whose chief excellence consists in softening the human heart, in cherishing and improving its finer feelings, should encourage a practice so totally repugnant to the first impressions of right and wrong? What adds to the wonder is, that this abominable practice has been introduced in the most enlightened ages. Times that seem to have pretensions to boast of high improvements in the arts and sciences; and refined morality, have brought into general use, and guarded by many laws, a species of violence and tyranny which our more rude and barbarous, but more honest ancestors detested. Is it not amazing that at a time when the rights of humanity are defined and understood with precision, in a country above all others fond of liberty, — that in such an age and in such a country we find men professing a religion the most mild, humane, gentle and generous, adopting such a principle, as repugnant to humanity as it is inconsistent with the Bible, and destructive to liberty! Every thinking, honest

man rejects it in speculation. How free in practice from conscientious motives!

Would any one believe that I am master of slaves of my own purchase? I am drawn along by the general inconvenience of living here without them. I will not, I cannot, justify it. However culpable my conduct, I will so far pay my devoir to virtue as to own the excellence and rectitude of her precepts, and lament my want of conformity to them.

I believe a time will come when an opportunity will be offered to abolish this lamentable evil. Everything we can do is to improve it, if it happens in our day; if not, let us transmit to our descendants, together with our slaves, a pity for their unhappy lot, and an abhorrence for slavery. If we cannot reduce this wished-for reformation to practice, let us treat the unhappy victims with lenity. It is the furthest advance we can make towards justice. It is a debt we owe to the purity of our religion, to show that it is at variance with that law which warrants slavery.

I know not when to stop. I could say many things on the subject, a serious view of which gives *a gloomy prospect to future times!*

What a sorrowful thing it is that such men live an inglorious life, drawn along by the general current of society, when they ought to be its regenerators! Has God endowed them with such nobleness of soul, such clearness of perception, for nothing? Should they, to whom he has given superior powers of insight and feeling, live as all the world live?

Southern men of this class have often risen up to reprove the men of the North, when they are drawn in to apologize for the system of slavery. Thus, on one occasion, a representative from one of the northern states, a gentleman now occupying the very highest rank of distinction and official station, used in Congress the following language:

The great relation of servitude, in some form or other, with greater or less departure from the theoretic equality of men, is inseparable from our nature. Domestic slavery is not, in my judgment, to be set down as an immoral or irreligious relation. The slaves of this country are better clothed and fed than the peasantry of some of the most prosperous states of Europe.

He was answered by Mr. Mitchell, of Tennessee, in these words:

Sir, I do not go the length of the gentleman from Massachusetts, and hold that the existence of slavery in this country is almost a blessing. On the contrary, I am firmly settled in the opinion that it is a great curse, — one of the greatest that could have been interwoven in our system. I, Mr. Chairman, am one of those whom these poor wretches call masters. I do not task them; I feed and clothe them well; but yet, alas! they are slaves, and slavery is a curse in any shape. It is no doubt true that there are persons in Europe far more degraded than our slaves, — worse fed, worse clothed, &c.; but, sir, this is far from proving that negroes ought to be slaves.

The celebrated John Randolph, of Roanoke, said in Congress, on one occasion:

Sir, I envy neither the heart nor the head of that man from the North who rises here to defend slavery on principle.

The following lines from the will of this eccentric man show that this clear sense of justice, which is a gift of superior natures, at last produced some appropriate fruits in practice:

I give to my slaves their freedom, to which my conscience tells me they are justly entitled. It has a long time been a matter of the deepest regret to me, that the circumstances under which I inherited them, and the obstacles thrown in the way by the laws of the land, have prevented my emancipating them in my life-time, which it is my full intention to do in case I can accomplish it.

The influence on such minds as these of that kind of theological teaching which prevails in the majority of pulpits at the South, and which justifies slavery directly from the Bible, cannot be sufficiently regretted. Such men are shocked to find their spiritual teachers less conscientious than themselves; and if the Biblical argument succeeds in bewildering them, it produces scepticism with regard to the Bible itself. Professor Stowe states that, during his residence in Ohio, he visited at the house of a gentleman who had once been a Virginian planter, and during the first years of his life was an avowed sceptic. He stated that his scepticism was entirely referable to this one cause,— that his minister had constructed a scriptural argument in defence of slavery which he was unable to answer, and that his moral sense was so shocked by the idea that the Bible defended such an atrocious system, that he became an entire unbeliever, and so continued until he came under the ministration of a clergyman in Ohio, who succeeded in presenting to him the true scriptural view of the subject. He immediately threw aside his scepticism, and became a member of a Christian church.

So we hear the *Baltimore Sun*, a paper in a slave state, and no way suspected of leaning towards abolitionism, thus scornfully disposing of the scriptural argument:

Messrs. Burgess, Taylor & Co., Sun Iron Building, send us a copy of a work of imposing exterior, a handsome work of nearly six hundred pages, from the pen of Rev. Josiah Priest, A.M., and published by Rev. W. S. Brown, M.D.,

at Glasgow, Kentucky, the copy before us conveying the assurance that it is the "fifth edition — stereotyped." And we have no doubt it is ; and the *fiftieth* edition may be published ; but it will amount to nothing, for there is nothing in it. The book comprises the usually quoted facts associated with the history of slavery as recorded in the Scriptures, accompanied by the opinions and arguments of *another* man in relation thereto. And this sort of thing may go on to the end of time. It can accomplish nothing towards the perpetuation of slavery. The book is called "Bible Defence of Slavery ; and Origin, Fortunes, and History, of the Negro Race." Bible defence of slavery! There is no such thing as a Bible defence of slavery at the present day. Slavery in the United States is a social institution, originating in the convenience and cupidity of our ancestors, existing by state laws and recognized to a certain extent — for the recovery of slave property — by the constitution. And nobody would pretend that, if it were inexpedient and unprofitable for any man or any state to continue to hold slaves, they would be bound to do so, on the ground of a "Bible defence" of it. Slavery is recorded in the Bible, and approved, with many degrading characteristics. War is recorded in the Bible, and approved, under what seems to us the extreme of cruelty. But are slavery and war to *endure* forever, because we find them in the Bible? Or, are they to *cease* at once and forever, because the Bible inculcates peace and brotherhood?

The book before us exhibits great research, but is obnoxious to severe criticism, on account of its gratuitous assumptions. The writer is constantly assuming this, that, and the other. In a work of this sort, a "doubtless" this, and "no doubt" the other, and "such is our belief," with respect to important premises, will not be acceptable to the intelligent reader. Many of the positions assumed are ludicrous ; and the fancy of the writer runs to exuberance in putting words and speeches into the mouths of the ancients, predicated upon the brief record of Scripture history. The argument from the *curse of Ham* is not worth the paper it is written upon. It is just equivalent to that of *Blackwood's Magazine*, we remember examining some years since, in reference to the admission of Rothschild to Parliament. The writer maintained the religious obligation of the *Christian* public to perpetuate the political disabilities of the Jews, because it would be resisting the Divine will to remove them, in view of the "curse" which the aforesaid Christian Pharisee understood to be levelled against the sons of Abraham. Admitting that God has cursed both the Jewish race and the descendants of Ham, He is able to fulfil His purpose, though the "rest of mankind" should in all things act up to the benevolent precepts of the "Divine law." *Man* may very safely cultivate the highest principles of the Christian dispensation, and leave God to work out the fulfilment of His *curse*.

According to the same book and the same logic, all mankind being under a "curse," none of us ought to work out any alleviation for ourselves, and we are sinning heinously in harnessing steam to the performance of manual labor, cutting wheat by McCormick's *diablerie*, and laying hold of the lightning to carry our messages for us, instead of footing it ourselves as our father Adam did. With a little more common sense, and much less of the uncommon sort, we should better understand Scripture, the institutions under which we live, the several rights of our fellow-citizens in all sections of the country, and the good, sound, practical, social relations, which ought to contribute infinitely more than they do to the happiness of mankind.

If the reader wishes to know what kind of preaching it is that St. Clare alludes to, when he says he can learn what is quite as much to the purpose from the *Picayune*, and that such scriptural expositions of their peculiar relations don't edify him much, he is referred to the following extract from a sermon preached in New Orleans, by the Rev. Theophilus Clapp. Let our reader now imagine that he sees St. Clare seated in the front slip, waggishly taking notes of the following specimen of ethics and humanity.

Let all Christian teachers show our servants the importance of being submissive, obedient, industrious, honest and faithful to the interests of their masters. Let their minds be filled with sweet anticipations of rest eternal beyond the grave. Let them be trained to direct their views to that fascinating and glorious futurity, where the sins, sorrows, and troubles of earth, will be contemplated under the aspect of means indispensable to our everlasting progress in knowledge, virtue and happiness. I would say to every slave in the United States, "You should realize that a wise, kind, and merciful Providence has appointed for you your condition in life; and, all things considered, you could not be more eligibly situated. The burden of your care, toils and responsibilities, is much lighter than that which God has imposed on your master. The most enlightened philanthropists, with unlimited resources, could not place you in a situation more favorable to your present and everlasting welfare than that which you now occupy. You have your troubles. So have all. Remember how evanescent are the pleasures and joys of human life."

But, as Mr. Clapp will not, perhaps, be accepted as a representation of orthodoxy, let him be supposed to listen to the following declarations of the Rev. James Smylie, a clergyman of great influence in the Presbyterian church, in a tract upon slavery, which he states in the introduction to have been written with particular reference to removing the conscientious scruples of religious people in Mississippi and Louisiana, with regard to its propriety.

If I believed, or was of opinion, that it was the legitimate tendency of the gospel to abolish slavery, how would I approach a man, possessing as many slaves as Abraham had, and tell him I wished to obtain his permission to preach to his slaves?

Suppose the man to be ignorant of the gospel, and that he would inquire of me what was my object. I would tell him candidly (and every minister ought to be candid) that I wished to preach the gospel, because its legitimate tendency is to make his slaves honest, trusty and faithful; not serving "with eye service, as men pleasers," "not purloining, but showing all good fidelity." "And is this," he would ask, "really the tendency of the gospel?" I would answer, Yes. Then I might expect that a man who had a thousand slaves, if he believed me, would not only permit me to preach to his slaves, but would do more. He would be willing to build me a house, furnish me a garden, and ample provision for a support. Because, he would conclude, *verily, that this preacher would be worth more to him than a dozen overseers*. But, suppose, then, he would tell me that he had understood that the tendency of the gospel was to abolish slavery, and inquire of me if that was the fact. Ah! this is the rub. He has now cornered me. What shall I say? Shall I, like a dishonest man, twist and dodge, and shift and turn, to evade an answer? No. I must, Kentuckian like, come out, *broad, flat-footed*, and tell him that *abolition is the tendency of the gospel*. What am I now to calculate upon? I have told the man that it is the tendency of the gospel to make him so poor as to oblige him to take hold of the maul and wedge himself; he must catch, curry, and saddle his own horse; he must black his own *brogans* (for he will not be able to buy boots). His wife must go, herself, to the washtub, take hold of the scrubbing-broom, wash the pots, and cook all that she and her rail mauler will eat.

Query. — Is it to be expected that a master ignorant heretofore of the tendency of the gospel would fall so desperately in love with it, from a knowledge of its tendency, that he would encourage the preaching of it among his slaves? Verily, NO.

But suppose, when he put the last question to me, as to its tendency, I *could* and *would*, without a twist or quibble, tell him, *plainly* and *candidly*, that it was a slander on the gospel to say that emancipation or abolition was its legitimate tendency. I would tell him that the commandments of *some* men, and not the commandments of God, made slavery a sin. — *Smylie on Slavery*, p. 71.

One can imagine the expression of countenance and tone of voice with which St. Clare would receive such expositions of the gospel. It is to be remarked that this tract does not contain the opinions of one man only, but that it has in its appendix a letter from two ecclesiastical bodies of the Presbyterian church, substantially endorsing its sentiments.

Can any one wonder that a man like St. Clare should put such questions as these? "Is what you hear at church religion? Is that which can bend and turn, and descend and ascend, to fit every crooked phase of selfish, worldly society, religion? Is *that* religion, which is less scrupulous, less generous, less just, less considerate for man, than even my own ungodly, worldly, blinded nature? No! When I look for a religion, I must look for something above me, and not something beneath."

The character of St. Clare was drawn by

the writer with enthusiasm and with hope. Will this hope never be realized? Will those men at the South, to whom God has given the power to perceive and the heart to feel the unutterable wrong and injustice of slavery, always remain silent and inactive? What nobler ambition to a Southern man than to deliver his country from this disgrace? From the South must the deliverer arise. How long shall he delay? There is a crown brighter than any earthly ambition has ever worn,— there is a laurel which will not fade: it is prepared and waiting for that hero who shall rise up for liberty at the South, and free that noble and beautiful country from the burden and disgrace of slavery.

CHAPTER X.

LEGREE.

As St. Clare and the Shelbys are the representatives of one class of masters, so Legree is the representative of another; and, as all good masters are not as enlightened, as generous, and as considerate, as St. Clare and Mr. Shelby, or as careful and successful in religious training as Mrs. Shelby, so all bad masters do not unite the personal ugliness, the coarseness and profaneness, of Legree.

Legree is introduced not for the sake of vilifying masters as a class, but for the sake of bringing to the minds of honorable Southern men, who are masters, a very important feature in the system of slavery, upon which, perhaps, they have never reflected. It is this: that *no Southern law requires any test of* CHARACTER *from the man to whom the absolute power of master is granted.*

In the second part of this book it will be shown that the legal power of the master amounts to an absolute despotism over body and soul; and that there is no protection for the slave's life or limb, his family relations, his conscience, nay, more, his eternal interests, but the CHARACTER of the master.

Rev. Charles C. Jones, of Georgia, in addressing masters, tells them that they have the power to open the kingdom of heaven or to shut it, to their slaves (*Religious Instruction of the Negroes,* p. 158), and a South Carolinian, in a recent article in *Fraser's Magazine,* apparently in a very serious spirit, thus acknowledges the fact of this awful power: "Yes, we would have the whole South to feel that the *soul* of the slave is in some sense in the master's keeping, and to be charged against him hereafter."

Now, it is respectfully submitted to men of this high class, who are the law-makers, whether this awful power to bind and to loose, to open and to shut the kingdom of heaven, ought to be intrusted to every man in the community, without any other qualification than that of property to buy. Let this gentleman of South Carolina cast his eyes around the world. Let him travel for one week through any district of country either in the South or the North, and ask himself how many of the men whom he meets are fit to be trusted with this power,— how many are fit to be trusted with their own souls, much less with those of others?

Now, in all the theory of government as it is managed in our country, just in proportion to the extent of power is the strictness with which qualification for the proper exercise of it is demanded. The physician may not meddle with the body, to prescribe for its ailments, without a certificate that he is properly qualified. The judge may not decide on the laws which relate to property, without a long course of training, and most abundant preparation. It is only this office of MASTER, which contains the power to bind and to loose, and to open and shut the kingdom of heaven, and involves responsibility for the soul as well as the body, that is thrown out to every hand, and committed without inquiry to any man of any character. A man may have made all his property by piracy upon the high seas, as we have represented in the case of Legree, and there is no law whatever to prevent his investing that property in acquiring this absolute control over the souls and bodies of his fellow-beings. To the half-maniac drunkard, to the man notorious for hardness and cruelty, to the man sunk entirely below public opinion, to the bitter infidel and blasphemer, the law confides this power, just as freely as to the most honorable and religious man on earth. And yet, men who make and uphold these laws think they are guiltless before God, because individually they do not perpetrate the wrongs which they allow others to perpetrate!

To the pirate Legree the law gives a power which no man of woman born, save One, ever was good enough to exercise.

Are there such men as Legree? Let any one go into the low districts and dens of New York, let them go into some of the lanes and alleys of London, and will they not there see many Legrees? Nay, take the purest district of New England, and let people cast about in their memory and see if there have not been men there, hard, coarse, unfeeling, brutal, who, if they had possessed the absolute power of Legree, would have used it in the same way; and that there should be Legrees in the Southern States, is only saying that human nature is the same there that it is everywhere. The only difference is this,—that in free states Legree is chained and restrained by law; in the slave states, the law makes him an absolute, irresponsible despot.

It is a shocking task to confirm by fact this part of the writer's story. One may well approach it in fear and trembling. It is so mournful to think that man, made in the image of God, and by his human birth a brother of Jesus Christ, can sink so low, can do such things as the very soul shudders to contemplate,—and to think that the very man who thus sinks is our brother,— is capable, like us, of the renewal by the Spirit of grace, by which he might be created in the image of Christ and be made equal unto the angels. They who uphold the laws which grant this awful power have another heavy responsibility, of which they little dream. How many souls of masters have been ruined through it! How has this absolute authority provoked and developed wickedness which otherwise might have been suppressed! How many have stumbled into everlasting perdition over this stumbling-stone of IRRESPONSIBLE POWER!

What facts do the judicial trials of slave-holding states occasionally develop! What horrible records defile the pages of the law-book, describing unheard-of scenes of torture and agony, perpetrated in this nineteenth century of the Christian era, by the irresponsible despot who owns the body and soul! Let any one read, if they can, the ninety-third page of Weld's *Slavery as It Is*, where the Rev. Mr. Dickey gives an account of a trial in Kentucky for a deed of butchery and blood too repulsive to humanity to be here described. The culprit was convicted, and *sentenced* to death. Mr. Dickey's account of the finale is thus:

The Court sat — Isham was judged to be guilty of a capital crime in the affair of George. He was to be hanged at Salem. The day was set. My good old father visited him in the prison — two or three times talked and prayed with him; I visited him once myself. We fondly hoped that he was a sincere penitent. Before the day of execution came, by some means, I never knew what, Isham

was *missing*. About two years after, we learned that he had gone down to Natchez, and had married a lady of some refinement and piety. I saw her letters to his sisters, who were worthy members of the church of which I was pastor. The last letter told of his death. He was in Jackson's army, and fell in the famous battle of New Orleans.   I am, sir, your friend,
                                            WM. DICKEY.

But the reader will have too much reason to know of the possibility of the existence of such men as Legree, when he comes to read the records of the trials and judicial decisions in Part II.

Let not the Southern country be taunted as the only country in the world which produces such men ;— let us in sorrow and in humility concede that such men are found everywhere ; but let not the Southern country deny the awful charge that she invests such men with absolute, irresponsible power over both the body and the soul.

With regard to that atrocious system of working up the human being in a given time, on which Legree is represented as conducting his plantation, there is unfortunately too much reason to know that it has been practised and is still practised.

In Mr. Weld's book, " Slavery as It Is," under the head of Labor, p. 39, are given several extracts from various documents, to show that this system has been pursued on some plantations to such an extent as to shorten life, and to prevent the increase of the slave population, so that, unless annually renewed, it would of itself die out. Of these documents we quote the following:

The Agricultural Society of Baton Rouge, La., in its report, published in 1829, furnishes a labored estimate of the amount of expenditure necessarily incurred in conducting "a well-regulated sugar estate." In this estimate, the annual net loss of slaves, over and above the supply by propagation, is set down at TWO AND A HALF PER CENT. ! The late Hon. Josiah S. Johnson, a member of Congress from Louisiana, addressed a letter to the Secretary of the United States' Treasury, in 1830, containing a similar estimate, apparently made with great care, and going into minute details. Many items in this estimate differ from the preceding ; but the estimate of the annual *decrease* of the slaves on a plantation was the same, — TWO AND A HALF PER CENT. !

In September, 1834, the writer of this had an interview with James G. Birney, Esq., who then resided in Kentucky, having removed, with his family, from Alabama, the year before. A few hours before that interview, and on the morning of the same day, Mr. B. had spent a couple of hours with Hon. Henry Clay, at his residence, near Lexington. Mr. Birney remarked that Mr. Clay had just told him he had lately been led to mistrust certain estimates as to the increase of the slave population in the far South-west, — estimates which he had presented, I think, in a speech before the Colonization Society. He now believed that the births among the slaves in that quarter were *not equal to the deaths;* and that, of course, the slave population, independent of immigration from the slave-selling states, was *not sustaining itself.*

Among other facts stated by Mr. Clay was the following, which we copy *verbatim* from the original memorandum made at the time by Mr. Birney, with which he has kindly furnished us.

"*Sept.* 16, 1834.—Hon. H. Clay, in a conversation at his own house on the subject of slavery, informed me that Hon. Outerbridge Horsey—formerly a senator in Congress from the State of Delaware, and the owner of a sugar plantation in Louisiana—declared to him that his overseer worked his hands so closely that one of the women brought forth a child whilst engaged in the labors of the field.

"Also that, a few years since, he was at a brick-yard in the environs of New Orleans, in which one hundred hands were employed; among them were from *twenty to thirty young women,* in the prime of life. He was told by the proprietor that there had *not been a child born among them for the last two or three years, although they all had husbands.*"

The late Mr. Samuel Blackwell, a highly-respected citizen of Jersey City, opposite the city of New York, and a member of the Presbyterian church, visited many of the sugar plantations in Louisiana a few years since; and having, for many years, been the owner of an extensive sugar refinery in England, and subsequently in this country, he had not only every facility afforded him by the planters for personal inspection of all parts of the process of sugar-making, but received from them the most unreserved communications as to their management of their slaves. Mr. B., after his return, frequently made the following statement to gentlemen of his acquaintance:—

"That the planters generally declared to him that they were *obliged* so to overwork their slaves, during the sugar-making season (from eight to ten weeks), as to *use them up* in seven or eight years. For, said they, after the process is commenced, it must be pushed, without cessation, night and day; and we cannot afford to keep a sufficient number of slaves to do the *extra* work at the time of sugar-making, as we could not profitably employ them the rest of the year."

Dr. Demming, a gentleman of high respectability, residing in Ashland, Richland County, Ohio, stated to Professor Wright, of New York city,

"That, during a recent tour at the South, while ascending the Ohio river, on the steamboat Fame, he had an opportunity of conversing with a Mr. Dickinson, a resident of Pittsburg, in company with a number of cotton-planters and slave-dealers from Louisiana, Alabama and Mississippi. Mr. Dickinson stated as a fact, that the sugar-planters upon the sugar-coast in Louisiana had ascertained that, as it was usually necessary to employ about *twice* the amount of labor during the boiling season that was required during the season of raising, they could, by excessive driving, day and night, during the boiling season, accomplish the whole labor *with one set of hands.* By pursuing this plan, they could afford *to sacrifice a set of hands once in seven years!* He further stated that this horrible system was now practised to a considerable extent. The correctness of this statement was substantially admitted by the slave-holders then on board."

The following testimony of Rev. Dr. Channing, of Boston, who resided some time in Virginia, shows that the over-working of slaves, to such an extent as to abridge life, and cause a decrease of population, is not confined to the far South and South-west.

"I heard of an estate managed by an individual who was considered as singularly successful, and who was able to govern the slaves without the use of the whip. I was anxious to see him; and trusted that some discovery had been made favorable to humanity. I asked him how he was able to dispense with corporal punishment. He replied to me, with a very determined look, 'The slaves know that the work *must* be done, and that it is better to do it without punishment than with it.' In other words, the certainty and dread of chastisement were so impressed on them that they never incurred it.

"I then found that the slaves on this well-managed estate *decreased* in number. I asked the cause. He replied, with perfect frankness and ease, 'The gang is not large enough for the estate.' In other words, they were not equal to the work of the plantation, and yet were *made to do it,* though with the certainty of abridging life.

"On this plantation the huts were uncommonly convenient. There was an unusual air of neatness. A superficial observer would have called the slaves happy. Yet they were living under a severe, subduing discipline, and were *over-worked* to a degree that *shortened life.*"—*Channing on Slavery,* page 162, first edition.

A friend of the writer—the Rev. Mr. Barrows, now officiating as teacher of Hebrew in Andover Theological Seminary—stated the following, in conversation with her:—That, while at New Orleans, some time since, he was invited by a planter to visit his estate, as he considered it to be a model one. He found good dwellings for the slaves, abundant provision distributed to them, all cruel punishments superseded by rational and reasonable ones, and half a day every week allowed to the negroes to cultivate their own grounds. Provision was also made for their moral and religious instruction. Mr. Barrows then asked the planter,

"Do you consider your estate a fair specimen?" The gentleman replied, "There are two systems pursued among us. One is, to make all we can out of a negro in a few years, and then supply his place with another; and the other is, to treat him as I do. My neighbor on the next plantation pursues the opposite system. His boys are hard worked and scantily fed; and I have had them come to me, and get down on their knees to beg me to buy them."

Mr. Barrows says he subsequently passed by this plantation, and that the woe-struck, dejected aspect of its laborers fully confirmed

the account. He also says that the gentleman who managed so benevolently told him,
"I do not make much money out of my
slaves."

It will be easy to show that such is the
nature of slavery, and the temptations of
masters, that such well-regulated plantations
are and must be infinitely in the minority,
and exceptional cases.

The Rev. Charles C. Jones, a man of the
finest feelings of humanity, and for many
years an assiduous laborer for the benefit of
the slave, himself the owner of a plantation,
and qualified, therefore, to judge, both by
experience and observation, says, after speaking of the great improvidence of the negroes,
engendered by slavery:

> And, indeed, once for all, I will here say that
> the wastes of the system are so great, as well as
> the fluctuation in prices of the staple articles for
> market, that it is *difficult, nay, impossible,* to in-
> dulge in large expenditures on plantations, and
> make them savingly profitable. — *Religious In-
> struction,* p. 116.

If even the religious and benevolent master feels the difficulty of uniting any great
consideration for the comfort of the slave
with prudence and economy, how readily
must the moral question be solved by minds
of the coarse style of thought which we have
supposed in Legree!

> "I used to, when I fust begun, have considera-
> ble trouble fussin' with 'em, and trying to make
> 'em hold out. — doctorin' on 'em up when they 's
> sick, and givin' on 'em clothes, and blankets, and
> what not, trying to keep 'em all sort o' decent
> and comfortable. Law, 't want no sort o' use : I
> lost money on 'em, and 't was heaps o' trouble.
> Now, you see, I just put 'em straight through,
> sick or well. When one nigger's dead, I buy
> another; and I find it comes cheaper and easier
> every way."

Added to this, the peculiar mode of labor
on the sugar plantation is such that the master, at a certain season of the year, must
over-work his slaves, unless he is willing to
incur great pecuniary loss. In that very
gracefully written apology for slavery, Professor Ingraham's "Travels in the South-
west," the following description of sugar-
making is given. We quote from him in
preference to any one else, because he speaks
as an apologist, and describes the thing with
the grace of a Mr. Skimpole.

> When the grinding has once commenced, there
> is no cessation of labor till it is completed. From
> beginning to end a busy and cheerful scene con-
> tinues. The negroes,
>
> "—— Whose sore task
> Does not divide the Sunday from the week,"
>
> work from eighteen to twenty hours,

> "And make the night joint laborer with the day ;"
>
> though, to lighten the burden as much as possi-
> ble, the gang is divided into two watches, one
> taking the first and the other the last part of the
> night ; and, notwithstanding this continued labor,
> the negroes improve in appearance, and appear
> fat and flourishing. They drink freely of cane-
> juice, and the sickly among them revive, and
> become robust and healthy.
> After the grinding is finished, the negroes have
> several holidays, when they are quite at liberty to
> dance and frolic as much as they please ; and the
> cane-song — which is improvised by one of the
> gang, the rest all joining in a prolonged and unin
> telligible chorus — now breaks, night and day,
> upon the ear, in notes "most musical, most mel-
> ancholy."

The above is inserted as a specimen of the
facility with which the most horrible facts
may be told in the genteelest phrase. In a
work entitled "Travels in Louisiana in
1802" is the following extract (see Weld's
"Slavery as It Is," p. 134), from which it
appears that this *cheerful* process of laboring night and day lasts *three months!*

Now, let any one learn the private history of seven hundred blacks,— men and
women,— compelled to work day and night,
under the lash of a driver, for a period of
three months.

Possibly, if the gentleman who wrote this
account were employed, with his wife and
family, in this "cheerful scene" of labor,—
if he saw the woman that he loved, the
daughter who was dear to him as his own
soul, forced on in the general gang, in this
toil which

> "Does not divide the Sabbath from the week,
> And makes the night joint laborer with the day,"

— possibly, if he saw all this, he might have
another opinion of its cheerfulness ; and it
might be an eminently salutary thing if
every apologist for slavery were to enjoy
some such privilege for a season, particularly
as Mr. Ingraham is careful to tell us that
its effect upon the general health is so excellent that the negroes improve in appearance,
and appear fat and flourishing, and that the
sickly among them revive, and become
robust and healthy. One would think it a
surprising fact, if working slaves night and
day, and giving them cane-juice to drink,
really produces such salutary results, that
the practice should not be continued the
whole year round ; though, perhaps, in this
case, the negroes would become so fat as to
be unable to labor. Possibly, it is because
this healthful process is not longer continued
that the agricultural societies of Louisiana
are obliged to set down an annual loss of
slaves on sugar plantations to the amount

of two and a half per cent. This ought to be looked into by philanthropists. Perhaps working them all night for six months, instead of three, might remedy the evil.

But this periodical pressure is not confined to the making of sugar. There is also a press in the cotton season, as any one can observe by reading the Southern newspapers. At a certain season of the year, the whole interest of the community is engaged in gathering in the cotton crop. Concerning this Mr. Weld says ("Slavery as It Is," page 34):

In the cotton and sugar region there is a fearful amount of desperate gambling, in which, though money is the ostensible stake and forfeit, *human life* is the real one. The length to which this rivalry is carried at the South and South-west, the multitude of planters who engage in it, and the recklessness of human life exhibited in driving the murderous game to its issue, cannot well be imagined by one who has not lived in the midst of it. Desire of gain is only one of the motives that stimulates them; the *éclat* of having made the largest crop with a given number of hands is also a powerful stimulant; the Southern newspapers, at the crop season, chronicle carefully the "cotton brag," and the "crack cotton-picking," and "unparalleled driving," &c. Even the editors of professedly religious papers cheer on the *mêlée*, and sing the triumphs of the victor. Among these we recollect the celebrated Rev. J. N. Maffit, recently editor of a religious paper at Natchez, Miss., in which he took care to assign a prominent place and capitals to "THE COTTON BRAG."

As a specimen, of recent date, of this kind of affair, we subjoin the following from the *Fairfield Herald*, Winsboro', S. C., Nov. 4, 1852.

COTTON-PICKING.

We find in many of our southern and western exchanges notices of the amount of cotton picked by hands, and the quantity by each hand; and, as we have received a similar account, which we have not seen excelled, so far as regards the quantity picked by one hand, we with pleasure furnish the statement, with the remark that it is from a citizen of this district, overseeing for Maj. H. W. Parr.

"Broad River, Oct. 12, 1852.

"MESSRS. EDITORS:—By way of contributing something to your variety (provided it meets your approbation), I send you the return of a day's picking of cotton, not by picked hands, but the fag end of a set of hands on one plantation, the able-bodied hands having been drawn out for other purposes. Now for the result of a day's picking, from sun-up until sun-down, by twenty-two hands, —women, boys, and two men:—four thousand eight hundred and eighty pounds of clean picked cotton, from the stalk.

"The highest, three hundred and fifty pounds, by several; the lowest, one hundred and fifteen pounds. One of the number has picked in the last seven and a half days (Sunday excepted), eleven

hours each day, nineteen hundred pounds clean cotton. When any of my agricultural friends beat this, in the same time, and during sunshine, I will try again. JAMES STEWARD."

It seems that this agriculturist professes to have accomplished all these extraordinary results with what he very elegantly terms the "fag end" of a set of hands; and, the more to exalt his glory in the matter, he distinctly informs the public that there were no "able-bodied" hands employed; that this whole triumphant result was worked out of women and children, and two disabled men; in other words, he boasts that out of women and children, and the feeble and sickly, *he* has extracted four thousand eight hundred and eighty pounds of clean picked cotton in a day; and that one of these same hands has been made to pick nineteen hundred pounds of clean cotton in a week! and adds, complacently, that, when any of his agricultural friends beat this, in the same time, and during sunshine, he "will try again."

Will any of our readers now consider the forcing up of the hands on Legree's plantation an exaggeration? Yet see how complacently this account is quoted by the editor, as a most praiseworthy and laudable thing!

"BEHOLD THE HIRE OF THE LABORERS WHO HAVE REAPED DOWN YOUR FIELDS, WHICH IS OF YOU KEPT BACK BY FRAUD, CRIETH! AND THE CRIES OF THEM WHICH HAVE REAPED ARE ENTERED INTO THE EARS OF THE LORD OF SABAOTH."

That the representations of the style of dwelling-house, modes of housekeeping, and, in short, the features of life generally, as described on Legree's plantation, are not wild and fabulous drafts on the imagination, or exaggerated pictures of exceptional cases, there is the most abundant testimony before the world, and has been for a long number of years. Let the reader weigh the following testimony with regard to the dwellings of the negroes, which has been for some years before the world, in the work of Mr. Weld. It shows the state of things in this respect, at least up to the year 1838.

Mr. Stephen E. Maltby, Inspector of Provisions, Skaneateles, N. Y., who has lived in Alabama. — "The huts where the slaves slept generally contained but *one* apartment, and that *without floor*."

Mr. George A. Avery, elder of the 4th Presbyterian Church, Rochester, N. Y., who lived four years in Virginia. — "Amongst all the negro cabins which I saw in Virginia, *I cannot call to mind one* in which there was any other floor than the *earth;* anything that a Northern laborer, or mechanic, white or colored, would call a *bed*, nor a solitary *partition*, to separate the sexes."

William Ladd, Esq., Minot, Maine, President of the American Peace Society, formerly a slaveholder in Florida. — "The dwellings of the slaves were palmetto huts, built by themselves of stakes and poles, thatched with the palmetto-leaf. The door, when they had any, was generally of the same materials, sometimes boards found on the beach. They had *no floors*, no separate apartments; except the Guinea negroes had sometimes a small enclosure for their 'god houses.' These huts the slaves built themselves after task and on Sundays."

Rev. Joseph M. Sadd, pastor Presbyterian Church, Castile, Greene Co., N. Y., who lived in Missouri five years previous to 1837. — "The slaves live *generally* in *miserable huts*, which are *without floors;* and have a single apartment only, where both sexes are herded promiscuously together."

Mr. George W. Westgate, member of the Congregational church in Quincy, Illinois, who has spent a number of years in slave states. — "On old plantations the negro quarters are of frame and clapboards, seldom affording a comfortable shelter from wind or rain ; their size varies from eight by ten to ten by twelve feet, and six or eight feet high ; sometimes there is a hole cut for a window, but I never saw a sash, or glass, in any. In the new country, and in the woods, the quarters are generally built of logs, of similar dimensions."

Mr. Cornelius Johnson, a member of a Christian church in Farmington, Ohio. Mr. J. lived in Mississippi in 1837–8. — "Their houses were commonly built of logs ; sometimes they were framed, often they had no floor ; some of them have two apartments, commonly but one ; each of those apartments contained a family. Sometimes these families consisted of a man and his wife and children, while in other instances persons of both sexes were thrown together, without any regard to family relationship."

The *Western Medical Reformer*, in an article on the Cachexia Africana, by a Kentucky physician, thus speaks of the huts of the slaves : "They are *crowded* together in a *small hut*, and sometimes having an imperfect and sometimes no floor, and seldom raised from the ground, ill ventilated, and surrounded with filth."

Mr. William Leftwich, a native of Virginia, but has resided most of his life in Madison Co., Alabama. — "The dwellings of the slaves are log huts, from ten to twelve feet square, often without windows, doors or floors ; they have neither chairs, table, or bedstead."

Reuben L. Macy, of Hudson, N. Y., a member of the religious society of Friends. He lived in South Carolina in 1818–19. — "The houses for the field-slaves were about fourteen feet square, built in the coarsest manner, with one room, *without any chimney or flooring, with a hole in the roof to let the smoke out.*"

Mr. Lemuel Sapington, of Lancaster, Pa., a native of Maryland, formerly a slave-holder. — "The descriptions generally given of negro quarters are correct ; the quarters are *without floors, and not sufficient to keep off the inclemency of the weather ;* they are uncomfortable both in summer and winter."

Rev. John Rankin, a native of Tennessee. — "When they return to their miserable huts at night, they find not there the means of comfort-

able rest ; but *on the cold ground they must lie without covering, and shiver while they slumber.*"

Philemon Bliss, Esq., Elyria, Ohio, who lived in Florida in 1835. — "The dwellings of the slaves are usually small *open* log huts, with but one apartment, and very generally *without floors.*"
Slavery as It Is, p. 43.

The Rev. C. C. Jones, to whom we have already alluded, when taking a survey of the condition of the negroes considered as a field for missionary effort, takes into account all the conditions of their external life. He speaks of a part of Georgia where as much attention had been paid to the comfort of the negro as in any part of the United States. He gives the following picture :

Their *general mode of living* is coarse and vulgar. Many negro houses are small, low to the ground, blackened with smoke, often with dirt floors, and the furniture of the plainest kind. On some estates the houses are framed, weatherboarded, neatly white-washed, and made sufficiently large and comfortable in every respect. The improvement in the size, material and finish, of negro houses, is extending. Occasionally they may be found constructed of tabby or brick.
Religious Instruction of the Negroes, p. 116.

Now, admitting what Mr. Jones says, to wit, that improvements with regard to the accommodation of the negroes are continually making among enlightened and Christian people, still, if we take into account how many people there are who are neither enlightened nor Christian, how unproductive of any benefit to the master all these improvements are, and how entirely, therefore, they must be the result either of native generosity or of Christian sentiment, the reader may fairly conclude that such improvements are the exception, rather than the rule.

A friend of the writer, travelling in Georgia during the last month, thus writes :

Upon the long line of rice and cotton plantations extending along the railroad from Savannah to this city, the negro quarters contain scarcely a single hut which a Northern farmer would deem fit shelter for his cattle. They are all built of poles, with the ends so slightly notched that they are almost as open as children's cob-houses (which they very much resemble), without a single glazed window, and with only one mud chimney to each cluster of from four to eight cabins. And yet our fellow-travellers were quietly expatiating upon the negro's strange inability to endure cold weather !

Let this modern picture be compared with the account given by the Rev. Horace Moulton, who spent five years in Georgia between 1817 and 1824, and it will be seen, in that state at least, there is some resemblance between the more remote and more recent practice :

The huts of the slaves are mostly of the poorest kind. They are not as good as those temporary shanties which are thrown up beside railroads. They are erected with posts and crotches, with but little or no frame-work about them. They have no stoves or chimneys; some of them have something like a fireplace at one end, and a board or two off at that side, or on the roof, to let off the smoke. Others have nothing like a fireplace in them; in these the fire is sometimes made in the middle of the hut. These buildings have but one apartment in them; the places where they pass in and out serve both for doors and windows; the sides and roofs are covered with coarse, and in many instances with refuse boards. In warm weather, especially in the spring, the slaves keep up a smoke, or fire and smoke, all night, to drive away the gnats and mosquitos, which are very troublesome in all the low country of the South; so much so that the whites sleep under frames with nets over them, knit so fine that the mosquitos cannot fly through them.

Slavery as It Is, p. 19.

The same Mr. Moulton gives the following account of the food of the slaves, and the mode of procedure on the plantation on which he was engaged. It may be here mentioned that at the time he was at the South he was engaged in certain business relations which caused him frequently to visit different plantations, and to have under his control many of the slaves. His opportunities for observation, therefore, were quite intimate. There is a homely matter-of-fact distinctness in the style that forbids the idea of its being a fancy sketch:

It was a general custom, wherever I have been, for the master to give each of his slaves, male and female, *one peck of corn per week* for their food. This, at fifty cents per bushel, which was all that it was worth when I was there, would amount to twelve and a half cents per week for board per head.

It cost me, upon an average, when at the South, one dollar per day for board; — the price of fourteen bushels of corn per week. This would make my board equal in amount to the board of *forty-six slaves!* This is all that good or bad masters allow their slaves, round about Savannah, on the plantations. One peck of gourd-seed corn is to be measured out to each slave once every week. One man with whom I labored, however, being desirous to get all the work out of his hands he could, before I left (about fifty in number), bought for them every week, or twice a week, a beef's head from market. With this they made a soup in a large iron kettle, around which the hands came at meal-time, and dipping out the soup, would mix it with their hominy, and eat it as though it were a feast. This man permitted his slaves to eat twice a day while I was doing a job for him. He promised me a beaver hat, and as good a suit of clothes as could be bought in the city, if I would accomplish so much for him before I returned to the North; giving me the entire control over his slaves. Thus you may see the temptations overseers sometimes have, to get all the work they can out of the poor slaves. The above is an exception to the general rule of feeding. For, in all other places where I worked and visited, the slaves had *nothing from their masters but the corn,* or its equivalent in potatoes or rice; and to this they were not permitted to come but *once a day.* The custom was to blow the horn early in the morning, as a signal for the hands to rise and go to work. When commenced, they continue work until about eleven o'clock A. M., when, at the signal, all hands left off, and went into their huts, made their fires, made their corn-meal into hominy or cake, ate it, and went to work again at the signal of the horn, and worked until night, or until their tasks were done. Some cooked their breakfast in the field while at work. Each slave must grind his own corn in a hand-mill after he has done his work at night. There is generally one hand-mill on every plantation for the use of the slaves.

Some of the planters have no corn; others often get out. The substitute for it is the equivalent of one peck of corn, either in rice or sweet potatoes, neither of which is as good for the slaves as corn. They complain more of being faint when fed on rice or potatoes than when fed on corn. I was with one man a few weeks who gave me his hands to do a job of work, and, to save time, one cooked for all the rest. The following course was taken: — Two crotched sticks were driven down at one end of the yard, and, a small pole being laid on the crotches, they swung a large iron kettle on the middle of the pole; then made up a fire under the kettle, and boiled the hominy; when ready, the hands were called around this kettle with their wooden plates and spoons. They dipped out and ate standing around the kettle, or sitting upon the ground, as best suited their convenience. When they had potatoes, they took them out with their hands, and ate them.

Slavery as It Is, p. 18.

Thomas Clay, Esq., a slave-holder of Georgia, and a most benevolent man, and who interested himself very successfully in endeavoring to promote the improvement of the negroes, in his address before the Georgia Presbytery, 1833, says of their food, " The quantity allowed by custom is a *peck of corn a week.*"

The *Maryland Journal and Baltimore Advertiser,* May 30, 1788, says, " A single peck of corn, or the same measure of rice, is the ordinary provision for a hard-working slave, to which a small quantity of meat is occasionally, though rarely, added."

Captain William Ladd, of Minot, Maine, formerly a slave-holder in Florida, says, " The usual allowance of food was a quart of corn a day to a full-task hand, with a modicum of salt; *kind* masters allowed a peck of corn a week."

The law of North Carolina provides that the master shall give his slave a quart of corn a day, which is less than a peck a week by one quart. — *Haywood's Manual.* 525; *Slavery as It Is,* p. 29. The master, therefore, who gave a peck a week would feel that he was going beyond the law, and giving a quart for generosity.

This condition of things will appear far more probable in the section of country where the scene of the story is laid. It is in the south-western states, where no provision is *raised* on the plantations, but the supply for the slaves is all purchased from the northern states.

Let the reader now imagine the various temptations which might occur to retrench the allowance of the slaves, under these circumstances ; — scarcity of money, financial embarrassment, high price of provisions, and various causes of the kind, bring a great influence upon the master or overseer.

At the time when it was discussed whether the State of Missouri should be admitted as a slave state, the measure, like all measures for the advancement of this horrible system, was advocated on the good old plea of humanity to the negroes; thus Mr. Alexander Smyth, in his speech on the slavery question, Jan. 21, 1820, says :

By confining the slaves to the Southern States, where crops are raised for exportation, and bread and meat are purchased, you *doom them to scarcity and hunger*. It is proposed to hem in the blacks where they are ILL FED.

Slavery as It Is, p. 28.

This is a simple recognition of the state of things we have adverted to. To the same purport, Mr. Asa A. Stone, a theological student, who resided near Natchez, Miss., in 1834–5, says :

On almost every plantation, the hands suffer more or less from hunger at some seasons of almost every year. There is always a *good deal of suffering* from hunger. On many plantations, and particularly in Louisiana, the slaves are in a condition of *almost utter famishment*, during a great portion of the year. — *Ibid*.

Mr. Tobias Baudinot, St. Albans, Ohio, a member of the Methodist Church, who for some years was a navigator on the Mississippi, says :

The slaves down the Mississippi are *half-starved*. The boats, when they stop at night, are constantly boarded by slaves, begging for something to eat.
Ibid.

On the whole, while it is freely and cheerfully admitted that many individuals have made most commendable advances in regard to the provision for the physical comfort of the slave, still it is to be feared that the picture of the accommodations on Legree's plantation has as yet too many counterparts. Lest, however, the author should be suspected of keeping back anything which might serve to throw light on the subject, she will insert in full the following incidents on the other side, from the pen of the accomplished Professor Ingraham. How far these may be regarded as exceptional cases, or as pictures of the general mode of providing for slaves, may safely be left to the good sense of the reader. The professor's anecdotes are as follows :

" What can you do with so much tobacco?" said a gentleman, — who related the circumstance to me, — on hearing a planter, whom he was visiting, give an order to his teamster to bring two hogsheads of tobacco out to the estate from the " Landing."

" I purchase it for my negroes ; it is a harmless indulgence, which it gives me pleasure to afford them."

" Why are you at the trouble and expense of having high-post bedsteads for your negroes ?" said a gentleman from the North, while walking through the handsome " quarters," or village, for the slaves, then in progress on a plantation near Natchez — addressing the proprietor.

" To suspend their ' bars ' from, that they may not be troubled with mosquitos."

" Master, me would like, if you please, a little bit gallery front my house."

" For what, Peter ?"

" 'Cause, master, the sun too hot [an odd reason for a negro to give] that side, and when he rain we no able to keep de door open."

" Well, well, when a carpenter gets a little leisure, you shall have one."

A few weeks after, I was at the plantation, and riding past the quarters one Sabbath morning, beheld Peter, his wife and children, with his old father, all sunning themselves in the new gallery.

" Missus, you promise me a Chrismus gif'."

" Well, Jane, there is a new calico frock for you."

" It werry pretty, Missus," said Jane, eying it at a distance without touching it, " but me prefer muslin, if you please : muslin de fashion dis Chrismus."

" Very well, Jane, call to-morrow, and you shall have a muslin."

The writer would not think of controverting the truth of these anecdotes. Any probable amount of high-post bedsteads and mosquito " bars," of tobacco distributed as gratuity, and verandas constructed by leisurely carpenters for the sunning of fastidious negroes, may be conceded, and they do in no whit impair the truth of the other facts. When the reader remembers that the " gang " of some opulent owners amounts to from five to seven hundred working hands, besides children, he can judge how extensively these accommodations are likely to be provided. Let them be safely thrown into the account, for what they are worth.

At all events, it is pleasing to end off so disagreeable a chapter with some more agreeable images. [See Appendix.]

CHAPTER XI.

SELECT INCIDENTS OF LAWFUL TRADE.

In this chapter of *Uncle Tom's Cabin* were recorded some of the most highly-wrought and touching incidents of the slave-trade. It will be well to authenticate a few of them.

One of the first sketches presented to view is an account of the separation of a very old, decrepit negro woman from her young son, by a sheriff's sale. The writer is sorry to say that not the slightest credit for invention is due to her in this incident. She found it, almost exactly as it stands, in the published journal of a young Southerner, related as a scene to which he was eye-witness. The only circumstance which she has omitted in the narrative was one of additional inhumanity and painfulness which he had delineated. He represents the boy as being bought by a planter, who fettered his hands, and tied a rope round his neck which he attached to the neck of his horse, thus compelling the child to trot by his side. This incident alone was suppressed by the author.

Another scene of fraud and cruelty, in the same chapter, is described as perpetrated by a Kentucky slave-master, who sells a woman to a trader, and induces her to go with him by the deceitful assertion that she is to be taken down the river a short distance, to work at the same hotel with her husband. This was an instance which occurred under the writer's own observation, some years since, when she was going down the Ohio river. The woman was very respectable both in appearance and dress. The writer recalls her image now with distinctness, attired with great neatness in a white wrapper, her clothing and hair all arranged with evident care, and having with her a prettily-dressed boy about seven years of age. She had also a hair trunk of clothing, which showed that she had been carefully and respectably brought up. It will be seen, in perusing the account, that the incident is somewhat altered to suit the purpose of the story, the woman being there represented as carrying with her a young infant.

The custom of unceremoniously separating the infant from its mother, when the latter is about to be taken from a Northern to a Southern market, is a matter of every-day notoriety in the trade. It is not done occasionally and sometimes, but always, when-

ever there is occasion for it; and the mother's agonies are no more regarded than those of a cow when her calf is separated from her.

The reason of this is, that the care and raising of children is no part of the intention or provision of a Southern plantation. They are a trouble; they detract from the value of the mother as a field-hand, and it is more expensive to raise them than to buy them ready raised; they are therefore left behind in the making up of a coffle. Not longer ago than last summer, the writer was conversing with Thomas Strother, a slave minister of the gospel in St. Louis, for whose emancipation she was making some effort. He incidentally mentioned to her a scene which he had witnessed but a short time before, in which a young woman of his acquaintance came to him almost in a state of distraction, telling him that she had been sold to go South with a trader, and leave behind her a nursing infant.

In Lewis Clark's narrative he mentions that a master in his neighborhood sold a woman and child to a trader, with the charge that he should not sell the child from its mother. The man, however, traded off the child in the very next town, in payment of his tavern-bill.

The following testimony is from a gentleman who writes from New Orleans to the *National Era*.

This writer says:

While at Robinson, or Tyree Springs, twenty miles from Nashville, on the borders of Kentucky and Tennessee, my hostess said to me, one day, "Yonder comes a gang of slaves, chained." I went to the road-side and viewed them. For the better answering my purpose of observation, I stopped the white man in front, who was at his ease in a one-horse wagon, and asked him if those slaves were for sale. I counted them and observed their position. They were divided by three one-horse wagons, each containing a man-merchant, so arranged as to command the whole gang. Some were unchained; sixty were chained in two companies, thirty in each, the right hand of one to the left hand of the other opposite one, making fifteen each side of a large ox-chain, to which every hand was fastened, and necessarily compelled to hold up, — men and women promiscuously, and about in equal proportions, — all young people. No children here, except a few in a wagon behind, which were the only children in the four gangs. I said to a respectable mulatto woman in the house, "Is it true that the negro-traders take mothers from their babies?" "Massa, it is true; for here, last week, such a girl [naming her], who lives about a mile off, was taken after dinner, — knew nothing of it in the morning, — sold, put into the gang, and her baby given away to a neighbor. She was a stout young woman, and brought a good price."

Nor is the pitiful lie to be regarded which says that these unhappy mothers and fathers, husbands and wives, do not feel when the most sacred ties are thus severed. Every day and hour bears living witness of the falsehood of this slander, the more false because spoken of a race peculiarly affectionate, and strong, vivacious and vehement, in the expression of their feelings.

The case which the writer supposed of the woman's throwing herself overboard is not by any means a singular one. Witness the following recent fact, which appeared under the head of

ANOTHER INCIDENT FOR "UNCLE TOM'S CABIN."

The editorial correspondent of the *Oneida*, (N. Y.) *Telegraph*, writing from a steamer on the Mississippi river, gives the following sad story :

"At Louisville, a gentleman took passage, having with him a family of blacks,—husband, wife and children. The master was bound for Memphis, Tenn., at which place he intended to take all except the man ashore. The latter was hand-cuffed, and although his master said nothing of his intention, the negro made up his mind, from appearances, as well as from the remarks of those around him, that he was destined for the *Southern market*. We reached Memphis during the night, and whilst within sight of the town, just before landing, the negro caused his wife to divide their things, as though resigned to the intended separation, and then, taking a moment when his master's back was turned, ran forward and jumped into the river. Of course he sank, and his master was several hundred dollars poorer than a moment before. That was all ; at least, scarcely any one mentioned it the next morning. I was obliged to get my information from the deck hands, and did not hear a remark concerning it in the cabin. In justice to the master, I should say, that after the occurrence he disclaimed any intention to separate them. Appearances, however, are quite against him, if I have been rightly informed. This sad affair needs no comment. It is an argument, however, that I might have used to-day, with some effect, whilst talking with a highly-intelligent Southerner of the evils of slavery. He had been reading *Uncle Tom's Cabin*, and spoke of it as a *novel*, which, like other romances, was well calculated to excite the sympathies, by the recital of heart-touching incidents which *never had an existence*, except in the imagination of the writer."

Instances have occurred where mothers, whose children were about to be sold from them, have, in their desperation, murdered their own offspring, to save them from this worst kind of orphanage. A case of this kind has been recently tried in the United States, and was alluded to, a week or two ago, by Mr. Giddings, in his speech on the floor of Congress.

An American gentleman from Italy, complaining of the effect of "Uncle Tom's Cabin" on the Italian mind, states that

images of fathers dragged from their families to be sold into slavery, and of babes torn from the breasts of weeping mothers, are constantly presented before the minds of the people as scenes of every-day life in America. The author can only say, sorrowfully, that it is *only the truth* which is thus presented.

These things *are*, every day, part and parcel of one of *the most thriving trades that is carried on in America*. The only difference between us and foreign nations is, that we have got used to it, and they have not. The thing has been done, and done again, day after day, and year after year, reported and lamented over in every variety of way; but it is *going on this day* with more briskness than ever before, and such scenes as we have described are enacted oftener, as the author will prove when she comes to the chapter on the internal slave-trade.

The incident in this same chapter which describes the scene where the wife of the unfortunate article, catalogued as "John aged 30," rushed on board the boat and threw her arms around him, with moans and lamentations, was a real incident. The gentleman who related it was so stirred in his spirit at the sight, that he addressed the trader in the exact words which the writer represents the young minister as having used in her narrative.

My friend, how can you, how dare you, carry on a trade like this! Look at those poor creatures! Here I am, rejoicing in my heart that I am going home to my wife and child ; and the same bell which is the signal to carry me onward towards them will part this poor man and his wife forever. Depend upon it, God will bring you into judgment for this.

If that gentleman has read the work,— as perhaps he has before now,— he has probably recognized his own words. One affecting incident in the narrative, as it really occurred, ought to be mentioned. The wife was passionately bemoaning her husband's fate, as about to be forever separated from all that he held dear, to be sold to the hard usage of a Southern plantation. The husband, in reply, used that very simple but sublime expression which the writer has placed in the mouth of Uncle Tom, in similar circumstances : "*There 'll be the same God there that there is here.*"

One other incident mentioned in "Uncle Tom's Cabin" may, perhaps, be as well verified in this place as in any other.

The case of old Prue w   related by a

brother and sister of the writer, as follows: She was the woman who supplied *rusks* and other articles of the kind at the house where they boarded. Her manners, appearance and character, were just as described. One day another servant came in her place, bringing the rusks. The sister of the writer inquired what had become of *Prue*. She seemed reluctant to answer for some time, but at last said that they had taken her into the cellar and beaten her, and that the flies had got at her, and she was dead!

It is well known that there are no *cellars*, properly so called, in New Orleans, the nature of the ground being such as to forbid digging. The slave who used the word had probably been imported from some state where cellars were in use, and applied the term to the place which was used for the ordinary purposes of a cellar. A cook who lived in the writer's family, having lived most of her life on a plantation, always applied the descriptive terms of the plantation to the very limited enclosures and retinue of a very plain house and yard.

This same lady, while living in the same place, used frequently to have her compassion excited by hearing the wailings of a sickly baby in a house adjoining their own, as also the objurgations and tyrannical abuse of a ferocious virago upon its mother. She once got an opportunity to speak to its mother, who appeared heart-broken and dejected, and inquired what was the matter with her child. Her answer was that she had had a fever, and that her milk was all dried away; and that her mistress was set against her child, and would not buy milk for it. She had tried to feed it on her own coarse food, but it pined and cried continually; and in witness of this she brought the baby to her. It was emaciated to a skeleton. The lady took the little thing to a friend of hers in the house who had been recently confined, and who was suffering from a redundancy of milk, and begged her to nurse it. The miserable sight of the little, famished, wasted thing affected the mother·so as to overcome all other considerations, and she placed it to her breast, when it revived, and took food with an eagerness which showed how much it had suffered. But the child was so reduced that this proved only a transient alleviation. It was after this almost impossible to get sight of the woman, and the violent temper of her mistress was such as to make it difficult to interfere in the case. The lady secretly afforded what aid she could, though, as she confessed, with a sort of mis-giving that it was a cruelty to try to hold back the poor little sufferer from the refuge of the grave; and it was a relief to her when at last its wailings ceased, and it went where the weary are at rest. This is one of those cases which go to show that the *interest* of the owner will not always insure kind treatment of the slave.

There is one other incident, which the writer interwove into the history of the mulatto woman who was bought by Legree for his plantation. The reader will remember that, in telling her story to Emmeline, she says:

"My Mas'r was Mr. Ellis, — lived on Levee-street. P'raps you 've seen the house."

"Was he good to you?" said Emmeline.

"Mostly, till he tuk sick. He 's lain sick, off and on, more than six months, and been orful oneasy. 'Pears like he warn't willin' to have nobody rest, day nor night; and got so cur'ous, there couldn't nobody suit him. 'Pears like he just grew crosser every day; kep me up nights till I got fairly beat out, and couldn't keep awake no longer; and 'cause I got to sleep one night, Lors! he talk so orful to me, and he tell me he'd sell me to just the·hardest master he could find; and he'd promised me my freedom, too, when he died."

An incident of this sort came under the author's observation in the following manner: A quadroon slave family, liberated by the will of the master, settled· on Walnut Hills, near her residence, and their children were received into her family school, taught in her house. In this family was a little quadroon boy, four or five years of age, with a sad, dejected appearance, who excited their interest.

The history of this child, as narrated by his friends, was simply this: His mother had been·the indefatigable nurse of her master, during a lingering and painful sickness, which at last terminated his life. She had borne all the fatigue of the nursing, both by night and by day, sustained in it by his promise that she should be rewarded for it by her liberty, at his death. Overcome by exhaustion and fatigue, she one night fell asleep, and he was unable to rouse her. The next day, after violently upbraiding her, he altered the directions of his will, and sold her to a man who was noted in all the region round as a cruel master, which sale, immediately on his death, took effect. The only mitigation of her sentence was that her child was not to be taken with her into this dreaded lot, but was·given to this quadroon family to be brought into a free state.

4

The writer very well remembers hearing this story narrated among a group of liberated negroes, and their comments on it. A peculiar form of grave and solemn irony often characterizes the communications of this class of people. It is a habit engendered in slavery to comment upon proceedings of this kind in language apparently respectful to the perpetrators, and which is felt to be irony only by a certain peculiarity of manner, difficult to describe. After the relation of this story, when the writer expressed her indignation in no measured terms, one of the oldest of the sable circle remarked, gravely,

"The man was a mighty great Christian, anyhow."

The writer warmly expressed her dissent from this view, when another of the same circle added,

"Went to glory, anyhow."

And another continued,

"Had the greatest kind of a time when he was a-dyin'; said he was goin' straight into heaven."

And when the writer remarked that many people thought so who never got there, a singular smile of grim approval passed round the circle, but no further comments were made. This incident has often recurred to the writer's mind, as showing the danger to the welfare of the master's soul from the possession of absolute power. A man of justice and humanity when in health, is often tempted to become unjust, exacting and exorbitant, in sickness. If, in these circumstances, he is surrounded by inferiors, from whom law and public opinion have taken away the rights of common humanity, how is he tempted to the exercise of the most despotic passions, and, like this unfortunate man, to leave the world with the weight of these awful words upon his head: "If ye forgive not men their trespasses, neither will your Father forgive your trespasses."

CHAPTER XII.

TOPSY.

Topsy stands as the representative of a large class of the children who are growing up under the institution of slavery,— quick, active, subtle and ingenious, apparently utterly devoid of principle and conscience, keenly penetrating, by an instinct which exists in the childish mind, the degradation of their condition, and the utter hopelessness

of rising above it; feeling the black skin on them, like the mark of Cain, to be a sign of reprobation and infamy, and urged on by a kind of secret desperation to make their "calling and election" in sin "sure."

Christian people have often been perfectly astonished and discouraged, as Miss Ophelia was, in the attempt to bring up such children decently and Christianly, under a state of things which takes away every stimulant which God meant should operate healthfully on the human mind.

We are not now speaking of the Southern States merely, but of the New England States; for, startling as it may appear, slavery is not yet wholly abolished in the free states of the North. The most unchristian part of it, that which gives to it all the bitterness and all the sting, is yet, in a great measure, unrepealed; it is the practical denial to the negro of the rights of human brotherhood. In consequence of this, Topsy is a character which may be found at the North as well as at the South.

In conducting the education of negro, mulatto and quadroon children, the writer has often observed this fact: — that, for a certain time, and up to a certain age, they kept equal pace with, and were often superior to, the white children with whom they were associated; but that there came a time when they became indifferent to learning, and made no further progress. This was invariably at the age when they were old enough to reflect upon life, and to perceive that society had no place to offer them for which anything more would be requisite than the rudest and most elementary knowledge.

Let us consider how it is with our own children; how few of them would ever acquire an education from the mere love of learning.

In the process necessary to acquire a handsome style of hand-writing, to master the intricacies of any language, or to conquer the difficulties of mathematical study, how often does the perseverance of the child flag, and need to be stimulated by his parents and teachers by such considerations as these: "It will be necessary for you, in such or such a position in life, to possess this or that acquirement or accomplishment. How could you ever become a merchant, without understanding accounts? How could you enter the learned professions, without understanding languages? If you are ignorant and uninformed, you cannot take rank as a gentleman in society."

Does not every one know that, without the stimulus which teachers and parents thus continually present, multitudes of children would never gain a tolerable education? And is it not the absence of all such stimulus which has prevented the negro child from an equal advance?

It is often objected to the negro race that they are frivolous and vain, passionately fond of show, and are interested only in trifles. And who is to blame for all this? Take away all high aims, all noble ambition, from any class, and what is left for them to be interested in *but* trifles?

The present attorney-general of Liberia, Mr. Lewis, is a man who commands the highest respect, for talent and ability in his position; yet, while he was in America, it is said that, like many other young colored men, he was distinguished only for foppery and frivolity. What made the change in Lewis after he went to Liberia? Who does not see the answer? Does any one wish to know what is inscribed on the seal which keeps the great stone over the sepulchre of African mind? It is this,— which was so truly said by poor Topsy,—"NOTHING BUT A NIGGER!"

It is this, burnt into the soul by the branding-iron of cruel and unchristian scorn, that is a sorer and deeper wound than all the physical evils of slavery together.

There never was a slave who did not feel it. Deep, deep down in the dark, still waters of his soul is the conviction, heavier, bitterer than all others, that he is *not regarded as a man*. On this point may be introduced the testimony of one who has known the wormwood and the gall of slavery by bitter experience. The following letter has been received from Dr. Pennington, in relation to some inquiries of the author:

{ 50 *Laurens-street*,
New York, Nov. 30, 1852.

MRS. H. B. STOWE.

ESTEEMED MADAM: I have duly received your kind letter in answer to mine of the 15th instant, in which you state that you " have an intense curiosity to know how far you have rightly divined the heart of the slave." You give me your idea in these words: " There lies buried down in the heart of the most seemingly careless and stupid slave a *bleeding spot*, that bleeds and aches, though he could scarcely tell why; and that this sore spot is the *degradation* of his position."

After escaping from the plantation of Dr. Tilghman, in Washington County, Md., where I was held as a slave, and worked as a blacksmith, I came to the State of Pennsylvania, and, after experiencing there some of the vicissitudes referred to in my little published narrative, I came into

New York State, bringing in my mind a certain indescribable feeling of wretchedness. They used to say of me at Dr. Tilghman's, " That blacksmith Jemmy is a 'cute fellow ; still water runs deep." But I confess that " blacksmith Jemmy" was not 'cute enough to understand the cause of his own wretchedness. The current of the still water may have run deep, but it did not reach down to that awful bed of lava.

At times I thought it occasioned by the lurking fear of betrayal. There was no Vigilance Committee at the time, — there were but anti-slavery men. I came North with my counsels in my own cautious breast. I married a wife, and did not tell her I was a fugitive. None of my friends knew it. I knew not the means of safety, and hence I was constantly in fear of meeting with some one who would betray me.

It was fully two years before I could hold up my head ; but still that feeling was in my mind. In 1846, after opening my bosom as a fugitive to John Hooker, Esq., I felt this much relief, — " Thank God there is one brother-man in hard old Connecticut that knows my troubles."

Soon after this, when I sailed to the island of Jamaica, and on landing there saw colored men in all the stations of civil, social, commercial life, where I had seen white men in this country, that feeling of wretchedness experienced a sensible relief, as if some feverish sore had been just reached by just the right kind of balm. There was before my eye evidence that a colored man is more than "a nigger." I went into the House of Assembly at Spanishtown, where fifteen out of forty-five members were colored men. I went into the courts, where I saw in the jury-box colored and white men together, colored and white lawyers at the bar. I went into the Common Council of Kingston ; there I found men of different colors. So in all the counting-rooms, &c. &c.

But still there was this drawback. Somebody says, " This is nothing but a nigger island." Now, then, my old trouble came back again ; " a nigger among niggers is but a nigger still."

In 1849, when I undertook my second visit to Great Britain, I resolved to prolong and extend my travel and intercourse with the best class of men, with a view to see if I could banish that trouble-some old ghost entirely out of my mind. In England, Scotland, Wales, France, Germany, Belgium and Prussia, my whole power he has been concentrated on this object. " I 'll be a man, and I 'll kill off this enemy which has haunted me these twenty years and more." I believe I have succeeded in some good degree ; at least, I have now no more trouble on the score of equal manhood with the whites. My European tour was certainly useful, because there the trial was fair and honorable. I had nothing to complain of. I got what was due to man, and I was expected to do what was due from man to man. I sought not to be treated as a pet. I put myself into the harness, and wrought manfully in the first pulpits, and the platforms in peace congresses, conventions, anniversaries, commencements, &c. ; and in these exercises that rusty old iron came out of my soul, and went " clean away."

You say again you have never seen a slave, how ever careless and merry-hearted, who had not this sore place, and that did not shrink or get angry if a finger was laid on it. I see that you have been a close observer of negro nature.

So far as I understand your idea, I think you are perfectly correct in the impression you have received, as explained in your note.

O, Mrs. Stowe, slavery is an awful system! It takes man, as God made him; it demolishes him, and then mis-creates him, or perhaps I should say mal-creates him!

Wishing you good health and good success in your arduous work,

I am yours, respectfully,
J. W. C. PENNINGTON.

People of intelligence, who have had the care of slaves, have often made this remark to the writer; "They are a singular whimsical people; you can do a great deal more with them by humoring some of their prejudices, than by bestowing on them the most substantial favors." On inquiring what these prejudices were, the reply would be, "They like to have their weddings elegantly celebrated, and to have a good deal of notice taken of their funerals, and to give and go to parties dressed and appearing like white people; and they will often put up with material inconveniences, and suffer themselves to be worked very hard, if they are humored in these respects."

Can any one think of this without compassion? Poor souls! willing to bear with so much for simply this slight acknowledgment of their common humanity. To honor their weddings and funerals is, in some sort, acknowledging that they are human, and therefore they prize it. Hence we see the reason of the passionate attachment which often exists in a faithful slave to a good master. It is, in fact, a transfer of his identity to his master. A stern law and an unchristian public sentiment has taken away his birthright of humanity, erased his name from the catalogue of men, and made him an anomalous creature — neither man nor brute. When a kind master recognizes his humanity, and treats him as a humble companion and a friend, there is no need to the devotion and gratitude which he thus excites. He is to the slave a deliverer and a saviour from the curse which lies on his hapless race. Deprived of all legal rights and privileges, all opportunity or hope of personal advancement or honor, he transfers, as it were, his whole existence into his master's, and appropriates his rights, his position, his honor, as his own; and thus enjoys a kind of reflected sense of what it might be to be a man himself. Hence it is that the appeal to the more generous part of the negro character is seldom made in vain.

An acquaintance of the writer was married to a gentleman in Louisiana, who was the proprietor of some eight hundred slaves. He, of course, had a large train of servants in his domestic establishment. When about to enter upon her duties, she was warned that the servants were all so thievish that she would be under the necessity, in common with all other housekeepers, of keeping everything under lock and key. She, however, announced her intention of training her servants in such a manner as to make this unnecessary. Her ideas were ridiculed as chimerical, but she resolved to carry them into practice. The course she pursued was as follows: She called all the family servants together; told them that it would be a great burden and restraint upon her to be obliged to keep everything locked from them; that she had heard that they were not at all to be trusted, but that she could not help hoping that they were much better than they had been represented. She told them that she should provide abundantly for all their wants, and then that she should leave her stores unlocked, and trust to their honor.

The idea that they were supposed capable of having any honor struck a new chord at once in every heart. The servants appeared most grateful for the trust, and there was much public spirit excited, the older and graver ones exerting themselves to watch over the children, that nothing might be done to destroy this new-found treasure of honor.

At last, however, the lady discovered that some depredations had been made on her cake by some of the juvenile part of the establishment; she, therefore, convened all the servants, and stated the fact to them. She remarked that it was not on account of the value of the cake that she felt annoyed, but that they must be sensible that it would not be pleasant for her to have it indiscriminately fingered and handled, and that, therefore, she should set some cake out upon a table, or some convenient place, and beg that all those who were disposed to take it would go there and help themselves, and allow the rest to remain undisturbed in the closet. She states that the cake stood upon the table and dried, without a morsel of it being touched, and that she never afterwards had any trouble in this respect.

A little time after, a new carriage was bought, and one night the leather boot of it was found to be missing. Before her husband had time to take any steps on the subject, the servants of the family called a convention among themselves, and instituted an inquiry into the offence. The boot was found and promptly restored, though they would not reveal to their master and mistress the name of the offender.

One other anecdote which this lady related illustrates that peculiar devotion of a slave to a good master, to which allusion has been made. Her husband met with his death by a sudden and melancholy accident. He had a personal attendant and confidential servant who had grown up with him from childhood. This servant was so overwhelmed with grief as to be almost stupefied. On the day of the funeral a brother of his deceased master inquired of him if he had performed a certain commission for his mistress. The servant said that he had forgotten it. Not perceiving his feelings at the moment, the gentleman replied, "I am surprised that you should neglect any command of your mistress, when she is in such affliction."

This remark was the last drop in the full cup. The poor fellow fell to the ground entirely insensible, and the family were obliged to spend nearly two hours employing various means to restore his vitality. The physician accounted for his situation by saying that there had been such a rush of all the blood in the body towards the heart, that there was actual danger of a rupture of that organ,—a literal death by a broken heart.

Some thoughts may be suggested by Miss Ophelia's conscientious but unsuccessful efforts in the education of Topsy.

Society has yet need of a great deal of enlightening as to the means of restoring the vicious and degraded to virtue.

It has been erroneously supposed that with brutal and degraded natures only coarse and brutal measures could avail; and yet it has been found, by those who have most experience, that their success with this class of society has been just in proportion to the delicacy and kindliness with which they have treated them.

Lord Shaftsbury, who has won so honorable a fame by his benevolent interest in the efforts made for the degraded lower classes of his own land, says, in a recent letter to the author:

You are right about Topsy; our ragged schools will afford you many instances of poor children, hardened by kicks, insults and neglect, moved to tears and docility by the first word of kindness. It opens new feelings, develops, as it were, a new

nature, and brings the wretched outcast into the family of man.

Recent efforts which have been made among unfortunate females in some of the worst districts of New York show the same thing. What is it that rankles deepest in the breast of fallen woman, that makes her so hopeless and irreclaimable? It is that burning consciousness of degradation which stings worse than cold or hunger, and makes her shrink from the face of the missionary and the philanthropist. They who have visited these haunts of despair and wretchedness have learned that they must touch gently the shattered harp of the human soul, if they would string it again to divine music; that they must encourage self-respect, and hope, and sense of character, or the bonds of death can never be broken.

Let us examine the gospel of Christ, and see on what principles its appeals are constructed. Of what nature are those motives which have melted *our* hearts and renewed *our* wills? Are they not appeals to the most generous and noble instincts of our nature? Are we not told of One fairer than the sons of men,— One reigning in immortal glory, who loved us so that he could bear pain, and want, and shame, and death itself, for our sake?

When Christ speaks to the soul, does he crush one of its nobler faculties? Does he taunt us with our degradation, our selfishness, our narrowness of view, and feebleness of intellect, compared with his own? Is it not true that he not only saves us from our sins, but saves us in a way most considerate, most tender, most regardful of our feelings and sufferings? Does not the Bible tell us that, in order to fulfil his office of Redeemer the more perfectly, he took upon him the condition of humanity, and endured the pains, and wants, and temptations of a mortal existence, that he might be to us a sympathizing, appreciating friend, " touched with the feeling of our infirmities," and cheering us gently on in the hard path of returning virtue?

O, when shall we, who have received so much of Jesus Christ, learn to repay it in acts of kindness to our poor brethren? When shall we be Christ-like, and not man-like, in our efforts to reclaim the fallen and wandering?

CHAPTER XIII.

THE QUAKERS.

THE writer's sketch of the character of this people has been drawn from personal observation. There are several settlements of these people in Ohio, and the manner of living, the tone of sentiment, and the habits of life, as represented in her book, are not at all exaggerated.

These settlements have always been refuges for the oppressed and outlawed slave. The character of Rachel Halliday was a real one, but she has passed away to her reward. Simeon Halliday, calmly risking fine and imprisonment for his love to God and man, has had in this country many counterparts among the sect.

The writer had in mind, at the time of writing, the scenes in the trial of Thomas Garret, of Wilmington, Delaware, for the crime of hiring a hack to convey a mother and four children from Newcastle jail to Wilmington, a distance of *five miles.*

The writer has received the facts in this case in a letter from John Garret himself, from which some extracts will be made :

Wilmington, Delaware,
1st month 18th, 1853.

MY DEAR FRIEND,

HARRIET BEECHER STOWE: I have this day received a request from Charles K. Whipple, of Boston, to furnish thee with a statement, authentic and circumstantial, of the trouble and losses which have been brought upon myself and others of my friends from the aid we had rendered to fugitive slaves, in order, if thought of sufficient importance, to be published in a work thee is now preparing for the press.

I will now endeavor to give thee a statement of what John Hunn and myself suffered by aiding a family of slaves, a few years since. I will give the facts as they occurred, and thee may condense and publish so much as thee may think useful in thy work, and no more :

"In the 12th month, year 1846, a family, consisting of Samuel Hawkins, a freeman, his wife Emeline, and six children, who were afterwards *proved slaves,* stopped at the house of a friend named John Hunn, near Middletown, in this state, in the evening about sunset, to procure food and lodging for the night. They were seen by some of Hunn's pro-slavery neighbors, who soon came with a constable, and had them taken before a magistrate. Hunn had left the slaves in his kitchen when he went to the village of Middletown, half a mile distant. When the officer came with a warrant for them, he met Hunn at the kitchen door, and asked for the blacks; Hunn, with truth, said he did not know where they were. Hunn's wife, thinking they would be safer, had sent them up stairs during his absence, where they were found. Hunn made no resistance, and they were taken before the magistrate, and from his office direct to Newcastle jail, where they arrived about one o'clock on 7th day morning.

The sheriff and his daughter, being kind, humane people, inquired of Hawkins and wife the facts of their case; and his daughter wrote to a lady here, to request me to go to Newcastle and inquire into the case, as her father and self really believed they were most of them, if not all, entitled to their *freedom.* Next morning I went to Newcastle : had the family of colored people brought into the parlor, and the sheriff and myself came to the conclusion that the parents and four youngest children were by law entitled to their freedom. I prevailed on the sheriff to show me the commitment of the magistrate, which I found was defective, and not in due form according to law. I procured a copy and handed it to a lawyer. He pronounced the commitment irregular, and agreed to go next morning to Newcastle and have the whole family taken before Judge Booth, Chief Justice of the state, by *habeas corpus,* when the following admission was made by Samuel Hawkins and wife : They admitted that the two eldest boys were held by one Charles Glaudin, of Queen Anne County, Maryland, as slaves ; that after the birth of these two children, Elizabeth Turner, also of Queen Anne, the mistress of their mother, had set her free, and permitted her to go and live with her husband, near twenty miles from her residence, after which the four youngest children were born ; that her mistress during all that time, eleven or twelve years, had never contributed one dollar to their support, or come to see them. After examining the commitment in their case, and consulting with my attorney, the judge set the whole family at liberty. The day was wet and cold ; one of the children, three years old, was a cripple from white swelling, and could not walk a step ; another, eleven months old, at the breast ; and the parents being desirous of getting to Wilmington, five miles distant, I asked the judge if there would be any risk or impropriety in my hiring a conveyance for the mother and four young children to Wilmington. His reply, in the presence of the sheriff and my attorney, was there would not be any. I then requested the sheriff to procure a hack to take them over to Wilmington."

The whole family escaped. John Hunn and John Garret were brought up to trial for having practically fulfilled those words of Christ which read, "I was a stranger and ye took me in, I was sick and in prison and ye came unto me." For John Hunn's part of this crime, he was fined two thousand five hundred dollars, and John Garret was fined five thousand four hundred. Three thousand five hundred of this was the fine for hiring a hack for them, and one thousand nine hundred was assessed on him as the value of the slaves! Our European friends will infer from this that it costs something to obey Christ in America, as well as in Europe.

After John Garret's trial was over, and this heavy judgment had been given against him, he calmly rose in the court-room, and requested leave to address a few words to the court and audience.

Leave being granted, he spoke as follows :

I have a few words which I wish to address to the court, jury and prosecutors, in the several suits that have been brought against me during the sittings of this court, in order to determine the amount of penalty I must pay for doing what my feelings prompted me to do as a lawful and meritorious act; a simple act of humanity and justice, as I believed, to eight of that oppressed race, the people of color, whom I found in the Newcastle jail, in the 12th month, 1845. I will now endeavor to state the facts of those cases, for your consideration and reflection after you return home to your families and friends. You will then have time to ponder on what has transpired here since the sitting of this court, and I believe that your verdict will then be unanimous, that the law of the United States, as explained by our venerable judge, when compared with the act committed by me, was cruel and oppressive, and needs remodelling.

Here follows a very brief and clear statement of the facts in the case, of which the reader is already apprized.

After showing conclusively that he had no reason to suppose the family to be slaves, and that they had all been discharged by the judge, he nobly adds the following words:

Had I believed every one of them to be slaves, I should have done the same thing. I should have done violence to my convictions of duty, had I not made use of all the lawful means in my power to liberate those people, and assist them to become men and women, rather than leave them in the condition of chattels personal.

I am called an Abolitionist; once a name of reproach, but one I have ever been proud to be considered worthy of being called. For the last twenty-five years I have been engaged in the cause of this despised and much-injured race, and consider their cause worth suffering for; but, owing to a multiplicity of other engagements, I could not devote so much of my time and mind to their cause as I otherwise should have done.

The impositions and persecutions practised on those unoffending and innocent brethren are extreme beyond endurance. I am now placed in a situation in which I have not so much to claim my attention as formerly; and I now pledge myself, in the presence of this assembly, to use all lawful and honorable means to lessen the burdens of this oppressed people, and endeavor, according to ability furnished, to burst their chains asunder, and set them free; not relaxing my efforts on their behalf while blessed with health, and a slave remains to tread the soil of the state of my adoption, — Delaware.

After mature reflection, I can assure this assembly it is my opinion at this time that the verdicts you have given the prosecutors against John Hunn and myself, within the past few days, will have a tendency to raise a spirit of inquiry throughout the length and breadth of the land, respecting this monster evil (slavery), in many minds that have not heretofore investigated the subject. The reports of those trials will be published by editors from Maine to Texas and the far West; and what must be the effect produced? It will, no doubt, add hundreds, perhaps 'thousands, to the present large and rapidly increasing army of abolitionists. The injury is great to us who are the immediate sufferers by your verdict; but I believe the verdicts you have given against us within the last few days will have a powerful effect in bringing about the abolition of slavery in this country, this land of boasted freedom, where not only the slave is fettered at the South by his lordly master, but the white man at the North is bound as in chains to do the bidding of his Southern masters.

In his letter to the writer John Garret adds, that after this speech a young man who had served as juryman came across the room, and taking him by the hand, said:

"Old gentleman, I believe every statement that you have made. I came from home prejudiced against you, and I now acknowledge that I have helped to do you injustice."

Thus calmly and simply did this Quaker confess Christ before men, according as it is written of them of old, —" He esteemed the reproach of Christ greater riches than all the treasures of Egypt."

Christ has said, "Whosoever shall be ashamed of me and my words, of him shall the Son of Man be ashamed." In our days it is not customary to be ashamed of Christ personally, but of *his words* many are ashamed. But when they meet Him in judgment they will have cause to remember them; for heaven and earth shall pass away, but His word shall not pass away.

Another case of the same kind is of a more affecting character.

Richard Dillingham was the son of a respectable Quaker family in Morrow County, Ohio. His pious mother brought him up in the full belief of the doctrine of St. John, that the love of God and the love of man are inseparable. He was diligently taught in such theological notions as implied in such passages as these: "Hereby perceive we the love of God, because he laid down his life for us; and we ought also to lay down our lives for the brethren. — But whoso hath this world's goods and seeth his brother have need and shutteth up his bowels of compassion from him, how dwelleth the love of God in him? — My little children, let us not love in word and in tongue, but in deed and in truth."

In accordance with these precepts, Richard Dillingham, in early manhood, was found in Cincinnati teaching the colored people, and visiting in the prisons and doing what in him lay to "love in deed and in truth."

Some unfortunate families among the colored people had dear friends who were slaves in Nashville, Tennessee. Richard was so interested in their story, that when he went into Tennessee he was actually taken up and caught in the very fact of helping certain poor people to escape to their friends.

He was seized and thrown into prison. In the language of this world he was imprisoned as a "negro-stealer." His own account is given in the following letter to his parents:

Nashville Jail, 12th mo. 15th, 1849.

DEAR PARENTS : I presume you have heard of my arrest and imprisonment in the Nashville jail, under a charge of aiding in an attempted escape of slaves from the city of Nashville, on the 5th inst. I was arrested by M. D. Maddox (district constable), aided by Frederick Marshal, watchman at the Nashville Inn, and the bridge-keeper, at the bridge across the Cumberland river. When they arrested me, I had rode up to the bridge on horseback and paid the toll for myself and for the hack to pass over, in which three colored persons, who were said to be slaves, were found by the men who arrested me. The driver of the hack (who is a free colored man of this city), and the persons in the hack, were also arrested ; and after being taken to the Nashville Inn and searched, we were all taken to jail. My arrest took place about eleven o'clock at night.

In another letter he says :

At the bridge, Maddox said to me, " You are just the man we wanted. We will make an example of you." As soon as we were safe in the bar-room of the inn, Maddox took a candle and looked me in the face, to see if he could recognize my countenance ; and looking intently at me a few moments, he said, " Well, you are too good-looking a young man to be engaged in such an affair as this." The bystanders asked me several questions, to which I replied that under the present circumstances I would rather be excused from answering any questions relating to my case ; upon which they desisted from further inquiry. Some threats and malicious wishes were uttered against me by the ruffian part of the assembly, being about twenty-five persons in it, and I can assure thee that they were very far from being agreeable companions to me, although they were kind. But thou knows that I do not relish cursing and swearing, and worst of all loathsome and obscene blasphemy ; and of such was most of the conversation of my prison mates when I was first put in here. The jailers are kind enough to me, but the jail is so constructed that it cannot be warmed, and we have to either warm ourselves by walking in our cell, which is twelve by fifteen feet, or by lying in bed. I went out to my trial on the 16th of last month, and put it off till the next term of the court, which will be commenced on the second of next 4th month. I put it off on the ground of excitement.

Dear brother, I have no hopes of getting clear of being convicted and sentenced to the penitentiary ; but do not think that I am without comfort in my afflictions, for I assure thee that I have many reflections that give me sweet consolation in the midst of my grief. I have a clear conscience

before my God, which is my greatest comfort and support through all my troubles and afflictions. An approving conscience none can know but those who enjoy it. It nerves us in the hour of trial to bear our sufferings with fortitude, and even with cheerfulness. The greatest affliction I have is the reflection of the sorrow and anxiety my friends will have to endure on my account. But I can assure thee, brother, that with the exception of this reflection, I am far, very far, from being one of the most miserable of men. Nay, to the contrary, I am not terrified at the prospect before me, though I am grieved about it ; but all have enough to grieve about in this unfriendly wilderness of sin and woe. My hopes are not fixed in this world, and therefore I have a source of consolation that will never fail me, so long as I slight not the offers of mercy, comfort and peace, which my blessed Saviour constantly privileges me with.

One source of almost constant annoyance to my feelings is the profanity and vulgarity, and the bad, disagreeable temper, of two or three fellow-prisoners of my cell. They show me considerable kindness and respect ; but they cannot do otherwise, when treated with the civility and kindness with which I treat them. If it be my fate to go to the penitentiary for eight or ten years, I can, I believe, meet my doom without shedding a tear. I have not yet shed a tear, though there may be many in store. My bail-bonds were set at seven thousand dollars. If I should be bailed out, I should return to my trial, unless my security were rich, and did not wish me to return ; for *I am Richard yet,* although I am in the prison of my enemy, and will not flinch from what I believe to be right and honorable. These are the principles which, in carrying out, have lodged me here ; for there was a time, at my arrest, that I might have, in all probability, escaped the police, but it would have subjected those who were arrested with me to punishment, perhaps even to death, in order to find out who I was, and if they had not told more than they could have done in truth, they would probably have been punished without mercy ; and I am determined no one shall suffer for me. I am now a prisoner, but those who were arrested with me are all at liberty, and I believe without whipping. I now stand alone before the Commonwealth of Tennessee to answer for the affair. Tell my friends I am in the midst of consolation here.

Richard was engaged to a young lady of amiable disposition and fine mental endowments.

To her he thus writes :

O, dearest ! Canst thou upbraid me ? canst thou call it crime ? wouldst thou call it crime, or couldst thou upbraid me, for rescuing, or attempting to rescue, *thy* father, mother, or brother and sister, or even friends, from a captivity among a cruel race of oppressors ? O, couldst thou only see what I have seen, and hear what I have heard, of the sad, vexatious, degrading, and soul-trying situation of as noble minds as ever the Anglo-Saxon race were possessed of, mourning in vain for that universal heaven-born boon of freedom, which an all-wise and beneficent Creator has designed for all, thou couldst not censure, but wouldst deeply sympathize with me ! Take all these things into consideration, and the thousands of poor mortals who are dragging out far more miserable lives than mine will be, even at ten years in the penitentiary, and thou wilt not look upon my fate with so much horror as thou would at first thought.

In another letter he adds :

I have happy hours here, and I should not be miserable if I could only know you were not sorrowing for me at home. It would give me more satisfaction to hear that you were not grieving about me than anything else.

The nearer I live to the principle of the commandment, " Love thy neighbor as thyself," the more enjoyment I have of this life. None can know the enjoyments that flow from feelings of good will towards our fellow-beings, both friends and enemies, but those who cultivate them. Even in my prison-cell I may be happy, if I will. For the Christian's consolation cannot be shut out from him by enemies or iron gates.

In another letter to the lady before alluded to he says :

By what I am able to learn, I believe thy " Richard" has not fallen altogether unlamented ; and the satisfaction it gives me is sufficient to make my prison life 'more pleasant and desirable than even a life of liberty without the esteem and respect of my friends. But it gives bitterness to the cup of my afflictions to think that my dear friends and relatives have to suffer such grief and sorrow for me.

* * * * * *

Though persecution ever so severe be my lot, yet I will not allow my indignation ever to ripen into revenge even against my bitterest enemies ; for there will be a time when all things must be revealed before Him who has said " Vengeance is mine, I will repay." Yes, my heart shall ever glow with love for my poor fellow-mortals, who are hastening rapidly on to their final destination —the awful tomb and the solemn judgment.

Perhaps it will give thee some consolation for me to tell thee that I believe there is a considerable sympathy existing in the minds of some of the better portion of the citizens here, which may be of some benefit to me. But all that can be done in my behalf will still leave my case a sad one. Think not, however, that it is all loss to me, for by my calamity I have learned many good and useful lessons, which I hope may yet prove both temporal and spiritual blessings to me.

> " Behind a frowning providence ·
> He hides a smiling face."

Therefore I hope thou and my dear distressed parents will be somewhat comforted about me, for I know you regard my spiritual welfare far more than anything else.

In his next 'letter to the same friend he says :

Since I wrote my last, I have had a severe moral conflict, in which I believe the right conquered, and has completely gained the ascendency. The matter was this : A man with whom I have become acquainted since my imprisonment offered to bail me out and let me stay away from my trial, and pay the bail-bonds for me, and was very

anxious to do it. [Here he mentions that the funds held by this individual had been placed in his hands by a person who obtained them by dishonest means.] But having learned the above facts, which he in confidence made known to me, I declined accepting his offer, giving him my reasons in full. The matter rests with him, my attorneys and myself. My attorneys do not know who he is, but, with his permission, I in confidence informed them of the nature of the case, after I came to a conclusion upon the subject, and had determined not to accept the offer ; which was approved by them. I also had an offer of iron saws and files and other tools by which I could break jail ; but I refused them also, as I do not wish to pursue any such underhanded course to extricate myself from my present difficulties ; for when I leave Tennessee — if I ever do — I am determined to leave it a free man. Thou need not fear that I shall ever stoop to dishonorable means to avoid my severe impending fate. When I meet thee again I want to meet thee with a clear conscience, and a character unspotted by disgrace.

In another place he says, in view of his nearly approaching trial :

O dear parents ! The principles of love for my fellow-beings which you have instilled into my mind are some of the greatest consolations I have in my imprisonment, and they give me resignation to bear whatever may be inflicted upon me without feeling any malice or bitterness toward my vigilant prosecutors. If they show me mercy, it will be accepted by me with gratitude ; but if they do not, I will endeavor to bear whatever they may inflict with Christian fortitude and resignation, and try not to murmur at my lot ; but it is hard to obey the commandment, " Love your enemies."

The day of his trial at length came.

His youth, his engaging manners, frank address, and invariable gentleness to all who approached him, had won many friends, and the trial excited much interest.

His mother and her brother, Asa Williams, went a distance of seven hundred and fifty miles to attend his trial. They carried with them a certificate of his character, drawn up by Dr. Brisbane, and numerously signed by his friends and acquaintances, and officially countersigned by civil officers. This was done at the suggestion of his counsel, and exhibited by them in court. When brought to the bar it is said that " his demeanor was calm, dignified and manly." His mother sat by his side. The prosecuting attorney waived his plea, and left the ground clear for Richard's counsel. Their defence was eloquent and pathetic. After they closed, Richard rose, and in a calm and dignified manner spoke extemporaneously as follows :

" By the kind permission of the Court, for which I am sincerely thankful, I avail myself of the privilege of adding a few words to the remarks already made by my counsel. And although I stand, by my own confession, as a criminal in the eyes of your violated laws, yet I feel confident that I am addressing those who have hearts to feel ; and in meting out the punishment that I am about to suffer I hope you ·will be lenient, for it is a new situation in which I am placed: Never before, in the whole course of my life, have I been charged with a dishonest act. And from my childhood kind parents, whose names I deeply reverence, have instilled into my mind a desire to be virtuous and honorable; and it has ever been my aim so to conduct myself as to merit the confidence and esteem of my fellow-men. But, gentlemen, I have violated your laws. This offence I did commit; and I now stand before you, to my sorrow and regret, as a criminal. But I was prompted to it by feelings of humanity. It has been suspected, as I was informed, that I am leagued with a fraternity who are combined for the purpose of committing such offences as the one with which I am charged. But, gentlemen, the impression is false. I alone am guilty, I alone committed the offence, and I alone must suffer the penalty. My parents, my friends, my relatives, are as innocent of any participation in or knowledge of my offence as the babe unborn. My parents are still living,* though advanced in years, and, in the course of nature, a few more years will terminate their earthly existence. In their old age and infirmity they will need a stay and protection; and if you can, consistently with your ideas of justice, make my term of imprisonment a short one, you will receive the lasting gratitude of a son who reverences his parents, and the prayers and blessings of an aged father and mother who love their child."

A great deal of sensation now appeared in the court-room, and most of the jury are said to have wept. They retired for a few moments, and returned a verdict for three years imprisonment in the penitentiary.

The *Nashville Daily Gazette* of April 13, 1849, contains the following notice:

"THE KIDNAPPING CASE.

"Richard Dillingham, who was arrested on the 5th day of December last, having in his possession three slaves whom he intended to convey with him to a free state, was arraigned yesterday and tried in the Criminal Court. The prisoner confessed his guilt, and made a short speech in palliation of his offence. He avowed that the act was undertaken by himself without instigation from any source, and he alone was responsible for the error into which his education had led him. He had, he said, no other motive than the good of the slaves, and did not expect to claim any advantage by freeing them. He was sentenced to three years imprisonment in the penitentiary, the least time the law allows for the offence committed. Mr. Dillingham is a Quaker from Ohio, and has been a teacher in that state. He belongs to a respectable family, and he is not without the sympathy of those who attended the trial. It was a foolhardy enterprise in which he embarked, and dearly has he paid for his rashness."

His mother, before leaving Nashville, visited the governor, and had an interview with him in regard to pardoning her son. He gave her some encouragement, but thought she had better postpone her petition for the present. After the lapse of several months, she wrote to him about it; but he seemed to have changed his mind, as the following letter will show:

"*Nashville, August* 29, 1849.

"DEAR MADAM: Your letter of the 6th of the 7th mo. was received, and would have been noticed

* R. D.'s father survived him only a few months.

earlier but for my absence from home. Your solicitude for your son is natural, and it would be gratifying to be able to reward it by releasing him, if it were in my power. But the offence for which he is suffering was clearly made out, and its tendency here is very hurtful to our rights, and our peace as a people. He is doomed to the shortest period known to our statute. And, at all events, I could not interfere with his case for some time to come; and, to be frank with you, I do not see how his time can be lessened at all. But my term of office will expire soon, and the governor elect, Gen. William Trousdale, will take my place. To him you will make any future appeal. "Yours, &c.   N. L. BROWN."

The warden of the penitentiary, John McIntosh, was much prejudiced against him. He thought the sentence was too light, and, being of a stern bearing, Richard had not much to expect from his kindness. But the same sterling integrity and ingenuousness which had ever, under all circumstances, marked his conduct, soon wrought a change in the minds of his keepers, and of his enemies generally. He became a favorite with McIntosh, and some of the guard. According to the rules of the prison, he was not allowed to write oftener than once in three months, and what he wrote had, of course, to be inspected by the warden.

He was at first put to sawing and scrubbing rock; but, as the delicacy of his frame unfitted him for such labors, and the spotless sanctity of his life won the reverence of his jailers, he was soon promoted to be steward of the prison hospital. In a letter to a friend he thus announces this change in his situation:

I suppose thou art, ere this time, informed of the change in my situation, having been placed in the hospital of the penitentiary as steward. . . I feel but poorly qualified to fill the situation they have assigned me, but will try to do the best I can. . . . . I enjoy the comforts of a good fire and a warm room, and am allowed to sit up evenings and read, which I prize as a great privilege. . . . . I have now been here nearly nine months, and have twenty-seven more to stay. It seems to me a long time in prospect. I try to be as patient as I can, but sometimes I get low-spirited. I throw off the thoughts of home and friends as much as possible; for, when indulged in, they only increase my melancholy feelings. And what wounds my feelings most is the reflection of what you all suffer of grief and anxiety for me. Cease to grieve for me, for I am unworthy of it; and it only causes pain for you, without availing aught for me. . . . As ever, thine in the bonds of affection,   R. D.

He had been in prison little more than a year when the cholera invaded Nashville, and broke out among the inmates; Richard was up day and night in attendance on the sick, his disinterested and sympathetic nature leading him to labors to which his delicate constitution, impaired by confinement, was altogether inadequate.

> "Beside the bed where parting life was laid,
> And sorrow, grief and pain, by turns dismayed,
> The youthful champion stood : at his control
> Despair and anguish fled the trembling soul,
> Comfort came down the dying wretch to raise,
> And his last faltering accents whispered praise."

Worn with these labors, the gentle, patient lover of God and of his brother, at last overwearied, and passed peacefully away to a world where all are lovely and loving.

Though his correspondence with her he most loved was interrupted, from his unwillingness to subject his letters to the surveillance of the warden, yet a note reached her, conveyed through the hands of a prisoner whose time was out. In this letter, the last which any earthly friend ever received, he says :

I ofttimes, yea, *all* times, think of thee ; — if I did not, I should cease to exist.

What must that system be which makes it necessary to imprison with convicted felons a man like this, because he loves his brother man " not wisely but too well " ?

On his death Whittier wrote the following :

> " Si crucem libenter portes, te portabit."— *Imit. Christ.*

> " The Cross, if freely borne, shall be
> No burthen, but support, to thee."
> So, moved of old time for our sake,
> The holy man of Kempen spake.

> Thou brave and true one, upon whom
> Was laid the Cross of Martyrdom,
> How didst thou, in thy faithful youth,
> Bear witness to this blessed truth !

> Thy cross of suffering and of shame
> A staff within thy hands became ; —
> In paths, where Faith alone could see
> The Master's steps, upholding thee.

> Thine was the seed-time : God alone
> Beholds the end of what is sown ;
> Beyond our vision, weak and dim,
> The harvest-time is hid with Him.

> Yet, unforgotten where it lies,
> That seed of generous sacrifice,
> Though seeming on the desert cast,
> Shall rise with bloom and fruit at last.
> J. G. WHITTIER.

Amesbury, Second mo. 18th, 1852.

CHAPTER XIV.

THE SPIRIT OF ST. CLARE.

THE general tone of the press and of the community in the slave states, so far as it has been made known at the North, has been loudly condemnatory of the representations of " Uncle Tom's Cabin." Still, it would be unjust to the character of the South to refuse to acknowledge that she has many sons with candor enough to perceive, and courage enough to avow, the evils of her " peculiar institutions." The manly independence exhibited by these men, in communities where popular sentiment rules despotically, either by law or in spite of law, should be duly honored. The sympathy of such minds as these is a high encouragement to philanthropic effort.

The author inserts a few testimonials from Southern men, not without some pride in being thus kindly judged by those who might have been naturally expected to read her book with prejudice against it.

The *Jefferson Inquirer*, published at Jefferson City, Missouri, Oct. 23, 1852, contains the following communication :

UNCLE TOM'S CABIN.

I have lately read this celebrated book, which, perhaps, has gone through more editions, and been sold in greater numbers, than any work from the American press, in the same length of time. It is a work of high literary finish, and its several characters are drawn with great power and truthfulness, although, like the characters in most novels and works of fiction, in some instances too highly colored. There is no attack on slave-holders as such, but, on the contrary, many of them are represented as highly noble, generous, humane and benevolent. Nor is there any attack upon them as a class. It sets forth many of the evils of slavery, as *an institution established by law*, but without charging these evils on those who hold the slaves, and seems fully to appreciate the difficulties in finding a remedy. Its effect upon the slave-holder is to make him a kinder and better master; to which none can object. This is said without any intention to endorse everything contained in the book, or, indeed, in any novel, or work of fiction. But, if I mistake not, there are few, excepting those who are greatly prejudiced, that will rise from a perusal of the book without being a truer and better Christian, and a more humane and benevolent man. As a slave-holder, I do not feel the least aggrieved. How Mrs. Stowe, the authoress, has obtained her extremely accurate knowledge of the negroes, their character, dialect, habits, &c., is beyond my comprehension, as she never resided — as appears from the preface — in a slave state, or among slaves or negroes. But they are certainly admirably delineated. The book is highly interesting and amusing, and will afford a rich treat to its reader.
THOMAS JEFFERSON.

The opinion of the editor himself is given in these words :

UNCLE TOM'S CABIN.

Well, like a good portion of " the world and the rest of mankind," we have read the book of Mrs. Stowe bearing the above title.

From numerous statements, newspaper paragraphs and rumors, we supposed the book was all that fanaticism and heresy could invent, and were therefore greatly prejudiced against it. But, on reading it, we cannot refrain from saying that it is a work of more than ordinary moral worth, and is entitled to consideration. We do not regard it as "a corruption of moral sentiment," and a gross "libel on a portion of our people." The authoress seems disposed to treat the subject fairly, though, in some particulars, the scenes are too highly colored, and too strongly drawn from the imagination. The book, however, may lead its readers at a distance to misapprehend some of the general and better features of "Southern life as it is" (which, by the way, we, as an individual, prefer to Northern life); yet it is a perfect mirror of several classes of people "we have in our mind's eye, who are not free from all the ills flesh is heir to." It has been feared that the book would result in injury to the slave-holding interests of the country; but we apprehend no such thing, and hesitate not to recommend it to the perusal of our friends and the public generally.

Mrs. Stowe has exhibited a knowledge of many peculiarities of Southern society which is really wonderful, when we consider that she is a Northern lady by birth and residence.

We hope, then, before our friends form any harsh opinions of the merits of "Uncle Tom's Cabin," and make up any judgment against us for pronouncing in its favor (barring some objections to it), that they will give it a careful perusal; and, in so speaking, we may say that we yield to no man in his devotion to Southern rights and interests.

The editor of the *St. Louis* (Missouri) *Battery* pronounces the following judgment:

We took up this work, a few evenings since, with just such prejudices against it as we presume many others have commenced reading it. We have been so much in contact with ultra abolitionists, — have had so much evidence that their benevolence was much more hatred for the master than love for the slave, accompanied with a profound ignorance of the circumstances surrounding both, and a most consummate, supreme disgust for the whole negro race, — that we had about concluded that anything but rant and nonsense was out of the question from a Northern writer upon the subject of slavery.

Mrs. Stowe, in these delineations of life among the lowly, has convinced us to the contrary. She brings to the discussion of her subject a perfectly cool, calculating judgment, a wide, all-comprehending intellectual vision, and a deep, warm, sea-like woman's soul, over all of which is flung a perfect iris-like imagination, which makes the light of her pictures stronger and more beautiful, as their shades are darker and terror-striking. We do not wonder that the copy before us is of the seventieth thousand. And seventy thousand more will not supply the demand, or we mistake the appreciation of the American people of the real merits of literary productions. Mrs. Stowe has, in "Uncle Tom's Cabin," set up for herself a monument more enduring than marble. It will stand amid the wastes of slavery as the Memnon stands amid the sands of the African desert, telling both the white man and the negro of the approach of morning. The book is not an abolitionist work, in the offensive sense of the word. It is, as we have intimated, free from everything like fanaticism, no matter what amount of enthusiasm vivifies every page, and runs like electricity along every thread of the story. It presents at one view the excellences and the evils of the system of slavery, and breathes the true spirit of Christian benevolence for the slave, and charity for the master.

The next witness gives his testimony in a letter to the *New York Evening Post:*

The subjoined communication comes to us postmarked New Orleans, June 19, 1852:

"I have just been reading 'Uncle Tom's Cabin, or, Scenes in Lowly Life,' by Mrs. Harriet Beecher Stowe. It found its way to me through the channel of a young student, who purchased it at the North, to read on his homeward passage to New Orleans. He was entirely unacquainted with its character; he was attracted by its title, supposing it might amuse him while travelling. Through his family it was shown to me, as something that I would probably like. I looked at the author's name, and said, 'O, yes; anything from that lady I will read;' otherwise I should have disregarded a work of fiction without such a title.

"The remarks from persons present were, that it was a most amusing work, and the scenes most admirably drawn to life. I accepted the offer of a perusal of it, and brought it home with me. Although I have not read every sentence, I have looked over the whole of it, and I now wish to bear my testimony to its just delineation of the position that the slave occupies. Colorings in the work there are, but no colorings of the actual and real position of the slave worse than really exist. Whippings to death do occur; I know it to be so. Painful separations of master and slave, under circumstances creditable to the master's feelings of humanity, do also occur. I know that, too. Many families, after having brought up their children in entire dependence on slaves to do everything for them, and after having been indulged in elegances and luxuries, have exhausted all their means; and the black people only being left, whom they must sell, for further support. Running away, everybody knows, is the worst crime a slave can commit, in the eyes of his master, except it be a humane master; and from such few slaves care to run away.

"I am a slave-holder myself. I have long been dissatisfied with the system; particularly since I have made the Bible my criterion for judging of it. I am convinced, from what I read there slavery is not in accordance with what God delights to honor in his creatures. I am altogether opposed to the system; and I intend always to use whatever influence I may have against it. I feel very bold in speaking against it, though living in the midst of it, because I am backed by a powerful arm, that can overturn and overrule the strongest efforts that the determined friends of slavery are now making for its continuance.

"I sincerely hope that more of Mrs. Stowes may be found, to show up the reality of slavery. It needs master minds to show it as it is, that it may rest upon its own merits.

"Like Mrs. Stowe, I feel that, since so many and good people, too, at the North, have quietly consented to leave the slave to his fate, by acquiescing in and approving the late measures of government, those who do feel differently should bestir themselves. Christian effort must do the work; and soon it would be done, if Christians would unite, not to destroy the Union states, but honestly to speak out, and speak freely, against that they know is wrong. They are not aware what countenance they give to slave-holders to hold on to their prey. Troubled consciences can be easily quieted by the sympathies of pious people, particularly when interest and inclination come in as aids.

"I am told there is to be a reply made to 'Uncle Tom's Cabin,' entitled 'Uncle Tom's Cabin as It Is.' I am glad of it. Investigation is what is wanted.

"You will wonder why this communication is made to you by an unknown. It is simply made to encourage your heart, and strengthen your determination to persevere, and do all you can to put the emancipation of the slave in progress. Who I am you will never know; nor do I wish you to know, nor any one else. I am a

"REPUBLICAN."

The following facts make the fiction of "Uncle Tom's Cabin" appear tame in the comparison. They are from the *New York Evangelist.*

UNCLE TOM'S CABIN.

MR. EDITOR : I see in your paper that some persons deny the statements of Mrs. Stowe. I have read her book, *every word of it.* I was born in East Tennessee, near Knoxville, and, *we thought,* in an enlightened part of the Union, much favored in our social, political and religious privileges, &c. &c. Well, I think about the year 1829, or, perhaps, '28, a good old German Methodist owned a black man named Robin, a Methodist preacher, and the manager of farm, distillery, &c., salesman and financier. This good old German Methodist had a son named Willey, a schoolmate of mine, and, as times were, a first-rate fellow. The old man also owned a keen, bright-eyed mulatto girl; and Willey — the naughty boy! — became enamored of the poor girl. The result was soon discovered; and our good German Methodist told his brother Robin to flog the girl for her wickedness. Brother Robin said he could not and would not perform such an act of cruelty as to flog the girl for what she could not help; and for that act of disobedience old Robin was flogged by the good old German brother, until he could not stand. He was carried to bed; and, some three weeks thereafter, when my father left the state, he was still confined to his bed from the effects of that flogging.

Again : in the fall of 1836 I went South, for my health, stopped at a village in Mississippi, and obtained employment in the largest house in the county, as a book-keeper, with a firm from Louisville, Ky. A man residing near the village — a bachelor, thirty years of age — became embarrassed, and executed a mortgage to my employer on a fine, likely boy, weighing about two hundred pounds, — quick-witted, active, obedient, and remarkably faithful, trusty and honest ; so much so, that he was held up as an example. He had a wife that he loved. His owner cast his eyes upon her, and she became his paramour. His boy remonstrated with his master ; told him that he tried faithfully to perform his every duty ; that he was a good and faithful "nigger" to him; and it was hard, after he had toiled hard all day, and till ten o'clock at night, for him to have his domestic relations broken up and interfered with. The white man denied the charge, and the wife also

denied it. One night, about the first of September, the boy came home earlier than usual, say about nine o'clock. It was a wet, dismal night; he made a fire in his cabin, went to get his supper, and found ocular demonstration of the guilt of his master. He became enraged, as I suppose any man would, seized a butcher-knife, and cut his master's throat, stabbed his wife in twenty-seven places, came to the village, and knocked at the office-door. I told him to come in. He did so, and asked for my employer. I called him. The boy then told him that he had killed his master and his wife, and what for. My employer locked him up, and he, a doctor and myself, went out to the house of the old bachelor, and found him dead, and the boy's wife nearly so. She, however, lived. We (my employer and myself) returned to the village, watched the boy until about sunrise, left him locked up, and went to get our breakfasts, intending to take the boy to jail (as it was my employer's interest, if possible, to save the boy, having one thousand dollars at stake in him). But, whilst we were eating, some persons who had heard of the murder broke open the door, took the poor fellow, put a log chain round his neck, and started him for the woods, at the point of the bayonet, marching by where we were eating, with a great deal of noise. My employer, hearing it, ran out, and rescued the boy. The mob again broke in and took the boy, and marched him, as before stated, out of town.

My employer then begged them not to disgrace their town in such a manner; but to appoint a jury of twelve *sober* men, to decide what should be done. And twelve as sober men as could be found (I was not sober) said he must be hanged. They then tied a rope round his neck, and set him on an old horse. He made a speech to the mob, which I, at the time, thought if it had come from some senator, would have been received with rounds of applause ; and, withal, he was more calm than I am now, in writing this. And, after he had told all about the deed, and its cause, he then kicked the horse out from under him, and was launched into eternity. My employer has often remarked that he never saw anything more noble, in his whole life, than the conduct of that boy.

Now, Mr. Editor, I have given you facts, and can give you names and dates. You can do what you think is best for the cause of humanity. I hope I have seen the evil of my former practices, and will endeavor to reform.

Very respectfully,
JAMES L. HILL.

Springfield, Ill., Sept. 17th, 1852.

"The Opinion of a Southerner," given below, appeared in the *National Era*, published at Washington. This is an anti-slavery journal, but by its generous tone and eminent ability it commands the respect and patronage of many readers in the slave states :

The following communication comes enclosed in an envelope from Louisiana. — *Ed. Era.*

THE OPINION OF A SOUTHERNER.

To the Editor of the National Era :

I have just been reading, in the *New York Observer* of the 12th of August, an article from the *Southern Free Press*, headed by an editorial one from the *Observer*, that has for its caption, "*Progress in the Right Quarter.*"

The editor of the *New York Observer* says that the *Southern Free Press* has been an able and earnest defender of Southern institutions; but that he now advocates the passage of a law to prohibit the separation of families, and recommends instruction to a portion of slaves that are most honest and faithful. The *Observer* further adds: "It was such language as this that was becoming common, before Northern fanaticism ruined the prospects of emancipation." It is not so! Northern fanaticism, as he calls it, has done everything that has been done for bettering the condition of the slave. Every one who knows anything of slavery for the last thirty years will recollect that about that time since, the condition of the slave in Louisiana — for about Louisiana only do I speak, because about Louisiana only do I know — was as depressed and miserable as any of the accounts of the abolitionists that ever I have seen have made it. I say abolitionists; I mean friends and advocates of freedom, in a fair and honorable way. If any doubt my assertion, let them seek for information. Let them get the black laws of Louisiana, and read them. Let them get facts from individuals of veracity, on whose statements they would rely.

This wretched condition of slaves roused the friends of humanity, who, like men, and Christian men, came fearlessly forward, and told truths, indignantly expressing their abhorrence of their oppressors. Such measures, of course, brought forth strife, which caused the cries of humanity to sound louder and louder throughout the land. The friends of freedom gained the ascendency in the hearts of the people, and the slave-holders were brought to a stand. Some, through fear of consequences, lessened their cruelties, while others were made to think, that, perhaps, were not unwilling to do so when it was urged upon them. Cruelties were not only refrained from, but the slave's comforts were increased. A retrograde treatment now was not practicable. Fears of rebellion kept them to it. The slave had found friends, and they were watchful. It was, however, soon discovered that too many privileges, too much leniency, and giving knowledge, would destroy the power to keep down the slave, and tend to weaken, if not destroy, the system. Accordingly, stringent laws had to be passed, and a penalty attached to them. No one must teach, or cause to be taught, a slave, without incurring the penalty. The law is now in force. These necessary laws, as they are called, are all put down to the account of the friends of freedom — to their interference. I do suppose that they do justly belong to their interference; for who that studies the history of the world's transactions does not know that in all contests with power the weak, until successful, will be dealt with more rigorously? Lose not sight, however, of their former condition. Law after law has since been passed to draw the cord tighter around the poor slave, and all attributed to the abolitionists. Well, anyhow, progress is being made. Here comes the *Southern Press*, and makes some honorable concessions. He says: "The assaults upon slavery, made for the last twenty years by the North, have increased the evils of it. The treatment of slaves has undoubtedly become a delicate and difficult question. The South has a great and

moral conflict to wage; and it is for her to put on *the most invulnerable moral panoply.*" He then thinks the availability of slave property would not be injured by passing a law to prohibit the separation of slave families; for he says, "Although cases sometimes occur which we observe are seized by these Northern fanatics as characteristic of the system," &c. Nonsense! there are no "cases sometimes" occurring — no such thing! They are every day's occurrences, though there are families that form the exception, and many, I would hope, that would not do it. While I am writing I can call before me three men that were brought here by negro traders from Virginia, each having left six or seven children, with their wives, from whom they have never heard. One other died here, a short time since, who left the same number in Carolina, from whom he had never heard.

I spent the summer of 1845 in Nashville. During the month of September, six hundred slaves passed through that place, in four different gangs, for New Orleans — final destination, probably, Texas. A goodly proportion were women; young women, of course; many mothers must have left not only their children, but their babies. One gang only had a few children. I made some excursions to the different watering places around Nashville; and while at Robinson, or Tyree Springs, twenty miles from Nashville, on the borders of Kentucky and Tennessee, my hostess said to me, one day, "Yonder comes a gang of slaves, chained." I went to the road-side, and viewed them. For the better answering my purpose of observation, I stopped the white man in front, who was at his ease in a one-horse wagon, and asked him if those slaves were for sale. I counted them and observed their position. They were divided by three one-horse wagons, each containing a man-merchant, so arranged as to command the whole gang. Some were unchained; sixty were chained, in two companies, thirty in each, the right hand of one to the left hand of the other opposite one, making fifteen each side of a large ox-chain, to which every hand was fastened, and necessarily compelled to hold up, — men and women promiscuously, and about in equal proportions, — all young people. No children here, except a few in a wagon behind, which were the only children in the four gangs. I said to a respectable mulatto woman in the house, "Is it true that the negro traders take mothers from their babies?" "Missis, it is true; for here, last week, such a girl [naming her], who lives about a mile off, was taken after dinner, — knew nothing of it in the morning, — sold, put into the gang, and her baby was given away to a neighbor. She was a stout young woman, and brought a good price."

The annexation of Texas induced the spirited traffic that summer. Coming down home in a small boat, water low, a negro trader on board had forty-five men and women crammed into a little spot, some handcuffed. One respectable-looking man had left a wife and seven children in Nashville. Near Memphis the boat stopped at a plantation by previous arrangement, to take in thirty more. An hour's delay was the stipulated time with the captain of the boat. Thirty young men and women came down the bank of the Mississippi, looking wretchedness personified — just from the field; in appearance dirty, disconsolate and op pressed; some with an old shawl under their arm a few had blankets; some had nothing at all—looked as though they cared for nothing. I calculated, while looking at them coming down the bank, that I could hold in a bundle all that the whole of them had. The short notice that was given them, when about to leave, was in consequence of the fears entertained that they would slip one side. They all looked distressed,—leaving all that was dear to them behind, to be put under the hammer, for the property of the highest bidder. No children here! The whole seventy-five were crammed into a little space on the boat, men and women all together.

I am happy to see that morality is rearing its head with advocates for slavery, and that a "most invulnerable moral panoply" is thought to be necessary. I hope it may not prove to be like Mr. Clay's compromises. The *Southern Press* says: "As for caricatures of slavery in 'Uncle Tom's Cabin' and the 'White Slave,' all founded in imaginary circumstances, &c., we consider them highly incendiary. He who undertakes to stir up strife between two individual neighbors, by detraction, is justly regarded, by all men and all moral codes, as a criminal." Then he quotes the ninth commandment, and adds : "But to bear false witness against whole states, and millions of people, &c., would seem to be a crime as much deeper in turpitude as the mischief is greater and the provocation less." In the first place, I will put the *Southern Press* upon proof that Mrs. Harriet Beecher Stowe has told one falsehood. If she has told truth, it is, indeed, a powerful engine of "assault on slavery," such as these Northern fanatics have made for the "last twenty years." The number against whom she offends, in the editor's opinion, seems to increase the turpitude of her crime. That is good reasoning! I hope the editor will be brought to feel that wholesale wickedness is worse than single-handed, and is infinitely harder to reach, particularly if of long standing. It gathers boldness and strength when it is sanctioned by the authority of time, and aided by numbers that are interested in supporting it. Such is slavery; and Mrs. Harriet Beecher Stowe deserves the gratitude of "states and millions of people" for her talented work, in showing it up in its true light. She has advocated truth, justice and humanity, and they will back her efforts. Her work will be read by "states and millions of people ;" and when the *Southern Press* attempts to malign her, by bringing forward her own avowal, "that the subject of slavery had been so painful to her, that she had abstained from conversing on it for several years," and that, in his opinion, "it accounts for the intensity of the venom of her book," his *really* envenomed shafts will fall harmless at her feet ; for readers will judge for themselves, and be very apt to conclude that more venom comes from the *Southern Press* than from her. She advocates what is right, and has a straight road, which "few get lost on ;" he advocates what is wrong, and has, consequently, to tack, concede, deny, slander, and all sorts of things.

With all due deference to whatever of just principles the *Southern Press* may have advanced in favor of the slave, I am a poor judge of human nature if I mistake in saying that Mrs. Stowe has done much to draw from him those concessions ; and the putting forth of this "*most invulnerable moral panoply*," that has just come into his head as a bulwark of safety for slavery, owes its impe-

tus to her, and other like efforts. I hope the *Southern Press* will not imitate the spoiled child, who refused to eat his pie for spite.

The "White Slave" I have not seen. I guess its character ; for I made a passage to New York, some fourteen or fifteen years since, in a packet-ship, with a young woman whose face was enveloped in a profusion of light brown curls, and who sat at the table with the passengers all the way as a white woman. When at the quarantine, Staten Island, the captain received a letter, sent by express mail, from a person in New Orleans, claiming her as his slave, and threatening the captain with the penalty of the existing law if she was not immediately returned. The streaming eyes of the poor, unfortunate girl told the truth, when the captain reluctantly broke it to her. She unhesitatingly confessed that she had run away, and that a friend had paid her passage. Proper measures were taken, and she was conveyed to a packet-ship that was at Sandy Hook, bound for New Orleans.

"Uncle Tom's Cabin," I think, is a just delineation of slavery. The incidents are colored, but the position that the slave is made to hold is just. I did not read every page of it, my object being to ascertain what position the slave occupied. I could state a case of whipping to death that would equal Uncle Tom's ; still, such cases are not very frequent.

The stirring up of strife between neighbors, that the *Southern Press* complains of, deserves notice. Who are neighbors? The most explicit answer to this question will be found in the reply Christ made to the lawyer, when he asked it of him. Another question will arise, Whether, in Christ's judgment, Mrs. Stowe would be considered a neighbor or an incendiary? As the Almighty Ruler of the universe and the Maker of man has said that He has made all the nations of the earth of one blood, and man in His own image, the black man, irrespective of his color, would seem to be a neighbor who has fallen among his enemies, that have deprived him of the fruits of his labor, his liberty, his right to his wife and children, his right to obtain the knowledge to read, or to anything that earth holds dear, except such portions of food and raiment as will fit him for his despoiler's purposes. Let not the apologists for slavery bring up the isolated cases of leniency, giving instruction, and affectionate attachment, that are found among some masters, as specimens of slavery ! It is unfair ! They form exceptions, and much do I respect them ; but they are not the rules of slavery. The strife that is being stirred up is not to take away anything that belongs to another, — neither their silver or gold, their fine linen or purple, their houses or land, their horses or cattle, or anything that is their property ; but to rescue a neighbor from their unmanly cupidity.   A REPUBLICAN.

No introduction is necessary to explain the following correspondence, and no commendation will be required to secure for it a respectful attention from thinking readers:

> *Washington City, D. C.,*
> *Dec. 6, 1852.*

D. R. GOODLOE, ESQ.

DEAR SIR : I understand that you are a North Carolinian, and have always resided in the South you must, consequently, be acquainted with the workings of the institution of slavery. You have doubtless also read that world-renowned book, "Uncle Tom's Cabin," by Mrs. Stowe. The apologists for slavery deny that this book is a truthful picture of slavery. They say that its representations are exaggerated, its scenes and incidents unfounded, and, in a word, that the whole book is a *caricature.* They also deny that families are separated, — that children are sold from their parents, wives from their husbands, &c. Under these circumstances, I am induced to ask your opinion of Mrs. Stowe's book, and whether or not, in your opinion, her statements are entitled to credit.   I have the honor to be,

Yours, truly,

A. M. Gangewer.

Washington, Dec. 8, 1852.

Dear Sir : Your letter of the 6th inst., asking my opinion of "Uncle Tom's Cabin," has been received ; and there being no reason why I should withhold it, unless it be the fear of public opinion (your object being, as I understand, the publication of my reply), I proceed to give it in some detail.

A book of fiction, to be worth reading, must necessarily be filled with rare and striking incidents, and the leading characters must be remarkable, some for great virtues, others, perhaps, for great vices or follies. A narrative of the ordinary events in the lives of commonplace people would be insufferably dull and insipid ; and a book made up of such materials would be, to the elegant and graphic pictures of life and manners which we have in the writings of Sir Walter Scott and Dickens, what a surveyor's plot of a ten-acre field is to a painted landscape, in which the eye is charmed by a thousand varieties of hill and dale, of green shrubbery and transparent water, of light and shade, at a glance. In order to determine whether a novel is a fair picture of society, it is not necessary to ask if its chief personages are to be met with every day ; but whether they are characteristic of the times and country, — whether they embody the prevalent sentiments, virtues, vices, follies, and peculiarities, — and whether the events, tragic or otherwise, are such as may and do occasionally occur.

Judging "Uncle Tom's Cabin" by these principles, I have no hesitation in saying that it is a faithful portraiture of Southern life and institutions. There is nothing in the book inconsistent with the laws and usages of the slave-holding states ; the virtues, vices, and peculiar hues of character and manners, are all Southern, and must be recognized at once by every one who reads the book. I may never have seen such depravity in one man as that exhibited in the character of Legree, though I have ten thousand times witnessed the various shades of it in different individuals. On the other hand, I have never seen so many perfections concentrated in one human being as Mrs. Stowe has conferred upon the daughter of a slave-holder. Evangeline is an image of beauty and goodness which can never be effaced from the mind, whatever may be its prejudices. Yet her whole character is fragrant of the South ; her generous sympathy, her beauty and delicacy, her sensibility, are all Southern. They are "to the manor born," and embodying as they do the Southern ideal of beauty and loveliness, cannot be ostracized from Southern hearts, even by the power of the vigilance committees.

The character of St. Clare cannot fail to inspire love and admiration. He is the *beau idéal* of a Southern gentleman, — honorable, generous and humane, of accomplished manners, liberal education, and easy fortune. In his treatment of his slaves, he errs on the side of lenity, rather than vigor ; and is always their kind protector, from a natural impulse of goodness, without much reflection upon what may befall them when death or misfortune shall deprive them of his friendship.

Mr. Shelby, the original owner of Uncle Tom, and who sells him to a trader, from the pressure of a sort of pecuniary necessity, is by no means a bad character ; his wife and son are whatever honor and humanity could wish ; and, in a word, the only white persons who make any considerable figure in the book to a disadvantage are the villain Legree, who is a Vermonter by birth, and the oily-tongued slave-trader Haley, who has the accent of a Northerner. It is, therefore, evident that Mrs. Stowe's object in writing "Uncle Tom's Cabin" has not been to disparage Southern character. A careful analysis of the book would authorize the opposite inference, — that she has studied to shield the Southern people from opprobrium, and even to convey an elevated idea of Southern society, at the moment of exposing the evils of the system of slavery. She directs her batteries against the institution, not against individuals ; and generously makes a renegade Vermonter stand for her most hideous picture of a brutal tyrant.

Invidious as the duty may be, I cannot withhold my testimony to the fact that families of slaves are often separated. I know not how any man can have the hardihood to deny it. The thing is notorious, and is often the subject of painful remark in the Southern States. I have often heard the practice of separating husband and wife, parent and child, defended, apologized for, palliated in a thousand ways, but have never heard it denied. How could it be denied, in fact, when probably the very circumstance which elicited the conversation was a case of cruel separation then transpiring ? No, sir ! the denial of this fact by mercenary scribblers may deceive persons at a distance, but it can impose upon no one at the South.

In all the slave-holding states the relation of matrimony between slaves, or between a slave and free person, is merely voluntary. There is no law sanctioning it, or recognizing it in any shape, directly or indirectly. In a word, it is illicit, and binds no one, — neither the slaves themselves nor their masters. In separating husband and wife, or parent and child, the trader or owner violates no law of the state — neither statute nor common law. He buys or sells at auction or privately that which the majesty of the law has declared to be property. The victims may writhe in agony, and the tender-hearted spectator may look on with gloomy sorrow and indignation, but it is to no purpose. The promptings of mercy and justice in the heart are only in rebellion against the law of the land.

The law itself not unfrequently performs the most cruel separations of families, almost without the intervention of individual agency. This happens in the case of persons who die insolvent, or who become so during lifetime. The estate, real and personal, must be disposed of at auction to the highest bidder, and the executor, administrator, sheriff, trustee, or other person whose duty it is to dispose of the property, although he may possess the most humane intentions in the world.

cannot prevent the final severance of the most endearing ties of kindred. The illustration given by Mrs. Stowe, in the sale of Uncle Tom by Mr. Shelby, is a very common case. Pecuniary embarrassment is a most fruitful source of misfortune to the slave as well as the master; and instances of family ties broken from this cause are of daily occurrence.

It often happens that great abuses exist in violation of law, and in spite of the efforts of the authorities to suppress them; such is the case with drunkenness, gambling, and other vices. But here is a law common to all the slave-holding states, which upholds and gives countenance to the wrongdoer, while its blackest terrors are reserved for those who would interpose to protect the innocent. Statesmen of elevated and honorable characters, from a vague notion of state necessity, have defended this law in the abstract, while they would, without hesitation, condemn every instance of its application as unjust.

In one respect I am glad to see it publicly denied that the families of slaves are separated; for while it argues a disreputable want of candor, it at the same time evinces a commendable sense of shame, and induces the hope that the public opinion at the South will not much longer tolerate this most odious, though not essential, part of the system of slavery.

In this connection I will call to your recollection a remark of the editor of the *Southern Press*, in one of the last numbers of that paper, which acknowledges the existence of the abuse in question, and recommends its correction. He says:

"The South has a great moral conflict to wage; and it is for her to put on the most invulnerable moral panoply. Hence it is her duty, as well as interest, to mitigate or remove whatever of evil that results incidentally from the institution. The separation of husband and wife, parent and child, is one of these evils, which we know is generally avoided and repudiated there — although cases sometimes occur which we observe are seized by these Northern fanatics as characteristic illustrations of the system. Now we can see no great evil or inconvenience, but much good, in the prohibition by law of such occurrences. Let the husband and wife be sold together, and the parents and minor children. Such a law would affect but slightly the general value or availability of slave property, and would prevent in some cases the violence done to the feelings of such connections by sales either compulsory or voluntary. We are satisfied that it would be beneficial to the master and slave to promote marriage, and the observance of all its duties and relations."

Much as I have differed with the editor of the *Southern Press* in his general views of public policy, I am disposed to forgive him past errors in consideration of his public acknowledgment of this "incidental evil," and his frank recommendation of its removal. A Southern newspaper less devoted than the *Southern Press* to the maintenance of slavery would be seriously compromised by such a suggestion, and its advice would be far less likely to be heeded. I think, therefore, that Mr. Fisher deserves the thanks of every good man, North and South, for thus boldly pointing out the necessity of reform.

The picture which Mrs. Stowe has drawn of slavery as an institution is anything but favorable. She has illustrated the frightful cruelty and oppression that must result from a law which gives

to one class of society almost absolute and irresponsible power over another. Yet the very machinery she has employed for this purpose shows that all who are parties to the system are not necessarily culpable. It is a high virtue in St. Clare to purchase Uncle Tom. He is actuated by no selfish or improper motive. Moved by a desire to gratify his daughter, and prompted by his own humane feelings, he purchases a slave, in order to rescue him from a hard fate on the plantations. If he had not been a slave-holder before, it was now his duty to become one. This, I think, is the moral to be drawn from the story of St. Clare; and the South have a right to claim the authority of Mrs. Stowe in defence of slave-holding, to this extent.

It may be said that it was the duty of St. Clare to emancipate Uncle Tom; but the wealth of the Rothschilds would not enable a man to act out his benevolent instincts at such a price. And if such was his duty, is it not equally the duty of every monied man in the free states to attend the New Orleans slave-mart with the same benevolent purpose in view? It seems to me that to purchase a slave with the purpose of saving him from a hard and cruel fate, and without any view to emancipation, is itself a good action. If the slave should subsequently become able to redeem himself, it would doubtless be the duty of the owner to emancipate him; and it would be but even-handed justice to set down every dollar of the slave's earnings, above the expense of his maintenance, to his credit, until the price paid for him should be fully restored. This is all that justice could exact of the slave-holder.

Those who have railed against "Uncle Tom's Cabin" as an incendiary publication have singularly (supposing that they have read the book) overlooked the moral of the hero's life. Uncle Tom is the most faithful of servants. He literally "obeyed in all things" his "masters according to the flesh; not with eye-service, as men-pleasers, but in singleness of heart, fearing God." If his conduct exhibits the slightest departure from a literal fulfilment of this injunction of Scripture, it is in a case which must command the approbation of the most rigid casuist; for the injunction of obedience extends, of course, only to lawful commands. It is only when the monster Legree commands him to inflict undeserved chastisement upon his fellow-servants, that Uncle Tom refuses obedience. He would not listen to a proposition of escaping into Ohio with the young woman Eliza, on the night after they were sold by Mr. Shelby to the trader Haley. He thought it would be bad faith to his late master, whom he had nursed in his arms, and might be the means of bringing him into difficulty. He offered no resistance to Haley, and obeyed even Legree in every legitimate command. But when he was required to be the instrument of his master's cruelty, he chose rather to die, with the courage and resolution of a Christian martyr, than to save his life by a guilty compliance. Such was Uncle Tom — not a bad example for the imitation of man or master. I am, sir, very respectfully,

Your ob't serv't,
DANIEL R. GOODLOE.

A. M. GANGEWER, Esq.,
Washington, D. C.

The writer has received permission to publish the following extract from a letter received by a lady at the North from the editor of a Southern paper. The mind and character of the author will speak for themselves, in the reading of it :

Charleston, Sunday, 25th July, 1852.
* * * The books, I infer, are Mrs. Beecher Stowe's "*Uncle Tom's Cabin.*" The book was furnished me by ——— ———, about a fortnight ago, and you may be assured I read it with an attentive interest. "Now, what is your opinion of it?" you will ask ; and, knowing my preconceived opinions upon the question of slavery, and the embodiment of my principles, which I have so long supported, in regard to that *peculiar* institution, you may be prepared to meet an indirect answer. This my own consciousness of truth would not allow, in the present instance. The book is a truthful picture of life, with the dark outlines beautifully portrayed. The life — the characteristics, incidents, and the dialogues — is life itself reduced to paper. In her appendix she rather evades the question whether it was taken from actual scenes, but says there are many counterparts. In this she is correct, beyond doubt. Had she changed the picture of Legree, on Red river, for ——— ———, on ——— Island, South Carolina, she could not have drawn a more admirable portrait. I am led to question whether she had not some knowledge of this beast, as he is known to be, and made the transposition for effect.

My position in connection with the extreme party, both in Georgia and South Carolina, would constitute a restraint to the full expression of my feelings upon several of the governing principles of the institution. I have studied slavery, in all its different phases, — have been thrown in contact with the negro in different parts of the world, and made it my aim to study his nature, so far as my limited abilities would give me light, — and, whatever my opinions have been, they were based upon what I supposed to be honest convictions.

During the last three years you well know what my opportunities have been to examine all the sectional bearings of an institution which now holds the great and most momentous question of our federal well-being. These opportunities I have not let pass, but have given myself, body and soul, to a knowledge of its vast intricacies, — to its constitutional compact, and its individual hardships. Its wrongs are in the constituted rights of the master, and the *blank letter* of those laws which pretend to govern the bondman's rights. What legislative act, based upon the construction of self-protection for the very men who contemplate the laws, — even though their intention was amelioration, — could be enforced, when the legislated object is held as the *bond property* of the legislator? The very fact of constituting a law for the amelioration of property becomes an absurdity, so far as carrying it out is concerned. A law which is intended to govern, and gives the governed no means of seeking its protection, is like the clustering together of so many useless words for vain show. But why talk of law!

That which is considered the popular rights of a people, and every tenacious prejudice set forth to protect its property interest, creates its own power, against every weaker vessel. Laws which interfere with this become unpopular, — repugnant to a forceable will, and a dead letter in effect. So long as the voice of the governed cannot be heard, and his wrongs are felt beyond the jurisdiction or domain of the law, as nine-tenths are, where is the hope of redress? The master is the powerful vessel ; the negro feels his dependence, and, fearing the consequences of an appeal for his rights, submits to the cruelty of his master, in preference to the dread of something more cruel. It is in those disputed cases of cruelty we find the wrongs of slavery, and in those governing laws which give power to bad Northern men to become the most cruel task-masters. Do not judge, from my observations, that I am seeking consolation for the abolitionists. Such is not my intention ; but truth to a course which calls loudly for reformation constrains me to say that humanity calls for some law to govern the force and absolute will of the master, and to reform no part is more requisite than that which regards the slave's food and raiment. A person must live years at the South before he can become fully acquainted with the many workings of slavery. A Northern man not prominently interested in the political and social weal of the South may live for years in it, and pass from town to town in his every-day pursuits, and yet see but the polished side of slavery. With me it has been different. Its effect upon the negro himself, and its effect upon the social and commercial well-being of Southern society, has been laid broadly open to me, and I have seen more of its workings within the past year than was disclosed to me all the time before. It is with these feelings that I am constrained to do credit to Mrs. Stowe's book, which I consider must have been written by one who derived the materials from a thorough acquaintance with the subject. The character of the slave-dealer, the bankrupt owner in Kentucky, and the New Orleans merchant, are simple every-day occurrences in these parts. Editors may speak of the dramatic effect as they please ; the tale is not told them, and the occurrences of common reality would form a picture more glaring. I could write a work, with date and incontrovertible facts, of abuses which stand recorded in the knowledge of the community in which they were transacted, that would need no dramatic effect, and would stand out ten-fold more horrible than anything Mrs. Stowe has described.

I have read two columns in the *Southern Press* of Mrs. Eastman's "*Aunt Phillis' Cabin*, or Southern Life as It Is," with the remarks of the editor. I have no comments to make upon it, that being done by itself. The editor might have saved himself being writ down an ass by the public, if he had withheld his nonsense. If the two columns are a specimen of Mrs. Eastman's book, I pity her attempt and her name as an author.

PART II.

CHAPTER I.

THE New York *Courier and Enquirer* of November 5th contained an article which has been quite valuable to the author, as summing up, in a clear, concise and intelligible form, the principal objections which may be urged to *Uncle Tom's Cabin*. It is here quoted in full, as the foundation of the remarks in the following pages.

The author of " Uncle Tom's Cabin," that writer states, has committed false-witness against thousands and millions of her fellow-men.

She has done it [he says] by attaching to them as slaveholders, in the eyes of the world, the guilt of the abuses of an institution of which they are absolutely guiltless. Her story is so devised as to present slavery in three dark aspects : first, the *cruel treatment* of the slaves ; second, *the separation of families ;* and, third, their *want of religious instruction.*

To show the first, she causes a reward to be offered for the recovery of a runaway slave, " dead or alive," when no reward with such an alternative was ever heard of, or dreamed of, south of Mason and Dixon's line, and it has been decided over and over again in Southern courts that " a slave who is merely flying away cannot be killed." She puts such language as this into the mouth of one of her speakers : — " The master who goes furthest and does the worst only uses within limits the power that the law gives him ;" when, in fact, the civil code of the very state where it is represented the language was uttered — Louisiana — declares that

" The slave is entirely subject to the will of his master, who may correct and chastise him, *though not with unusual rigor, nor so as to maim or mutilate him, or to expose him to the danger of loss of life, or to cause his death.*"

And provides for a compulsory sale

" When the master shall be convicted of cruel treatment of his slaves, and the judge shall deem proper to pronounce, besides the penalty established for such cases, that the slave be sold at public auction, *in order to place him out of the reach of the power which the master has abused.*"

" If any person whatsoever shall wilfully kill his slave, or the slave of another person, the said person, being convicted thereof, shall be tried and condemned agreeably to the laws."

In the General Court of Virginia, last year, in the case of Souther v. the Commonwealth, it was held that the killing of a slave by his master and owner, by wilful and excessive whipping, is murder in the first degree, *though it may not have been the purpose of the master and owner to kill the slave !* And it is not six months since Governor Johnston, of Virginia, pardoned a slave who killed his master, who was beating him with brutal severity.

And yet, in the face of such laws and decisions as these, Mrs. Stowe winds up a long series of cruelties upon her other black personages, by causing her faultless hero, Tom, to be literally whipped to death in Louisiana, by his master, Legree ; and these acts, which the laws make criminal, and punish as such, she sets forth in the most repulsive colors, to illustrate the institution of slavery !

So, too, in reference to the separation of children from their parents. A considerable part of the plot is made to hinge upon the selling, in Louisiana, of the child Eliza, " eight or nine years old," away from her mother ; when, had its inventor looked in the statute-book of Louisiana, she would have found the following language :

" Every person is expressly prohibited from selling separately from their mothers *the children who shall not have attained the full age of ten years.*"

" *Be it further enacted,* That if any person or persons shall sell the mother of any slave child or children *under the age of ten years, separate from said child or children, or shall, the mother living, sell any slave child or children of ten years of age, or under, separate from said mother,* said person or persons shall be fined not less than one thousand nor more than two thousand dollars, and be imprisoned in the public jail for a period of not less than six months nor more than one year."

The privation of religious instruction, as represented by Mrs. Stowe, is utterly unfounded in fact. The largest churches in the Union consist entirely of slaves. The first African church in Louisville, which numbers fifteen hundred persons, and the first African church in Augusta, which numbers thirteen hundred, are specimens. On multitudes of the large plantations in the different parts of the South the ordinances of the gospel are as regularly maintained, by competent ministers, as in any other communities, north or south. A larger proportion of the slave population are in communion with some Christian church, than of the white population in any part of the country. A very considerable portion of every southern congregation, either in city or country, is sure to consist of blacks ; whereas, of our northern churches, not a colored person is to be seen in one out of fifty.

The peculiar falsity of this whole book consists in making exceptional or impossible cases the representatives of the system. By the same process which she has used, it would not be difficult to frame a fatal argument against the relation of husband and wife, or parent and child, or of guardian and ward; for thousands of wives and children and wards have been maltreated, and even murdered. It is wrong, unpardonably wrong, to impute to any relation of life those enormities which spring only out of the worst depravity of human nature. A ridiculously extravagant spirit of generalization pervades this fiction from beginning to end. The Uncle Tom of the authoress is a perfect angel, and her blacks generally are half angels; her Simon Legree is a perfect demon, and her whites generally are half demons. She has quite a peculiar spite against the clergy; and, of the many she introduces at different times into the scenes, all, save an insignificant exception, are Pharisees or hypocrites. One who could know nothing of the United States and its people, except by what he might gather from this book, would judge that it was some region just on the confines of the infernal world. We do not say that Mrs. Stowe was actuated by wrong motives in the preparation of this work, but we do say that she has done a wrong which no ignorance can excuse and no penance can expiate.

A much-valued correspondent of the author, writing from Richmond, Virginia, also uses the following language:

I will venture this morning to make a few suggestions which have occurred to me in regard to future editions of your work, "Uncle Tom's Cabin," which I desire should have all the influence of which your genius renders it capable, not only abroad, but in the local sphere of slavery, where it has been hitherto repudiated. Possessing already the great requisites of artistic beauty and of sympathetic affection, it may yet be improved in regard to accuracy of statement without being at all enfeebled. For example, you do less than justice to the formalized laws of the Southern States, while you give more credit than is due to the virtue of public or private sentiment in restricting the evil which the laws permit.

I enclose the following extracts from a southern paper:

"'I'll manage that ar; they's young in the business, and must spect to work cheap,' said Marks, as he continued to read. 'Thar's three on 'em easy cases, 'cause all you've got to do is to shoot 'em, or swear they is shot; they could n't, of course, charge much for that.'"

"The reader will observe that two charges against the South are involved in this precious discourse; — one that it is the habit of Southern masters to offer a reward, with the alternative of 'dead or alive,' for their fugitive slaves; and the other, that it is usual for pursuers to shoot them. Indeed, we are led to infer that, as the shooting is the easier mode of obtaining the reward, it is the more frequently employed in such cases. Now, when a Southern master offers a reward for his runaway slave, it is because he has lost a certain amount of property, represented by the negro which he wishes to recover. What man of Vermont, having an ox or an ass that had gone astray, would forthwith offer half the full value of the animal, not for the carcass, which might be turned to some useful purpose, but for the unavailing satisfaction of its head? Yet are the two cases exactly parallel. With regard to the assumption that

men are permitted to go about, at the South, with double-barrelled guns, shooting down runaway negroes, in preference to apprehending them, we can only say that it is as wicked and wilful as it is ridiculous. Such Thugs there may have been as Marks and Loker, who have killed negroes in this unprovoked manner; but, if they have escaped the gallows, they are probably to be found within the walls of our state penitentiaries, where they are comfortably provided for at public expense. The laws of the Southern States, which are designed, as in all good governments, for the protection of persons and property, have not been so loosely framed as to fail of their object where person and property are one.

"The law with regard to the killing of runaways is laid down with so much clearness and precision by a South Carolina judge, that we cannot forbear quoting his dictum, as directly in point. In the case of Witsell v. Earnest and Parker, Colcock J. delivered the opinion of the court:

"'By the statute of 1740, any white man may apprehend, and moderately correct, any slave who may be found out of the plantation at which he is employed; and if the slave assaults the white person, he may be killed; but a slave who is merely flying away cannot be killed. Nor can the defendants be justified by the common law, if we consider the negro as a person; for Jan. term, 1818. they were not clothed with the authority of the law to apprehend him 1 Nott & McCord's S. C. Rep. 182. as a felon, and without such authority he could not be killed.'

"'It's commonly supposed that the *property* interest is a sufficient guard in these cases. If people choose to ruin their possessions, I don't know what's to be done. It seems the poor creature was a thief and a drunkard; and so there won't be much hope to get up sympathy for her.'

"'It is perfectly outrageous, — it is horrid, Augustine! It will certainly bring down vengeance upon you.'

"'My dear cousin, I did n't do it, and I can't help it; I would, if I could. If low-minded, brutal people will act like themselves, what am I to do? *They have absolute control*; *they are irresponsible despots*. There would be no use in interfering; *there is no law, that amounts to anything practically, for such a case*. The best we can do is to shut our eyes and ears, and let it alone. It's the only resource left us.'

"In a subsequent part of the same conversation, St. Clare says:

"'For pity's sake, for shame's sake, because we are men born of women, and not savage beasts, many of us do not, and dare not, — we would *scorn* to use the full power which our savage laws put into our hands. *And he who goes furthest and does the worst only uses within limits the power that the law gives him.*'

"Mrs. Stowe tells us, through St. Clare, that 'there is no law that amounts to anything' in such cases, and that he who goes furthest in severity towards his slave, — that is, to the deprivation of an eye or a limb, or even the destruction of life, — 'only uses within limits the power that the law gives him.' This is an awful and tremendous charge, which, lightly and unwarrantably made, must subject the maker to a fearful accountability. Let us see how the matter stands upon the statute-book of Louisiana. By referring to the civil code of that state, chapter 3d, article 173, the reader will find this general declaration:

"'The slave is entirely subject to the will of his master, who may correct and chastise him, *though not with unusual rigor, nor so as to maim or mutilate him, or to expose him to the danger of loss of life, or to cause his death.*'

"On a subsequent page of the same volume and chapter, article 192, we find provision made for the slave's protection against his master's cruelty, in the statement that one of two cases, in which a master can be compelled to sell his slave, is

"'When the master shall be convicted of cruel treatment of his slave, and the judge shall deem proper to pronounce, *besides the penalty established for such cases*, that the slave shall be sold at public auction, *in order to place him out of the reach of the power which the master has abused.*'

"A code thus watchful of the negro's safety in life and limb confines not its guardianship to inhibitory clauses, but proscribes extreme penalties in case of their infraction. In the Code Noir (Black Code) of Louisiana, under head of Crimes and Offences, No. 55, § xvi., it is laid down, that

"'If any person whatsoever shall wilfully kill his slave, or the slave of another person, the said person, being convicted thereof, shall be tried and condemned agreeably to the laws.'

"And because negro testimony is inadmissible in the courts of the state, and therefore the evidence of such crimes might be with difficulty supplied, it is further provided that,

"'If any slave be mutilated, beaten or illtreated, contrary to the true intent and meaning of this act, when no one shall be present, in such case the owner, or other person having the management of said slave thus mutilated, shall be deemed responsible and guilty of the said offence, and shall be prosecuted without further evidence, unless the said owner, or other person so as aforesaid, can prove the contrary by means of good and sufficient evidence, or can clear himself by his own oath, which said oath every court, under the cognizance of which such offence shall Code Noir.
Crimes and Offences, 56, xvii. have been examined and tried, is by this act authorized to administer.'

"Enough has been quoted to establish the utter falsity of the statement, made by our authoress through St. Clare, that brutal masters are 'irresponsible despots,'—at least in Louisiana. It would extend our review to a most unreasonable length, should we undertake to give the law, with regard to the murder of slaves, as it stands in each of the Southern States. The crime is a rare one, and therefore the reporters have had few cases to record. We may refer, however, to two. In *Fields v. the State of Tennessee*, the plaintiff in error was indicted in the circuit court of Maury county for the murder of a negro slave. He pleaded not guilty; and at the trial was found guilty of wilful and felonious slaying of the slave. From this sentence he prosecuted his writ of error, which was disallowed, the court affirming the original judgment. The opinion of the court, as given by Peck J., overflows with the spirit of enlightened humanity. He concludes thus:

"'It is well said by one of the judges of North Carolina, that the master has a right to exact the labor of his slave; that far, the rights of the slave are suspended; but this gives the master no right over the life of his slave. I add to the saying of the judge, that law which says thou shalt not kill, 1 Yerger's Tenn. Rep. 156 protects the slave; and he is within its very letter. Law, reason, Christianity, and common humanity, all point but one way.'

"In the General Court of Virginia, June term, 1851, in *Souther v. the Commonwealth*, it was held that 'the killing of a slave by his master and owner, by wilful and excessive whipping, is murder in the first degree; *though it may not have been*

the purpose of the master and owner to kill the slave.' The writer shows, 7 Grattan's Rep. 673. also, an ignorance of the law of contracts, as it affects slavery in the South, in making George's master take him from the factory against the proprietor's consent. George, by virtue of the contract of hiring, had become the property of the proprietor for the time being, and his master could no more have taken him away forcibly than the owner of a house in Massachusetts can dispossess his lessee, at any moment, from mere whim or caprice. There is no court in Kentucky where the hirer's rights, in this regard, would not be enforced.

"'No. Father bought her once, in one of his trips to New Orleans, and brought her up as a present to mother. She was about eight or nine years old, then. Father would never tell mother what he gave for her; but, the other day, in looking over his old papers, we came across the bill of sale. He paid an extravagant sum for her, to be sure. I suppose, on account of her extraordinary beauty.'

"George sat with his back to Cassy, and did not see the absorbed expression of her countenance, as he was giving these details.

"At this point in the story, she touched his arm, and, with a face perfectly white with interest, said, 'Do you know the names of the people he bought her of?'

"'A man of the name of Simmons, I think, was the principal in the transaction. At least, I think that was the name in the bill of sale.'

"'O, my God!' said Cassy, and fell insensible on the floor of the cabin.''

"Of course Eliza turns out to be Cassy's child, and we are soon entertained with the family meeting in Montreal, where George Harris is living, five or six years after the opening of the story, in great comfort.

"Now, the reader will perhaps be surprised to know that such an incident as the sale of Cassy apart from Eliza, upon which the whole interest of the foregoing narrative hinges, never could have taken place in Louisiana, and that the bill of sale for Eliza would not have been worth the paper it was written on. Observe. George Shelby states that Eliza was *eight or nine years old*, at the time his father purchased her in New Orleans. Let us again look at the statute-book of Louisiana.

"In the *Code Noir* we find it set down that

"'Every person is expressly prohibited from selling separately from their mothers *the children who shall not have attained the full age of ten years.*'

"And this humane provision is strengthened by a statute, one clause of which runs as follows:

"'Be it further enacted, That if any person or persons shall sell the mother of any slave child or children *under the age of ten years, separate from said child or children, or shall, the mother living, sell any slave child or children of ten years of age, or under, separate from said mother,* such person or persons shall incur the penalty of the sixth section of this act.'

"This penalty is a fine of not less than one thousand nor more than two thousand dollars, and imprisonment in the public jail for a period of not less than six months nor more than one year.— *Vide Acts of Louisiana,* 1 *Session,* 9th *Legislature,* 1828, 1829, No. 24, Section 16.''

The author makes here a remark. Scattered through all the Southern States are slaveholders who are such only in name. They have no pleasure in the system, they consider it one of wrong altogether, and they hold the legal relation still, only because not yet clear with regard to the best way of changing it, so as to better the condition of those held. Such are most earnest advocates for state emancipation, and are friends of anything, written in a right spirit, which tends in that direction. From such the author ever receives criticisms with pleasure.

She has endeavored to lay before the world, in the fullest manner, all that can be objected to her work, that both sides may have an opportunity of impartial hearing.

When writing "Uncle Tom's Cabin," though entirely unaware and unexpectant of the importance which would be attached to its statements and opinions, the author of that work was anxious, from love of consistency, to have some understanding of the laws of the slave system. She had on hand for reference, while writing, the Code Noir of Louisiana, and a sketch of the laws relating to slavery in the different states, by Judge Stroud, of Philadelphia. This work, professing to have been compiled with great care from the latest editions of the statute-books of the several states, the author supposed to be a sufficient guide for the writing of a work of fiction.* As the accuracy of those statements which relate to the slave-laws has been particularly contested, a more especial inquiry has been made in this direction. Under the guidance and with the assistance of legal gentlemen of high standing, the writer has proceeded to examine the statements of Judge Stroud with regard to statute-law, and to follow them up with some inquiry into the decisions of courts. The result has been an increasing conviction on her part that the impressions first derived from Judge Stroud's work were correct; and the author now can only give the words of St. Clare, as the best possible expression of the sentiments and opinion which this course of reading has awakened in her mind.

This cursed business, accursed of God and man, — what is it? Strip it of all its ornament, run it down to the root and nucleus of the whole, and what is it? Why, because my brother Quashy is ignorant and weak, and I am intelligent and strong, — because I know how, and *can* do it, — therefore I may steal all he has, keep it, and give him only such and so much as suits my fancy! Whatever is too hard, too dirty, too disagreeable for me, I may set Quashy to doing. Because I don't like work, Quashy shall work. Because the sun burns me, Quashy shall stay in the sun. Quashy shall earn the money, and I will spend it.

* In this connection it may be well to state that the work of Judge Stroud is now out of print, but that a work of the same character is in course of preparation by William I. Bowditch, Esq., of Boston, which will bring the subject out, by the assistance of the latest editions of statutes, and the most recent decisions of courts.

Quashy shall lie down in every puddle, that I may walk over dry shod. Quashy shall do my will, and not his, all the days of his mortal life, and have such a chance of getting to heaven at last as I find convenient. This I take to be about what slavery is. I defy anybody on earth to read our slave-code, as it stands in our law-books, and make anything else of it. Talk of the *abuses* of slavery! Humbug! The *thing itself* is the essence of all abuse. And the only reason why the land don't sink under it, like Sodom and Gomorrah, is because it is *used* in a way infinitely better than it is. For pity's sake, for shame's sake, because we are men born of women, and not savage beasts, many of us do not, and dare not, — we would *scorn* to use the full power which our savage laws put into our hands. And he who goes the furthest, and does the worst, only uses within limits the power that the law gives him!

The author still holds to the opinion that slavery in itself, as legally defined in law-books and expressed in the records of courts, *is* the SUM AND ESSENCE OF ALL ABUSE; and she still clings to the hope that there are *many* men at the South *infinitely* better than their laws; and after the reader has read all the extracts which she has to make, for the sake of a common humanity they will hope the same. The author must state, with regard to some passages which she must quote, that the language of certain enactments was so incredible that she would not take it on the authority of any compilation whatever, but copied it with her own hand from the latest edition of the statute-book where it stood and still stands.

CHAPTER II.

WHAT IS SLAVERY?

THE author will now enter into a consideration of slavery as it stands revealed in slave law.

What is it, according to the definition of law-books and of legal interpreters? "A slave," says the law of Louisiana, "is one who is in the power of a master, to whom he belongs. The master may sell him, dispose of his person, his industry and his labor; he can do nothing, possess nothing, nor acquire anything, but what must belong to his master." South Carolina says ^{Art. 35.} "slaves shall be deemed, sold, taken, reputed and adjudged in law, to be chattels personal in the hands of their owners and possessors, and their executors, administrators, and assigns, TO ALL INTENTS, CONSTRUCTIONS AND PURPOSES WHAT- ^{2 Brev. Dig.} SOEVER." The law of Georgia is ^{Digest, 446.} similar.

Let the reader reflect on the extent of the meaning in this last clause. Judge

Ruffin, pronouncing the opinion of the Supreme Court of North Carolina, says, a slave is "one doomed in his own person, and his posterity, to live without knowledge, and without the capacity to make anything his own, and to toil that another may reap the fruits."

^{Wheeler's Law of Slavery, 246. State v. Mann.}

This is what slavery *is*,— this is what it is to be a slave! The slave-code, then, of the Southern States, is designed to keep millions of human beings in the condition of chattels personal: to keep them in a condition in which the master may sell them, dispose of their time, person and labor: in which they can do nothing, possess nothing, and acquire nothing, except for the benefit of the master: in which they are doomed in themselves and in their posterity to live without knowledge, without the power to make anything their own,— to toil that another may reap. The laws of the slave-code are designed to work out this problem, consistently with the peace of the community, and the safety of that superior race which is constantly to perpetrate this outrage.

From this simple statement of what the laws of slavery are designed to do,—from a consideration that the class thus to be reduced, and oppressed, and made the subjects of a perpetual robbery, are *men* of like passions with our own, men originally made in the image of God as much as ourselves, men partakers of that same humanity of which Jesus Christ is the highest ideal and expression, — when we consider that the material thus to be acted upon is that fearfully explosive element, the soul of man; that soul elastic, upspringing, immortal, whose free will even the Omnipotence of God refuses to coerce, — we may form some idea of the tremendous force which is necessary to keep this mightiest of elements in the state of repression which is contemplated in the definition of slavery.

Of course, the system necessary to consummate and perpetuate such a work, from age to age, must be a fearfully stringent one; and our readers will find that it is so. Men who make the laws, and men who interpret them, may be fully sensible of their terrible severity and inhumanity; but, if they are going to preserve the THING, they have no resource but to make the laws, and to execute them faithfully after they are made. They may say, with the honorable Judge Ruffin, of North Carolina, when solemnly from the bench announcing this great foundation principle of slavery, that "THE POWER OF THE MASTER MUST BE ABSO-LUTE, TO RENDER THE SUBMISSION OF THE SLAVE PERFECT," — they may say, with him, "I most freely confess my sense of the harshness of this proposition; I feel it as deeply as any man can; and, as a principle of moral right, every person in his retirement must repudiate it;" — but they will also be obliged to add, with him, "But, in the *actual condition* of things, it MUST BE SO. * * This discipline belongs to the state of slavery. * * * It is INHERENT in the relation of master and slave."

And, like Judge Ruffin, men of honor, men of humanity, men of kindest and gentlest feelings, are *obliged* to interpret these severe laws with inflexible severity. In the perpetual reaction of that awful force of human passion and human will, which necessarily meets the compressive power of slavery, — in that seething, boiling tide, never wholly repressed, which rolls its volcanic stream underneath the whole frame-work of society so constituted, ready to find vent at the least rent or fissure or unguarded aperture, — there is a constant necessity which urges to severity of law and inflexibility of execution. So Judge Ruffin says, "We cannot allow the *right* of the matter to be brought into discussion in the courts of justice. The slave, to remain a slave, must be made sensible that there is NO APPEAL FROM HIS MASTER." Accordingly, we find in the more southern states, where the slave population is most accumulated, and slave property most necessary and valuable, and, of course, the determination to abide by the system the most decided, *there* the enactments are most severe, and the interpretation of courts the most inflexible.* And, when legal decisions of a contrary character begin to be made, it would appear that it is a symptom of leaning towards emancipation. So abhorrent is the slave-code to every feeling of humanity, that just as soon as there is any hesitancy in the community about perpetuating the institution of slavery, judges begin to listen to the voice of their more honorable nature, and by favorable interpretations to soften its necessary severities.

Such decisions do not commend themselves to the professional admiration of legal gentlemen. But in the workings of the slave system, when the irresponsible power which it guarantees comes to be used by men

* We except the State of Louisiana. Owing to the influence of the French code in that state, more really humane provisions prevail there. How much these provisions avail in point of fact, will be shown when we come to that part of the subject.

of the most brutal nature, cases sometimes arise for trial where the consistent exposition of the law involves results so loathsome and frightful, that the judge prefers to be illogical, rather than inhuman. Like a spring outgushing in the desert, some noble man, now and then, from the fulness of his own better nature, throws out a legal decision, generously inconsistent with every principle and precedent of slave jurisprudence, and we bless God for it. All we wish is that there were more of them, for then should we hope that the day of redemption was drawing nigh.

The reader is now prepared to enter with us on the proof of this proposition: That the slave-code is designed *only for the security of the master, and not with regard to the welfare of the slave.*

This is implied in the whole current of law-making and law-administration, and is often asserted in distinct form, with a precision and clearness of legal accuracy which, in a literary point of view, are quite admirable. Thus, Judge Ruffin, after stating that considerations restricting the power of the master had often been drawn from a comparison of slavery with the relation of parent and child, master and apprentice, tutor and pupil, says distinctly:

The court does not recognize their application. There is no likeness between the cases. They are in opposition to each other, and there is an impassable gulf between them.   *   *   *   *
In the one [case], the end in view is the *happiness of the youth,* born to equal rights with that governor, on whom the duty devolves of training the young to usefulness, in a station which he is afterwards to assume among freemen. * * * * With slavery it is far otherwise. The *end* _{Wheeler's Law of Slavery, page 246.} *is the profit of the master,* his security and the public safety.

Not only is this principle distinctly asserted in so many words, but it is more distinctly implied in multitudes of the arguings and reasonings which are given as grounds of legal decisions. Even such provisions as seem to be for the benefit of the slave we often find carefully interpreted so as to show that it is only on account of his property value to his master that he is thus protected, and not from any consideration of humanity towards himself. Thus it has been decided that a master can bring no action for assault _{Wheeler's Law of Slavery, p. 239.} and battery on his slave, *unless the injury be such as to produce a loss of service.*

The spirit in which this question is discussed is worthy of remark. We give a brief statement of the case, as presented in Wheeler, p. 239.

It was an action for assault and battery committed by Dale on one Cornfute's slave. It was contended by Cornfute's counsel that it was not necessary to *prove loss of service,* in order that the action should be sustained; that an action might be supported for beating plaintiff's *horse;* and that the lord might have an action for the battery of his villein, which is founded on this principle, that, as the villein could not support the action, *the injury would be without redress, unless the lord could.* On the other side it was said that Lord Chief Justice Raymond had decided that an assault on a horse was no cause of action, unless accompanied with *a special damage* which would impair his value.

_{Cornfute v. Dale, April Term, 1800. 1 Har. & Johns. Rep. 4.}
_{2 Lutw. 1481 ; 20 Viner's Abr. 454.}

Chief Justice Chase decided that no redress could be obtained in the case, because the value of the slave had not been impaired, and *without injury or wrong to the master* no action could be sustained; and assigned this among other reasons for it, that there was no reciprocity in the case, as the master was not liable for assault and battery committed by his slave, neither could he gain redress for one committed upon his slave.

Let any reader now imagine what an amount of wanton cruelty and indignity may be heaped upon a slave man or woman or child without actually impairing their power to do service to the master, and he will have a full sense of the cruelty of this decision.

In the same spirit it has been held in North Carolina that patrols (night watchmen) are not liable to the master for inflicting punishment on the slave, unless their conduct clearly demonstrates *malice against the master.*

_{Tate v. O'Neal, 1 Hawks, 418. U. S. Dig. Sup. 2, p. 797, § 121.}

The cool-bloodedness of some of these legal discussions is forcibly shown by two decisions in Wheeler's Law of Slavery, p. 243. On the question whether the criminal offence of assault and battery can be committed on a slave, there are two decisions of the two States of South and North Carolina; and it is difficult to say which of these decisions has the preëminence for cool legal inhumanity. That of South Carolina reads thus.

_{State v. Maner, 2 Hill's Rep. 453. Wheeler's Law of Slavery, page 243.}

Judge O'Neill says:

The criminal offence of assault and battery can not, at common law, be committed upon the person of a slave. For notwithstanding (for some purposes) a slave is regarded by law as a *person,* yet generally he is a mere chattel personal, and his right of personal protection belongs to his master, who can maintain an action of the battery of his slave. There can be therefore no offence against the state for a *mere beating of a slave unaccompanied with any circumstances of cruelty* (!!), *or an attempt to kill and murder.* The peace of the state *is not thereby broken; for a slave* is not generally regarded as legally capable of being within the peace of the state. He is not a citizen, and is not in that character entitled to her protection.

What declaration of the utter indifference of the state to the sufferings of the slave could be more elegantly cool and clear?

See State v. Hale. Wheeler, p. 239. 2 Hawk. N. C. Rep. 582.

But in North Carolina it appears that the case is argued still more elaborately.

Chief Justice Taylor thus shows that, after all, there are reasons why an assault and battery upon the slave may, on the whole, have some such general connection with the comfort and security of the community, that it may be construed into a breach of the peace, and should be treated as an indictable offence.

The instinct of a slave may be, and generally is, tamed into subservience to his master's will, and from him he receives chastisement, whether it be merited or not, with perfect submission; for he knows the extent of the dominion assumed over him, and that the law ratifies the claim. But when the same authority is wantonly usurped by a stranger, nature is disposed to assert her rights, and to prompt the slave to a resistance, often momentarily successful, sometimes fatally so. The public peace is thus broken, as much as if a free man had been beaten; for the party of the aggressor is always the strongest, and such contests usually terminate by overpowering the slave, and inflicting on him a severe chastisement, without regard to the original cause of the conflict. There is, consequently, as much reason for making such offences indictable as if a white man had been the victim. A wanton injury committed on a slave *is a great provocation to the owner, awakens his resentment, and has a direct tendency to a breach of the peace, by inciting him to seek immediate vengeance.* If resented in the heat of blood, it would probably extenuate a homicide to manslaughter, upon the same principle with the case stated by Lord Hale, that if A riding on the road, B had whipped his horse out of the track, and then A had alighted and killed B. These offences are usually committed by men of dissolute habits, hanging loose upon society, *who, being repelled from association with well-disposed citizens, take refuge in the company of colored persons and slaves, whom they deprave by their example, embolden by their familiarity, and then beat, under the expectation that a slave dare not resent a blow from a white man.* If such offences may be committed with impunity, the public peace will not only be rendered extremely insecure, but *the value of slave property must be much impaired,* for the offenders can seldom make any reparation in damages. Nor is it necessary, in any case, that a person who has received an injury, real or imaginary, from a slave, should carve out his own justice;

for the law has made ample and summary provision for the punishment of all trivial offences committed by slaves, by carrying them before a justice, who is authorized to pass sentence for their being publicly whipped. This provision, while it excludes the necessity of private vengeance, would seem to forbid its legality, since it effectually protects all persons from the insolence of slaves, even where their masters are unwilling to correct them upon complaint being made. The common law has often been called into efficient operation, for the punishment of public cruelty inflicted *upon animals,* for needless and wanton barbarity exercised even by masters upon their slaves, and for various violations of *decency, morals, and comfort.* Reason and analogy seem to require that a human being, *although the subject of property,* should be *so far protected as the public might be injured through him.*

1 Rev. Code, 448.

For all purposes necessary to enforce the obedience of the slave, and to render him useful as property, the law secures to the master a complete authority over him, and it will not lightly interfere with the relation thus established. *It is a more effectual guarantee of his right of property, when the slave is protected from wanton abuse from those who have no power over him;* for it cannot be disputed that a slave is rendered less capable of performing his master's service when he finds himself exposed by the law to the capricious violence of every turbulent man in the community.

If this is not a scrupulous disclaimer of all humane intention in the decision, as far as the slave is concerned, and an explicit declaration that he is protected only out of regard to the comfort of the community, and his property value to his master, it is difficult to see how such a declaration could be made. After all this cool-blooded course of remark, it is somewhat curious to come upon the following certainly most unexpected declaration, which occurs in the very next paragraph:

Mitigated as slavery is by the *humanity of our laws,* the refinement of manners, and by *public opinion, which revolts at every instance of cruelty towards* them, it would be an anomaly in the system of police which affects them, if the offence stated in the verdict were not indictable.

The reader will please to notice that this remarkable declaration is made of the State of North Carolina. We shall have occasion again to refer to it by and by, when we extract from the statute-book of North Carolina some specimens of these humane laws.

In the same spirit it is decided, under the law of Louisiana, that if an individual injures another's slave so as to make him *entirely useless,* and the owner recovers from him the full value of the slave, the slave by that act becomes thenceforth the property of the person who injured him. A decision to this effect is given in Wheeler's Law

Jourdain v. Patton, July term, 1818. 5 Martin's Louis. Rep. 615.

of Slavery, p. 249. A woman sued for an injury done to her slave by the slave of the defendant. The injury was such as to render him entirely useless, his *only* eye being put out. The parish court decreed that she should recover twelve hundred dollars, that the defendant should pay a further sum of twenty-five dollars a month from the time of the injury; also the physician's bill, and two hundred dollars for the sustenance of the slave during his life, and that he should remain forever in the possession of his mistress.

The case was appealed. The judge reversed the decision, and delivered the slave into the possession of the man whose slave had committed the outrage. In the course of the decision, the judge remarks, with that calm legal explicitness for which many decisions of this kind are remarkable, that

The principle of humanity, which would lead us to suppose that the mistress, whom he had long served, would treat her miserable blind slave with more kindness than the defendant, to whom the judgment ought to transfer him, cannot be taken into consideration in deciding this case.

Jan. term, 1828. Another case, reported in Wheel-
9 Martin La. er's Law, page 198, the author
Rep. 350. thus summarily abridges. It is Dorothee v. Coquillon *et al.* A young girl, by will of her mistress, was to have her freedom at twenty-one; and it was required by the will that in the mean time she should be educated in such a manner as to enable her to earn her living when free, her services in the mean time being bequeathed to the daughter of the defendant. Her mother (a free woman) entered complaint that no care was taken of the child's education, and that she was cruelly treated. The prayer of the petition was that the child be declared free at twenty-one, and in the mean time hired out by the sheriff. The suit was decided against the mother, on this ground, — that she could not sue *for* her daughter in a case where the daughter could not sue for herself were she of age, — the object of the suit being *relief from ill-treatment during the time of her slavery, which a slave cannot sue for.*

Jan. term, 1827. Observe, now, the following
4 M'Cord's Rep. case of Jennings v. Fundeberg.
161. Wheeler's It seems Jennings brings an ac-
Law of Slavery, tion of trespass against Funde-
p. 201. berg for killing his slave. The case was thus: Fundeberg with others, being out hunting runaway negroes, surprised them in their camp, and, as the report says, "*fired his gun towards them* as they were run-

ning away, *to induce them to stop.*" One of them, being shot through the head, was thus *induced to stop*, — and the master of the boy brought action for trespass against the firer for killing his slave.

The decision of the inferior court was as follows :

The court "thought the killing accidental, and that the defendant ought not to be made answerable as a trespasser." * * * * "When one is lawfully interfering with the property of another, and accidentally destroys it, he is no trespasser, and ought not to be answerable for the value of the property. In this case, the defendant was engaged in a lawful and *meritorious* service, and if he really fired his gun in the manner stated it was an allowable act."

The superior judge reversed the decision, on the ground that in dealing with another person's property one is responsible for any injury which he could have avoided by any degree of circumspection. "The firing . . . . was *rash* and *incautious.*"

Does not the whole spirit of this discussion speak for itself ?

See also the very next case in Jan. T. 1827. 4
Wheeler's Law. Richardson v. M'Cord's Rep.
Dukes, p. 202. 156.

Trespass for killing the plaintiff's slave. It appeared the slave was stealing potatoes from a bank near the defendant's house. The defendant fired upon him with a gun loaded with buckshot, and killed him. The jury found a verdict for plaintiff for one dollar. Motion for a new trial.

The Court. Nott J. held, there must be a new trial; that the jury ought to have given the plaintiff the value of the slave. That if the jury were of opinion the slave was of bad character, some deduction from the usual price ought to be made, but the plaintiff was certainly entitled to his actual damage for killing his slave. Where property is in question, the value of the article, as nearly as it can be ascertained, furnishes a rule from which they are not at liberty to depart.

It seems that the value of this unfortunate piece of property was somewhat reduced from the circumstance of his "stealing potatoes." Doubtless he had his own best reasons for this; so, at least, we should infer from the following remark, which Wheeler's Law occurs in one of the reasonings of Slavery, 220. of Judge Taylor, of N. Carolina.

"The act of 1786 (Iredell's Revisal, p. 588) does, in the preamble, recognize the fact, that many persons, *by cruel treatment to* their *slaves, cause* them to commit crimes for which they are executed. * * The cruel treatment here alluded to must consist in *withholding from them the necessaries of life;* and the crimes thus resulting are such as are calculated to *furnish them with food and raiment.*"

Perhaps "stealing potatoes" in this case was one of the class of crimes alluded to.

Again we have the following case:

Whitsell v. Earnest & Parker. Wheeler, p. 202.

The defendants went to the plantation of Mrs. Witsell for the purpose of hunting for runaway negroes; there being many in the neighborhood, and the place in considerable alarm. As they approached the house with loaded guns, a negro ran from the house, or near the house, towards a swamp, when they fired and killed him.

The judge charged the jury, that such circumstances might exist, by the excitement and alarm of the neighborhood, as to authorize the killing of a negro without the sanction of a magistrate.

This decision was reversed in the Superior Court, in the following language:

By the statute of 1740, any white man may apprehend and moderately correct any slave who may be found out of the plantation at which he is employed, and if the slave assaults the white person, *he may be killed;* but a slave who is merely flying away cannot be killed. Nor can the defendants be justified by common law, IF *we consider the negro as a person;* for they were not clothed with the authority of the law to apprehend him as a felon, and without such authority he could not be killed.

IF *we consider the negro a person,* says the judge; and, from his decision in the case, he evidently intimates that he has a strong leaning to this opinion, though it has been contested by so many eminent legal authorities that he puts forth his sentiment modestly, and in an hypothetical form. The reader, perhaps, will need to be informed that the question whether the slave is to be considered a person or a human being in any respect has been extensively and ably argued on both sides in legal courts, and it may be a comfort to know that the balance of legal opinion inclines in favor of the slave. Judge Clarke, of Mississippi, is quite clear on the point, and argues very ably and earnestly, though, as he confesses, against very respectable legal authorities, that the slave *is* a person,— that he *is* a reasonable creature.

The reasoning occurs in the case State of Mississippi *v.* Jones, and is worthy of attention as a literary curiosity.

Wheeler, p. 252. June T., 1820. Walker's Rep. 83.

It seems that a case of murder of a slave had been clearly made out and proved in the lower court, and that judgment was arrested and the case appealed on the ground whether, in that state, murder could be committed on a slave. Judge Clarke thus ably and earnestly argues:

The question in this case is, whether murder can be committed on a slave. Because individuals may have been deprived of many of their rights by society, it does not follow, that they have been deprived of all their rights. In some respects, slaves may be considered as chattels; but in others, they are regarded as men. The law views them as capable of committing crimes. This can only be upon the principle, that they are *men* and rational beings. The Roman law has been much relied on by the counsel of the defendant. That law was confined to the Roman empire, giving the power of life and death over captives in war, as slaves; but it no more extended here, than the similar power given to parents over the lives of their children. Much stress has also been laid by the defendant's counsel on the case cited from Taylor's Reports, decided in North Carolina; yet, in that case, two judges against one were of opinion, that killing a slave was murder. Judge Hall, who delivered the dissenting opinion in the above case, based his conclusions, as we conceive, upon erroneous principles, by considering the laws of Rome applicable here. His inference, also, that a person cannot be condemned capitally, because he may be liable in a civil action, is not sustained by reason or authority, but appears to us to be in direct opposition to both. At a very early period in Virginia, the power of life over slaves was given by statute; but Tucker observes, that as soon as these statutes were repealed, it was at once considered by their courts that the killing of a slave might be murder. Commonwealth *v.* Dolly Chapman: indictment for maliciously stabbing a slave, under a statute. It has been determined in Virginia that slaves are persons. In the constitution of the United States, slaves are expressly designated as "persons." In this state the legislature have considered slaves as reasonable and accountable beings; and it would be a stigma upon the character of the state, and a reproach to the administration of justice, if the life of a slave could be taken with impunity, or if he could be murdered in cold blood, without subjecting the offender to the highest penalty known to the criminal jurisprudence of the country. Has the slave no rights, because he is deprived of his freedom? He is still a human being, and possesses all those rights of which he is not *deprived by the positive provisions of the law;* but in vain shall we look for any law passed by the enlightened and philanthropic legislature of this state, giving even to the master, much less to a stranger, power over the life of a slave. Such a statute would be worthy the age of Draco or Caligula, and would be condemned by the unanimous voice of the people of this state, where even cruelty to slaves, much [more] the taking away of life, meets with universal reprobation. By the provisions of our law, a slave may commit murder, and be punished with death; why, then, is it not murder to kill a slave? Can a mere chattel commit murder, and be subject to punishment!

* * * * * *

The right of the master exists not by force of the law of nature or nations, but by virtue only of the positive law of the state; and although that gives to the master the right to command the services of the slave, requiring the master to feed and clothe the slave from infancy till death, yet it gives the master no right to take the life of the slave; and, if the offence be not murder, it is not a crime, and subjects the offender to no punishment.

The taking away the life of a reasonable creature, under the king's peace, with malice afore-thought, express or implied, is murder at common law. Is not a slave a reasonable creature!—is he not a human being! And the meaning of this phrase, *reasonable creature*, is, a human being. For the killing a lunatic, an idiot, or even a child unborn, is murder, as much as the killing a philosopher; and has not the slave as much reason as a lunatic, an idiot, or an unborn child!

Thus triumphantly, in this nineteenth century of the Christian era and in the State of Mississippi, has it been made to appear that the slave is a reasonable creature,— a human being!

What sort of system, what sort of a public sentiment, was that which made this argument *necessary?*

And let us look at some of the admissions of this argument with regard to the *nature* of slavery. According to the judge, it is depriving human beings of *many of their rights*. Thus he says: "Because individuals may have been deprived of many of their rights by society, it does not follow that they have been deprived of *all* their rights." Again, he says of the slave: "He is still a human being, and possesses all those *rights* of which he is not deprived by the *positive provisions of the law*." Here he admits that the provisions of law deprive the slave of natural *rights*. Again he says: "The right of the master exists not by force of the law of nature or of nations, but by virtue only of the positive law of the state." According to the decision of this judge, therefore, slavery exists by the same right that robbery or oppression of any kind does, — the right of *ability*. A gang of robbers associated into a society have rights over all the neighboring property that they can acquire, of precisely the same kind.

With the same unconscious serenity does the law apply that principle of force and robbery which is the essence of slavery, and show how far the master may proceed in appropriating another human being as his property.

The question arises, May a master give a woman to one person, and her *unborn children* to another one? Let us hear the case argued. The unfortunate mother selected as the test point of this interesting legal principle comes to our view in the will of one Samuel Marksbury, under the style and denomination of "my negro wench Pen." Said Samuel states in his will that, for the good will and love he bears to his *own* children, he gives said negro wench Pen to son Samuel, and all her future increase to

Wheeler, p. 28.
Banks, Adm'r,
p. Marksbury.
Spring T. 1823.
5 Little's Rep.
— 275.

daughter Rachael. When daughter Rachael, therefore, marries, her husband sets up a claim for this increase,— as it is stated, quite off-hand, that the "wench had several children." Here comes a beautifully interesting case, quite stimulating to legal acumen. Inferior court decides that Samuel Marksbury could not have given away unborn children on the strength of the legal maxim, "*Nemo dat quod non habet*,"— i. e., "Nobody can give what he has not got,"— which certainly one should think sensible and satisfactory enough. The case, however, is appealed, and reversed in the superior court; and now let us hear the reasoning.

The judge acknowledges the force of the maxim above quoted,— says, as one would think any man might say, that it is quite a correct maxim,— the only difficulty being that it does not at all apply to the present case. Let us hear him:

He who is the absolute owner of a *thing* owns all its faculties for profit or increase; and he may, no doubt, grant the profits or increase, as well as the *thing* itself. Thus, it is every day's practice to grant the future rents or profits of real estate; and it is held that a man may grant the wool of a flock of sheep for years.

See also p. 33, Fanny *v.* Bryant, 4 J. J. Marshall's Rep., 368. In this almost precisely the same language is used. If the reader will proceed, he will find also this principle applied with equal clearness to the hiring, selling, mortgaging of unborn children; and the perfect legal nonchalance of these discussions is only comparable to running a dissecting-knife through the course of all the heart-strings of a living subject, for the purpose of demonstrating the laws of nervous contraction.

Judge Stroud, in his sketch of the slave-laws, page 99, lays down for proof the following assertion: That the penal codes of the slave states bear much more severely on slaves than on white persons. He introduces his consideration of this proposition by the following humane and sensible remarks:

A being, ignorant of letters, unenlightened by religion, and deriving but little instruction from good example, cannot be supposed to have right conceptions as to the nature and extent of moral or political obligations. This remark, with but a slight qualification, is applicable to the condition of the slave. It has been just shown that the benefits of education are not conferred upon him, while his *chance* of acquiring a knowledge of the precepts of the gospel is so remote as scarcely to be appreciated. He may be regarded, therefore as almost without the capacity to comprehend the force of laws; and, on this account, such as are designed for his government should be recommended by their simplicity and mildness.

His condition suggests another motive for tenderness on his behalf in these particulars. *He is unable to read*, and holding little or no communication with those who are better informed than himself; how is he to become acquainted with the fact that a law for his observance has been made? To exact obedience to a law which has not been promulgated, — which is unknown to the subject of it, — has ever been deemed most unjust and tyrannical. The reign of Caligula, were it obnoxious to no other reproach than this, would never cease to be remembered with abhorrence.

The lawgivers of the slaveholding states seem, in the formation of their penal codes, to have been uninfluenced by these claims of the slave upon their compassionate consideration. The *hardened convict* moves their sympathy, and is to be *taught* the laws *before* he is expected to obey them; yet the *guiltless slave* is subjected to an extensive system of cruel enactments, of no part of which, probably, has he ever heard.

Parts of this system apply to the slave exclusively, and for every infraction a large retribution is demanded; while, with respect to offences for which whites as well as slaves are amenable, *punishments of much greater severity are inflicted upon the latter* than upon the former.

This heavy charge of Judge Stroud is sustained by twenty pages of proof, showing the very great disproportion between the number of offences made capital for slaves, and those that are so for whites. Concerning this, we find the following cool remark in Wheeler's Law of Slavery, page 222, note.

Much has been said of the disparity of punishment between the white inhabitants and the slaves and negroes of the same state; that slaves are punished with much more severity, for the commission of similar crimes, by white persons, than the latter. The charge is undoubtedly true to a considerable extent. It must be remembered that the primary object of the enactment of penal laws, is the protection and security of those who make them. The slave has no agency in making them. He is indeed one cause of the apprehended evils to the other class, which those laws are expected to remedy. That he should be held amenable for a violation of those rules established for the security of the other, is the natural result of the state in which he is placed. And the severity of those rules will always bear a relation to that danger, real or ideal, of the other class. It has been so among all nations, and will ever continue to be so, while the disparity between bond and free remains.

A striking example of a legal decision to this purport is given in Wheeler's Law of Slavery, page 224. The case, apart from legal technicalities, may be thus briefly stated:

The State v. Mann. Dec. Term, 1829. Devereaux's North Carolina Rep. 263.

The defendant, Mann, had hired a slave-woman for a year. During this time the slave committed some slight offence, for which the defendant undertook to chastise her. While in the act of doing so the slave ran off, whereat he shot at and wounded her. The judge in the inferior court charged the jury that if they believed the punishment was cruel and unwarrantable, and disproportioned to the offence, in law the defendant was guilty, *as he had only a special property in the slave.* The jury finding evidence that the punishment *had* been cruel, unwarrantable and *disproportioned to the offence,* found verdict against the defendant. But on what ground? — Because, according to the law of North Carolina, cruel, unwarrantable, disproportionate punishment of a slave from a master, is an indictable offence? No. They decided against the defendant, not because the punishment was cruel and unwarrantable, but because *he* was not the person who had the right to inflict it, "as he had only a SPECIAL *right of property in the slave.*"

The defendant appealed to a higher court, and the decision was reversed, on the ground that the hirer has for the time being all the rights of the master. The remarks of Judge Ruffin are so characteristic, and so strongly express the conflict between the feelings of the humane judge and the logical necessity of a strict interpreter of slave-law, that we shall quote largely from it. One cannot but admire the unflinching calmness with which a man, evidently possessed of honorable and humane feelings, walks through the most extreme and terrible results and conclusions, in obedience to the laws of legal truth. Thus he says:

A judge cannot but lament, when such cases as the present are brought into judgment. It is impossible that the reasons on which they go can be appreciated, but where institutions similar to our own exist, and are *thoroughly understood.* The struggle, too, in the judge's own breast, between the feelings of the man and the duty of the magistrate, is a severe one, presenting strong temptation to put aside such questions, if it be possible. It is useless, however, to complain of things inherent in our political state. And it is criminal in a court to avoid any responsibility which the laws impose. With whatever reluctance, therefore, it is done, the court is compelled to express an opinion upon the extent of the dominion of the master over the slave in North Carolina. The indictment charges a battery on Lydia, a slave of Elizabeth Jones. . . . . The inquiry here is, whether a cruel and unreasonable battery on a slave by the hirer is indictable. The judge below instructed the jury that it is. He seems to have put it on the ground, that the defendant had but a special property. Our laws uniformly treat the master, or other person having the possession and command of the slave, as entitled to the same extent of authority. *The object is the same, the service of the slave;* and the same powers must be confided. In a criminal proceeding, and, indeed, in reference to all other persons but the general owner, the hirer and possessor of the slave, in relation to both rights and duties, is, for the time being, the owner. . . . . But, upon the general question, whether the owner is answerable *criminaliter,* for a battery upon his own slave, or other exercise of authority of force, not forbidden by statute, the court entertains but little doubt. That he is so liable, has never been decided; nor, as far as is known, been hitherto contended. There has been no prosecution of the sort. The established habits and uniform practice of the country, in this respect, is the best evidence of the portion of power deemed by the whole community requisite to the preservation of the master's dominion. If we thought differently, we could not set our notions in array against the judgment of everybody else, and say that this or that authority may be safely lopped off. This has indeed been assimilated at the bar to the other domestic relations; and arguments drawn from the well-established principles, which *confer* and *restrain* the authority of the parent over the child, the tutor over the pupil, the master over the apprentice, have been pressed on us.

. The court does not recognize their application. There is no likeness between the cases. They are in opposition to each other, and there is an impassable gulf between them. The difference is that which exists between freedom and slavery; and a greater cannot be imagined. In the one, the end in view is the happiness of the youth born to equal rights with that governor on whom the duty devolves of training the young to usefulness, in a station which he is afterwards to assume among freemen. To such an end, and with such a subject, moral and intellectual instruction seem the natural means; and, for the most part, they are found to suffice. Moderate force is superadded only to make the others effectual. If that fail, it is better to leave the party to his own headstrong passions, and the ultimate correction of the law, than to allow it to be immoderately inflicted by a private person. With slavery it is far otherwise. The end is the profit of the master, his security and the public safety; the subject, one doomed, in his own person and his posterity, to live without knowledge, and without the capacity to make anything his own, and to toil that another may reap the fruits. What moral considerations shall be addressed to such a being, to convince him what it is impossible but that the most stupid must feel and know can never be true, — that he is thus to labor upon a principle of natural duty, or for the sake of his own personal happiness? Such services can only be expected from one who has no will of his own; who surrenders his will in implicit obedience to that of another. Such obedience is the consequence only of uncontrolled authority over the body. There is nothing else which can operate to produce the effect. THE POWER OF THE MASTER MUST BE ABSOLUTE, TO RENDER THE SUBMISSION OF THE SLAVE PERFECT. I most freely confess my sense of the harshness of this proposition. I feel it as deeply as any man can. And, as a principle of moral right, every person in his retirement must repudiate it. But, in the actual condition of things, it must be so. There is no remedy. This discipline belongs to the state of

slavery. They cannot be disunited without abrogating at once the rights of the master, and absolving the slave from his subjection. It constitutes the curse of slavery to both the bond and the free portions of our population. But it is *inherent in the relation* of master and slave. That there may be particular instances of cruelty and deliberate barbarity, where in conscience the law might properly interfere, is most probable. The difficulty is to determine where *a court* may properly begin. Merely in the abstract, it may well be asked which power of the master accords with right. The answer will probably sweep away all of them. But we cannot look at the matter in that light. The truth is that we are forbidden to enter upon a train of general reasoning on the subject. We cannot allow the right of the master to be brought into discussion in the courts of justice. The slave, to remain a slave, must be made sensible that there is no appeal from his master; that his power is, in no instance, usurped, but is conferred by the laws of man, at least, if not by the law of God. The danger would be great, indeed, if the tribunals of justice should be called on to graduate the punishment appropriate to every temper and every dereliction of menial duty.

No man can anticipate the many and aggravated provocations of the master which the slave would be constantly stimulated by his own passions, or the instigation of others, to give; or the consequent wrath of the master, prompting him to bloody vengeance upon the turbulent traitor; a vengeance *generally practised with impunity, by reason of its privacy.* The court, therefore, disclaims the power of changing the relation in which these parts of our people stand to each other.

*   *   *   *   *

I repeat, that I would gladly have avoided this ungrateful question. But, being brought to it, the court is compelled to declare that while slavery exists amongst us in its present state, or until it shall seem fit to the legislature to interpose express enactments to the contrary, it will be the imperative *duty* of the judges *to recognize the full dominion of the owner over the slave,* except where the exercise of it is forbidden by statute.

And this we do upon the ground that *this dominion is essential to the value of slaves as property, to the security of the master and the public tranquillity, greatly dependent upon their subordination;* and, in fine, as most effectually securing the general protection and comfort of the slaves themselves. Judgment below reversed; and judgment entered for the defendant.

No one can read this decision, so fine and clear in expression, so dignified and solemn in its earnestness, and so dreadful in its results, without feeling at once deep respect for the man and horror for the system. The man, judging him from this short specimen, which is all the author knows,[*] has one of that high order of minds, which looks straight through all verbiage and sophistry to the heart of every subject which it encounters. He has, too, that noble

---

[*] More recently the author has met with a passage in a North Carolina newspaper, containing some further par-

scorn of dissimulation, that straightforward determination not to call a bad thing by a good name, even when most popular and reputable and legal, which it is to be wished could be more frequently seen, both in our Northern and Southern States. There is but one sole regret; and that is that such a man, with such a mind, should have been merely an *expositor*, and not a *reformer* of law.

CHAPTER III.

SOUTHER *v.* THE COMMONWEALTH — THE NE PLUS ULTRA OF LEGAL HUMANITY.

" Yet in the face of such laws and decisions as these!
Mrs. Stowe, &c."— *Courier & Enquirer.*

THE case of Souther *v.* the Commonwealth has been cited by the *Courier & Enquirer* as a particularly favorable speci-

ticulars of the life of Judge Ruffin, which have proved interesting to her, and may also to the reader.

From the Raleigh (N. C.) Register.
RESIGNATION OF THE CHIEF JUSTICE OF THE STATE OF NORTH CAROLINA.

We publish below the letter of Chief Justice Ruffin, of the Supreme Court, resigning his seat on the bench.

This act takes us, and no less will it take the state, by surprise. The public are not prepared for it; and we doubt not there will scarcely be an exception to the deep and general regret which will be felt throughout the state. Judge Ruffin's great and unsurpassed legal learning, his untiring industry, the ease with which he mastered the details and comprehended the whole of the most complicated cases, were the admiration of the bar; and it has been a common saying of the ablest lawyers of the state, for a long time past, that his place on the bench could be supplied by no other than himself.

He is now, as we learn, in the sixty-fifth year of his age, in full possession of his usual excellent health, unaffected, so far as we can discover, in his natural vigor and strength, and certainly without any symptom of mental decay. Forty-five years ago he commenced the practice of the law. He has been on the bench twenty-eight years, of which time he has been one of the Supreme Court twenty-three years. During this long public career he has, in a pecuniary point of view, sacrificed many thousands; for there has been no time of it in which he might not, with perfect ease, have doubled, by practice, the amount of his salary as judge.

" To the Honorable the General Assembly of North Carolina,
now in session.

"Gentlemen: I desire to retire to the walks of private life, and therefore pray your honorable body to accept the resignation of my place on the bench of the Supreme Court. In surrendering this trust, I would wish to express my grateful sense of the confidence and honors so often and so long bestowed on me by the General Assembly. But I have no language to do it suitably. I am very sensible that they were far beyond my deserts, and that I have made an insufficient return of the service. Yet I can truly aver that, to the best of my ability, I have administered the law as I understood it, and to the ends of suppressing crime and wrong, and upholding virtue, truth and right; aiming to give confidence to honest men, and to confirm in all good citizens love for our country, and a pure trust in her law and magistrates.

"In my place I hope I have contributed to these ends; and I firmly believe that our laws will, as heretofore, be executed, and our people happy in the administration of justice, honest and contented, as long as they keep, and only so long as they keep, the independent and sound judiciary now established in the constitution; which, with

men of judicial proceedings under the slave-code, with the following remark:

And yet, in the face of such laws and decisions as these, Mrs. Stowe winds up a long series of cruelties upon her other black personages, by causing her faultless hero, Tom, to be literally whipped to death in Louisiana, by his master, Legree; and these acts, which the laws make criminal, and punish as such, she sets forth in the most repulsive colors, to illustrate the institution of slavery!

By the above language the author was led into the supposition that this case had been conducted in a manner so creditable to the feelings of our common humanity as to present a fairer side of criminal jurisprudence in this respect. She accordingly took the pains to procure a report of the case, designing to publish it as an offset to the many barbarities which research into this branch of the subject obliges one to unfold. A legal gentleman has copied the case from Grattan's Reports, and it is here given. If the reader is astounded at it, he cannot be more so than was the writer.

Souther v. The Commonwealth. 7 Grattan, 673, 1851.

The killing of a slave by his master and owner, by wilful and excessive whipping, is murder in the first degree: though it may not have been the purpose and intention of the master and owner to kill the slave.

Simeon Souther was indicted at the October Term, 1850, of the Circuit Court for the County of Hanover, for the murder of his own slave. The indictment contained fifteen counts, in which the various modes of punishment and torture by which the homicide was charged to have been committed were stated singly, and in various combinations, The fifteenth count unites them all: and, as the court certifies that the *indictment was sustained by the evidence*, the giving the facts stated in 'that count will show what was the charge against the prisoner, and what was the proof to sustain it.

The count charged that on the 1st day of September, 1849, the prisoner tied his negro slave, Sam, with ropes about his wrists, neck, body, legs and ankles, to a tree. That whilst so tied, the prisoner next beat and cobbed the slave with a shingle, and compelled two of his slaves, a man and a woman, also to cob the deceased with the shingle. That whilst the deceased was so tied to the tree, the prisoner did strike, knock, kick, stamp and beat him upon various parts of his head, face and body; that he applied fire to his body; * * * * that he then washed his body with warm water, in which pods of red pepper had been put and steeped; and he compelled his two slaves aforesaid also to wash him with this same preparation of warm water and red pepper. That after the tying, whipping, cobbing, striking, beating, knocking, kicking, stamping, wounding, bruising, lacerating, burning, washing and torturing, as

all other blessings, I earnestly pray may be perpetuated to the people of North Carolina.

"I have the honor to be, gentlemen, your most obliged and obedient servant,   THOMAS RUFFIN.
"*Raleigh, November* 10, 1852."

aforesaid, the prisoner untied the deceased from the tree in such way as to throw him with violence to the ground; and he then and there did knock, kick, stamp and beat the deceased upon his head, temples, and various parts of his body. That the prisoner then had the deceased carried into a-shed-room of his house, and there he compelled one of his slaves, in his presence, to confine the deceased's feet in stocks, by making his legs fast to a piece of timber, and to tie a rope about the neck of the deceased, and fasten it to a bed-post in the room, thereby strangling, choking and suffocating the deceased. And that whilst the deceased was thus made fast in stocks as aforesaid, the prisoner did kick, knock, stamp and beat him upon his head, face, breast, belly, sides, back and body; and he again compelled his two slaves to apply fire to the body of the deceased, whilst he was so made fast as aforesaid. And the count charged that from these various modes of punishment and torture the slave Sam then and there died. It appeared that the prisoner commenced the punishment of the deceased in the morning, and that it was continued throughout the day: and that the deceased died in the presence of the prisoner, and one of his slaves, and one of the witnesses, whilst the punishment was still progressing.

Field J. delivered the opinion of the court.

The prisoner was indicted and convicted of *murder in the second degree*, in the Circuit Court of Hanover, at its April term last past, and was sentenced to the *penitentiary for five years*, the period of time ascertained by the jury. The murder consisted in the killing of a negro man-slave by the name of Sam, the property of the prisoner, by cruel and excessive whipping and torture, inflicted by Souther, aided by two of his other slaves, on the 1st day of September, 1849. The prisoner moved for a new trial, upon the ground that the offence, *if any*, amounted only to manslaughter. The motion for a new trial was overruled, and a bill of exceptions taken to the opinion of the court, setting forth the facts proved, or as many of them as were deemed material for the consideration of the application for a new trial. The bill of exception states: That the slave Sam, in the indictment mentioned, was the slave and property of the prisoner. That for the purpose of chastising the slave for the offence of getting drunk, and dealing as the slave confessed and alleged with Henry and Stone, two of the witnesses for the Commonwealth, he caused him to be tied and punished in the presence of the said witnesses, with the exception of slight whipping with peach or apple-tree switches, before the said witnesses arrived at the scene after they were sent for by the prisoner (who were present by request from the defendant), and of several slaves of the prisoner, in the manner and by the means charged in the indictment; and the said slave died under and from the infliction of the said punishment, in the presence of the prisoner, one of his slaves, and of one of the witnesses for the Commonwealth. But it did not appear that it was the design of the prisoner to kill the said slave, unless such design be properly inferable from the manner, means and duration of the punishment. And, on the contrary, it did appear that the prisoner frequently declared, while the said slave was undergoing the punishment, that he believed the said slave was feigning, and pretending to be suffering and injured when he was not. The judge certifies that the slave was punished in the *manner and by the means*

charged in the indictment. The indictment contains fifteen counts, and sets forth a case of the most cruel and excessive whipping and torture.*

*　　*　　*　　*　　*　　*　　*

It is believed that the records of criminal jurisprudence do not contain a case of more atrocious and wicked cruelty than was presented upon the trial of Souther; and yet it has been gravely and earnestly contended here by his counsel that his offence amounts to manslaughter only.

It has been contended by the counsel of the prisoner that a man cannot be indicted and prosecuted for the cruel and excessive whipping of his own slave. That it is lawful for the master to chastise his slave, and that if death ensues from such chastisement, unless it was intended to produce death, it is like the case of homicide which is committed by a man in the performance of a lawful act, which is manslaughter only. It has been decided by this court in Turner's case, 5 Rand, that the owner of a slave, for the malicious, cruel and excessive beating of his own slave, cannot be indicted; yet it by no means follows, when such malicious, cruel and excessive beating results in death, though not intended and premeditated, that the beating is to be regarded as lawful for the purpose of reducing the crime to manslaughter, when the whipping is inflicted for the sole purpose of chastisement. *It is the policy of the law, in respect to the relation of master and slave, and for the sake of securing proper subordination and obedience on the part of the slave, to protect the master from prosecution in all such cases, even if the whipping and punishment be malicious, cruel and excessive.* But in so inflicting punishment for the sake of punishment, the owner of the slave acts at his peril; and if death ensues in consequence of such punishment, the relation of master and slave affords no ground of excuse or palliation. The principles of the common law, in relation to homicide, apply to his case without qualification or exception; and according to those principles, the act of the prisoner, in the case under consideration, amounted to murder. *　*　* The crime of the prisoner is not manslaughter, but murder in the first degree.

On the case now presented there are some remarks to be made.

This scene of torture, it seems, occupied about twelve hours. It occurred in the State of Virginia, in the County of Hanover. Two white men were witnesses to nearly the whole proceeding, and, so far as we can see, made no effort to arouse the neighborhood, and bring in help to stop the outrage. What sort of an education, what habits of thought, does this presuppose in these men?

The case was brought to trial. It re-

* The following is Judge Field's statement of the punishment:

The negro was tied to a tree and whipped with switches. When Souther became fatigued with the labor of whipping, he called upon a negro man of his, and made him cob Sam with a shingle. He also made a negro woman of his help to cob him. And, after cobbing and whipping, he applied fire to the body of the slave. *　*　*　* He then caused him to be washed down with hot water, in which pods of red pepper had been steeped. The negro was also tied to a log and to the bed-post with ropes, which choked him, and he was kicked and stamped by Souther. This sort of punishment was continued and repeated until the negro died under its infliction.

quires no ordinary nerve to read over the counts of this indictment. Nobody, one would suppose, could willingly read them twice. One would think that it would have laid a cold hand of horror on every heart; — that the community would have risen, by an universal sentiment, to shake out the man, as Paul shook the viper from his hand. It seems, however, that they were quite self-possessed; that lawyers calmly sat, and examined, and cross-examined, on particulars known before only in the records of the Inquisition; that it was "ably and earnestly argued" by educated, intelligent, American men, that this catalogue of horrors did not amount to a murder! and, in the cool language of legal precision, that "the offence, IF ANY, amounted to manslaughter;" and that an American jury found that the offence was murder *in the second degree.* Any one who reads the indictment will certainly think that, if this be murder in the *second degree,* in Virginia, one might earnestly pray to be murdered in the first degree, to begin with. Had Souther walked up to the man, and shot him through the head with a pistol, before white witnesses, *that* would have been murder in the *first* degree. As he preferred to spend *twelve hours* in killing him by torture, under the name of "*chastisement,*" that, says the verdict, is murder in the second degree; "*because,*" says the bill of exceptions, with admirable coolness, "*it did not appear that it was the design of the prisoner to kill the slave,* UNLESS SUCH DESIGN BE PROPERLY INFERABLE FROM THE MANNER, MEANS AND DURATION, OF THE PUNISHMENT.

The bill evidently seems to have a leaning to the idea that twelve hours spent in beating, stamping, scalding, burning and mutilating a human being, might possibly be considered as presumption of something beyond the limits of lawful chastisement. So startling an opinion, however, is expressed cautiously, and with a becoming diffidence, and is balanced by the very striking fact, which is also quoted in this remarkable paper, that the prisoner frequently declared, while the slave was undergoing the punishment, that he believed the slave was feigning and pretending to be suffering, when he was not. This view appears to have struck the court as eminently probable, — as going a long way to prove the propriety of Souther's intentions, making it at least extremely probable that only *correction* was intended.

It seems, also, that Souther, so far from

being crushed by the united opinion of the community, found those to back him who considered five years in the penitentiary an unjust severity for his crime, and hence the bill of exceptions from which we have quoted, and the appeal to the Superior Court; and hence the form in which the case stands in law-books, "*Souther v. the Commonwealth.*" Souther evidently considers himself an ill-used man, and it is in this character that he appears before the Superior Court.

As yet there has been no particular overflow of humanity in the treatment of the case. The manner in which it has been discussed so far reminds one of nothing so much as of some discussions which the reader may have seen quoted from the records of the Inquisition, with regard to the propriety of roasting the feet of children who have not arrived at the age of thirteen years, with a view to eliciting evidence.

Let us now come to the decision of the Superior Court, which the editor of the *Courier & Enquirer* thinks so particularly enlightened and humane. Judge Field thinks that the case is a very atrocious one, and in this respect he seems to differ materially from judge, jury and lawyers, of the court below. Furthermore, he doubts whether the annals of jurisprudence furnish a case of equal atrocity, wherein certainly he appears to be not far wrong; and he also states unequivocally the principle that killing a slave by torture under the name of correction is murder in the first degree; and here too, certainly, everybody will think that he is also right; the only wonder being that any man could ever have been called to express such an opinion, judicially. But he states, quite as unequivocally as Judge Ruffin, that awful principle of slavelaws, that the law cannot interfere with the master for any amount of torture inflicted on his slave which does not result in death. The decision, if it establishes anything, establishes this principle quite as strongly as it does the other. Let us hear the words of the decision :

It has been decided by this court, in Turner's case, that *the owner of a slave, for the malicious, cruel and excessive beating of his own slave, cannot be indicted.*   * * * * * *It is the policy of the law, in respect to the relation of master and slave, and for the sake of securing proper subordination and obedience on the part of the slave, to protect the master from prosecution in all such cases, even if the whipping and punishment be malicious, cruel and excessive.*

What follows as a corollary from this remarkable declaration is this, — that if the victim of this twelve hours' torture had only possessed a little stronger constitution, and had not actually died under it, there is no law in Virginia by which Souther could even have been indicted for misdemeanor.

If this is not filling out the measure of the language of St. Clare, that "he who goes the furthest and does the worst only uses within limits the power which the law gives him," how could this language be verified? Which is "*the worst*," death outright, or torture indefinitely prolonged? This decision, in so many words, gives every master the power of indefinite torture, and takes from him only the power of terminating the agony by merciful death. And this is the judicial decision which the *Courier & Enquirer* cites as a perfectly convincing specimen of legal humanity. It must be hoped that the editor never read the decision, else he never would have cited it. Of all who knock at the charnel-house of legal precedents, with the hope of disinterring any evidence of humanity in the slave system, it may be said, in the awful words of the Hebrew poet :

"He knoweth not that the dead are there,
And that her guests are in the depths of hell."

The upshot of this case was, that Souther, instead of getting off from his five years' imprisonment, got simply a judicial *opinion* from the Superior Court that he ought to be hung ; but he could not be tried over again, and, as we may infer from all the facts in the case that he was a man of tolerably resolute nerves and not very exquisite sensibility, it is not likely that the *opinion* gave him any very serious uneasiness. He has probably made up his mind to get over his five years with what grace he may. When he comes out, there is no law in Virginia to prevent his buying as many more negroes as he chooses, and going over the same scene with any one of them at a future time, if only he profit by the information which has been so explicitly conveyed to him in this decision, that he must take care and stop his tortures short of the point of death,—a matter about which, as the history of the Inquisition shows, men, by careful practice, can be able to judge with considerable precision. Probably, also, the next time, he will not be so foolish as to send out and request the attendance of two white witnesses, even though they may be so complacently interested in the proceedings as to spend the whole day in witnessing them without effort at prevention.

Slavery, as defined in American law, is no more capable of being regulated in its administration by principles of humanity, than the torture system of the Inquisition. Every act of humanity of every individual owner is an illogical result from the legal definition ; and the reason why the slave-code of America is more atrocious than any ever before exhibited under the sun, is that the Anglo-Saxon race are a more coldly and strictly logical race, and have an unflinching courage to meet the consequences of every premise which they lay down, and to work out an accursed principle, with mathematical accuracy, to its most accursed results. The decisions in American law-books show nothing so much as this severe, unflinching accuracy of logic. It is often and evidently, not because judges are inhuman or partial, but because they are logical and truthful, that they announce from the bench, in the calmest manner, decisions which one would think might make the earth shudder, and the sun turn pale.

The French and the Spanish nations are, by constitution, more impulsive, passionate and poetic, than logical ; hence it will be found that while there may be more instances of individual barbarity, as might be expected among impulsive and passionate people, there is in their slave-code more exhibition of humanity. The code of the State of Louisiana contains more really humane provisions, were there any means of enforcing them, than that of any other state in the Union.

It is believed that there is no code of laws in the world which contains such a perfect cabinet crystallization of every tear and every drop of blood which can be wrung from humanity, so accurately, elegantly and scientifically arranged, as the slave-code of America. It is a case of elegant surgical instruments for the work of dissecting the living human heart ; — every instrument wrought with exactest temper and polish, and adapted with exquisite care, and labelled with the name of the nerve or artery or muscle which it is designed to sever. The instruments of the anatomist are instruments of earthly steel and wood, designed to operate at most on perishable and corruptible matter ; but these are instruments of keener temper, and more ethereal workmanship, designed in the most precise and scientific manner to DESTROY THE IMMORTAL SOUL, and carefully and gradually to reduce man from the high position of a free agent, a social, religious, accountable being, down to the condition of the brute, or of inanimate matter.

CHAPTER IV.

PROTECTIVE STATUTES.

Apprentices protected. — Outlawry. — Melodrama of Prue in the Swamp. — Harry the Carpenter, a Romance of Real Life.

BUT the question now occurs, Are there not protective statutes, the avowed object of which is the protection of the life and limb of the slave? We answer, there are; and these protective statutes are some of the most remarkable pieces of legislation extant. That they were dictated by a spirit of humanity, charity, which hopeth *all* things, would lead us to hope; but no newspaper stories of bloody murders and shocking outrages convey to the mind so dreadful a picture of the numbness of public sentiment caused by slavery as these so-called protective statutes. The author copies the following from the statutes of North Carolina. Section 3d of the act passed in 1798 runs thus :

Whereas by another Act of the Assembly, passed in 1774, the killing of a slave, however wanton, cruel and deliberate, is only punishable in the first instance by imprisonment and paying the value thereof to the owner, which *distinction of criminality between the murder of a white person and one who is equally a human creature, but merely of a different complexion, is* DISGRACEFUL TO HUMANITY, AND DEGRADING IN THE HIGHEST DEGREE TO THE LAWS AND PRINCIPLES OF A FREE, CHRISTIAN AND ENLIGHTENED COUNTRY, Be it enacted, &c., That if any person shall hereafter be guilty of wilfully and maliciously killing a slave, such offender shall, upon the first conviction thereof, be adjudged guilty of murder, and shall suffer the same punishment as if he had killed a free man : *Provided always, this act shall not extend to the person killing a slave* OUTLAWED BY VIRTUE OF ANY ACT OF ASSEMBLY OF THIS STATE, *or to any slave in the act of resistance to his lawful owner or master, or to any slave dying under moderate correction.*"

A law with a like proviso, except the outlawry clause, exists in Tennessee. *See Caruthers and Nicholson's Compilation,* 1836. p. 676.

The language of the constitution of Georgia, art. iv., sec. 12, is as follows :

Any person who shall maliciously dismember or deprive a slave of life shall suffer such punishment as would be inflicted in case the like offence had been committed on a free white person, and on the like proof, except in case of insurrection by such slave, and *unless such death should happen by accident in giving such slave moderate correction.* —*Cobb's Dig.* 1851, p. 1125.

Let now any Englishman or New Englander imagine that such laws with regard to apprentices had ever been proposed in Parliament or State Legislature under the head of *protective acts;* — laws which in so many words permit the killing of the subject in three cases, and those comprising all the acts which would generally occur under the law ; namely, if the slave resist; if he be outlawed, or if he die under *moderate* correction.

What rule in the world will ever prove correction immoderate, if the fact that the subject *dies* under it is not held as proof ? How many such "accidents" would have to happen in Old England or New England, before Parliament or Legislature would hear from such a protective law.

"But," some one may ask, "what is the *outlawry* spoken of in this act?" The question is pertinent, and must be answered. The author has copied the following from the Revised Statutes of North Carolina, chap. cxi, sec. 22. It may be remarked in passing that the preamble to this law presents rather a new view of slavery to those who have formed their ideas from certain pictures of blissful contentment and Arcadian repose, which have been much in vogue of late.

Whereas, MANY TIMES *slaves run away and lie out, hid and lurking in swamps, woods, and other obscure places,* killing cattle and hogs, and committing other injuries to the inhabitants of this state ; in all such cases, upon intelligence of any slave or slaves lying out as aforesaid, any two justices of the peace for the county wherein such slave or slaves is or are supposed to lurk or do mischief, shall, and they are hereby empowered and required to issue proclamation against such slave or slaves (reciting his or their names, and the name or names of the owner or owners, if known), thereby requiring him or them, and every of them, forthwith to surrender him or themselves; and also to empower and require the sheriff of the said county to take such power with him as he shall think fit and necessary for going in search and pursuit of, and effectually apprehending, such outlying slave or slaves ; which proclamation shall be published at the door of the court-house, and at such other places as said justices shall direct. And if any slave or slaves against whom proclamation hath been thus issued stay out, and do not immediately return home, it shall be lawful for any person or persons whatsoever to kill and destroy such slave or slaves by *such ways and means as he shall think fit,* without accusation or impeachment of any crime for the same.

What ways and means *have been* thought fit, in actual experience, for the destruction of the slave ? What was done with the negro McIntosh, in the streets of St. Louis. in open daylight, and endorsed at the next sitting of the Supreme Court of the state, as transcending the sphere of law, because it was "an act of the majority of her most respectable citizens"? ** If these things are done in the green tree, what will be done in the dry? If these things have once been

---

* This man was burned alive.

done in the open streets of St. Louis, by "a majority of her most respectable citizens," what will be done in the lonely swamps of North Carolina, by men of the stamp of Souther and Legree?

This passage of the Revised Statutes of North Carolina is more terribly suggestive to the imagination than any particulars into which the author of Uncle Tom's Cabin has thought fit to enter. Let us suppose a little melodrama quite possible to have occurred under this act of the legislature. Suppose some luckless Prue or Peg, as in the case we have just quoted, in State *v.* Mann, getting tired of the discipline of whipping, breaks from the overseer, clears the dogs, and gets into the swamp, and there "lies out," as the act above graphically says. The act which we are considering says that *many* slaves do this, and doubtless they have their own best reasons for it. We all know what fascinating places to "lie out" in these Southern swamps are. What with alligators and moccasin snakes, mud and water, and poisonous vines, one would be apt to think the situation not particularly eligible; but still, Prue "lies out" there. Perhaps in the night some husband or brother goes to see her, taking a hog, or some animal of the plantation stock, which he has ventured his life in killing, that she may not perish with hunger. Master overseer walks up to master proprietor, and reports the accident; master proprietor mounts his horse, and assembles to his aid two justices of the peace.

In the intervals between drinking brandy and smoking cigars a proclamation is duly drawn up, summoning the contumacious Prue to surrender, and requiring sheriff of said county to take such power as he shall think fit to go in search and pursuit of said slave; which proclamation, for Prue's further enlightenment, is solemnly published at the door of the court-house, and "at such other places as said justices shall direct." * Let us suppose, now, that Prue, given over to hardness of heart and blindness of mind, pays no attention to all these means of grace, put forth to draw her to the protective shadow of the patriarchal roof. Suppose, further, as a final effort of long-suffering, and to leave her utterly without excuse, the

worthy magistrate rides forth in full force,— man, horse, dog and gun,— to the very verge of the swamp, and there proclaims aloud the merciful mandate. Suppose that, hearing the yelping of the dogs and the proclamation of the sheriff mingled together, and the shouts of Loker, Marks, Sambo and Quimbo, and other such posse, black and white, as a sheriff can generally summon on such a hunt, this very ignorant and contumacious Prue only runs deeper into the swamp, and continues obstinately "lying out," as aforesaid;— now she is by act of the assembly *outlawed*, and, in the astounding words of the act, "it shall be lawful for any person or persons whatsoever to kill and destroy her, by such ways and means as he shall think fit, without accusation or impeachment of any crime for the same." What awful possibilities rise to the imagination under the fearfully suggestive clause "*by such ways and means as he shall think fit!*" Such ways and means as ANY man shall think fit, of *any* character, of *any* degree of fiendish barbarity!! Such a permission to kill even a dog, by "any ways and means which,anybody should think fit," never ought to stand on the law-books of a Christian nation; and yet this stands against one bearing that same humanity which Jesus Christ bore,— against one, perhaps, who, though blinded, darkened and ignorant, he will not be ashamed to own, when he shall come in the glory of his Father, and all his holy angels with him!

That this law has not been a dead letter there is sufficient proof. In 1836 the following proclamation and advertisement appeared in the "Newbern (N. C.) Spectator:"

STATE OF NORTH CAROLINA, LENOIR COUNTY. — Whereas complaint hath been this day made to us, two of the justices of the peace for the said county, by William D. Cobb, of Jones County, that two negro-slaves belonging to him, named Ben (commonly known by the name of Ben Fox) and Rigdon, have absented themselves from their said master's service, and are lurking about in the Counties of Lenoir and Jones, committing acts of felony; these are, in the name of the state, to command the said slaves forthwith to surrender themselves, and turn home to their said master. And we do hereby also require the sheriff of said County of Lenoir to make diligent search and pursuit after the above-mentioned slaves. . . And we do hereby, by virtue of an act of assembly of this state concerning servants and slaves, intimate and declare, if the said slaves do not surrender themselves and return home to their master immediately after the publication of these presents, that any person may kill or destroy said slaves by such means as he or they think fit, without accusation or impeachment of any crime or offence

---

* The old statute of 1741 had some features still more edifying. That provides that said "proclamation shall be published on a Sabbath day, at the door of every church or chapel, or, for want of such, at the place where divine service shall be performed in the said county, by the parish clerk or reader, *immediately* after divine service." *Potter's Revisal,* i. 166. What a peculiar appropriateness there must have been in this proclamation, particularly after a sermon on the love of Christ, or an exposition of the text "thou shalt love thy neighbor as thyself!"

for so doing, or without incurring any penalty or forfeiture thereby.

Given under our hands and seals, this 12th of November, 1836. B. COLEMAN, J. P. [Seal.]
JAS. JONES, J. P. [Seal.]

$200 REWARD. — Ran away from the subscriber, about three years ago, a certain negro-man, named Ben, commonly known by the name of Ben Fox; also one other negro, by the name of Rigdon, who ran away on the 8th of this month.

I will give the reward of $100 for each of the above negroes, to be delivered to me, or confined in the jail of Lenoir or Jones County, *or for the killing of them, so that I can see them.*

Nov. 12, 1836 W. D. COBB.

That this act was *not* a dead letter, also, was plainly implied in the protective act first quoted. If slaves were not, as a matter of fact, ever outlawed, why does the act formally recognize such a class? — "provided that this act shall not extend to the killing of any slave *outlawed* by any act of the assembly." This language sufficiently indicates the existence of the custom.

Further than this, the statute-book of 1821 contained two acts: the first of which provides that all masters in certain counties, who have had slaves killed in consequence of outlawry, shall have a claim on the treasury of the state for their value, unless cruel treatment of the slave be proved on the part of the master: the second act extends the benefits of the latter provision to all the counties in the state.*

Finally, there is evidence that this act of outlawry was executed so recently as the year 1850, — the year in which "Uncle Tom's Cabin" was written. See the following from the Wilmington Journal of December 13, 1850:

STATE OF NORTH CAROLINA, NEW HANOVER COUNTY.—Whereas complaint upon oath hath this day been made to us, two of the justices of the peace for the said state and county aforesaid, by Guilford Horn, of Edgecombe County, that a certain male slave belonging to him, named Harry, a carpenter by trade, about forty years old, five feet four inches high, or thereabouts; yellow complexion; stout built; with a scar on his left leg (from the cut of an axe); has very thick lips; eyes deep sunk in his head; forehead very square; tolerably

* Be it further enacted, That when any slave shall be legally outlawed in any of the counties within mentioned, Potter's Revisal, ch. 467, § 2. the owner of which shall reside in one of the said counties, and the said slave shall be killed in consequence of such outlawry, the value of such slave shall be ascertained by a jury which shall be empanelled at the succeeding court of the county where the said slave was killed, and a certificate of such valuation shall be given by the clerk of the court to the owner of said slave, who shall be entitled to receive two-thirds of such valuation from the sheriff of the county wherein the slave was killed. [Extended to other counties in 1797. — Potter, ch. 480, § 1.] now obsolete.

loud voice; has lost one or two of his upper teeth; and has a very dark spot on his jaw, supposed to be a mark, — hath absented himself from his master's service, and is supposed to be lurking about in this county, committing acts of felony or other misdeeds; these are, therefore, in the name of the state aforesaid, to command the said slave forthwith to surrender himself and return home to his said master; and we do hereby, by virtue of the act of assembly in such cases made and provided, intimate and declare that if the said slave Harry doth not surrender himself and return home immediately after the publication of these presents, that any person or persons may KILL and DESTROY the said slave by such means as he or they may think fit, without accusation or impeachment of any crime or offence for so doing, and without incurring any penalty or forfeiture thereby.

Given under our hands and seals, this 29th day of June, 1850.

JAMES T. MILLER, J. P. [Seal.]
W. C. BETTENCOURT, J. P. [Seal.]

ONE HUNDRED AND TWENTY-FIVE DOLLARS REWARD will be paid for the delivery of the said Harry to me at Tosnott Depot, Edgecombe County, or for his confinement in any jail in the state, so that I can get him; or *One Hundred and Fifty Dollars will be given for his head.*

He was lately heard from in Newbern, where he called himself Henry Barnes (or Burns), and will be likely to continue the same name, or assume that of Copage or Farmer. He has a free mulatto woman for a wife, by the name of Sally Bozeman, who has lately removed to Wilmington, and lives in that part of the town called Texas, where he will likely be lurking.

Masters of vessels are particularly cautioned against harboring or concealing the said negro on board their vessels, as the full penalty of the law will be rigorously enforced.

June 29th, 1850. GUILFORD HORN.

There is an inkling of history and romance about the description of this same Harry, who is thus publicly set up to be killed in any way that any of the negro-hunters of the swamps may think the most piquant and enlivening. It seems he is a carpenter, — a powerfully made man, whose thews and sinews might be a profitable acquisition to himself. It appears also that he has a wife, and the advertiser intimates that possibly he may be caught prowling about somewhere in her vicinity. This indicates sagacity in the writer, certainly. Married men generally have a way of liking the society of their wives; and it strikes us, from what we know of the nature of carpenters here in New England, that Harry was not peculiar in this respect. Let us further notice the portrait of Harry: "*Eyes deep sunk in his head; — forehead very square.*" This picture reminds us of what a persecuting old ecclesiastic once said in the days of the Port-Royalists, of a certain truculent abbess, who stood obstinately to a certain course, in the face of the whole power, temporal and spiritual, of the Romish church, in spite of fining, imprisoning, starving, whipping, beating, and other enlightening argumentative processes, not wholly peculiar, it seems, to that age. "You will never subdue that woman," said the ecclesiastic, who was a phrenologist before his age; "she's got a *square head*, and I have always noticed that people with *square heads* never can be turned out of their course." We think it very probable that Harry, with his "square head," is just one of this sort. He is probably one of those articles which would be extremely valuable, if the owner could only get the use of him. His head is well enough, but he will use it for himself. It is of no use to any one but the wearer; and the master seems to symbolize this state of things, by offering twenty-five dollars more for the head without the body, than he is willing to give for head, man and all. Poor Harry! We wonder whether they have caught him yet; or whether the impenetrable thickets, the poisonous miasma, the deadly snakes, and the unwieldy alligators of the swamps, more humane than the slave-hunter, have interposed their uncouth and loathsome forms to guard the only fastness in Carolina where a slave can live in freedom.

It is not, then, in mere poetic fiction that the humane and graceful pen of Longfellow has drawn the following picture:

"In the dark fens of the Dismal Swamp
  The hunted negro lay;
He saw the fire of the midnight camp,
And heard at times the horse's tramp,
  And a bloodhound's distant bay.

"Where will-o'-the-wisps and glow-worms shine,
  In bulrush and in brake;
Where waving mosses shroud the pine,
And the cedar grows, and the poisonous vine
  Is spotted like the snake;

"Where hardly a human foot could pass,
  Or a human heart would dare, —
On the quaking turf of the green morass
He crouched in the rank and tangled grass,
  Like a wild beast in his lair.

"A poor old slave! infirm and lame,
  Great scars deformed his face;
On his forehead he bore the brand of shame,
And the rags that hid his mangled frame
  Were the livery of disgrace.

"All things above were bright and fair,
  All things were glad and free;
Lithe squirrels darted here and there,
And wild birds filled the echoing air
  With songs of liberty!

"On him alone was the doom of pain,
  From the morning of his birth;
On him alone the curse of Cain *
Fell like the flail on the garnered grain,
  And struck him to the earth."

* Gen. 4 : 14. — "And it shall come to pass that every one that findeth me shall slay me."

The civilized world may and will ask, in what state this law has been drawn, and passed, and revised, and allowed to appear at the present day on the revised statute-book, and to be executed in the year of our Lord 1850, as the above-cited extracts from its most respectable journals show. Is it some heathen, Kurdish tribe, some nest of pirates, some horde of barbarians, where destructive gods are worshipped, and libations to their honor poured from human skulls? The civilized world will not believe it, — but it is actually a fact, that this law has been made, and is still kept in force, by men in every other respect than what relates to their slave-code as high-minded, as enlightened, as humane, as any men in Christendom; — by citizens of a state which glories in the blood and hereditary Christian institutions of Scotland. Curiosity to know what sort of men the legislators of North Carolina might be, led the writer to examine with some attention the proceedings and debates of the convention of that state, called to amend its constitution, which assembled at Raleigh, June 4th, 1835. It is but justice to say that in these proceedings, in which all the different and perhaps conflicting interests of the various parts of the state were discussed, there was an exhibition of candor, fairness and moderation, of gentlemanly honor and courtesy in the treatment of opposing claims, and of an over-ruling sense of the obligations of law and religion, which certainly have not always been equally conspicuous in the proceedings of deliberative bodies in such cases. It simply goes to show that one can judge nothing of the religion or of the humanity of individuals from what seems to us objectionable práctice, where they have been educated under a system entirely incompatible with both. Such is the very equivocal character of what we call virtue.

It could not be for a moment supposed that such men as Judge Ruffin, or many of the gentlemen who figure in the debates alluded to, would ever think of availing themselves of the savage permissions of such a law. But what then? It follows that the law is a direct permission, letting loose upon the defenceless slave that class of men who exist in every community, who have no conscience, no honor, no shame, — who are too far below public opinion to be restrained by that, and from whom accordingly this provision of the law takes away the only available restraint of their fiendish natures. Such men are not peculiar to the

South. It is unhappily too notorious that they exist everywhere,—in England, in New England, and the world over; but they can only arrive at full maturity in wickedness under a system where the law clothes them with absolute and irresponsible power.

CHAPTER V.

PROTECTIVE ACTS OF SOUTH CAROLINA AND LOUISIANA.—THE IRON COLLAR OF LOUISIANA AND NORTH CAROLINA.

THUS far by way of considering the protective acts of North Carolina, Georgia and Tennessee.

Certain miscellaneous protective acts of various other states will now be cited, merely as specimens of the spirit of legislation.

In South Carolina, the act of 1740 punished the wilful, deliberate murder of a slave by disfranchisement, and by a fine of seven hundred pounds current money, or, in default of payment, imprisonment for seven years. But the wilful murder of a slave, in the sense contemplated in this law, is a crime which would not often occur. The kind of murder which was most frequent among masters or overseers was guarded against by another section of the same act, — *how· adequately* the reader will judge for himself, from the following quotation :

<small>Stroud's Sketch, p. 40. 2 Brevard's Digest, 241. James' Digest, 392.</small> If any person shall, on a sudden heat or passion, or by *undue correction,* kill his own slave, or the slave of any other person, he shall forfeit the sum of *three hundred and fifty pounds* current money.

In 1821 the act punishing the wilful murder of the slave only with fine or imprisonment was mainly repealed, and it was enacted that such crime should be punished by death; but the latter section, which relates to killing the slave in sudden heat or passion, or by undue correction, has been altered only by *diminishing* the pecuniary penalty to a fine of five hundred dollars, authorizing also imprisonment for six months.

The next protective statute to be noticed is the following from the act of 1740, South Carolina.

<small>Stroud, p. 40. 2 Brevard's Digest, 241.</small> In case any person shall wilfully cut out the tongue, put out the eye, * * * or cruelly scald, burn, or deprive any slave of any limb, or member, or shall inflict any other cruel punishment, oth.r *than* by whipping or beating with a horse-whip, cowskin, switch

or small stick, or by putting irons on, or confining or imprisoning such slave, every such person shall, for every such offence, forfeit the sum of one hundred pounds, current money.

The language of this law, like many other of these protective enactments, is exceedingly suggestive ; the first suggestion that occurs is, What sort of an institution, and what sort of a state of society is it, that called out a law worded like this ? Laws are generally not made against practices that do not exist, and exist with some degree of frequency.

The advocates of slavery are very fond of comparing it to the apprentice system of England and America. Let us suppose that in the British Parliament, or in a New England Legislature, the following law is proposed, under the title of An Act for the Protection of Apprentices, &c. &c.

In case any person shall wilfully cut out the tongue, put out the eye, or cruelly scald, burn, or deprive any apprentice of any limb or member, or shall inflict any other cruel punishment, other than by whipping or beating with a horse-whip, cowskin, switch or small stick, or by putting irons on or confining or imprisoning such apprentice, every such person shall, for every such offence, forfeit the sum of one hundred pounds, current money.

What a sensation such a proposed law would make in England may be best left for Englishmen to say ; but in New England it would simply constitute the proposer a candidate for Bedlam. Yet that such a statute is necessary in South Carolina is evident enough, if we reflect that, because there is no such statute in Virginia, it has been decided that a wretch who perpetrates all these enormities on a slave cannot even be indicted for it, unless the slave dies.

But let us look further : —What is to be the penalty when any of these fiendish things are done ?

Why, the man forfeits a hundred pounds, current money. Surely he ought to pay as much as that for doing so very unnecessary an act, when the Legislature bountifully allows him to inflict any torture which revengeful ingenuity could devise, by means of horse-whip, cowskin, switch or small stick, or putting irons on, or confining and imprisoning. One would surely think that here was sufficient scope and variety of legalized means of torture to satisfy any ordinary appetite for vengeance. It would appear decidedly that any more piquant varieties of agony ought to be an extra charge. The advocates of slavery are fond of comparing the situation of the slave with that of the English laborer. We are not aware that the English laborer has been so unfortunate as to be protected by any enactment like this, since the days of villeinage.

Judge Stroud says, that the same law, substantially, has been adopted in Louisiana. It is true that the civil code of Louisiana thus expresses its humane intentions.

<small>Stroud's Sketch, p. 41. 1 Mar. Digest, 654.</small>

The slave is entirely subject to the will of his master, who may correct and chastise him, though not with unusual rigor, nor so as to maim or mutilate him, or to expose him to the danger of loss of life, or to cause his death. — *Civil Code of Louisiana, Article 173.*

The expression "unusual rigor" is suggestive, again. It will afford large latitude for a jury, in states where slaves are in the habit of *dying* under *moderate* correction ; where outlawed slaves may be killed by any means which any person thinks fit; and where laws have to be specifically made against scalding, burning, cutting out the tongue, putting out the eye, &c. What will be thought unusual rigor? This is a question, certainly, upon which persons in states not so constituted can have no means of forming an opinion.

In one of the newspaper extracts with which we prefaced our account, the following protective act of Louisiana is alluded to, as being particularly satisfactory and efficient. We give it, as quoted by Judge Stroud in his Sketch, page 58, giving his reference.

No master shall be compelled to sell his slave, but in one of two cases, to wit: the first, when, being only co-proprietor of the slave, his co-proprietor demands the sale, in order to make partition of the property ; *second,* when the master shall be CONVICTED of cruel treatment of his slave, AND THE JUDGE SHALL DEEM IT PROPER TO PRONOUNCE, besides the penalty established for such cases, that the slave shall be sold at public auction, in order to place him out of the reach of the power which his master has abused.—*Civil Code, Art.* 192.

The question for a jury to determine in this case is, What is cruel treatment of a slave ? Now, if all these barbarities which have been sanctioned by the legislative acts which we have quoted are not held to be cruel treatment, the question is, What *is* cruel treatment of a slave ?

Everything that fiendish barbarity could desire can be effected under the protection of the law of South Carolina, which, as we have just shown, exists also in Louisiana. It is true the law restrains from some particular forms of cruelty. If any person has a mind to scald or burn his slave,—- and it seems, by the statute, that there have been such people,— these statutes merely pro-

vide that he shall do it in decent privacy; for, as the very keystone of Southern jurisprudence is the rejection of colored testimony, such an outrage, if perpetrated most deliberately in the presence of hundreds of slaves, could not be proved upon the master.

It is to be supposed that the fiendish people whom such statutes have in view will generally have enough of common sense not to perform it in the presence of white witnesses, since this simple act of prudence will render them entirely safe in doing whatever they have a mind to. We are told, it is true, as we have been reminded by our friend in the newspaper before quoted, that in Louisiana the deficiency caused by the rejection of negro testimony is supplied by the following most remarkable provision of the Code Noir :

If any slave be mutilated, beaten, or ill treated, contrary to the true intent and meaning of this section, when no one shall be present. in such case the owner, or other person having the charge or management of said slave thus mutilated, shall be deemed responsible and guilty of the said offence, and shall be prosecuted without further evidence, unless the said owner, or other person so as aforesaid, can prove the contrary by means of good and sufficient evidence, or can clear himself by his own oath, which said oath every court under the cognizance of which such offence shall have been examined and tried is by this act authorized to administer. — *Code Noir. Crimes and Offences*, 56. xvii. *Rev. Stat.* 1852, p. 550, § 141.

Would one have supposed that sensible people could ever publish as a law such a specimen of utter legislative nonsense — so ridiculous on the very face of it !

The object is to bring to justice those fiendish people who burn, scald, mutilate, &c. How is this done ? Why, it is enacted that the fact of finding the slave in this condition shall be held presumption against the owner or overseer, unless — unless what ? Why, unless he will prove to the contrary, — or swear to the contrary, it is no matter which — either will answer the purpose. The question is, If a man is bad enough to do these things, will he not be bad enough to swear falsely? As if men who are the incarnation of cruelty, as supposed by the deeds in question, would not have sufficient intrepidity of conscience to compass a false oath !

What was this law ever made for ? Can any one imagine ?

Upon this whole subject, we may quote the language of Judge Stroud, who thus sums up the whole amount of the protective laws for the slave, in the United States of America :

Upon a fair review of what has been written on the subject of this proposition, the result is found to be — that the master's power to inflict corporal punishment to any extent, short of life and limb, is fully sanctioned by law, in *all* the slave-holding states; that the master, in at least two states, is *expressly* protected in using the horse-whip and cowskin as instruments for *beating* his slave; that he may with entire impunity, in the same states, load his slave with irons, or subject him to perpetual imprisonment, whenever he may so choose; that, for cruelly scalding, wilfully cutting out the tongue, putting out an eye, and for any other dismemberment, if proved, a fine of one hundred pounds currency only is incurred in South Carolina; that, though in all the states the wilful, deliberate and malicious murder of the slave is now *directed* to be punished with death, yet, as in the case of a *white* offender none except whites can give evidence, a conviction can seldom, if ever, take place. — *Stroud's Sketch*, p. 43.

One very singular antithesis of two laws of Louisiana will still further show that deadness of public sentiment on cruelty to the slave which is an inseparable attendant on the system. It will be recollected that the remarkable *protective* law of South Carolina, with respect to scalding, burning, cutting out the tongue, and putting out the eye of the slave, has been substantially enacted in Louisiana; and that the penalty for a man's doing these things there, if he has not sense enough to do it privately, is not more than five hundred dollars.

Now, compare this other statute of Louisiana, (Rev. Stat., 1852, p. 552, § 151):

If any person or persons, &c., shall cut or break any iron chain or collar, which any master of
Stroud, p. 41. slaves should have used, in order to prevent the running away or escape of any such slave or slaves, such person or persons so offending shall, on conviction, &c., be fined not less than two hundred dollars, nor exceeding one thousand dollars; and suffer imprisonment for a term not exceeding two years, nor less than six months. — *Act of Assembly of March* 6, 1819. *Pamphlet, page* 64.

Some Englishmen may naturally ask, "What is this iron collar which the Legislature have thought worthy of being protected by a special act?" On this subject will be presented the testimony of an unimpeachable witness, Miss Sarah M. Grimké, a personal friend of the author. "Miss Grimké is a daughter of the late Judge Grimké, of the Supreme Court of South Carolina, and sister of the late Hon. Thomas S. Grimké." She is now a member of the Society of Friends, and resides in Bellville, New Jersey. The statement given is of a kind that its author did not mean to give, nor wish to give, and never would have given, had it not been made necessary to illustrate this passage in the slave-law. The account occurs in a statement which

Miss Grimké furnished to her brother-in-law, Mr. Weld, and has been before the public ever since 1839, in his work entitled *Slavery as It Is*, p. 22.

A handsome mulatto woman, about eighteen or twenty years of age, whose independent spirit could not brook the degradation of slavery, was in the habit of running away: for this offence she had been repeatedly sent by her master and mistress to be whipped by the keeper of the Charleston workhouse. This had been done with such inhuman severity as to lacerate her back in a most shocking manner; a finger could not be laid between the cuts. But the love of liberty was too strong to be annihilated by torture; and, as a last resort, she was whipped at several different times, and kept a close prisoner. A heavy iron collar, with three long prongs projecting from it, was placed round her neck, and a strong and sound front tooth was extracted, to serve as a mark to describe her, in case of escape. Her sufferings at this time were agonizing; she could lie in no position but on her back, which was sore from scourgings, as I can testify from personal inspection; and her only place of rest was the floor, on a blanket. These outrages were committed in a family where the mistress daily read the Scriptures, and assembled her children for family worship. She was accounted, and was really, so far as almsgiving was concerned, a charitable woman, and tender-hearted to the poor; and yet this suffering slave, who was the seamstress of the family, was continually in her presence, sitting in her chamber to sew, or engaged in her other household work, with her lacerated and bleeding back, her mutilated mouth, and heavy iron collar, without, so far as appeared, exciting any feelings of compassion.

This iron collar the author has often heard of from sources equally authentic.[*] That one will meet with it every day in walking the streets, is not probable: but that it must have been used with some great degree of frequency, is evident from the fact of a law being thought necessary to protect it. But look at the penalty of the two *protective* laws! The fiendish cruelties described in the act of South Carolina cost the perpetrator not more than five hundred dollars, if he does them before white people. The act of humanity costs from two hundred to one thousand dollars, and imprisonment from six months to two years, according to discretion of court! What public sentiment was it which made these laws?

<hr/>

[*] The iron collar was also in vogue in North Carolina, as the following extract from the statute-book will show. The wearers of this article of apparel certainly have some reason to complain of the "tyranny of fashion."
"When the keeper of the said public jail shall, by direction of such court as aforesaid, let out any negro or runaway to hire, to any person or persons whomsoever, the said keeper shall, at the time of his delivery, cause an iron collar to be put on the neck of such negro or runaway, with the letters P. G. stamped thereon; and thereafter the said keeper shall not be answerable for any escape of the said negro or runaway."— *Potter's Revisal*, i. 162.

CHAPTER VI.

PROTECTIVE ACTS WITH REGARD TO FOOD
AND RAIMENT, LABOR, ETC.

Illustrative Drama of Tom v. Legree, under the Law of
South Carolina. — Separation of Parent and Child.

HAVING finished the consideration of the
laws which protect the life and limb of the
slave, the reader may feel a curiosity to
know something of the provisions by which
he is protected in regard to food and clothing,
and from the exactions of excessive labor.
It is true, there are multitudes of men in the
Northern States who would say, at once, that
such enactments, on the very face of them,
must be superfluous and absurd. "What!"
they say, "are not the slaves property?
and is it likely that any man will impair
the market value of his own property by not
giving them sufficient food or clothing, or
by overworking them?" This process of
reasoning appears to have been less convincing to the legislators of Southern States
than to gentlemen generally at the North;
since, as Judge Taylor says, "the act of
1786 (Iredell's Revisal, p. 588)
does, in the preamble, recognize
the fact, that *many* persons, by
cruel treatment of their slaves,
cause them to commit crimes for which
they are executed;" and the judge further
explains this language, by saying, "The
cruel treatment here alluded to must consist
in withholding from them the necessaries of
life; and the crimes thus resulting are such
as are necessary to furnish them with food
and raiment."

Wheeler, p.
220. State v.
Sue, Cameron
& Norwood's
C. Rep. 54.

The State of South Carolina, in the act
of 1740 (see Stroud's Sketch, p. 28), had
a section with the following language in its
preamble:

Whereas *many* owners of slaves, and *others* who
have the care, management, and overseeing of
slaves, *do confine them so closely to hard
labor that they have not sufficient time
for natural rest;* —

Stroud, p. 29.

And the law goes on to enact that the
slave shall not work more than fifteen hours
a day in summer, and fourteen in winter.
Judge Stroud makes it appear that in
three of the slave states the time allotted for
work to convicts in prison, whose punishment is to consist in hard labor, cannot exceed *ten* hours, even in the summer months.

This was the protective act of South
Carolina, designed to reform the abusive
practices of masters who confined their
slaves so closely that they had not time for

natural rest! What sort of habits of thought
do these humane provisions show, in the
makers of them? In order to protect the
slave from what they consider undue exac-
tion, they humanely provide that he shall
be obliged to work only four or five hours
longer than the convicts in the prison of the
neighboring state! In the Island of Jamaica,
besides many holidays which were accorded
by law to the slave, ten hours a day was the
extent to which he was compelled by law
ordinarily to work. — See *Stroud*, p. 29.

With regard to protective acts concerning
food and clothing, Judge Stroud gives the
following example from the legislation of
South Carolina. The author gives it as
quoted by Stroud, p. 32.

In case any person, &c., who shall be the
owner, or who shall have the care, government or
charge, of any slave or slaves, shall deny, neglect
or refuse to allow, such slave or slaves, &c.,
sufficient clothing, covering or food, it shall and
may be lawful for any person or persons, on behalf
of such slave or slaves, to make complaint to the
next neighboring justice in the parish where such
slave or slaves live, or are usually employed, * * *
and the said justice shall summons the party
against whom such complaint shall be made, and
shall inquire of, hear and determine, the same;
and, if the said justice shall find the said complaint
to be true, or that such person will not exculpate
or clear himself from the charge, by his or her own
oath, which *such person shall be at liberty to do in
all cases* where positive proof is not given of the
offence, such justice shall and may make such
orders upon the same, for the relief of such slave
or slaves, as he in his discretion shall think fit;
and shall and may set and impose a fine or
penalty on any person who shall offend in the
premises, in any sum not exceeding twenty
pounds current money, for each offence. — 2 Brevard's, Dig. 241. Also Cobb's Dig. 827.

A similar law obtains in Louisiana. —
Rev. Stat. 1852, p. 557, § 166.

Now, would not anybody think, from the
virtuous solemnity and gravity of this act,
that it was intended in some way to amount
to something? Let us give a little sketch,
to show how much it does amount to. Ange-
lina Grimké Weld, sister to Sarah Grimké,
before quoted, gives the following account
of the situation of slaves on plantations : *

And here let me say, that the treatment of
plantation slaves cannot be fully known, except by
the poor sufferers themselves, and their drivers
and overseers. In a multitude of instances, even
the master can know very little of the actual condition of his own field-slaves, and his wife and
daughters far less. A few facts concerning my
own family will show this. Our permanent residence was in Charleston; our country-seat (Bellemont) was two hundred miles distant, in the

* Slavery as It Is ; Testimony of a Thousand Witnesses.
New York, 1839. pp. 52, 53.

north western part of the state, where, for some years, our family spent a few months annually. Our *plantation* was three miles from this family mansion. There all the field-slaves lived and worked. Occasionally, — once a month, perhaps, —some of the family would ride over to the plantation ; but I never visited the *fields where the slaves were at work*, and knew almost nothing of their condition ; but this I do know, that the overseers who had charge of them were generally unprincipled and intemperate men. But I rejoice to know that the general treatment of slaves in that region of country was far milder than on the plantations in the lower country.

Throughout all the eastern and middle portions of the state, the planters very rarely reside permanently on their plantations. They have almost invariably *two* residences, and spend less than half the year on their estates. Even while spending a few months on them, politics, field-sports, races, speculations, journeys, visits, company, literary pursuits, &c., absorb so much of their time, that they must, to a considerable extent, take the condition of their slaves on *trust*, from the reports of their overseers. I make this statement, because these slaveholders (the wealthier class) are, I believe, almost the only ones who visit the North with their families ; and Northern opinions of slavery are based chiefly on their testimony.

With regard to overseers, Miss Grimké's testimony is further borne out by the universal acknowledgment of Southern owners. A description of this class of beings is furnished by Mr. Wirt, in his Life of Patrick Henry, page 34. "Last and lowest," he says, [of different classes in society] "a *feculum* of beings called overseers,— a most abject, degraded, unprincipled race." Now, suppose, while the master is in Charleston, enjoying literary leisure, the slaves on some Bellemont or other plantation, getting tired of being hungry and cold, form themselves into a committee of the whole, to see what is to be done. A broad-shouldered, courageous fellow, whom we will call Tom, declares it is too bad, and he won't stand it any longer ; and, having by some means become acquainted with this benevolent protective act, resolves to make an appeal to the horns of this legislative altar. Tom talks stoutly, having just been bought on to the place, and been used to better quarters elsewhere. The women and children perhaps admire, but the venerable elders of the plantation,— Sambo, Cudge, Pomp and old Aunt Dinah, — tell him he better mind himself, and keep clar o' dat ar. Tom, being young and progressive, does not regard these conservative maxims ; he is determined that, if there is such a thing as justice to be got, he will have it. After considerable research, he finds some white man in the neighborhood verdant enough to enter the complaint for him.

Master Legree finds himself, one sunshiny, pleasant morning, walked off to some Justice Dogberry's, to answer to the charge of not giving his niggers enough to eat and wear. We will call the infatuated white man who has undertaken this fool's errand Master Shallow. Let us imagine a scene : — Legree, standing carelessly with his hands in his pockets, rolling a quid of tobacco in his mouth ; Justice Dogberry, seated in all the majesty of law, reinforced by a decanter of whiskey and some tumblers, intended to assist in illuminating the intellect ·in such obscure cases.

Justice Dogberry. Come, gentlemen, take a little something, to begin with. Mr. Legree, sit down ; sit down, Mr. — a' what 's-your-name ? — Mr. Shallow.

Mr. Legree and Mr. Shallow each sit down, and take their tumbler of whiskey and water. After some little conversation, the justice introduces the business as follows :

"Now, about this nigger business. Gentlemen, you know the act of —— um — um,— where the deuce *is* that act ? [Fumbling an old law-book.] How plagued did you ever hear of that act, Shallow ? I'm sure I'm forgot all about it ; — O ! here 't is. Well, Mr. Shallow, the act says you must make proof, you observe.

Mr. Shallow. [Stuttering and hesitating.] Good land ! why, don't everybody see that them ar niggers are most starved ? Only see how ragged they are !

Justice. I can't say as I've observed it particular. Seem to be very well contented.

Shallow. [Eagerly.] But just ask Pomp, or Sambo, or Dinah, or Tom !

Justice Dogberry. [With dignity.] I'm astonished at you, Mr. Shallow ! You think of producing negro testimony ? I hope I know the law better than that ! We must have direct proof, you know.

Shallow is posed ; Legree significantly takes another tumbler of whiskey and water, and Justice Dogberry gives a long ahe-a-um. After a few moments the justice speaks :

"Well, after all, I suppose, Mr. Legree, you would n't have any objections to swarin' off ; that settles it all, you know."

As swearing is what Mr. Legree is rather more accustomed to do than anything else that could be named, a more appropriate termination of the affair could not be suggested ; and he swears, accordingly, to any extent, and with any fulness and variety of oath that could be desired ; and thus the little affair terminates. But it does not terminate thus for Tom or Sambo, Dinah, or any others who have been alluded to for authority. What will happen to them, when Mr. Legree comes home, had better be left to conjecture.

It is claimed, by the author of certain paragraphs quoted at the commencement of Part II., that there exist in Louisiana ample protective acts to prevent the separation of young children from their mothers. This writer appears to be in the enjoyment of an amiable ignorance and unsophisticated innocence with regard to the workings of human society generally, which is, on the whole, rather refreshing. For, on a certain incident in "Uncle Tom's Cabin," which represented Cassy's little daughter as having been sold from her, he makes the following naïf remark:

Now, the reader will perhaps be surprised to know that such an incident as the sale of Cassy apart from Eliza, upon which the whole interest of the foregoing narrative hinges, never could have taken place in Louisiana, and that the bill of sale for Eliza would not have been worth the paper it was written on. — Observe. George Shelby states that Eliza was *eight or nine years old* at the time his father purchased her in New Orleans. Let us again look at the statute-book of Louisiana.

In the *Code Noir* we find it set down that

" Every person is expressly prohibited from selling separately from their mothers *the children who shall not have attained the full age of ten years.*"

And this humane provision is strengthened by a statute, one clause of which runs as follows:

" Be it further enacted, that if any person or persons shall sell the mother of any slave child or children *under the age of ten years, separate from said child or children, or shall, the mother living, sell any slave child or children of ten years of age or under, separate from said mother,* such person or persons shall incur the penalty of the sixth section of this act."

This penalty is a fine of not less than one thousand nor more than two thousand dollars, and imprisonment in the public jail for a period of not less than six months nor more than one year. — *Vide Acts of Louisiana*, 1 *Session, 9th Legislature*, 1828–9, No. 24, Section 16. (*Rev. Stat.* 1852, p. 550, § 143.)

What a charming freshness of nature is suggested by this assertion! A thing could not have happened in a certain state, because there is a law against it!

Has there not been for two years a law forbidding to succor fugitives, or to hinder their arrest? — and has not this thing been done thousands of times in all the Northern States, and is not it more and more likely to be done every year? What is a law, against the whole public sentiment of society? — and will anybody venture to say that the public sentiment of Louisiana

practically goes against separation of families?

But let us examine a case more minutely, remembering the bearing on it of two great foundation principles of slave jurisprudence: namely, that a slave cannot bring a suit in any case, except in a suit for personal freedom, and this in some states must be brought by a guardian; and that a slave cannot bear testimony in any case in which whites are implicated.

Suppose Butler wants to sell Cassy's child of nine years. There is a statute forbidding to sell under ten years; — what is Cassy to do? She cannot bring suit. Will the state prosecute? Suppose it does, — what then? Butler says the child is ten years old; if he pleases, he will say she is ten and a half, or eleven. What is Cassy to do? She cannot testify; besides, she is utterly in Butler's power. He may tell her that if she offers to stir in the affair, he will whip the child within an inch of its life; and she knows he can do it, and that there is no help for it; — he may lock her up in a dungeon, sell her on to a distant plantation, or do any other despotic thing he chooses, and there is nobody to say Nay.

How much does the protective statute amount to for Cassy? It may be very well as a piece of advice to the public, or as a decorous expression of opinion; but one might as well try to stop the current of the Mississippi with a bulrush as the tide of trade in human beings with such a regulation.

We think that, by this time, the reader will agree with us, that the less the defenders of slavery say about protective statutes, the better.

CHAPTER VII.

THE EXECUTION OF JUSTICE.

State *v.* Eliza Rowand. — The " Ægis of Protection " to the Slave's Life.

" We cannot but regard the fact of this trial as a salutary occurrence."— *Charleston Courier.*

HAVING given some account of what sort of statutes are to be found on the law-books of slavery, the reader will hardly be satisfied without knowing what sort of trials are held under them. We will quote one specimen of a trial, reported in the *Charleston Courier* of May 6th, 1847. The *Charleston Courier* is one of the leading papers of South Carolina, and the case is reported with the utmost apparent innocence that there was any-thing about the trial that could reflect in the least on the character of the state for the utmost legal impartiality. In fact, the *Charleston Courier* ushers it into public view with the following flourish of trumpets, as something which is forever to confound those who say that South Carolina does not protect the life of the slave :

THE TRIAL FOR MURDER.

Our community was deeply interested and ex-cited, yesterday, by a case of great importance, and also of entire novelty in our jurisprudence. It was the trial of a lady of respectable family, and the mother of a large family, charged with the murder of her own or her husband's slave. The court-house was thronged with spectators of the exciting drama, who remained, with unabated interest and undiminished numbers, until the ver-dict was rendered acquitting the prisoner. We cannot but regard the fact of this trial as a salu-tary, although in itself lamentable occurrence, as it will show to the world that, however panoplied in station and wealth, and although challenging those sympathies which are the right and inher-itance of the female sex, no one will be suffered, in this community, to escape the most sifting scru-tiny, at the risk of even an ignominious death, who stands charged with the suspicion of murder-ing a slave,— to whose life our law now extends the ægis of protection, in the same manner as it does to that of the white man, *save only in the character of the evidence necessary for conviction or defence.* While evil-disposed persons at home are thus taught that they may expect rigorous trial and condign punishment, when, actuated by ma-lignant passions, they invade the life of the hum-ble slave, the enemies of our domestic institution abroad will find, their calumnies to the contrary notwithstanding, that we are resolved, in this particular, to do the full measure of our duty to the laws of humanity. We subjoin a report of the case.

The proceedings of the trial are thus given :

TRIAL FOR THE MURDER OF A SLAVE.

State v. *Eliza Rowand.* — *Spring Term, May 5,* 1847.

Tried before his Honor Judge O'Neall.

The prisoner was brought to the bar and ar-raigned, attended by her husband and mother, and humanely supported, during the trying scene, by the sheriff, J. B. Irving, Esq. On her arraign-ment, she pleaded " Not Guilty," and for her trial, placed herself upon " God and her country." After challenging John M. Deas, James Bancroft, H. F. Harbers, C. J. Beckman, E. R. Cowperth-waite, Parker J. Holland, Moses D. Hyams, Thomas Glaze, John Lawrence, B. Archer, J. S. Addison, B. P. Colburn, B. M. Jenkins, Carl Houseman, Geo. Jackson, and Joseph Coppen-berg, the prisoner accepted the subjoined panel, who were duly sworn, and charged with the case : 1. John L. Nowell, foreman. 2. Elias Whilden. 3. Jesse Coward. 4. Effington Wagner. 5. Wm. Whaley. 6. James Culbert. 7. R. L. Baker. 8. S. Wiley. 9. W. S. Chisolm. 10. T. M. Howard. 11. John Bickley. 12. John Y. Stock.

The following is the indictment on which the prisoner was arraigned for trial :

The State v. *Eliza Rowand* — *Indictment for mur-der of a slave.*

STATE OF SOUTH CAROLINA,
  Charleston District, } to wit :

At a Court of General Sessions, begun and holden in and for the district of Charleston, in the State of South Carolina, at Charleston, in the district and state aforesaid, on Monday, the third day of May, in the year of our Lord one thousand eight hundred and forty-seven :

The jurors of and for the district of Charleston, aforesaid, in the State of South Carolina, afore-said, upon their oaths present, that Eliza Rowand, the wife of Robert Rowand, Esq., not having the fear of God before her eyes, but being moved and seduced by the instigation of the devil, on the 6th day of January, in the year of our Lord one thou-sand eight hundred and forty-seven, with force and arms, at Charleston, in the district of Charles-ton, and state aforesaid, in and upon a certain female slave of the said Robert Rowand, named Maria, in the peace of God, and of the said state, then and there being, feloniously, maliciously, wilfully, deliberately, and of her malice afore-thought, did make an assault ; and that a certain other slave of the said Robert Rowand, named Richard, then and there, being then and there in the presence and by the command of the said Eliza Rowand, with a certain piece of wood, which he the said Richard in both his hands then and there had and held, the said Maria did beat and strike, in and upon the head of her the said Maria, then and there giving to her the said Maria, by such striking and beating, as aforesaid, with the piece of wood aforesaid, divers mortal bruises on the top, back, and sides of the head of her the said Maria, of which several mortal bruises she, the said Maria, then and there instantly died ; and that the said Eliza Rowand was then and there present, and then and there feloniously, mali-ciously, wilfully, deliberately, and of her malice aforethought, did order, command, and require, the said slave named Richard the murder and fel-ony aforesaid, in manner and form aforesaid, to do and commit. And as the jurors aforesaid, up-on their oaths aforesaid, do say, that the said Eliza Rowand her the said slave named Maria, in the manner and by the means aforesaid, felo-niously, maliciously, wilfully, deliberately, and of her malice aforethought, did kill and murder, against the form of the act of the General As-sembly of the said state in such case made and provided, and against the peace and dignity of the same state aforesaid.

And the jurors aforesaid, upon their oaths aforesaid, do further present, that the said Eliza Rowand, not having the fear of God before her eyes, but being moved and seduced by the insti-gation of the devil, on the sixth day of January, in the year of our Lord one thousand eight hun-dred and forty-seven, with force and arms, at Charleston, in the district of Charleston, and state aforesaid, in and upon a certain other fe-male slave of Robert Rowand, named Maria, in the peace of God, and of the said state, then and there being, feloniously, maliciously, wilfully, deliberately, and of her malice aforethought, did make an assault ; and that the said Eliza Row-and, with a certain piece of wood, which she, the said Eliza Rowand, in both her hands then and there had and held, her the said last-mentioned slave named Maria did then and there strike, and beat, in and upon the head of her the said Maria, then and there giving to her the said Maria, by such striking and beating aforesaid, with the piece of wood aforesaid, divers mortal bruises, on the top, back, and side of the head, of her the said Maria, of which said several mortal bruises she the said Maria then and there instantly died. And so the jurors aforesaid, upon their oaths aforesaid, do say, that the said Eliza Rowand her the said last-mentioned slave named Maria, in the manner and by the means last mentioned, feloniously, maliciously, wilfully, deliberately, and of her malice aforethought, did kill and murder, against the form of the act of the General Assembly of the said state in such case made and provided, and against the peace and dignity of the same state aforesaid.

H. BAILEY, *Attorney-general.*

As some of our readers may not have been in the habit of endeavoring to extract anything like common sense or information from documents so very concisely and luminously worded, the author will just state her own opinion that the above document is intended to charge Mrs. Eliza Rowand with having killed her slave Maria, in one of two ways: either with beating her on the head with her own hands, or having the same deed performed by proxy, by her slave-man Richard. The whole case is now presented. In order to make the reader clearly understand the arguments, it is necessary that he bear in mind that the law of 1740, as we have before shown, punished the murder of the slave only with fine and disfranchisement, while the law of 1821 punishes it with death.

On motion of Mr. Petigru, the prisoner was allowed to remove from the bar, and take her place by her counsel; the judge saying he granted the motion only because the prisoner was a woman, but that no such privilege would have been extended by him to any man.

The Attorney-general, Henry Bailey, Esq., then rose and opened the case for the state, in substance, as follows: He said that, after months of anxiety and expectation, the curtain had at length risen, and he and the jury were about to bear their part in the sad drama of real life, which had so long engrossed the public mind. He and they were called to the discharge of an important, painful, and solemn duty. They were to pass between the prisoner and the state — to take an inquisition of blood; on their decision hung the life or death, the honor or ignominy, of the prisoner; yet he trusted he and they would have strength and ability to perform their duty faithfully; and, whatever might be the result, their consciences would be consoled and quieted by that reflection. He bade the jury pause and reflect on the great sanctions and solemn responsibilities under which they were acting. The constitution of the state invested them with power over all that affected the life and was dear to the family of the unfortunate lady on trial before them.

They were charged, too, with the sacred care of the law of the land; and to their solution was submitted one of the most solemn questions ever intrusted to the arbitrament of man. They should pursue a direct and straight-forward course, turning neither to the right hand nor to the left —influenced neither by prejudice against the prisoner, nor by a morbid sensibility in her behalf. Some of them might practically and personally be strangers to their present duty; but they were all familiar with the laws, and must be aware of the responsibilities of jurymen. It was scarcely necessary to tell them that, if evidence fixed guilt on this prisoner, they should not hesitate to record a verdict of guilty, although they should write that verdict in tears of blood. They should let no sickly sentimentality, or morbid feeling on the subject of capital punishments, deter them from the discharge of their plain and obvious duty. They were to administer, not to make, the law; they were called on to enforce the law, by sanctioning the highest duty to God and to their country. If any of them were disturbed with doubts or scruples on this point, he scarcely supposed they would have gone into the jury-box. The law had awarded capital punishment as the meet retribution for the crime under investigation, and they were sworn to administer that law. It had, too, the full sanction of Holy Writ; we were there told that " the land cannot be cleansed of the blood shed therein, except by the blood of him that shed it." He felt assured, then, that they would be swayed only by a firm resolve to act on this occasion in obedience to the dictates of sound judgments and enlightened consciences. The prisoner, however, had claims on them, as well as the community; she was entitled to a fair and impartial trial. By the wise and humane principles of our law, they were bound to hold the prisoner *innocent*, and she stood *guiltless* before them, until proved guilty, by legal, competent, and satisfactory evidence. Deaf alike to the voice of sickly humanity and heated prejudice, they should proceed to their task with minds perfectly equipoised and impartial; they should weigh the circumstances of the case with a nice and careful hand; and if, by legal evidence, circumstantial and satisfactory, although not positive, guilt be established, they should unhesitatingly, fearlessly and faithfully, record the result of their convictions. He would next call their attention to certain legal distinctions, but would not say a word of the facts; he would leave *them* to the lips of the witnesses, unaffected by any previous comments of his own. The prisoner stood indicted for the murder of a slave. This was supposed not to be murder at common law. At least, it was not murder by our former statute; but the act of 1821 had placed the killing of the white man and the black man on the same footing. He here read the act of 1821, declaring that "any person who shall wilfully, deliberately, and maliciously murder a slave, shall, on conviction thereof, suffer death without benefit of clergy." The rules applicable to murder at common law were generally applicable, however, to the present case. The inquiries to be made may be reduced to two: 1. Is the party charged guilty of the fact of killing? This must be clearly made out by proof. If she be not guilty of killing, there is an end of the case. 2. The character of that killing, or of the offence. Was it done with malice aforethought? Malice is the essential ingredient of the crime. Where killing takes place, malice is presumed, unless the contrary appear; and this must be gathered from the attending circumstances. Malice is a technical term, importing a different meaning from that conveyed by the same word in common parlance. According to the learned Michael Foster, it consists not in " malevolence to particulars," it does not mean hatred to any particular individual, but is general in its import and application. But even killing, with intention to kill, is not always murder; there may be justifiable and excusable homicide, and killing in sudden heat and passion is so modified to manslaughter. Yet there may be murder when there is no ill-feeling, — nay, perfect indifference to the slain, — as in the case of the robber who slays to conceal his crime. Malice aforethought is that depraved feeling of the heart, which makes one regardless of social duty, and fatally bent on mischief. It is fulfilled by that recklessness of law and human life which is indicated by shooting into a crowd, and thus doing murder on even an unknown object. Such a feeling the law regards as hateful, and visits, in its practical exhibition, with condign punishment, because opposed to the very existence of law and society. One may do fatal mischief without this recklessness; but when the act is done, regardless of consequences, and death ensues, it is murder in the eye of the law. If the facts to be proved in this case should not come up to these requisitions, he implored the jury to acquit the accused, as at once due to law and justice. They should note every fact with scrutinizing eye, and ascertain whether the fatal result proceeded from passing accident or from brooding revenge, which the law stamped with the odious name of malice. He would make no further preliminary remarks, but proceed at once to lay the facts before them, from the mouths of the witnesses.

Evidence.

J. *Porteous Deveaux* sworn. — He is the coroner of Charleston district; held the inquest, on the seventh of January last, on the body of the deceased slave, *Maria*, the slave of Robert Rowand, at the residence of Mrs. T. C. Bee (the mother of the prisoner), in Logan-street. The body was found in an outbuilding — a kitchen; it was the body of an old and emaciated person, between fifty and sixty years of age; it was not examined in his presence by physicians; saw some few scratches about the face; adjourned to the City Hall. Mrs. Rowand was examined; her examination was in writing; it was here produced, and read, as follows:

" Mrs. *Eliza Rowand* sworn. — Says Maria is her nurse, and had misbehaved on yesterday morning; deponent sent Maria to Mr. Rowand's house, to be corrected by Simon; deponent sent Maria from the house about seven o'clock, A. M.; she returned to her about nine o'clock; came into her chamber; Simon did not come into the chamber at any time previous to the death of Maria; deponent says Maria fell down in the chamber; deponent had her seated up by Richard, who was then in the chamber, and deponent gave Maria some asafœtida; deponent then left the room; Richard came down and said Maria was dead; deponent says Richard did not strike Maria, nor did any one else strike her, in deponent's chamber. Richard left the chamber immediately with deponent; Maria was about fifty-two years of age;

deponent sent Maria by Richard to Simon, to Mr. Rowand's house, to be corrected; Mr. Rowand was absent from the city; Maria died about twelve o'clock; Richard and Maria were on good terms; deponent was in the chamber all the while that Richard and Maria were there together.
" ELIZA ROWAND.
" Sworn to before me this seventh January, 1847.
" J. P. DEVEAUX, *Coroner, D. C.*"

Witness went to the chamber of prisoner, where the death occurred; saw nothing particular; some pieces of wood in a box, set in the chimney; his attention was called to one piece, in particular, eighteen inches long, three inches wide, and about one and a half inch thick; did not measure it; the jury of inquest did; it was not a light-wood knot; thinks it was of oak; there was some pine wood and some split oak. Dr. Peter Porcher was called to examine the body professionally, who did so out of witness' presence.

Before this witness left the stand, B. F. Hunt, Esq., one of the counsel for the prisoner, rose and opened the defence before the jury, in substance as follows:

He said that the scene before them was a very novel one; and whether for good or evil, he would not pretend to prophesy. It was the first time in the history of this state, that a lady of good character and respectable connections stood arraigned at the bar, and had been put on trial for her life, on facts arising out of her domestic relations to her own slave. It was a spectacle consoling, and cheering, perhaps, to those who owed no good will to the institutions of our country; but calculated only to excite pain and regret among ourselves. He would not state a proposition so revolting to humanity as that crime should go unpunished; but judicial interference between the slave and the owner was a matter at once of delicacy and danger. It was the first time he had ever stood between a slave-owner and the public prosecutor, and his sensations were anything but pleasant. *This is an entirely different case from homicide between equals in society.* Subordination is indispensable where slavery exists; and in this there is no new principle involved. The same principle prevails in every country; on shipboard and in the army a large discretion is always left to the superior. Charges by inferiors against their superiors were always to be viewed with great circumspection at least, and especially when the latter are charged with cruelty or crime against subordinates. In the relation of owner and slave there is an absence of the usual motives for murder, and strong inducements against it on the part of the former. Life is usually taken from avarice or passion. The master gains nothing, but loses much, by the death of his slave; and when he takes the life of the latter deliberately, there must be more than ordinary malice to instigate the deed. The policy of altering the old law of 1740, which punished the killing of a slave with fine and political disfranchisement, was more than doubtful. It was the law of our colonial ancestors; it conformed to their policy and was approved by their wisdom, and it continued undisturbed by their posterity until the year 1821. It was engrafted on our policy in counteraction of the schemes and machinations, or in deference to the clamors, of those who formed plans for our improvement, although not interested in nor understanding our institutions, and whose interference led to the tragedy of 1822. He here adverted to the views of Chancellor Harper on this subject, who, in his able and philosophical memoir on slavery, said : " It is a somewhat singular fact, that when there existed in our state no law for punishing the murder of a slave, other than a pecuniary fine, there were, I will venture to say, at least ten murders of freemen for one murder of a slave. Yet it is supposed that they are less protected than their masters." " The change was made in subserviency to the opinions and clamor of others, who were utterly incompetent to form an opinion on the subject ; and a wise act is seldom the result of legislation in this spirit. From the fact I have stated, it is plain they need less protection. Juries are, therefore, less willing to convict, and it may sometimes happen that the guilty will escape all punishment. Security is one of the compensations of their humble position. We challenge the comparison, that with us there have been fewer murders of slaves than of parents, children, apprentices, and other murders, cruel and unnatural, in society where slavery does not exist."

Such was the opinion of Chancellor Harper on this subject, who had profoundly studied it, and whose views had been extensively read on this continent and in Europe. Fortunately, the jury, he said, were of the country, acquainted with our policy and practice ; composed of men too independent and honorable to be led astray by the noise and clamor out of doors. All was now as it should be ; — at least, a court of justice had assembled, to which his client had fled for refuge and safety ; its threshold was sacred ; no profane clamors entered there ; but legal investigation was had of facts, derived from the testimony of sworn witnesses ; and this should teach the community to shut their bosoms against sickly humanity, and their ears to imaginary tales of blood and horror, the food of a depraved appetite. *He warned the jury that they were to listen to no testimony but that of free white persons, given on oath in open court.* They were to *imagine* none that came not from them. It was for this that they were selected, — their intelligence putting them beyond the influence of unfounded accusations, unsustained by legal proof ; of legends of aggravated cruelty, founded on the evidence of negroes, and arising from weak and wicked falsehoods. Were slaves permitted to testify against their owner, it would cut the cord that unites them in peace and harmony, and enable them to sacrifice their masters to their ill will or revenge. Whole crews had been often leagued to charge captains of vessels with foulest murder, but judicial trial had exposed the falsehood. Truth has been distorted in this case, and murder manufactured out of what was nothing more than *ordinary domestic discipline.* Chastisement must be inflicted until subordination is produced ; and the extent of the punishment is not to be judged of by one's neighbors, but by himself. The event in this case has been unfortunate and sad ; but there was no motive for the taking of life. There is no pecuniary interest in the owner to destroy his slave ; the murder of his slave can only happen from ferocious passions of the master, filling his own bosom with anguish and contrition. This case has no other basis but unfounded rumor, commonly believed, *on evidence that will not venture here,* the offspring of that passion and depravity which make up falsehood.

The hope of freedom, of change of owners, revenge, are all motives with slave witnesses to malign their owners ; and to credit such testimony would be to dissolve human society. Where deliberate, wilful, and malicious murder is done, whether by male or female, the retribution of the law is a debt to God and man ; but the jury should beware lest it fall upon the innocent. The offence charged was not strictly murder at common law. The act of 1740 was founded on the practical good sense of our old planters, and its spirit still prevails. The act of 1821 is, by its terms, an act only to increase the punishment of persons convicted of murdering a slave, — *and this is a refinement in humanity of doubtful policy.* But, by the act of 1821, the murder must be wilful, deliberate and malicious ; and, when punishment is due to the slave, the master must not be held to strict account for going *an inch beyond the mark;* whether for doing so he shall be a felon, is a question for the jury to solve. The master must conquer a refractory slave ; and deliberation, so as to render clear the existence of malice, is necessary to bring the master within the provision of the act. He bade the jury remember the words of Him who spake as never man spake, — " *Let him that has never sinned throw the first stone.*" *They, as masters, might regret excesses to which they have themselves carried punishment.* He was not at all surprised at the course of the attorney-general ; it was his wont to treat every case with perfect fairness. He (Colonel H.) agreed that the inquiry should be —

1. Into the fact of the death.
2. The character or motive of the act.

The examination of the prisoner showed conclusively that the slave died a natural death, and not from personal violence. She was chastised with a lawful weapon, — was in weak health, nervous, made angry by her punishment, — excited. The story was then a plain one ; the community had been misled by the creations of imagination, or the statements of interested slaves. The negro came into her mistress' chamber ; fell on the floor ; medicine was given her ; it was supposed she was asleep, but she slept the sleep of death. To show the wisdom and policy of the old act of 1740 (this indictment is under both acts, — the punishment only altered by that of 1821), he urged that a case like this was not murder at common law ; nor is the same evidence applicable at common law. There, murder was presumed from killing ; not so in the case of a slave. The act of 1740 permits a master, when his slave is killed in his presence, there being no other white person present, to exculpate himself by his own oath ; and this exculpation is complete, unless clearly contravened by the evidence of two white witnesses. This is exactly what the prisoner has done ; she has, as the law permits, by calling on God, exculpated herself. And her oath is good, at least against the slander of her own slaves. Which, then, should prevail, the clamors of others, or the policy of the law established by our colonial ancestors? There would not be a tittle of positive evidence against the prisoner, nothing but circumstantial evidence ; and ingenious combination might be made to lead to any conclusion. Justice was all that his client asked. She appealed to liberal and high-minded men, — and she rejoiced in the privilege of doing so, — to accord her that justice they would demand for themselves.

Mr. Deveaux was not cross-examined.

Evidence resumed.

Dr. E. W. North sworn. — (Cautioned by attorney-general to avoid hearsay evidence.) Was the family physician of Mrs. Rowand. Went on the 6th January, at Mrs. Rowand's request, to see her at her mother's, in Logan-street; found her down stairs. in sitting-room. She was in a nervous and excited state; had been so for a month before; he had attended her; she said nothing to witness of slave Maria; found Maria in a chamber, up stairs, about one o'clock, P. M.; she was dead; she appeared to have been dead about an hour and a half; his attention was attracted to a piece of pine wood on a trunk or table in the room; it had a large knot on one end; had it been used on Maria, it must have caused considerable contusion; other pieces of wood were in a box, and much smaller ones; the corpse was lying one side in the chamber; it was not laid out; presumed she died there; the marks on the body were, to witness' view, very slight; some scratches about the face; he purposely avoided making an examination; observed no injuries about the head; had no conversation with Mrs. Rowand about Maria; left the house; it was on the 6th January last, — the day before the inquest; knew the slave before, but had never attended her.

Cross-examined. — Mrs. Rowand was in feeble health, and nervous; the slave Maria was weak and emaciated in appearance; sudden death of such a person, in such a state, from apoplexy or action of nervous system, not unlikely; her sudden death would not imply violence; had prescribed asafœtida for Mrs. Rowand on a former visit; it is an appropriate remedy for nervous disorders. Mrs. Rowand was not of bodily strength to handle the pine knot so as to give a severe blow; Mrs. Rowand has five or six children, the elder of them large enough to have carried pieces of the wood about the room; there must have been a severe contusion, and much extravasation of blood, to infer death from violence in this case; apoplexy is frequently attended with extravasation of blood; there were two Marias in the family.

In reply. — Mrs. Rowand could have raised the pine knot, but could not have struck a blow with it; such a piece of wood could have produced death, but it would have left its mark; saw the fellow Richard; he was quite capable of giving such a blow.

Dr. Peter Porcher. — Was called in by the coroner's jury to examine Maria's body; found it in the wash-kitchen; it was the corpse of one feeble and emaciated; partly prepared for burial; had the clothes removed; the body was lacerated with stripes; abrasions about face and knuckles; skin knocked off; passed his hand over the head; no bone broken: on request, opened her thorax, and examined the viscera; found them healthy; heart unusually so for one of her age; no particular odor; some undigested food; no inflammation; removed the scalp, and found considerable extravasation between scalp and skull: scalp bloodshot; just under the scalp, found the effects of a single blow, just over the right ear; after removing the scalp, lifted the bone; no rupture of any bloodvessel; some softening of the brain in the upper hemisphere; there was considerable extravasation under the scalp, the result of a succession of blows on the top of the head; this extravasation was general, but that over the ear was a single spot;

the butt-end of a cowhide would have sufficed for this purpose; an ordinary stick, a heavy one, would have done it; a succession of blows on the head, in a feeble woman, would lead to death, when, in a stronger one, it would not; saw no other appearance about her person, to account for her death, except those blows.

Cross-examined. — To a patient in this woman's condition, the blows would probably cause death; they were not such as were calculated to kill an ordinary person; witness saw the body twenty-four hours after her death: it was winter, and bitter cold; no disorganization, and the examination was therefore to be relied on; the blow behind the ear might have resulted from a fall, but not the blow on the top of the head, unless she fell head foremost; came to the conclusion of a succession of blows, from the extent of the extravasation; a single blow would have shown a distinct spot, with a gradual spreading or diffusion; one large blow could not account for it, as the head was spherical; no blood on the brain; the softening of the brain did not amount to much; in an ordinary dissection would have passed it over; anger sometimes produces apoplexy, which results in death; blood between the scalp and the bone of the skull; it was evidently a fresh extravasation; twenty-four hours would scarcely have made any change; knew nothing of this negro before; even after examination, the cause of death is sometimes inscrutable, — not usual, however.

In reply. — Does not attribute the softening of the brain to the blows; it was slight, and might have been the result of age; it was some evidence of impairment of vital powers by advancing age.

Dr. A. P. Hayne. — At request of the coroner, acted with Dr. Porcher; was shown into an outhouse; saw on the back of the corpse evidences of contusion; arms swollen and enlarged; laceration of body; contusions on head and neck; between scalp and skull extravasation of blood, on the top of head, and behind the right ear; a burn on the hand; the brain presented healthy appearance; opened the body, and no evidences of disease in the chest or viscera; attributed the extravasation of blood to external injury from blows, — blows from a large and broad and blunt instrument; attributes the death to those blows; supposes they were adequate to cause death, as she was old, weak and emaciated.

Cross-examined. — Would not have caused death in a young and robust person.

The evidence for the prosecution here closed, and no witnesses were called for the defence.

The jury were then successively addressed, ably and eloquently, by J. L. Petigru and James S. Rhett, Esqrs., on behalf of the prisoner, and H. Bailey, Esq., on behalf of the state, and by B. F. Hunt, Esq., in reply. Of those speeches, and also of the judge's charge, we have taken full notes, but have neither time nor space to insert them here.

His Honor, Judge O'Neall, then charged the jury eloquently and ably on the facts, vindicating the existing law, making death the penalty for the murder of a slave; but, on the law, intimated to the jury that he held the act of 1740 so far still in force as to admit of the prisoner's exculpation by her own oath, unless clearly disproved by the oaths of two witnesses; and that they were, therefore, in his opinion, bound to acquit, — although he left it to them, wholly, to say whether the prisoner was guilty of murder, killing in sudden heat and passion, or not guilty.

The jury then retired, and, in about twenty or thirty minutes, returned with a verdict of "Not Guilty."

There are some points which appear in this statement of the trial, especially in the plea for the defence. Particular attention is called to the following passage:

"Fortunately," said the lawyer, "the jury were of the country; —acquainted with our policy and practice; composed of men too honorable to be led astray by the *noise and clamor out of doors*. All was now as it should be; at least, a court of justice had assembled to which his client had fled for refuge and safety; its threshold was sacred; *no profane clamors entered there;* but legal investigation was had of facts."

From this it plainly appears that the case was a notorious one: so notorious and atrocious as to break through all the apathy which slave-holding institutions tend to produce, and to surround the court-house with noise and clamor.

From another intimation in the same speech, it would appear that there was abundant testimony of slaves to the direct fact,— testimony which left no kind of doubt on the popular mind. Why else does he thus earnestly warn the jury?

He warned the jury that they were to listen to no evidence but that of free white persons, given on oath in open court; they were to imagine none that came not from them. It was for this that they were selected; — their intelligence putting them beyond the influence of unfounded accusations, unsustained by legal proof; of legends of aggravated cruelty, founded on the evidence of negroes, and arising from weak and wicked falsehoods.

See also this remarkable admission: — "Truth had been distorted in this case, and murder manufactured out of what was nothing more than ORDINARY DOMESTIC DISCIPLINE." If the reader refers to the testimony, he will find it testified that the woman appeared to be about sixty years old; that she was much emaciated; that there had been a succession of blows on the top of her head, and one violent one over the ear; and that, in the opinion of a surgeon, these blows were sufficient to cause death. Yet the lawyer for the defence coolly remarks that "murder had been *manufactured* out of what was *ordinary domestic discipline.*" Are we to understand that beating feeble old women on the head, in this manner, is a specimen of *ordinary domestic discipline* in Charleston?

What would have been said if any antislavery newspaper at the North had made such an assertion as this? Yet the *Charleston Courier* reports this statement without comment or denial. But let us hear the lady's lawyer go still further in vindication of this ordinary domestic discipline: "Chastisement must be inflicted until subordination is produced; and the extent of the punishment is not to be judged by one's neighbors, but by himself. The event, IN THIS CASE, has been unfortunate and sad." The lawyer admits that the result of thumping a feeble old woman on the head has, *in this case*, been "unfortunate and sad." The old thing had not strength to bear it, and had no greater regard for the convenience of the family, and the reputation of "the institution," than to die, and so get the family and the community generally into trouble. It will appear from this that in most cases where old women are thumped on the head they have stronger constitutions — or more consideration.

Again he says, "When punishment is due to the slave, the master must not be held to strict account *for going an inch beyond the mark.*" And finally, and most astounding of all, comes this: "*He bade the jury remember the words of him who spake as never man spake,*— 'LET HIM THAT HATH NEVER SINNED THROW THE FIRST STONE.' They, as masters, might regret excesses to which they themselves might have carried punishment."

What sort of an insinuation is this? Did he mean to say that almost all the jurymen had probably done things of the same sort, and therefore could have nothing to say in this case? and did no member of the jury get up and resent such a charge? From all that appears, the jury acquiesced in it as quite a matter of course; and the *Charleston Courier* quotes it without comment, in the record of a trial which it says "will show to the world HOW the law extends the ægis of her protection alike over the white man and the humblest slave."

Lastly, notice the decision of the judge, which has become law in South Carolina. What point does it establish? That the simple oath of the master, in face of all circumstantial evidence to the contrary, may clear him, when the murder of a slave is the question. And this trial is paraded as a triumphant specimen of legal impartiality and equity! "If the *light* that is in thee be darkness, how great is that darkness!"

CHAPTER VIII.

THE GOOD OLD TIMES.

"A refinement in humanity of doubtful policy."
B. F. HUNT.

THE author takes no pleasure in presenting to her readers the shocking details of the following case. But it seems necessary to exhibit what were the actual workings of the ancient law of South Carolina, which has been characterized as one "conformed to the policy, and approved by the wisdom," of the fathers of that state, and the reform of which has been called "a refinement in humanity of doubtful policy."

It is well, also, to add the charge of Judge Wilds, partly for its intrinsic literary merit, and the nobleness of its sentiments, but principally because it exhibits such a contrast as could scarcely be found elsewhere, between the judge's high and indignant sense of justice, and the shameful impotence and imbecility of the laws under which he acted.

The case was brought to the author's knowledge by a letter from a gentleman of Pennsylvania, from which the following is an extract:

Some time between the years 1807 and 1810, there was lying in the harbor of Charleston a ship commanded by a man named Slater. His crew were slaves: one of them committed some offence, not specified in the narrative. The captain ordered him to be bound and laid upon the deck; and there, in the harbor of Charleston, in the broad day-light, compelled another slave-sailor to chop off his head. The affair was public — notorious. A prosecution was commenced against him; the offence was proved beyond all doubt, — perhaps, indeed, it was not denied, — and the judge, in a most eloquent charge or rebuke of the defendant, expressed his sincere regret that he could inflict no punishment, under the laws of the state.

I was studying law when the case was published in "Hall's American Law Journal, vol. I." I have not seen the book for twenty-five or thirty years. I may be in error as to names, &c., but while I have life and my senses the facts of the case cannot be forgotten.

The following is the "charge" alluded to in the above letter. It was pronounced by the Honorable Judge Wilds, of South Carolina, and is copied from Hall's Law Journal, I. 67.

John Slater! You have been convicted by a jury of your country of the wilful murder of your own slave; and I am sorry to say, the short, impressive, uncontradicted testimony, on which that conviction was founded, leaves but too little room to doubt its propriety.

The annals of human depravity might be safely challenged for a parallel to this unfeeling, bloody and diabolical transaction.

You caused your unoffending, unresisting slave to be bound hand and foot, and, by a refinement in cruelty, compelled his companion, perhaps the friend of his heart, to chop his head with an axe, and to cast his body, yet convulsing with the agonies of death, into the water! And this deed you dared to perpetrate in the very harbor of Charleston, within a few yards of the shore, unblushingly, in the face of open day. Had your murderous arm been raised against your equals, whom the laws of self-defence and the more efficacious law of the land unite to protect, your crimes would not have been without precedent, and would have seemed less horrid. Your personal risk would at least have proved, that though a murderer, you were not a coward. But you too well knew that this unfortunate man, whom chance had subjected to your caprice, had not, like yourself, chartered to him by the laws of the land the sacred rights of nature; and that a stern, but necessary policy, had disarmed him of the rights of self-defence. Too well you knew that to you alone he could look for protection; and that your arm alone could shield him from oppression, or avenge his wrongs; yet, that arm you cruelly stretched out for his destruction.

The counsel, who generously volunteered his services in your behalf, shocked at the enormity of your offence, endeavored to find a refuge, as well for his own feelings as for those of all who heard your trial, in a derangement of your intellect. Several witnesses were examined to establish this fact; but the result of their testimony, it is apprehended, was as little satisfactory to his mind, as to those of the jury to whom it was addressed. I sincerely wish this defence had proved successful, not from any desire to save you from the punishment which awaits you, and which you so richly merit, but from the desire of saving my country from the foul reproach of having in its bosom so great a monster.

From the peculiar situation of this country, our fathers felt themselves justified in subjecting to a very slight punishment him who murders a slave. Whether the present state of society require a continuation of this policy, so opposite to the apparent rights of humanity, it remains for a subsequent legislature to decide. Their attention would ere this have been directed to this subject, but, for the honor of human nature, such hardened sinners as yourself are rarely found, to disturb the repose of society. The grand jury of this district, deeply impressed with your daring outrage against the laws both of God and man, have made a very strong expression of their feelings on the subject to the legislature; and, from the wisdom and justice of that body, the friends of humanity may confidently hope soon to see this blackest in the catalogue of human crimes pursued by appropriate punishment.

In proceeding to pass the sentence which the law provides for your offence, I confess I never felt more forcibly the want of power to make respected the laws of my country, whose minister I am. You have already violated the majesty of those laws. You have profanely pleaded the law under which you stand convicted, as a justification of your crime. You have held that law in one hand, and brandished your bloody axe in the other, impiously contending that the *one* gave a license to the unrestrained use of the *other*.

But, though you will go off unhurt in person, by the present sentence, expect not to escape with impunity. Your bloody deed has set a mark upon you, which I fear the good actions of your future life will not efface. You will be held in abhorrence by an impartial world, and shunned as a monster by every honest man. Your unoffending posterity will be visited, for your iniquity, by the stigma of deriving their origin from an unfeeling murderer. Your days, which will be but few, will be spent in wretchedness; and, if your conscience be not steeled against every virtuous emotion, if you be not entirely abandoned to hardness of heart, the mangled, mutilated corpse of your murdered slave will ever be present in your imagination, obtrude itself into all your amusements, and haunt you in the hours of silence and repose.

But, should you disregard the reproaches of an offended world, should you hear with callous insensibility the gnawings of a guilty conscience, yet remember, I charge you, remember, that an awful period is fast approaching, and with you is close at hand, when you must appear before a tribunal whose want of power can afford you no prospect of impunity; when you must raise your bloody hands at the bar of an impartial omniscient Judge! Remember, I pray you, remember, whilst yet you have time, that God is just, and that his vengeance will not sleep forever!

The penalty that followed this solemn denunciation was a fine of *seven hundred pounds*, current money, or, in default of payment, imprisonment for seven years.

And yet it seems that there have not been wanting those who consider the reform of this law "*a refinement in humanity of doubtful policy*"! To this sentiment, so high an authority as that of Chancellor Harper is quoted, as the reader will see by referring to the speech of Mr. Hunt, in the last chapter. And, as is very common in such cases, the old law is vindicated, as being, on the whole, a surer protection to the life of the slave than the new one. From the results of the last two trials, there would seem to be a fair show of plausibility in the argument. For under the old law it seems that Slater had at least to pay seven hundred pounds, while under the new Eliza Rowand comes off with only the penalty of "a most sifting scrutiny."

Thus, it appears, the penalty of the law goes with the murderer of the slave.

How is it executed in the cases which concern the life of the master? Look at this short notice of a recent trial of this kind, which is given in the *Alexandria* (Va.) *Gazette*, of Oct. 23, 1852, as an extract from the *Charlestown* (Va.) *Free Press.*

TRIAL OF NEGRO HENRY.

The trial of this slave for an attack, with intent to kill, on the person of Mr. Harrison Anderson, was commenced on Monday and concluded on Tuesday evening. His Honor, Braxton Daven-

port, Esq., chief justice of the county, with four associate gentlemen justices, composed the court.

The commonwealth was represented by its attorney, Charles B. Harding, Esq., and the accused ably and eloquently defended by Wm. C. Worthington and John A. Thompson, Esqs. The evidence of the prisoner's guilt was conclusive. A majority of the court thought that he ought to suffer the extreme penalty of the law; but, as this required a unanimous agreement, he was sentenced to receive five hundred lashes, not more than thirty-nine at one time. The physician of the jail was instructed to see that they should not be administered too frequently, and only when, in his opinion, he could bear them.

In another paper we are told that the *Free Press* says:

. A majority of the court thought that he ought to suffer the extreme penalty of the law; but, as this required a unanimous agreement, he was sentenced to receive five hundred lashes, not more than thirty-nine at any one time. The physician of the jail was instructed to see that they should not be administered too 'frequently, and *only* when, in his opinion, he could bear them. This *may seem* to be a harsh and inhuman punishment; but, when we take into consideration that it is in accordance with the *law of the land*, and the further fact that the insubordination among the slaves of that state has become truly alarming, we cannot question the righteousness of the judgment.

Will anybody say that the master's life is in more danger from the slave than the slave's from the master, that this disproportionate retribution is meted out? Those who countenance such legislation will do well to ponder the solemn words of an ancient book, inspired by One who is no respecter of persons:

"If I have refused justice to my man-servant or maid-servant,
When they had a cause with me,
What shall I do when God riseth up?
And when he visiteth, what shall I answer him?
Did not he that made me in the womb make him?
Did not the same God fashion us in the womb?"
Job 31 : 13—15.

CHAPTER IX.

MODERATE CORRECTION AND ACCIDENTAL
DEATH — STATE *v.* CASTLEMAN.

THE author remarks that the record of the following trial was read by her a little time before writing the account of the death of Uncle Tom. The shocking particulars haunted her mind and were in her thoughts when the following sentence was written:

What man has nerve to do, man has not nerve to hear. What brother man and brother Christian must suffer, cannot be told us, even in our secret chamber, it so harrows up the soul. And yet, O my country, these things are done under the shadow of thy laws! O Christ, thy church sees them almost in silence!

It is given precisely as prepared by Dr. G. Bailey, the very liberal and fair-minded editor of the National Era.

From the National Era, Washington, November 6, 1851.

HOMICIDE CASE IN CLARKE COUNTY, VIRGINIA.

Some time since, the newspapers of Virginia contained an account of a horrible tragedy, enacted in Clarke County, of that state. A slave of Colonel James Castleman, it was stated, had been chained by the neck, and whipped to death by his master, on the charge of stealing. The whole neighborhood in which the transaction occurred was incensed; the Virginia papers abounded in denunciations of the cruel act; and the people of the North were called upon to bear witness to the justice which would surely be meted out in a slave state to the master of a slave. We did not publish the account. The case was horrible; it was, we were confident, exceptional; it should not be taken as evidence of the general treatment of slaves; we chose to delay any notice of it till the courts should pronounce their judgment, and we could announce at once the crime and its punishment, so that the state might stand acquitted of the foul deed.

Those who were so shocked at the transaction will be surprised and mortified to hear that the actors in it have been tried and *acquitted;* and when they read the following account of the trial and verdict, published at the instance of the friends of the accused, their mortification will deepen into bitter indignation:

From the "Spirit of Jefferson."

"COLONEL JAMES CASTLEMAN. — The following statement, understood to have been drawn up by counsel, since the trial, has been placed by the friends of this gentleman in our hands for publication:

"At the Circuit Superior Court of Clarke County, commencing on the 13th of October, Judge Samuels presiding, James Castleman and his son Stephen D. Castleman were indicted jointly for the murder of negro Lewis, property of the latter. By advice of their counsel, the parties elected to be tried separately, and the attorney for the commonwealth directed that James Castleman should be tried first.

"It was proved, on this trial, that for many months previous to the occurrence the money-drawer of the tavern kept by Stephen D. Castleman, and the liquors kept in large quantities in his cellar, had been pillaged from time to time, until the thefts had attained to a considerable amount. Suspicion had, from various causes, been directed to Lewis, and another negro, named Reuben (a blacksmith), the property of James Castleman; but by the aid of two of the house-servants they had eluded the most vigilant watch.

"On the 20th of August last, in the afternoon, S. D. Castleman accidentally discovered a clue, by means of which, and through one of the house-servants implicated, he was enabled fully to detect the depredators, and to ascertain the manner in which the theft had been committed. He im-

mediately sent for his father, living near him, and after communicating what he had discovered, it was determined that the offenders should be punished at once, and before they should know of the discovery that had been made.

"Lewis was punished first; and in a manner, as was fully shown, to preclude all risk of injury to his person, by stripes with a broad leathern strap. He was punished severely, but to an extent by no means disproportionate to his offence; nor was it pretended, in any quarter, that this punishment implicated either his life or health. He confessed the offence, and admitted that it had been effected by false keys, furnished by the blacksmith, Reuben.

"The latter servant was punished immediately afterwards. It was believed that he was the principal offender, and he was found to be more obdurate and contumacious than Lewis had been in reference to the offence. Thus it was proved, both by the prosecution and the defence, that he was punished with greater severity than his accomplice. It resulted in a like confession on his part, and he produced the false key, one fashioned by himself, by which the theft had been effected.

"It was further shown, on the trial, that Lewis was whipped in the upper room of a warehouse, connected with Stephen Castleman's store, and near the public road, where he was at work at the time; that after he had been flogged, to secure his person, whilst they went after Reuben, he was confined by a chain around his neck, which was attached to a joist above his head. The length of this chain, the breadth and thickness of the joist, its height from the floor, and the circlet of chain on the neck, were accurately measured; and it was thus shown that the chain unoccupied by the circlet and the joist was a foot and a half longer than the space between the shoulders of the man and the joist above, or to that extent the chain hung loose above him; that the circlet (which was fastened so as to prevent its contraction) rested on the shoulders and breast, the chain being sufficiently drawn only to prevent being slipped over his head, and that there was no other place in the room to which he could be fastened, except to one of the joists above. His hands were tied in front; a white man, who had been at work with Lewis during the day, was left with him by the Messrs. Castleman, the better to insure his detention, whilst they were absent after Reuben. It was proved by this man (who was a witness for the prosecution) that Lewis asked for a box to stand on, or for something that he could jump off from; that after the Castlemans had left him he expressed a fear that when they came back he would be whipped again; and said, if he had a knife, and could get one hand loose, he would cut his throat. The witness stated that the negro 'stood firm on his feet,' that he could turn freely in whatever direction he wished, and that he made no complaint of the mode of his confinement. This man stated that he remained with Lewis about half an hour, and then left there to go home.

"After punishing Reuben, the Castlemans returned to the warehouse, bringing him with them; their object being to confront the two men, in the hope that by further examination of them jointly all their accomplices might be detected.

"They were not absent more than half an hour. When they entered the room above, Lewis was found hanging by the neck, his feet thrown behind him, his knees a few inches from the floor, and his head thrown forward — the body warm and supple (or relaxed), but life was extinct.

"It was proved by the surgeons who made a post-mortem examination before the coroner's inquest that the death was caused by strangulation by hanging; and other eminent surgeons were examined to show, from the appearance of the brain and its blood-vessels after death (as exhibited at the post-mortem examination), that the subject could not have fainted before strangulation.

"After the evidence was finished on both sides, the jury from their box, and of their own motion, without a word from counsel on either side, informed the court that they had agreed upon the verdict. The counsel assented to its being thus received, and a verdict of "not guilty" was immediately rendered. The attorney for the commonwealth then informed the court that all the evidence for the prosecution had been laid before the jury; and as no new evidence could be offered on the trial of Stephen D. Castleman, he submitted to the court the propriety of entering a nolle prosequi. The judge replied that the case had been fully and fairly laid before the jury upon the evidence; that the court was not only satisfied with the verdict, but, if any other had been rendered, it must have been set aside; and that if no further evidence was to be adduced on the trial of Stephen, the attorney for the commonwealth would exercise a proper discretion in entering a nolle prosequi as to him, and the court would approve its being done. A nolle prosequi was entered accordingly, and both gentlemen discharged.

"It may be added that two days were consumed in exhibiting the evidence, and that the trial was by a jury of Clarke County. Both the parties had been on bail from the time of their arrest, and were continued on bail whilst the trial was depending."

Let us admit that the evidence does not prove the legal crime of homicide : what candid man can doubt, after reading this ex parte version of it, that the slave died in consequence of the punishment inflicted upon him?

In criminal prosecutions the federal constitution guarantees to the accused the right to a public trial by an impartial jury; the right to be informed of the nature and cause of the accusation ; to be confronted with the witnesses against him ; to have compulsory process for obtaining witness in his favor ; and to have the assistance of counsel ; guarantees necessary to secure innocence against hasty or vindictive judgment, — absolutely necessary to prevent injustice. Grant that they were not intended for slaves ; every master of a slave must feel that they are still morally binding upon him. He is the sole judge ; he alone determines the offence, the proof requisite to establish it, and the amount of the punishment. The slave then has a peculiar claim upon him for justice. When charged with a crime, common humanity requires that he should be informed of it, that he should be confronted with the witnesses against him, that he should be permitted to show evidence in favor of his innocence.

But how was poor Lewis treated ! The son of Castleman said he had discovered who stole the money ; and it was forthwith "determined that the offenders should be punished at once, and before they should know of the discovery that had been made." Punished without a hearing ! Punished

on the testimony of a house-servant, the nature of which does not appear to have been inquired into by the court ! Not a word is said which authorizes the belief that any careful examination was made, as it respects their guilt. Lewis and Reuben were assumed, on loose evidence, without deliberate investigation, to be guilty ; and then, without allowing them to attempt to show their evidence, they were whipped, until a confession of guilt was extorted by bodily pain.

Is this Virginia justice?

Lewis was punished with "a broad leathern strap," — he was "punished severely :" this we do not need to be told. A "broad leathern strap" is well adapted to severity of punishment. "Nor was it pretended," the account says, "in any quarter, that this punishment implicated either his life or his health." This is false ; it was expressly stated in the newspaper accounts at the time, and such was the general impression in the neighborhood, that the punishment did very severely implicate his life. But more of this anon.

Lewis was left. A chain was fastened around his neck, so as not to choke him, and secured to the joist above, leaving a slack of about a foot and a half. Remaining in an upright position, he was secure against strangulation, but he could neither sit nor kneel ; and should he faint, he would be choked to death. The account says that they fastened him thus for the purpose of securing him. If this had been the sole object, it could have been accomplished by safer and less cruel methods, as every reader must know. This mode of securing him was intended probably to intimidate him, and, at the same time, afforded some gratification to the vindictive feeling which controlled the actors in this foul transaction. The man whom they left to watch Lewis said that, after remaining there about half an hour, he went home ; and Lewis was then alive. The Castlemans say that, after punishing Reuben, they returned, having been absent not more than half an hour, and they found him hanging by the neck, dead. We direct attention to this part of the testimony, to show how loose the statements were which went to make up the evidence.

Why was Lewis chained at all, and a man left to watch him ? "To secure him," say the Castlemans. Is it customary to chain slaves in this manner, and set a watch over them, after severe punishment, to prevent their running away ? If the punishment of Lewis had not been unusual, and if he had not been threatened with another infliction on their return, there would have been no necessity for chaining him.

The testimony of the man left to watch represents him as desperate, apparently, with pain and fright. "Lewis asked for a box to stand on :" why ? Was he not suffering from pain and exhaustion, and did he not wish to rest himself, without danger of slow strangulation ? Again : he asked for "something he could jump off from ;" "after the Castlemans left, he expressed a fear when they came back that he would be whipped again ; and said, if he had a knife, and could get one hand loose, he would cut his throat."

The punishment that could drive him to such desperation must have been horrible.

How long they were absent we know not, for the testimony on this point is contradictory. They found him hanging by the neck, dead, "his feet thrown behind him, his knees a few inches from the floor, and his head thrown forward," —

just the position he would naturally fall into, had he sunk from exhaustion. They wish it to appear that he hung himself. Could this be proved (we need hardly say that it is not), it would relieve but slightly the dark picture of their guilt. The probability is that he sank, exhausted by suffering, fatigue and fear. As to the testimony of "surgeons," founded upon a post-mortem examination of the brain and blood-vessels, "that the subject could not have fainted before strangulation," it is not worthy of consideration. We know something of the fallacies and fooleries of such examinations.

From all we can learn, the only evidence relied on by the prosecution was that white man employed by the Castlemans. He was dependent upon them for work. Other evidence might have been obtained; why it was not is for the prosecuting attorney to explain. To prove what we say, and to show that justice has not been done in this horrible affair, we publish the following communication from an old and highly-respectable citizen of this place, and who is very far from being an Abolitionist. The slave-holders whom he mentions are well known here, and would have promptly appeared in the case, had the prosecution, which was aware of their readiness, summoned them.

" *To the Editor of the Era:*

" I see that Castleman, who lately had a trial for whipping a slave to death, in Virginia, was '*triumphantly acquitted*,' — as many expected. There are three persons in this city, with whom I am acquainted, who staid at Castleman's the same night in which this awful tragedy was enacted. They heard the dreadful lashing and the heart-rending screams and entreaties of the sufferer. They implored the only white man they could find on the premises, not engaged in the bloody work, to interpose; but for a long time he refused, on the ground that he was a dependent, and was afraid to give offence; and that, moreover, they had been drinking, and he was in fear for his own life, should he say a word that would be displeasing to them. He did, however, venture, and returned and reported the cruel manner in which the slaves were chained, and lashed, and secured in a blacksmith's vice. In the morning, when they ascertained that one of the slaves was dead, they were so shocked and indignant that they refused to eat in the house, and reproached Castleman with his cruelty. He expressed his regret that the slave had died, and especially as he had ascertained that he *was innocent* of the accusation for which he had suffered. The idea was that he had fainted from exhaustion; and, the chain being round his neck, he was strangled. The persons I refer to are themselves slave-holders, — but their feelings were so harrowed and lacerated that they could not sleep (two of them are ladies); and for many nights afterwards their rest was disturbed, and their dreams made frightful, by the appalling recollection.

" These persons would have been material witnesses, and would have willingly attended on the part of the prosecution. The knowledge they had of the case was communicated to the proper authorities, yet their attendance was not required. The only witness was that dependent who considered his own life in danger.

" Yours, &c., J. F.' "

The account, as published by the friends of the accused parties, shows a case of extreme cruelty. The statements made by our correspondent prove that the truth has not been fully revealed, and that justice has been baffled. The result of the trial shows how irresponsible is the power of a master over his slave; and that whatever security the latter has is to be sought in the humanity of the former, not in the guarantees of law. Against the cruelty of an inhuman master he has really no safeguard.

Our conduct in relation to this case, deferring all notice of it in our columns till a legal investigation could be had, shows that we are not disposed to be captious towards our slave-holding countrymen. In no unkind spirit have we examined this lamentable case; but we must expose the utter repugnance of the slave system to the proper administration of justice. The newspapers of Virginia generally publish the account from the *Spirit of Jefferson*, without comment. They are evidently not satisfied that justice was done; they doubtless will deny that the accused were guilty of homicide, legally; but they will not deny that they were guilty of an atrocity which should brand them forever, in a Christian country.

CHAPTER X.

PRINCIPLES ESTABLISHED. — STATE *v.* LEGREE; A CASE NOT IN THE BOOKS.

FROM a review of all the legal cases which have hitherto been presented, and of the principles established in the judicial decisions upon them, the following facts must be apparent to the reader :

First, That masters do, now and then, kill slaves by the torture.

Second, That the fact of so killing a slave is not of itself held presumption of murder, in slave jurisprudence.

Third, That the slave in the act of resistance to his master may always be killed.

From these things it will be seen to follow, that, if the facts of the death of Tom had been fully proved by two white witnesses, in open court, Legree could not have been held by any *consistent* interpreter of slave-law to be a murderer; for Tom was in the act of resistance to the will of his master. His master had laid a command on him, in the presence of other slaves. Tom had deliberately refused to obey the command. The master commenced chastisement, to reduce him to obedience. And it is evident, at the first glance, to every one, that, if the law does not sustain him in enforcing obedience in such a case, there is an end of the whole slave power. No Southern court would dare to decide that Legree did wrong to continue the punishment, as long as Tom continued the insubordination. Legree stood by him every moment of the time, pressing him to yield, and offering to let him go as soon as he did yield. Tom's resistance was *insurrection.* It was an example which could not be allowed, for a moment, on any Southern plantation. By the express words of the constitution of Georgia, and by the understanding and usage of all slave-law, the power of life and death is always left in the hands of the master, in exigences like this. This is not a case·like that of Souther *v.* The Commonwealth. The victim of Souther was not in a state of resistance or insurrection. The punishment, in his case, was a simple vengeance for a past offence, and not an attempt to reduce him to subordination.

There is no principle of slave jurisprudence by which a man could be pronounced a murderer, for acting as Legree did, in his circumstances. Everybody must see that such an admission would strike at the foundations of the slave system. To be sure, Tom was in a state of insurrection for conscience' sake. But the law does not, and cannot,· contemplate that the negro shall have a conscience independent of his master's. To allow that the negro may refuse to obey his master whenever he thinks that obedience would be wrong, would be to produce universal anarchy. If Tom had been allowed to disobey his master in this case, for conscience' sake, the next day Sambo would have had a case of conscience, and Quimbo the next. Several of them might very justly have thought that it was a sin to work as they did. The mulatto woman would have remembered that the command of God forbade her to take another husband. Mothers might have considered that it was more their duty to stay at home and take care of their children, when they were young and feeble, than to work for Mr. Legree in the cotton-field. There would be no end to the havoc made upon cotton-growing operations, were the negro allowed the right of maintaining his own conscience on moral subjects. If the slave system is a right system, and ought to be maintained, Mr. Legree ought not to be blamed for his conduct in this case; for he did only what was absolutely essential to maintain the system; and Tom died in fanatical and foolhardy resistance to "the powers that be, which are ordained of God.". He followed a sentimental impulse of his desperately depraved heart, and neglected those "solid teachings of the written word," which, as recently elucidated, have proved so refreshing to eminent political men.

CHAPTER XI.

THE TRIUMPH OF JUSTICE OVER LAW.

HAVING been obliged to record so many trials in which justice has been turned away backward by the hand of law, and equity and common humanity have been kept out by the bolt and bar of logic, it is a relief to the mind to find one recent trial recorded, in North Carolina, in which the nobler feelings of the human heart have burst over formalized limits, and where the prosecution appears to have been conducted by *men,* who were not ashamed of possessing in their bosoms that very dangerous and most illogical agitator, a human heart. It is true that, in giving this trial, very sorrowful, but inevitable, inferences will force themselves upon the mind, as to that state of public feeling which allowed such outrages to be perpetrated in open daylight, in the capital of North Carolina, upon a hapless woman. It would seem that the public were too truly instructed in the awful doctrine pronounced by Judge Ruffin, that "THE POWER OF THE MASTER MUST BE ABSOLUTE," to think of interfering while the poor creature was dragged, barefoot and bleeding, at a horse's neck, at the rate of five miles an hour, through the streets of Raleigh. It seems, also, that the most horrible brutalities and enormities that could be conceived of were *witnessed,* without any efficient interference, by a number of the citizens, among whom we see the name of the Hon. W. H. Haywood, of Raleigh. It is a comfort to find the attorney-general, in this case, speaking as a man ought to speak. Certainly there can be no occasion to wish to pervert or overstate the dread workings of the slave system, or to leave out·the few comforting and encouraging features, however small the encouragement of them may be.

The case˙ is now presented, as narrated from the published reports, by Dr. Bailey, editor of the *National Era ;* a man whose candor and fairness need no indorsing, as every line that he writes speaks for itself. The reader may at first be surprised to find slave testimony in the court, till he recollects that it is a slave that is on trial, the testimony of slaves being only null when it concerns whites.

AN INTERESTING TRIAL.

We find in one of the Raleigh (North Carolina) papers, of June 5, 1851, a report of an interesting trial, at the spring term of the Superior Court. Mima, a slave, was indicted for the murder of her master, William Smith, of Johnston County, on the night of the 29th of November, 1850. The evidence for the prosecution was Sidney, a slave-boy, twelve years old, who testified that, in the night, he and a slave-girl, named Jane, were roused from sleep by the call of their master, Smith, who had returned home. They went out, and found Mima tied to his horse's neck, with two ropes, one round her neck, the other round her hands. Deceased carried her into the house, jerking the rope fastened to her neck, and tied her to a post. He called for something to eat, threw her a piece of bread, and, after he had done, beat her on her naked back with a large piece of light-wood, giving her many hard blows. In a short time, deceased went out of the house, for a special purpose, witness accompanying him with a torch-light, and hearing him say that he intended " to use the prisoner up." The light was extinguished, and he reëntered the house for the purpose of lighting it. Jane was there; but the prisoner had been untied, and was not there. While lighting his torch, he heard blows outside, and heard the deceased cry out, two or three times, " O, Leah! O, Leah!" Witness and Jane went out, saw the deceased bloody and struggling, were frightened, ran back, and shut themselves up. Leah, it seems, was mother of the prisoner, and had run off two years, on account of cruel treatment by the deceased.

Smith was speechless and unconscious till he died, the following morning, of the wounds inflicted on him.

It was proved on the trial that Carroll, a white man, living about a mile from the house of the deceased, and whose wife was said to be the illegitimate daughter of Smith, had in his possession, the morning of the murder, the receipt given the deceased by sheriff High, the day before, for jail fees, and a note for thirty-five dollars, due deceased from one Wiley Price, which Carroll collected a short time thereafter; also the chest-keys of the deceased; and no proof was offered to show how Carroll came into possession of these articles.

The following portion of the testimony discloses facts so horrible, and so disgraceful to the people who tolerated, in broad daylight, conduct which would have shamed the devil, that we copy it just as we find it in the Raleigh paper. The scene, remember, is the city of Raleigh.

" The defence was then opened. James Harris, C. W. D. Hutchings, and Hon. W. H. Haywood, of Raleigh; John Cooper, of Wake; Joseph Hane and others, of Johnston, were examined for the prisoner. The substance of their testimony was as follows: On the forenoon of Friday, 29th of November last, deceased took prisoner from Raleigh jail, tied her round the neck and wrist; ropes were then latched to the horse's neck; he cursed the prisoner several times, got on his horse, and started off; when he got opposite the Telegraph office, on Fayetteville-street, he pulled her shoes and stockings off, cursed her again, went off in a swift trot, the prisoner running after him, doing apparently all she could to keep up; passed round by Peck's store; prisoner seemed very humble and submissive; took down the street east of the capitol, going at the rate of five miles an hour; continued this gait until he passed O. Rork's corner, about half or three-quarters of a mile from the capitol: that he reached Cooper's (one of the witnesses), thirteen miles from Ra-

leigh, about four o'clock, P. M.: that it was raining very hard; deceased got off his horse, turned it loose with prisoner tied to its neck; witness went to take deceased's horse to stable; heard great lamentations at the house; hurried back; saw his little daughter running through the rain from the house, much frightened; got there; deceased was gouging prisoner in the eyes, and she making outcries; made him stop; became vexed, and insisted upon leaving; did leave in a short time, in the rain, sun about an hour high; when he left, prisoner was tied as she was before; her arms and fingers were very much swollen; the rope around her wrist was small, and had sunk deep into the flesh, almost covered with it; that around the neck was large, and tied in a slip-knot; deceased would jerk it every now and then; when jerked, it would choke prisoner; she was barefoot and bleeding; deceased was met some time after dark, in about six miles of home, being twenty-four or twenty-five from Raleigh."

Why did they not strike the monster to the earth, and punish him for his infernal brutality?

The attorney-general conducted the prosecution with evident loathing. The defence argued, first, that the evidence was insufficient to fasten the crime upon the prisoner; secondly, that, should the jury be satisfied beyond a rational doubt that the prisoner committed the act charged, it would yet be only manslaughter.

" A single blow between equals would mitigate a killing instanter from murder to manslaughter. It could not, in law, be anything more, if done under the furor brevis of passion. But the rule was different as between master and slave. It was necessary that this should be, to preserve the subordination of the slave. The prisoner's counsel then examined the authorities at length, and contended that the prisoner's case came within the rule laid down in The State v. Will (1 Dev. and Bat. 121). The rule there given by Judge Gaston is this: 'If a slave, in defence of his life, and under circumstances strongly calculated to excite his passions of terror and resentment, kill his overseer or master, the homicide is, by such circumstances, mitigated to manslaughter.' The cruelties of the deceased to the prisoner were grievous and long-continued. They would have shocked a barbarian. The savage loves and thirsts for blood; but the acts of civilized life have not afforded him such refinement of torture as was here exhibited."

The attorney-general, after discussing the law, appealed to the jury " not to suffer the prejudice which the counsel for the defence had attempted to create against the deceased (whose conduct, he admitted, was disgraceful to human nature) to influence their judgments in deciding whether the act of the prisoner was criminal or not, and what degree of criminality attached to it. He desired the prisoner to have a fair and impartial trial. He wished her to receive the benefit of every rational doubt. It was her right, however humble her condition; he hoped he had not that heart, as he certainly had not the right by virtue of his office, to ask in her case for anything more than he would ask from the highest and proudest of the land on trial, that the jury should decide according to the evidence, and vindicate the violated law."

These were honorable sentiments.

After an able charge by Judge Ellis, the jury retired, and, after having remained out several hours, returned with a verdict of NOT GUILTY. Of course, we see not how they could hesitate to come to this verdict at once.

The correspondent who furnishes the *Register* with a report of the case says:

"It excited an intense interest in the community in which it occurred, and, although it develops a series of cruelties shocking to human nature, the result of the trial, nevertheless, vindicates the benignity and justice of our laws towards that class of our population whose condition Northern fanaticism has so carefully and grossly misrepresented, for their own purposes of selfishness, agitation, and crime."

We have no disposition to misrepresent the condition of the slaves, or to disparage the laws of North Carolina; but we ask, with a sincere desire to know the truth, Do the *laws* of North Carolina allow a master to practise such horrible cruelties upon his slaves as Smith was guilty of, and would the *public sentiment* of the city of Raleigh permit a repetition of such enormities as were perpetrated in its streets, in the light of day, by that miscreant?

In conclusion, as the accounts of these various trials contain so many shocking incidents and particulars, the author desires to enter a caution against certain mistaken uses which may be made of them, by well-intending persons. The crimes themselves, which form the foundation of the trials, are not to be considered and spoken of as specimens of the *common* working of the slave system. They are, it is true, the logical and legitimate fruits of a system which makes every individual owner an irresponsible despot. But the actual number of them, compared with the whole number of masters, we take pleasure in saying, is small. It is an injury to the cause of freedom to ground the argument against slavery upon the *frequency* with which such scenes as these occur. It misleads the popular mind as to the real issue of the subject. To hear many men talk, one would think that they supposed that unless negroes actually were whipped or burned alive at the rate of two or three dozen a week, there was no harm in slavery. They seem to see nothing in the system but its gross bodily abuses. If these are absent, they think there is no harm in it. They do not consider that the twelve hours' torture of some poor victim, bleeding away his life, drop by drop, under the hands of a SOUTHER, is only a symbol of that more atrocious process by which the divine, immortal soul is mangled, burned, lacerated, thrown down, stamped upon, and suffocated, by the fiend-like force of the tyrant Slavery. And as, when the torturing work was done, and the poor soul flew up to the judgment-seat, to stand there in awful witness, there was not a vestige of humanity left in that dishonored body, nor anything by which it could be said, "See, this was a man!" — so, when Slavery has finished her legitimate work upon the soul, and trodden out every spark of manliness, and honor, and self-respect, and natural affection, and conscience, and religious sentiment, then there is nothing left *in the soul*, by which to say, "This was a man!" and it becomes necessary for judges to construct grave legal arguments to prove that the slave is a human being.

Such *extreme* cases of bodily abuse from the despotic power of slavery are comparatively rare. Perhaps they may be paralleled by cases brought to light in the criminal jurisprudence of other countries. They might, perhaps, have happened anywhere; at any rate, we will concede that they might. But where under the sun did *such* TRIALS, of such cases, ever take place, in any nation professing to be free and Christian? The reader of English history will perhaps recur to the trials under Judge Jeffries, as a parallel. A moment's reflection will convince him that there is no parallel between the cases. The decisions of Jeffries were the decisions of a monster, who violently wrested law from its legitimate course, to gratify his own fiendish nature. The decisions of American slave-law have been, for the most part, the decisions of honorable and humane men, who have wrested from their natural course the most humane feelings, to fulfil the mandates of a cruel law.

In the case of Jeffries, the sacred forms of the administration of justice were violated. In the case of the American decisions, every form has been maintained. Revolting to humanity as these decisions appear, they are strictly logical and legal.

Therefore, again, we say, Where, ever, in any nation professing to be civilized and Christian, did *such* TRIALS, of *such cases*, take place? When were ever *such* legal arguments made? When, ever, such legal principles judicially affirmed? Was ever such a trial held in England as that in Virginia, of SOUTHER *v.* THE COMMONWEALTH? Was it ever necessary in England for a judge to declare on the bench, contrary to the opinion of a lower court, that the death of an apprentice, by twelve hours' torture from his master, *did* amount to murder in the first degree? Was such a decision, if given, accompanied by the affirmation of the principle, that any amount of torture inflicted by the master, *short of* the point of death, was not indictable? Not being read in English law, the writer cannot say;· but there is strong impression from within that such a decision as this would have shaken the whole island of Great Britain; and that such a case as *Souther* v. *The Commonwealth* would never have been forgotten under the sun. Yet it is probable that very few persons in the United States ever heard of the case, or ever would have heard of it, had it not been quoted by the New York *Courier and Enquirer* as an overwhelming example of legal humanity.

The horror of the whole matter is, that more than one such case should ever need to happen in a country, in order to make the whole community feel, as one man, that such power ought not to be left in the hands of a master. How many such cases do people *wish* to have happen?— how many *must* happen, before they will learn that utter despotic power is not to be trusted in any hands? If one white man's son or brother had been treated in this way, under the law of *apprenticeship*, the whole country would have trembled, from Louisiana to Maine, till that law had been altered. They forget that the black man has also a father. It is "He that sitteth upon the circle of the heavens, who bringeth the princes to nothing, and maketh the judges of the earth as vanity." He hath said that "When he maketh inquisition for blood, he FORGETTETH NOT the cry of the humble." That blood which has fallen so despised to the earth,—that blood which lawyers have quibbled over, ·in the quiet of legal nonchalance, discussing in great ease whether it fell by murder in the first or second degree,— HE will one day reckon for as the blood of his own child. He "is not slack concerning his promises, as some men count slackness, but is long-suffering to usward;" but the day of vengeance is surely coming, and the year of his redeemed is in his heart.

Another court will sit upon these trials, when the Son of Man shall come in his glory. It will be not alone Souther, and such as he, that will be arraigned there; but all those in this nation, north and south, who have abetted the system, and made the laws which MADE Souther what he was. In *that* court negro testimony will be received, if never before; and the judges and the counsellors, and the chief men, and the mighty men, marshalled to that awful bar, will say to the mountains and the rocks, "Fall on us and hide us from the face of Him that sitteth on the throne, and from the wrath of the Lamb."

The wrath of the Lamb! Think of it! Think that Jesus Christ has been present, a witness,—a silent witness through every such scene of torture and anguish,— a silent witness in every such court, calmly hearing the evidence given in, the lawyers pleading, the bills filed, and cases appealed! And think what a heart Jesus Christ has, and with what age-long patience he has suffered! What awful depths are there in that word, LONG-SUFFERING! and what must be that wrath, when, after ages of endurance, this dread accumulation of wrong and anguish comes up at last to judgment!

CHAPTER XI.

A COMPARISON OF THE ROMAN LAW OF SLAVERY WITH THE AMERICAN.

THE writer has expressed the opinion that the American law of slavery, taken throughout, is a more severe one than that of any other civilized nation, ancient or modern, if we except, perhaps, that of the Spartans. She has not at hand the means of comparing French and Spanish slave-codes; but, as it is a common remark that Roman slavery was much more severe than any that has ever existed in America, it will be well to compare the Roman with the American law. We therefore present a description of the Roman slave-law, as quoted by William Jay, Esq., from Blair's "*Inquiry into the State of Slavery among the Romans*," giving such references to *American authorities* as will enable the reader to make his own comparison, and to draw his own inferences.

I. *The slave had no protection against the avarice, rage, or lust of the master, whose authority was founded in absolute property; and the bondman was viewed less as a human being subject to arbitrary dominion, than as an inferior animal, dependent wholly on the will of his owner.*

See law of South Carolina, in Stroud's "*Sketch of the Laws of Slavery*," p. 23.

Slaves shall be deemed, sold, taken, reputed and adjudged in law to be *chattels personal* in the hands of their owners and possessors, and their executors, administrators and assigns, to all intents, constructions, and purposes whatever. 2 Brev. Dig. 229. Prince's Dig. 446. Cobb's Dig. 971.

A slave is one who is in the power of a master to whom he belongs. Lou. Civil Code, art. 35. Stroud's Sketch, p. 22.

—— Such obedience is the consequence only
Judge Ruf-
fin's Decision
in the case of
The State v.
Mann. Whee-
ler's Law of
Slavery, 246. of uncontrolled authority over the body. There is nothing else which can operate to produce the effect. The power of the master must be *absolute*, to render the submission of the slave perfect.

II. *At first, the master possessed the uncontrolled power of life and death.*

Judge Clarke, in case of
State of Miss. v. Jones.
Wheeler, 252. At a very early period in Virginia, the power of life over slaves was *given by statute.*

III. *He might kill, mutilate or torture his slaves, for any or no offence; he might force them to become gladiators or prostitutes.*

The privilege of killing is now somewhat abridged; as to mutilation and torture, see the case of *Souther* v. *The Commonwealth,* 7 *Grattan,* 673, quoted in Chapter III., above. Also *State* v. *Mann,* in the same chapter, from *Wheeler,* p. 244.

IV. *The temporary unions of male with female slaves were formed and dissolved at his command; families and friends were separated when he pleased.*

See the decision of Judge Mathews in the case of *Girod* v. *Lewis,* Wheeler, 199:

It is clear, that slaves have no legal capacity to assent to any contract. With the consent of their master, they may marry, and their moral power to agree to such a contract or connection as that of marriage cannot be doubted; but whilst in a state of slavery it cannot produce any civil effect, because slaves are deprived of all civil rights.

See also the chapter below on "the separation of families," and the files of *any* southern newspaper, *passim.*

V. *The laws recognized no obligation upon the owners of slaves, to furnish them with food and clothing, or to take care of them in sickness.*

The extent to which this deficiency in the Roman law has been supplied in the American, by "*protective acts,*" has been exhibited above.*

VI. *Slaves could have no property but by the sufferance of their master, for whom they acquired everything, and with whom they could form no engagements which could be binding on him.*

The following chapter will show how far American legislation is in advance of that of the Romans, in that it makes it a penal offence on the part of the master to permit his slave to hold property, and a crime on the part of the slave to be so permitted. For the present purpose, we give an extract from the Civil code of Louisiana, as quoted by Judge Stroud :

A slave is one who is in the power of a master to whom he belongs. The master may sell him, dispose of his person, his industry, Civil Code, Article 35. and his labor ; he can do nothing, possess nothing, nor acquire anything Stroud, p. 22. but what must belong to his master.

According to Judge Ruffin, a slave is "one doomed in his own person, and his posterity, to live without knowledge, and without the capacity to Wh'ler's Law of Slavery, p. 246. State v. Mann. make anything his own, and to toil that another may reap the fruits."

With reference to the binding power of engagements between master and slave, the following decisions from the United States Digest are in point (7, p. 449) :

All the acquisitions of the slave in possession are the property of his master, notwithstanding the promise of his master that the slave shall have certain of Gist v. Toohey, 2 Rich. 424. them.

A slave paid money which he had earned over and above his wages, for the purchase of his children into the hands of B, and B purchased such children with the money. Held that Ibid. the master of such slave was entitled to recover the money of B.

VII. *The master might transfer his rights by either sale or gift, or might bequeath them by will.*

Slaves shall be deemed, sold, taken, reputed and adjudged in law, to be chattels Law of S. Carolina. Cobb's Digest, 971. personal in the hands of their owners and possessors, and their executors, administrators, and assigns, to all intents, constructions, and purposes whatsoever.

VIII. *A master selling, giving, or bequeathing a slave, sometimes made it a provision that he should never be carried abroad, or that he should be manumitted on a fixed day; or that, on the other hand, he should never be emancipated, or that he should be kept in chains for life.*

We hardly think that a provision that a slave should never be emancipated, or that Williams v. Ash, 1 How. U. S. Rep. 1. 5 U. S. Dig. 792, § 5. he should be kept in chains for life, would be sustained. A provision that the slave should not be carried out of the state, and that on the happening of either event he should be free, has been sustained.

The remainder of Blair's account of Roman slavery is devoted rather to the practices of masters than to the state of the law itself. Surely, the writer is not called upon to exhibit in the society of enlightened, republican and Christian America, in the nineteenth century, a parallel to the atrocities committed in pagan Rome, under the sceptre of the persecuting Cæsars, when the amphitheatre was the favorite resort of the most refined of her citizens, as well as the great "school of morals" for the multitude.

---

* See also the case of *State* v. *Abram,* 10 *Ala.* 928. 7*U. S. Dig.* p. 449. "The master or overseer, and not the slave, is the proper judge whether the slave is too sick to be able to labor. The latter cannot, therefore, resist the order of the former to go to work."

A few references only will show, as far as we desire to show, how much safer it is now to trust man with absolute power over his fellow, than it was then.

IX. *While slaves turned the handmill they were generally chained, and had a broad wooden collar, to prevent them from eating the grain. The* FURCA, *which in later language means a gibbet, was, in older dialect, used to denote a wooden fork or collar, which was made to bear upon their shoulders, or around their necks, as a mark of disgrace, as much as an uneasy burden.*

The reader has already seen, in Chapter V., that this instrument of degradation has been in use, in our own day, in certain of the slave states, under the express sanction and protection of statute laws; although the material is different, and the construction doubtless improved by modern ingenuity.

X. *Fetters and chains were much used for punishment or restraint, and were, in some instances, worn by slaves during life, through the sole authority of the master. Porters at the gates of the rich were generally chained. Field laborers worked for the most part in irons posterior to the first ages of the republic.*

The Legislature of South Carolina specially sanctions the same practices, by excepting them in the *"protective enactment,"* which inflicts the penalty of *one hundred pounds* "in case any person shall wilfully cut out the tongue," &c., of a slave, "or shall inflict *any other cruel* punishment, *other than* by whipping or beating with a horse-whip, cowskin, switch, or small stick, *or by putting irons on, or confining or imprisoning such slave."*

XI. *Some persons made it their business to catch runaway slaves.*

That such a profession, constituted by the highest legislative authority in the nation, and rendered respectable by the commendation expressed or implied of statesmen and divines, and of newspapers political and religious, exists in our midst, *especially in the free states,* is a fact which is, day by day, making itself too apparent to need testimony. The matter seems, however, to be managed in a more perfectly open and business-like manner in the State of Alabama than elsewhere. Mr. Jay cites the following advertisement from the *Sumpter County* (Ala.) *Whig :*

NEGRO DOGS.

The undersigned having bought the entire pack of Negro Dogs (of the Hay and Allen stock), he now proposes to catch runaway negroes. His charges will be Three Dollars per day for hunting, and Fifteen Dollars for catching a runaway. He resides three and one half miles north of Livingston, near the lower Jones' Bluff road.

WILLIAM GAMBEL.

Nov. 6, 1845. — 6m.

The following is copied, *verbatim et literatim,* and with the pictorial embellishments, from *The Dadeville* (Ala.) *Banner,* of November 10th, 1852. *The Dadeville Banner* is *"devoted to politics, literature, education, agriculture, &c."*

NOTICE.

The undersigned having an excellent pack of HOUNDS, for trailing and catching runaway slaves, informs the public that his prices in future will be as follows for such services :

For each day employed in hunting or trailing,	$2.50
For catching each slave,	10.00
For going over ten miles and catching slaves,	20.00

If sent for, the above prices will be exacted in cash. The subscriber resides one mile and a half south of Dadeville, Ala.

B. BLACK.

Dadeville, Sept. 1, 1852. 1tf

XII. *The runaway, when taken, was severely punished by authority of the master, or by the judge, at his desire; sometimes with crucifixion, amputation of a foot, or by being sent to fight as a gladiator with wild beasts; but most frequently by being branded on the brow with letters indicative of his crime.*

That severe punishment would be the lot of the recaptured runaway, every one would suppose, from the *"absolute power"* of the master to inflict it. That it *is* inflicted in many cases, it is equally easy and needless to prove. The peculiar forms of punishment mentioned above are now very much out of vogue, but the following advertisement by Mr. Micajah Ricks, in the *Raleigh* (N. C.) *Standard* of July 18th, 1838, shows that something of classic taste in torture still lingers in our degenerate days.

Ran away, a negro woman and two children ; a few days before she went off, I burnt her with a hot iron, on the left side of her face. I tried to make the letter M.

It is charming to notice the *naïf* betrayal of literary pride on the part of Mr. Ricks. He did not wish that letter M to be taken as a specimen of what he could do in the way of writing. The creature would not hold still, and he fears the M may be ilegible.

The above is only one of a long list of advertisements of maimed, cropped and branded negroes, in the book of Mr. Weld, entitled *American Slavery as It Is,* p. 77.

XIII. *Crue. masters sometimes hired torturers by profession, or had such persons in their establishments, to assist them in punishing their slaves. The noses and ears and teeth of slaves were often in danger from an enraged owner; and sometimes the eyes of a great offender were put out. Crucifixion was very frequently made the fate of a wretched slave for a trifling misconduct, or from mere caprice.*

For justification of such practices as these, we refer again to that horrible list of maimed and mutilated men, advertised by slaveholders themselves, in Weld's *American Slavery as It Is*, p. 77. We recall the reader's attention to the evidence of the monster Kephart, given in Part I. As to crucifixion, we presume that there are wretches whose religious scruples would deter them from this particular form of torture, who would not hesitate to inflict equal cruelties by other means; as the Greek pirate, during a massacre in the season of Lent, was conscience-stricken at having tasted a drop of blood. We presume?—Let any one but read again, if he can, the sickening details of that twelve hours' torture of Souther's slave, and say how much more merciful is American slavery than Roman.

The last item in Blair's description of Roman slavery is the following:

By a decree passed by the Senate, if a master was murdered when his slaves might possibly have aided him, all his household within reach were held as implicated, and deserving of death: and Tacitus relates an instance in which a family of four hundred were all executed.

To this alone, of all the atrocities of the slavery of old heathen Rome, do we fail to find a parallel in the slavery of the United States of America.

There are other respects, in which American legislation has reached a refinement in tyranny of which the despots of those early days never conceived. The following is the language of Gibbon:

Hope, the best comfort of our imperfect condition, was not denied to the Roman slave; and if he had any opportunity of rendering himself either useful or agreeable, he might very naturally expect that the diligence and fidelity of a few years would be rewarded with the inestimable gift of freedom. * * * Without destroying the distinction of ranks, a distant prospect of freedom and honors was presented even to those whom pride and prejudice almost disdained to number among the human species.[*]

The youths of promising genius were instructed in the arts and sciences, and their ·price was ascertained by the degree of their skill and talents. Almost every profession, either liberal or mechanical, might be found in the household of an opulent senator.[†]

---

[*] Gibbon's "Decline and Fall," Chap. II.   [†] Ibid.

The following chapter will show how "the best comfort" which Gibbon knew for human adversity is taken away from the American slave; how he is denied the commonest privileges of education and mental improvement, and how the whole tendency of the unhappy system, under which he is in bondage, is to take from him the consolations of religion itself, and to degrade him from our common humanity, and common brotherhood with the Son of God.

CHAPTER XIII.

THE MEN BETTER THAN THEIR LAWS.

Judgment is turned away backward,
And Justice standeth afar off;
For Truth is fallen in the street,
And Equity cannot enter.
Yea, Truth faileth;
And HE THAT DEPARTETH FROM EVIL MAKETH HIMSELF A
     PREY.   ISAIAH 59: 14, 15.

THERE is one very remarkable class of laws yet to be considered.

So full of cruelty and of unmerciful severity is the slave-code,— such an atrocity is the institution of which it is the legal definition,— that there are multitudes of individuals too generous and too just to be willing to go to the full extent of its restrictions and deprivations.

A generous man, instead of regarding the poor slave as a piece of property, dead, and void of rights, is tempted to regard him rather as a helpless younger brother, or as a defenceless child, and to extend to him, by his own good right arm, that protection and those rights which the law denies him. A religious man, who, by the theory of his belief, regards all men as brothers, and considers his Christian slave, with himself, as a member of Jesus Christ,— as of one body, one spirit; and called in one hope of his calling,—cannot willingly see him "doomed to live without knowledge," without the power of reading the written Word, and to raise up his children after him in the same darkness.

Hence, if left to itself, individual humanity would, in many cases, practically abrogate the slave-code. Individual humanity would teach the slave to read and write, — would build school-houses for his children, and would, in very, very many cases, enfranchise him.

The result of all this has been foreseen. It has been foreseen that the result of education would be general intelligence; that the result of intelligence would be a knowledge of personal rights; and that an inquiry into the doctrine of personal rights would be fatal to the system. It has been foreseen, also, that the example of disinterestedness and generosity, in emancipation, might carry with it a generous contagion, until it should become universal; that the example of educated and emancipated slaves would prove a dangerous excitement to those still in bondage.

For this reason, the American slave-code, which, as we have already seen, embraces, substantially, all the barbarities of that of ancient Rome, has had added to it a set of laws more cruel than any which ancient and heathen Rome ever knew, — laws designed to shut against the slave his last refuge, — the humanity of his master. The master, in ancient Rome, might give his slave whatever advantages of education he chose, or at any time emancipate him, and the state did not interfere to prevent.*

But in America the laws, throughout all the slave states, most rigorously forbid, in the first place, the *education* of the slave. We do not profess to give all these laws, but a few striking specimens may be presented. Our authority is Judge Stroud's "Sketch of the Laws of Slavery."

The legislature of South Carolina, in 1740, enounced the following preamble : — Stroud's Sketch, "Whereas, the having of slaves p. 88. taught to write, or suffering them to be employed in writing, may be attended with *great inconveniences ;*" and enacted that the crime of teaching a slave to write, or of employing a slave as a scribe, should be punished by a fine of *one hundred pounds*, current money. If the reader will turn now to the infamous "protective" statute, enacted by the same legislature, in the same year, he will find that the *same penalty* has been appointed for the cutting out of the tongue, putting out of the eye, cruel scalding, &c., of any slave, as for the offence of teaching him to write ! That is to say, that to teach him to write, and to put out his eyes, are to be regarded as equally reprehensible.

That there might be no doubt of the "great and fundamental policy" of the state, and that there might be full security against the "*great inconveniences*" of "having of slaves taught to write," it was

enacted, in 1800, "That assemblies of slaves, free negroes, &c., * * * * for the purpose of *mental instruction*, in a confined or secret place, &c. &c., is [are] declared to be an unlawful meeting ;" and the officers are required to enter such confined places, and disperse the "unlawful assemblage," inflicting, at their discretion, "*such corporal punishment*, not exceeding twenty lashes, upon such slaves, free negroes, &c., as they may judge p. 89. 2 Brenecessary for deterring them varil's Digest, pp. 254-5. *from the like unlawful assemblage in future.*"

The statute-book of Virginia is adorned with a law similar to the one last Stroud, pp. quoted. 88, 89.

The offence of teaching a slave to write was early punished, in Georgia, as in South Carolina, by a pecuniary fine. But the city of Savannah seems to have found this penalty insufficient to protect it from "*great inconveniences*," and we learn, by a quotation in the work of Judge Stroud from a number of "The Portfolio,'" that " the city has passed an ordinance, by which any person that teaches any person of color, *slave or free*, to *read or write*, or causes such person to be so taught, is Stroud's Sketch, subjected to a fine of thirty dol- pp. 89, 90. lars for *each* offence ; and every person of color who shall keep a school, to teach reading or writing, is subject to a fine of thirty dollars, or to be imprisoned ten days, and whipped thirty-nine lashes."

Secondly. In regard to religious privileges :

The State of Georgia has enacted a law, " To *protect* religious societies in- the exercise of their religious duties." This law, after appointing rigorous penalties for the offence of interrupting or disturbing a congregation of *white persons*, concludes in the following words :

No congregation, or company of *negroes*, shall, under *pretence of divine worship,* Stroud, p. 92. assemble themselves, contrary to the Prince's Digest, act regulating patrols. p. 342.

" The act regulating patrols," as quoted by the editor of Prince's Digest, empowers *every justice of the peace to disperse* ANY *assembly or meeting of slaves* which *may* disturb the peace, Stroud, p. 93. &c., of his majesty's subjects, Prince's Digest, p. 447. and permits that every slave found at such a meeting shall " *immediately* be corrected, WITHOUT TRIAL, *by receiving on the bare back twenty-five stripes with a whip, switch, or cowskin.*"

---

* In and after the reign of Augustus, certain restrictive regulations were passed, designed to prevent an increase of unworthy citizens by emancipation. They had, however, nothing like the stringent force of American laws.

The history of legislation in South Carolina is significant. An act was passed in 1800, containing the following section:

It shall not be lawful for any number of slaves, free negroes, mulattoes or mestizoes, even in company with white persons, to meet together ^{Stroud, p. 93.} and assemble for the purpose of men- ^{2 Brevard's} tal instruction *or religious worship,* ^{Dig. 254, 255.} either before the rising of the sun, or after the going down of the same. And all magistrates, sheriffs, militia officers, &c. &c., are hereby vested with power, &c., for dispersing such assemblies, &c.

The law just quoted seems somehow to have had a prejudicial effect upon the religious interests of the "slaves, free negroes," &c., specified in it: for, three years afterwards, on the petition of certain religious societies, a "*protective act*" was passed, which should secure them this *great religious privilege ;* to wit, that it should be unlawful, before nine o'clock, " to break into a place of meeting, wherein shall be assembled the members of any religious society of this state, *provided a majority of them shall be white persons,* or otherwise to disturb their devotion, *unless* such person shall have first obtained * * * * a warrant, &c."

Thirdly. It appears that many masters, who are disposed to treat their slaves generously, have allowed them to accumulate property, to raise domestic animals for their own use, and, in the case of intelligent servants, to go at large, to hire their own time, and to trade upon their own account. Upon all these practices the law comes down, with unmerciful severity. A penalty is inflicted on the owner, but, with a rigor quite accordant with the tenor of slave-law the offence is considered, in law, as that of the slave, rather than that of the master ; so that, if the master is generous enough not to regard the penalty which is imposed upon himself, he may be restrained by the fear of bringing a greater evil upon his dependent. These laws are, in some cases, so constructed as to make it for the interest of the lowest and most brutal part of society that they be enforced, by offering half the profits to the informer. We give the following, as specimens of slave legislation on this subject :

The law of South Carolina :

It shall not be lawful for any slave to buy, sell, trade, &c., for any goods, &c., without a license from the owner, &c.; nor shall any slave be permitted to keep any boat, periauger,* or canoe,

or raise and breed, for the benefit of such slave, any horses, mares, cattle, sheep, or hogs, under pain of forfeiting all the goods, &c., and all the boats, periaugers, or canoes, horses, mares, cattle, sheep or hogs. And it shall be law- ^{Stroud, pp. 46, 47. James' Di gest, 355. 386. Act of 1740.} ful for any person whatsoever to seize and take away from any slave all such goods, &c., boats, &c. &c., and to deliver the same into the hands of any justice of the peace, nearest to the place where the seizure shall be made ; and such justice shall take the oath of the person making such seizure, concerning the manner thereof ; and if the said justice shall be satisfied that such seizure has been made according to law, he shall pronounce and declare the goods so seized to be forfeited, and order the same to be sold at public outcry, one half of the moneys arising from such sale to go to the state, and the other half to him or them that sue for the same.

The laws in many other states are similar to the above; but the State of Georgia has an additional provision, against per- ^{2 Cobb's} mitting the slave to hire himself to ^{Dig. 284.} another for his own benefit; a penalty of thirty dollars is imposed for every weekly offence, on the part of the master, unless the labor be done on his own premises. Savannah, Augusta, and Sunbury, are places excepted.

In Virginia, "if the master shall permit his slave to hire himself out," the ^{Stroud, p. 47.} *slave* is to be apprehended, ·&c., and the *master* to be fined.

In an early act of the legislature of the orthodox and Presbyterian State of North Carolina, it is gratifying to see how the judicious course of public policy is made to subserve the interests of Christian charity, — how, in a single ingenious sentence, provision is made for punishing the offender against society, rewarding the patriotic informer, and feeding the poor and destitute :

All horses, cattle, hogs or sheep, that, one month after the passing of this act, shall belong to any slave, or be of any slave's ^{Stroud's Sketch, 47.} mark, in this state, shall be seized and sold by the county wardens, and by them applied, the one-half to the support of the poor ·of the county, and the other half to the informer.

In Mississippi a fine of fifty dollars is imposed upon the master who permits his slave to cultivate cotton for his own use ; or who licenses his slave to ^{Stroud, p. 48.} go at large and trade as a freeman ; or who is *convicted* of permitting his slave to keep " *stock of any description.*"

To show how the above law has been interpreted by the highest judicial tribunal of the sovereign State of Mississippi, we repeat here a portion of a decision of Chief Justice Sharkey, which we have elsewhere given more in full.

---

* *i. e.* Periagua.

Independent of the principles laid down in adjudicated cases, our statute-law prohibits slaves from owning certain kinds of property; and it may be inferred that the legislature supposed they were extending the act as far as it could be necessary to exclude them from owning *any* property, as the prohibition includes that kind of property which they would most likely be permitted to own without interruption, to wit: hogs, horses, cattle, &c. They cannot be prohibited from holding such property in consequence of its being of a dangerous or offensive character, but because *it was deemed impolitic for them to hold property of any description.*

It was asserted, at the beginning of this head, that the permission of the master to a slave to hire his own time is, by law, considered the offence of the slave; the slave being subject to prosecution therefor, not the master. This is evident from the tenor of some of the laws quoted and alluded to above. It will be still further illustrated by the following decisions of the courts of North Carolina. They are copied from the Supplement to the U. S. Digest, vol. II. p. 798:

139. An indictment charging that a certain negro did hire her own time, contrary to the form of the statute, &c., is defective and must be quashed, because it was omitted to be charged that *she was permitted by her master to go at large, which is one essential part of the offence.*

The State v. Clarissa.
5 Iredell, 221.

140. Under the first clause of the thirty-first section of the 111th chapter of the Revised Statutes, prohibiting masters from hiring to slaves their own time, the master is not *indictable;* he is only subject to a penalty of forty dollars. Nor is the master indictable under the second clause of that section; the process being *against the slave,* not against the master. — Ib.

142. To constitute the offence under section 32 (Rev. Stat. c. cxi. § 32) it is not necessary that the slave should have hired his time; it is sufficient if the master permits him to go at large as a freeman.

This is maintaining the ground that *"the master can do no wrong"* with great consistency and thoroughness. But it is in perfect keeping, both in form and spirit, with the whole course of slave-law, which always upholds the supremacy of the master, and always depresses the slave.

Fourthly. Stringent laws against emancipation exist in nearly all the slave states. In four of the states, — South Carolina, Georgia, Alabama, and Mississippi, — emancipation cannot be effected, except by a special act of the legislature of the state.

Stroud, 147. Prince's Dig. 456. James' Dig. 393. Toulmin's Dig. 632. Miss. Rev. Code, 386.

In Georgia, the *offence* of setting free "any slave, or slaves, in any other manner and form than the one prescribed," was punishable, according to the law of 1801, by

the forfeiture of two hundred dollars, to be recovered by action *or indictment;* the slaves in question still remaining, "*to all intents and purposes, as much in a state of slavery as before they were manumitted.*"

Believers in human progress will be interested to know that since the law of 1801 there has been a reform introduced into this part of the legislation of the republic of Georgia. In 1818, a new law was passed, which, as will be seen, contains a grand remedy for the abuses of the old. In this it is provided, with endless variety of specifications and synonyms, as if to "let suspicion double-lock the door" against any possible evasion, that, "All and every will, testament and deed; whether by way of trust or otherwise, contract, or agreement, or stipulation, or other instrument in writing or by parol, made and executed for the purpose of effecting, or endeavoring to effect, the manumission of any slave or slaves, either directly . . . or indirectly, or virtually, &c. &c., shall be, and the same are hereby, declared to be utterly null and void." And the guilty author of the outrage against the peace of the state, contemplated in such deed, &c. &c., "and all and every person or persons concerned in giving or attempting to give effect thereto, . . . in any way or manner whatsoever, shall be severally liable to a penalty not exceeding one thousand dollars."

It would be quite anomalous in slave-law, and contrary to the "great and fundamental policy" of slave states, if the negroes who, not having the fear of God before their eyes, but being instigated by the devil, should be guilty of being thus manumitted, were suffered to go unpunished; accordingly, the law very properly and judiciously provides that "each and every slave or slaves in whose behalf such will or testament, &c. &c. &c., shall have been made, shall be liable to be *arrested* by warrant, &c.; and, *being thereof convicted,* &c., shall be liable to be sold as a slave or slaves by public outcry; and the proceeds of such slaves shall be appropriated, &c. &c."

Stroud's Sketch, pp. 147—8. Prince's Dig. 466.

Judge Stroud gives the following account of the law of Mississippi:

The emancipation must be by an *instrument in writing,* a last will or deed, &c., under seal, attested by at least *two credible witnesses,* or *acknowledged in the court* of the county or corporation where the emancipator resides; *proof satisfactory to the General Assembly* must be ad-

Stroud's Sketch, 149. Miss. Rev. Code, 385 —6 (Act June 18, 1822).

duced that the slave has done *some meritorious act for the benefit of his master*, or rendered *some distinguished service to the state;* all which circumstances are but *pre-requisites*, and are of no efficacy until a *special act of assembly* sanctions the emancipation; to which may be added, as has been already stated, a saving of the *rights of creditors*, and the protection of *the widow's thirds.*

The same *pre-requisite* of "*meritorious services*, to be adjudged of and allowed by the county court," is exacted by an act of the General Assembly of North Carolina; and all slaves emancipated contrary to the provisions of this act are to be committed to the jail of the county, and at the next court held for that county are to be sold to the highest bidder.

But the law of North Carolina does not refuse opportunity for repentance, even after the crime has been proved: accordingly,

The sheriff is directed, five days before the time for the sale of the *emancipated* negro, to give notice, in writing, to the person by whom the emancipation was made, to the end, Stroud's Sketch, 148. Haywood's Manual, 525, 526, 529, 537.

and with the hope that, smitten by remorse of conscience, and brought to a sense of his guilt before God and man,

such person may, if he thinks proper, renew his claim to the negro so emancipated by him; on failure to do which, the sale is to be made by the sheriff, and one-fifth part of the net proceeds is to become the property of the freeholder by whom the apprehension was made, and the remaining four-fifths are to be paid into the public treasury.

It is proper to add that we have given examples of the laws of states whose legislation on this subject has been most severe. The laws of Virginia, Maryland, Missouri, Kentucky and Louisiana, are much less stringent. Stroud, pp. 148—154.

A striking case, which shows how inexorably the law contends with the kind designs of the master, is on record in the reports of legal decisions in the State of Mississippi. The circumstances of the case have been thus briefly stated in the *New York Evening Post*, edited by Mr. William Cullen Bryant. They are a romance of themselves.

A man of the name of Elisha Brazealle, a planter in Jefferson County, Mississippi, was attacked with a loathsome disease. During his illness he was faithfully nursed by a mulatto slave, to whose assiduous attentions he felt that he owed his life. He was duly impressed by her devotion, and soon after his recovery took her to Ohio, and had her educated. She was very intelligent, and improved her advantages so rapidly that when he visited her again he determined to marry her. He executed a deed for her emancipation, and had it

recorded both in the States of Ohio and Mississippi, and made her his wife.

Mr. Brazealle returned with her to Mississippi, and, in process of time had a son. After a few years he sickened and died, leaving a will, in which, after reciting the deed of emancipation, he declared his intention to ratify it, and devised all his property to this lad, acknowledging him in the will to be such.

Some poor and distant relations in North Carolina, whom he did not know, and for whom he did not care, hearing of his death, came on to Mississippi, and claimed the property thus devised. They instituted a suit to recover the case (it is reported in Howard's Mississippi Reports, vol. II., p. 837) came before Judge Sharkey, our new consul at Havana. He decided it, and in that decision declared the act of emancipation *an offence against morality*, and pernicious and detestable as an example. He set *aside the will; gave the property of Brazealle to his distant relations, condemned Brazealle's son, and his wife, that* son's mother, again to bondage, and made them the slaves of these North Carolina kinsmen, as part of the assets of the estate.

Chief Justice Sharkey, after narrating the circumstances of the case, declares the validity of the deed of emancipation to be the main question in the controversy. He then argues that, although according to principles of national comity "contracts are to be construed according to the laws of the country or state where they are made," yet these principles are not to be followed when they lead to conclusions in conflict with "the great and fundamental policy of the state." What this "great and fundamental policy" is, in Mississippi, may be gathered from the remainder of the decision, which we give in full.

Let us apply these principles to the deed of emancipation. To give it validity would be, in the first place, a violation of the declared policy, and contrary to a positive law of the state.

The policy of a state is indicated by the general course of legislation on a given subject: and we find that free negroes are deemed offensive, because they are not permitted to emigrate to or remain in the state. They are allowed few privileges, and subject to heavy penalties for offences. They are required to leave the state within thirty days after notice, and in the mean time give security for good behavior; and those of them who can lawfully remain must register and carry with them their certificates, or they may be committed to jail. It would also violate a positive law, passed by the legislature, expressly to maintain this settled policy, and to prevent emancipation. No owner can emancipate his slave, but by a deed or will properly attested, or acknowledged in court, and proof to the legislature that such slave has performed some meritorious act for the benefit of the master, or some distinguished service for the state; and the deed or will can have no validity until ratified by special act of legislature. It is believed that this law and policy are too essentially important to the interests of our citizens to permit them to be evaded.

The state of the case shows conclusively that the contract had its origin in an offence against morality, pernicious and detestable as an example. But, above all, it seems to have been planned and executed with a fixed design to evade the rigor of the laws of this state. The acts of the party in going to Ohio with the slaves, and there executing the deed, and his immediate return with them to this state, point with unerring certainty to his purpose and object. The laws of this state cannot be thus defrauded of their operation by one of our own citizens. If we could have any doubts about the principle, the case reported in 1 Randolph, 15, would remove them.

As we think the validity of the deed must depend upon the laws of this state, it becomes unnecessary to inquire whether it could have any force by the laws of Ohio. If it were even valid there, it can have no force here. The consequence is, that the negroes, John Monroe and his mother, are still slaves, and a part of the estate of Elisha Brazealle. They have not acquired a right to their freedom under the will; for, even if the clause in the will were sufficient for that purpose, their emancipation has not been consummated by an act of the legislature.

John Monroe, being a slave, cannot take the property as devisee; and I apprehend it is equally clear that it cannot be held in trust for him. 4 Desans. Rep. 266. Independent of the principles laid down in adjudicated cases, our statute law prohibits slaves from owning certain kinds of property; and it may be inferred that the legislature supposed they were extending the act as far as it could be necessary to exclude them from owning any property, as the prohibition includes that kind of property which they would most likely be permitted to own without interruption, to wit, hogs, horses, cattle, &c. They cannot be prohibited from holding such property in consequence of its being of a dangerous or offensive character, but because it was deemed impolitic for them to hold property of any description. It follows, therefore, that his heirs are entitled to the property.

As the deed was void, and the devisee could not take under the will, the heirs might, perhaps, have had a remedy at law; but, as an account must be taken for the rents and profits, and for the final settlement of the estate, I see no good reason why they should be sent back to law. The remedy is, doubtless, more full and complete than it could be at law. The decree of the chancellor overruling the demurrer must be affirmed, and the cause remanded for further proceedings.

The Chief Justice Sharkey who pronounced this decision is stated by the *Evening Post* to have been a principal agent in the passage of the severe law under which this horrible inhumanity was perpetrated.

Nothing more forcibly shows the absolute despotism of the slave-law over all the kindest feelings and intentions of the master, and the determination of courts to carry these severities to their full lengths, than this cruel deed, which precipitated a young man who had been educated to consider himself free, and his mother, an educated woman, back into the bottomless abyss of slavery. Had this case been chosen for the theme of a novel, or a tragedy, the world would have cried out upon it as a plot of monstrous improbability. As it stands in the law-book, it is only a specimen of that awful kind of truth, stranger than fiction, which is all the time evolving, in one form or another, from the workings of this anomalous system.

This view of the subject is a very important one, and ought to be earnestly and gravely pondered by those in foreign countries, who are too apt to fasten their condemnation and opprobrium rather on the *person* of the slave-holder than on the horrors of the legal system. In some slave states it seems as if there was very little that the benevolent owner could do which should permanently benefit his slave, unless he should seek to *alter the laws*. Here it is that the highest obligation of the Southern Christian lies. Nor will the world or God hold *them* guiltless who, with the elective franchise in their hands, and the full power to speak, write and discuss, suffer this monstrous system of legalized cruelty to go on from age to age.

CHAPTER XIV.

THE HEBREW SLAVE-LAW COMPARED WITH THE AMERICAN SLAVE-LAW.

HAVING compared the American law with the Roman, we will now compare it with one other code of slave-laws, to wit, the Hebrew.

This comparison is the more important, because American slavery has been defended on the ground of God's permitting Hebrew slavery.

The inquiry now arises, What kind of slavery was it that was permitted among the Hebrews? for in different nations very different systems have been called by the general name of slavery.

That the patriarchal state of servitude which existed in the time of Abraham was a very different thing from American slavery, a few graphic incidents in the scripture narrative show; for we read that when the angels came to visit Abraham, although he had three hundred servants born in his house, it is said that *Abraham* hasted, and took a calf, and killed it, and gave it to a young man to dress; and that he told *Sarah* to take three measures of meal and knead it into cakes; and that, when all was done, he himself set it before his guests.

From various other incidents which appear in the patriarchal narrative, it would seem that these servants bore more the relation of the members of a Scotch clan to their feudal lord than that of an American slave to his master; —'thus it seems that if Abraham had died without children, his head servant would have been his heir.— Gen. 15 : 3.

Of what species, then, was the slavery which God permitted among the Hebrews? By what laws was it regulated?

In the New Testament the whole Hebrew system of administration is spoken of as a relatively imperfect one, and as superseded by the Christian dispensation.— Heb. 8 : 13.

We are taught thus to regard the Hebrew system as an educational system, by which a debased, half-civilized race, which had been degraded by slavery in its worst form among the Egyptians, was gradually elevated to refinement and humanity.

As they went from the land of Egypt, it would appear that the most disgusting personal habits, the most unheard-of and unnatural impurities, prevailed among them; so that it was necessary to make laws with relation to things of which Christianity has banished the very name from the earth.

Beside all this, polygamy, war and slavery, were the universal custom of nations. It is represented in the New Testament that God, in educating this people, proceeded in the same gradual manner in which a wise father would proceed with a family of children.

He selected a few of the most vital points of evil practice, and forbade them by positive statute, under rigorous penalties.

The worship of any other god was, by the Jewish law, constituted high treason, and rigorously punished with death.

As the knowledge of the true God and religious instruction could not then, as now, be afforded by printing and books, one day in the week had to be set apart for preserving in the minds of the people a sense of His being, and their obligations to Him. The devoting of this day to any other purpose was also punished with death; and the reason is obvious, that its sacredness was the principal means relied on for preserving the allegiance of the nation to their king and God, and its desecration, of course, led directly to high treason against the head of the state.

With regard to many other practices which prevailed among the Jews, as among other heathen nations, we find the Divine Being taking the same course which wise human legislators have taken.

When Lycurgus wished to banish money and its attendant luxuries from Sparta, he did not forbid it by direct statute-law, but he instituted a currency so clumsy and uncomfortable that, as we are informed by Rollin, it took a cart and pair of oxen to carry home the price of a very moderate estate.

In the same manner the Divine Being surrounded the customs of polygamy, war, blood-revenge and slavery, with regulations which gradually and certainly tended to abolish them entirely.

No one would pretend that the laws which God established in relation to polygamy, cities of refuge, &c., have any application to Christian nations now.

The following summary of some of these laws of the Mosaic code is given by Dr. C. E. Stowe, Professor of Biblical Literature in Andover Theological Seminary:

1. It commanded a Hebrew, even though a married man, with wife and children living, to take the childless widow of a deceased brother, and beget children with her. — Deut. 25 : 5—10.

2. The Hebrews, under certain restrictions, were allowed to make concubines, or wives for a limited time, of women taken in war. — Deut. 21 : 10—19.

3. A Hebrew who already had a wife was allowed to take another also, provided he still continued his intercourse with the first as her husband, and treated her kindly and affectionately. — Exodus 21 : 9—11.

4. By the Mosaic law, the nearest relative of a murdered Hebrew could pursue and slay the murderer, unless he could escape to the city of refuge; and the same permission was given in case of accidental homicide. — Num. 35 : 9—30.

5. The Israelites were commanded to exterminate the Canaanites, men, women and children. — Deut. 9 : 12; 20 : 16,—18.

Any one, or all, of the above practices, can be justified by the Mosaic law, as well as the practice of slave-holding.

Each of these laws, although in its time it was an ameliorating law, designed to take the place of some barbarous abuse, and to be a connecting link by which some higher state of society might be introduced, belongs confessedly to that system which St. Paul says made nothing perfect. They are a part of the commandment which he says was annulled for the weakness and unprofitableness thereof, and which, in the time which he wrote, was waxing old, and ready to vanish away. And Christ himself says, with regard to certain permissions of this system, that they were given on account of the "hardness of their hearts,"— because the attempt to enforce a more stringent system at that time, owing to human depravity, would have only produced greater abuses.

The following view of the Hebrew laws of slavery is compiled from Barnes' work on slavery, and from Professor Stowe's manuscript lectures.

The legislation commenced by making the great and common source of slavery — kidnapping — a capital crime.

The enactment is as follows: " He that stealeth a man and selleth him, or if he be found in his hand, he shall surely be put to death." —Exodus 21 : 16.

The sources from which slaves were to be obtained were thus reduced to two : first, the voluntary sale of an individual by himself, which certainly does not come under the designation of involuntary servitude ; second, the appropriation of captives taken in war, and the buying from the heathen.

With regard to the servitude of the Hebrew by a voluntary sale of himself, such servitude, by the statute-law of the land, came to an end once in seven years ; so that the worst that could be made of it was that it was a voluntary contract to labor for a certain time.

With regard to the servants bought of the heathen, or of foreigners in the land, there was a statute by which their servitude was annulled once in fifty years.

It has been supposed, from a disconnected view of one particular passage in the Mosaic code, that God directly countenanced the treating of a slave, who was a stranger and foreigner, with more rigor and severity than a Hebrew slave. That this was not the case will appear from the following enactments, which have express reference to strangers :

The stranger that dwelleth with you shall be unto you as one born among you, and thou shalt love him as thyself. — Lev. 19 : 34.

Thou shalt neither vex a stranger nor oppress him ; for ye were strangers in the land of Egypt. —Exodus 22 : 21.

Thou shalt not oppress a stranger, for ye know the heart of a stranger. — Exodus 23 : 9.

The Lord your God regardeth not persons. He doth execute the judgment of the fatherless and the widow, and loveth the stranger in giving him food and raiment ; love ye therefore the stranger. — Deut. 10 : 17—19.

Judge righteously between every man and his brother, and the stranger that is with him. — Deut. 1 : 16.

Cursed be he that perverteth the judgment of the stranger. — Deut. 27 : 19.

Instead of making slavery an oppressive institution with regard to the stranger, it was made by God a system within which heathen were adopted into the Jewish state, educated and instructed in the worship of the true God, and in due time emancipated.

In the first place, they were protected by law from personal violence. The loss of an eye or a tooth, through the violence of his master. took the slave out of that master's power entirely, and gave him his liberty. Then, further than this, if a master's conduct towards a slave was such as to induce him to run away, it was enjoined that nobody should assist in retaking him, and that he should dwell wherever he chose in the land, without molestation. Third, the law secured to the slave a very considerable portion of time, which was to be at his own disposal. Every seventh year was to be at his own disposal.— Lev. 25 : 4—6. Every seventh day was, of course, secured to him. — Ex. 20 : 10.

The servant had the privilege of attending the three great national festivals, when all the males of the nation were required to appear before God in Jerusalem. — Ex. 34 : 23.

Each of these festivals, it is computed, took up about three weeks.

The slave also was to be a guest in the family festivals. In Deut. 12 : 12, it is said, " Ye shall rejoice before the Lord your God, ye, and your sons, and your daughters, and your men-servants, and your maid-servants, and the Levite that is within your gates."

Dr. Barnes estimates that the whole amount of time which a servant could have to himself would amount to about twenty-three years out of fifty, or nearly one-half his time.

Again, the servant was placed on an exact equality with his master in all that concerned his religious relations.

Now, if we recollect that in the time of Moses the God and the king of the nation were one and the same person, and that the civil and religious relation were one and the same, it will appear that the slave and his master stood on an equality in their civil relation with regard to the state.

Thus, in Deuteronomy 29, is described a solemn national convocation, which took place before the death of Moses, when the whole nation were called upon, after a solemn review of their national history, to renew their constitutional oath of allegiance to their supreme Magistrate and Lord.

On this occasion, Moses addressed them thus : — " Ye stand this day, all of you. before the Lord your God ; your captains of your tribes, your elders, and your officers, with all the men of Israel, your little ones, your wives, and thy stranger that is in thy camp, *from the hewer of thy wood unto the drawer of thy water ;* that *thou* shouldest enter into covenant with the Lord thy God, and into his oath, which the Lord thy God maketh with thee this day."

How different is this from the cool and explicit declaration of South Carolina with regard to the position of the American slave :— " A slave is not generally regarded as legally *capable of being* Wheeler's law *within the peace of the state.* of Slavery, p. 243. He is not a citizen, and is not in that character entitled to her protection."

In all the religious services, which, as we have seen by the constitution of the nation, were civil services, the slave and the master mingled on terms of strict equality. There was none of the distinction which appertains to a distinct class or caste. " There was no special service appointed for them at unusual seasons. There were no particular seats assigned to them, to keep up the idea that they were a degraded class. There was no withholding from them the instruction which the word of God gave about the equal rights of mankind."

Fifthly. It was always contemplated that the slave would, as a matter of course, choose the Jewish religion, and the service of God, and enter willingly into all the obligations and services of the Jewish polity.

Mr. Barnes cites the words of Maimonides, to show how this was commonly understood by the Hebrews.— *Inquiry into the Scriptural Views of Slavery.* By Albert Barnes. p. 132.

Whether a servant be born in the power of an Israelite, or whether he be purchased from the heathen, the master is to bring them both into the covenant.

But he that is in the *house* is entered on the eighth day ; and he that is bought with money, on the day on which his master receives him, unless the slave be *unwilling.* For, if the master receive a grown slave, and he be *unwilling*, his master is to bear with him, to seek to win him over by instruction, and by love and kindness, for one year. After which, should he refuse so long, it is forbidden to keep him longer than a year. And the master must send him back to the strangers from whence he came. For the God of Jacob will not accept any other than the worship of a *willing* heart.— *Maimon. Hilcoth Miloth*, chap. i., sec. 8.

A sixth fundamental arrangement with regard to the Hebrew slave was that he *could never be sold.* Concerning this Mr. Barnes remarks :

A man, in certain circumstances, *might be bought* by a Hebrew ; but when once bought, that was an end of the matter. There is not the slightest evidence that any Hebrew ever sold a slave ; and any provision contemplating that was unknown to the constitution of the Commonwealth. It is said of Abraham that he had " servants bought with money ;" but there is no record of his having ever sold one, nor is there any account of its ever having been done by Isaac or

Jacob. The only instance of a *sale* of this kind among the patriarchs is that act of the brothers of Joseph, which is held up to so strong reprobation, by which they sold him to the Ishmaelites. Permission is given in the law of Moses to *buy* a servant, but none is given to *sell* him again ; and the fact that no such permission is given is full proof that it was not contemplated. When he entered into that relation, it became certain that there could be no change, unless it was voluntary on his part (comp. Ex. 21 : 5, 6), or unless his master gave him his freedom, until the not distant period fixed by law when he could be free. There is no arrangement in the law of Moses by which servants were to be taken in payment of their master's debts, by which they were to be given as pledges, by which they were to be consigned to the keeping of others, or by which they were to be given away as presents. There are no instances occurring in the Jewish history in which any of these things were done. This law is positive in regard to the Hebrew servant, and the principle of the law would apply to all others. Lev. 25 : 42. — " They shall not be sold as bondmen." In all these respects there was a marked difference, and there was doubtless intended to be, between the estimate affixed to servants and to property.— *Inquiry*, &c., p. 133—4.

As to the practical workings of this system, as they are developed in the incidents of sacred history, they are precisely what we should expect from such a system of laws. For instance, we find it mentioned incidentally in the ninth chapter of the first book of Samuel, that when Saul and his servant came to see Samuel, that Samuel, in anticipation of his being crowned king, made a great feast for him ; and in verse twenty-second the history says : " And Samuel took Saul *and his servant*, and brought them into the parlor, and made *them* sit in the chiefest place."

We read, also, in 2 Samuel 9 : 10, of a servant of Saul who had large estates, and twenty servants of his own.

We find, in 1 Chron. 2 : 34, the following incident related : " Now, Sheshan had no sons, but daughters. And Sheshan had a servant, an Egyptian, whose name was Jarha. And Sheshan gave his daughter to Jarha, his servant, to wife."

Does this resemble American slavery ?

We find, moreover, that this connection was not considered at all disgraceful, for the son of this very daughter was enrolled among the valiant men of David's army. — 1 Chron. 2 : 41.

In fine, we are not surprised to discover that the institutions of Moses in effect so obliterated all the characteristics of slavery, that it had ceased to exist among the Jews long before the time of Christ. Mr. Barnes asks :

On what evidence would a man rely to prove

that slavery existed at all in the land in the time of the later prophets of the Maccabees, or when the Saviour appeared? There are abundant proofs, as we shall see, that it existed in Greece and Rome ; but what is the evidence that it existed in Judea? So far as I have been able to ascertain, there are no declarations that it did to be found in the canonical books of the Old Testament, or in Josephus. There are no allusions to laws and customs which imply that it was prevalent. There are no coins or medals which suppose it. There are no facts which do not admit of an easy explanation on the supposition that slavery had ceased. — *Inquiry*, &c., p. 226.

Two objections have been urged to the interpretations which have been given of two of the enactments before quoted.

1. It is said that the enactment, " Thou shalt not return to his master the servant that has escaped," &c., relates only to servants escaping from heathen masters to the Jewish nation.

The following remarks on this passage are from Prof. Stowe's lectures:

Deuteronomy 23: 15, 16.— These words make a statute which, like every other statute, is to be strictly construed. There is nothing in the language to limit its meaning ; there is nothing in the connection in which it stands to limit its meaning ; nor is there anything in the history of the Mosaic legislation to limit the application of this statute to the case of servants escaping from foreign masters. The assumption that it is thus limited is wholly gratuitous, and, so far as the Bible is concerned, unsustained by any evidence whatever. It is said that it would be absurd for Moses to enact such a law while servitude existed among the Hebrews. It would indeed be absurd, were it the object of the Mosaic legislation to sustain and perpetuate slavery ; but, if it were the object of Moses to limit and to restrain, and finally to extinguish slavery, this statute was admirably adapted to his purpose. That it was the object of Moses to extinguish, and not to perpetuate, slavery, is perfectly clear from the whole course of his legislation on the subject. Every slave was to have all the religious privileges and instruction to which his master's children were entitled. Every seventh year released the Hebrew slave, and every fiftieth year produced universal emancipation. If a master, by an accidental or an angry blow, deprived the slave of a tooth, the slave, by that act, was forever free. And so, by the statute in question, if the slave felt himself oppressed, he could make his escape, and, though the master was not forbidden to retake him if he could,

every one was forbidden to aid his master in doing it. This statute, in fact, made the servitude voluntary, and that was what Moses intended.

Moses dealt with slavery precisely as he dealt with polygamy and with war: without directly prohibiting, he so restricted as to destroy it ; instead of cutting down the poison-tree, he girdled it, and left it to die of itself. There is a statute in regard to military expeditions precisely analogous to this celebrated fugitive slave law. Had Moses designed to perpetuate a warlike spirit among the Hebrews, the statute would have been preëminently absurd ; but, if it was his design to crush it, and to render foreign wars almost impossible, the statute was exactly adapted to his purpose. It rendered foreign military service, in effect, entirely voluntary, just as the fugitive law rendered domestic servitude, in effect, voluntary.

The law may be found at length in Deuteronomy 20: 5—10 ; and let it be carefully read and compared with the fugitive slave law already adverted to. Just when the men are drawn up ready for the expedition,— just at the moment when even the hearts of brave men are apt to fail them,— the officers are commanded to address the soldiers thus :

" What man of you is there that hath built a new house, and hath not dedicated it? Let him go and return to his house, lest he die in the battle, and another man dedicate it.

" And what man is he that hath planted a vineyard and hath not yet eaten of it? Let him also go and return to his house, lest he die in the battle, and another man eat of it.

" And what man is there that hath betrothed a wife, and hath not taken her? Let him go and return unto his house, lest he die in the battle, and another man take her."

And the officers shall speak further unto the people, and they shall say, " What man is there that is fearful and faint-hearted? Let him go and return unto his house, lest his brethren's heart faint, as well as his heart."

Now, consider that the Hebrews were exclusively an agricultural people, that warlike parties necessarily consist mainly of young men, and that by this statute every man who had built a house which he had not yet lived in, and every man who had planted a vineyard from which he had not yet gathered fruit, and every man who had engaged a wife whom he had not yet married, and every one who felt timid and faint-hearted, was permitted and commanded to go home,— how many would there probably be left? Especially when the officers, instead of exciting their military ardor by visions of glory and of splendor, were commanded to repeat it over and over again that they would probably die in the battle and never get home, and hold this idea up before them as if it were the only idea suitable for their purpose, how excessively absurd is the whole statute considered as a military law,— just as absurd as the Mosaic fugitive law, understood in its widest application, is, considered as a slave law!

It is clearly the object of this military law to put an end to military expeditions; for, with this law in force, such expeditions must always be entirely volunteer expeditions. Just as clearly was it the object of the fugitive slave law to put an end to compulsory servitude; for, with that law in force, the servitude must, in effect, be, to a great extent, voluntary,— and that is just what the legislator intended. There is no possibility of limiting the law, on account of its absurdity, when understood in its widest sense, except by proving that the Mosaic legislation was designed to perpetuate and not to limit slavery; and this certainly cannot be proved, for it is directly contrary to the plain matter of fact.

I repeat it, then, again : there is nothing in the language of this statute, there is nothing in the connection in which it stands, there is nothing in the history of the Mosaic legislation on this subject, to limit the application of the law to the case of servants escaping from foreign masters; but every consideration, from every legitimate source, leads us to a conclusion directly the opposite. Such a limitation is the arbitrary, unsupported *stet voluntas pro ratione* assumption of the commentator, and nothing else. The only shadow of a philological argument that I can see, for limiting the statute, is found in the use of the words *to thee*, in the fifteenth verse. It may be said it that the pronoun *thee* is used in a *national* and not *individual* sense, implying an escape from some other nation to the Hebrews. But, examine the statute immediately preceding this, and observe the use of the pronoun *thee* in the thirteenth verse. Most obviously, the pronouns in these statutes are used with reference to the *individuals* addressed, and not in a collective or national sense exclusively ; very rarely, if ever, can this sense be given to them in the way claimed by the argument referred to.

2. It is said that the proclamation, "Thou shalt proclaim liberty through the land to

all the inhabitants thereof," related only to Hebrew slaves. This assumption is based entirely on the supposition that the slave was not considered, in Hebrew law, as a person, as an inhabitant of the land, and a member of the state; but we have just proved that in the most solemn transaction of the state the hewer of wood and drawer of water is expressly designated as being just as much an actor and participator as his master; and it would be absurd to suppose that, in a statute addressed to all the inhabitants of the land, he is not included as an inhabitant.

Barnes enforces this idea by some pages of quotations from Jewish writers, which will fully satisfy any one who reads his work.

From a review, then, of all that relates to the Hebrew slave-law, it will appear that it was a very well-considered and wisely-adapted system of education and gradual emancipation. No rational man can doubt that if the same laws were enacted and the same practices prevailed with regard to slavery in the United States, that the system of American slavery might be considered, to all intents and purposes, practically at an end. If there is any doubt of this fact, and it is still thought that the permission of slavery among the Hebrews justifies American slavery, in all fairness the experiment of making the two systems alike ought to be tried, and we should then see what would be the result.

CHAPTER XV.

SLAVERY IS DESPOTISM.

IT is always important, in discussing a thing, to keep before our minds exactly what it is.

The only means of understanding precisely what a civil institution is are an examination of the laws which regulate it. In different ages and nations, very different things have been called by the name of slavery. Patriarchal servitude was one thing, Hebrew servitude was another, Greek and Roman servitude still a third ; and these institutions differed very much from each other. What, then, is American slavery, as we have seen it exhibited by law, and by the decisions of courts ?

Let us begin by stating what it is not.

1. It is not apprenticeship.
2. It is not guardianship.

3. It is in no sense a system for the education of a weaker race by a stronger.

4. The happiness of the governed is in no sense its object.

5. The temporal improvement or the eternal well-being of the governed is in no sense its object.

The object of it has been distinctly stated in one sentence, by Judge Ruffin,—"The end is the profit of the master, his security, and the public safety."

Slavery, then, is absolute despotism, of the most unmitigated form.

It would, however, be doing injustice to the absolutism of any *civilized* country to liken American slavery to it. The absolute governments of Europe none of them pretend to be founded on a *property* right of the governor to the persons and entire capabilities of the governed.

This is a form of despotism which exists only in some of the most savage countries of the world; as, for example, in Dahomey.

The European absolutism or despotism, now, does, to some extent, recognize the happiness and welfare of the *governed* as the foundation of government; and the ruler is considered as invested with power *for the benefit of the people ;* and his right to rule is supposed to be in somewhat predicated upon the idea that he better understands how to promote the good of the people than they themselves do. No government in the *civilized* world now presents the pure despotic idea, as it existed in the old days of the Persian and Assyrian rule.

The arguments which defend slavery must be substantially the same as those which defend despotism of any other kind; and the objections which are to be urged against it are precisely those which can be urged against despotism of any other kind. The customs and practices to which it gives rise are precisely those to which despotisms in all ages have given rise.

Is the slave suspected of a crime? His master has the power to examine him by torture (see State *v.* Castleman). His master has, in fact, in most cases, the power of life and death, owing to the exclusion of the slave's evidence. He has the power of banishing the slave, at any time, and without giving an account to anybody, to an exile as dreadful as that of Siberia, and to labors as severe as those of the galleys. He has also unlimited power over the character of his slave. He can accuse him of any crime, yet withhold from him all right of trial or investigation; and sell him into captivity, with his name blackened by an unexamined imputation.

These are all abuses for which despotic governments are blamed. They are powers which good men who are despotic rulers are beginning to disuse ; but, under the flag of every slave-holding state, and under the flag of the whole United States in the District of Columbia, they are committed indiscriminately to men of any character.

But the worst kind of despotism has been said to be that which extends alike over the body and over the soul ; which can bind the liberty of the conscience, and deprive a man of all right of choice in respect to the manner in which he shall learn the will of God, and worship Him. In other days, kings on their thrones, and cottagers by their firesides, alike trembled before a despotism which declared itself able to bind and to loose, to open and to shut the kingdom of heaven.

Yet this power to control the conscience, to control the religious privileges, and all the opportunities which man has of acquaintanceship with his Maker, and of learning to do his will, is, under the flag of every slave state, and under the flag of the United States, placed in the hands of any men, of any character, who can afford to pay for it.

It is a most awful and most solemn truth that the greatest republic in the world does sustain under her national flag the worst system of despotism which can possibly exist.

With regard to one point to which we have adverted,— the power of the master to deprive the slave of a legal trial while accusing him of crime,— a very striking instance has occurred in the District of Columbia, within a year or two. The particulars of the case, as stated, at the time, in several papers, were briefly these : A gentleman in Washington, our national capital,— an elder in the Presbyterian church,— held a female slave, who had, for some years, supported a good character in a Baptist church of that city. He accused her of an attempt to poison his family, and immediately placed her in the hands of a slave-dealer, who took her over and imprisoned her in the slave-pen at Alexandria, to await the departure of a coffle. The poor girl had a mother, who felt as any mother would naturally feel.

When apprized of the situation of her daughter, she flew to the pen, and, with tears, besought an interview with her only child ; but she was cruelly repulsed, and told to be gone ! She then tried to see the elder, but failed. She had the promise of money sufficient to purchase her daughter, but the owner would listen to no terms of compromise.

In her distress, the mother repaired to a lawyer in the city, and begged him to give form to her petition in writing. She stated to him what she wished to have said, and he arranged it for her in such a form as she herself might have presented it in, had not the benefits of education been denied her. The following is the letter:

Washington, July 25, 1851.

Mr. ——.

Sir : I address you as a rich Christian freeman and father, while I am myself but a poor slavemother ! I come to plead with you for an only child whom I love, who is a professor of the Christian religion with yourself, and a member of a Christian church ; and who, by your act of ownership, now pines in her imprisonment in a loathsome man-warehouse, where she is held for sale ! I come to plead with you for the exercise of that blessed law, "Whatsoever ye would that men should do unto you, do ye even so to them."

With great labor, I have found friends who are willing to aid me in the purchase of my child, to save us from a cruel separation. You, as a *father*, can judge of my feelings when I was told that you had decreed her banishment to *distant* as well as to *hopeless* bondage !

For nearly six years my child has done for you the hard labor of a slave ; from the age of sixteen to twenty-two, she has done the hard work of your chamber, kitchen, cellar, and stables. By night and by day, your will and your commands have been her highest law ; and all this has been unrequited toil. If in all this time her scanty allowance of tea and coffee has been sweetened, it has been at the cost of her slave-mother, and not at yours.

You are an office-bearer in the church, and a man of *prayer*. As such, and as the absolute owner of my child, I ask candidly whether she has enjoyed such mild and gentle treatment, and amiable example, as she ought to have had, to encourage her in her monotonous bondage? Has she received at your hands, in faithful religious instruction in the Word of God, a full and fair compensation for all her toil ? It is not to me alone that you must answer these questions. You acknowledge the high authority of His laws who preached a deliverance to the captive, and who commands you to give to your servant "that which is just and equal." O ! I entreat you, withhold not, at this trying hour, from my child that which will cut off her last hope, and which may endanger your own soul !

It has been said that you charge my daughter with crime. Can this be really so? Can it be that you would set aside the obligations of honor and good citizenship, — that you would dare to sell the guilty one away for money, rather than bring her to trial, which you *know* she is ready to meet ? What would you say, if you were accused of guilt, and refused a trial ? Is not her fair name as precious to her, in the church to which she belongs, as yours can be to you ?

Suppose, now, for a moment, that *your* daughter, whom you love, instead of mine, was in these hot days incarcerated in a *negro-pen*, subject to my control, fed on the coarsest food, committed to the entire will of a brute, denied the privilege commonly allowed even to the murderer — that of seeing the face of his friends ? O ! then, you would FEEL ! Feel soon, then, for a poor slavemother and her child, and do for us as you shall wish you had done when we shall meet before the Great Judge, and when it shall be your greatest joy to say, "I *did* let the oppressed free."

ELLEN BROWN.

The girl, however, was sent off to the Southern market.

The writer has received these incidents from the gentleman who wrote the letter. Whether the course pursued by the master was strictly legal is a point upon which we are not entirely certain ; that it was a course in which the law did not in fact interfere is quite plain, and it is also very apparent that it was a course against which public sentiment did not remonstrate. The man who exercised this power was a professedly religious man, enjoying a position of importance in a Christian church ; and it does not appear, from any movements in the Christian community about him, that they did not consider his course a justifiable one.

Yet is not this kind of power the very one at which we are so shocked when we see it exercised by foreign despots ?

Do we not read with shuddering that in Russia, or in Austria, a man accused of crime is seized upon, separated from his friends, allowed no opportunities of trial or of self-defence, but hurried off to Siberia, or some other dreaded exile ?

Why is despotism any worse in the governor of a state than in a private individual ?

There is a great controversy now going on in the world between the despotic and the republican principle. All the common arguments used in support of slavery are arguments that apply with equal strength to despotic government, and there are some arguments in favor of despotic governments that do not apply to individual slavery.

There are arguments, and quite plausible ones, in favor of despotic government. Nobody can deny that it possesses a certain kind of efficiency, compactness, and promptness of movement, which cannot, from the nature of things, belong to a republic. Despotism has established and sustained much more efficient systems of police than ever a republic did. The late King of Prussia, by the possession of absolute despotic power, was enabled to carry out a much more efficient system of popular education than we ever have succeeded in carrying out in America. He districted his kingdom in the most thorough manner, and obliged every parent, whether he would or not, to have his children thoroughly educated.

If we reply to all this, as we do, that the possession of absolute power in a man qualified to use it right is undoubtedly calculated for the good of the state, but that there are so few men that know how to use it, that this form of government is not, on the whole, a safe one, then we have stated an argument that goes to overthrow slavery as much as it does a despotic government; for certainly the chances are much greater of finding one man, in the course of fifty years, who is capable of wisely using this power, than of finding thousands of men every day in our streets, who can be trusted with such power. It is a painful and most serious fact, that America trusts to the hands of the most brutal men of her country, equally with the best, that despotic power which she thinks an unsafe thing even in the hands of the enlightened, educated and cultivated Emperor of the Russias.

With all our republican prejudices, we cannot deny that Nicholas is a man of talent, with a mind liberalized by education; we have been informed, also, that he is a man of serious and religious character; — he certainly, acting as he does in the eye of all the world, must have great restraint upon him from public opinion, and a high sense of character. But who is the man to whom American laws intrust powers more absolute than those of Nicholas of Russia, or Ferdinand of Naples? He may have been a pirate on the high seas; he may be a drunkard; he may, like Souther, have been con-victed of a brutality at which humanity turns pale; but, for all that, American slave-law will none the less trust him with this irresponsible power,— power over the body, and power over the soul.

On which side, then, stands the American nation, in the great controversy which is now going on between self-government and despotism? On which side does America stand, in the great controversy for liberty of conscience?

Do foreign governments exclude their population from the reading of the Bible? — The slave of America is excluded by the most effectual means possible. Do we say, "Ah! but we read the Bible to our slaves, and present the gospel orally?" — This is precisely what religious despotism in Italy says. Do we say that we have no objection to our slaves reading the Bible, if they will stop there; but that with this there will come in a flood of general intelligence, which will upset the existing state of things? — This is precisely what is said in Italy.

Do we say we should be willing that the slave should read his Bible, but that he, in his ignorance, will draw false and erroneous conclusions from it, and for that reason we prefer to impart its truths to him orally? — This, also, is precisely what the religious despotism of Europe says.

Do we say, in our vain-glory, that despotic government dreads the coming in of anything calculated to elevate and educate the people? — And is there not the same dread through all the despotic slave governments of America?

On which side, then, does the American nation stand, in the great, last QUESTION of the age?

PART III.

CHAPTER I.

The utter inefficiency of the law to protect the slave in any respect has been shown.

But it is claimed that, precisely because the law affords the slave no protection, therefore public opinion is the more strenuous in his behalf.

Nothing more frequently strikes the eye, in running over judicial proceedings in the courts of slave states, than announcements of the utter inutility of the law to rectify some glaring injustice towards this unhappy race, coupled with congratulatory remarks on that beneficent state of *public sentiment* which is to supply entirely this acknowledged deficiency of the law.

On this point it may, perhaps, be sufficient to ask the reader, whether North or South, to review in his own mind the judicial documents which we have presented, and ask himself what inference is to be drawn, as to the state of public sentiment, from the cases there presented, — from the pleas of lawyers, the decisions of judges, the facts sworn to by witnesses, and the general style and spirit of the whole proceedings.

In order to appreciate this more fully, let us compare a trial in a free state with a trial in a slave state.

In the free State of Massachusetts, a man of standing, learning and high connections, murdered another man. He did not torture him, but with one blow sent him in a moment from life. The murderer had every advantage of position, of friends; it may be said, indeed, that he had the sympathy of the whole United States; yet how calmly, with what unmoved and awful composure, did the judicial examination proceed! The murderer was condemned to die — what a sensation shook the country! Even sovereign states assumed the attitude of petitioners for him.

There was a voice of entreaty, from Maine to New Orleans. There were remonstrances, and there were threats; but still, with what passionless calmness retributive justice held on its way! Though the men who were her instruments were men of merciful and bleeding hearts, yet they bowed in silence to her sublime will. In spite of all that influence and wealth and power could do, a cultivated and intelligent man, from the first rank of society, suffered the same penalty that would fall on any other man who violated the sanctity of human life.

Now, compare this with a trial in a slave state. In Virginia, Souther also murdered a man; but he did not murder him by one merciful blow, but by twelve hours of torture so horrible that few readers could bear even the description of it. It was a mode of death which, to use the language that Cicero in his day applied to crucifixion, "ought to be forever removed from the sight, hearing, and from the very thoughts of mankind." And to this horrible scene two white men were WITNESSES!

Observe the mode in which these two cases were tried, and the general sensation they produced. Hear the lawyers, in this case of Souther, coolly debating whether it can be considered any crime at all. Hear the decision of the inferior court, that it is murder in the *second degree*, and apportioning as its reward five years of imprisonment. See the horrible butcher coming up to the Superior Court in the attitude of an injured man! See the case recorded as that of *Souther* VERSUS *The Commonwealth*, and let us ask any intelligent man, North or South, what sort of public sentiment does this show!

Does it show a belief that the negro is a man? Does it not show decidedly that he is *not* considered as a man? Consider further the horrible principle which, reaffirmed in the case, is the law of the land in Virginia. *It is the policy of the law, in respect to the relation of master and slave, and for the sake of securing proper subordination on the part of the slave, to protect the master from prosecution in all such cases, even if the whipping and punishment be malicious, cruel and excessive!*

When the most cultivated and intelligent men in the state formally, calmly and without any apparent perception of saying anything inhuman, utter such an astounding decision as this, what *can* be thought of it? If they do not consider this cruel, what is cruel? And, if their feelings are so blunted as to see no cruelty in such a decision, what hope is there of any protection to the slave?

This law is a plain and distinct permission to such wretches as Souther to inflict upon the helpless slave any torture they may choose, without any accusation or impeachment of crime. It distinctly tells Souther, and the white witnesses who saw his deed, and every other low, unprincipled man in the court, that it is the policy of the law to protect him in malicious, cruel and excessive punishments.

What sort of an education is this for the intelligent and cultivated men of a state to communicate to the lower and less-educated class? Suppose it to be solemnly announced in Massachusetts, with respect to free laborers or apprentices, that it is the policy of the law, for the sake of producing subordination, to protect the master in inflicting any punishment, however cruel, malicious and excessive, short of death. We cannot imagine such a principle declared, without a rebellion and a storm of popular excitement to which that of Bunker Hill was calmness itself; — but, supposing the State of Massachusetts were so "twice dead and plucked up by the roots" as to allow such a decision to pass without comment concerning her working classes, — suppose it did pass, and become an active, operative reality, what kind of an educational influence would it exert upon the commonwealth? What kind of an estimate of the working classes would it show in the minds of those who make and execute the law?

What an immediate development of villany and brutality would be brought out by such a law, avowedly made to protect men in cruelty! Cannot men be cruel enough, without all the majesty of law being brought into operation to sanction it, and make it reputable?

And suppose it were said, in vindication of such a law, " O, of course, no respectable, humane man would ever think of taking advantage of it." Should we not think the

old State of Massachusetts sunk very low, to have on her legal records direct assurances of protection to deeds which no decent man would ever do?

And, when this shocking permission is brought in review at the judgment-seat of Christ, and the awful Judge shall say to its makers, aiders, and abettors, Where is thy brother? — when all the souls that have called from under the altar, "How long, O Lord, dost thou not judge and avenge our blood," shall rise around the judgment-seat as a great cloud of witnesses, and the judgment is set and the books are opened, — what answer will be made for such laws and decisions as these?

Will they tell the great Judge that it was necessary to preserve the slave system, — that it could not be preserved without them?

Will they dare look upon those eyes, which are as a flame of fire, with any such avowal?

Will He not answer, as with a voice of thunders, "Ye have killed the poor and needy, and ye have forgotten that the Lord was his helper"?

The deadly sin of slavery is its denial of humanity to man. This has been the sin of oppression, in every age. To tread down, to vilify and crush, the image of God, in the person of the poor and lowly, has been the great sin of man since the creation of the world. Against this sin all the prophets of ancient times poured forth their thunders. A still stronger witness was borne against this sin when God, in Jesus Christ, took human nature, and made each human being a brother of the Lord. But the last and most sublime witness shall be borne when a MAN shall judge the whole earth — a Man who shall acknowledge for His brother the meanest slave, equally with the proudest master.

In most singular and affecting terms it is asserted in the Bible that the Father hath committed all judgment to the Son, BECAUSE HE IS THE SON OF MAN. That human nature, which, in the person of the poor slave, has been despised and rejected, scoffed and scorned, scourged and tortured, shall in that day be glorified; and it shall appear the most fearful of sins to have made light of the sacredness of humanity, as these laws and institutions of slavery have done. The fact is, that the whole system of slave-law, and the whole practice of the slave system, and the public sentiment that is formed by it, are alike based on the greatest of all heresies, *a denial of equal human brotherhood.* A whole race has been thrown out of the range of human existence, their immortality disregarded, their dignity as children of God scoffed at, their brotherhood with Christ treated as a fable, and all the law and public sentiment and practice with regard to them such as could be justified only on supposition that they were a race of inferior animals.

It is because the negro is considered an *inferior animal,* and not worthy of any better treatment, that the system which relates to him and the treatment which falls to him are considered humane.

Take any class of white men, however uneducated, and place them under the same system of laws, and make their civil condition in all respects like that of the negro, and would it not be considered the most outrageous cruelty?

Suppose the slave-law were enacted with regard to all the Irish in our country, and they were parcelled off as the property of any man who had money enough to buy them. Suppose their right to vote, their right to bring suit in any case, their right to bear testimony in courts of justice, their right to contract a legal marriage, their right to hold property or to make contracts of any sort, were all by one stroke of law blotted out. Furthermore, suppose it was forbidden to teach them to read and write, and that their children to all ages were "doomed to live without knowledge." Suppose that, in judicial proceedings, it were solemnly declared, with regard to them, that the *mere beating* of an Irishman, "apart from any circumstances of cruelty, or any attempt to kill," was no offence against the peace of the state. Suppose that it were declared that, for the better preservation of subjection among them, the law would protect the master in any kind of punishment inflicted, even if it should appear to be malicious, cruel and excessive; and suppose that monsters like Souther, in availing themselves of this permission, should occasionally torture Irishmen to death, but still this circumstance should not be deemed of sufficient importance to call for any restriction on the part of the master. Suppose it should be coolly said, " O yes, Irishmen are occasionally tortured to death, we know; but it is not by any means a *general* occurrence; in fact, no men of position in society would do it; and when cases of the kind do occur, they are indignantly frowned upon."

Suppose it should be stated that the reason that the law restraining the power of the master cannot be made any more stringent is, that the general system cannot be maintained without allowing this extent of power to the master.

Suppose that, having got all the Irishmen in the country down into this condition, they should maintain that such was the public sentiment of humanity with regard to them as abundantly to supply the want of all legal rights, and to make their condition, on the whole, happier than if they were free. Should we not say that a public sentiment which saw no cruelty in thus depriving a whole race of every right dear to manhood could see no cruelty in anything, and had proved itself wholly unfit to judge upon the subject? What man would not rather see his children in the grave than see them slaves? What man, who, should he wake to-morrow morning in the condition of an American slave, would not wish himself in the grave? And yet all the defenders of slavery start from the point that this legal condition is not *of itself* a cruelty! They would hold it the last excess of cruelty with regard to themselves, or any white man; why do they call it no cruelty at all with regard to the negro?

The writer in defence of slavery in *Fraser's Magazine* justifies this depriving of a whole class of any legal rights, by urging that " the good there is in human nature will supply the deficiencies of human legislation." This remark is one most significant, powerful index of the state of public sentiment, produced even in a generous mind, by the slave system. This writer thinks the good there is in human nature will supply the absence of all legal rights to thousands and millions of human beings. He thinks it right to risk their bodies and their souls on the good there is in human nature; yet this very man would not send a fifty-dollar bill through the post-office, in an unsealed letter, trusting to " the good there is in human nature."

Would this man dare to place his children in the position of slaves, and trust them to " the good in human nature " ?

Would he buy an estate from the most honorable man of his acquaintance, and have no legal record of the deed, trusting to "the good in human nature"? And if " the good in human nature" will not suffice for him and his children, how will it suffice for his brother and his brother's children? Is his happiness of any more importance in God's sight than his brother's happiness, that his must be secured by legal bolts, and bonds, and bars, and his brother's left to "the good there is in human nature"? Never are we so impressed with the utter deadness of public sentiment to protect the slave, as when we see such opinions as these uttered by men of a naturally generous and noble character.

The most striking and the most painful examples of the perversion of public sentiment, with regard to the negro race, are often given in the writings of men of humanity, amiableness and piety.

That devoted laborer for the slave, the Rev. Charles C. Jones, thus expresses his sense of the importance of one African soul:

> Were it now revealed to us that the most extensive system of instruction which we could devise, requiring a vast amount of labor and protracted through ages, would result in the tender mercy of our God in the salvation of the soul of *one poor African*, we should feel warranted in cheerfully entering upon our work, with all its costs and sacrifices.

What a noble, what a sublime spirit, is here breathed! Does it not show a mind capable of the very highest impulses?

And yet, if we look over his whole writings, we shall see painfully how the moral sense of the finest mind may be perverted by constant familiarity with such a system.

We find him constructing an appeal to masters to have their slaves *orally* instructed in religion. In many passages he speaks of oral instruction as confessedly an imperfect species of instruction, very much inferior to that which results from personal reading and examination of the Word of God. He says, in one place, that in order to do much good it must be begun very early in life, and intimates that people in advanced years can acquire very little from it; and yet he decidedly expresses his opinion that slavery is an institution with which no Christian has cause to interfere.

The slaves, according to his own showing, are cut off from the best means for the salvation of their souls, and restricted to one of a very inferior nature. They are placed under restriction which makes their souls as dependent upon others for spiritual food as a man without hands is dependent upon others for bodily food. He recognizes the fact, which his own experience must show him, that the slave is at all times liable to pass into the hands of those who will not take the trouble thus to feed his soul; nay, if we may judge from his urgent appeals to masters, he perceives around him many who,

having spiritually cut off the slave's hands, refuse to feed him. He sees that, by the operation of this law as a matter of fact, thousands are placed in situations where the perdition of the soul is almost certain, and yet he declares that he does not feel called upon at all to interfere with their civil condition!

But, if the soul of every poor African is of that inestimable worth which Mr. Jones believes, does it not follow that he ought to have the very best means for getting to heaven which it is possible to give him? And is not he who can read the Bible for himself in a better condition than he who is dependent upon the reading of another? If it be said that such teaching cannot be afforded, because it makes them unsafe property, ought not a clergyman like Mr. Jones to meet this objection in his own expressive language:

> Were it now revealed to us that the most extensive system of instruction which we could devise, requiring a vast amount of labor and protracted through ages, would result in the tender mercy of our God in the salvation of the soul of *one poor African*, we should feel warranted in cheerfully entering upon our work, with all its costs and sacrifices.

Should not a clergyman, like Mr. Jones, tell masters that they should risk the loss of all things seen and temporal, rather than incur the hazard of bringing eternal ruin on these souls? All the arguments which Mr. Jones so eloquently used with masters, to persuade them to give their slaves oral instruction, would apply with double force to show their obligation to give the slave the power of reading the Bible for himself.

Again, we come to hear Mr. Jones telling masters of the power they have over the souls of their servants, and we hear him say,

> We may, according to the power lodged in our hands, forbid religious meetings and religious instruction on our own plantations; we may forbid our servants going to church at all, or only to such churches as we may select for them. We may literally shut up the kingdom of heaven against men, and suffer not them that are entering to go in.

And, when we hear Mr. Jones say all this, and then consider that he must see and know this awful power is often lodged in the hands of wholly irreligious men, in the hands of men of the most profligate character, we can account for his thinking such a system right only by attributing it to that blinding, deadening influence which the public sentiment of slavery exerts even over the best-constituted minds.

Neither Mr. Jones nor any other Christian minister would feel it right that the eternal happiness of their own children should be thus placed in the power of any man who should have money to pay for them. How, then, can they think it right that this power be given in the case of their African brother?

Does this not show that, even in case of the most humane and Christian people, who theoretically believe in the equality of all souls before God, a constant familiarity with slavery works a practical infidelity on this point; and that they give their assent to laws which practically declare that the salvation of the servant's soul is of less consequence than the salvation of the property relation?

Let us not be thought invidious or uncharitable in saying, that where slavery exists there are so many causes necessarily uniting to corrupt public sentiment with regard to the slave, that the best-constituted minds cannot trust themselves in it. In the northern and free states public sentiment has been, and is, to this day, fatally infected by the influence of a past and the proximity of a present system of slavery. Hence the injustice with which the negro in many of our states is treated. Hence, too, those apologies for slavery, and defences of it, which issue from Northern presses, and even Northern pulpits. If even at the North the remains of slavery can produce such baleful effects in corrupting public sentiment, how much more must this be the case where this institution is in full force!

The whole American nation is, in some sense, under a paralysis of public sentiment on this subject. It was said by a heathen writer that the gods gave us a fearful power when they gave us the faculty of becoming accustomed to things. This power has proved a fearful one indeed in America. We have got used to things which might stir the dead in their graves.

When but a small portion of the things daily done in America has been told in England, and France, and Italy, and Germany, there has been a perfect shriek and outcry of horror. America alone remains cool, and asks, "What is the matter?"

Europe answers back, "Why, we have heard that men are *sold* like cattle in your country."

"Of course they are," says America; "but what then?"

"We have heard," says Europe, "that millions of men are forbidden to read and write in your country."

"We know that," says America; "but what is this outcry about?"

"We have heard," says Europe, "that Christian girls are sold to shame in your markets!"

"That is n't quite as it should be," says America; "but still what is this *excitement* about?"

"We hear that three millions of your people can have no legal marriage ties," says Europe.

"Certainly that is true," returns America; "but you made such an outcry, we thought you saw some great *cruelty* going on."

"And you profess to be a free country!" says indignant Europe.

"Certainly we are the freest and most enlightened country in the world, — what are you talking about?" says America.

"You send your missionaries to Christianize us," says Turkey; "and our religion has abolished this horrible system."

"You! you are all heathen over there, — what business have you to talk?" answers America.

Many people seem really to have thought that nothing but horrible exaggerations of the system of slavery could have produced the sensation which has recently been felt in all modern Europe. They do not know that the thing they have become accustomed to, and handled so freely in every discussion, seems to all other nations the sum and essence of villany. Modern Europe, opening her eyes and looking on the legal theory of the slave system, on the laws and interpretations of law which define it, says to America, in the language of the indignant Othello, If thou wilt justify a thing like this,

"Never pray more; abandon all remorse;
On Horror's head horrors accumulate;
Do deeds to make heaven weep, all earth amazed;
For nothing canst thou to damnation add
Greater than this."

There is an awful state of familiarity with evil which the apostle calls being "dead in trespasses and sins," where truth has been resisted, and evil perseveringly defended, and the convictions of conscience stifled, and the voice of God's Holy·Spirit bidden to depart. There is an awful paralysis of the moral sense, when deeds unholiest and crimes most fearful cease any longer to affect the nerve. That paralysis, always a fearful

KEY TO UNCLE TOM'S CABIN. 129

indication of the death and dissolution of nations, is a doubly dangerous disease in a republic, whose only power is in intelligence, justice and virtue.

CHAPTER II.

PUBLIC OPINION FORMED BY EDUCATION.

REV. CHARLES C. JONES, in his interesting work on the Religious Instruction of Negroes, has a passage which so peculiarly describes that influence of public opinion which we have been endeavoring to illustrate, that we shall copy it.

Habits of feeling and prejudices in relation to any subject are wont to take their rise out of our *education* or circumstances. Every man knows their influence to be great in shaping opinions and conduct, and ofttimes how unwittingly they are formed ; that while we may be unconscious of their existence, they may grow with our growth and strengthen with our strength. Familiarity converts deformity into comeliness. Hence we are not always the best judges of our condition. Another may remark inconveniences, and, indeed, real evils, in it, of which we may be said to have been all our lives scarcely conscious. So, also, evils which, upon first acquaintance, revolted our whole nature, and appeared intolerable, custom almost makes us forget even to see. Men passing out of one state of society into another encounter a thousand things to which they feel that they can never be reconciled ; yet, shortly after, their sensibilities become dulled, — a change passes over them, they scarcely know how. They have accommodated themselves to their new circumstances and relations, — they are Romans in Rome.

Let us now inquire what are the educational influences which bear upon the mind educated in constant familiarity with the slave system.

Take any child of ingenuous mind and of generous heart, and educate him under the influences of slavery, and what are the things which go to form his character ? An anecdote which a lady related to the writer may be in point in this place. In giving an account of some of the things which induced her to remove her family from under the influence of slavery, she related the following incident : Looking out of her nursery window one day, she saw her daughter, about three years of age, with her little carriage, with six or eight young negro children harnessed into it for horses. Two or three of the older slaves were standing around their little mistress, and one of them, putting a whip into her hand, said, "There, Misse, whip 'em well ; make 'em go,—they're all your niggers."

9

What a moral and religious lesson was this for that young soul ! The mother was a judicious woman, who never would herself have taught such a thing ; but the whole influence of slave society had burnt it into the soul of every negro, and through them it was communicated to the child.

As soon as a child is old enough to read the newspapers, he sees in every column such notices as the following from a late *Richmond Whig*, and other papers.

LARGE SALE OF NEGROES, HORSES, MULES, CATTLE, &c.

The subscriber, under a decree of the Circuit Superior Court for Fluvanna County, will proceed to sell, by public auction, at the late residence of William Galt, deceased, on TUESDAY, the 30th day of November, and WEDNESDAY, the 1st day of December next, beginning at 11 o'clock, the negroes, stock, &c., of all kinds, belonging to the estate, consisting of 175 *negroes, amongst whom are* SOME CARPENTERS AND BLACKSMITHS, — 10 horses, 33 mules, 100 head of cattle, 100 sheep, 200 hogs, 1500 barrels corn, oats, fodder, &c., the plantation and shop tools of all kinds.

The Negroes will be sold for cash ; the other property on a credit of nine months, the purchaser giving bond, with approved security.

JAMES GALT, *Administrator of*
Oct. 19.   *William Galt, deceased.*

From the *Nashville Gazette*, Nov. 23, 1852 :

GREAT SALE OF NEGROES, MULES, CATTLE, &c.

On TUESDAY, the 21st day of December next, at the Plantation of the late N. A. McNAIRY, on the Franklin Turnpike, on account of Mrs. C. B. McNairy, Executrix, we will offer at Public Sale

FIFTY VALUABLE NEGROES.

These Negroes are good Plantation Negroes, and will be sold in families. Those wishing to purchase will do well to see them before the day of sale.

Also, TEN FINE WORK MULES, TWO JACKS AND ONE JENNET, MILCH COWS AND CALVES, Cattle, Stock Hogs, 1200 barrels Corn, Oats, Hay, Fodder, &c. Two Wagons, One Cart, Farming Utensils, &c.

From the *Newberry Sentinel :*

FOR SALE.

The subscriber will sell at Auction, on the 15th of this month, at the Plantation on which he resides, distant eleven miles from the Town of Newberry, and near the Laurens Railroad,

22 Young and Likely Negroes ;

comprising able-bodied field-hands, good cooks, house-servants, and an excellent blacksmith ; — about 1500 bushels of corn, a quantity of fodder, hogs, mules, sheep, neat cattle, household and kitchen furniture, and other property. — *Terms made public on day of Sale.*

M. C. GARY.
Dec. 1.
☞ *Laurensville Herald* copy till day of sale.

From the *South Carolinian*, Oct. 21, 1852:

ESTATE SALE OF VALUABLE PROPERTY.

The undersigned, as Administrator of the Estate of Col. T. Randell, deceased, will sell, on MONDAY, the 20th December next, all the personal property belonging to said estate, consisting of 56 NEGROES, STOCK, CORN, FODDER, &c. &c. The sale will take place at the residence of the deceased, on Sandy River, 10 miles West of Chesterville.

Terms of Sale : The negroes on a credit of 12 months, with interest from day of sale, and two good sureties. The other property will be sold for cash.   SAMUEL J. RANDELL.
Sept. 2.

See, also, *New Orleans Bee*, Oct. 28. After advertising the landed estate of Madeline Lanoux, deceased, comes the following enumeration of chattels :

Twelve slaves, men and women ; a small, quite new schooner ; a ferrying flat-boat ; some cows, calves, heifers and sheep ; a lot of household furniture ; the contents of a store, consisting of hardware, crockery ware, groceries, dry goods, etc.

Now, suppose all parents to be as pious and benevolent as Mr. Jones,— a thing not at all to be hoped for, as things are ; — and suppose them to try their very best to impress on the child a conviction that all souls are of equal value in the sight of God ; that the negro soul is as truly beloved of Christ, and ransomed with his blood, as the master's ; and is there any such thing as making him believe or realize it ? Will he believe that that which he sees, every week, advertised with hogs, and horses, and fodder, and cotton-seed, and refuse furniture, — bedsteads, tables and chairs,— is indeed so divine a thing ? We will suppose that the little child knows some pious slave ; that he sees him at the communion-table, partaking, in a far-off, solitary manner, of the sacramental bread and wine. He sees his pious father and mother recognize the slave as a Christian brother ; they tell him that he is an " heir of God, a joint heir with Jesus Christ ;" and the next week he sees him advertised in the paper, in company with a lot of hogs, stock and fodder. Can the child possibly believe in what his Christian parents have told him, when he sees this ? We have spoken now of only the common advertisements of the paper ; but suppose the child to live in some districts of the country, and advertisements of a still more degrading character meet his eye. In the State of Alabama, a newspaper devoted to politics, literature and EDUCATION, has a

standing weekly advertisement of which this is a copy :

NOTICE.

The undersigned having an excellent pack of HOUNDS, for trailing and catching runaway slaves, informs the public that his prices in future will be as follows for such services :

For each day employed in hunting or
trailing, - - - - - - - $2.50
For catching each slave, - - - 10.00
For going over ten miles, and catching
slaves, - - - - - - - 20.00

If sent for, the above prices will be exacted in cash. The subscriber resides one mile and a half south of Dadeville, Ala.
                                                B. BLACK.
Dadeville, Sept. 1, 1852.   1-tf

The reader will see, by the printer's sign at the bottom, that it is a season advertisement, and, therefore, would meet the eye of the child week after week. The paper from which we have cut this contains among its extracts passages from Dickens' *Household Words*, from Professor Felton's article in the *Christian Examiner* on the relation of the sexes, and a most beautiful and chivalrous appeal from the eloquent senator Soulé on the legal rights of women. Let us now ask, since this paper is devoted to education, what sort of an educational influence such advertisements have. And, of course, such an establishment is not kept up without patronage. Where there are negro-hunters advertising in a paper, there are also negro-hunts, and there are dogs being trained to hunt ; and all this process goes on before the eyes of children ; and what sort of an education is it ?

The writer has received an account of the way in which dogs are trained for this business. The information has been communicated to the gentleman who writes it by a negro man, who, having been always accustomed to see it done, described it with as little sense of there being anything out of the way in it as if the dogs had been trained to catch raccoons. It came to the writer in a recent letter from the South.

The way to train 'em (says the man) is to take these yer pups, — any kind o' pups will do, — fox-hounds, bull-dogs, most any ; — but take the pups, and keep 'em shut up, and don't let 'em never see a nigger till they get big enough to be larned. When the pups gits old enough to be set on to things, then make 'em run after a nigger ; and when they cotches him, give 'em meat. Tell the nigger to run as hard as he can, and git up in a tree, so as to larn the dogs to tree 'em ; then take the shoe of a nigger, and larn 'em to find the nigger it belongs to ; then a rag of his clothes ; and so on. Allers be carful to tree the nigger, and teach the dog to wait and bark under the tree till you come up and give him his meat.

See also the following advertisement from the *Ouachita Register*, a newspaper dated "Monroe, La., Tuesday evening, June 1, 1852."

NEGRO DOGS.

The undersigned would respectfully inform the citizens of Ouachita and adjacent parishes, that he has located about 2½ miles east of John White's, on the road leading from Monroe to Bastrop, and that he has a fine pack of Dogs for catching negroes. Persons wishing negroes caught will do well to give him a call. He can always be found at his stand when not engaged in hunting, and even then information of his whereabouts can always be had of some one on the premises.

Terms. — Five dollars per day and found, when there is no track pointed out. When the track is shown, twenty-five dollars will be charged for catching the negro.

M. C. GOFF.

Monroe, Feb. 17, 1852. 15-3m

Now, do not all the scenes likely to be enacted under this head form a fine education for the children of a Christian nation? and can we wonder if children so formed see no cruelty in slavery? Can children realize that creatures who are thus hunted are the children of one heavenly Father with themselves?

But suppose the boy grows up to be a man, and attends the courts of justice, and hears intelligent, learned men declaring from the bench that "the mere beating of a slave, unaccompanied by any circumstances of cruelty, or an attempt to kill, is no breach of the peace of the state." Suppose he hears it decided in the same place that no insult or outrage upon any slave is considered worthy of legal redress, unless it impairs his property value. Suppose he hears, as he would in Virginia, that it is the policy of the law to protect the master even in inflicting cruel, malicious and excessive punishment upon the slave. Suppose a slave is murdered, and he hears the lawyers arguing that it cannot be considered a murder, because the slave, in law, is not considered a human being; and then suppose the case is appealed to a superior court, and he hears the judge expending his forces on a long and eloquent dissertation to prove that the slave *is* a human being; at least, that he is as much so as a lunatic, an idiot, or an unborn child, and that, therefore, he can be murdered. (See Judge Clark's speech, on p. 75.) Suppose he sees that all the administration of law with regard to the slave proceeds on the idea that he is absolutely

nothing more than a bale of merchandise. Suppose he hears such language as this, which occurs in the reasonings of the Brazealle case, and which is a fair sample of the manner in which such subjects are ordinarily discussed. "The slave has no more political capacity, no more right to purchase, hold or transfer property, than the mule in his plough; he is in himself but a mere chattel, — the subject of absolute ownership." Suppose he sees on the statute-book such sentences as these, from the civil code of Louisiana:

Art. 2500. The latent defects of slaves and animals are divided into two classes, — vices of body and vices of character.

Art. 2501. The vices of body are distinguished into absolute and relative.

Art. 2502. The absolute vices of slaves are leprosy, madness and epilepsy.

Art. 2503. The absolute vices of horses and mules are short wind, glanders, and founder.

The influence of this language is made all the stronger on the young mind from the fact that it is not the language of contempt, or of passion, but of calm, matter-of-fact, legal statement.

What effect must be produced on the mind of the young man when he comes to see that, however atrocious and however well-proved be the murder of a slave, the murderer uniformly escapes; and that, though the cases where the slave has fallen a victim to passions of the white are so multiplied, yet the fact of an execution for such a crime is yet almost unknown in the country? Does not all this tend to produce exactly that estimate of the value of negro life and happiness which Frederic Douglass says was expressed by a common proverb among the white boys where he was brought up: "It's worth sixpence to kill a nigger, and sixpence more to bury him"?

We see the public sentiment which has been formed by this kind of education exhibited by the following paragraph from the *Cambridge Democrat*, Md., Oct. 27, 1852. That paper quotes the following from the *Woodville Republican*, of Mississippi. It seems a Mr. Joshua Johns had killed a slave, and had been sentenced therefor to the penitentiary for two years. The *Republican* thus laments his hard lot:

STATE *v.* JOSHUA JOHNS.

This cause resulted in the conviction of Johns, and his sentence to the penitentiary for two years. Although every member of the jury, together with the bar, and the public generally, signed a petition to the governor for young Johns' pardon, yet there was no fault to find with the verdict of the jury. The extreme youth of Johns, and the circumstances in which the killing occurred, enlisted universal sympathy in his favor. There is no doubt that the negro had provoked him to the deed by the use of insolent language ; but how often must it be told that words are no justification for blows ? There are *many* persons — and we regret to say it — *who think they have the same right to shoot a negro, if he insults them, or even runs from them, that they have to shoot down a dog ;* but there are laws for the protection of the slave as well as the master, and the sooner the *error above alluded to is removed,* the better will it be for both parties.

The unfortunate youth who has now entailed upon himself the penalty of the law, we doubt not, had no idea that there existed such penalty ; and even if he was aware of the fact, the repeated insults and taunts of the negro go far to mitigate the crime. Johns was defended by I. D. Gildart, Esq., who probably did all that could have been effected in his defence.

The *Democrat* adds :

We learn from Mr. Curry, deputy sheriff, of Wilkinson County, that Johns has been pardoned by the governor. We are gratified to hear it.

This error above alluded to, of thinking it is as innocent to shoot down a negro as a dog, is one, we fairly admit, for which young Johns ought not to be very severely blamed. He has been educated in a system of things of which this opinion is the inevitable result; and he, individually, is far less guilty for it, than are those men who support the system of laws, and keep up the educational influences, which lead young Southern men directly to this conclusion. Johns may be, for aught we know, as generous-hearted and as just naturally as any young man living; but the horrible system under which he has been educated has rendered him incapable of distinguishing what either generosity or justice is, as applied to the negro.

The public sentiment of the slave states is the sentiment of men who have been thus educated, and in all that concerns the negro it is utterly blunted and paralyzed. What would seem to them injustice and horrible wrong in the case of white persons, is the coolest matter of course in relation to slaves.

As this educational influence descends from generation to generation, the moral sense becomes more and more blunted, and the power of discriminating right from wrong, in what relates to the subject race, more and more enfeebled.

Thus, if we read the writings of distinguished men who were slave-holders about the time of our American Revolution, what clear views do we find expressed of the injustice of slavery, what strong language of reprobation do we find applied to it ! Nothing more forcible could possibly be said in relation to its evils than by quoting the language of such men as Washington, Jefferson, and Patrick Henry. In those days there were no men of that high class of mind who thought of such a thing as defending slavery on principle ; now there are an abundance of the most distinguished men, North and South, statesmen, civilians, men of letters, even clergymen, who in various degrees palliate it, apologize for or openly defend it. And what is the cause of this, except that educational influences have corrupted public sentiment, and deprived them of the power of just judgment? *The public opinion even of free America, with regard to slavery, is behind that of all other civilized nations.*

When the holders of slaves assert that they are, as a general thing, humanely treated, what do they mean ? Not that they would consider such treatment humane if given to themselves and their children,— no, indeed ! — but it is humane *for slaves.*

They do, in effect, place the negro below the range of humanity, and on a level with brutes, and then graduate all their ideas of humanity accordingly.

They would not needlessly kick or abuse a dog or a negro. They may pet a dog, and they often do a negro. Men have been found who fancied having their horses elegantly lodged in marble stables, and to eat out of sculptured mangers, but they thought them horses still ; and, with all the indulgences with which good-natured masters sometimes surround the slave, he is to them but a negro still, and *not* a man.

In what has been said in this chapter, and in what appears incidentally in all the facts cited throughout this volume, there is abundant proof that, notwithstanding there be frequent and most noble instances of generosity towards the negro, and although the sentiment of honorable men and the voice of Christian charity does everywhere protest against what it *feels* to be inhumanity, yet the popular sentiment engendered by the system must *necessarily* fall deplorably short of giving anything like sufficient protection to the rights of the slave. It will appear in the succeeding chapters, as it must already have appeared to reflecting minds, that the whole course of educational influence upon the mind of the slave-master is such as to deaden his mind to those appeals which come from the negro as a fellow-man and a brother.

CHAPTER III.

SEPARATION OF FAMILIES

"What must the difference be," said Dr. Worthington, with startling energy, "between Isabel and her servants! To her it is loss of position, fortune, the fair hopes of life, perhaps even health; for she must inevitably break down under the unaccustomed labor and privations she will have to undergo. But to them it is *merely a change of masters*"!

"Yes, for the neighbors won't allow any of the families to be separated."

"Of course not. We read of such things in *novels* sometimes. But I have yet to see it in real life, except in rare cases, or where the slave has been guilty of some misdemeanor, or crime, for which, in the North, he would have been imprisoned, perhaps for life."— *Cabin and Parlor*, by J. Thornton Randolph, p. 39.

* * * * * * * * *

"But they're going to sell us all to Georgia, I say. How are we to escape that?"

"Spec dare some mistake in dat," replied Uncle Peter, stoutly. "I nebber knew of sich a ting in dese parts, 'cept where some niggar'd been berry bad."— *Ibid.*

BY such graphic touches as the above does Mr. Thornton Randolph represent to us the patriarchal stability and security of the slave population in the Old Dominion. Such a thing as a slave being sold out of the state has never been heard of by Dr. Worthington, except in rare cases for some crime; and old Uncle Peter never heard of such a thing in his life.

Are these representations true?

The worst abuse of the system of slavery is its outrage upon the family; and, as the writer views the subject, it is one which is more notorious and undeniable than any other.

Yet it is upon this point that the most stringent and earnest denial has been made to the representations of "Uncle Tom's Cabin," either indirectly, as by the romance-writer above, or more directly in the assertions of newspapers, both at the North and at the South. When made at the North, they indicate, to say the least, very great ignorance of the subject; when made at the South, they certainly do very great injustice to the general character of the Southerner for truth and honesty. All sections of country have faults peculiar to themselves. The fault of the South, as a general thing, has not been cowardly evasion and deception. It was with utter surprise that the author read the following sentences in an article in *Fraser's Magazine*, professing to come from a South Carolinian.

Mrs. Stowe's favorite illustration of the master's power to the injury of the slave is the separation of families. We are told of infants of ten months old being sold from the arms of their mothers, and of men whose habit it is to raise children to sell away from their mother as soon as they are old enough to be separated. Were our views of this feature of slavery derived from Mrs. Stowe's book, we should regard the families of slaves as utterly unsettled and vagrant.

And again:

We feel confident that, if statistics could be had to throw light upon this subject, we should find that there is less separation of families among the negroes than occurs with almost any other class of persons.

As the author of the article, however, is evidently a man of honor, and expresses many most noble and praiseworthy sentiments, it cannot be supposed that these statements were put forth with any view to misrepresent or to deceive. They are only to be regarded as evidences of the facility with which a sanguine mind often overlooks the most glaring facts that make against a favorite idea or theory, or which are unfavorable in their bearings on one's own country or family. Thus the citizens of some place notoriously unhealthy will come to believe, and assert, with the utmost sincerity, that there is actually less sickness in their town than any other of its size in the known world. Thus parents often think their children perfectly immaculate in just those particulars in which others see them to be most faulty. This solution of the phenomena is a natural and amiable one, and enables us to retain our respect for our Southern brethren.

There is another circumstance, also, to be taken into account, in reading such assertions as these. It is evident, from the pamphlet in question, that the writer is one of the few who regard the possession of absolute irresponsible power as the highest of motives to moderation and temperance in its use. Such men are commonly associated in friendship and family connection with others of similar views, and are very apt to fall into the error of judging others by themselves, and thinking that a thing may do for all the world because it operates well in their immediate circle. Also it cannot but be a fact that the various circumstances which from infancy conspire to degrade and depress the negro in the eyes of a Southern-born man,— the constant habit of speaking of them, and hearing them spoken of, and seeing them advertised, as mere articles of property, often in connection with horses, mules, fodder, swine, &c., as are almost daily in every Southern paper,— must tend, even in the best-constituted minds, to produce a certain obtuseness with regard to the interests, sufferings and affections, of such as do not particularly belong to himself,

---

which will peculiarly unfit him for estimating their condition. The author has often been singularly struck with this fact, in the letters of Southern friends; in which, upon one page, they will make some assertion regarding the condition of Southern negroes, and then go on, and in other connections state facts which apparently contradict them all. We can all be aware how this familiarity would operate with ourselves. Were we called upon to state how often our neighbors' cows were separated from their calves, or how often their household furniture and other effects are scattered and dispersed by executor's sales, we should be inclined to say that it was not a misfortune of very common occurrence.

But let us open two South Carolina papers, published in the very state where this gentleman is residing, and read the advertisements FOR ONE WEEK. The author has slightly abridged them.

COMMISSIONER'S SALE OF 12 LIKELY NEGROES.

FAIRFIELD DISTRICT.

R. W. Murray and wife and others
    v.
William Wright and wife and others.
} In Equity.

In pursuance of an Order of the Court of Equity made in the above case at July Term, 1852, I will sell at public outcry, to the highest bidder, before the Court House in Winnsboro, on the first Monday in January next, on

12 VERY LIKELY NEGROES,

belonging to the estate of Micajah Mobley, deceased, late of Fairfield District.

These Negroes consist chiefly of young boys and girls, and are said to be very likely.

Terms of Sale, &c.

W. R. ROBERTSON,
C. E. F. D.

Commissioner's Office,
Winnsboro, Nov. 30, 1852.
Dec. 2   42   x4.

ADMINISTRATOR'S SALE.

Will be sold at public outcry, to the highest bidder, on Tuesday, the 21st day of December next, at the late residence of Mrs. M. P. Rabb, deceased, all of the personal estate of said deceased, consisting in part of about
2,000 Bushels of Corn.
25,000 pounds of Fodder.
Wheat — Cotton Seed.
Horses, Mules, Cattle, Hogs, Sheep.
There will, in all probability, be sold at the same time and place *several likely Young Negroes.*
The Terms of Sale will be — all sums under Twenty-five Dollars, Cash. All sums of Twenty-five Dollars and over, twelve months' credit, with interest from day of Sale, secured by note and two approved sureties. WILLIAM S. RABB,
Administrator.

Nov. 11.   39   x2

COMMISSIONER'S SALE OF LAND AND NEGROES.

FAIRFIELD DISTRICT.

James E. Caldwell,
Admr., with the Will
annexed, of Jacob Gibson,
deceased,
    v.
Jason D. Gibson
and others.
} In Equity.

In pursuance of the order of sale made in the above case, I will sell at public outcry, to the highest bidder, before the Court House in Winnsboro, on the first Monday in January next, and the day following, the following real and personal estate of Jacob Gibson, deceased, late of Fairfield District, to wit:

The Plantation on which the testator lived at the time of his death, containing 661 Acres, more or less, lying on the waters of Wateree Creek, and bounded by lands of Samuel Johnston, Theodore S. DuBose, Edward P. Mobley, and B. R. Cockrell. This plantation will be sold in two separate tracts, plats of which will be exhibited on the day of sale:

46 PRIME LIKELY NEGROES,

consisting of *Wagoners, Blacksmiths, Cooks, House Servants, &c.*   W. R. ROBERTSON,
C. E. F. D.

Commissioner's Office,
Winnsboro, 29th Nov. 1852.
}

ESTATE SALE.—FIFTY PRIME NEGROES. BY J. & L. T. LEVIN.

On the first Monday in January next I will sell, before the Court House in Columbia, 50 of as Likely NEGROES as have ever been exposed to public sale, belonging to the estate of A. P. Vinson, deceased. The Negroes have been well cared for, and well managed in every respect. Persons wishing to purchase will not, it is confidently believed, have a better opportunity to supply themselves.
J. H. ADAMS,
Executor.

Nov. 18   40   x3

ADMINISTRATOR'S SALE.

Will be sold on the 15th December next, at the late residence of Samuel Moore, deceased, in York District, all the personal property of said deceased, consisting of:

35 LIKELY NEGROES,

a quantity of Cotton and Corn, Horses and Mules, Farming Tools, Household and Kitchen Furniture, with many other articles.
SAMUEL E. MOORE,
Administrator.

Nov. 18   40   x4t.

ADMINISTRATOR'S SALE.

Will be sold at public outcry, to the highest bidder, on Tuesday, the 14th day of December next, at the late residence of Robert W. Durham, deceased, in Fairfield District, all of the personal estate of said deceased: consisting in part as follows:

50 PRIME LIKELY NEGROES.

About 3,000 Bushels of Corn.
A large quantity of Fodder.

Wheat, Oats, Cow Peas, Rye, Cotton Seed, Horses, Mules, Cattle, Hogs, Sheep.

C. H. DURHAM,
Nov. 23. Administrator.

SHERIFF'S SALE.

By virtue of sundry executions to me directed, I will sell at Fairfield Court House, on the first Monday, and the day following, in December next, within the legal hours of sale, to the highest bidder, for cash, the following property. Purchasers to pay for titles:

2 NEGROES, levied upon as the property of Allen R. Crankfield, at the suit of Alexander Brodie, et al.

2 Horses and 1 Jennet, levied upon as the property of Allen R. Crankfield, at the suit of Alexander Brodie.

2 Mules, levied upon as the property of Allen R. Crankfield, at the suit of Temperance E. Miller and J. W. Miller.

1 pair of Cart Wheels, levied upon as the property of Allen R. Crankfield, at the suit of Temperance E. Miller and J. W. Miller.

1 Chest of Drawers, levied upon as the property of Allen R. Crankfield, at the suit of Temperance E. Miller and J. W. Miller.

1 Bedstead, levied upon as the property of Allen R. Crankfield, at the suit of Temperance E. Miller and J. W. Miller.

1 NEGRO, levied upon as the property of R. J. Gladney, at the suit of James Camak.

1 NEGRO, levied upon as the property of Geo. McCormick, at the suit of W. M. Phifer.

1 Riding Saddle, to be sold under an assignment of G. W. Boulware to J. B. Mickle, in the case of Geo. Murphy, Jr., v. G. W. Boulware.

R. E. ELLISON,
Sheriff's Office, } S. F. D.
Nov. 19 1852. }
Nov. 20   37   †xtf

COMMISSIONER'S SALE.

John A. Crumpton, and others, }
v. } In Equity.
Zachariah C. Crumpton. }

In pursuance of the Decretal order made in this case, I will sell at public outcry to the highest bidder, before the Court House door in Winnsboro, on the first Monday in December next, three separate tracts or parcels of land, belonging to the estate of Zachariah Crumpton, deceased.

I will also sell, at the same time and place, FIVE OR SIX LIKELY YOUNG NEGROES, sold as the property of the said Zachariah Crumpton, deceased, by virtue of the authority aforesaid.

The Terms of sale are as follows, &c. &c.

W. R. ROBERTSON,
Commissioner's Office, } C. E. F. D.
Winnsboro, Nov. 8, 1852. }
Nov 11   30   x3

ESTATE SALE OF VALUABLE PROPERTY.

The undersigned, as Administrator of the Estate of Col. T. Randell, deceased, will sell, on Monday the 20th December next, all the personal property belonging to said estate, consisting of

56 NEGROES,
STOCK, CORN, FODDER, ETC. ETC.

Terms of sale, &c. &c.

SAMUEL J. RANDELL.
Sep. 2   29   x16

The *Tri-weekly South Carolinian*, published at Columbia, S. C., has this motto:

" BE JUST AND FEAR NOT ; LET ALL THE ENDS THOU AIM'ST AT BE THY COUNTRY'S, THY GOD'S, AND TRUTH'S."

In the number dated December 23d, 1852, is found a " Reply of the Women of Virginia to the Women of England," containing this sentiment:

Believe us, we deeply, prayerfully, *study God's holy word;* we are fully persuaded that our institutions are in accordance with it.

After which, in other columns, come the ten advertisements following :

SHERIFF'S SALES FOR JANUARY 2, 1853.

By virtue of sundry writs of *fieri facias*, to me directed, will be sold before the Court House in Columbia, within the legal hours, on the first Monday and Tuesday in January next,

Seventy-four acres of Land, more or less, in Richland District, bounded on the north and east by Lorick's, and on the south and west by Thomas Trapp.

Also, Ten Head of Cattle, Twenty-five Head of Hogs, and Two Hundred Bushels of Corn, levied on as the property of M. A. Wilson, at the suit of Samuel Gardner v. M. A. Wilson.

SEVEN NEGROES, named Grace, Frances, Edmund, Charlotte, Emuline, Thomas and Charles, levied on as the property of Bartholomew Turnipseed, at the suit of A. F. Dubard, J. S. Lever, Bank of the State and others, v. B. Turnipseed.

450 acres of Land, more or less, in Richland District, bounded on the north, &c. &c.

LARGE SALE OF REAL AND PERSONAL PROPERTY.—ESTATE SALE.

On Monday, the (7th) seventh day of February next, I will sell at Auction, without reserve, at the Plantation, near Linden, all the Horses, Mules, Wagons, Farming Utensils, Corn, Fodder, &c.

And on the following Monday (14th), the fourteenth day of February next, at the Court House, at Linden, in Marengo County, Alabama, I will sell at public auction, without reserve, to the highest bidder,

110 PRIME AND LIKELY NEGROES,
belonging to the Estate of the late John Robinson, of South Carolina.

Among the Negroes are *four valuable Carpenters, and a very superior Blacksmith.*

NEGROES FOR SALE.

By permission of Peter Wylie, Esq., Ordinary for Chester District, I will sell, at public auction, before the Court House, in Chesterville, on the first Monday in February next,

FORTY LIKELY NEGROES,
belonging to the Estate of F. W. Davie.

W. D. DESAUSSURE, Executor.
Dec. 23.   56   †tds.

ESTATE SALE OF FURNITURE, &c., BY J. & L. T. LEVIN.

Will be sold, at our store, on Thursday, the 6th day of January next, all the Household and Kitch en Furniture, belonging to the Estate of B. L. McLaughlin, deceased, consisting in part of Hair Seat Chairs, Sofas and Rockers, Piano, Mahogany Dining, Tea, and Card Tables ; Carpets, Rugs, Andirons, Fenders, Shovel and Tongs, Mantel Ornaments, Clocks, Side Board, Bureaus, Mahogany Bedsteads, Feather Beds and Mattresses, Wash Stands, Curtains, fine Cordial Stand, Glassware, Crockery, and a great variety of articles for family use.

Terms cash.

ALSO,

A NEGRO MAN, named *Leonard, belonging to same.*

Terms, &c.

ALSO,

At same time, a quantity of New Brick, belonging to Estate of A. S. Johnstone, deceased.

Dec. 21.		53		‡tds.

GREAT SALE OF NEGROES AND THE SALUDA FACTORY, BY J. & L. T. LEVIN.

On Thursday, December 30, at 11 o'clock, will be sold at the Court House in Columbia,

ONE HUNDRED VALUABLE NEGROES.

It is seldom such an opportunity occurs as now offers. Among them are only four beyond 45 years old, and none above 50. There are twenty-five prime young men, between sixteen and thirty ; forty of the most likely young women, and *as fine a set of children as can be shown!!*

Terms, &c.		Dec. 18, '52.

NEGROES AT AUCTION.— BY J. & L. T. LEVIN.

Will be sold, on Monday, the 3d January next, at the Court House, at 10 o'clock,

22 LIKELY NEGROES, the larger number of which are young and desirable. Among them are Field Hands, Hostlers and Carriage Drivers, House Servants, &c., and of the following ages : Robinson 40, Elsey 34, Yanaky 13, Sylla 11, Anikee 8, Robinson 6, Candy 3, Infant 9, Thomas 35, Die 38, Amey 18, Eldridge 13, Charles 6, Sarah 60, Baket 50, Mary 18, Betty 16, Guy 12, Tilla 9, Lydia 24, Rachel 4, SCIPIO 2.

The above Negroes are sold for the purpose of making some other investment of the proceeds ; the sale will, therefore, be positive.

Terms. — A credit of one, two, and three years, for notes payable at either of the Banks, with two or more approved endorsers, with interest from date. Purchasers to pay for papers.	Dec 8 43

☞ *Black River Watchman* will copy the above, and forward bill to the auctioneers for payment.

Poor little Scip!

LIKELY AND VALUABLE GIRL, AT PRIVATE SALE.

A LIKELY GIRL, about seventeen years old (raised in the up-country), a good Nurse and House Servant, can wash and iron, and do plain cooking, and is warranted sound and healthy. She may be seen at our office, where she will remain until sold.		ALLEN & PHILLIPS,

Dec. 15, '49.		Auctioneers & Com. Agents.

PLANTATION AND NEGROES FOR SALE.

The subscriber, having located in Columbia, offers for sale his Plantation in St. Matthew's

Parish, six miles from the Railroad, containing 1,500 acres. now in a high state of cultivation, with Dwelling House and all necessary Out-buildings.

ALSO,

50 Likely NEGROES, with provisions, &c.

The terms will be accommodating. Persons desirous to purchase can call upon the subscriber in Columbia, or on his son at the Plantation.

Dec. 6 41.		T. J. GOODWYN.

FOR SALE.

A LIKELY NEGRO BOY, about twenty-one years old, a good wagoner and field hand. Apply at this office.		Dec. 20 52.

Now, it is scarcely possible that a person who has been accustomed to see such advertisements from boyhood, and to pass them over with as much indifference as we pass over advertisements of sofas and chairs for sale, could possibly receive the shock from them which one wholly unaccustomed to such a mode of considering and disposing of human beings would receive. They make no impression upon him. His own family servants, and those of his friends, are not in the market, and he does not realize that any are. Under the advertisements, a hundred such scenes as those described in "Uncle Tom" may have been acting in his very vicinity. When Mr. Dickens drew pictures of the want and wretchedness of London life, perhaps a similar incredulity might have been expressed within the silken curtains of many a brilliant parlor. *They* had never seen such things, and they had always lived in London. But, for all that, the writings of Dickens awoke in noble and aristocratic bosoms the sense of a common humanity with the lowly, and led them to feel how much misery might exist in their immediate vicinity, of which they were entirely unaware. They have never accused him as a libeller of his country, though he did make manifest much of the suffering, sorrow and abuse, which were in it. The author is led earnestly to entreat that the writer of this very paper *would* examine the "statistics" of the American internal slave-trade ; that he would look over the exchange files of some newspaper, and, for a month or two, endeavor to keep some inventory of the number of human beings, with hearts, hopes and affections, like his own, who are constantly subjected to all the uncertainties and mutations of property relation. The writer is sure that he could not do it long without a generous desire being excited in his bosom to become, not an apologist for, but a reformer of, these institutions of his country.

These papers of South Carolina are not exceptional ones; they may be matched by hundreds of papers from any other state.

Let the reader now stop one minute, and look over again these two weeks' advertisements. This is not novel-writing — *this* is fact. See these human beings tumbled promiscuously out before the public with horses, mules, second-hand buggies, cottonseed, bedsteads, &c. &c.; and Christian ladies, in the same newspaper, saying that they prayerfully study God's word, and believe their institutions have his sanction! Does he suppose that here, in these two weeks, there have been no scenes of suffering? Imagine the distress of these families — the nights of anxiety of these mothers and children, wives and husbands, when these sales are about to take place! Imagine the scenes of the sales! A young lady, a friend of the writer, who spent a winter in Carolina, described to her the sale of a woman and her children. When the little girl, seven years of age, was put on the block, she fell into spasms with fear and excitement. She was taken off — recovered and put back — the spasms came back — three times the experiment was tried, and at last the sale of the *child* was deferred!

See also the following, from Dr. Elwood Harvey, editor of a western paper, to the *Pennsylvania Freeman*, Dec. 25, 1846.

We attended a sale of land and other property, near Petersburg, Virginia, and unexpectedly saw slaves sold at public auction. The slaves were told they would not be sold, and were collected in front of the quarters, gazing on the assembled multitude. The land being sold, the auctioneer's loud voice was heard, "Bring up the *niggers!*" A shade of astonishment and affright passed over their faces, as they stared first at each other, and then at the crowd of purchasers, whose attention was now directed to them. When the horrible truth was revealed to their minds that they were to be sold, and nearest relations and friends parted forever, the effect was indescribably agonizing. Women snatched up their babes, and ran screaming into the huts. Children hid behind the huts and trees, and the men stood in mute despair. The auctioneer stood on the portico of the house, and the "men and boys" were ranging in the yard for inspection. It was announced that no warranty of *soundness* was given, and purchasers must examine for themselves. A few old men were sold at prices from thirteen to twenty-five dollars, and it was painful to see old men, bowed with years of toil and suffering, stand up to be the jest of brutal tyrants, and to hear them tell their disease and worthlessness, fearing that they would be bought by traders for the southern market.

A white boy, about fifteen years old, was placed on the stand. His hair was brown and straight, his skin exactly the same hue as other white persons, and no discernible trace of negro features in his countenance.

Some vulgar jests were passed on his color, and two hundred dollars was bid for him; but the audience said "that it was not enough to begin on for such a likely young nigger." Several remarked that they "would not have him as a gift." Some said a white nigger was more trouble than he was worth. One man said it was wrong to sell *white* people. I asked him if it was more wrong than to sell black people. He made no reply. Before he was sold, his mother rushed from the house upon the portico, crying, in frantic grief, "My son, O! my boy, they will take away my dear —" Here her voice was lost, as she was rudely pushed back and the door closed. The sale was not for a moment interrupted, and none of the crowd appeared to be in the least affected by the scene. The poor boy, afraid to cry before so many strangers, who showed no signs of sympathy or pity, trembled, and wiped the tears from his cheeks with his sleeves. He was sold for about two hundred and fifty dollars. During the sale, the quarters resounded with cries and lamentations that made my heart ache. A woman was next called by name. She gave her infant one wild embrace before leaving it with an old woman, and hastened mechanically to obey the call; but stopped, threw her arms aloft, screamed and was unable to move.

One of my companions touched my shoulder and said, "Come, let us leave here; I can bear no more." We left the ground. The man who drove our carriage from Petersburg had two sons who belonged to the estate — small boys. He obtained a promise that they should not be sold. He was asked if they were his only children; he answered, "All that 's left of eight." Three others had been sold to the south, and he would never see or hear from them again.

As Northern people do not see such things, they should hear of them often enough to keep them awake to the sufferings of the victims of their indifference.

Such are the *common* incidents, not the *admitted cruelties*, of an institution which people have brought themselves to feel is in accordance with God's word!

Suppose it be conceded now that "the family relation is protected, *as far as possible*." The question still arises, *How far is it possible?* Advertisements of sales to the number of those we have quoted, more or less, appear from week to week in the same papers, in the same neighborhood; and professional traders make it their business to attend them, and buy up victims. Now, if the inhabitants of a given neighborhood charge themselves with the care to see that no families are separated in this whirl of auctioneering, one would fancy that they could have very little else to do. It *is* a fact, and a most honorable one to our common human nature, that the distress and anguish of these poor, helpless creatures does often raise up for them friends among the generous-hearted. Southern men often go to the extent of their means, and beyond their means, to arrest the cruel operations of trade, and relieve cases of individual distress. There are men at the South who could tell, if they would, how, when they have spent the last dollar that they thought they could afford on one week, they have been importuned by precisely such a case the next, and been unable to meet it. There are masters at the South who could tell, if they would, how they have stood and bid against a trader, to redeem some poor slave of their own, till the bidding was perfectly ruinous, and they have been obliged to give up by sheer necessity. Good-natured auctioneers know very well how they have often been entreated to connive at keeping a poor fellow out of the trader's clutches; and how sometimes they succeed, and sometimes they do not.

The very struggle and effort which generous Southern men make to stop the regular course of trade only shows them the hopelessness of the effort. We fully concede that many of them do as much or more than any of us would do under similar circumstances; and yet *they know* that what they do amounts, after all, to the merest trifle.

But let us still further reason upon the testimony of advertisements. What is to be understood by the following, of the *Memphis Eagle and Inquirer*, Saturday, Nov. 13, 1852? Under the editorial motto, "*Liberty* and Union, now and forever," come the following illustrations:

NO. I.

75 NEGROES.

I have just received from the East 75 assorted A No. 1 negroes. Call soon, if you want to get the first choice.

BENJ. LITTLE.

NO. II.

CASH FOR NEGROES.

I will pay as high cash prices for a few likely young negroes as any trader in this city. Also, will receive and sell on commission at Byrd Hill's, old stand, on Adams-street, Memphis.   BENJ. LITTLE.

NO. III.

500 NEGROES WANTED.

We will pay the highest cash price for all good negroes offered. We invite all those having negroes for sale to call on us at our Mart, opposite the lower steamboat landing. We will also have a large lot of Virginia negroes for sale in the Fall. We have as safe a jail as any in the' country, where we can keep negroes safe for those that wish them kept.   BOLTON, DICKINS & Co.

Under the head of advertisements No. 1, let us humbly inquire what "*assorted A No. 1 Negroes*" means. Is it likely that

it means negroes sold in families? What is meant by the invitation, "*Call soon if you want to get the first choice*"?

So much for Advertisement No. 1. Let us now propound a few questions to the initiated on No. 2. What does Mr. Benjamin Little mean by saying that he "*will pay as high a cash price for a few likely young negroes as any trader in the city*"? Do *families* commonly consist exclusively of "*likely young negroes*"?

On the third advertisement we are also desirous of some information. Messrs. BOLTON, DICKINS & Co. state that they expect to receive a large lot of *Virginia* negroes in the fall.

Unfortunate Messrs. Bolton, Dickins & Co.! Do you suppose that Virginia families will sell their negroes? Have you read Mr. J. Thornton Randolph's last novel, and have you not learned that old Virginia families *never* sell to traders? and, more than that, that they *always* club together and buy up the negroes that are for sale in their neighborhood, and the traders when they appear on the ground are hustled off with very little ceremony? One would really think that you had got your impressions on the subject from "Uncle Tom's Cabin." For we are told that all who derive their views of slavery from this book "regard the families of slaves as utterly unsettled and vagrant." *

But, before we recover from our astonishment on reading this, we take up the *Natchez* (Mississippi) *Courier* of Nov. 20th, 1852, and there read:

NEGROES.

The undersigned would respectfully state to the public that he has leased the stand in the Forks of the Road, near Natchez, for a term of years, and that he intends to keep a large lot of NEGROES on hand during the year. He will sell as low or lower than any other trader at this place or in New Orleans.

He has just arrived from Virginia with a very likely lot of Field Men and Women; also, House Servants, three Cooks, and a Carpenter. Call and see.

A fine Buggy Horse, a Saddle Horse and a Carryall, on hand, and for sale.

THOS. G. JAMES.

Natchez, Sept. 28, 1852.

Where in the world did this lucky Mr. THOS. G. JAMES get this likely Virginia "assortment"? Probably in some county which Mr. Thornton Randolph never visited. And had no families been separated to form

* Article in *Fraser's Magazine* for October, by a South Carolinian.

the assortment? We hear of a lot of field men and women. Where are their children? We hear of a lot of house-servants, — of " three cooks," and " one carpenter," as well as a " fine buggy horse." Had these unfortunate cooks and carpenters no relations? Did no sad natural tears stream down their dark cheeks, when they were being "assorted" for the Natchez market? Does no mournful heart among them yearn to the song of

"O, carry me back to old Virginny"?

Still further, we see in the same paper the following :

SLAVES! SLAVES! SLAVES!

FRESH ARRIVALS WEEKLY. — Having established ourselves at the Forks of the Road, near Natchez, for a term of years, we have now on hand, and intend to keep throughout the entire year, a large and well-selected stock of Negroes, consisting of field-hands, house servants, mechanics, cooks, seamstresses, washers, ironers, etc., which we can and will sell as low or lower than any other house here or in New Orleans.

Persons wishing to purchase would do well to call on us before making purchases elsewhere, as our regular arrivals will keep us supplied with a good and general assortment. Our terms are liberal. Give us a call.
GRIFFIN & PULLAM.
Natchez, Oct. 15, 1852.–6m.
Free Trader and *Concordia Intelligencer* copy as above.

Indeed! Messrs. Griffin and Pullam, it seems, are equally fortunate! They are having fresh supplies weekly, and are going to keep a large, well-selected stock constantly on hand, to wit, "field-hands, house-servants, mechanics, cooks, seamstresses, washers, ironers, etc."

Let us respectfully inquire what is the process by which a trader acquires a well-selected stock. He goes to Virginia to *select.* He has had orders, say, for one dozen cooks, for half a dozen carpenters, for so many house-servants, &c. &c. Each one of these individuals have their own ties; besides being cooks, carpenters and house-servants, they are also fathers, mothers, husbands, wives; but what of that? They must be *selected*—it is an *assortment* that is wanted. The gentleman who has ordered a cook does not, of course, want her five children ; and the planter who has ordered a carpenter does not want the cook, his wife. A carpenter is an expensive article, at any rate, as they cost from a thousand to fifteen hundred dollars ; and a man who has to pay out this sum for him cannot always afford himself the luxury of indulging his humanity; and

as to the children, they must be left in the slave-raising state. For, when the ready-raised article is imported *weekly* into Natchez or New Orleans, is it likely that the inhabitants will encumber themselves with the labor of raising children? No, there must be division of labor in all well-ordered business. The northern slave states raise the article, and the southern ones consume it.

The extracts have been taken from the papers of the more southern states. If, now, the reader has any curiosity to explore the *selecting* process in the northern states, the daily prints will further enlighten him. In the *Daily Virginian* of Nov. 19, 1852, Mr. J. B. McLendon thus announces to the Old Dominion that he has settled himself down to attend to the selecting process :

NEGROES WANTD.

The subscriber, having located in Lynchburg, is giving the highest cash prices for negroes *between the ages of* 10 *and* 30 *years.* Those having negroes for sale may find it to their interest to call on him at the Washington Hotel, Lynchburg, or address him by letter.

All communications will receive prompt attention.
J. B. McLENDON.
nov. 5-d1y.

Mr. McLendon distinctly announces that he is not going to take any children under ten years of age, nor any grown people over thirty. Likely *young* negroes are what he is after : — families, of course, never separated !

Again, in the same paper, Mr. Seth Woodroof is desirous of keeping up the recollection in the community that he also is in the market, as it would appear he has been, some time past. He, likewise, wants negroes between ten and thirty years of age ; but his views turn rather on mechanics, blacksmiths, and carpenters,— witness his hand :

NEGROES WANTED.

The subscriber continues in market for Negroes, of both sexes, *between the ages of* 10 *and* 30 years, including Mechanics, such as Blacksmiths, Carpenters, and will pay the highest market prices in cash. His office is a newly erected brick building on 1st or Lynch street, immediately in rear of the Farmers' Bank, where he is prepared (having erected buildings with that view) to board negroes sent to Lynchburg for sale or otherwise on as moderate terms, and keep them as secure, as if they were placed in the jail of the Corporation.
aug 26.
SETH WOODROOF.

There is no manner of doubt that this Mr. Seth Woodroof is a gentleman of humanity, and wishes to avoid the separation of families *as much as possible.* Doubtless he ardently wishes that all his blacksmiths and carpenters would be considerate, and never have any children under ten years of age; but, if the thoughtless dogs have got them, what's a humane man to do? He has to fill out Mr. This, That, and the Other's order,— that's a clear case; and therefore John and Sam must take their last look at their babies, as Uncle Tom did of his when he stood by the rough trundle-bed and dropped into it great, useless tears.

Nay, my friends, don't curse poor Mr. Seth Woodroof, because he does the horrible, loathsome work of tearing up the living human heart, to make twine and shoe-strings for you! It's disagreeable business enough, he will tell you, sometimes; and, if you must have him to do it for you, treat him civilly, and don't pretend that you are any better than he.

But the good trade is not confined to the Old Dominion, by any means. See the following extract from a Tennessee paper, the *Nashville Gazette,* Nov. 23, 1852, where Mr. A. A. McLean, general agent in this kind of business, thus makes known his wants and intentions:

WANTED.

I want to purchase immediately 25 likely NEGROES,— male and female,— *between the ages of 15 and 25 years;* for which I will pay the highest price in cash.
           A. A. McLEAN, *General Agent,*
nov 9   *Cherry Street.*

Mr. McLean, it seems, only wants those between the ages of fifteen and twenty-five. This advertisement is twice repeated in the same paper, from which fact we may conjecture that the gentleman is very much in earnest in his wants, and entertains rather confident expectations that somebody will be willing to sell. Further, the same gentleman states another want.

WANTED.

I want to purchase, immediately, a Negro man, Carpenter, and will give a good price.
sept 29   A. A. McLEAN, *Gen'l Agent.*

Mr. McLean does not advertise for his wife and children, or where this same carpenter is to be sent,— whether to the New Orleans market, or up the Red River, or off to some far bayou of the Mississippi, never to look upon wife or child again. But, again, Mr. McLean in the same paper tells us of another want:

WANTED IMMEDIATELY.

A Wet Nurse. Any price will be given for one of good character, constitution, &c. Apply to
           A. A. McLEAN, *Gen'l Agent.*

And what is to be done with the baby of this wet nurse? Perhaps, at the moment that Mr. McLean is advertising for her, she is hushing the little thing in her bosom, and thinking, as many another mother has done, that it is about the brightest, prettiest little baby that ever was born; for, singularly enough, even black mothers do fall into this delusion sometimes. No matter for all this, — she is wanted for a wet nurse! Aunt Prue can take her baby, and *raise it* on corn-cake, and what not. Off with her to Mr. McLean!

See, also, the following advertisement of the good State of Alabama, which shows how the trade is thriving there. Mr. S. N. Brown, in the *Advertiser and Gazette,* Montgomery, Alabama, holds forth as follows:

NEGROES FOR SALE.

S. N. BROWN takes this method of informing his old patrons, and others waiting to purchase Slaves, that he has now on hand, of his own selection and purchasing, a lot of likely young *Negroes,* consisting of Men, Boys, and Women, Field Hands, and superior House Servants, which he offers and will sell as low as the times will warrant. Office on Market-street, above the Montgomery Hall, at Lindsay's Old Stand, where he intends to keep slaves for sale on his own account, and not on commission,— therefore thinks he can give satisfaction to those who patronize him.
     Montgomery, Ala., Sept. 13, 1852.   twtf (J)

Where were these boys and girls of Mr. Brown *selected,* let us ask. How did their fathers and mothers feel when they were *"selected"?* Emmeline was taken out of one family, and George out of another. The judicious trader has travelled through wide regions of country, leaving in his track wailing and anguish. A little incident, which has recently been the rounds of the papers, may perhaps illustrate some of the scenes he has occasioned:

INCIDENT OF SLAVERY.

A negro woman belonging to Geo. M. Garrison, of Polk Co., killed four of her children, by cutting their throats while they were asleep, on Thursday night, the 2d inst., and then put an end to her own existence by cutting her throat. Her master knows of no cause for the horrid act, unless it be that she heard him speak of selling her and two of her children, and keeping the others.

The uncertainty of the master in this case is edifying. He knows that negroes cannot be expected to have the feelings of cultivated people; — and yet, here is a case where the creature really acts unaccountably, and he can't think of any cause except that he was going to sell her from her children.

But, compose yourself, dear reader; there was no great harm done. These were all *poor* people's children, and some of them, though not all, were black; and that makes all the difference in the world, you know!

But Mr. Brown is not alone in Montgomery. Mr. J. W. Lindsey wishes to remind the people of his dépôt.

100 NEGROES FOR SALE,

At my depot, on Commerce-street, immediately between the Exchange Hotel and F. M. Gilmer, Jr.'s Warehouse, where I will be receiving, from time to time, large lots of Negroes during the season, and will sell on as accommodating terms as any house in this city. I would respectfully request my old customers and friends to call and examine my stock. Jno. W. Lindsey.
Montgomery, Nov. 2, 1852.

Mr. Lindsey is going to be receiving, from time to time, all the season, and will sell as cheap as anybody; so there's no fear of the supply's falling off. And, lo! in the same paper, Messrs. Sanders & Foster press their claims also on the public notice.

NEGROES FOR SALE.

The undersigned have bought out the well-known establishment of Eckles & Brown, where they have now on hand a large lot of likely young Negroes, to wit: Men, Women, Boys and Girls, good field-hands. Also, several good House Servants and Mechanics of all kinds. The subscribers intend to keep constantly on hand a large assortment of Negroes, comprising every description. Persons wishing to purchase will find it much to their interest to call and examine previous to buying elsewhere. Sanders & Foster.
April 13.

Messrs. Sanders & Foster are going to have an *assortment* also. All their negroes are to be young and likely; the trashy old fathers and mothers are all thrown aside like a heap of pig-weed, after one has been weeding a garden.

Query: Are these Messrs. Sanders & Foster, and J. W. Lindsey, and S. N. Brown, and McLean, and Woodroof, and McLendon, all members of the church, in good and regular standing? Does the question shock you? Why so? Why should they not be? The Rev. Dr. Smylie, of Mississippi, in a document endorsed by two presbyteries, says distinctly that the Bible gives a right to buy and sell slaves.*

If the Bible guarantees this right, and sanctions this trade, why should it shock you to see the slave-trader at the communion-

table? Do you feel that there is blood on his hands,— the blood of human hearts, which he has torn asunder? Do you shudder when he touches the communion-bread, and when he drinks the cup which "whosoever drinketh unworthily drinketh damnation to himself"? But who makes the trader? Do not you? Do you think that the trader's profession is a healthy one for the soul? Do you think the scenes with which he must be familiar, and the deeds he must do, in order to keep up an *assortment* of negroes for your convenience, are such things as Jesus Christ approves? Do you think they tend to promote his growth in grace, and to secure his soul's salvation? Or is it so important for you to have *assorted* negroes that the traders must not only be turned out of good society in this life, but run the risk of going to hell forever, for your accommodation?

But let us search the Southern papers, and see if we cannot find some evidence of that humanity which avoids the separation of families, *as far as possible.* In the *Argus,* published at Weston, Missouri, Nov. 5, 1852, see the following:

A NEGRO FOR SALE.

I wish to sell a black girl about 24 years old, a good cook and washer, handy with a needle, can spin and weave. I wish to sell her in the neighborhood of Camden Point; if not sold there in a short time, I will hunt the best market; or I will trade her for two small ones, a boy and girl.
M. Doyal.

Considerate Mr. Doyal! He is opposed to the separation of families, and, therefore, wishes to sell this woman in the neighborhood of Camden Point, where her family ties are,— perhaps her husband and children, her brothers or sisters. He will not separate her from her family if it is possible to avoid it; that is to say, if he can get as much for her without; but, if he can't, he will *"hunt the best market."* What more would you have of Mr. Doyal?

How speeds the blessed trade in the State of Maryland?— Let us take the *Baltimore Sun* of Nov. 23, 1852.

Mr. J. S. Donovan thus advertises the Christian public of the accommodations of his jail:

CASH FOR NEGROES.

The undersigned continues, at his old stand, No. 13 Camden St., to pay the highest price for Negroes. Persons bringing Negroes by railroad or steamboat will find it very convenient to secure their Negroes, as my Jail is adjoining the Railroad Depot and near the Steamboat Landings. Negroes received for safe keeping.
J. S. Donovan.

* "If language can convey a clear and definite meaning at all, I know not how it can more unequivocally or more plainly present to the mind any thought or idea than the twenty-fifth chapter of Leviticus clearly or unequivocally establishes the fact that slavery or bondage was sanctioned by God himself; and that *'buying, selling, holding and bequeathing'* slaves, as property, are regulations which were established by himself." — *Smylie, on Slavery.*

Messrs. B. M. & W. L. Campbell, in the respectable old stand of Slatter, advertise as follows:

SLAVES WANTED.

We are at all times purchasing SLAVES, paying the highest CASH prices. Persons wishing to sell will please call at 242 PRATT ST. (Slatter's old stand). Communications attended to.

B. M. & W. L. CAMPBELL.

In another column, however, Mr. John Denning has his season advertisement, in terms which border on the sublime:

5000 NEGROES WANTED.

I will pay the highest prices, in cash, for 5000 NEGROES, with good titles, slaves for life or for a term of years, in large or small families, or single negroes. I will also purchase Negroes restricted to remain in the State, that sustain good characters. Families never separated. Persons having Slaves for sale will please call and see me, as I am always in the market with the cash. Communications promptly attended to, and liberal commissions paid, by JOHN N. DENNING, No. 18 S. Frederick street, between Baltimore and Second streets, Baltimore, Maryland. Trees in front of the house.

Mr. John Denning, also, is a man of humanity. He never separates families. Don't you see it in his advertisement? If a man offers him a wife without her husband, Mr. John Denning won't buy her. O, no! His five thousand are all unbroken families; he never takes any other; and he transports them whole and entire. This is a comfort to reflect upon, certainly.

See, also, the *Democrat*, published in Cambridge, Maryland, Dec. 8, 1852. A gentleman gives this pictorial representation of himself, with the proclamation to the slave-holders of Dorchester and adjacent counties that he is again in the market:

NEGROES WANTED.

I wish to inform the slave-holders of Dorchester and the adjacent counties that I am again in the Market. Persons having negroes that are slaves for life to dispose of will find it to their interest to see me before they sell, as I am determined to pay the highest prices in cash that the Southern market will justify. I can be found at A. Hall's Hotel in Easton, where I will remain until the first day of July next. Communications addressed to me at Easton, or information given to Wm. Bell in Cambridge, will meet with prompt attention.

WM. HARKER.

Mr. Harker is very accommodating. He keeps himself informed as to the state of the southern market, and will give the very highest price that it will justify. Moreover, he will be on hand till July, and will answer any letters from the adjoining country on the subject. On one point he ought to be spoken to. He has not advertised that he does not separate families. It is a mere matter of taste, to be sure; but then some well-disposed people like to see it on a trader's card, thinking it has a more creditable appearance; and, probably, Mr. Harker, if he reflects a little, will put it in next time. It takes up very little room, and makes a good appearance.

We are occasionally reminded, by the advertisements for runaways, to how small an extent it is found *possible to avoid* the separation of families; as in the *Richmond Whig* of Nov. 5, 1852:

$10 REWARD.

We are requested by Henry P. Davis to offer a reward of $10 for the apprehension of a negro man named HENRY, who ran away from the said Davis' farm near Petersburg, on Thursday, the 27th October. Said slave came from near Lynchburg, Va., purchased of —— Cock, and has a wife in Halifax county, Va. He has recently been employed on the South Side Railroad. He may be in the neighborhood of his wife.

PULLIAM & DAVIS, *Aucts.*, *Richmond.*

It seems to strike the advertiser as *possible* that Henry may be in the neighborhood of his wife. We should not at all wonder if he were.

The reader, by this time, is in possession of some of those statistics of which the South Carolinian speaks, when he says,

We feel confident, if statistics could be had, to throw light upon the subject, we should find that there is less separation of families among the negroes than occurs with almost any other class of persons.

In order to give some little further idea of the extent to which this kind of property is continually changing hands, see the following calculation, which has been made from sixty-four Southern newspapers, taken very much at random. The papers were all published in the last two weeks of the month of November, 1852.

The negroes are advertised sometimes by name, sometimes in definite numbers, and sometimes in "lots," "assortments," and other indefinite terms. We present the result of this estimate, far as it must fall from a fair representation of the facts, in a tabular form.

Here is recorded, in *only eleven papers*, the sale of eight hundred forty-nine slaves in *two weeks* in Virginia; the state where Mr. J. Thornton Randolph describes such an event as a separation of families being a thing that "we read of in *novels* sometimes."

States where published.	No. of Papers consulted.	No. of Negroes advertised.	No. of Lots.	No. of Runaways described.
Virginia,	11	849	7	15
Kentucky,	5	238	1	7
Tennessee,	8	385	4	17
S. Carolina,	12	852	2	7
Georgia,	6	98	2	0
Alabama,	10	549	5	5
Mississippi,	8	669	5	6
Louisiana,	4	460	4	35
	64	4100	30	92

In South Carolina, where the writer in *Fraser's Magazine* dates from, we have during these same two weeks a sale of eight hundred and fifty-two recorded by one dozen papers. Verily, we must apply to the newspapers of his state the same language which he applies to "Uncle Tom's Cabin:" "Were our views of the system of slavery to be derived from *these papers*, we should regard the families of slaves as utterly unsettled and vagrant."

The total, in *sixty-four papers*, in different states, for only two weeks, is four thousand one hundred, besides ninety-two *lots*, as they are called.

And now, who is he who compares the hopeless, returnless separation of the negro from his family, to the voluntary separation of the freeman, whom necessary business interest takes for a while from the bosom of his family? Is not the lot of the slave bitter enough, without this last of mockeries and worst of insults? Well may they say, in their anguish, "Our soul is exceedingly filled with the scorning of them that are at ease, and with the contempt of the proud!"

From the poor negro, exposed to bitterest separation, the law jealously takes away the power of writing. For him the gulf of separation yawns black and hopeless, with no redeeming signal. Ignorant of geography, he knows not whither he is going, or where he is, or how to direct a letter. To all intents and purposes, it is a separation hopeless as that of death, and as final.

CHAPTER IV.

THE SLAVE-TRADE.

WHAT is it that constitutes the vital force of the institution of slavery in this country?

Slavery, being an unnatural and unhealthful condition of society, being a most wasteful and impoverishing mode of cultivating the soil, would speedily run itself out in a community, and become so unprofitable as to fall into disuse, were it not kept alive by some unnatural process.

What has that process been in America? Why has that healing course of nature which cured this awful wound in all the northern states stopped short on Mason & Dixon's line? In Delaware, Maryland, Virginia and Kentucky, slave labor long ago impoverished the soil almost beyond recovery, and became entirely unprofitable. In all these states it is well known that the question of emancipation has been urgently presented. It has been discussed in legislatures, and Southern men have poured forth on the institution of slavery such anathemas as only Southern men can pour forth. All that has ever been said of it at the North has been said in four-fold thunders in these Southern discussions. The State of Kentucky once came within one vote, in her legislature, of taking measures for gradual emancipation. The State of Virginia has come almost equally near, and Maryland has long been waiting at the door. There was a time when no one doubted that all these states would soon be free states; and what is now the reason that they are not? Why are these discussions now silenced, and why does this noble determination now retrograde? The answer is in a word. It is the extension of slave territory, the opening of a great southern slave-market, and the organization of a great internal slave-trade, that has arrested the progress of emancipation.

While these states were beginning to look upon the slave as one who might possibly yet become a man, while they meditated giving to him and his wife and children the inestimable blessings of liberty, this great southern slave-mart was opened. It began by the addition of Missouri as slave territory, and the votes of two Northern men were those which decided this great question. Then, by the assent and concurrence of Northern men, came in all the immense acquisition of slave territory which now opens so boundless a market to tempt the avarice and cupidity of the northern slave-raising states.

This acquisition of territory has deferred perhaps for indefinite ages the emancipation of a race. It has condemned to sorrow and heart-breaking separation, to groans and wailings, hundreds of thousands of slave families; it has built, through all the Southern States, slave-warehouses, with all their ghastly furnishings of gags, and thumbscrews, and cowhides; it has organized unnumbered slave-coffles, clanking their chains and filing in mournful march through this land of liberty.

This accession of slave territory hardened the heart of the master. It changed what was before, in comparison, a kindly relation, into the most horrible and inhuman of trades.

The planter whose slaves had grown up around him, and whom he had learned to look upon almost as men and women, saw on every sable forehead now nothing but its market value. This man was a thousand dollars, and this eight hundred. The black baby in its mother's arms was a hundred-dollar bill, and nothing more. All those nobler traits of mind and heart which should have made the slave a brother became only -so many stamps on his merchandise. Is the slave intelligent? — Good! that raises his price two hundred dollars. Is he conscientious and faithful? — Good! stamp it down in his certificate; it's worth two hundred dollars more. Is he religious? Does that Holy Spirit of God, whose name we mention with reverence and fear, make that despised form His temple? — Let that also be put down in the estimate of his market value; and the gift of the Holy Ghost shall be sold for money. Is he a minister of God? — Nevertheless, he has his price in the market. From the church and from the communiontable the Christian brother and sister are taken to make up the slave-coffle. And woman, with her tenderness, her gentleness, her beauty,— woman, to whom mixed blood of the black and the white have given graces perilous for a slave, — what is her accursed lot, in this dreadful commerce? — The next few chapters will disclose facts on this subject which ought to wring the heart of every Christian mother, if, indeed, she be worthy of that holiest name.

But we will not deal in assertions merely. We have stated the thing to be proved; let us show the facts which prove it.

The existence of this fearful traffic is known to many,— the particulars and dreadful extent of it realized but by few.

Let us enter a little more particularly on them. The slave-exporting states are Maryland, Virginia, Kentucky, North Carolina, Tennessee and Missouri. These are slave-raising states, and the others are slave-con-

suming states. We have shown, in the preceding chapters, the kind of advertisements which are usual in those states; but, as we wish to produce on the minds of our readers something of the impression which has been produced on our own mind by their multiplicity and abundance, we shall add a few more here. For the State of VIRGINIA, see all the following:

Kanawha Republican, Oct. 20, 1852, Charleston, Va. At the head — Liberty, with a banner, "*Drapeau sans Tæche.*"

CASH FOR NEGROES.

The subscriber wishes to purchase a few young NEGROES, *from* 12 *to* 25 *years of age*, for which the highest market price will be paid in cash. A few lines addressed to him through the Post Office, Kanawha C. H., or a personal application, will be promptly attended to.   JAS. L. FICKLIN.
Oct. 20, '53. — 3t

Alexandria Gazette, Oct. 28th:

CASH FOR NEGROES.

I wish to purchase immediately, for the South, any number of NEGROES, *from* 10 *to* 30 *years of age*, for which I will pay the very highest cash price. All communications promptly attended to.
        JOSEPH BRUIN.
West End, Alexandria, Va., Oct. 26. — tf

Lynchburg Virginian, Nov. 18:

NEGROES WANTED.

The subscriber, having located in Lynchburg, is giving the highest cash prices for negroes, *between the ages of* 10 *and* 30 *years*. Those having negroes for sale may find it to their interest to call on him at the Washington Hotel, Lynchburg, or address him by letter.

All communications will receive prompt attention.   J. B. McLENDON.
Nov. 5. — dly

Rockingham Register, Nov. 13:

CASH FOR NEGROES.

I wish to purchase a number of NEGROES of both sexes and all ages, for the Southern market, for which I will pay the highest cash prices. Letters addressed to me at Winchester, Virginia, will be promptly attended to.
        H. J. McDANIEL, Agent
Nov. 24, 1846. — tf   for Wm. Crow.

Richmond Whig, Nov. 16:

PULLIAM & DAVIS,
AUCTIONEERS FOR THE SALE OF NEGROES.

D. M. PULLIAM.   HECTOR DAVIS.

The subscribers continue to sell Negroes, at their office, on Wall-street. From *their experience in the business*, they can safely insure the highest prices for all negroes intrusted to their care. They will make sales of negroes in estates, and would say to Commissioners, Executors and Administrators, that they will make their sales on favorable terms. They are prepared to board and lodge negroes comfortably at 25 cents per day.

NOTICE. — CASH FOR SLAVES.

Those who wish to sell slaves in Buckingham and the adjacent counties in Virginia, by application to ANDERSON D. ABRAHAM, Sr., or his son, ANDERSON D. ABRAHAM, Jr., they will find sale, at the highest cash prices, for one hundred and fifty to two hundred slaves. One or the other of the above parties will be found, for the next eight months, at their residence in the aforesaid county and state. Address ANDERSON D. ABRAHAM, Sr., Maysville Post Office, White Oak Grove, Buckingham County, Va.

Winchester Republican, June 29, 1852:

NEGROES WANTED.

The subscriber having located himself in Winchester, Va., wishes to purchase a large number of SLAVES of both sexes, for which he will give the highest price in cash. Persons wishing to dispose of Slaves will find it to their advantage to give him a call before selling.

All communications addressed to him at the *Taylor Hotel, Winchester, Va.,* will meet with prompt attention.   ELIJAH McDOWEL,
       Agent for B. M. & Wm. L. Campbell,
Dec. 27, 1851. — 1y   of Baltimore.

For MARYLAND :

Port Tobacco Times, Oct., '52 :

SLAVES WANTED.

The subscriber is permanently located at MIDDLEVILLE, Charles County (immediately on the road from Port Tobacco to Allen's Fresh), where he will be pleased to buy any SLAVES that are for sale. The extreme value will be given at all times, and liberal commissions paid for information leading to a purchase. Apply personally, or by letter addressed to Allen's Fresh, Charles County.   JOHN G. CAMPBELL.
Middleville, April 14, 1852.

Cambridge (Md.) *Democrat,* October 27, 1852 :

NEGROES WANTED.

I wish to inform the slave-holders of Dorchester and the adjacent counties that I am again in the market. Persons having negroes that are slaves for life to dispose of will find it to their interest to see me before they sell, as I am determined to pay the highest prices in cash that the Southern market will justify. I can be found at A. Hall's Hotel, in Easton, where I will remain until the first day of July next. Communications addressed to me at Easton, or information given to Wm. Bell, in Cambridge, will meet with prompt attention.

I will be at John Bradshaw's Hotel, in Cambridge, every Monday.   WM. HARKER.
Oct. 6, 1852. — 3m.

The Westminster Carroltonian, Oct. 22, 1852 :

25 NEGROES WANTED.

The undersigned wishes to purchase 25 LIKELY YOUNG NEGROES, for which the highest cash

10

prices will be paid. All communications addressed to me in Baltimore will be punctually attended to.   LEWIS WINTERS.
Jan. 2. — tf

For TENNESSEE the following :

Nashville True Whig, Oct. 20th, '52 :

FOR SALE.

21 likely Negroes, of different ages.
Oct. 6.   A. A. McLEAN, Gen. Agent.

WANTED.

I want to purchase, immediately, a Negro man, Carpenter, and will give a good price.
Oct. 6.   A. A. McLEAN, Gen. Agent.

Nashville Gazette, October 22 :

FOR SALE.

SEVERAL likely girls from 10 to 18 years old, a woman 24, a very valuable woman 25 years old, with three very likely children.
       WILLIAMS & GLOVER.
Oct. 16th, 1852.   A. B. U.

WANTED.

I want to purchase Twenty-five LIKELY NEGROES, between the ages of 18 and 25 years, male and female, for which I will pay the highest price IN CASH.   A. A. McLEAN.
Oct. 20.   Cherry Street.

The Memphis Daily Eagle and Enquirer :

500 NEGROES WANTED.

We will pay the highest cash price for all good negroes offered. We invite all those having negroes for sale to call on us at our mart, opposite the lower steamboat landing. We will also have a large lot of Virginia negroes for sale in the Fall. We have as safe a jail as any in the country, where we can keep negroes safe for those that wish them kept.   BOLTON, DICKINS & Co.
je 13 — d & w

LAND AND NEGROES FOR SALE.

A good bargain will be given in about 400 acres of Land ; 200 acres are in a fine state of cultivation, fronting the Railroad about ten miles from Memphis. Together with 18 or 20 likely negroes, consisting of men, women, boys and girls. Good time will be given on a portion of the purchase money.   J. M. PROVINE.
Oct. 17. — 1m.

Clarksville Chronicle, Dec. 3, 1852:

NEGROES WANTED.

We wish to hire 25 good Steam Boat hands for the New Orleans and Louisville trade. We will pay very full prices for the Season, commencing about the 15th November.
       McCLURE & CROZIER, Agents
Sept. 10th, 1852. — 1m   S. B. Bellpoor.

MISSOURI:

The *Daily St. Louis Times*, October 14, 1852:

REUBEN BARTLETT,

On Chesnut, between Sixth and Seventh streets, near the city jail, will pay the highest price in cash for all good negroes offered. There are also other buyers to be found in the office very anxious to purchase, who will pay the highest prices given in cash.

Negroes boarded at the lowest rates.

jy 15 — 6m.

NEGROES.

BLAKELY and McAFEE having dissolved co-partnership by mutual consent, the subscriber will at all times pay the highest cash prices for negroes of every description. Will also attend to the sale of negroes on commission, having a jail and yard fitted up expressly for boarding them.

☞ Negroes for sale at all times.

3   A. B. McAFEE, 93 Olive street.

ONE HUNDRED NEGROES WANTED.

Having just returned from Kentucky, I wish to purchase, as soon as possible, one hundred likely negroes, consisting of men, women, boys and girls, for which I will pay at all times from fifty to one hundred dollars on the head more money than any other trading man in the city of St. Louis, or the State of Missouri. I can at all times be found at Barnum's City Hotel, St. Louis, Mo.

je12d&w1y.   JOHN MATTINGLY.

From another St. Louis paper:

NEGROES WANTED.

I will pay at all times the highest price in cash for all good negroes offered. I am buying for the Memphis and Louisiana markets, and can afford to pay, and will pay, as high as any trading man in this State. All those having negroes to sell will do well to give me a call at No. 210, corner of Sixth and Wash streets, St Louis, Mo.

      THOS. DICKINS,

      of the firm of Bolton, Dickins & Co.

o18 — 6m*

ONE HUNDRED NEGROES WANTED.

Having just returned from Kentucky, I wish to purchase one hundred likely Negroes, consisting of men and women, boys and girls, for which I will pay in cash from fifty to one hundred dollars more than any other trading man in the city of St. Louis or the State of Missouri. I can at all times be found at Barnum's City Hotel, St. Louis, Mo.   JOHN MATTINGLY.

je14d&w1y

B. M. LYNCH,

No. 104 Locust street, St. Louis, Missouri, Is prepared to pay the highest prices in cash for good and likely negroes, or will furnish boarding for others, in comfortable quarters and under secure fastenings. He will also attend to the sale and purchase of negroes on commission.

☞ Negroes for sale at all times.   &w

We ask you, Christian reader, we beg you to think, what sort of scenes are going on in Virginia under these advertisements? You see that they are carefully worded so as to take only the young people; and they are only a specimen of the standing, season advertisements which are among the most common things in the Virginia papers. A succeeding chapter will open to the reader the interior of these slave-prisons, and show him something of the daily incidents of this kind of trade. Now let us look at the corresponding advertisements in the southern states. The coffles made up in Virginia and other states are thus announced in the southern market.

From the *Natchez* (Mississippi) *Free Trader*, Nov. 20 :

NEGROES FOR SALE.

The undersigned have just arrived, direct from Richmond, Va., with a large and likely lot of Negroes, consisting of Field Hands, House Servants, Seamstresses, Cooks, Washers and Ironers, a first-rate brick mason, and other mechanics, which they now offer for sale at the Forks of the Road, near Natchez (Miss.), on the most accommodating terms.

They will continue to receive fresh supplies from Richmond, Va., during the season, and will be able to furnish to any order any description of Negroes sold in Richmond.

Persons wishing to purchase would do well to give us a call before purchasing elsewhere.

nov20–6m   MATTHEWS, BRANTON & Co.

To The Public.
NEGROES BOUGHT AND SOLD.

ROBERT S. ADAMS & MOSES J. WICKS have this day associated themselves under the name and style of ADAMS & WICKS, for the purpose of buying and selling Negroes, in the city of Aberdeen, and elsewhere. They have an Agent who has been purchasing Negroes for them in the Old States for the last two months. One of the firm, Robert S. Adams, leaves this day for North Carolina and Virginia, and will buy a large number of negroes for this market. They will keep at their depot in Aberdeen, during the coming fall and winter, a large lot of choice Negroes, which they will sell *low for cash*, or for bills on Mobile.

      ROBERT S. ADAMS,

      MOSES J. WICKS.

Aberdeen, Miss. May 7th, 1852.

SLAVES! SLAVES! SLAVES!

FRESH ARRIVALS WEEKLY. — Having established ourselves at the Forks of the Road, near Natchez, for a term of years, we have now on hand, and intend to keep throughout the entire year, a large and well-selected stock of Negroes, consisting of field-hands, house servants, mechanics, cooks, seamstresses, washers, ironers, etc., which we can sell and will sell as low or lower than any other house here or in New Orleans.

Persons wishing to purchase would do well to call on us before making purchases elsewhere, as our regular arrivals will keep us supplied with a good and general assortment. Our terms are liberal. Give us a call.

GRIFFIN & PULLUM.
Natchez, Oct. 16, 1852. 6m

NEGROES FOR SALE.

I have just returned to my stand, at the Forks of the Road, with fifty likely young NEGROES for sale. R. H. ELAM.
sept 22

NOTICE.

The undersigned would respectfully state to the public that he has leased the stand in the Forks of the Road, near Natchez, for a term of years, and that he intends to keep a large lot of NEGROES on hand during the year. He will sell as low, or lower, than any other trader at this place or in New Orleans.

He has just arrived from Virginia, with a very likely lot of field men and women and house servants, three cooks, a carpenter and a fine buggy horse, and a saddle-horse and carryall. Call and see. THOS. G. JAMES.

Daily Orleanian, Oct. 19, 1852 :

W. F. TANNEHILL,

No. 159 GRAVIER STREET.

SLAVES! SLAVES! SLAVES!

Constantly on hand, bought and sold on commission, at most reasonable prices.— Field hands, cooks, washers and ironers, and general house servants. City reference given, if required.
oct 14

DEPOT D'ESCLAVES

DE LA NOUVELLE-ORLEANS.

No. 68, RUE BARONNE.

WM. F. TANNEHILL & Co. ont constamment en mains un assortiment complet d'ESCLAVES bien choisis A VENDRE. Aussi, vente et achat d'esclaves par commission.

Nous avons actuellement en mains un grand nombre de NEGRES à louer aux mois, parmi lesquels se trouvent des jeunes garcons, domestiques de maison, cuisinières, blanchisseuses et repasseuses, nourices, etc.

REFERENCES :
Wright, Williams & Co.   Moon, Titus & Co.
Williams, Phillips & Co.   S. O. Nelson & Co.
Moses Greenwood.   E. W. Diggs. 3ms

New Orleans Daily Crescent, Oct. 21, 1852 :

SLAVES.

JAMES WHITE, No. 73 Baronne street, New Orleans, will give strict attention to receiving, boarding and selling SLAVES consigned to him. He will also buy and sell on commission. References : Messrs. Robson & Allen, McRea, Coffman & Co., Pregram, Bryan & Co. sep 23

NEGROES WANTED.

Fifteen or twenty good Negro Men wanted to go on a Plantation. The best of wages will be given until the first of January, 1853.
Apply to THOMAS G. MACKEY & Co.,
5 Canal street, corner of Magazine,
sep11 * up stairs.

From another number of the *Mississippi Free Trader* is taken the following :

NEGROES.

The undersigned would respectfully state to the public that he has a lot of about forty-five now on hand, having this day received a lot of twenty-five *direct from Virginia*, two or three good cooks, a carriage driver, a good house boy, *a fiddler, a fine seamstress* and a likely lot of *field men and women ;* all of whom he will sell at a small profit. He wishes to close out and *go on to Virginia after a lot for the fall trade.* Call and see.
THOMAS G. JAMES.

The slave-raising business of the northern states has been variously alluded to and recognized, both in the business statistics of the states, and occasionally in the speeches of patriotic men, who have justly mourned over it as a degradation to their country. In 1841, the British and Foreign Anti-Slavery Society addressed to the executive committee of the American Anti-Slavery Society some inquiries on the internal American slave-trade.

A labored investigation was made at that time, the results of which were published in London; and from that volume are made the following extracts :

The *Virginia Times* (a weekly newspaper, published at Wheeling, Virginia) estimates, in 1836, the number of slaves exported for sale from that state alone, during " the twelve months preceding," at *forty thousand*, the aggregate value of whom is computed at twenty-four millions of dollars.

Allowing for Virginia one-half of the whole exportation during the period in question, and we have the appalling sum total of *eighty thousand slaves* exported in a single year from the breeding states. We cannot decide with certainty what proportion of the above number was furnished by each of the breeding states, but Maryland ranks next to Virginia in point of numbers, North Carolina follows Maryland, Kentucky North Carolina, then Tennessee and Delaware.

The *Natchez* (Mississippi) *Courier* says " that the States of Louisiana, Mississippi, Alabama and Arkansas, imported *two hundred and fifty thousand* slaves from the more northern states in the year 1836."

This seems absolutely incredible, but it probably includes all the slaves introduced by the immigration of their masters. The following, from the *Virginia Times*, confirms this supposition. In the same paragraph which is referred to under the second query, it is said :

" We have heard intelligent men estimate the number of slaves exported from Virginia, within the last twelve months, at a hundred and twenty thousand, each slave averaging at least six hundred dollars, making an aggregate of seventy-two million dollars. Of the number of slaves exported, not more than *one-third* have been sold ; the others having been carried by their masters, who have removed."

Assuming one-third to be the proportion of the

sold, there are more than eighty thousand imported for sale into the four States of Louisiana, Mississippi, Alabama and Arkansas. Supposing one-half of eighty thousand to be sold into the other buying states, — S. Carolina, Georgia, and the territory of Florida, — and we are brought to the conclusion that more than a hundred and twenty thousand slaves were, for some years previous to the great pecuniary pressure in 1837, exported from the breeding to the consuming states.

The *Baltimore American* gives the following from a Mississippi paper of 1837 :

" The report made by the committee of the citizens of Mobile, appointed at their meeting held on the 1st instant, on the subject of the existing pecuniary pressure, states that so large has been the return of slave labor, that purchases by Alabama of that species of property from other states, since 1833, have amounted to about *ten million dollars annually.*"

" Dealing in slaves," says the *Baltimore* (Maryland) *Register* of 1829, has become a large business ; establishments are made in several places in Maryland and Virginia, at which they are sold like cattle. These places of deposit are strongly built, and well supplied with iron thumbscrews and gags, and ornamented with cowskins and other whips, oftentimes bloody."

Professor Dew, now President of the University of William and Mary, in Virginia, in his review of the debate in the Virginia legislature in 1831—2, says (p. 120) :

" A full equivalent being left in the place of the slave (the purchase-money), this emigration becomes an advantage to the state, and does not check the black population as much as at first view we might imagine ; because it furnishes every inducement to the master to attend to the negroes, *to encourage breeding, and to cause the greatest number possible to be raised.*" Again : " *Virginia is, in fact, a negro-raising state for the other states.*"

Mr. Goode, of Virginia, in his speech before the Virginia legislature, in January, 1832, said : " The superior usefulness of the slaves in the South will constitute an *effectual demand,* which will remove them from our limits. We shall send them from our state, because it will be *our interest* to do so. But gentlemen are alarmed *lest the markets of other states* be closed against the introduction of our slaves. Sir, the demand for *slave labor must increase,*" &c.

In the debates of the Virginia Convention, in 1829, Judge Upshur said : " The value of slaves as an article of property depends much on the state of the market abroad. In this view, it is the value of land *abroad,* and not of land here, which furnishes the ratio. Nothing is more fluctuating than the value of slaves. A late law of Louisiana reduced their value twenty-five per cent. in two hours after its passage was known. *If it should be our lot, as I trust it will be, to acquire the country of Texas, their price will rise again.*"

Hon. Philip Doddridge, of Virginia, in his speech in the Virginia Convention, in 1829 (Debates p. 89), said : " The acquisition of Texas will greatly enhance the value of the property in question (Virginia slaves)."

Rev. Dr. Graham, of Fayetteville, North Carolina, at a Colonization meeting held at that place in the fall of 1837, said :

" There were nearly seven thousand slaves offered in New Orleans market, last winter. From Virginia alone six thousand were annually sent to the South, and from Virginia and North Carolina there had gone to the South, in the last twenty years, THREE HUNDRED THOUSAND SLAVES."

Hon. Henry Clay, of Kentucky, in his speech before the Colonization Society, in 1829, says : " It is believed that nowhere in the farming portion of the United States would slave labor be generally employed, if the proprietor were not tempted to *raise slaves by the high price of the southern markets,* which keeps it up in his own."

The *New York Journal of Commerce* of October 12th, 1835, contains a letter from a Virginian, whom the editor calls " a very good and sensible man," asserting that *twenty thousand* slaves had been driven to the South from Virginia that year, but little more than three-fourths of which had then elapsed.

Mr. Gholson, of Virginia, in his speech in the legislature of that state, January 18, 1831 (see *Richmond Whig*), says :

" It has always (perhaps erroneously) been considered, by steady and old-fashioned people, that the owner of land had a reasonable right to its annual profits ; the owner of orchards to their annual fruits ; the owner of brood mares to their product ; and the owner of *female slaves to their increase.* We have not the fine-spun intelligence nor legal acumen to discover the technical distinctions drawn by gentlemen (that is, the distinction between *female slaves* and *brood mares*). The legal maxim of *partus sequitur ventrem* is coëval with the existence of the right of property itself, and is founded in wisdom and justice. It is on the justice and inviolability of this maxim that the master foregoes the service of the female slave, has her nursed and attended during the period of her gestation, and raises the helpless infant offspring. The value of the property *justifies the expense,* and I do not hesitate to say that in its *increase consists much of our wealth.*"

Can any comment on the state of public sentiment produced by slavery equal the simple reading of this extract, if we remember that it was spoken in the Virginia legislature ? One would think the cold cheek of Washington would redden in its grave for shame, that his native state had sunk so low. That there were Virginian hearts to feel this disgrace is evident from the following reply of Mr. Faulkner to Mr. Gholson, in the Virginia House of Delegates, 1832. See *Richmond Whig :*

" But he (Mr. Gholson) has labored to show that the abolition of slavery would be impolitic, because your slaves constitute the entire wealth of the state, all *the productive capacity* Virginia possesses ; and, sir, as things are, *I believe he is correct.* He says that the slaves constitute the entire available wealth of Eastern Virginia. Is it true that for two hundred years the only increase in the wealth and resources of Virginia has been a remnant of the natural increase of this miserable race ! Can it be that on this increase she places her sole dependence ! Until I heard these declarations, I had not fully conceived the horrible extent of this evil. These gentlemen state the fact, which the history and *present aspect of the commonwealth* but too well sustain. What, sir! have you lived for two hundred years without personal effort or productive industry, in extravagance and indolence, sustained alone by the return from the sales of the increase of slaves, and retaining merely such a number as your now impoverished lands can sustain as STOCK!"

Mr. Thomas Jefferson Randolph in the Virginia legislature used the 'following language (*Liberty Bell*, p. 20):

"I agree with gentlemen in the necessity of arming the state for internal defence. I will unite with them in any effort to restore confidence to the public mind, and to conduce to the sense of the safety of our wives and our children. Yet, sir, I must ask upon whom is to fall the burden of this defence? Not upon the lordly masters of their hundred slaves, who will never turn out except to retire with their families when danger threatens. No, sir; it is to fall upon the *less wealthy class of our citizens, chiefly upon* the non-slaveholder. I have known patrols turned out where *there was not a slave-holder among them;* and this is the practice of the country. I have slept in times of alarm quiet in bed, without having a thought of care, while these individuals, owning none of this property themselves, were patrolling under a compulsory process, for a pittance of seventy-five cents per twelve hours, the very curtilage of my house, and guarding that property which was alike dangerous to them and myself. After all, this is but an expedient. As this population becomes more numerous, it becomes less productive. Your guard must be increased, until finally its profits will not pay for the expense of its subjection. Slavery has the effect of lessening the free population of a country.

"The gentleman has spoken of the increase of the female slaves being a part of the profit. It is admitted; but no great evil can be averted, no good attained, without some inconvenience. It may be questioned how far it is desirable to foster and encourage this branch of profit. It is a practice, and an increasing practice, in parts of Virginia, to rear slaves for market. How can an honorable mind, a patriot, and a lover of his country, bear to see this Ancient Dominion, rendered illustrious by the noble devotion and patriotism of her sons in the cause of liberty, converted into one grand menagerie, where men are to reared for the market, like oxen for the shambles? Is it better, is it not worse, than the slave-trade;— that trade which enlisted the labor of the good and wise of every creed, and every clime, to abolish it? The trader receives the slave, a stranger in language, aspect and manners, from the merchant who has brought him from the interior. The ties of father, mother, husband and child, have all been rent in twain; before he receives him, his soul has become callous. But here, sir, individuals whom the master has known from infancy, whom he has seen sporting in the innocent gambols of childhood, who have been accustomed to look to him for protection, he tears from the mother's arms, and sells into a strange country, among strange people, subject to cruel taskmasters.

"He has attempted to justify slavery here because it exists in Africa, and has stated that it exists all over the world. Upon the same principle, he could justify Mahometanism, with its

plurality of wives, petty wars for plunder, robbery and murder, or any other of the abominations and enormities of savage tribes. Does slavery exist in any part of civilized Europe?—No, sir, in no part of it."

The calculations in the volume from which we have been quoting were made in the year 1841. Since that time, the area of the southern slave-market has been doubled, and the trade has undergone a proportional increase. Southern papers are full of its advertisements. It is, in fact, the great trade of the country. From the single port of Baltimore, in the last two years, a thousand and thirty-three slaves have been shipped to the southern market, as is apparent from the following report of the custom-house officer:

ABSTRACT OF THE NUMBER OF VESSELS CLEARED IN THE DISTRICT OF BALTIMORE FOR SOUTHERN PORTS, HAVING SLAVES ON BOARD, FROM JAN. 1, 1851, TO NOVEMBER 20, 1852.

Date.	Denomina'n	Names of Vessels.	Where Bound.	Nos.
1851				
Jan. 6	Sloop,	Georgia,	Norfolk, Va.	16
" 10	"		"	6
" 11	Bark,	Elizabeth,	New Orleans.	92
" 14	Sloop,	Georgia,	Norfolk, Va.	9
" 17	"		"	6
" 20	Bark,	Cora,	New Orleans.	14
Feb. 6	"	E. H. Chapin,	"	31
" 8	"	Sarah Bridge,	"	34
" 12	Sloop,	Georgia,	Norfolk, Va.	5
" 24	Schooner,	H. A. Barling,	New Orleans.	37
" 26	Sloop,	Georgia,	Norfolk, Va.	3
" 28	"		"	42
Mar. 10	Ship,	Edward Everett,	New Orleans.	20
" 17	Sloop,	Georgia,	Norfolk, Va.	11
" 19	Bark,	Baltimore,	Savannah.	13
Apr. 1	Sloop,	Herald,	Norfolk, Va.	7
" 2	Brig,	Waverley,	New Orleans.	31
" 18	Sloop,	Baltimore,	Arquia Creek, Va.	4
" 23	Ship,	Charles,	New Orleans.	25
" 28	Sloop,	Georgia,	Norfolk, Va.	5
May 15	"	Herald,	"	27
" 17	Schooner,	Brilliant,	Charleston.	1
June 10	Sloop,	Herald,	Norfolk, Va.	3
" 16	"	Georgia,	"	4
" 20	Schooner,	Truth,	Charleston.	5
" 21	Ship,	Herman,	New Orleans.	10
July 19	Schooner,	Aurora S.,	Charleston.	1
Sept. 6	Bark,	Kirkwood,	New Orleans.	2
Oct. 4	"	Abbott Lord,	"	1
" 11	"	Elizabeth,	"	70
" 18	"	Edward Everett,	"	12
Oct. 20	Sloop,	Georgia,	Norfolk, Va.	1
Nov. 13	Ship,	Eliza F. Mason,	New Orleans.	57
" 18	Bark,	Mary Broughtons,	"	47
Dec. 4	Ship,	Timalean,	"	22
" 18	Schooner,	H. A. Barling,	"	45
1852.				
Jan. 5	Bark,	Southerner,	"	52
Feb. 7	Ship,	Nathan Hooper,	"	51
" 21	"	Dumbarton,	"	22
Mar. 27	Sloop,	Palmetto,	Charleston.	36
" 4	"	Jewess,	Norfolk, Va.	34
Apr. 24	"	Palmetto,	Charleston.	8
" 25	Bark,	Abbott Lord,	New Orleans.	36
May 15	Ship,	Charles,	"	2
June 12	Sloop,	Pampero,	"	1
July 3	"	Palmetto,	Charleston.	3
" 6	"	Herald,	Norfolk, Va.	7
" 6	"	Maryland,	Arquia Creek, Va.	4
Sept. 14	"	North Carolina,	Norfolk, Va.	15
" 23	Ship,	America,	New Orleans.	1
Oct. 15	"	Brandywine,	"	6
" 18	Sloop,	Isabel,	Charleston.	1
" 28	Schooner,	Maryland,	"	12
Nov. 1	Ship,	H. M. Gambrill,	Savannah.	11
" 6	Sloop,	Jane Henderson,	New Orleans.	18
		Palmetto,	Charleston.	3
				1033

If we look back to the advertisements, we shall see that the traders take only the younger ones, between the ages of ten and thirty. But this is only one port, and only one mode of exporting; for multitudes of them are sent in coffles over land; and yet Mr. J. Thornton Randolph represents the negroes of Virginia as living in pastoral security, smoking their pipes under their own vines and fig-trees, the venerable patriarch of the flock declaring that "he nebber hab hear such a ting as a nigger sold to Georgia all his life, unless dat nigger did someting very bad."

An affecting picture of the consequences of this traffic upon both master and slave is drawn by the committee of the volume from which we have quoted.

The writer cannot conclude this chapter better than by the language which they have used.

This system bears with extreme severity upon the slave. It subjects him to a perpetual fear of being sold to the "soul-driver," which to the slave is the realization of all conceivable woes and horrors, more dreaded than death. An awful apprehension of this fate haunts the poor sufferer by day and by night, from his cradle to his grave. SUSPENSE hangs like a thunder-cloud over his head. He knows that there is not a passing hour, whether he wakes or sleeps, which may not be THE LAST that he shall spend with his wife and children. Every day or week some acquaintance is snatched from his side, and thus the consciousness of his own danger is kept continually awake. "Surely my turn will come next," is his harrowing conviction; for he knows that he was reared for this, as the ox for the yoke, or the sheep for the slaughter. In this aspect, the slave's condition is truly indescribable. *Suspense*, even when it relates to an event of no great moment, and "endureth but for a night," is hard to bear. But when it broods over all, absolutely all that is dear, chilling the present with its deep shade, and casting its awful gloom over the future, it *must* break the heart! Such is the suspense under which every slave in the breeding states lives. It poisons all his little lot of bliss. If a father, he cannot go forth to his toil without bidding a mental farewell to his wife and children. He cannot return, weary and worn, from the field, with any certainty that he shall not find his home robbed and desolate. Nor can he seek his bed of straw and rags without the frightful misgiving that his wife may be torn from his arms before morning. Should a white stranger approach his master's mansion, he fears that the *soul-driver* has come, and awaits in terror the overseer's mandate, "You are sold; follow that man." There is no being on earth whom the slaves of the breeding states regard with so much horror as the *trader*. He is to them what the prowling kidnapper is to their less wretched brethren in the wilds of Africa. The master knows this, and that there is no punishment so effectual to secure labor, or deter from misconduct, as the threat of being delivered to the soul-driver.*

* This horribly expressive appellation is in common use among the slaves of the breeding states.

Another consequence of this system is the prevalence of licentiousness. This is indeed one of the foul features of slavery everywhere; but it is especially prevalent and indiscriminate where *slave-breeding* is conducted as a business. It grows directly out of the system, and is inseparable from it. * * * The pecuniary inducement to general pollution must be very strong, since the larger the slave increase the greater the master's gains, and especially since the *mixed blood* demands a considerably *higher price than the pure black.*

The remainder of the extract contains specifications too dreadful to be quoted. We can only refer the reader to the volume, p. 13.

The poets of America, true to the holy soul of their divine art, have shed over some of the horrid realities of this trade the pathetic light of poetry. Longfellow and Whittier have told us, in verses beautiful as strung pearls, yet sorrowful as a mother's tears, some of the incidents of this unnatural and ghastly traffic. For the sake of a common humanity, let us hope that the first extract describes no *common* event.

THE QUADROON GIRL.

The Slaver in the broad lagoon
　Lay moored with idle sail;
He waited for the rising moon,
　And for the evening gale.

Under the shore his boat was tied,
　And all her listless crew
Watched the gray alligator slide
　Into the still bayou.

Odors of orange-flowers and spice
　Reached them, from time to time,
Like airs that breathe from Paradise
　Upon a world of crime.

The Planter, under his roof of thatch,
　Smoked thoughtfully and slow;
The Slaver's thumb was on the latch,
　He seemed in haste to go.

He said, "My ship at anchor rides
　In yonder broad lagoon;
I only wait the evening tides,
　And the rising of the moon."

Before them, with her face upraised,
　In timid attitude,
Like one half curious, half amazed,
　A Quadroon maiden stood.

Her eyes were large, and full of light,
　Her arms and neck were bare;
No garment she wore, save a kirtle bright,
　And her own long raven hair.

And on her lips there played a smile
　As holy, meek, and faint,
As lights in some cathedral aisle
　The features of a saint.

"The soil is barren, the farm is old,"
　The thoughtful Planter said;
Then looked upon the Slaver's gold,
　And then upon the maid.

His heart within him was at strife
　With such accursed gains;
For he knew whose passions gave her life,
　Whose blood ran in her veins.

But the voice of nature was too weak ;
  He took the glittering gold !
Then pale as death grew the maiden's cheek,
  Her hands as icy cold.

The Slaver led her from the door,
  He led her by the hand,
To be his slave and paramour
  In a strange and distant land !

THE FAREWELL

OF A VIRGINIA SLAVE MOTHER TO HER DAUGHTERS, SOLD INTO
SOUTHERN BONDAGE.

Gone, gone, — sold and gone,
  To the rice-swamp dank and lone.
Where the slave-whip ceaseless swings,
Where the noisome insect stings,
Where the fever demon strews
Poison with the falling dews,
Where the sickly sunbeams glare
Through the hot and misty air, —
  Gone, gone, — sold and gone,
  To the rice-swamp dank and lone,
  From Virginia's hills and waters, —
  Woe is me, my stolen daughters !

Gone, gone, — sold and gone,
  To the rice-swamp dank and lone.
There no mother's eye is near them,
There no mother's ear can hear them ;
Never, when the torturing lash
Seams their back with many a gash,
Shall a mother's kindness bless them,
Or a mother's arms caress them.
  Gone, gone, &c.

Gone, gone, — sold and gone,
  To the rice-swamp dank and lone.
O, when weary, sad, and slow,
From the fields at night they go,
Faint with toil, and racked with pain,
To their cheerless homes again, —
There no brother's voice shall greet them,
There no father's welcome meet them.
  Gone, gone, &c.

Gone, gone, — sold and gone,
  To the rice-swamp dank and lone.
From the tree whose shadow lay
On their childhood's place of play ; ,
From the cool spring where they drank ;
Rock, and hill, and rivulet bank ;
From the solemn house of prayer,
And the holy counsels there, —
  Gone, gone, &c.

Gone, gone, — sold and gone,
  To the rice-swamp dank and lone ;
Toiling through the weary day,
And at night the spoiler's prey.
O, that they had earlier died,
Sleeping calmly, side by side,
Where the tyrant's power is o'er,
And the fetter galls no more !
  Gone, gone, &c.

Gone, gone, — sold and gone,
  To the rice-swamp dank and lone.
By the holy love He beareth,
By the bruised reed He spareth,
O, may He, to whom alone
All their cruel wrongs are known,
Still their hope and refuge prove,
With a more than mother's love !
  Gone, gone, &c.

            JOHN G. WHITTIER.

  The following extract from a letter of
Dr. Bailey, in the *Era*, 1847, presents a view
of this subject more creditable to some Virginia families. May the number that refuse

to part with slaves except by emancipation
increase !

  The sale of slaves to the south is carried to a
great extent. The slave-holders do not, so far as
I can learn, raise them for that special purpose.
But, here is a man with a score of slaves, located
on an exhausted plantation. It must furnish support for all ; but, while they increase, its capacity
of supply decreases. The result is, he must emancipate or sell. But he has fallen into debt, and
he sells to relieve himself from debt, and also from
an excess of mouths. Or, he requires money to
educate his children ; or, his negroes are sold under execution. From these and other causes, large
numbers of slaves are continually disappearing
from the state, so that the next census will undoubtedly show a marked diminution of the slave
population.

  The season for this trade is generally from November to April ; and some estimate that the average number of slaves passing by the southern
railroad weekly, during that period of six months,
is at least two hundred. A slave-trader told me
that he had known one hundred pass in a single
night. But this is only one route. Large numbers are sent off westwardly, and also by sea,
coastwise. The Davises, in Petersburg, are the
great slave-dealers. They are Jews, who came to
that place many years ago as poor pedlers ; and,
I am informed, are members of a family which
has its representatives in Philadelphia, New York,
&c. ! These men are always in the market, giving the highest price for slaves. During the summer and fall they buy them up at low prices, trim,
shave, wash them, fatten them so that they may
look sleek, and sell them to great profit. It might
not be unprofitable to inquire how much Northern capital, and what firms in some of the Northern cities, are connected with this detestable
business.

  There are many planters here who cannot be
persuaded to sell their slaves. They have far
more than they can find work for, and could at
any time obtain a high price for them. The temptation is strong, for they want more money and
fewer dependants. But they resist it, and nothing can induce them to part with a single slave,
though they know that they would be greatly the
gainers in a pecuniary sense, were they to sell
one-half of them. Such men are too good to be
slave-holders. Would that they might see it their
duty to go one step further, and become emanci-
pators ! The majority of this class of planters
are religious men, and this is the class to which
generally are to be referred the various cases of
emancipation *by will*, of which from time to time
we hear accounts.

<hr>

CHAPTER V.

SELECT INCIDENTS OF LAWFUL TRADE, OR
FACTS STRANGER THAN FICTION.

  THE atrocious and sacrilegious system of
breeding human beings for sale, and trading
them like cattle in the market, fails to produce the impression on the mind that it
ought to produce, because it is lost in
generalities.

It is like the account of a great battle, in which we learn, in round numbers, that ten thousand were killed and wounded, and throw the paper by without a thought.

So, when we read of sixty or eighty thousand human beings being raised yearly and sold in the market, it passes through our mind, but leaves no definite trace.

Sterne says that when he would realize the miseries of captivity, he had to turn his mind from the idea of hundreds of thousands languishing in dungeons, and bring before himself the picture of one poor, solitary captive pining in his cell. In like manner, we cannot give any idea of the horribly cruel and demoralizing effect of this trade, except by presenting facts in detail, each fact being a specimen of a class of facts.

For a specimen of the public sentiment and the kind of morals and manners which this breeding and trading system produces, both in slaves and in their owners, the writer gives the following extracts from a recent letter of a friend in one of the Southern States.

DEAR MRS. S:—The sable goddess who presides over our bed and wash-stand is such a queer specimen of her race, that I would give a good deal to have you see her. Her whole appearance, as she goes giggling and curtseying about, is perfectly comical, and would lead a stranger to think her really deficient in intellect. This is, however, by no means the case. During our two months' acquaintance with her, we have seen many indications of sterling good sense, that would do credit to many a white person with ten times her advantages.

She is disposed to be very communicative;—seems to feel that she has a claim upon our sympathy, in the very fact that we come from the North; and we could undoubtedly gain no little knowledge of the practical workings of the "peculiar institution," if we thought proper to hold any protracted conversation with her. This, however, would insure a visit from the authorities, requesting us to leave town in the next train of cars; so we are forced to content ourselves with gleaning a few items, now and then, taking care to appear quite indifferent to her story, and to cut it short by despatching her on some trifling errand;—being equally careful, however, to note down her peculiar expressions, as soon as she has disppeared. A copy of these I have thought you would like to see, especially as illustrating the views of the marriage institution which is a necessary result of the great human property relation system.

A Southern lady, who thinks "negro sentiment" very much exaggerated in "Uncle Tom's Cabin," assures us that domestic attachments cannot be very strong, where one man will have two or three wives and families, on as many different plantations. (!) And the lady of our hotel tells us of her cook having received a message from her husband, that he has another wife, and she may get another husband, with perfect indifference;

simply expressing a hope that "she won't find another here during the next month, as she must then be sent to her owner, in Georgia, and would be more unwilling to go." And yet, both of these ladies are quite religious, and highly resent any insinuation that the moral character of the slaves is not far above that of the free negroes at the North.

With Violet's story, I will also enclose that of one of our waiters; in which, I think, you will be interested.

Violet's father and mother both died, as she says, "'fore I had any sense," leaving eleven children—all scattered. "To sabe my life, Missis, could n't tell dis yer night where one of dem is. Massa lib in Charleston. My first husband,—when we was young,—nice man; he had seven children; den he sold off to Florida—neber hear from him 'gain. Ole folks die. O, dat's be my boderation, Missis,—when ole people be dead, den we be scattered all 'bout. Den I sold up here—now hab 'noder husband—hab four children up here. I lib bery easy when my young husband 'libe—and we had children bery fast. But now dese yer ones tight fellers. Massa don't 'low us to raise noting; no pig—no goat—no dog—no noting; won't allow us raise a bit of corn. *We has to do jist de best we can.* Dey don't gib us a single grain but jist two homespun frocks—no coat 't all.

"Can't go to meetin, 'cause, Missis, get dis work done—den get dinner. In summer, I goes ebery Sunday ebening; but dese yer short days, time done get dinner dishes washed, den time get supper. Gen'lly goes Baptist church."

"Do your people usually go there?"

"Dere bees tree shares ob dem—Methodist gang, Baptist gang, 'Piscopal gang. Last summer, use to hab right smart* meetins in our yard, Sunday night. Massa Johnson preach to us. Den he said could n't hab two meetins—we might go to church."

"Why?"

"Gracious knows. I lubs to go to meetin allers—'specially when dere 's good preaching—lubs to hab people talk good to me—likes to hab people read to me, too. 'Cause don't b'long to church, no reason why I shan't."

"Does your master like to have others read to you?"

"He won't hinder—I an't bound tell him when folks reads to me. I hab *my* soul to sabe—he hab *his* soul to sabe. Our owners won't stand few minutes and read to us—dey tink it too great honor—dey 's bery hard on us. Brack preachers sometimes talk good to us, and pray wid us,—and *pray a heap for* DEM *too.*

"I jest done hab great quarrel wid Dinah, down in de kitchen. I tells Dinah, ' De way you goes on spile all de women's character.'—She say she did n't care, she do what she please wid herself. Dinah, she slip away somehow from her first husband, and hab 'noder child by Sambo (he b'long to Massa D.); so she and her first husband dey fall out somehow. Dese yer men, yer know, is so queer, Missis, dey don't neber like sich tings.

"Ye know, Missis, tings we lub, we don't like, hab anybody else hab 'em. Such a ting as dat, Missis, tetch your heart so, ef you don't mind, 't will fret you almost to death. Ef my husband

_____

* *Right smart of* — that is, a great many of — an idiom of Anglo-Ethiopia.

was to slip away from me, Missis, dat ar way, it ud wake me right up. I'm brack, but I would n't do so to my husband, neider. What I hide behind de curtain now, I can't hide it behind de curtain when I stand before God—de whole world know it den.

"Dinah's (second) husband say what she do for her first husband noting to him;—now, my husband don't feel so. He say he would n't do as Daniel do—he would n't buy tings for de oder children—dem as has de children might buy de tings for dem. Well, so dere dey is.—Dinah's first husband come up whenever he can, to see his children,—and Sambo, he come up to see his child, and gib Dinah tings for it.

"You know, Missis, Massa hab no nigger but me and one yellow girl, when he bought me and my four children. Well, den Massa, he want me to breed; so he say, 'Violet, you must take some nigger here in C.'

"Den I say, 'No, Massa, I can't take any here.' Den he say, 'You must, Violet;' 'cause you see he want me breed for him; so he say plenty young fellers here, but I say I can't hab any ob dem. Well, den, Missis, he go down Virginia, and he bring up two niggers,—and dey was pretty ole men,—and Missis say, 'One of dem's for you, Violet;' but I say, 'No, Missis, I can't take one of dem, 'cause I don't lub 'em, and I can't hab one I don't lub.' Den Massa, he say, 'You must take one of dese—and den, ef you can't lub him, you must find somebody else you can lub.' Den I say, 'O, no, Massa! I can't do dat—I can't hab one ebery day.' Well, den, by-and-by, Massa he buy tree more, and den Missis say, 'Now, Violet, ones dem is for you.' I say, 'I do'no—maybe I can't lub one dem neider;' but she say, 'You must hab one ob dese.' Well, so Sam and I we lib along two year—he watchin my ways, and I watchin his ways.

"At last, one night, we was standin' by de wood-pile togeder, and de moon bery shine, and I do'no how 't was, Missis, he answer me, he wan't a wife, but he did n't know where he get one. I say, plenty girls in G. He say, 'Yes—but maybe I shan't find any I like so well as you.' Den I say maybe he would n't like my ways, 'cause I 'se an ole woman, and I hab four children by my first husband; and anybody marry me, must be jest kind to dem children as dey was to me, else I could n't lub him. Den he say, 'Ef he had a woman 't had children,'—mind you, he did n't say me,—' he would be jest as kind to de children as he was to de moder, and dat 's 'cordin to how she do by him.' Well, so we went on from one ting to anoder, till at last we say we 'd take one anoder, and so we 've libed togeder eber since—and I 's had four children by him—and he neber slip away from me, nor I from him."

"How are you married in your yard?"

"We jest takes one anoder—we asks de white folks' leave—and den takes one anoder. Some folks, dey 's married by de book; but den, what 's de use! Dere 's my fus husband, we 'se married by de book, and he sold way off to Florida, and I 's here. Dey wants to do what dey please wid us, so dey don't want us to be married. Dey don't care what we does, so we jest makes money for dem.

"My fus husband,—he young, and he bery kind to me,—O, Missis, he bery kind indeed. He set up all night and work, so as to make me comfortable. O, we got 'long bery well when I had

him; but he sold way off Florida, and, sence then, Missis, I jest gone to noting. Dese yer white people dey hab here, dey won't 'low us noting—noting at all—jest gibs us food, and two suits a year—a broad stripe and a narrow stripe; you 'll see 'em, Missis."—

And we did "see 'em;" for Violet brought us the "narrow stripe," with a request that we would fit it for her. There was just enough to cover her, but no hooks and eyes, cotton, or even lining; these extras she must get as she can; and yet her master receives from our host eight dollars per month for her services. We asked how she got the "broad stripe" made up.

"O, Missis, my husband,—he working now out on de farm,—so he hab 'lowance four pounds bacon and one peck of meal ebery week; so he stinge heself, so as to gib me four pounds bacon to pay for making my frock." [Query.—Are there any husbands in refined circles who would do more than this!]

Once, finding us all three busily writing, Violet stood for some moments silently watching the mysterious motion of our pens, and then, in a tone of deepest sadness, said,

"O! dat be great comfort, Missis. You can write to your friends all 'bout ebery ting, and so hab dem write to you. Our people can't do so. Wheder dey be 'live or dead, we can't neber know—only sometimes we hears dey be dead."

What more expressive comment on the cruel laws that forbid the slave to be taught to write!

The history of the serving-man is thus given:

George's father and mother belonged to somebody in Florida. During the war, two older sisters got on board an English vessel, and went to Halifax. His mother was very anxious to go with them, and take the whole family; but her husband persuaded her to wait until the next ship sailed, when he thought he should be able to go too. By this delay opportunity of escape was lost, and the whole family were soon after sold for debt. George, one sister, and their mother, were bought by the same man. He says, "My old boss cry powerful when she (the mother) die; say he 'd rather lost two thousand dollars. She was part Indian—hair straight as yourn—and she was white as dat ar pillow." George married a woman in another yard. He gave this reason for it: "'Cause, when a man sees his wife 'bused, he can't help feelin' it. When he hears his wife 's 'bused, 'tan't like as how it is when he sees it. Then I can fadge for her better than when she 's in my own yard." This wife was sold up country, but after some years became "lame and sick—could n't do much—so her massa gabe her her time, and paid 'her fare to G.''—[The sick and infirm are always provided for, you know.]— "Had n't seen her for tree years," said George; "but soon as I heard of it, went right down;— hired a house, and got some one to take care ob her,—and used to go to see her ebery tree months." He is a mechanic, and worked sometimes all night to earn money to do this. His master asks twenty dollars per month for his services, and allows him fifty cents per week for clothes, etc. J. says, if he could only save, by working nights, money enough to buy himself, he would get some one he could trust to buy him; " den work hard as eber, till I could buy my children, den I'd get away from dis yer."—

" Where ?"

" O ! Philadelphia — New York — somewhere North."

" Why, you'd freeze to death."

" O, no, Missis ! I can bear cold. I want to go *where I can belong to myself*, and do as I want to."

The following communication has been given to the writer by Captain Austin Bearse, ship-master in Boston. Mr. Bearse is a native of Barnstable, Cape Cod. He is well known to our Boston citizens and merchants.

I am a native of the State of Massachusetts. Between the years 1818 and 1830 I was, from time to time, mate on board of different vessels engaged in the coasting trade on the coast of South Carolina. It is well known that many New England vessels are in the habit of spending their winters on the southern coast in pursuit of this business. Our vessels used to run up the rivers for the rough rice and cotton of the plantations, which we took to Charleston.

We often carried gangs of slaves to the plantations, as they had been ordered. These slaves were generally collected by slave-traders in the slave-pens in Charleston, — brought there by various causes, such as the death of owners and the division of estates, which threw them into the market. Some were sent as punishment for insubordination, or because the domestic establishment was too large, or because persons moving to the North or West preferred selling their slaves to the trouble of carrying them. We had on board our vessels, from time to time, numbers of these slaves, — sometimes two or three, and sometimes as high as seventy or eighty. They were separated from their families and connections with as little concern as calves and pigs are selected out of a lot of domestic animals. Our vessels used to lie in a place called Poor Man's Hole, not far from the city. We used to allow the relations and friends of the slaves to come on board and stay all night with their friends, before the vessel sailed.

In the morning it used to be my business to pull off the hatches and warn them that it was time to separate ; and the shrieks and heart-rending cries at these times were enough to make anybody's heart ache.

In the year 1828, while mate of the brig Milton, from Boston, bound to New Orleans, the following incident occurred, which I shall never forget :

The traders brought on board four quadroon men in handcuffs, to be stowed away for the New Orleans market. An old negro woman, more than eighty years of age, came screaming after them, " My son, O, my son, my son !" She seemed almost frantic, and when we had got more than a mile out in the harbor we heard her screaming yet.

When we got into the Gulf Stream, I came to the men, and took off their handcuffs. They were resolute fellows, and they told me that I would see that they would never live to be slaves in New Orleans. One of the men was a carpenter, and one a blacksmith. We brought them into New Orleans, and consigned them over to the agent. The agent told the captain afterwards that in forty-eight hours after they came to New Orleans they were all dead men, having every one killed themselves, as they said they should. One of them, I know, was bought for a fireman on the steamer Post Boy, that went down to the Balize. He jumped over, and was drowned.

The others, — one was sold to a blacksmith, and one to a carpenter. The particulars of their death I didn't know, only that the agent told the captain that they were all dead.

There was a plantation at Coosahatchie, back of Charleston, S. C., kept by a widow lady, who owned eighty negroes. She sent to Charleston, and bought a quadroon girl, very nearly white, for her son. We carried her up. She was more delicate than our other slaves, so that she was not put with them, but was carried up in the cabin.

I have been on the rice-plantations on the river, and seen the cultivation of the rice. In the fall of the year, the plantation hands, both men and women, work all the time above their knees in water in the rice-ditches, pulling out the grass, to fit the ground for sowing the rice. Hands sold here from the city, having been bred mostly to house-labor, find this very severe. The plantations are so deadly that white people cannot remain on them during the summer-time, except at a risk of life. The proprietors and their families are there only through the winter, and the slaves are left in the summer entirely under the care of the overseers. Such overseers as I saw were generally a brutal, gambling, drinking set.

I have seen slavery, in the course of my wanderings, in almost all the countries in the world. I have been to Algiers, and seen slavery there. I have seen slavery in Smyrna, among the Turks. I was in Smyrna when our American consul ransomed a beautiful Greek girl in the slave-market. I saw her come aboard the brig Suffolk, when she came on board to be sent to America for her education. I have seen slavery in the Spanish and French ports, though I have not been on their plantations.

My opinion is that American slavery, as I have seen it in the internal slave-trade, as I have seen it on the rice and sugar plantations, and in the city of New Orleans, is *full as bad* as slavery in any country of the world, heathen or Christian. People who go for visits or pleasure through the Southern States cannot possibly know those things which can be seen of slavery by ship-masters who run up into the back plantations of countries, and who transport the slaves and produce of plantations.

In my past days the system of slavery was not much discussed. I saw these things as others did, without interference. Because I no longer think it right to see these things in silence, I trade no more south of Mason & Dixon's line.

AUSTIN BEARSE.

The following account was given to the writer by Lewis Hayden. Hayden was a fugitive slave, who escaped from Kentucky by the assistance of a young lady named Delia Webster, and a man named Calvin Fairbanks. Both were imprisoned. Lewis Hayden has earned his own character as a free citizen of Boston, where he can find an abundance of vouchers for his character.

I belonged to the Rev. Adam Rankin, a Presbyterian minister in Lexington, Kentucky.

My mother was of mixed blood, — white and Indian. She married my father when he was working in a bagging factory near by. After a while my father's owner moved off and took my father with him, which broke up the marriage. She was a very handsome woman. My master kept a large dairy, and she was the milk-woman. Lexington was a small town in those days, and the dairy was in the town. Back of the college was the Masonic lodge. A man who belonged to the lodge saw my mother when she was about her work. He made proposals of a base nature to her. When she would have nothing to say to him, he told her that she need not be so independent, for if money could buy her he would have her. My mother told old mistress, and begged that master might not sell her. But he did sell her. My mother had a high spirit, being part Indian. She would not consent to live with this man, as he wished; and he sent her to prison, and had her flogged, and punished her in various ways, so that at last she began to have crazy turns. When I read in "Uncle Tom's Cabin" about Cassy, it put me in mind of my mother, and I wanted to tell Mrs. S—— about her. She tried to kill herself several times, once with a knife and once by hanging. She had long, straight black hair, but after this it all turned white, like an old person's. When she had her raving turns she always talked about her children. The jailer told the owner that if he would let her go to her children, perhaps she would get quiet. They let her out one time, and she came to the place where we were. I might have been seven or eight years old, — don't know my age exactly. I was not at home when she came. I came in and found her in one of the cabins near the kitchen. She sprung and caught my arms, and seemed going to break them, and then said, "I 'll fix you so they 'll never get you!" I screamed, for I thought she was going to kill me; they came in and took me away. They tied her, and carried her off. Sometimes, when she was in her right mind, she used to tell me what things they had done to her. At last her owner sold her, for a small sum, to a man named Lackey. While with him she had another husband and several children. After a while this husband either died or was sold, I do not remember which. The man then sold her to another person, named Bryant. My own father's owner now came and lived in the neighborhood of this man, and brought my mother with him. He had had another wife and family of children where he had been living. He and my mother came together again, and finished their days together. My mother almost recovered her mind in her last days.

I never saw anything in Kentucky which made me suppose that ministers or professors of religion considered it any more wrong to separate the families of slaves by sale than to separate any domestic animals.

There may be ministers and professors of religion who think it is wrong, but I never met with them. My master was a minister, and yet he sold my mother, as I have related.

When he was going to leave Kentucky for Pennsylvania, he sold all my brothers and sisters at auction. I stood by and saw them sold. When I was just going up on to the block, he swapped me off for a pair of carriage-horses. I looked at those horses with strange feelings. I had indulged hopes that master would take me into Pennsylvania with him, and I should get free. How I looked at those horses, and walked round them, and thought for them I was sold!

It was commonly reported that my master had said in the pulpit that there was no more harm in separating a family of slaves than a litter of pigs. I did not hear him say it, and so cannot say whether this is true or not.

It may seem strange, but it is a fact, — I had more sympathy and kind advice, in my efforts to get my freedom, from gamblers and such sort of men, than Christians. Some of the gamblers were very kind to me:

I never knew a slave-trader that did not seem to think, in his heart, that the trade was a bad one. I knew a great many of them, such as Neal, McAnn, Cobb, Stone, Pulliam and Davis, &c. They were like Haley, — they meant to repent when they got through.

Intelligent colored people in my circle of acquaintance, as a general thing, felt no security whatever for their family ties. Some, it is true, who belonged to rich families, felt some security; but those of us who looked deeper, and knew how many were not rich that seemed so, and saw how fast money slipped away, were always miserable. The trader was all around, the slave-pens at hand, and we did not know what time any of us might be in it. Then there were the rice-swamps, and the sugar and cotton plantations; we had had them held before us as terrors, by our masters and mistresses, all our lives. We knew about them all; and when a friend was carried off, why, it was the same as death, for we could not write or hear, and never expected to see them again.

I have one child who is buried in Kentucky, and that grave is pleasant to think of. I 've got another that is sold nobody knows where, and that I never can bear to think of. LEWIS HAYDEN.

The next history is a long one, and part of it transpired in a most public manner, in the face of our whole community.

The history includes in it the whole account of that memorable capture of the Pearl, which produced such a sensation in Washington in the year 1848. The author, however, will preface it with a short history of a slave woman who had six children embarked in that ill-fated enterprise.

CHAPTER VI.

MILLY EDMONDSON is an aged woman, now upwards of seventy. She has received the slave's inheritance of entire ignorance. She cannot read a letter of a book, nor write her own name; but the writer must say that she was never so impressed with any presentation of the Christian religion as that which was made to her in the language and appearance of this woman during the few interviews that she had with her. The circumstances of the interviews will be detailed at length in the course of the story.

Milly is above the middle height, of a large, full figure. She dresses with the greatest attention to neatness. A plain

Methodist cap shades her face, and the plain white Methodist handkerchief is folded across the bosom. A well-preserved 'stuff apron, and clean white apron, with a white pocket-handkerchief pinned to her side, completes the inventory of the costume in which the writer usually saw her. She is a mulatto, and must once have been a very handsome one. Her eyes and smile are still uncommonly beautiful, but there are deep-wrought lines of patient sorrow and weary endurance on her face, which tell that this lovely and noble-hearted woman has been all her life a slave.

Milly Edmondson was kept by her owners and allowed to live with her husband, with the express understanding and agreement that her service and value was to consist in breeding up her own children to be sold in the slave-market. Her legal owner was a maiden lady of feeble capacity, who was set aside by the decision of court as incompetent to manage her affairs.

The estate — that is to say, Milly Edmondson and her children —, was placed in the care of a guardian. It appears that Milly's poor, infirm mistress was fond of her, and that Milly exercised over her much of that ascendency which a strong mind holds over a weak one. Milly's husband, Paul Edmondson was a free man. A little of her history, as she related it to the writer, will now be given in her own words:

"Her mistress," she said, "was always kind to her 'poor thing!' but then she had n't *sperit* ever to speak for herself, and her friends would n't let her have her own way. It always laid on my mind," she said, "that I was a slave. When I wan't more than fourteen years old, Missis was doing some work one day that she thought she could n't trust me with, and she says to me, 'Milly, now you see it 's I that am the slave, and not you.' I says to her, 'Ah, Missis, I am a poor slave, for all that.' I 's sorry afterwards I said it, for I thought it seemed to hurt her feelings.

"Well, after a while, when I got engaged to Paul, I loved Paul very much; but I thought it wan't right to bring children into the world to be slaves, and I told our folks that I was never going to marry, though I did love Paul. But that wan't to be allowed," she said, with a mysterious air. "What do you mean?" said I.

"Well, they told me I must marry, or I should be turned out of the church — so it was," she added, with a significant nod. — "Well, Paul and me, we was married, and

we was happy enough, if it had n't been for that; but when our first child was born I says to him, 'There 't is, now, Paul, our troubles is begun; this child is n't ours.' And every child I had, it grew worse and worse. 'O, Paul,' says I, 'what a thing it is to have children that is n't ours!' Paul he says to me, 'Milly, my dear, if they be God's children, it an't so much matter whether they be ours or no; they may be heirs of the kingdom, Milly, for all that.' Well, when Paul's mistress died, she set him free, and he got him a little place out about fourteen miles from Washington; and they let me live out there with him, and take home my tasks; for they had that confidence in me that they always know'd that what I said I 'd do was as good done as if they 'd seen it done. I had mostly sewing; sometimes a shirt to make in a day, — it was coarse like, you know, — or a pair of sheets, or some such; but, whatever 't was, I always got it done. Then I had all my house-work and babies to take care of; and many 's the time, after ten o'clock, I 've took my children's clothes and washed 'em all out and ironed 'em late in the night, 'cause I could n't never bear to see my children dirty, — always wanted to see 'em sweet and clean, and I brought 'em up and taught 'em the very best ways I was able. But nobody knows what I suffered; I never see a white man come on to the place that I did n't think, 'There, now, he 's coming to look at my children;' and when I saw any white man going by, I 've called in my children and hid 'em, for fear he 'd see 'em and want to buy 'em. O, ma'am, mine 's been a long sorrow, a long sorrow! I 've borne this heavy cross a great many years."

"But," said I, "the Lord has been with you."

She answered, with very strong emphasis, "Ma'am, if the Lord had n't held me up, I should n't have been alive this day. O, sometimes my heart 's been so heavy, it seemed as if I *must* die; and then I 've been to the throne of grace, and when I 'd poured out all my sorrows there, I came away *light*, and felt that I could live a little longer."

This language is exactly her own. She had often a forcible and peculiarly beautiful manner of expressing herself, which impressed what she said strongly.

Paul and Milly Edmondson were both devout communicants in the Methodist Episcopal Church at Washington, and the testimony to their blamelessness of life and the consistence of their piety is unanimous from all who know them. In their simple cottage, made respectable by neatness and order, and hallowed by morning and evening prayer, they trained up their children, to the best of their poor ability, in the nurture and admonition of the Lord, to be sold in the slave-market. They thought themselves only too happy, as one after another arrived at the age when they were to be sold, that they were hired to families in their vicinity, and not thrown into the trader's pen to be drafted for the dreaded southern market!

The mother, feeling, with a constant but repressed anguish, the weary burden of slavery which lay upon her, was accustomed, as she told the writer, thus to warn her daughters:

"Now, girls, don't you never come to the sorrows that I have. Don't you never marry till you get your liberty. Don't you marry, to be mothers to *children that an't your own.*"

As a result of this education, some of her older daughters, in connection with the young men to whom they were engaged, raised the sum necessary to pay for their freedom before they were married. One of these young women, at the time that she paid for her freedom, was in such feeble health that the physician told her that she could not live many months, and advised her to keep the money, and apply it to making herself as comfortable as she could.

She answered, " If I had only two hours to live, I would pay down that money to die free."

If this was setting an extravagant value on liberty, it is not for an American to say so.

All the sons and daughters of this family were distinguished both for their physical and mental developments, and therefore were priced exceedingly high in the market. The whole family, rated by the market prices which have been paid for certain members of it, might be estimated as an estate of fifteen thousand dollars. They were distinguished for intelligence, honesty and faithfulness, but above all for the most devoted attachment to each other. These children, thus intelligent, were all held as slaves in the city of Washington, the very capital where our national government is conducted. Of course, the high estimate which their own mother taught them to place upon liberty was in the way of being constantly strengthened and reinforced by such addresses, celebrations and speeches,

on the subject of liberty, as every one knows are constantly being made, on one occasion or another, in our national capital.

On the 13th day of April, the little schooner PEARL, commanded by Daniel Drayton, came to anchor in the Potomac river, at Washington.

The news had just arrived of a revolution in France, and the establishment of a democratic government, and all Washington was turning out to celebrate the triumph of Liberty.

The trees in the avenue were fancifully hung with many-colored lanterns,— drums beat, bands of music played, the houses of the President and other high officials were illuminated, and men, women and children, were all turned out to see the procession, and to join in the shouts of liberty that rent the air. Of course, all the slaves of the city, lively, fanciful and sympathetic, most excitable as they are by music and by dazzling spectacles, were everywhere listening, seeing, and rejoicing, in ignorant joy. All the heads of department, senators, representatives, and dignitaries of all kinds, marched in procession to an open space on Pennsylvania Avenue, and there delivered congratulatory addresses on the progress of universal freedom. With unheard-of imprudence, the most earnest defenders of slave-holding institutions poured down on the listening crowd, both of black and white, bond and free, the most inflammatory and incendiary sentiments. Such, for example, as the following language of Hon. Frederick P. Stanton, of Tennessee:

We do not, indeed, propagate our principles with the sword of power; but there is one sense in which we are propagandists. We cannot help being so. Our example is contagious. In the section of this great country where I live, on the banks of the mighty Mississippi river, we have the true emblem of the tree of liberty. There you may see the giant cotton-wood spreading his branches widely to the winds of heaven. Sometimes the current lays bare his roots, and you behold them extending far around, and penetrating to an immense depth in the soil. When the season of maturity comes, the air is filled with a cotton-like substance, which floats in every direction, bearing on its light wings the living seeds of the mighty tree. Thus the seeds of freedom have emanated from the tree of our liberties. They fill the air. They are wafted to every part of the habitable globe. And even in the barren sands of tyranny they are destined to take root. The tree of liberty will spring up everywhere, and nations shall recline in its shade.

Senator Foote, of Mississippi, also, used this language:

Such has been the extraordinary course of events

in France, and in Europe, within the last two months, that the more deliberately we survey the scene which has been spread out before us, and the more rigidly we scrutinize the conduct of its actors, the more confident does our conviction become that the *glorious work* which has been so well begun cannot possibly fail of complete accomplishment; that the age of TYRANTS AND SLAVERY is rapidly drawing to a close; and that the happy period to be signalized by the *universal emancipation of man* from the *fetters of civil oppression*, and the recognition *in all countries* of the great principles of *popular sovereignty, equality, and* BROTHERHOOD, is, at this moment, visibly commencing.

Will any one be surprised, after this, that seventy-seven of the most intelligent young slaves, male and female, in Washington city, honestly taking Mr. Foote and his brother senators at their word, and believing that the age of tyrants and slavery was drawing to a close, banded together, and made an effort to obtain their part in this reign of universal brotherhood?

The schooner Pearl was lying in the harbor, and Captain Drayton was found to have the heart of a man. Perhaps he, too, had listened to the addresses on Pennsylvania Avenue, and thought, in the innocence of his heart, that a man who really *did* something to promote universal emancipation was no worse than the men who only made speeches about it.

At any rate, Drayton was persuaded to allow these seventy-seven slaves to secrete themselves in the hold of his vessel, and among them were six children of Paul and Milly Edmondson. The incidents of the rest of the narrative will now be given as obtained from Mary and Emily Edmondson, by the lady in whose family they have been placed by the writer for an education.

Some few preliminaries may be necessary, in order to understand the account.

A respectable colored man, by the name of Daniel Bell, who had purchased his own freedom, resided in the city of Washington. His wife, with her eight children, were set free by her master, when on his death-bed. The heirs endeavored to break the will, on the ground that he was not of sound mind at the time of its preparation. The magistrate, however, before whom it was executed, by his own personal knowledge of the competence of the man at the time, was enabled to defeat their purpose;—the family, therefore, lived as free for some years. On the death of this magistrate, the heirs again brought the case into court, and, as it seemed likely to be decided against the family, they resolved to secure their legal rights by flight,

and engaged passage on board the vessel of Captain Drayton. Many of their associates and friends, stirred up, perhaps, by the recent demonstrations in favor of liberty, begged leave to accompany them, in their flight. The seeds of the cotton-wood were flying everywhere, and springing up in all hearts; so that, on the eventful evening of the 15th of April, 1848, not less than seventy-seven men, women and children, with beating hearts, and anxious secrecy, stowed themselves away in the hold of the little schooner, and Captain Drayton was so wicked that he could not, for the life of him, say "Nay" to one of them.

Richard Edmondson had long sought to buy his liberty; had toiled for it early and late; but the price set upon him was so high that he despaired of ever earning it. On this evening, he and his three brothers thought, as the reign of universal brotherhood had begun, and the reign of tyrants and slavery come to an end, that they would take to themselves and their sisters that sacred gift of liberty, which all Washington had been informed, two evenings before, it was the peculiar province of America to give to all nations. Their two sisters, aged sixteen and fourteen, were hired out in families in the city. On this evening Samuel Edmondson called at the house where Emily lived, and told her of the projected plan.

"But what will mother think?" said Emily.

"Don't stop to think of her; she would rather we'd be free than to spend time to talk about her."

"Well, then, if Mary will go, I will."

The girls give as a reason for wishing to escape, that though they had never suffered hardships or been treated unkindly, yet they knew they were liable at any time to be sold into rigorous bondage, and separated far from all they loved.

They then all went on board the Pearl, which was lying a little way off from the place where vessels usually anchor. There they found a company of slaves, seventy-seven in number.

At twelve o'clock at night the silent wings of the little schooner were spread, and with her weight of fear and mystery she glided out into the stream. A fresh breeze sprang up, and by eleven o'clock next night they had sailed two hundred miles from Washington, and began to think that liberty was gained. They anchored in a place called Cornfield Harbor, intending to wait for daylight. All laid down to sleep in peaceful security, lulled by the gentle rock of the vessel and the rippling of the waters.

But at two o'clock at night they were roused by terrible noises on deck, scuffling, screaming, swearing and groaning. A steamer had pursued and overtaken them, and the little schooner was boarded by an infuriated set of armed men. In a moment, the captain, mate and all the crew, were seized and bound, amid oaths and dreadful threats. As they, swearing and yelling, tore open the hatches on the defenceless prisoners below, Richard Edmondson stepped forward, and in a calm voice said to them, "Gentlemen, do yourselves no harm, for we are all here." With this exception, all was still among the slaves as despair could make it; not a word was spoken in the whole company. The men were all bound and placed on board the steamer; the women were left on board the schooner, to be towed after.

The explanation of their capture was this: In the morning after they had sailed, many families in Washington found their slaves missing, and the event created as great an excitement as the emancipation of France had, two days before. At that time they had listened in the most complacent manner to the announcement that the reign of slavery was near its close, because they had not the slightest idea that the language meant anything; and they were utterly confounded by this practical application of it. More than a hundred men, mounted upon horses, determined to push out into the country, in pursuit of these new disciples of the doctrine of universal emancipation. Here a colored man, by the name of Judson Diggs, betrayed the whole plot. He had been provoked, because, after having taken a poor woman, with her luggage, down to the boat, she was unable to pay the twenty-five cents that he demanded. So he told these admirers of universal brotherhood that they need not ride into the country, as their slaves had sailed down the river, and were far enough off by this time. A steamer was immediately manned by two hundred armed men, and away they went in pursuit.

When the cortege arrived with the captured slaves, there was a most furious excitement in the city. The men were driven through the streets bound with ropes, two and two. Showers of taunts and jeers rained upon them from all sides. One man asked one of the girls if she "didn't feel pretty to be caught running away," and another asked her "if she wasn't sorry." She answered, "No, if it was to do again to-morrow, she would do the same." The man turned to a bystander and said, "Han't she got good spunk?"

But the most vehement excitement was against Drayton and Sayres, the captain and mate of the vessel. Ruffians armed with dirk-knives and pistols crowded around them, with the most horrid threats. One of them struck so near Drayton as to cut his ear, which Emily noticed as bleeding. Meanwhile there mingled in the crowd multitudes of the relatives of the captives, who, looking on them as so many doomed victims, bewailed and lamented them. A brother-in-law of the Edmondsons was so overcome when he saw them that he fainted away and fell down in the street, and was carried home insensible. The sorrowful news spread to the cottage of Paul and Milly Edmondson; and, knowing that all their children were now probably doomed to the southern market, they gave themselves up to sorrow. "O! what a day that was!" said the old mother when describing that scene to the writer. "Never a morsel of anything could I put into my mouth. Paul and me we fasted and prayed before the Lord, night and day, for our poor children."

The whole public sentiment of the community was roused to the most intense indignation. It was repeated from mouth to mouth that they had been kindly treated and never abused; and what could have induced them to try to get their liberty? All that Mr. Stanton had said of the insensible influence of American institutions, and all his pretty similes about the cotton-wood seeds, seemed entirely to have escaped the memory of the community, and they could see nothing but the most unheard-of depravity in the attempt of these people to secure freedom. It was strenuously advised by many that their owners should not forgive them, — that no mercy should be shown, but that they should be thrown into the hands of the traders, forthwith, for the southern market, — that Siberia of the irresponsible despots of America.

When all the prisoners were lodged in jail, the owners came to make oath to their property, and the property also was required to make oath to their owners. Among them came the married sisters of Mary and Emily, but were not allowed to enter the prison. The girls looked through the iron grates of the third-story windows, and saw their sisters standing below in the yard weeping.

The guardian of the Edmondsons, who acted in the place of the real owner, apparently touched with their sorrow, promised their family and friends, who were anxious to purchase them, if possible, that they should have an opportunity the next morning. Perhaps he intended at the time to give them one; but, as Bruin and Hill, the keepers of the large slave warehouse in Alexandria, offered him four thousand five hundred dollars for the six children, they were irrevocably sold before the next morning. Bruin would listen to no terms which any of their friends could propose. The lady with whom Mary had lived offered a thousand dollars for her; but Bruin refused, saying he could get double that sum in the New Orleans market. He said he had had his eye upon the family for twelve years, and had the promise of them should they ever be sold.

While the girls remained in the prison they had no beds or chairs, and only one blanket each, though the nights were chilly; but, understanding that the rooms below, where their brothers were confined, were still colder, and that no blankets were given them, they sent their own down to them. In the morning they were allowed to go down into the yard for a few moments; and then they used to run to the window of their brothers' room, to bid them good-morning, and kiss them through the grate.

At ten o'clock, Thursday night, the brothers were handcuffed, and, with their sisters, taken into carriages by their new owners, driven to Alexandria, and put into a prison called a Georgia Pen. The girls were put into a large room alone, in total darkness, without bed or blanket, where they spent the night in sobs and tears, in utter ignorance of their brothers' fate. At eight o'clock in the morning they were called to breakfast, when, to their great comfort, they found their four brothers all in the same prison.

They remained here about four weeks, being usually permitted by day to stay below with their brothers, and at night to return to their own rooms. Their brothers had great anxieties about them, fearing they would be sold south. Samuel, in particular, felt very sadly, as he had been the principal actor in getting them away. He often said he would gladly *die* for them, if that would save them from the fate he feared. He used to weep a great deal, though he endeavored to restrain his tears in their presence.

While in the slave-prison they were required to wash for thirteen men, though their brothers performed a great share of the labor. Before they left, their size and height were measured by their owners. At length they were again taken out, the brothers handcuffed, and all put on board a steamboat, where were about forty slaves, mostly men, and taken to Baltimore. The voyage occupied one day and a night. When arrived in Baltimore, they were thrown into a slave-pen kept by a partner of Bruin and Hill. He was a man of coarse habits, constantly using the most profane language, and grossly obscene and insulting in his remarks to women. Here they were forbidden to pray together, as they had previously been accustomed to do. But, by rising very early in the morning, they secured to themselves a little interval which they could employ, uninterrupted, in this manner. They, with four or five other women in the prison, used to meet together, before daybreak, to spread their sorrows before the Refuge of the afflicted; and in these prayers the hard-hearted slave-dealer was daily remembered. The brothers of Mary and Emily were very gentle and tender in their treatment of their sisters, which had an influence upon other men in their company.

At this place they became acquainted with Aunt Rachel, a most godly woman, about middle age, who had been sold into the prison away from her husband. The poor husband used often to come to the prison and beg the trader to sell her to *his* owners, who he thought were willing to purchase her, if the price was not too high. But he was driven off with brutal threats and curses. They remained in Baltimore about three weeks.

The friends in Washington, though hitherto unsuccessful in their efforts to redeem the family, were still exerting themselves in their behalf; and one evening a message was received from them by telegraph, stating that a person would arrive in the morning train of cars prepared to bargain for the family, and that a part of the money was now ready. But the trader was inexorable, and in the morning, an hour before the cars were to arrive, they were all put on board the brig *Union*, ready to sail for New Orleans. The messenger came, and brought nine hundred dollars in money, the gift of a grandson of John Jacob Astor. This was finally appropriated to the ransom of Richard Edmondson, as his wife and children were said to be suffering in Washington; and the trader would not sell the girls to them upon any consideration, nor would he even suffer Richard to be brought back from the brig, which had not yet sailed. The bargain was, however, made, and the money deposited in Baltimore.

On this brig the eleven women were put in one small apartment, and the thirty or forty men in an adjoining one. Emily was very sea-sick most of the time, and her brothers feared she would die. They used to come and carry her out on deck and back again, buy little comforts for their sisters, and take all possible care of them.

Frequently head winds blew them back, so that they made very slow progress; and in their prayer-meetings, which they held every night, they used to pray that head winds might blow them to New York; and one of the sailors declared that if they could get within one hundred miles of New York, and the slaves would stand by him, he would make way with the captain, and pilot them into New York himself.

When they arrived near Key West, they hoisted a signal for a pilot, the captain being aware of the dangers of the place, and yet not knowing how to avoid them. As the pilot-boat approached, the slaves were all fastened below, and a heavy canvas thrown over the grated hatchway door, which entirely excluded all circulation of air, and almost produced suffocation. The captain and pilot had a long talk about the price, and some altercation ensued, the captain not being willing to give the price demanded by the pilot; during which time there was great suffering below. The women became so exhausted that they were mostly helpless; and the situation of the men was not much better, though they managed with a stick to break some holes through the canvas on their side, so as to let in a little air, but a few only of the strongest could get there to enjoy it. Some of them shouted for help as long as their strength would permit; and at length, after what seemed to them an almost interminable interview, the pilot left, refusing to assist them; the canvas was removed, and the brig obliged to turn tack, and take another course. Then, one after another, as they got air and strength, crawled out on deck. Mary and Emily were carried out by their brothers as soon as they were able to do it.

Soon after this the stock of provisions ran low, and the water failed, so that the slaves were restricted to a gill a day. The sailors were allowed a quart each, and often gave a pint of it to one of the Edmondsons for their sisters; and they divided it with

the other women, as they always did every nice thing they got in such ways.

The day they arrived at the mouth of the Mississippi a terrible storm arose, and the waves rolled mountain high, so that, when the pilot-boat approached, it would sometimes seem to be entirely swallowed by the waves, and again it would emerge, and again appear wholly buried. At length they were towed into and up the river by a steamer, and there, for the first time, saw cotton plantations, and gangs of slaves at work on them.

They arrived at New Orleans in the night, and about ten the next day were landed and marched to what they called the show-rooms, and, going out into the yard, saw a great many men and women sitting around, with such sad faces that Emily soon began to cry, upon which an overseer stepped up and struck her on the chin, and bade her "stop crying, or he would give her something to cry about." Then pointing, he told her "there was the calaboose, where they whipped those who did not behave themselves!" As soon as he turned away, a slave-woman came and told her to look cheerful, if she possibly could, as it would be far better for her. One of her brothers soon came to inquire what the woman had been saying to her; and when informed, encouraged Emily to follow the advice, and endeavored to profit by it himself.

That night all the four brothers had their hair cut close, their mustaches shaved off, and their usual clothing exchanged for a blue jacket and pants, all of which so altered their appearance that at first their sisters did not know them. Then, for three successive days, they were all obliged to stand in an open porch fronting the street, for passers by to look at, except, when one was tired out, she might go in for a little time, and another take her place. Whenever buyers called, they were paraded in the auction-room in rows, exposed to coarse jokes and taunts. When any one took a liking to any girl in the company, he would call her to him, take hold of her, open her mouth, look at her teeth, and handle her person rudely, frequently making obscene remarks; and she must stand and bear it, without resistance. Mary and Emily complained to their brothers that they could not submit to such treatment. They conversed about it with Wilson, a partner of Bruin and Hill, who had the charge of the slaves at this prison. After this they were treated with more decency.

Another brother of the girls, named Hamilton, had been a slave in or near New Orleans for sixteen years, and had just purchased his own freedom for one thousand dollars; having once before earned that sum for himself, and then had it taken from him. Richard being now really free, as the money was deposited in Baltimore for his ransom, found him out the next day after their arrival at New Orleans, and brought him to the prison to see his brothers and sisters. The meeting was overpoweringly affecting.

He had never before seen his sister Emily, as he had been sold away from his parents before her birth.

The girls' lodging-room was occupied at night by about twenty or thirty women, who all slept on the bare floor, with only a blanket each. After a few days, word was received (which was *really incorrect*), that half the money had been raised for the redemption of Mary and Emily. After this they were allowed, upon their brothers' earnest request, to go to their free brother's house and spend their nights, and return in the mornings, as they had suffered greatly from the mosquitos and other insects, and their feet were swollen and sore.

While at this prison, some horrible cases of cruelty came to their knowledge, and some of them under their own observation. Two persons, one woman and one boy, were whipped to death in the prison while they were there, though they were not in the same pen, or owned by the same trader, as themselves.

None of the slaves were allowed to sleep in the day-time, and sometimes little children sitting or standing idle all day would become so sleepy as not to be able to hold up their eyelids; but, if they were caught thus by the overseer, they were cruelly beaten. Mary and Emily used to watch the little ones, and let them sleep until they heard the overseers coming, and then spring and rouse them in a moment.

One young woman, who had been sold by the traders for the worst of purposes, was returned, not being fortunate (?) enough to suit her purchaser; and, as is their custom in such cases, was most cruelly flogged,—so much so that some of her flesh mortified, and her life was despaired of. When Mary and Emily first arrived at New Orleans they saw and conversed with her. She was then just beginning to sit up; was quite small, and very fine-looking, with beautiful straight hair, which was formerly long, but had been cut off short by her brutal tormentors.

The overseer who flogged her said, in their hearing, that he would never flog another girl in that way — it was too much for any one to bear. They suggest that perhaps the reason why he promised this was because he was obliged to be her nurse, and of course saw her sufferings. She was from Alexandria, but they have forgotten her name.

One young man and woman of their company in the prison, who were engaged to be married, and were sold to different owners, felt so distressed at their separation that they could not or did not labor well; and the young man was soon sent back, with the complaint that he would not answer the purpose. Of course, the money was to be refunded, and he flogged. He was condemned to be flogged each night for a week; and, after about two hundred lashes by the overseer, each one of the male slaves in the prison was required to come and lay on five lashes with all his strength, upon penalty of being flogged himself. The young woman, too, was soon sent there, with a note from her new mistress, requesting that she might be whipped a certain number of lashes, and enclosing the money to pay for it; which request was readily complied with.

While in New Orleans they saw gangs of women cleaning the streets, chained together, some with a heavy iron ball attached to the chain; a form of punishment frequently resorted to for household servants who had displeased their mistresses.

Hamilton Edmondson, the brother who had purchased his own freedom, made great efforts to get good homes for his brothers and sisters in New Orleans, so that they need not be far separated from each other. One day, Mr. Wilson, the overseer, took Samuel away with him in a carriage, and returned without him. The brothers and sisters soon found that he was sold, and gone they knew not whither; but they were not allowed to weep, or even look sad, upon pain of severe punishment. The next day, however, to their great joy, he came to the prison himself, and told them he had a good home in the city with an Englishman, who had paid a thousand dollars for him.

After remaining about three weeks in this prison, the Edmondsons were told that, in consequence of the prevalence of the yellow fever in the city, together with the fact of their not being acclimated, it was deemed dangerous for them to remain there longer; — and, besides this, purchasers were loth to give good prices under these circumstances.

Some of the slaves in the pen were already sick; some of them old, poor or dirty, and for these reasons greatly exposed to sickness. Richard Edmondson had already been ransomed, and must be sent back; and, upon the whole, it was thought best to fit out and send off a gang to Baltimore, without delay.

The Edmondsons received these tidings with joyful hearts, for they had not yet been undeceived with regard to the raising of the money for their ransom. Their brother who was free procured for them many comforts for the voyage, such as a mattress, blankets, sheets and different kinds of food and drink; and, accompanied to the vessel by their friends there, they embarked on the brig Union just at night, and were towed out of the river. The brig had nearly a full cargo of cotton, molasses, sugar, &c., and, of course, the space for the slaves was exceedingly limited. The place allotted the females was a little close, filthy room, perhaps eight or ten feet square, filled with cotton within two or three feet of the top of the room, except the space directly under the hatchway door. Richard Edmondson kept his sisters upon deck with him, though without a shelter; prepared their food himself, made up their bed at night on the top of barrels, or wherever he could find a place, and then slept by their side. Sometimes a storm would arise in the middle of the night, when he would spring up and wake them, and, gathering up their bed and bedding, conduct them to a little kind of a pantry, where they could all three just stand, till the storm passed away. Sometimes he contrived to make a temporary shelter for them out of bits of boards, or something else on deck.

After a voyage of sixteen days, they arrived at Baltimore, fully expecting that their days of slavery were numbered. Here they were conducted back to the same old prison from which they had been taken a few weeks before, though they supposed it would be but for an hour or two. Presently Mr. Bigelow, of Washington, came for Richard. When the girls found that they were not to be set free too, their grief and disappointment were unspeakable. But they were *separated*,—Richard to go to his home, his wife and children, and they to remain in the slave-prison. Wearisome days and nights again rolled on. In the mornings they were obliged to march round the yard to the music of fiddles, banjoes, &c.; in the day-time they washed and ironed for the male slaves, slept some, and wept a great deal. After a few weeks their father came to visit them, accompanied by their sister.

His object was partly to ascertain what were the very lowest terms upon which their keeper would sell the girls, as he indulged a faint hope that in some way or other the money might be raised, if time enough were allowed. The trader declared he should soon send them to some other slave-market, but he would wait two weeks, and, if the friends could raise the money in that time, they might have them.

The night their father and sister spent in the prison with them, he lay in the room over their heads; and they could hear him groan all night, while their sister was weeping by their side. None of them closed their eyes in sleep.

In the morning came again the wearisome routine of the slave-prison. Old Paul walked quietly into the yard, and sat down to see the poor slaves marched around. He had never seen his daughters in such circumstances before, and his feelings quite overcame him. The yard was narrow, and the girls, as they walked by him, almost brushing him with their clothes, could just hear him groaning within himself, " O, my children, my children ! "

After the breakfast, which none of them were able to eat, they parted with sad hearts, the father begging the keeper to send them to New Orleans, if the money could not be raised, as perhaps their brothers there might secure for them kind masters.

Two or three weeks afterwards Bruin & Hill visited the prison, dissolved partnership with the trader, settled accounts, and took the Edmondsons again in their own possession.

The girls were roused about eleven o'clock at night, after they had fallen asleep, and told to get up directly, and prepare for going home. They had learned that the word of a slave-holder is not to be trusted, and feared they were going to be sent to Richmond, Virginia, as there had been talk of it. They were soon on their way in the cars with Bruin, and arrived at Washington at a little past midnight.

Their hearts throbbed high when, after these long months of weary captivity, they found themselves once more in the city where were their brothers, sisters and parents. But they were permitted to see none of them, and were put into a carriage and driven immediately to the slave-prison at Alexandria, where, about two o'clock at night, they found themselves in the same forlorn old room in which they had begun their term of captivity !

This was the latter part of August. Again they were employed in washing, ironing and sewing by day, and always locked up by night. Sometimes they were allowed to sew in Bruin's house, and even to eat there. After they had been in Alexandria two or three weeks, their eldest married sister, not having heard from them for some time, came to see Bruin, to learn, if possible, something of their fate; and her surprise and joy were great to see them once more, even there. After a few weeks their old father came again to see them. Hopeless as the idea of their emancipation seemed, he still clung to it. He had had some encouragement of assistance in Washington, and he purposed to go North to see if anything could be done there; and he was anxious to obtain from Bruin what were the very lowest possible terms for which he would sell the girls. Bruin drew up his terms in the following document, which we subjoin:

Alexandria, Va., Sept. 5, 1848.

The bearer, Paul Edmondson, is the father of two girls, Mary Jane and Emily Catharine Edmondson. These girls have been purchased by us, and once sent to the south; and, upon the positive assurance that the money for them would be raised if they were brought back, they were returned. Nothing, it appears, has as yet been done in this respect by those who promised, and we are on the very eve of sending them south the second time; and we are candid in saying that, if they go again, we will not regard any promises made in relation to them. The father wishes to raise money to pay for them; and intends to appeal to the liberality of the humane and the good to aid him, and has requested us to state in writing *the conditions upon which we will sell his daughters.*

We expect to start our servants to the south in a few days; if the sum of twelve hundred ($1200) dollars be raised and paid to us in fifteen days, or we be assured of that sum, then we will retain them for twenty-five days more, to give an opportunity for the raising of the other thousand and fifty ($1050) dollars; otherwise we shall be compelled to send them along with our other servants.

BRUIN & HILL.

Paul took his papers, and parted from his daughters sorrowfully. After this, the time to the girls dragged on in heavy suspense. Constantly they looked for letter or message, and prayed to God to raise them up a deliverer from some quarter. But day after day and week after week passed, and the dreaded time drew near. The preliminaries for fitting up the gang for South Carolina commenced. Gay calico was bought for them to make up into "show dresses," in which they were to be exhibited on sale. They made them up with far sadder feelings than they would have sewed on their own shrouds. Hope had almost died out of their bosoms. A few days before the gang were to be sent

off, their sister made them a sad farewell visit. They mingled their prayers and tears, and the girls made up little tokens of remembrance to send by her as parting gifts to their brothers and sisters and aged father and mother, and with a farewell sadder than that of a death-bed the sisters parted.

The evening before the coffle was to start drew on. Mary and Emily went to the house to bid Bruin's family good-by. Bruin had a little daughter who had been a pet and favorite with the girls. She clung round them, cried, and begged them not to go. Emily told her that, if she wished to have them stay, she must go and ask her father. Away ran the little pleader, full of her errand; and was so very earnest in her importunities, that he, to pacify her, said he would consent to their remaining, if his partner, Captain Hill, would do so. At this time Bruin, hearing Mary crying aloud in the prison, went up to see her. With all the earnestness of despair, she made her last appeal to his feelings. She begged him to make the case his own, to think of his own dear little daughter,— what if she were exposed to be torn away from every friend on earth, and cut off from all hope of redemption, at the very moment, too, when deliverance was expected! Bruin was not absolutely a man of stone, and this agonizing appeal brought tears to his eyes. He gave some encouragement that, if Hill would consent, they need not be sent off with the gang. A sleepless night followed, spent in weeping, groaning and prayer. Morning at last dawned, and, according to orders received the day before, they prepared themselves to go, and even put on their bonnets and shawls, and stood ready for the word to be given. When the very last tear of hope was shed, and they were going out to join the gang, Bruin's heart relented. He called them to him, and told them they might remain! O, how glad were their hearts made by this, as they might now hope on a little longer! Either the entreaties of little Martha or Mary's plea with Bruin had prevailed.

Soon the gang was started on foot,— men, women and children, two and two, the men all handcuffed together, the right wrist of one to the left wrist of the other, and a chain passing through the middle from the handcuffs of one couple to those of the next. The women and children walked in the same manner throughout, handcuffed or chained. Drivers went before and at the side, to take up those who were sick or lame. They were obliged to set off *singing!* accompanied with fiddles and banjoes!—"*For they that carried us away captive required of us a song, and they that wasted us required of us mirth.*" And this is a scene of daily occurrence in a Christian country!—and Christian ministers say that the right to do these things is *given by God himself!!*

Meanwhile poor old Paul Edmondson went northward to supplicate aid. Any one who should have travelled in the cars at that time might have seen a venerable-looking black man, all whose air and attitude indicated a patient humility, and who seemed to carry a weight of overwhelming sorrow, like one who had long been acquainted with grief. That man was Paul Edmondson.

Alone, friendless, unknown, and, worst of all, black, he came into the great bustling city of New York, to see if there was any one there who could give him twenty-five hundred dollars to buy his daughters with. Can anybody realize what a poor man's feelings are, who visits a great, bustling, rich city, alone and unknown, for such an object? The writer has now, in a letter from a slave father and husband who was visiting Portland on a similar errand, a touching expression of it:

I walked all day, till I was tired and discouraged. O! Mrs. S——, when I see so many people who seem to have so many more things than they want or know what to do with, and then think that I have worked hard, till I am past forty, all my life, and don't own even my own wife and children, it makes me feel sick and discouraged!

So sick at heart and discouraged felt Paul Edmondson. He went to the Anti-Slavery Office, and made his case known. The sum was such a large one, and seemed to many so exorbitant, that, though they pitied the poor father, they were disheartened about raising it. They wrote to Washington to authenticate the particulars of the story, and wrote to Bruin and Hill to see if there could be any reduction of price. Meanwhile, the poor old man looked sadly from one adviser to another. He was recommended to go to the Rev. H. W. Beecher, and tell his story. He inquired his way to his door,—ascended the steps to ring the door-bell, but his heart failed him,—he sat down on the steps weeping!

There Mr. Beecher found him. He took him in, and inquired his story. There was to be a public meeting that night, to raise money. The hapless father begged him to go and plead for his children. He did go, and spoke as if he were pleading for his own father and sisters. Other clergymen fol-lowed in the same strain,—the meeting became enthusiastic, and the money was raised on the spot, and poor old Paul laid his head that night on a grateful pillow,—not to sleep, but to give thanks!

Meanwhile the girls had been dragging on anxious days in the slave-prison. They were employed in sewing for Bruin's family, staying sometimes in the prison and sometimes in the house.

It is to be stated here that Mr. Bruin is a man of very different character from many in his trade. He is such a man as never would have been found in the profession of a slave-trader, had not the most respectable and religious part of the community defended the right to buy and sell, as being conferred by God himself. It is a fact, with regard to this man, that he was one of the earliest subscribers to the *National Era*, in the District of Columbia; and, when a certain individual there brought himself into great peril by assisting fugitive slaves, and there was no one found to go bail for him, Mr. Bruin came forward and performed this kindness.

While we abhor the horrible system and the horrible trade with our whole soul, there is no harm, we suppose, in wishing that such a man had a better occupation. Yet we cannot forbear reminding all such that, when we come to give our account at the judgment-seat of Christ, every man must speak *for himself alone;* and that Christ will not accept as an apology for sin the word of all the ministers and all the synods in the country. He has given fair warning, "Beware of false prophets;" and if people will not beware of them, their blood is upon their own heads.

The girls, while under Mr. Bruin's care, were treated with as much kindness and consideration as could possibly consist with the design of selling them. There is no doubt that Bruin was personally friendly to them, and really wished most earnestly that they might be ransomed; but then he did not see how he was to lose two thousand five hundred dollars. He had just the same difficulty on this subject that some New York members of churches have had, when they have had slaves brought into their hands as security for Southern debts. He was sorry for them, and wished them well, and hoped Providence would provide for them when they were sold, but still he could not afford to lose his money; and while such men remain elders and communicants in churches in New York, we must not be surprised that there remain slave-traders in Alexandria.

It is one great art of the enemy of souls to lead men to compound for their participation in one branch of sin by their righteous horror of another. The slave-trader has been the general scape-goat on whom all parties have vented their indignation, while buying of him and selling to him.

There is an awful warning given in the fiftieth Psalm to those who in word have professed religion and in deed consented to iniquity, where from the judgment-seat Christ is represented as thus addressing them : " What hast *thou* to do to declare my statutes, or that thou shouldst take my covenant into thy mouth, seeing thou hatest instruction, and castest my words behind thee ? When thou sawest a thief, then thou consentedst with him, and hast been partaker with adulterers."

One thing is certain, that all who do these things, openly or secretly, must, at last, make up their account with a Judge who is no respecter of persons, and who will just as soon condemn an elder in the church for slave-trading as a professed trader ; nay, He may make it more tolerable for the Sodom and Gomorrah of the trade than for them,— for it may be, if the trader had the means of grace that they have had, that he would have repented long ago.

But to return to our history.— The girls were sitting sewing near the open window of their cage, when Emily said to Mary, " There, Mary, is that white man we have seen from the North." They both looked, and in a moment more saw their own dear father. They sprang and ran through the house and the office, and into the street, shouting as they ran, followed by Bruin, who said he thought the girls were crazy. In a moment they were in their father's arms, but observed that he trembled exceedingly, and that his voice was unsteady. They eagerly inquired if the money was raised for their ransom. Afraid of exciting their hopes too soon, before their free papers were signed, he said he would talk with them soon, and went into the office with Mr. Bruin and Mr. Chaplin. Mr. Bruin professed himself sincerely glad, as undoubtedly he was, that they had brought the money ; but seemed much hurt by the manner in which he had been spoken of by the Rev. H. W. Beecher at the liberation meeting in New York, thinking it hard that no difference should be made between him and other traders, when he had shown himself so much more considerate and humane than the great body of them. He, however, counted over the money and signed

the papers with great good will, taking out a five-dollar gold piece for each of the girls, as a parting present.

The affair took longer than they supposed, and the time seemed an age to the poor girls, who were anxiously walking up and down outside the room, in ignorance of their fate. Could their father have brought the money ? Why did he tremble so ? Could he have failed of the money, at last ? Or could it be that their dear mother was dead, for they had heard that she was very ill !

At length a messenger came shouting to them, " You are free, you are free ! " Emily thinks she sprang nearly to the ceiling overhead. They jumped, clapped their hands, laughed and shouted aloud. Soon their father came to them, embraced them tenderly and attempted to quiet them, and told them to prepare them to go and see their mother. This they did they know not how, but with considerable help from the family, who all seemed to rejoice in their joy. Their father procured a carriage to take them to the wharf, and, with joy overflowing all bounds, they bade a most affectionate farewell to each member of the family, not even omitting Bruin himself. The " good that there is in human nature " for once had the upper hand, and all were moved to tears of sympathetic joy. Their father, with subdued tenderness, made great efforts to soothe their tumultuous feelings, and at length partially succeeded. When they arrived at Washington, a carriage was ready to take them to their sister's house. People of every rank and description came running together to get a sight of them. Their brothers caught them up in their arms, and ran about with them, almost frantic with joy. Their aged and venerated mother, raised up from a sick bed by the stimulus of the glad news, was there, weeping and giving thanks to God. Refreshments were prepared in their sister's house for all who called, and amid greetings and rejoicings, tears and gladness, prayers and thanksgivings, but without sleep, the night passed away, and the morning of November 4, 1848, dawned upon them free and happy.

This last spring, during the month of May, as the writer has already intimated, the aged mother of the Edmondson family came on to New York, and the reason of her coming may be thus briefly explained. She had still one other daughter, the guide and support of her feeble age, or, as she calls her in her own expressive language, " the last drop of blood in her heart." She had also a son, twenty-one years of age, still a slave on a neighboring plantation. The infirm woman in whose name the estate was held was supposed to be drawing near to death, and the poor parents were distressed with the fear that, in case of this event, their two remaining children would be sold for the purpose of dividing the estate, and thus thrown into the dreaded southern market. No one can realize what a constant horror the slave-prisons and the slave-traders are to all the unfortunate families in the vicinity. Everything for which other parents look on their children with pleasure and pride is to these poor souls a source of anxiety and dismay, because it renders the child so much more a merchantable article.

It is no wonder, therefore, that the light in Paul and Milly's cottage was overshadowed by this terrible idea.

The guardians of these children had given their father a written promise to sell them to him for a certain sum, and by hard begging he had acquired a hundred dollars towards the twelve hundred which were necessary. But he was now confined to his bed with sickness. After pouring out earnest prayers to the Helper of the helpless, Milly says, one day she said to Paul, " I tell ye, Paul, I'm going up to New York myself, to see if I can't get that money."

"Paul says to me, ' Why, Milly dear, how can you ? Ye an't fit to be off the bed, and ye 's never in the cars in your life.'

" ' Never you fear, Paul,' says I; ' I shall go trusting in the Lord; and the Lord, He'll take me, and He'll bring me,— that I know.'

"So I went to the cars and got a white man to put me aboard ; and, sure enough, there I found two Bethel ministers; and one set one side o' me, and one set the other, all the way; and they got me my tickets, and looked after my things, and did every thing for me. There did n't anything happen to me all the way. Sometimes, when I went to set down in the sitting-rooms, people looked at me and moved off so scornful ! Well, I thought, I wish the Lord would give you a better mind."

Emily and Mary, who had been at school in New York State, came to the city to meet their mother, and they brought her directly to the Rev. Henry W. Beecher's house, where the writer then was.

The writer remembers now the scene when she first met this mother and daughters. It must be recollected that they had not seen each other before for four years.

One was sitting each side the mother, holding her hand ; and the air of pride and filial affection with which they presented her was touching to behold. After being presented to the writer, she again sat down between them, took a hand of each, and looked very earnestly first on one and then on the other; and then, looking up, said, with a smile, " O, these children,— how they do lie round our hearts ! "

She then explained to the writer all her sorrows and anxieties for the younger children. " Now, madam," she says, " that man that keeps the great trading-house at Alexandria, *that man*," she said, with a strong, indignant expression, " has sent to know if there's any more of my children to be sold. That man said he wanted to see *me !* Yes, má'am, he said he'd give twenty dollars to see me. I would n't see him, if he'd give me a hundred ! He sent for me to come and see him, when he had my daughters in his prison. I would n't go to see him,— I did n't want to see them there ! "

The two daughters, Emily and Mary, here became very much excited, and broke out in some very natural but bitter language against all slave-holders. " Hush, children ! you must forgive your enemies," she said. " But they 're so wicked ! " said the girls. " Ah, children, you must hate the *sin*, but love the *sinner*." " Well," said one of the girls, " mother, if I was taken again and made a slave of, I 'd kill myself." " I trust not, child,— that would be wicked." " But, mother, I *should ;* I know I never could bear it." " Bear it, my child ?" she answered, " it 's they that bears the sorrow here is they that has the glories there."

There was a deep, indescribable pathos of voice and manner as she said these words, — a solemnity and force, and yet a sweetness, that can never be forgotten.

This poor slave-mother, whose whole life had been one long outrage on her holiest feelings,— who had been kept from the power to read God's Word, whose whole pilgrimage had been made one day of sorrow by the injustice of a Christian nation, — she had yet learned to solve the highest problem of Christian ethics, and to do what so few reformers can do,— hate the *sin*, but love the *sinner !*

A great deal of interest was excited among the ladies in Brooklyn by this history. Several large meetings were held in different parlors, in which the old mother related her history with great simplicity and pathos, and a subscription for the redemption of the remaining two of her family was soon on foot. It may be interesting to know that the subscription list was headed by the lovely and benevolent Jenny Lind Goldschmidt.

Some of the ladies who listened to this touching story were so much interested in Mrs. Edmondson personally, they wished to have her daguerreotype taken; both that they might be strengthened and refreshed by the sight of her placid countenance, and that they might see the beauty of true goodness beaming there.

She accordingly went to the rooms with them, with all the simplicity of a little child. "O," said she, to one of the ladies, "you can't think how happy it's made me to get here, where everybody is *so kind* to me! Why, last night, when I went home, I was so happy I could n't sleep. I had to go and tell my Saviour, over and over again, how happy I was."

A lady spoke to her about reading something. "Law bless you, honey! I can't read a letter."

"Then," said another lady, "how have you learned so much of God, and heavenly things?"

"Well, 'pears like a *gift* from above."

"Can you have the Bible read to you?"

"Why, yes; Paul, he reads a little, but then he has so much work all day, and when he gets home at night he's so tired! and his eyes is bad. But then the *Sperit* teaches us."

"Do you go much to meeting?"

"Not much now, we live so far. In winter I can't never. But, O! what meetings I have had, alone in the corner,— my Saviour and only me!" The smile with which these words were spoken was a thing to be remembered. A little girl, daughter of one of the ladies, made some rather severe remarks about somebody in the daguerreotype rooms, and her mother checked her.

The old lady looked up, with her placid smile. "That puts me in mind," she said, "of what I heard a preacher say once. 'My friends,' says he, 'if you know of anything that will make a brother's heart glad, *run quick and tell it;* but if it is something that will only cause a sigh, 'bottle it up, bottle it up!' O, I often tell my children, 'Bottle it up, bottle it up!'"

When the writer came to part with the old lady, she said to her: "Well, good-by, my dear friend; remember and pray for me."

"Pray for *you!*" she said, earnestly. "Indeed I shall,— I can't help it." She then, raising her finger, said, in an emphatic tone, peculiar to the old of her race, "Tell you what! we never gets no good bread ourselves till we begins *to ask for our brethren.*"

The writer takes this opportunity to inform all those friends, in different parts of the country, who generously contributed for the redemption of these children, that they are *at last free!*

The following extract from the letter of a lady in Washington may be interesting to them:

I have seen the Edmondson parents, — Paul and his wife Milly. I have seen the *free* Edmondsons,— mother, son, and daughter,— the very day after the great era of *free life* commenced, while yet the inspiration was on them, while the mother's face was all light and love, the father's eyes moistened and glistening with tears, the son calm in conscious manhood and responsibility, the daughter (not more than fifteen years old, I think) smiling a delightful appreciation of joy in the present and hope in the future, thus suddenly and completely unfolded.

Thus have we finished the account of one of the families who were taken on board the *Pearl.* We have another history to give, to which we cannot promise so fortunate a termination.

CHAPTER VII.

AMONG those unfortunates guilty of loving freedom too well, was a beautiful young quadroon girl, named Emily Russell, whose mother is now living in New York. The writer has seen and conversed with her. She is a pious woman, highly esteemed and respected, a member of a Christian church.

By the avails of her own industry she purchased her freedom, and also redeemed from bondage some of her children. Emily was a resident of Washington, D. C., a place which belongs not to any state, but to the United States; and there, under the laws of the United States, she was held as a slave. She was of a gentle disposition and amiable manners; she had been early touched with a sense of religious things, and was on the very point of uniting herself with a Christian church; but her heart yearned after her widowed mother and after freedom, and so, on the fatal night when all the other poor victims sought the Pearl, the child Emily went also among them.

How they were taken has already been

told. The sin of the poor girl was inexpiable. Because she longed for her mother's arms and for liberty, she could not be forgiven. Nothing would do for such a sin, but to throw her into the hands of the trader. She also was thrown into Bruin & Hill's jail, in Alexandria. Her poor mother in New York received the following letter from her. Read it, Christian mother, and think what if your daughter had written it to you !

To Mrs. NANCY CARTWRIGHT, New York.
Alexandria, Jan. 22, 1850.

MY DEAR MOTHER : I take this opportunity of writing you a few lines, to inform you that I am in *Bruin's Jail*, and Aunt Sally and all of her children, and Aunt Hagar and all her children, and grandmother is almost crazy. My dear mother, will you please to come on as soon as you can ? I expect to go away very shortly. O, mother ! my dear mother ! come now and see your distressed and heart-broken daughter once more. Mother ! my dear mother ! do not forsake me, for I feel desolate ! Please to come now.
Your daughter,
EMILY RUSSELL.

P. S. — If you do not come as far as Alexandria, come to Washington, and do what you can.

That letter, blotted and tear-soiled, was brought by this poor washerwoman to some Christian friends in New York, and shown to them. "What do you suppose they will ask for her ? " was her question. All that she had, — her little house, her little furniture, her small earnings, — all these poor Nancy was willing to throw in ; but all these were but as a drop to the bucket.

The first thing to be done, then, was to ascertain what Emily could be redeemed for; and, as it may be an interesting item of American trade, we give the reply of the traders in full :

Alexandria, Jan. 31, 1850.

DEAR SIR : When I received your letter I had not bought the negroes you spoke of, but since that time I have bought them. All I have to say about the matter is, that we paid very high for the negroes, and cannot afford to sell the girl Emily for less than EIGHTEEN HUNDRED DOLLARS. This may seem a high price to you, but, cotton being very high, consequently slaves are high. We have two or three offers for Emily from *gentlemen* from the south. *She is said to be the finest-looking woman in this country.* As for Hagar and her seven children, we will take two thousand five hundred dollars for them. Sally and her four children, we will take for them two thousand eight hundred dollars. You may seem a little surprised at the difference in prices, but the difference in the negroes makes the difference in price. We expect to start south with the negroes on the 8th February, and if you intend to do anything, you had better do it soon. Yours, respectfully,
BRUIN & HILL.

This letter came to New York before the

case of the Edmondsons had called the attention of the community to this subject. The enormous price asked entirely discouraged effort, and before anything of importance was done they heard that the coffle had departed, with Emily in it.

Hear, O heavens ! and give ear, O earth ! Let it be known, in all the countries of the earth, that the market-price of a beautiful Christian girl in America is from EIGHTEEN HUNDRED to TWO THOUSAND DOLLARS; and yet, judicatories in the church of Christ have said, in solemn conclave, that AMERICAN SLAVERY AS IT IS IS NO EVIL ! *

From the table of the sacrament and from the sanctuary of the church of Christ this girl was torn away, because her beauty was a salable article in the slave-market in New Orleans !

Perhaps some Northern apologist for slavery will say she was kindly treated here — not handcuffed by the wrist to a chain, and forced to walk, as articles less choice are ; that a wagon was provided, and that she rode; and that food abundant was given her to eat, and that her clothing was warm and comfortable, and therefore no harm was done. We have heard it told us, again and again, that there is no harm in slavery, if one is only warm enough, and full-fed, and comfortable. It is true that the slave-woman has no protection from the foulest dishonor and the utmost insult that can be offered to womanhood, — none whatever in law or gospel; but, so long as she has enough to eat and wear, our Christian fathers and mothers tell us it is not so bad !

Poor Emily could not think so. There was no eye to pity, and none to help. The food of her accursed lot did not nourish her; the warmest clothing could not keep the chill of slavery from her heart. In the middle of the overland passage, sick, weary, heart-broken, the child laid her down and died. By that lonely pillow there was no mother. But there was one Friend, who loveth at all times, who is closer than a brother. Could our eyes be touched by the seal of faith, where others see only the lonely wilderness and the dying girl, we, perhaps, should see one clothed in celestial beauty, waiting for that short agony to be over, that He might redeem her from all iniquity, and present her faultless before the presence of his Grace with exceeding joy !

* The words of the Georgia Annual Conference : *Resolved,* "That slavery, *as it exists* in the United States, is not a moral evil."

Even the hard-hearted trader was touched with her sad fate, and we are credibly informed that he said he was sorry he had taken her.

Bruin & Hill wrote to New York that the girl Emily was dead. The Quaker, William Harned, went with the letter, to break the news to her mother. Since she had given up all hope of redeeming her daughter from the dreadful doom to which she had been sold, the helpless mother had drooped like a stricken woman. She no longer lifted up her head, or seemed to take any interest in life.

When Mr. Harned called on her, she asked, eagerly,

"Have you heard anything from my daughter?"

"Yes, I have," was the reply, "a letter from Bruin & Hill."

"And what is the news?"

He thought best to give a direct answer, —"Emily is dead."

The poor mother clasped her hands, and, looking upwards, said, "The Lord be thanked! He has heard my prayers at last!"

And, now, will it be said this is an exceptional case — it happens one time in a thousand? Though we know that this is the foulest of falsehoods, and that the case is only a specimen of what is acting every day in the American slave-trade, yet, for argument's sake, let us, for once, admit it to be true. If only once in this nation, under the protection of our law, a Christian girl had been torn from the altar and the communion-table, and sold to foulest shame and dishonor, would that have been a light sin? Does not Christ say, "Inasmuch as ye have done it unto *one of the least of* these, ye have done it unto me"? O, words of woe for thee, America! — words of woe for thee, church of Christ! Hast thou trod them under foot and trampled them in the dust so long that Christ has forgotten them? In the day of judgment every one of these words shall rise up, living and burning, as accusing angels to witness against thee. Art thou, O church of Christ! praying daily, "Thy kingdom come"? Darest thou pray, "Come, Lord Jesus, come quickly"? O, what if He should come? What if the Lord, whom ye seek, should *suddenly* come into his temple? If his soul was stirred within him when he found within his temple of old those that changed money, and sold sheep and oxen and doves, what will he say now,

when he finds them selling body, blood and bones, of his own people? And is the Christian church, which justifies this enormous system, — which has used the awful name of her Redeemer to sanction the buying, selling and trading in the souls of men, — is this church the bride of Christ? Is she one with Christ, even as Christ is one with the Father? O, bitter mockery! Does this church believe that every Christian's body is a temple of the Holy Ghost? Or does she think those solemn words were idle breath, when, a thousand times, every day and week, in the midst of her, is this temple set up and sold at auction, to be bought by any godless, blasphemous man, who has money to pay for it!

As to poor Daniel Bell and his family, whose contested claim to freedom was the beginning of the whole trouble, a few members of it were redeemed, and the rest were plunged into the abyss of slavery. It would seem as if this event, like the sinking of a ship, drew into its maëlstrom the fate of every unfortunate being who was in its vicinity. A poor, honest, hard-working slaveman, of the name of Thomas Ducket, had a wife who was on board the *Pearl*. Tom was supposed to know the men who countenanced the enterprise, and his master, therefore, determined to sell him. He brought him to Washington for the purpose. Some in Washington doubted his legal right to bring a slave from Maryland for the purpose of selling him, and commenced legal proceedings to test the matter. While they were pending, the counsel for the master told the men who brought action against his client that Tom was anxious to be sold; that he preferred being sold to the man who had purchased his wife and children, rather than to have his liberty. It was well known that Tom did not wish to be separated from his family, and the friends here, confiding in the representations made to them, consented to withdraw the proceedings.

Some time after this, they received letters from poor Tom Ducket, dated ninety miles above New Orleans, complaining sadly of his condition, and making piteous appeals to hear from them respecting his wife and children. Upon inquiry, nothing could be learned respecting them. They had been sold and gone,— sold and gone,— no one knew whither; and as a punishment to Tom for his contumacy in refusing to give the name of the man who had projected the expedition of the *Pearl*, he was denied the privilege of going off the place, and was not allowed to talk with the other servants, his master fearing a conspiracy. In one of his letters he says, "I have seen more trouble here in one day than I have in all my life." In another, "I would be glad to hear from her [his wife], but I should be more glad to hear of her death than for her to come here."

In his distress, Tom wrote a letter to Mr. Bigelow, of Washington. People who are not in the habit of getting such documents have no idea of them. We give a *fac simile* of Tom's letter, with all its poor spelling, all its ignorance, helplessness, and misery.

february 18 1850

Mr Begelow dr sor I rit to you to let you no how i am get in a long had times her I have not Had one oyr to goout sid of the place sence I have bin on et i put my trust in the lord to halp me I long to hear from you all I ret ten to hear frem yoall Mr Beg elow i hop yo will not for me you no et was not my folt that I am hear I hop you will nam me to Mr Geden Mr chaplen Mr Baly to healp me out of et I be leve that if Would mak the les move to et that et cod be Don i

long to hear from my famaly
how the ar Geten a long you
will ples to rit to me jest
to let me no how thear geten
a long you can rit to me J re
main yours yo umbil servent

       thomas Ducket

you can Ded rec you let ters
to thomas Duck in car of
Mr sam ul t harisin
lusana nan lyagoler of is
for god sake let me hear
from you all my wife and
children ar not out of my
mine day nor night

[*February* 18, 1852.
Mr. Bigelow. Dear Sir:—I write to let you know how I am getting along. Hard times here. I have not had one hour to go outside the place since I have been on it. I put my trust in the Lord to help me. I long to hear from you all.

I written to hear from you all. Mr. Bigelow, I hope you will not forget me. You know it was not my fault that I am here. I hope you will name me to Mr. Geden, Mr. Chaplin, Mr. Bailey, to help me out of it. I believe that if they would make the least move to it that it could be done. I long to hear from my family how they are getting along. You will please to write to me just to let me know how they are getting along. You can write to me.

I remain your humble servant,
THOMAS DUCKET.

You can direct your letters to Thomas Ducket, in care of Mr. Samuel T. Harrison, Louisiana, near Bayou Goula. For God's sake let me hear from you all. My wife and children are not out of my mind day nor night.]

CHAPTER VIII.

KIDNAPPING.

THE principle which declares that one human being may lawfully hold another as property leads directly to the trade in human beings; and that trade has, among its other horrible results, the temptation to the crime of kidnapping.

The trader is generally a man of coarse nature and low associations, hard-hearted, and reckless of right or honor. He who is not so is an exception, rather than a specimen. If he has anything good about him when he begins the business, it may well be seen that he is in a fair way to lose it.

Around the trader are continually passing and repassing men and women who would be worth to him thousands of dollars in the way of trade,— who belong to a class whose rights nobody respects, and who, if reduced to slavery, could not easily make their word good against him. The probability is that hundreds of free men and women and children are all the time being precipitated into slavery in this way.

The recent case of *Northrop*, tried in Washington, D. C., throws light on this fearful subject. The following account is abridged from the *New York Times:*

Solomon Northrop is a free colored citizen of the United States ; he was born in Essex county, New York, about the year 1808 ; became early a resident of Washington county, and married there in 1829. His father and mother resided in the county of Washington about fifty years, till their decease, and were both free. With his wife and children he resided at Saratoga Springs in the winter of 1841, and while there was employed by two gentlemen to drive a team South, at the rate of a dollar a day. In fulfilment of his employ-

ment, he proceeded to New York, and, having taken out free papers, to show that he was a citizen, he went on to Washington city, where he arrived the second day of April, the same year, and put up at Gadsby's Hotel. Soon after he arrived he felt unwell, and went to bed.

While suffering with severe pain, some persons came in, and, seeing the condition he was in, proposed to give him some medicine, and did so. This is the last thing of which he had any recollection, until he found himself chained to the floor of Williams' slave-pen in this city, and handcuffed. In the course of a few hours, James H. Burch, a slave-dealer, came in, and the colored man asked him to take the irons off from him, and wanted to know why they were put on. Burch told him it was none of his business. The colored man said he was free, and told where he was born. Burch called in a man by the name of Ebenezer Rodbury, and they two stripped the man and laid him across a bench, Rodbury holding him down by his wrists. Burch whipped him with a paddle until he broke that, and then with a cat-o'-nine-tails, giving him a hundred lashes ; and he swore he would kill him if he ever stated to any one that he was a free man. From that time forward the man says he did not communicate the fact from fear, either that he was a free man, or what his name was, until the last summer. He was kept in the slave-pen about ten days, when he, with others, was taken out of the pen in the night by Burch, handcuffed and shackled, and taken down the river by a steamboat, and then to Richmond, where he, with forty-eight others, was put on board the brig *Orleans*. There Burch left them. The brig sailed for New Orleans, and on arriving there, before she was fastened to the wharf, Theophilus Freeman, another slave-dealer, belonging in the city of New Orleans, and who in 1833 had been a partner with Burch in the slave-trade, came to the wharf, and received the slaves as they were landed, under his direction. This man was immediately taken by Freeman and shut up in his pen in that city. He was taken sick with the small-pox immediately after getting there, and was sent to a hospital, where he lay two or three weeks. When he had sufficiently recovered to leave the hospital, Freeman declined to sell him to any person in that vicinity, and sold him to a Mr. Ford, who resided in Rapides Parish, Louisiana, where he was taken and lived more than a year, and worked as a carpenter, working with Ford at that business.

Ford became involved, and had to sell him. A Mr. Tibaut became the purchaser. He, in a short time, sold him to Edwin Eppes, in Bayou Beouf, about one hundred and thirty miles from the mouth of Red river, where Eppes has retained him on a cotton plantation since the year 1843.

To go back a step in the narrative, the man wrote a letter, in June, 1841, to Henry B. Northrop, of the State of New York, dated and postmarked at New Orleans, stating that he had been kidnapped and was on board a vessel, but was unable to state what his destination was ; but requesting Mr. N. to aid him in recovering his freedom, if possible. Mr. N. was unable to do anything in his behalf, in consequence of not knowing where he had gone, and not being able to find any trace of him. His place of residence remained unknown until the month of September last, when the following letter was received by his friends :

Bayou Beouf, August, 1852.

Mr. WILLIAM PENY, or MR. LEWIS PARKER.

GENTLEMEN : It having been a long time since I have seen or heard from you, and not knowing that you are living, it is with uncertainty that I write to you ; but the necessity of the case must be my excuse. Having been born free just across the river from you, I am certain you know me ; and I am here now a slave. I wish you to obtain free papers for me, and forward them to me at Marksville, Louisiana, Parish of Avovelles, and oblige   Yours,   SOLOMON NORTHROP.

On receiving the above letter, Mr. N. applied to Governor Hunt, of New York, for such authority as was necessary for him to proceed to Louisiana as an agent to procure the liberation of Solomon. Proof of his freedom was furnished to Governor Hunt by affidavits of several gentlemen, General Clarke among others. Accordingly, in pursuance of the laws of New York, Henry B. Northrop was constituted an agent, to take such steps, by procuring evidence, retaining counsel, &c., as were necessary to secure the freedom of Solomon, and to execute all the duties of his agency.

The result of Mr. Northrop's agency was the establishing of the claim of Solomon Northrop to freedom, and the restoring him to his native land.

It is a singular coincidence that this man was carried to a plantation in the Red river country, that same region where the scene of Tom's captivity was laid ; and his account of this plantation, his mode of life there, and some incidents which he describes, form a striking parallel to that history. We extract them from the article of the *Times :*

The condition of this colored man during the nine years that he was in the hands of Eppes was of a character nearly approaching that described by Mrs. Stowe as the condition of "Uncle Tom" while in that region. During that whole period his hut contained neither a floor, nor a chair, nor a bed, nor a mattress, nor anything for him to lie upon, except a board about twelve inches wide, with a block of wood for his pillow, and with a single blanket to cover him, while the walls of his hut did not by any means protect him from the inclemency of the weather. He was sometimes compelled to perform acts revolting to humanity, and outrageous in the highest degree. On one occasion, a colored girl belonging to Eppes, about seventeen years of age, went one Sunday, without the permission of her master, to the nearest plantation, about half a mile distant, to visit another colored girl of her acquaintance. She returned in the course of two or three hours, and for that offence she was called up for punishment, which Solomon was required to inflict. Eppes compelled him to drive four stakes into the ground at such distances that the hands and ankles of the girl might be tied to them, as she lay with her face upon the ground ; and, having thus fastened her down, he compelled him, while standing by himself, to inflict one hundred lashes upon her bare flesh, she being stripped naked. Having inflicted the hundred blows, Solomon refused to proceed any further. Eppes tried to compel him to go on, but

he absolutely set him at defiance, and refused to murder the girl. Eppes then seized the whip, and applied it until he was too weary to continue it. Blood flowed from her neck to her feet, and in this condition she was compelled the next day to go into the field to work as a field-hand. She bears the marks still upon her body, although the punishment was inflicted four years ago.

When Solomon was about to leave, under the care of Mr. Northrop, this girl came from behind her hut, unseen by her master, and, throwing her arms around the neck of Solomon, congratulated him on his escape from slavery, and his return to his family ; at the same time, in language of despair, exclaiming, " But, O God! what will become of me ?"

These statements regarding the condition of Solomon while with Eppes, and the punishment and brutal treatment of the colored girls, are taken from Solomon himself. It has been stated that the nearest plantation was distant from that of Eppes a half-mile, and of course there could be no interference on the part of neighbors in any punishment, however cruel, or however well disposed to interfere they might be.

Had not Northrop been able to write, as few of the free blacks in the slave states are, his doom might have been sealed for life in this den of misery.

Two cases recently tried in Baltimore also unfold facts of a similar nature.

The following is from

THE CASE OF RACHEL PARKER AND HER SISTER.

It will be remembered that more than a year since a young colored woman, named Mary Elizabeth Parker, was abducted from Chester county and conveyed to Baltimore, where she was sold as a slave, and transported to New Orleans. A few days after, her sister, Rachel Parker, was also abducted in like manner, taken to Baltimore, and detained there in consequence of the interference of her Chester county friends. In the first case, Mary Elizabeth was, by an arrangement with the individual who had her in charge, brought back to Baltimore, to await her trial on a petition for freedom. So also with regard to Rachel. Both, after trial, — the proof in their favor being so overwhelming, — were discharged, and are now among their friends in Chester county. In this connection we give the narratives of both females, obtained since their release.

Rachel Parker's Narrative.

" I was taken from Joseph C. Miller's about twelve o'clock on Tuesday (Dec. 30th, 1851), by two men who came up to the house by the *back* door. One came in and asked Mrs. Miller where Jesse McCreary lived, and then seized me by the arm, and pulled me out of the house. Mrs. Miller called to her husband, who was in the *front* porch, and he ran out and seized the man by the collar, and tried to stop him. The other, with an oath, then told him to take his hands off, and if he touched me he would kill him. He then told Miller that I belonged to Mr. Schoolfield, in Baltimore. They then hurried me to a wagon, where there was another large man, put me in, and drove off.

" Mr. Miller ran across the field to head the wagon, and picked up a stake to run through the wheel, when one of the men pulled out a sword (I think it was a sword, I never saw one), and threatened to cut Miller's arm off. Pollock's wagon being in the way, and he refusing to get out of the road, we turned off to the left. After we rode away, one of the men tore a hole in the back of the carriage, to look out to see if they were coming after us, and they said they wished they had given Miller and Pollock a blow.

"We stopped at a tavern near the railroad, and I told the landlord (I think it was) that I was free. I also told several persons at the car-office; and a very nice-looking man at the car-office was talking at the door, and he said he thought that they had better take me back again. One of the men did not come further than the tavern. I was taken to Baltimore, where we arrived about seven o'clock the same evening, and I was taken to jail.

"The next morning, a man with large light-colored whiskers took me away by myself, and asked me if I was not Mr. Schoolfield's slave. I told him I was not; he said that I was, and that if I did not say I was he would 'cowhide me and salt me, and put me in a dungeon.' I told him I was free, and that I would say nothing but the truth."

Mary E. Parker's Narrative.

"I was taken from Matthew Donnelly's on Saturday night (Dec. 6th, or 13th, 1851); was caught whilst out of doors, soon after I had cleared the supper-table, about seven o'clock, by two men, and put into a wagon. One of them got into the wagon with me, and rode to Elkton, Md., where I was kept until Sunday night at twelve o'clock, when I left there in the cars for Baltimore, and arrived there early on Monday morning.

"At Elkton a man was brought in to see me, by one of the men, who said that I was not his father's slave. Afterwards, when on the way to Baltimore in the cars, a man told me that I must say that I was Mr. Schoolfield's slave, or he would shoot me, and pulled a 'rifle' out of his pocket and showed it to me, and also threatened to whip me.

"On Monday morning, Mr. Schoolfield called at the jail in Baltimore to see me; and on Tuesday morning he brought his wife and several other ladies to see me. I told them I did not know them, and then Mr. C. took me out of the room, and told me who they were, and took me back again, so that I might appear to know them. On the next Monday I was shipped to New Orleans.

"It took about a month to get to New Orleans. After I had been there about a week, Mr. C. sold me to Madame C., who keeps a large flower-garden. She sends flowers to sell to the theatres, sells milk in market, &c. I went out to sell candy and flowers for her, when I lived with her. One evening, when I was coming home from the theatre, a watchman took me up, and I told him I was not a slave. He put me in the calaboose, and next morning took me before a magistrate, who sent for Madame C., who told him she bought me. He then sent for Mr. C., and told him he must account for how he got me. Mr. C. said that my mother and all the family were free, except me. The magistrate told me to go back to Madame C., and he told Madame C. that she must not let me go out at night; and he told Mr. C. that he must prove how he came by me. The magistrate afterwards called on Mrs. C., at her house, and had a long talk with her in the parlor. I do not know what he said, as they were by themselves. About a month afterwards, I was sent back to Baltimore. I lived with Madame C. about six months.

"There were six slaves came in the vessel with me to Baltimore, who belonged to Mr. D., and were returned because they were sickly.

"A man called to see me at the jail after I came back to Baltimore, and told me that I must say I was Mr. Schoolfield's slave, and that if I did not do it he would kill me the first time he got a chance. He said Rachel [her sister] said she came from Baltimore and was Mr. Schoolfield's slave. Afterwards some gentlemen called on me [Judge Campbell and Judge Bell, of Philadelphia, and William H. Norris, Esq., of Baltimore], and I told them I was Mr. Schoolfield's slave. They said they were my friends, and I must tell them the truth. I then told them who I was, and all about it.

"When I was in New Orleans Mr. C. whipped me because I said that I was free."

Elizabeth, by her own account above, was seized and taken from Pennsylvania, Dec. 6th or 13th, 1851, which is confirmed by other testimony.

It is conceded that such cases, when brought into Southern courts, are generally tried with great fairness and impartiality. The agent for Northrop's release testifies to this, and it has been generally admitted fact. But it is probably only one case in a hundred that can get into court;—of the multitudes who are drawn down in the ever-widening maëlstrom only now and then one ever comes back to tell the tale.

The succeeding chapter of advertisements will show the reader how many such victims there may probably be.

CHAPTER IX.

SLAVES AS THEY ARE, ON TESTIMONY OF OWNERS.

THE investigation into the actual condition of the slave population at the South is beset with many difficulties. So many things are said pro and con,— so many said in one connection and denied in another, — that the effect is very confusing.

Thus, we are told that the state of the slaves is one of blissful contentment; that they would not take freedom as a gift: that their family relations are only now and then invaded; that they are a stupid race, almost sunk to the condition of animals; that generally they are kindly treated, &c. &c.

In reading over some two hundred Southern newspapers this fall, the author has been struck with the very graphic and circumstantial pictures, which occur in all of them, describing fugitive slaves. From these descriptions one may learn a vast many things. The author will here give an assortment of them, taken at random. It is a commentary on the contented state of the slave population that the writer finds two or three always, and often many more, in every one of the hundreds of Southern papers examined.

In reading the following little sketches of "slaves as they are," let the reader notice:

1. The color and complexion of the majority of them.

2. That it is customary either to describe slaves by some *scar*, or to say "*No scars recollected.*"

3. The *intelligence* of the parties advertised.

4. The number that *say they are free* that are to be *sold to pay jail-fees.*

Every one of these slaves has a history,— a history of woe and crime, degradation, endurance, and wrong. Let us open the chapter:

South-side Democrat, Oct. 28, 1852. Petersburgh, Virginia:

REWARD.

Twenty-five dollars, with the payment of all necessary expenses, will be given for the apprehension and delivery of my man CHARLES, if taken on the Appomattox river, or within the precincts of Petersburgh. He ran off about a week ago, and, if he leaves the neighborhood, will no doubt make for Farmville and Petersburgh. He is *a mulatto*, rather below the medium height and size, but well proportioned, and very active and sensible. He is aged about 27 years, has a mild, submissive look, *and will, no doubt, show the marks of a recent whipping, if taken.* He must be delivered to the care of Peebles, White, Davis & Co.

R. H. DeJARNETT,
Oct. 25 — 3t. Lunenburgh.

Poor Charles! — *mulatto!* — has a mild, submissive look, and will probably show marks of a recent whipping!

Kosciusko Chronicle, Nov. 24, 1852:

COMMITTED

To the Jail of Attila County, on the 8th instant, a negro boy, who calls his name GREEN, and says he belongs to James Gray, of Winston County. Said boy is about 20 years old, *yellow complexion*, round face, *has a scar on his face, one on his left thigh, and one in his left hand*, is about 5 feet 6 inches high. Had on when taken up a cotton check shirt, Linsey pants, new cloth cap, and was riding a large roan horse about 12 or 14 years old and thin in order. The owner is requested to come forward, prove property, pay charges, and take him away, or he will be sold to pay charges.

E. B. SANDERS, Jailer A. C.
Oct. 12, 1842. n12tf.

Capitolian Vis-a-Vis, West Baton Rouge, Nov. 1, 1852:

$100 REWARD.

RUNAWAY from the subscriber, in Randolph County, on the 18th of October, a *yellow* boy, named JIM. This boy is 19 years old, *a light mulatto with dirty sunburnt hair, inclined to be straight;* he is just 5 feet 7 inches high, and slightly made. He had on when he left a black cloth cap, black cloth pantaloons, a plaided sack coat, a fine shirt, and brogan shoes. One hundred dollars will be paid for the recovery of the above-described boy, if taken out of the State, or fifty dollars if taken in the State.

MRS. S. P. HALL,
Nov. 4, 1852. Huntsville, Mo.

American Baptist, Dec. 20, 1852:

TWENTY DOLLARS REWARD FOR A PREACHER.

The following paragraph, headed "Twenty Dollars Reward," appeared in a recent number of the *New Orleans Picayune:*

"Run away from the plantation of the undersigned the negro man Shedrick, a preacher, 5 feet 9 inches high, about 40 years old, but looking not over 23, *stamped N. E. on the breast, and having both small toes cut off.* He is of a very dark complexion, with eyes small but bright, *and a look quite insolent.* He dresses good, and was arrested as a runaway at Donaldsonville, some three years ago. The above reward will be paid for his arrest, by addressing Messrs. Armant Brothers, St. James parish, or A. Miltenberger & Co., 30 Carondelet-street."

Here is a preacher who is branded on the breast and has both toes cut off,— and *will* look insolent yet! There's depravity for you!

Jefferson Inquirer, Nov. 27, 1852:

$100 DOLLARS REWARD.

RANAWAY from my plantation, in Bolivar County, Miss., a negro man named MAY, aged 40 years, 5 feet 10 or 11 inches high, *copper colored*, and very straight; his front teeth are good and stand a little open; stout through the shoulders, *and has some scars on his back that show above the skin plain, caused by the whip;* he frequently hiccups when eating, if he has not got water handy; he was pursued into Ozark County, Mo., and there left. I will give the above reward for his confinement in jail, so that I can get him.

JAMES H. COUSAR,
Victoria, Bolivar County, Mississippi.
Nov. 13, 1m.

Delightful master to go back to, this man must be!

The Alabama Standard has for its motto:

"RESISTANCE TO TYRANTS IS OBEDIENCE TO GOD."

Date of Nov. 29th, this advertisement:

COMMITTED

To the Jail of Choctaw County, by Judge Young, of Marengo County, a RUNAWAY SLAVE, who calls his name BILLY, and says he belongs to the late William Johnson, and was in the employment of John Jones, near Alexandria, La. He is about 5 feet 10 inches high, black, about 40 years old, *much scarred on the face and head*, and *quite intelligent*.

The owner is requested to come forward, prove his property, and take him from Jail, or he will be disposed of according to law.

S. S. HOUSTON, Jailer C. C.

December 1, 1852. 44-tf

Query: Whether this "quite intelligent" Billy had n't been corrupted by hearing this incendiary motto of the *Standard*?

Knoxville (Tenn.) *Register*, Nov. 3d:

LOOK OUT FOR RUNAWAYS!!
$25 REWARD!

RANAWAY from the subscriber, on the night of the 26th July last, a negro woman named HARRIET. Said woman is about five feet five inches high, has prominent cheek-bones, large mouth and good front teeth, tolerably spare built, about 25 years old. We think it probable she is harbored by some negroes not far from John Mynatt's, in Knox County, where she and they are likely making some arrangements to get to a free state; or she may be concealed by some negroes (her connections) in Anderson County, near Clinton. I will give the above reward for her apprehension and confinement in any prison in this state, or I will give fifty dollars for her confinement in any jail out of this state, so that I get her. H. B. GOENS,

Nov. 3. 4m Clinton, Tenn.

The Alexandria Gazette, November 29, 1852, under the device of Liberty trampling on a tyrant, motto "*Sic semper tyrannis*," has the following:

TWENTY-FIVE DOLLARS REWARD.

Ranaway from the subscriber, living in the County of Rappahannock, on Tuesday last, DANIEL, *a bright mulatto*, about 5 feet 8 inches high, about 35 years old, *very intelligent*, has been a wagoner for several years, and is pretty well acquainted from Richmond to Alexandria. He calls himself *DANIEL TURNER; his hair curls, without showing black blood, or wool; he has a scar on one cheek, and his left hand has been seriously injured by a pistol-shot*, and he was shabbily dressed when last seen. I will give the above reward if taken out of the county, and secured in jail, so that I get him again, or $10 if taken in the county.

A. M. WILLIS.

Rappahannock Co., Va., Nov. 29. — eolm.

Another "very intelligent," straight-haired man. Who was his father?

The New Orleans Daily Crescent, office No. 93 St. Charles-street; Tuesday morning, December 13, 1852:

BROUGHT TO THE FIRST DISTRICT POLICE PRISON.

NANCY, a griffe, about 34 years old, 5 feet 1¾ inch high, *a scar on left wrist;* says she belongs to Madame Wolf.

CHARLES HALL, a black, about 13 years old, 5 feet 6 inches high; *says he is free*, but supposed to be a slave.

PHILOMONIA, a mulattress, about 10 years old, 4 feet 3 inches high; *says she is free*, but supposed to be a slave.

COLUMBUS, a griffe, about 21 years old, 5 feet 5¾ inches high; *says he is free*, but supposed to be a slave.

SEYMOUR, a black, about 21 years old, 5 feet 1¾ inch high; *says he is free*, but supposed to be a slave

The owners will please comply with the law respecting them. J WORRALL, Warden.

New Orleans, Dec. 14, 1852.

What chance for any of these poor fellows who *say they are free?*

$50 REWARD.

RANAWAY from the subscriber, living in Unionville, Frederick County, Md., on Sunday morning, the 17th instant, a DARK MULATTO GIRL, about 18 years of age, 5 feet 4 or 5 inches high, *looks pleasant generally*, talks very quick, *converses tolerably well*, and can *read*. It is supposed she had on, when she left, a red Merino dress, black Visette or plaid Shawl, and a purple calico Bonnet, as those articles are missing.

A reward of Twenty-five Dollars will be given for her, if taken in the State, or Fifty Dollars if taken out of the State, and lodged in jail, so that I get her again. G. R. SAPPINGTON.

Oct. 13. — 2m.

Kosciusko Chronicle, Mississippi:

TWENTY DOLLARS REWARD

Will be paid for the delivery of the boy WALKER, aged about 28 years, about 5 feet 8 or 9 inches high, black complexion, loose make, smiles when spoken to, has a mild, sweet voice, and fine teeth. Apply at 25 Tchoupitoulas-street, up stairs. o12 6t.

Walker has walked off, it seems. Peace be with him!

$25 REWARD.

RANAWAY from the subscriber, living near White's Store, Anson County, on the 3d of May last, a *bright mulatto boy*, named BOB. Bob is about 5 feet high, will weigh 130 pounds, is about 22 years old, and has some beard on his upper lip. His left leg is somewhat shorter than his right, causing him to hobble in his walk; has a very broad face, *and will show color like a white man*. It is probable he has gone off with some wagoner or trader, or he may have free papers and be passing as a free man. *He has straight hair.*

I will give a reward of TWENTY-FIVE DOLLARS for the apprehension and delivery to me of said boy, or for his confinement in any jail, so that I get him again. CLARA LOCKHART,

By Adam Lockhart.

June 30, 1852. 698:5

Southern Standard, Oct. 16, 1852:

$50 REWARD!!!

RANAWAY, or stolen, from the subscriber, living near Aberdeen, Miss., a light mulatto woman, of small size, and about 23 years old. She has *long, black, straight hair, and she usually keeps*

it in good order. When she left she had on either a white dress, or a brown calico one with white spots or figures, and took with her a red handkerchief, and a red or pink sun-bonnet. *She generally dresses very neatly.* She generally calls herself Mary Ann Paine, — can *read print*, — has some freckles on her face and hands, — shoes No. 4, — had a ring or two on her fingers. She is very intelligent, and converses well. The above reward will be given for her, if taken out of the State, and $25 if taken within the State.
U. McALLISTER.

Memphis (weekly) *Appeal* will insert to the amount of $5, and send account to this office.
October 6th, 1853.   20 — tf.

Much can be seen of this Mary Ann in this picture. The black, straight hair, usually kept in order,— the general neatness of dress,— the ring or two on the fingers,— the ability to read,— the fact of being intelligent and conversing well, are all to be noticed.

$20 REWARD.

Ranaway, on the 9th of last August, my servant boy *HENRY:* he is 14 or 15 years old, a *bright mulatto*, has dark eyes, stoops a little, and stutters when confused. Had on, when he went away, white pantaloons, long blue summer coat, and a palm-leaf hat. I will give the above reward if he should be taken in the State of Virginia, or $30 if taken in either of the adjoining States, but in either case he must be so secured that I get him again.   EDWIN C. FITZHUGH.
Oct. 7. — eotf.

Poor Henry ! — only 14 or 15.

COMMITTED

To the Jail of Lowndes County, Mississippi, on the 9th of May, by Jno. K. Peirce, Esq., and taken up as a runaway slave by William S. Cox, a negro man, who says his name is ROLAND, and that he belongs to Maj. Cathey, of Marengo Co., Ala., was sold to him by Henry Williams, a negro trader from North Carolina.
Said negro is about 35 years old, 5 feet 6 or 8 inches high, dark complexion, weighs about 150 pounds, *middle finger on the right hand off at the second joint*, and had on, when committed, a black silk hat, black *drap d'ete* dress coat, and white linsey pants.
The owner is requested to come forward, prove property, pay charges, and take him away, or he will be dealt with according to law.
L. H. WILLEFORD,
June 6, 1852.   19 — tf.   Jailer.

Richmond Semi-weekly Examiner, October 29, 1852 :

FIFTY DOLLARS REWARD.

Ranaway from the subscriber, residing in the County of Halifax, about the middle of last August, a Negro Man, Ned, aged some thirty or forty years, of medium height, *copper color*, full forehead, and cheek bones a little prominent. *No scars recollected,* except one of his fingers — the

little one, probably — is stiff and crooked. The man Ned was purchased in Richmond, of Mr. Robert Goodwin, who resides near Frederick-Hall, in Louisa County, *and has. a wife in that vicinity.* He has been seen in the neighborhood, and is supposed to have gone over the Mountains, and to be now at work as a free man at some of the Iron Works; some one having given him free papers. The above reward will be given for the apprehension of the slave Ned, and his delivery to R. H. Dickinson & Bro., in Richmond, or to the undersigned, in Halifax, Virginia, or twenty-five if confined in any jail in the Commonwealth, so that I get him.   JAS. M. CHAPPELL,
[Firm of Chappell & Tucker.]
Aug. 10. — tf.

This unfortunate copper-colored article is supposed to have gone after his *wife.*

Kentucky Whig, Oct. 22, '52 :

$200 REWARD.

Ranaway from the subscriber, near Mount Sterling, Ky., on the night of the 20th of October, a negro man named PORTER. Said boy is black, about 22 years old, very stout and active, weighs about 165 or 170 pounds. *He is a smart fellow, converses well, without the negro accent ; no particular scars recollected.* He had on a pair of coarse boots about half worn, no other clothing recollected. He was raised near Sharpsburg, in Bath county, by Harrison Caldwell, and may be lurking in that neighborhood, but will probably endeavor to reach Ohio.
I will pay the above-mentioned reward for him, if taken out of the State ; $50, if taken in any county bordering on the Ohio river ; or $25, if taken in this or any adjoining county, and secured so that I can get him.
He is supposed to have ridden a yellow Horse, 15 hands and one inch high, mane and tail both yellow, five years old, and paces well.
October 21st, 1852.   G. W. PROCTOR.

"No particular scars recollected*"* !

St. Louis Times, Oct. 14, 1852 :

NOTICE.

Taken up and committed to Jail in the town of Rockbridge, Ozark county, Mo., on the 31st of August last, a runaway slave, who calls his name MOSES. Had on, when taken, a brown Jeanes pantaloons, old cotton shirt, blue frock-coat, an old rag tied round his head. He is about six feet high, dark complexion, *a scar over the left eye,* supposed to be about 27 years old. The owner is hereby notified to come forward, prove said negro, and pay all lawful charges incurred on his account, or the said negro will be sold at public auction for ready money at the Court House door in the town of Rockbridge, on MONDAY, the 13th of December next, according to law in such cases made and provided, this 9th of September, 1852.
s23d & w.   ROBERT HICKS, Sh'ff.

Charleston Mercury, Oct. 15, 1852 :

FIFTY DOLLARS REWARD.

Runaway on Sunday the 6th inst., from the South Carolina Railroad Company, their negro man SAM, recently bought by them, with others, at Messrs. Cothran & Sproull's sale, at Aiken. He was raised in Cumberland County, North Carolina, and last brought from Richmond, Va. In height he is 5 feet 6¾ inches. Complexion copper color; *on the left arm and right leg somewhat scarred.* Countenance good. The above reward will be paid for his apprehension and lodgment in any one of the Jails of this or any neighboring State.

J. D. PETSCH,
June 12. Sup't Transportation.

Kosciusko Chronicle, Nov. 24, '52:

COMMITTED

To the Jail of Attila County, Miss., October the 7th, 1852, a negro boy, who calls his name HAMBLETON, and says he belongs to Parson William Young, of Pontotoc County; is about 26 or 27 years old, about 5 feet 8 inches high, rather dark complexion, *has two or three marks on his back, a small scar on his left hip.* Had on, when taken up, a pair of blue cotton pants, white cotton drawers, a new cotton shirt, a pair of kip boots, an old cloth cap and wool hat. The owner is requested to come forward, prove property, pay charges and take him away, or he will be dealt with as provided in such case.

E. B. SANDERS, Jailer A. C.
Oct. 12, 1852. n 12tf.

Frankfort Commonwealth, October 21, 1852:

COMMITTED TO JAIL.

A negro boy, who calls his name ADAM, was committed to the Muhlenburg Jail on the 24th of July, 1852. Said boy is black; about 16 or 17 years old; 5 feet 8 or 9 inches high; will weigh about 150 lbs. He has *lost a part of the finger next to his little finger on the right hand; also the great toe on his left foot.* This boy says he belongs to Wm. Mosley; that said Mosley was moving to Mississippi from Virginia. He further states that he is lost, and not a runaway. His owner is requested to come forward, prove property, pay expenses, and take him away, or he will be disposed of as the law directs.

S. H. DEMPSEY, J. M. C.
Greenville, Ky., Oct. 20, 1852.

RUNAWAY SLAVE.

A negro man arrested and placed in the Barren County Jail, Ky., on the 21st instant, calling himself HENRY, about 22 years old; says he ran away from near Florence, Alabama, and belongs to John Calaway. He is about five feet eight inches high, dark, but not very black, rather thin visage, pointed nose, *no scars perceivable,* rather spare built; says he has been runaway nearly three months. The owner can get him by applying and paying the reward and expenses; if not, he will be proceeded against according to law. This 24th of August, 1852. SAMUEL ADWELL, Jailer.
Aug. 25, 1852. — 6m

In the same paper are two more poor fellows, who probably have been sold to pay jail-fees, before now.

NOTICE.

Taken up by M. H. Brand, as a runaway slave,

on the 22d ult., in the city of Covington, Kenton county, Ky., a negro man calling himself CHARLES WARFIELD, about 30 years old, but looks older, about 6 feet high; no particular marks: had no free papers, but he *says he is free,* and *was born in Pennsylvania,* and in *Fayette county.* Said negro was lodged in jail on the said 22d ult., and the owner or owners, if any, are hereby notified to come forward, prove property, and pay charges, and take him away.

C. W. HULL, J. K. C.
August 3, 1852. — 6m.

COMMITTED

To the Jail of Graves county, Ky., on the 4th inst., a negro man calling himself DAVE or DAVID. He *says he is free,* but formerly belonged to Samuel Brown, of Prince William county, Virginia. He is of black color, about 5 feet 10 inches high, weighs about 180 lbs.; supposed to be about 45 years old; had on brown pants and striped shirt. He had in his possession an old rifle gun, an old pistol, and some old clothing. He also informs me that he has escaped from the Dyersburg Jail, Tennessee, where he had been confined some eight or nine months. The owner is hereby notified to come forward, prove property, pay charges, &c.

L. B. HOLEFIELD, Jailer G. C.
June 28, 1852. — w6m.

Charleston Mercury, Oct. 29, 1852:

$200 REWARD.

Ranaway from the subscriber, some time in March last, his servant LYDIA, and is suspected of being in Charleston. I will give the above reward to any person who may apprehend her, and furnish evidence to conviction of the person supposed to harbor her, or $50 for having her lodged in any Jail so that I get her. Lydia is a *Mulatto woman,* twenty-five years of age, four feet eleven inches high, with *straight black hair, which inclines to curl,* her front teeth defective, and has been plugged; the gold distinctly seen when talking; round face, *a scar under her chin, and two fingers on one hand stiff at the first joints.*
June 16. tuths C. T. SCAIFE.

$25 REWARD.

Runaway from the subscriber, on or about the first of May last, his negro boy GEORGE, about 18 years of age, about 5 feet high, *well set, and speaks properly.* He formerly belonged to Mr. J. D. A. Murphy, living in Blackville; *has a mother belonging to a Mr. Lorrick, living in Lexington District.* He is supposed to have a pass, and is likely to be lurking about Branchville or Charleston.

The above reward will be paid to any one lodging George in any Jail in the State, so that I can get him.

J. J. ANDREWS, Orangeburg C. H.
Orangeburg, Aug. 7, 1852. sw Sept 11

NOTICE.

Committed to the Jail at Colleton District as a runaway, JORDAN, a negro man about thirty years of age, who says he belongs to Dobson

Coely, of Pulaski County, Georgia. The owner has notice to prove property and take him away.
L. W. McCants, Sheriff Colleton Dist.
Walterboro, So. Ca., Sept. 7; 1852.

The following are selected by the *Commonwealth* mostly from New Orleans papers. The characteristics of the slaves are interesting.

TWENTY-FIVE DOLLARS REWARD

Will be paid by the undersigned for the apprehension and delivery to any Jail in this city of the negro woman MARIAH, who ran away from the Phœnix House about the 15th of October last. She is about 45 years old, 5 feet 4 inches high, stout built, *speaks French and English.* Was purchased from Chas. Deblanc.
H. Bidwell & Co., 16 Front Levee.

FIFTY DOLLARS REWARD.

Ranaway about the 25th ult., ALLEN, *a bright mulatto, aged about* 22 years, 6 feet high, very well dressed, has an extremely careless gait, of slender build, and wore a moustache when he left; the property of J. P. Harrison, Esq., of this city. The above reward will be paid for his safe delivery at any safe place in the city. For further particulars apply at 10 Bank Place.

ONE HUNDRED DOLLARS REWARD.

We will give the above reward for the apprehension of the *light mulatto boy SEABOURN,* aged 20 years, about 5 feet 4 inches high; is stout, well made, and remarkably active. He is somewhat of a circus actor, by which he may easily be detected, as he is always showing his gymnastic qualifications. The said boy absented himself on the 3d inst. Besides the above reward, all reasonable expenses will be paid.
W. & H. Stackhouse, 70 Tchoupitoulas.

TWENTY-FIVE DOLLARS REWARD.

The above reward will be paid for the apprehension of the mulatto boy SEVERIN, aged 25 years, 5 feet 6 or 8 inches high; *most of his front teeth are out, and the letters C. V. are marked on either of his arms with India Ink* He speaks French, English and Spanish, and *was formerly* owned by Mr. Courcell, in the Third District. I will pay, in addition to the above reward, $50 for such information as will lead to the conviction of any person harboring said slave.
·John Ermon, corner Camp and Race sts.

TWENTY-FIVE DOLLARS REWARD.

Ran away from the Chain Gang in New Orleans, First Municipality, in February last, a negro boy named STEPHEN. He is about 5 feet 7 inches in height, a very light mulatto, *with blue eyes and brownish hair,* stoops a little in the shoulders, has a cast-down look, and is very strongly built and muscular. He will not acknowledge his name or owner, is an habitual runaway, and *was shot somewhere in the ankle while endeavoring to escape from Baton Rouge Jail.* The above reward, with all

attendant expenses, will be paid on his delivery to me, or for his apprehension and commitment to any Jail from which I can get him.
A. L. Bingaman.

TWENTY-FIVE DOLLARS REWARD.

The above reward will be given to the person who will lodge in one of the Jails of this city the slave SARAH, belonging to Mr. Guisonnet, corner St. John Baptiste and Race streets; said slave is aged about 28 years, 5 feet high, *benevolent face, fine teeth, and speaking French and English.* Captains of vessels and steamboats are hereby cautioned not to receive her on board, under penalty of the law. Ayet Brothers,
Corner Bienville and Old Levee streets.

Lynchburg Virginian, Nov. 6th:

TWENTY DOLLARS REWARD.

Ranaway from the subscriber on the Virginia and Tennessee Railroad, in the county of Wythe, on the 20th of June, 1852, a negro man named CHARLES, 6 feet high, *copper color, with several teeth out in front,* about 35 years of age, rather slow to reply, *but pleasing appearance when spoken to.* He wore, when he left, a cloth cap and a blue cloth sack coat; he was purchased in Tennessee, 14 months ago, by Mr. M. Connell, of Lynchburg, and carried to that place, where he remained until I purchased him 4 months ago. *It is more than probable that he will make his way to Tennessee, as he has a wife now living there;* or he may perhaps return to Lynchburg, and lurk about there, as he has acquaintances there. The above reward will be paid if he is taken in the State and confined so that I get him again; or I will pay a reward of $40, if taken out of the State and confined in Jail. George W. Kyle.
July 1. — d&c2twts

Winchester Republican (Va.), Nov. 26:

ONE HUNDRED DOLLARS REWARD.

Ranaway from the subscriber, near Culpepper Ct. House, Va., about the 1st of October, a negro man named ALFRED, about five feet seven inches in height, about twenty-five years of age, uncommonly muscular and active, complexion dark but not black, countenance mild and rather pleasant. He had a boil last winter on the middle joint of the middle or second finger of the right hand, which left the finger stiff in that joint, more visible in opening his hand than in shutting it. *He has a wife at Mr. Thomas G. Marshall's, near Farrowsville, in Fauquier County,* and may be in that neighborhood, where he wishes to be sold, and where I am willing to sell him.
I will give the above reward if he is taken out of the State and secured, so that I get him again; or $50 if taken in the State, and secured in like manner. W. B. Slaughter.
October 29, 1852.

From the *Louisville Daily Journal,* Oct. 23, 1852:

$100 REWARD.

Ran away from the subscriber, in this city, on Friday, May 28th, a negro boy named WYATT.

Said boy is copper colored, 25 or 26 years old, about 5 feet 11 inches high, of large frame, slow and heavy gait, has very large hands and feet, small side-whiskers, a full head of hair which he combs to the side, quite a pleasing look, and is very likely. I recently purchased Wyatt from Mr. Garrett, of Garrett's Landing, Ky., and *his wife is the property of Thos. G. Rowland, Esq.,* of this city. I will pay the above reward for the apprehension and delivery of the boy to me if taken out of the State, or $50 if taken in the State.
June 2 d&wtf   DAVID W. YANDELL.

$200 REWARD.

TWO NEGROES. Ranaway from the subscriber, living in Louisville, on the 2d, one negro man and girl. The man's name is MILES. He is about 5 feet 8 inches high, dark-brown color, *with a large scar upon his head, as if caused from a burn;* age about 25 years ; and had with him two carpet sacks, one of cloth, the other enamelled leather, also a pass from Louisville to Owenton, Owen county, Ky., and back. The girl's name is JULIA, and she is of light-brown color, short and heavy set, rather good looking, *with a scar upon her forehead;* had on a plaid silk dress when she left, and took other clothes with her ; looks to be about 16 years of age.

The above reward will be paid for the man, if taken out of the State, or $100 for the girl; $100 for the man, if taken in the State, or $50 for the girl. In either event, they are to be secured, so I get them.   JOHN W. LYNN.
oct 5 d&wtf

The following advertisements are all dated Shelby Co., Kentucky.

JAILER'S NOTICE.

Was committed to the Jail of Shelby county a negro woman, who says her name is JUDA ; dark complexion ; twenty years of age ; some five feet high ; weighs about one hundred and twenty pounds ; *no scars recollected,* and says she belongs to James Wilson, living in Denmark, Tennessee. The owner of said slave is requested to come forward, prove property, pay charges, and take her away, or she will be dealt with as the law directs.
     W. H. EANES,
oct27 — w4t   Jailer Shelby county.

JAILER'S NOTICE.

Was committed to the Jail of Shelby county, on the 28th ult., a negro boy, who says his name is JOHN W. LOYD ; of a bright complexion, 25 years of age, will weigh about one hundred and fifty pounds, about five feet nine or ten inches high, *three scars on his left leg, which was caused by a dog-bite. The said boy John claims to be free.* If he has any master, he is hereby notified to come forward, prove property, pay charges, and take him away, or he will be dealt with as the law directs.   [nov3 — w4t

ALSO — Committed at the same time a negro boy, who says his name is PATRICK, of a bright complexion, about 30 years of age, will weigh about one hundred and forty-five or fifty pounds ; about six feet high ; his face is very badly scarred, which he says was caused by being salivated.

The disease caused him to lose the bone out of his nose, and his jaw-bone, also. Says he belongs to Dr. Wm. Cheathum, living in Nashville, Tenn. The owner of said slave is requested to come forward, prove property, pay charges, and take him away, or he will be dealt with as the law directs.
     [nov3 — w4t

ALSO — Committed at the same time a negro boy, who says his name is CLAIBORNE ; dark complexion, 22 years of age, will weigh about one hundred and forty pounds, about five feet high ; *no scars recollected;* says he belongs to Col. Rousell, living in De Soto county, Miss. The owner of said slave is requested to come forward, prove property, pay charges, and take him away, or he will be dealt with as the law directs.
     W. H. EANES,
nov3 — w4t   Jailer of Shelby county.

JAILER'S NOTICE.

Was committed to the Jail of Shelby county a negro boy, who says his name is GEORGE ; dark complexion, about twenty-five or thirty years of age, some five feet nine or ten inches high ; will weigh about one hundred and forty pounds, *no scars,* and says he belongs to Malley Bradford, living in Issaqueen county, Mississippi. The owner of said slave is requested to come forward, prove property, pay charges, and take him away, or he will be dealt with as the law directs.
     W. H. EANES,
nov10. — w4t   Jailer of Shelby county.

JAILER'S NOTICE.

Was committed to the Jail of Shelby county, on the 30th ult., a negro woman, who says her name is NANCY, of a bright complexion, some twenty or twenty-one years of age, will weigh about one hundred and forty pounds, about five feet high, *no scars,* and says she belongs to John Pittman, living in Memphis, Tenn. The owner of said slave is requested to come forward, prove property, pay charges, and take her away, or she will be dealt with as the law directs.
     W. H. EANES,
nov10. — w4t   Jailer of Shelby county.

Negro property is decidedly "brisk" in this county.

Natchez (Miss.) *Free Trader,* November 6, 1852 :

25 DOLLARS REWARD.

Ranaway from the undersigned, on the 17th day of October, 1852, a negro man by the name of ALLEN, about 23 years old, near 6 feet high, of dark mulatto color, *no marks, save one, and that caused by the bite of a dog;* had on, when he left, lowell pants, and cotton shirt ; reads imperfect, can make a short calculation correctly, and can write some few words ; said negro has run away heretofore, and when taken up was in possession of a free pass. He is quick-spoken, lively, and smiles when in conversation.

I will give the above reward to any one who will confine said negro in any Jail, so that I can get him.   THOS R. CHEATHAM.
nov6. — 3t

Newberry Sentinel (S. C.), Nov. 17, 1852 :

NOTICE!

RANAWAY from the subscriber, on the 9th of July last, my Boy WILLIAM, a bright mulatto, about 26 years old, 5 feet 9 or 10 inches high, of slender make, quite intelligent, speaks quick when spoken to, and walks briskly. *Said boy was brought from Virginia, and will probably attempt to get back.* Any information of said boy will be thankfully received. JOHN M. MARS.
Near Mollohon P. O., Newberry Dist., S. C.
Nov. 3.   414t.
☞ *Raleigh Register* and *Richmond Enquirer* will copy four times weekly, and send bills to this office.

Greensboro' Patriot (N. C.), Nov. 6 :

10 DOLLARS REWARD.

·RANAWAY from my service, in February, 1851, a colored man named EDWARD WINSLOW, low, *thick-set, part Indian*, and a first rate fiddler. Said Winslow was sold out of Guilford jail, at February court, 1851, for his prison charges, for the term of five years. It is supposed that he is at work on the Railroad, somewhere in Davidson county. The above reward will be paid for his apprehension and confinement in the jail of Guilford or any of the adjoining counties, so that I get him, or for his delivery to me in the south-east corner of Guilford. My post-office is Long's Mills, Randolph, N. C.   P. C. SMITH.
October 27, 1852.   702 — 5w.

The New Orleans *True Delta,* of the 11th ult., 1853, has the following editorial notice·:

THE GREAT RAFFLE OF A TROTTING HORSE AND A NEGRO SERVANT. — The enterprising and go-a-head Col. Jennings has got a raffle under way now, which eclipses all his previous undertakings in that line. The prizes are the celebrated trotting horse "Star," buggy and harness, and a valuable negro servant, — the latter valued at nine hundred dollars. See his advertisement in another column.

The advertisement is as follows :

RAFFLE.

MR. JOSEPH JENNINGS

Respectfully informs his friends and the public, that, at the request of many of his acquaintances, he has been induced to purchase from Mr. Osborn, of Missouri, the celebrated dark bay horse "Star," age five years, square trotter, and warranted sound, with a new light trotting Buggy and Harness ; *also the stout mulatto girl "Sarah," aged about twenty years, general house servant*, valued at nine hundred dollars, and guaranteed ; will be raffled for at 4 o'clock, P. M., February 1st, at any hotel selected by the subscribers.

The above is as represented, and those persons who may wish to engage in the usual practice of raffling will, I assure them, be perfectly satisfied with their destiny in this affair.

Fifteen hundred chances, at $1 each.
The whole is valued at its just worth, fifteen hundred dollars.
·The raffle will be conducted by gentlemen selected by the interested subscribers present. Five

nights allowed to complete the raffle. Both of above can be seen at my store, No. 78 Common-street, second door from Camp, at from 9 o'clock A. M., till half-past 2 P. M.

Highest throw takes the first choice ; the lowest throw the remaining prize, and the fortunate winners to pay Twenty Dollars each, for the refreshments furnished for the occasion.
Jan. 9. 2w.   J. JENNINGS.

Daily Courier (Natchez, Miss.), Nov. 20, 1852 :

TWENTY-FIVE DOLLARS REWARD.

THE above reward will be given for the apprehension and confinement in any jail of the negro man HARDY, who ran away from the subscriber, residing on Lake St. John, near Rifle Point, Concordia parish, La., on the 9th August last. Hardy is a remarkably likely negro, *entirely free from all marks, scars or blemishes*, when he left home ; about six feet high, of black complexion (though quite light), *fine countenance*, unusually smooth skin, good head of hair, *fine eyes and teeth.*

Address the subscriber at Rifle Point, Concordia Parish, La.   ROBERT Y. JONES.
Oct. 30. — 1m.

What an unfortunate master — lost an article entirely free from " marks, scars or blemishes " ! Such a rarity ought to be choice !

Savannah Daily Georgian, 6th Sept., 1852 :

ARRESTED,

ABOUT three weeks ago, under suspicious circumstances, a negro woman, who calls herself PHEBE, or PHILLIS. *Says she is free*, and lately from Beaufort District, South Carolina. Said woman is about 50 years of age, stout in stature, mild-spoken, 5 feet 4 inches high, and weighs about 140 pounds. Having made diligent inquiry by letter, and from what I can learn, said woman is a runaway. Any person owning said slave can get her by making application to me, properly authenticated.   WARING RUSSELL,
                    County Constable.
Savannah, Oct. 25, 1852.   6   oct. 26.

250 DOLLARS REWARD.

RANAWAY from Sparta, Ga., about the first of last year my boy GEORGE. He is a good carpenter, about 35 years : a bright mulatto, tall and quite likely. *He was brought about three years ago from St. Mary's, and had, when he ran away, a wife there, or near there, belonging to a Mr. Holzendorff.* I think he has told me he has been about Macon also. He had, and perhaps still has, a brother in Savannah. *He is very intelligent.* I will give the above reward for his confinement in some jail in the State, so that I can get him. Refer, for any further information, to Rabun & Whitehead, Savannah, Ga.
                    W. J. SASSNETT.
Oxford, Ga., Aug. 13th, 1852.   tuths3m. a17.

From these advertisements, and hundreds of similar ones, one may learn the following things :

1. That the arguments for the enslaving of the *negro* do not apply to a large part of the actual slaves.

2. That they are not, in the estimation of their masters, very stupid.

3. That they are not remarkably contented.

4. That they have no particular reason to be so.

5. That multitudes of men claiming to be free are constantly being sold into slavery.

In respect to the complexion of these slaves, there are some points worthy of consideration. The writer adds the following advertisements, published by Wm. I. Bowditch, Esq., in his pamphlet " Slavery and the Constitution."

From the *Richmond* (Va.) *Whig:*

100 DOLLARS REWARD

WILL be given for the apprehension of my negro (!) Edmund Kenney. *He has straight hair, and complexion so nearly white that it is believed a stranger would suppose there was no African blood in him.* He was with my boy Dick a short time since in Norfolk, *and offered him for sale,* and was apprehended, *but escaped under pretence of being a white man!* ANDERSON BOWLES.
January 6, 1836.

From the *Republican Banner and Nashville Whig* of July 14, 1849:

200 DOLLARS REWARD.

RANAWAY from the subscriber, on the 23d of June last, a bright mulatto woman, named Julia, about 25 years of age. She is of common size, *nearly white,* and very likely. She is a good seamstress, and can read a little. *She may attempt to pass for white,* — dresses fine. She took with her Anna, her child, 8 or 9 years old, and considerably darker than her mother. . . . . She once belonged to a Mr. Helm, of Columbia, Tennessee.

I will give a reward of $50 for said negro and child, if delivered to me, or confined in any jail in this state, so I can get them ; $100, if caught in any other Slave state, and confined in a jail so that I can get them ; and $200, if caught in any Free state, and put in any good jail in Kentucky or Tennessee, so I can get them.
A. W. JOHNSON.
Nashville, July 9, 1849.

The following three advertisements are taken from Alabama papers :

RANAWAY

From the Subscriber, working on the plantation of Col. H. Tinker, a bright mulatto boy, named Alfred. Alfred is about 18 years old, pretty well grown, *has blue eyes, light flaxen hair, skin disposed to freckle. He will try to pass as free-born.*
Green County, Ala. S. G. STEWART.

100 DOLLARS REWARD.

Ran away from the subscriber, a bright mulatto man-slave, named Sam. *Light, sandy hair, blue eyes, ruddy complexion, — is so white as very easily to pass for a free white man.* EDWIN PECK.
Mobile, April 22, 1837.

RANAWAY,

On the 15th of May, from me, a negro woman, named Fanny. Said woman is 20 years old ; is rather tall ; can read and write, and so forge passes for herself. Carried away with her a pair of ear-rings, — a Bible with a red cover ; is very pious. She prays a great deal, and was, as supposed, contented and happy. *She is as white as most white women, with straight, light hair, and blue eyes, and can pass herself for a white woman.* I will give $500 for her apprehension and delivery to me. She is very intelligent.
Tuscaloosa, May 29, 1845. JOHN BALCH.

From the *Newbern* (N. C.) *Spectator:*

50 DOLLARS REWARD

Will be given for the apprehension and delivery to me of the following slaves : — Samuel, and Judy his wife, with their four children, belonging to the estate of Sacker Dubberly, deceased.

I will give $10 for the apprehension of *William Dubberly,* a slave belonging to the estate. William is about 19 years old, *quite white, and would not readily be taken for a slave.* JOHN J. LANE.
March 13, 1837.

The next two advertisements we cut from the *New Orleans Picayune* of Sept. 2, 1846 :

25 DOLLARS REWARD.

Ranaway from the plantation of Madame Fergus Duplantier, on or about the 27th of June, 1846, a bright mulatto named Ned, very stout built, about 5 feet 11 inches high, *speaks English and French,* about 35 years old, waddles in his walk. *He may try to pass himself for a white man, as he is of a very clear color, and has sandy hair.* The above reward will be paid to whoever will bring him to Madame Duplantier's plantation, Manchac, or lodge him in some jail where he can be conveniently obtained.

200 DOLLARS REWARD.

Ran away from the subscriber, last November, *a white negro* man, about 35 years old, height about 5 feet 8 or 10 inches, *blue eyes, has a yellow woolly head, very fair skin.*

These are the characteristics of three races. The copper-colored complexion shows the Indian blood. The others are the mixed races of negroes and whites. It is known that the poor remains of Indian races have been in many cases forced into slavery. It is no less certain that white children have sometimes been kidnapped and sold into slavery. Rev. George Bourne, of Virginia, Presbyterian minister, who wrote against slavery there as early as 1816, gives an account of a boy who was stolen from his parents at seven years of age, immersed in a tan-vat to change his complexion, tattooed and sold, and, after a captivity of fourteen years, succeeded in escaping. The tanning process is not necessary now, as a fair skin is no presumption against slavery. There is reason to think that the grandmother of poor Emily Russell was a *white child*, stolen by kidnappers. That kidnappers may steal and sell white children at the South now, is evident from these advertisements.

The writer, within a week, has seen a fugitive quadroon mother, who had with her two children,— a boy of ten months, and a girl of three years. Both were surpassingly fair, and uncommonly beautiful. The girl had blue eyes and golden hair. The mother and those children were about to be sold for the division of an estate, which was the reason why she fled. When the mind once becomes familiarized with the process of slavery,— of enslaving first black, then Indian, then mulatto, then quadroon, and when blue eyes and golden hair are advertised as properties of *negroes*,— what protection will there be for poor white people, especially as under the present fugitive law they can be carried away without a jury trial?

A Governor of South Carolina openly declared, in 1835, that the laboring population of any country, bleached or unbleached, were a *dangerous element*, unless reduced to slavery. Will not this be the result, then?

CHAPTER VIII.

"POOR WHITE TRASH."

WHEN the public sentiment of Europe speaks in tones of indignation of the system of American slavery, the common reply has been, "*Look at your own lower classes.*" The apologists of slavery have pointed England to *her own poor*. They have spoken of the heathenish ignorance, the vice, the darkness, of her crowded cities,— nay, even of her agricultural districts.

Now, in the first place, a country where the population is not crowded, where the resources of the soil are more than sufficient for the inhabitants,— a country of recent origin, not burdened with the worn-out institutions and clumsy lumber of past ages, —ought not to be satisfied to do *only* as well as countries which have to struggle against all these evils.

It is a poor defence for America to say to older countries, "We are no worse than you are." She ought to be infinitely better.

But it will appear that the institution of slavery has produced not only heathenish, degraded, miserable slaves, but it produces a class of white people who are, by universal admission, more heathenish, degraded, and miserable. The institution of slavery has accomplished the double feat, in America, not only of degrading and brutalizing her black working classes, but of producing, notwithstanding a fertile soil and abundant room, a poor white population as degraded and brutal as ever existed in any of the most crowded districts of Europe.

The way that it is done can be made apparent in a few words. 1. The distribution of the land into large plantations, and the consequent sparseness of settlement, make any system of common-school education impracticable. 2. The same cause operates with regard to the preaching of the gospel. 3. The degradation of the idea of labor, which results inevitably from enslaving the working class, operates to a great extent in preventing respectable working men of the middling classes from settling or remaining in slave states. Where carpenters, blacksmiths and masons, are advertised every week with their own tools, or in company with horses, hogs and other cattle, there is necessarily such an estimate of the laboring class that intelligent, self-respecting mechanics, such as abound in the free states, must find much that is annoying and disagreeable. They may endure it for a time, but with much uneasiness ; and they are glad of the first opportunity of emigration.

Then, again, the filling up of all branches of mechanics and agriculture with slave labor necessarily depresses free labor. Suppose, now, a family of poor whites in Carolina or Virginia, and the same family in Vermont or Maine ; how different the influences that come over them ! In Vermont or Maine, the children have the means of education at hand in public schools, and they have all around them in society avenues of success that require only industry to make them available. The boys have their choice among all the different trades, for which the organization of free society makes a steady demand. The girls, animated by the spirit of the land in which they are born, think useful labor no disgrace, and find, with true female ingenuity, a hundred ways of adding to the family stock. If there be one member of a family in whom diviner gifts and higher longings seem a call for a more finished course of education, then cheerfully the whole family unites its productive industry to give that one the wider education which his wider genius demands ; and thus have been given to the world such men as Roger Sherman and Daniel Webster.

But take this same family and plant them in South Carolina or Virginia — how different the result! No common school opens its doors to their children; the only church, perhaps, is fifteen miles off, over a bad road. The whole atmosphere of the country in which they are born associates degradation and slavery with useful labor; and the only standard of gentility is ability to live without work. What branch of useful labor opens a way to its sons? Would he be a black-smith? — The planters around him prefer to *buy* their blacksmiths in Virginia. Would he be a carpenter? — Each planter in his neighborhood owns one or two now. And so coopers and masons. Would he be a shoe-maker? — The plantation shoes are made in Lynn and Natick, towns of New England. In fact, between the free labor of the North and the slave labor of the South, there is nothing for a poor white to do. Without schools or churches, these miserable families grow up heathen on a Christian soil, in idleness, vice, dirt and discomfort of all sorts. They are the pest of the neighborhood, the scoff and contempt or pity even of the slaves. The expressive phrase, so common in the mouths of the negroes, of "poor white trash," says all for this luckless race of beings that can be said. From this class spring a tribe of keepers of small grog-geries, and dealers, by a kind of contraband trade, with the negroes, in the stolen produce of plantations. Thriving and promising sons may perhaps hope to grow up into negro-traders, and thence be exalted into overseers of plantations. The utmost stretch of ambition is to compass money enough, by any of a variety of nondescript measures, to "buy a *nigger* or two," and begin to appear like other folks. Woe betide the unfortunate negro man or woman, carefully raised in some good religious family, when an execution or the death of their proprietors throws them into the market, and they are bought by a master and mistress of this class! Oftentimes the slave is infinitely the superior, in every respect, — in person, manners, education and morals; but, for all that, the law guards the despotic authority of the owner quite as jealously.

From all that would appear, in the case of Souther, which we have recorded, he must have been one of this class. We have certain indications, in the evidence, that the two white witnesses, who spent the whole day in gaping, unresisting survey of his diabolical proceedings, were men of this order. It appears that the crime alleged against the poor victim was that of getting drunk and trading with these two very men, and that they were sent for probably by way of showing them "what a nigger would get by trading with them." This circumstance at once marks them out as belonging to that band of half-contraband traders who spring up among the mean whites, and occasion owners of slaves so much inconvenience by dealing with their hands. Can any words so forcibly show what sort of white men these are, as the idea of their standing in stupid, brutal curiosity, a whole day, as *witnesses* in such a hellish scene?

Conceive the misery of the slave who falls into the hands of such masters! A clergyman, now dead, communicated to the writer the following anecdote: In travelling in one of the Southern States, he put up for the night in a miserable log shanty, kept by a man of this class. All was dirt, discomfort and utter barbarism. The man, his wife, and their stock of wild, neglected children, drank whiskey, loafed and predominated over the miserable man and woman who did all the work and bore all the caprices of the whole establishment. He — the gentleman — was not long in discovering that these slaves were in person, language, and in every respect, superior to their owners; and all that he could get of comfort in this miserable abode was owing to their ministrations. Before he went away, they contrived to have a private interview, and begged him to buy them. They told him that they had been decently brought up in a respectable and refined family, and that their bondage was therefore the more inexpressibly galling. The poor creatures had waited on him with most assiduous care, tending his horse, brushing his boots, and anticipating all his wants, in the hope of inducing him to buy them. The clergyman said that he never so wished for money as when he saw the dejected visages with which they listened to his assurances that he was too poor to comply with their desires.

This miserable class of whites form, in all the Southern States, a material for the most horrible and ferocious of mobs. Utterly ignorant, and inconceivably brutal, they are like some blind, savage monster, which, when aroused, tramples heedlessly over everything in its way.

Singular as it may appear, though slavery is the cause of the misery and degradation of this class, yet they are the most vehement and ferocious advocates of slavery.

The reason is this. They feel the scorn

of the upper classes, and their only means of consolation is in having a class below them, whom they may scorn in turn. To set the negro at liberty would deprive them of this last comfort; and accordingly no class of men advocate slavery with such frantic and unreasoning violence, or hate abolitionists with such demoniac hatred. Let the reader conceive of a mob of men as brutal and callous as the two white witnesses of the Souther tragedy, led on by men like Souther himself, and he will have some idea of the materials which occur in the worst kind of Southern mobs.

The leaders of the community, those men who play on other men with as little care for them as a harper plays on a harp, keep this blind, furious monster of the MOB, very much as an overseer keeps plantation-dogs, as creatures to be set on to any man or thing whom they may choose to have put down.

These leading men have used the cry of "abolitionism" over the mob, much as a huntsman uses the "set on" to his dogs. Whenever they have a purpose to carry, a man to put down, they have only to raise this cry, and the monster is wide awake, ready to spring wherever they shall send him.

Does a minister raise his voice in favor of the slave? — Immediately, with a whoop and hurra, some editor starts the mob on him, as an abolitionist. Is there a man teaching his negroes to read? — The mob is started upon him — he must promise to give it up, or leave the state. Does a man at a public hotel-table express his approbation of some anti-slavery work? — Up come the police, and arrest him for seditious language; * and on the heels of the police, thronging round the justice's office, come the ever-ready mob,— men with clubs and bowie-knives, swearing that they will have his heart's blood. The more respectable citizens in vain try to compose them; it is quite as hopeful to reason with a pack of hounds, and the only way is to smuggle the suspected person out of the state as quickly as possible. All these are scenes of common occurrence at the South. Every Southern man knows them to be so, and they know, too, the reason *why* they are so; but, so much do they fear the monster, that they dare not say what they know.

This brute monster sometimes gets beyond the power of his masters, and then results ensue most mortifying to the patriot-

* The writer is describing here a scene of recent occurrence in a slave state, of whose particulars she has the best means of knowledge. The work in question was " Uncle Tom's Cabin."

ism of honorable Southern men, but which they are powerless to prevent. Such was the case when the Honorable Senator Hoar, of Massachusetts, with his daughter, visited the city of Charleston. The senator was appointed by the sovereign State of Massachusetts to inquire into the condition of her free colored citizens detained in South Carolina prisons. We cannot suppose that men of honor and education, in South Carolina, can contemplate without chagrin the fact that this honorable gentleman, the representative of a sister state, and accompanied by his daughter, was obliged to flee from South Carolina, because they were told that the constituted authorities would not be powerful enough to protect them from the ferocities of a mob. This is not the only case in which this mob power has escaped from the hands of its guiders, and produced mortifying results. The scenes of Vicksburg, and the succession of popular whirlwinds which at that time flew over the south-western states, have been forcibly painted by the author of " The White Slave."

They who find these popular outbreaks useful when they serve their own turns are sometimes forcibly reminded of the consequences

"Of letting rapine loose, and murder,
    To go *just so far*, and no further ;
    And setting all the land on fire,
    To burn *just so high*, and no higher."

The statements made above can be substantiated by various documents,— mostly by the testimony of residents in slave states, and by extracts from their newspapers.

Concerning the class of poor whites, Mr. William Gregg, of Charleston, South Carolina, in a pamphlet, called " Essays on Domestic Industry, or an Inquiry into the expediency of establishing Cotton Manufactories in South Carolina, 1845," says, p. 22 :

Shall we pass unnoticed the thousands of poor, ignorant, degraded white people among us, who, in this land of plenty, live in comparative nakedness and starvation? Many a one is reared in *proud* South Carolina, from birth to manhood, who has never passed a month in which he has not, some part of the time, been stinted for meat. Many a mother is there who will tell you that her children are but scantily provided with bread, and much more scantily with meat; and, if they be clad with comfortable raiment, it is at the expense of these scanty allowances of food. These may be startling statements, but they are nevertheless true; and if not believed in Charleston, the members of our legislature who have traversed the state in electioneering campaigns can attest their truth."

The Rev. Henry Duffner, D.D., President of Lexington College, Va., himself a slave-holder, published in 1847 an address to the people of Virginia, showing that slavery is injurious to public welfare, in which he shows the influence of slavery in producing a decrease of the white population. He says:

It appears that, in the ten years from 1830 to 1840, Virginia lost by emigration no fewer than three hundred and seventy-five thousand of her people; of whom East Virginia lost three hundred and four thousand, and West Virginia seventy-one thousand. At this rate, Virginia supplies the West, every ten years, with a population equal in number to the population of the State of Mississippi in 1840. * * * * * She has sent — or, we should rather say, she has driven — from her soil at least one-third of all the emigrants who have gone from the old states to the new. More than another third have gone from the other old slave states. Many of these multitudes, who have left the slave states, have shunned the regions of slavery, and settled in the free countries of the West. These were generally industrious and enterprising white men, who found, by sad experience, that a country of slaves was not the country for them. It is a truth, a certain truth, *that slavery drives free laborers — farmers, mechanics and all, and some of the best of them, too — out of the country, and fills their places with negroes.* * * * * * Even the common mechanical trades do not flourish in a slave state. Some mechanical operations must, indeed, be performed in every civilized country; but the general rule in the South is, to import from abroad every fabricated thing that can be carried in ships, such as household furniture, boats, boards, laths, carts, ploughs, axes, and axe-helves; besides innumerable other things, which free communities are accustomed to make for themselves. What is most wonderful is, that the forests and iron mines of the South supply, in great part, the materials out of which these things are made. The Northern freemen come with their ships, carry home the timber and pig-iron, work them up, supply their own wants with a part, and then sell the rest at a good profit in the Southern markets. Now, although mechanics, by setting up their shops in the South, could save all these freights and profits, yet so it is that Northern mechanics will not settle in the South, and the Southern mechanics are undersold by their Northern competitors.

In regard to education, Rev. Theodore Parker gives the following statistics, in his " Letters on Slavery," p. 65:

In 1671, Sir William Berkely, Governor of Virginia, said, "I thank God that there are no free schools nor printing-presses (in Virginia), and I hope we shall not have them these hundred years." In 1840, in the fifteen slave states and territories, there were at the various primary schools 201,085 scholars; at the various primary schools of the free states, 1,626,028. The State of Ohio alone had, at her primary schools, 17,524 more scholars than all the fifteen slave states. New York alone had 301,282 more.

In the slave states there are 1,368,325 free white children between the ages of five and twenty; in the free states, 3,536,689 such children. In the slave states, at schools and colleges, there are 301,172 pupils; in the free states, 2,212,444 pupils at schools or colleges. Thus, in the slave states, out of twenty-five free white children between five and twenty, there are not quite five at any school or college; while out of twenty-five such children in the free states, there are more than fifteen at school or college.

In the slave states, of the free white population that is over twenty years of age, there is almost one-tenth part that are unable to read and write; while in the free states there is not quite one in one hundred and fifty-six who is deficient to that degree.

In New England there are but few born therein, and more than twenty years of age, who are unable to read and write; but many foreigners arrive there with no education, and thus swell the number of the illiterate, and diminish the apparent effect of her free institutions. The South has few such emigrants; the ignorance of the Southern States, therefore, is to be ascribed to other causes. The Northern men who settle in the slave-holding states have perhaps about the average culture of the North, and more than that of the South. The South, therefore, gains educationally from immigration, as the North loses.

Among the Northern States Connecticut, and among the Southern States South Carolina, are to a great degree free from disturbing influences of this character. A comparison between the two will show the relative effects of the respective institutions of the North and South. In Connecticut there are 163,843 free persons over twenty years of age; in South Carolina, but 111,663. In Connecticut there are but 526 persons over twenty who are unable to read and write, while in South Carolina there are 20,615 free white persons over twenty years of age unable to read and write. In South Carolina, out of each 626 free whites more than twenty years of age there are more than 53 wholly unable to read or write; out of that number of such persons in Connecticut, not quite two! More than the sixth part of the adult freemen of South Carolina are unable to read the vote which will be deposited at the next election. It is but fair to infer that at least one-third of the adults of South Carolina, if not of much of the South, are unable to read and understand even a newspaper. Indeed, in one of the slave states this is not a matter of mere inference; for in 1837 Gov. Clarke, of Kentucky, declared in his message to the legislature that "one-third of the adult population were unable to write their names;" yet Kentucky has a "school-fund," valued at $1,221,819, while South Carolina has none.

One sign of this want of ability even to read, in the slave states, is too striking to be passed by. The staple reading of the least-cultivated Americans is the newspapers, one of the lowest forms of literature, though one of the most powerful, read even by men who read nothing else. In the slave states there are published but 377 newspapers, and in the free 1135. These numbers do not express the entire difference in the case; for, as a general rule, the circulation of the Southern newspapers is 50 to 75 per cent. less than that of the North. Suppose, however, that each Southern newspaper has two-thirds the circulation of a Northern journal, we have then but 225 newspapers for the slave states! The more valuable journals — the monthlies and quarterlies — are published almost entirely in the free States.

The number of churches, the number and character of the clergy who labor for these churches, are other measures of the intellectual and moral condition of the people. The scientific character of the Southern clergy has been already touched on. Let us compare the more external facts.

In 1830, South Carolina had a population of 581,185 souls; Connecticut, 297,675. In 1836, South Carolina had 364 ministers; Connecticut, 498.

In 1834, there were in the slave states but 82,532 scholars in the Sunday-schools; in the free states, 504,835; in the single State of New York, 161,768.

The fact of constant emigration from slave states is also shown by such extracts from papers as the following, from the *Raleigh* (N. C.) *Register*, quoted in the columns of the *National Era :*

THEY WILL LEAVE NORTH CAROLINA.

Our attention was arrested, on Saturday last, by quite a long train of wagons, winding through our streets, which, upon inquiry, we found to belong to a party emigrating from Wayne county, in this state, to the "far West.". This is but a repetition of many similar scenes that we and others have witnessed during the past few years; and such spectacles will be still more frequently witnessed, unless something is done to retrieve our fallen fortunes at home.

If there be any one "consummation devoutly to be wished" in our policy, it is that our young men should remain at home, and not abandon their native state. From the early settlement of North Carolina, the great drain upon her prosperity has been the spirit of emigration, which has so prejudicially affected all the states of the South. Her sons, hitherto neglected (if we must say it) by an unparental government, have wended their way, by hundreds upon hundreds, from the land of their fathers, — that land, too, to make it a paradise, wanting nothing but a market, — to bury their bones in the land of strangers. We firmly believe that this emigration is caused by the laggard policy of our people on the subject of internal improvement, for man is not prone by nature to desert the home of his affections.

The editor of the *Era* also quotes the following from the *Greensboro* (Ala.) *Beacon :*

"An unusually large number of movers have passed through this village, within the past two or three weeks. On one day of last week, upwards of thirty wagons and other vehicles belonging to emigrants, mostly from Georgia and South Carolina, passed through on their way, most of them bound to Texas and Arkansas."

This tide of emigration does not emanate from an overflowing population. Very far from it. Rather it marks an abandonment of a soil which, exhausted by injudicious culture, will no longer repay the labor of tillage. The emigrant, turning his back upon the homes of his childhood, leaves a desolate region, it may be, and finds that he can indulge in his feelings of local attachment only at the risk of starvation.

How are the older states of the South to keep their population? We say nothing of an increase, but how are they to hold their own? It is useless to talk about strict construction, state rights, or Wilmot Provisos. Of what avail can such things be to a sterile desert, upon which people cannot subsist!

In the columns of the *National Era,*

Oct. 2, 1851, also is the following article, by its editor :

STAND YOUR GROUND.

A citizen of Guilford county, N. C., in a letter to the *True Wesleyan,* dated August 20th, 1851, writes :

"You may discontinue my paper for the present, as I am inclined to go Westward, where I can enjoy religious liberty, and have my family in a free country. Mobocracy has the ascendency here, and there is no law. Brother Wilson had an appointment on Liberty Hill, on Sabbath, 24th inst. The mob came armed, according to mob law, and commenced operations on the meeting-house. They knocked all the weather-boarding off, destroying doors, windows, pulpit, and benches; and I have no idea that, if the mob was to kill a Wesleyan, or one of their friends, that they would be hung.

"There is more moving this fall to the far West than was ever known in one year. People do not like to be made slaves, and they are determined to go where it is no crime to plead the cause of the poor and oppressed. They have become alarmed at seeing the laws of God trampled under foot with impunity; and that, too, by legislators, sworn officers of the peace, and professors of religion. And even ministers (so called) are justifying mobocracy. They think that such a course of conduct will lead to a dissolution of the Union, and then every man will have to fight in defence of slavery, or be killed. This is an awful state of things, and, if the people were destitute of the Bible, and the various means of information which they possess, there might be some hope of reform. But there is but little hope, under existing circumstances."

We hope the writer will reconsider his purpose. In his section of North Carolina there are very many anti-slavery men, and the majority of the people have no interest in what is called slave property. Let them stand their ground, and maintain the right of free discussion. How is the despotism of Slavery to be put down, if those opposed to it abandon their rights, and flee their country? Let them do as the indomitable Clay does in Kentucky, and they will make themselves respected.

The following is quoted, without comment, in the *National Era,* in 1851, from the columns of the *Augusta Republic* (Georgia):

FREEDOM OF SPEECH IN GEORGIA.

          {   *Warrenton (Ga.),*
          { *Thursday, July* 10, 1851.

This day the citizens of the town and county met in the court-house at eight o'clock, A. M. On motion, Thomas F. Parsons, Esq., was called to the chair, and Mr. Wm. H. Pilcher requested to act as secretary.

The object of the meeting was stated by the chairman, as follows :

Whereas, our community has been thrown into confusion by the presence among us of one Nathan Bird Watson, who hails from New Haven (Conn.), and who has been promulgating abolition sentiments, publicly and privately, among our people, — sentiments at war with our institutions, and intolerable in a slave community, — and also been detected in visiting suspicious negro houses, as we suppose for the purpose of inciting our slaves and free negro population to insurrection and insubordination.

The meeting having been organized, Wm. Gibson, Esq., offered the following resolution, which, after various expressions of opinion, was unanimously adopted, to wit:

Resolved, That a committee of ten be appointed by the chairman for the purpose of making arrangements to expel Nathan Bird Watson, an avowed abolitionist, who has been in our village for three or four weeks, by twelve o'clock this day, by the Georgia Railroad cars; and that it shall be the duty of said committee to escort the said Watson to Camak, for the purpose of shipment to his native land.

The following gentlemen were named as that committee:

William Gibson, E. Cody, J. M. Roberts, J. B. Huff, E. H. Pottle, E. A. Brinkley, John C. Jennings, George W. Dickson, A. B. Rogers, and Dr. R. W. Hubert.

On motion, the chairman was added to that committee.

It was, on motion,

Resolved, That the proceedings of this meeting, with a minute description of the said Watson, be forwarded to the publishers of the Augusta papers, with the request that they, and all other publishers of papers in the slave-holding states, publish the same for a sufficient length of time.

DESCRIPTION.—The said Nathan Bird Watson is a man of dark complexion, hazel eyes, black hair, and wears a heavy beard; measures five feet eleven and three-quarter inches; has a quick step, and walks with his toes inclined inward, and a little stooped-shouldered; now wears a checked coat and white pants; says he is twenty-three years of age, but will pass for twenty-five or thirty.

On motion, the meeting was adjourned.

THOMAS F. PARSONS, *Chairman.*
WILLIAM H. PILCHER, *Secretary.*

This may be regarded as a specimen of that kind of editorial halloo which is designed to rouse and start in pursuit of a man the bloodhounds of the mob.

The following is copied by the *National Era* from the *Richmond Times:*

LYNCH LAW.

On the 13th inst. the vigilance committee of the county of Grayson, in this state, arrested a man named John Cornutt [a friend and follower of Bacon, the Ohio abolitionist], and, after examining the evidence against him, required him to renounce his abolition sentiments. This Cornutt refused to do; thereupon, he was stripped, tied to a tree, and whipped. After receiving a dozen stripes, he caved in, and promised, not only to recant, but to sell his property in the county [consisting of land and negroes], and leave the state. Great excitement prevailed throughout the country, and the *Wytheville Republican* of the 20th instant states that the vigilance committee of Grayson were in hot pursuit of other obnoxious persons.

On this outrage the *Wytheville Republican* makes the following comments:

Laying aside the white man, humanity to the negro, the slave, demands that these abolitionists be dealt with summarily, and above the law.

On Saturday, the 13th, we learn that the committee of vigilance of that county, to the number of near two hundred, had before them one John Cornutt, a citizen, a friend and backer of Bacon, and promulgator of his abolition doctrines. They required him to renounce abolitionism, and promise obedience to the laws. He refused. They stripped him, tied him to a tree, and appealed to him again to renounce, and promise obedience to the laws. He refused. The rod was brought; one, two, three, and on to twelve, on the bare back, and he cried out; he promised — and, more, he said he would sell and leave.

This Mr. Cornutt owns land, negroes and money, say fifteen to twenty thousand dollars. He has a wife, but no *white* children. He has among his negroes some born on his farm, of mixed blood. He is believed to be a friend of the negro, even to amalgamation. He intends to set his negroes free, and make them his heirs. It is hoped he will retire to Ohio, and there finish his operations of amalgamation and emancipation.

The vigilance committees were after another of Bacon's men on Thursday; we have not heard whether they caught him, nor what followed. There are not more than six of his followers that adhere; the rest have renounced him, and are much outraged at his imposition.

Mr. Cornutt appealed for redress to the law. The result of his appeal is thus stated in the *Richmond* (Va.) *Times,* quoted by the *National Era:*

MORE TROUBLE IN GRAYSON.

The clerk of Grayson County Court having, on the 1st inst. (the first day of Judge Brown's term) tendered his resignation, and there being no applicant for the office, and it being publicly stated at the bar that no one would accept said appointment, Judge Brown found himself unable to proceed with business, and accordingly adjourned the court until the first day of the next term.

Immediately upon the adjournment of the court, a public meeting of the citizens of the county was held, when resolutions were adopted expressive of the determination of the people to maintain the stand recently taken; exhorting the committees of vigilance to increased activity in ferreting out all persons tinctured with abolitionism in the county, and offering a reward of one hundred dollars for the apprehension and delivery of one Jonathan Roberts to any one of the committees of vigilance.

We have a letter from a credible correspondent in Carroll county, which gives to the affair a still more serious aspect. Trusting that there may be some error about it, we have no comments to make until the facts are known with certainty. Our correspondent, whose letter bears date the 13th inst., says:

"I learn, from an authentic source, that the Circuit Court that was to sit in Grayson county during last week was dissolved by violence. The circumstances were these. After the execution of the negroes in that county, some time ago, who had been excited to rebellion by a certain Methodist preacher, by the name of Bacon, of which you have heard, the citizens held a meeting, and instituted a sort of inquisition, to find out, if possible, who were the accomplices of said Bacon. Suspicion soon rested on a man by the name of Cornutt, and, on being charged with being an accomplice, he acknowledged the fact, and declared his intention of persevering in the cause; upon which he was severely lynched. Cornutt then instituted suit against the parties, who afterwards *held a meeting and passed resolutions, notifying the court and lawyers not to undertake the case, upon pain of a coat of tar and feathers.* The court, however, convened at the appointed time; and, true to their promise, *a band of armed men marched around the court-house, fired their guns by platoons, and dispersed the court in confusion. There was no blood shed.* This county and the county of Wythe have held meetings and passed resolutions sustaining the movement of the citizens of Grayson."

Is it any wonder that people emigrate from states where such things go on?

The following accounts will show what ministers of the gospel will have to encounter who undertake faithfully to express their sentiments in slave states. The first is an article by Dr. Bailey, of the *Era* of April 3, 1852:

LYNCHING IN KENTUCKY.

The *American Baptist*, of Utica, New York, publishes letters from the Rev. Edward Matthews, giving an account of his barbarous treatment in Kentucky.

Mr. Matthews, it seems, is an agent of the American Free Mission Society, and, in the exercise of his agency, visited that state, and took occasion to advocate from the pulpit anti-slavery sentiments. Not long since, in the village of Richmond, Madison county, he applied to several churches for permission to lecture on the moral and religious condition of the slaves, but was unsuccessful. February 1st, in the evening, he preached to the colored congregation of that place, after which he was assailed by a mob, and driven from the town. Returning in a short time, he left a communication respecting the transaction at the office of the *Richmond Chronicle*, and again departed; but had not gone far before he was overtaken by four men, who seized him, and led him to an out-of-the-way place, where they consulted as to what they should do with him. They resolved to duck him, ascertaining first that he could swim. Two of them took him and threw him into a pond, as far as they could, and, on his rising to the surface, bade him come out. He did so, and, on his refusing to promise never to come to Richmond, they flung him in again. This operation was repeated four times, when he yielded. They next demanded of him a promise that he would never leave Kentucky, and never return again. He refused to give it, and they threw him in the water six times more, when, his strength failing, and they threatening to whip him, he gave the pledge required, and left the state.

We do not know anything about Mr. Matthews, or his mode of promulgating his views. The laws in Kentucky for the protection of what is called "slave property" are stringent enough, and nobody can doubt the readiness of public sentiment to enforce their heaviest penalties against offenders. If Mr. Matthews violated the law, he should have been tried by the law; and he would have been, had he committed an illegal act. No charge of the kind is made against him.

He was, then, the victim of Lynch law, administered in a ruffianly manner, and without provocation; and the parties concerned in the transaction, whatever their position in society, were guilty of conduct as cowardly as it was brutal.

As to the manner in which Mr. Matthews has conducted himself in Kentucky we know nothing. We transfer to our columns the following extract from an editorial in the *Journal and Messenger* of Cincinnati, a Baptist paper, and which, it may be presumed, speaks intelligently on the subject:

"Mr. Matthews is likewise a Baptist minister, whose *ostensible* mission is one of love. If he has violated that mission, or *any law*, he is amenable to God and *law*, and not to LAWLESS VIOLENCE. His going to Kentucky is a matter of conscience to him, in which he has a right to indulge. Many good anti-slavery men would question the wisdom of such a step. None would doubt his RIGHT. Many, as a matter of taste and propriety, cannot admire the way in which he is reputed to do his work. But they believe he is conscientious, and they know that 'oppression maketh even a wise man mad.' We do not think, in obedience to Christ's commands, he sufficiently counted the cost. For no one in his position should go to Kentucky to agitate the question of slavery, unless he EXPECTS TO DIE. No man in this position, which Mr. Matthews occupies, can do it, without falling a martyr. Liberty of speech and thought is not, *cannot* be, enjoyed in slave states. Slavery could not exist for a moment, if it did. It is, doubtless, the duty of the Christian not to surrender his life cheaply, for the sake of being a martyr. This would be an unholy motive. It is his duty to preserve it until the last moment. So Christ enjoins. It is no mark of cowardice to flee. 'When they persecute you in one city, flee into another,' said the Saviour. But he did not say, Give a *pledge* that you will not exercise your *rights*. Hence, he nor his disciples never did it. But it *is a question*, after one has deliberated, and conscientiously entered a community in the exercise of his constitutional and religious rights, whether he should give a *pledge*, under the influence of a *love of life, never to return*. If he does, he has not counted the cost. A Christian should be as conscientious in pledging solemnly not to do what he has an undoubted *right* to do, as he is in laboring for the emancipation of the slave."

The following is from the *National Era*, July 10, 1851.

Mr. McBride wished to form a church of non-slaveholders.

CASE OF REV. JESSE M'BRIDE.

This missionary, it will be remembered, was expelled lately from the State of North Carolina. We give below his letter detailing the conduct of the mob. His letter is dated Guilford, May 6. After writing that he is suffering from temporary illness, he proceeds:

"I would have kept within doors this day, but

for the fact that I mistrusted a mob would be out to disturb my congregation, though such a hint had not been given me by a human being. About six o'clock this morning I crawled into my carriage and drove eighteen miles, which brought me to my meeting place, eight miles east of Greensboro', — the place I gave an account of a few weeks since, — where some seven or eight persons gave their names to go into the organization of a Wesleyan Methodist church. Well, sure enough, just before meeting time (twelve o'clock) I was informed that a pack of rioters were on hand, and that they had sworn I should not fulfil my appointment this day. As they had heard nothing of this before, the news came upon some of my friends like a clap of thunder from a clear sky; they scarcely knew what to do. I told them I should go to meeting or die in the attempt, and, like 'good soldiers,' they followed. Just before I got to the arbor, I saw a man leave the crowd and approach me at the left of my path. As I was about to pass, he said:

"'Mr. McBride, here's a letter for you.'

"I took the letter, put it into my pocket, and said, 'I have not time to read it until after meeting.'

"'No, you must read it now.'

"Seeing that I did not stop, he said, 'I want to speak to you,' beckoning with his hand, and turning, expecting me to follow.

"'I will talk to you after meeting,' said I, pulling out my watch; 'you see I have no time to spare — it is just twelve.'

"As I went to go in at the door of the stand, a man who had taken his seat on the step rose up, placed his hand on me, and said, in a very excited tone,

"'Mr. McBride, you can't go in here!'

"Without offering any resistance, or saying a word, I knelt down outside the stand, on the ground, and prayed to my 'Father;' plead His promises, such as, 'When the enemy comes in like a flood, I will rear up a standard against' him; 'I am a present help in trouble;' 'I will fight all your battles for you;' prayed for grace, victory, my enemies, &c. Rose perfectly calm. Meantime my enemies cursed and swore some, but most of the time they were rather quiet. Mr. Hiatt, a slave-holder and merchant from Greensboro', said,

"'You can't preach here to-day; we have come to prevent you. We think you are doing harm — violating our laws,' &c.

"'From what authority do you thus command and prevent me from preaching? Are you authorized by the civil authority to prevent me?'

"'No, sir.'

"'Has God sent you, and does he enjoin it on you as a duty to stop me?'

"'I am unacquainted with Him.'

"'Well, 'acquaint now thyself with Him, and be at peace;' and he will give you a more honorable business than stopping men from preaching his gospel. The judgment-day is coming on, and I summon you there, to give an account of this day's conduct. And now, gentlemen, if I have violated the laws of North Carolina, by them I am willing to be judged, condemned, and punished; to go to the whipping-post, pillory or jail, or even to hug the stake. But, gentlemen, you are not generally a pack of ignoramuses; your good sense teaches you the impropriety of your course; you know that you are doing wrong; you

know that it is not right to trample all law, both human and divine, in the dust, out of professed love for it. You must see that your course will lead to perfect anarchy and confusion. The time may come when Jacob Hiatt may be in the minority, when his principles may be as unpopular as Jesse McBride's are now. What then? Why, if your course prevails, he must be lynched — whipped, stoned, tarred and feathered, dragged from his own house, or his house burned over his head, and he perish in the ruins. The persons became food for the beasts they threw Daniel to; the same fire that was kindled for the 'Hebrew children' consumed those who kindled it; Haman stretched the same rope he prepared for Mordecai. Yours is a dangerous course, and you must reap a retribution, either here or hereafter. We will sing a hymn,' said I.

"'O yes,' said H., 'you may sing.'

"'The congregation will please assist me, as I am quite unwell;' and I lined off the hymn, 'Father, I stretch my hands to thee,' &c., rioters and all helping to sing. All seemed in good humor, and I almost forgot their errand. When we closed, I said, 'Let us pray.'

"'G——d d——n it, that's not singing!' said one of the company, who stood back pretty well.

"While we invoked the divine blessing, I think many could say, 'It is good for us to be here.' Before I rose from my knees, after the friends rose, I delivered an exhortation of some ten or fifteen minutes, in which I urged the brethren to steadfastness, prayer, &c., some of the mob crying, 'Lay hold of him!' 'Drag him out!' 'Stop him!' &c."

"My voice being nearly drowned by the tumult, I left off. I was then called to have some conversation with H., who repeated some of the charges he preferred at first, — said I was bringing on insurrection, causing disturbance, &c.; wishing me to leave the state; said he had some slaves, and he himself was the most of a slave of any of them, had harder times than they had, and he would like to be shut of them, and that he was my true friend.

"'As to your friendship, Mr. H., you have acted quite friendly, remarkably so — fully as much so as Judas when he kissed the Saviour. As to your having to be so much of a slave, I am sorry for you; you ought to be freed. As to insurrection, I am decidedly opposed to it, have no sympathy with it whatever. As to raising disturbance and leaving the state, I left a little motherless daughter in Ohio, over whom I wished to have an oversight and care. When I left, I only expected to remain in North Carolina one year; but the people dragged me up before the court under the charge of felony, put me in bonds, and kept me; and now would you have me leave my securities to suffer, have me lie and deceive the court!'

"'O! if you will leave, your bail will not have to suffer; that can, I think, be settled without much trouble,' said Mr H.

"'They shall not have trouble on my account,' said I.

"After talking with Mr. H. and one or two more on personal piety, &c., I went to the arbor, took my seat in the door of the stand for a minute; then rose, and, after referring to a few texts of Scripture, to show that all those who will live godly shall suffer persecution, I inquired, 1st, What is persecution? 2ndly, noticed the fact, 'shall suffer;' gave a synoptical history of persecution, by showing that Abel was the first martyr for the right — the Israelites' sufferings. The prophets were stoned, were sawn asunder, were tempted, were slain with the sword, had to wander in deserts, mountains, dens and caves of the earth, were driven from their houses, given to ferocious beasts, lashed to the stake, and destroyed in different ways. Spoke of John the Baptist; showed how he was persecuted, and what the charge. Christ was persecuted for doing what John was persecuted for not doing. Spoke of the sufferings of the apostles, and their final death; of Luther and his coadjutors; of the Wesleys and early Methodists; of Fox and the early Quakers; of the early settlers in the colonies of the United States. Noticed why the righteous were persecuted, the advantages thereof to the righteous themselves, and how they should treat their persecutors — with kindness, &c. Spoke, I suppose, some half an hour, and dismissed. Towards the close, some of the rioters got quite angry, and yelled, 'Stop him!' 'Pull him out!' 'The righteous were never persecuted for d——d abolitionism,' &c. Some of them paid good attention to what I said. And thus we spent the time from twelve to three o'clock, and thus the meeting passed by.

"Brother dear, I am more and more confirmed in the righteousness of our cause. I would rather, much rather, die for good principles, than to have applause and honor for propagating false theories and abominations, You perhaps would like to know how I feel. Happy, most of the time; a religion that will not stand persecution will not

take us to heaven. Blessed be God, that I have not, thus far, been suffered to deny Him. Sometimes I have thought that I was nearly home. I generally feel a calmness of soul, but sometimes my enjoyments are rapturous. I have had a great burden of prayer for the dear flock; help me pray for them. Thank God, I have not heard of one of them giving up or turning; and I believe some, if not most of them, would go to the stake rather than give back. I forgot to say I read a part of the fifth chapter of the Acts of the Apostles to the rioters, commencing at the 17th verse. I told them, if their institutions were of God, I could not harm them; that if our cause was of God, *they could not stop it* — that they could kill me, but they could *not kill* the truth. Though I talked plainly, I talked and felt kindly to them.

"I have had to write in such haste, and being fatigued and unwell, my letter is disconnected. I meant to give you a copy of the letter of the mob. Here it is :

"'Mr. McBRIDE :

"'We, the subscribers, very and most respectfully request you not to attempt to fulfil your appointment at this place. If you do, you will surely be interrupted.

"'*May* 6, 1851.'   [Signed by 32 persons.]

"Some were professors of religion — Presbyterians, Episcopal Methodists, and Methodist Protestants. One of the latter was an 'exhorter.' I understand some of the crowd were negro-traders.
                              "Farewell,   J. McBRIDE.'"

PART IV.

CHAPTER I.

THE INFLUENCE OF THE AMERICAN CHURCH ON SLAVERY.

THERE is no country in the world where the religious influence has a greater ascendency than in America. There is no country where the clergy are more powerful. This is the more remarkable, because in America religion is entirely divorced from the state, and the clergy have none of those artificial means for supporting their influence which result from rank and wealth. Taken as a body of men, the American clergy are generally poor. The salaries given to them afford only a bare support, and yield them no means of acquiring property. Their style of living can be barely decent and respectable, and no more. The fact that, under these circumstances, the American clergy are probably the most powerful body of men in the country, is of itself a strong presumptive argument in their favor. It certainly argues in them, as a class, both intellectual and moral superiority.

It is a well-known fact that the influence of the clergy is looked upon by our statesmen as a most serious element in making up their political combinations; and that that influence is so great, that no statesman would ever undertake to carry a measure against which all the clergy of the country should unite. Such a degree of power, though it be only a power of opinion, argument and example, is not without its dangers to the purity of any body of men. To be courted by political partisans is always a dangerous thing for the integrity and spirituality of men who profess to be governed by principles which are not of this world. The possession, too, of so great a power as we have described, involves a most weighty responsibility; since, if the clergy do possess the power to rectify any great national immorality, the fact of its not being done seems in some sort to bring the sin of the omission to their door.

We have spoken, thus far, of the clergy alone; but in America, where the clergyman is, in most denominations, elected by the church, and supported by its voluntary contributions, the influence of the church and that of the clergy are, to a very great extent, identical. The clergyman is the very ideal and expression of the church. They choose him, and retain him, because he expresses more perfectly than any other man they can obtain, their ideas of truth and right. The clergyman is supported, in all cases, by his church, or else he cannot retain his position in it. The fact of his remaining there is generally proof of identity of opinion, since, if he differed very materially from them, they have the power to withdraw from him, and choose another.

The influence of a clergyman, thus retained by the free consent of the understanding and heart of his church, is in some respects greater even than that of a papal priest. The priest can control only by a blind spiritual authority, to which, very often, the reason demurs, while it yields an outward assent; but the successful free minister takes captive the affections of the heart by his affections, overrules the reasoning powers by superior strength of reason, and thus, availing himself of affection, reason, conscience, and the entire man, possesses a power, from the very freedom of the organization, greater than can ever result from blind spiritual despotism. If a minister cannot succeed in doing this to some good extent in a church, he is called unsuccessful; and he who realizes this description most perfectly has the highest and most perfect kind of power, and expresses the idea of a successful American minister.

In speaking, therefore, of this subject, we shall speak of the church and the clergy as identical, using the word church in the American sense of the word, for that class

13

of men, of all denominations, who are *organized* in bodies distinct from nominal Christians, as professing to be actually controlled by the precepts of Christ.

What, then, is the influence of the church on this great question of slavery?

Certain things are evident on the very face of the matter.

1. It has not put an end to it.
2. It has not prevented the increase of it.
3. It has not occasioned the repeal of the laws which forbid education to the slave.
4. It has not attempted to have laws passed forbidding the separation of families and legalizing the marriage of slaves.
5. It has not stopped the internal slave-trade.
6. It has not prevented the extension of this system, with all its wrongs, over new territories.

With regard to these assertions it is presumed there can be no difference of opinion.

What, then, have they done?

In reply to this, it can be stated,

1. That almost every one of the leading denominations have, at some time, in their collective capacity, expressed a decided disapprobation of the system, and recommended that something should be done with a view to its abolition.

2. One denomination of Christians has pursued such a course as entirely, and in fact, to free every one of its members from any participation in slave-holding. We refer to the Quakers. The course by which this result has been effected will be shown by a pamphlet soon to be issued by the poet J. G. Whittier, one of their own body.

3. Individual members, in all denominations, animated by the spirit of Christianity, have in various ways entered their protest against it.

It will be well now to consider more definitely and minutely the sentiments which some leading ecclesiastical bodies in the church have expressed on this subject

It is fair that the writer should state the sources from which the quotations are drawn. Those relating to the action of Southern judicatories are principally from a pamphlet compiled by the Hon. James G. Birney, and entitled "The Church the Bulwark of Slavery." The writer addressed a letter to Mr. Birney, in which she inquired the sources from which he compiled. His reply was, in substance, as follows: That the pamphlet was compiled from original documents, or files of newspapers, which had recorded these transactions at the time of their occurrence. It was

compiled and published in England, in 1842, with a view of leading the people there to understand the position of the American church and clergy. Mr. Birney says that, although the statements have long been before the world, he has never known one of them to be disputed; that, knowing the extraordinary nature of the sentiments, he took the utmost pains to authenticate them.

We will first present those of the Southern States.

1. The Presbyterian Church.

HARMONY PRESBYTERY, OF SOUTH CAROLINA.

Whereas, sundry persons in Scotland and England, and others in the north, east and west of our country, have denounced slavery as obnoxious to the laws of God, some of whom have presented before the General Assembly of our church, and the Congress of the nation, memorials and petitions, with the avowed object of bringing into disgrace slave-holders, and abolishing the relation of master and slave : And whereas, from the said proceedings, and the statements, reasonings and circumstances connected therewith, it is most manifest that those persons " know not what they say, nor whereof they affirm;" and with this ignorance discover a spirit of self-righteousness and exclusive sanctity, &c., therefore,

1. *Resolved*, That as the kingdom of our Lord is not of this world, His church, as such, has no right to abolish, alter, or affect any institution or ordinance of men, political or civil, &c.

2. *Resolved*, That slavery has existed from the days of those good old slave-holders and patriarchs, Abraham, Isaac and Jacob (who are now in the kingdom of heaven), to the time when the apostle Paul sent a runaway home to his master Philemon, and wrote a Christian and fraternal letter to this slave-holder, which we find still stands in the canon of the Scriptures ; and that slavery has existed ever since the days of the apostle, and does now exist.

3. *Resolved*, That as the relative duties of master and slave are taught in the Scriptures, in the same manner as those of parent and child, and husband and wife, the existence of slavery itself is not opposed to the will of God ; and whosoever has a conscience too tender to recognize this relation as lawful is "righteous over much," is " wise above what is written," and has submitted his neck to the yoke of men, sacrificed his Christian liberty of conscience, and leaves the infallible word of God for the fancies and doctrines of men.

THE CHARLESTON UNION PRESBYTERY.

It is a principle which meets the views of this body, that slavery, as it exists among us, is a political institution, with which ecclesiastical judicatories have not the smallest right to interfere ; and in relation to which, any such interference, especially at the present momentous crisis, would be *morally wrong*, and fraught with the most dangerous and pernicious consequences. The sentiments which *we* maintain, *in common with Christians at the South of every denomination*, are sentiments which so fully approve themselves to our consciences, are so identified with our solemn convictions of duty, that we should maintain them under any circumstances.

Resolved, That in the opinion of this Presbytery, the holding of slaves, so far from being a SIN in the sight of God, is nowhere condemned in his holy word; that it is in accordance with the example, is consistent with the precepts, of patriarchs, apostles and prophets, and that it is compatible with the most fraternal regard to the best good of those servants whom God may have committed to our charge.

The New-school Presbyterian Church in Petersburgh, Virginia, Nov. 16, 1838, passed the following :

Whereas, the General Assembly did, in the year 1818, pass a law which contains provisions for slaves irreconcilable with our civil institutions, and solemnly declaring slavery to be sin against God — a law at once offensive and insulting to the whole Southern community,

1. *Resolved,* That, as slave-holders, we cannot consent longer to remain in connection with any church where there exists a statute conferring the right upon slaves to arraign their masters before the judicatory of the church —*and that, too, for the act of selling them without their consent first had and obtained.*

2. *Resolved,* That, as the Great Head of the church has recognized the relation of *master and slave,* we conscientiously believe that slavery is not a sin against God, as declared by the General Assembly.

This sufficiently indicates the opinion of the Southern Presbyterian Church. The next extracts will refer to the opinions of Baptist Churches. In 1835 the Charleston Baptist Association addressed a memorial to the Legislature of South Carolina, which contains the following :

The undersigned would further represent that the said association does not consider that the Holy Scriptures have made the fact of slavery *a question of morals at all.* The Divine Author of our holy religion, in particular, found slavery a part of the existing institutions of society ; with which, if not sinful, it was not his design to *intermeddle,* but to leave them entirely to the control of men. Adopting this, therefore, as one of the allowed arrangements of society, he made it the province of his religion only to prescribe the reciprocal duties of the relation. The question, it is believed, is purely one of political economy. It amounts, in effect, to this, — *Whether the operatives of a country shall be bought and sold, and themselves become property, as in this state ; or whether they shall be hirelings, and their labor only become property, as in some other states.* In other words, whether an employer may buy the whole time of laborers at once, of those who have a right to dispose of it, with a permanent relation of protection and care over them ; or whether he shall be restricted to buy it in certain portions only, subject to their control, and with no such permanent relation of care and protection. *The right of masters to dispose of the time of their slaves has been distinctly recognized by the Creator of all things,* who is surely at liberty to vest the right of property over any object in whomsoever he pleases. That the lawful possessor should retain this right at will, is no more against the laws of society and good morals, than that he should retain the personal endowments with which his Creator has blessed him, or the money and lands inherited from his ancestors, or acquired by his industry. And neither society nor individuals have any more authority to demand a relinquishment, without an equivalent, in the one case, than in the other.

As it is a question purely of political economy, and one which in this country is reserved to the cognizance of the state governments severally, it is further believed, that the State of South Carolina alone has the right to regulate the existence and condition of slavery within her territorial limits ; and we should resist to the utmost every invasion of this right, come from what quarter and under whatever pretence it may.

The Methodist Church is, in some respects, peculiarly situated upon this subject, because its constitution and book of discipline contain the most vehement denunciations against slavery of which language is capable, and the most stringent requisitions that all members shall be disciplined for the holding of slaves ; and these denunciations and requisitions have been reäffirmed by its General Conference.

It seemed to be necessary, therefore, for the Southern Conference to take some notice of this fact, which they did, with great coolness and distinctness, as follows :

THE GEORGIA ANNUAL CONFERENCE.

Resolved, unanimously, That, whereas there is a clause in the discipline of our church which states that we are as much as ever convinced of the great evil of *slavery ;* and whereas the said clause has been *perverted* by some, and used in such a manner as to produce the impression that the Methodist Episcopal Church believed *slavery* to be a *moral evil ;* —

Therefore *Resolved,* That it is the sense of the Georgia Annual Conference that slavery, as it exists in the United States, *is not a moral evil.*

Resolved, That we view *slavery* as a civil and domestic institution, and one with which, as ministers of Christ, we have nothing to do, further than to ameliorate the condition of the slave, by endeavoring to impart to him and his master the benign influences of the religion of Christ, and aiding both on their way to heaven.

On motion, it was *Resolved,* unanimously, That the Georgia Annual Conference regard with feelings of profound respect and approbation the dignified course pursued by *our several superintendents,* or bishops, *in suppressing* the attempts that have been made by various individuals to get up and protract an excitement in the churches and country on the subject of *abolitionism.*

Resolved, further, That they shall have our cordial and zealous support in sustaining them in the ground they have taken.

SOUTH CAROLINA CONFERENCE.

The Rev. W. Martin introduced resolutions similar to those of the Georgia Conference.

The Rev. W. Capers, D.D., after expressing his conviction that "the sentiment of the resolutions was universally held, not only by the ministers of that conference, but of the whole South;" and after stating that the only true doctrine was, "it belongs to Cæsar, and not to the church," offered the following as a substitute:

* Whereas, we hold that the subject of slavery in these United States is not one proper for the action of the church, but is exclusively appropriate to the civil authorities,
Therefore *Resolved,* That this conference will not intermeddle with it, further than to express our regret that it has ever been introduced, in any form, into any one of the judicatures of the church.

Brother Martin accepted the substitute.

Brother Betts asked whether the substitute was intended *as implying that slavery, as it exists among us, was not a moral evil? He understood it as equivalent to such a declaration.*

· Brother Capers explained *that his intention was to convey that sentiment fully and unequivocally;* and that he had chosen the form of the substitute for the purpose, *not only of reproving some wrong doings at the North,* but with reference also to the General Conference. If slavery were a moral evil (that is, *sinful*), *the church would be bound to take cognizance of it;* but our affirmation is, that it is not a matter for *her* jurisdiction, but is exclusively appropriate to the *civil government,* and *of course not sinful.*

The substitute was then unanimously adopted.

In 1836, an Episcopal clergyman in North Carolina, of the name of Freeman, preached, in the presence of his bishop (Rev. Levi. S. Ives, D.D., a native of a free state), two sermons on the rights and duties of slave-holders. In these he essayed to justify from the Bible the slavery both of white men and negroes, and insisted that "*without a new revelation from heaven, no man was authorized to pronounce slavery* WRONG." The sermons were printed in a pamphlet, prefaced with a letter to Mr. Freeman from the Bishop of North Carolina, declaring that he had "listened with most unfeigned pleasure" to his discourses, and advised their publication, as being "urgently called for at the present time."

"The Protestant Episcopal Society for the advancement of Christianity (!) in South Carolina" thought it expedient to republish Mr. Freeman's pamphlet as *a religious tract !* *

Afterwards, when the addition of the new State of Texas made it important to organize the Episcopal Church there, this Mr. Freeman was made Bishop of Texas.

The question may now arise,— it must arise to every intelligent thinker in Christendom,— Can it be possible that American slavery, *as defined by its laws,* and the decisions of its courts, including all the horrible abuses that the laws recognize and sanction, is considered to be a right and proper institution? Do these Christians merely recognize the relation of slavery, in the abstract, as one that, under proper legislation, might be made a good one, or do they justify it *as it actually exists* in America?

It is a fact that there is a large party at the South who justify not only slavery in the abstract, but slavery just as it exists in America, in whole and in part, and even its worst abuses.

There are four legalized parts or results of the system, which are of especial atrocity. They are,—

1. *The prohibition of the testimony of colored people in cases of trial.*
2. The forbidding of education.
3. The internal slave-trade.
4. The consequent separation of families.

We shall bring evidence to show that every one of these practices has been either defended on principle, or recognized without condemnation, by decisions of judicatories of churches, or by writings of influential clergymen, without any expression of dissent being made to their opinions by the bodies to which they belong.

In the first place, the exclusion of colored testimony in the church. In 1840, the General Conference of the Methodist Episcopal Church passed the following resolution: "THAT IT IS INEXPEDIENT AND UNJUSTIFIABLE FOR ANY PREACHER TO PERMIT COLORED PERSONS TO GIVE TESTIMONY AGAINST WHITE PERSONS IN ANY STATE WHERE THEY ARE DENIED THAT PRIVILEGE BY LAW."

This was before the Methodist Church had separated on the question of slavery, as they subsequently did, into Northern and Southern Conferences. Both Northern and Southern members voted for this resolution.

After this was passed, the conscience of many Northern ministers was aroused; and they called for a reconsideration. The Southern members imperiously demanded that it should remain as a compromise and test of union. The spirit of the discussion may be inferred from one extract.

Mr. Peck, of New York, who moved the reconsideration of the resolution, thus expressed himself:

That resolution (said he) was introduced under peculiar circumstances, during considerable excitement, and he went for it *as a peace-offering to the South*, without sufficiently reflecting upon the precise import of its phraseology; but, after a little deliberation, he was sorry; and he had been sorry but once, and that was all the time; he was convinced that, if that resolution remain upon the journal, *it would be disastrous to the whole Northern church.*

Rev. Dr. A. J. Few, of Georgia, the mover of the original resolution, then rose. The following are extracts from his speech. The Italics are the writers.

Look at it! What do you declare to us, in taking this course? Why, simply, as much as to say, "We cannot sustain you in the condition which you cannot avoid!" We cannot sustain you in the *necessary conditions* of slave-holding; one of its *necessary conditions* being the rejection of negro testimony! If it is not sinful to hold slaves, under all circumstances, *it is not sinful to hold them in the only condition, and under the only circumstances, which they can be held.* The rejection of negro testimony is one of the necessary circumstances under which slave-holding can exist; indeed, it is utterly impossible for it to exist without it; therefore it is not sinful to hold slaves *in the condition and under the circumstances which they are held at the South, inasmuch as they can be held under no other circumstances.* * * * If you believe that slave-holding is necessarily sinful, come out with the abolitionists, and honestly say so. If you believe that slave-holding is necessarily sinful, you believe we are necessarily sinners: and, if so, come out and honestly declare it, *and let us leave you.* * * * We want to know distinctly, precisely and honestly, the position which you take. We cannot be tampered with by you any longer. We have had enough of it. We are tired of your sickly sympathies. * * * If you are not opposed to the principles which it involves, unite with us, *like honest men*, and go home, and boldly meet the consequences. We say again, you are responsible for this state of things; for it is *you* who have driven us to the alarming point where we find ourselves. * * * *You* have made that resolution absolutely necessary to the quiet of the South! But *you* now revoke that resolution! And you pass the Rubicon! Let me not be misunderstood. I say, *you* pass the Rubicon! If you revoke, you revoke the principle which that resolution involves, and you array the whole South against you, *and we must separate!* * * * If you accord to the principles which it involves, arising from the necessity of the case, stick by it, "though the heavens perish!" But, if you persist on reconsideration, I ask in what light will your course be regarded in the South? What will be the conclusion, there, in reference to it? Why, that you cannot sustain us as long as we hold slaves! It will declare, in the face of the sun, "We cannot sustain you, gentlemen, while you retain your slaves!" Your opposition to the resolution is based upon your opposition to slavery; you cannot, therefore, maintain your consistency, unless you come out with the abolitionists, and condemn us at once and forever; or else refuse to reconsider.

The resolution was therefore left in force, with another resolution appended to it, expressing *the undiminished regard of the General Conference for the colored population.*

It is quite evident that it *was undiminished*, for the best of reasons. That the colored population were not properly impressed with this last act of condescension, appears from the fact that "the official members of the Sharp-street and Asbury Colored Methodist Church in Baltimore" protested and petitioned against the motion. The following is a passage from their address:

The adoption of such a resolution, by our highest ecclesiastical judicatory, — a judicatory composed of the most experienced and wisest brethren in the church, the choice selection of twenty-eight Annual Conferences, — has inflicted, we fear, an irreparable injury upon eighty thousand souls for whom Christ died — souls, who, by this act of your body, have been stripped of the dignity of Christians, degraded in the scale of humanity, and treated as criminals, for no other reason than the color of their skin! Your resolution has, in our humble opinion, *virtually* declared, that a mere physical peculiarity, the handiwork of our all-wise and benevolent Creator, is *prima facie* evidence of incompetency to tell the truth, or is an unerring indication of unworthiness to bear testimony against a fellow-being whose skin is denominated white. * * *

Brethren, out of the abundance of the heart we have spoken. *Our grievance is before you!* If you have any regard for the salvation of the eighty thousand immortal souls committed to your care; if you would not *thrust* beyond the pale of the church *twenty-five hundred souls in this city*, who have felt determined never to leave the church that has nourished and brought them up; if you regard us as children of one common Father, and can, upon reflection, sympathize with us as members of the body of Christ, — if you would not incur the fearful, the tremendous responsibility of offending not only one, but many thousands of his "little ones," we conjure you to wipe from your journal the odious resolution which is ruining our people.

"A Colored Baltimorean," writing to the editor of *Zion's Watchman*, says:

The address was presented to one of the secretaries, a delegate of the Baltimore Conference, and subsequently given by him to the bishops. How many of the members of the conference saw it, I know not. One thing is certain, *it was not read to the conference.*

With regard to the second head, — of defending the laws which prevent the slave from being taught to read and write, — we have the following instance.

In the year 1835, the Chillicothe Presbytery, Ohio, addressed a Christian remonstrance to the presbytery of Mississippi on the subject of slavery, in which they specifically enumerated the respects in which they considered it to be unchristian. The eighth resolution was as follows:

That any member of our church, who shall advocate or speak in favor of such laws as have been or may yet be enacted, for the purpose of keeping the slaves in ignorance, and preventing them from learning to read the word of God, is guilty of a great sin, and ought to be dealt with as for other scandalous crimes.

This remonstrance was answered by Rev. James Smylie, stated clerk of the Mississippi Presbytery, and afterwards of the Amity Presbytery of Louisiana, in a pamphlet of eighty-seven pages, in which he defended slavery generally and particularly, in the same manner in which all other abuses have always been defended — by the word of God. The tenth section of this pamphlet is devoted to the defence of this law. He devotes seven pages of fine print to this object. He says (p. 63):

There are laws existing in both states, Mississippi and Louisiana, accompanied with heavy penal sanctions, prohibiting the teaching of the slaves to read, *and meeting the approbation of the religious part of the reflecting community.*
* * * * *

He adds, still further:

The laws preventing the slaves from learning to read are a fruitful source of much ignorance and immorality among the slaves. The printing, publishing, and circulating of abolition and emancipatory principles in those states, was the cause of the passage of those laws.

He then goes on to say that the ignorance and vice which are the consequence of those laws do not properly belong to those who made the laws, but to those whose emancipating doctrines rendered them necessary. Speaking of these consequences of ignorance and vice, he says:

Upon whom must they be saddled? If you will allow me to answer the question, I will answer by saying, Upon such great and good men as John Wesley, Jonathan Edwards, Bishop Porteus, Paley, Horsley, Scott, Clark, Wilberforce, Sharpe, Clarkson, Fox, Johnson, Burke, and other great and good men, who, without examining the word of God, have concluded that it is a true maxim that slavery is in itself sinful.

He then illustrates the necessity of these laws by the following simile. He supposes that the doctrine had been promulgated that the authority of parents was an unjust usurpation, and that it was getting a general hold of society; that societies were being formed for the emancipation of children from the control of their parents; that all books

were beginning to be pervaded by this sentiment; and that, under all these influences, children were becoming restless and fractious. He supposes that, under these circumstances, parents meet and refer the subject to legislators. He thus describes the dilemma of the legislators:

These meet, and they take the subject seriously and solemnly into consideration. On the one hand, they perceive that, if their children had access to these doctrines, they were ruined forever. To let them have access to them was unavoidable, if they taught them to read. To prevent their being taught to read was cruel, and would prevent them from obtaining as much knowledge of the laws of Heaven as otherwise they might enjoy. In this sad dilemma, sitting and consulting in a legislative capacity, they must, of two evils, choose the least. With indignant feelings towards those, who, under the influence of "seducing spirits," had sent and were sending among them "doctrines of devils," but with aching hearts towards their children, they resolved that their children should not be taught to read, until the storm should be overblown; hoping that Satan's being let loose will be but for a little season. And during this season they will have to teach them orally, and thereby guard against their being contaminated by these wicked doctrines.

So much for that law.

Now, as for the internal slave-trade, — the very essence of that trade is the buying and selling of human beings *for the mere purposes of gain.*

A master who has slaves transmitted to him, or a master who buys slaves with the purpose of retaining them on his plantation or in his family, can be supposed to have some object in it besides the *mere purpose of gain.* He may be supposed, in certain cases, to have some regard to the happiness or well-being of the slave. The trader buys and sells *for the mere purpose of gain.*

Concerning this abuse the Chillicothe Presbytery, in the document to which we have alluded, passed the following resolution:

Resolved, That the buying, selling, or holding of a slave, *for the sake of gain,* is a heinous sin and scandal, requiring the cognizance of the judicatories of the church.

In the reply from which we have already quoted, Mr. Smylie says (p. 13):

If the buying, selling and holding of a slave for the sake of gain, is, as you say, a heinous sin and scandal, then verily three-fourths of all Episcopalians, Methodists, Baptists and Presbyterians, in the eleven states of the Union, are of the devil.
* * * * *

Again:

To question whether slave-holders or slave-buyers are of the devil, seems to me like calling in question whether God is or is not a true witness; that is, provided it is God's testimony, and not merely the testimony of the Chillicothe Presbytery, that it is a " heinous sin and scandal" to buy, sell and hold slaves.

Again (p. 21):

If language can convey a clear and definite meaning at all, I know not how it can more plainly or unequivocally present to the mind any thought or idea, than the twenty-fifth chapter of Leviticus clearly and unequivocally establishes the fact that slavery was sanctioned by God himself, and that buying, selling, holding and bequeathing slaves, *as property, are regulations which are established by himself.*

* * * * * * *

What language can more explicitly show, not that God winked at slavery merely, but that, to say the least, he gave a *written permit* to the Hebrews, then the best people in the world, to *buy, hold and bequeath, men and women,* to perpetual servitude? What, now, becomes of the position of the Chillicothe Presbytery? * * * * Is it, indeed, a fact, that God once gave a written permission to his own dear people [" *ye shall buy* "] to do that which is in itself sinful? Nay, to do that which the Chillicothe Presbytery says " is a heinous sin and scandal " ?

* * * * * * *

God resolves that his own children may, or rather " *shall,*" " *buy, possess and hold,*" bondmen and bond-women, in bondage, *forever.* But the Chillicothe Presbytery resolves that " *buying, selling, or holding slaves,* for the sake of gain, is a *heinous sin and scandal.*"

We do not mean to say that Mr. Smylie had the internal slave-trade directly in his mind in writing these sentences; but we do say that no slave-trader would ask for a more explicit justification of his trade than this.

Lastly, in regard to that dissolution of the marriage relation, which is the necessary consequence of this kind of trade, the following decisions have been made by judicatories of the church.

The Savannah River (Baptist) Association, in 1835, in reply to the question,

Whether, in a case of involuntary separation, of such a character as to preclude all prospect of future intercourse, the parties ought to be allowed to marry again ?

answered,

That such a separation, among persons situated as our slaves are, is *civilly* a separation by *death,* and they believe that, in the sight of God, it would be so viewed. To forbid second marriages, in such cases, would be to expose the parties, not only to stronger hardships and strong temptation, but to *church censure,* for acting in obedience to their masters, who cannot be expected to acquiesce in a regulation at variance with justice to the slaves, and to the spirit of that command which regulates marriage among Christians. *The slaves are not free agents,* and a dissolution by death is

not more entirely without their consent, and beyond their control, than by such separation.

At the Shiloh Baptist Association, which met at Gourdvine, a few years since, the following query, says the *Religious Herald,* was presented from Hedgman church, viz:

Is a servant, whose husband or wife has been sold by his or her master into a distant country, to be permitted to marry again ?

The query was referred to a committee, who made the following report; which, after discussion, was adopted :

That, in view of the circumstances in which servants in this country are placed, the committee are unanimous in the opinion that it is better to permit servants thus circumstanced to take another husband or wife.

The Reverend Charles C. Jones, who was an earnest and indefatigable laborer for the good of the slave, and one who, it would be supposed, would be likely to feel strongly on this subject, if any one would, simply remarks, in estimating the moral condition of the negroes, that, as husband and wife are subject to all the vicissitudes of property, and may be separated by division of estate, debts, sales or removals, &c. &c., the marriage relation naturally loses much of its sacredness, and says:

It is a contract of convenience, profit or pleasure, that may be entered into and dissolved at the will of the parties, and that without heinous sin, or injury to the property interests of any one.

In this sentence he is expressing, as we suppose, the *common* idea of slaves and masters of the nature of this institution, and not his own. We infer this from the fact that he endeavors in his catechism to impress on the slave the sacredness and perpetuity of the relation. But, when the most pious and devoted men that the South has, and those professing to spend their lives for the service of the slave, thus calmly, and without any reprobation, contemplate this state of things as a state with which Christianity does not call on them to interfere, what can be expected of the world in general ?

It is to be remarked, with regard to the sentiments of Mr. Smylie's pamphlet, that they are endorsed in the appendix by a document in the name of two presbyteries, which document, though with less minuteness of investigation, takes the same ground with Mr. Smylie. This Rev. James Smylie

was one who, in company with the Rev.
John L. Montgomery, was appointed by the
synod of Mississippi, in 1839, to write or
compile a catechism for the instruction of
the negroes.

Mr. Jones says, in his "History of the
Religious Instruction of the Negroes" (p.
83): "The Rev. James Smylie and the
Rev. C. Blair are engaged in this good
work (of enlightening the negroes) sys-
tematically and constantly in Mississippi."
The former clergyman is characterized as
an "aged and indefatigable father." "His
success in enlightening the negroes has been
very great. A large proportion of the
negroes in his old church can recite both
Williston's and the Westminster Catechism
very accurately." The writer really wishes
that it were in her power to make copious
extracts from Mr. Smylie's pamphlet. A
great deal could be learned from it as to what
style of mind, and habits of thought, and
modes of viewing religious subjects, are
likely to grow up under such an institution.
The man is undoubtedly and heartily sincere in his opinions, and appears to maintain them with a most abounding and triumphant joyfulness, as the very latest
improvement in theological knowledge. We
are tempted to present a part of his *Introduction*, simply for the light it gives us on
the style of thinking which is to be found
on our south-western waters:

In presenting the following review to the public, the author was not entirely or mainly influenced by a desire or hope to correct the views of
the Chillicothe Presbytery. He hoped the publication would be of essential service to others, as
well as to the presbytery.

From his intercourse with religious societies of
all denominations, in Mississippi and Louisiana, he
was aware that the abolition maxim, namely, *that
slavery is in itself sinful*, had gained on and entwined itself among the religious and conscientious scruples of many in the community so far
as not only to render them unhappy, but to draw
off the attention from the great and important
duty of a householder to his household. The eye
of the mind, resting on slavery itself as a corrupt
fountain, from which, of necessity, nothing but
corrupt streams could flow, was incessantly employed in search of some plan by which, with
safety, the fountain could, in some future time, be
entirely dried up; never reflecting, or dreaming,
that slavery, in itself considered, was an innox-
ious relation, and that the whole error rested in
the neglect of the relative duties of the relation.

If there be a consciousness of guilt resting on
the mind, it is all the same, as to the effect,
whether the conscience is or is not right. Although the word of God alone ought to be the
guide of conscience, yet it is not always the case.
Hence, conscientious scruples sometimes exist for
neglecting to do that which the word of God condemns.

The Bornean who neglects to kill his father,
and to eat him with his dates, when he has become
old, is sorely tortured by the wringings of a guilty
conscience, when his filial tenderness and sympathy have gained the ascendency over his apprehended duty of killing his parent. In like manner, many a slave-holder, whose conscience is
guided, not by the word of God, but by the doctrines of men, is often suffering the lashes of a
guilty conscience, even when he renders to his
slave " that which is just and equal," according
to the Scriptures, simply because he does not
emancipate his slave, irrespective of the benefit
or injury done by such an act.

"How beautiful upon the mountains," in the
apprehension of the reviewer, "would be the feet
of him that would bring" to the Bornean " the
glad tidings" that his conduct, in sparing the life
of his tender and affectionate parent, was no sin!
* * * * Equally beautiful and delightful,
does the reviewer trust, will it be, to an honest,
scrupulous and conscientious slave-holder, to learn,
from the word of God, the glad tidings that slavery itself is not sinful. Released now from an
incubus that paralyzed his energies in discharge
of duty towards his slaves, he goes forth cheerfully to energetic action. It is not now as formerly, when he viewed slavery as in itself sinful.
He can now pray, with the hope of being heard,
that God will bless his exertions to train up his
slaves " in the nurture and admonition of the
Lord :" whereas, before, he was retarded by this
consideration, — " If I regard iniquity in my
heart, the Lord will not hear me." Instead of
hanging down his head, moping and brooding over
his condition, as formerly, without action, he
raises his head, and moves on cheerfully, in the
plain path of duty.

He is no more tempted to look askance at the
word of God, and saying, " Hast thou found me,
O mine enemy," come to " filch from me" my
slaves, which, "while not enriching" them, "leaves
me poor indeed ?" Instead of viewing the word of
God, as formerly, come with whips and scorpions
to chastise him into paradise, he feels that its
" ways are ways of pleasantness, and its paths
peace." Distinguishing now between the real
word of God and what are only the doctrines and
commandments of men, the mystery is solved,
which was before insolvable, namely, " The statutes of the Lord are right, rejoicing the heart."

If you should undertake to answer such
a man by saying that his argument proves
too much,— that neither Christ nor his
apostles bore any explicit testimony against
the gladiatorial shows and the sports of the
arena, and, therefore, it would be right to
get them up in America,— the probability
seems to be that he would heartily assent to
it, and think, on the whole, that it might be a
good speculation. As a further specimen of
the free-and-easy facetiousness which seems
to be a trait in this production, see, on p. 58,
where the Latin motto *Facilis descensus
Averni sed revocare*, &c., receives the following quite free and truly Western trans-
lation, which, he good-naturedly says, is
given for the benefit of those who do not

understand Latin,— "It is easy to go to the devil, but the devil to get back."

Some uncharitable people might, perhaps, say that the preachers of such doctrines are as likely as anybody to have an experimental knowledge on this point. The idea of this jovial old father instructing a class of black "Sams" and young "Topsys" in the mysteries of the Assembly's Catechism is truly picturesque !

That Mr. Smylie's opinions on the subject of slavery have been amply supported and carried out by leading clergymen in every denomination, we might give volumes of quotations to show.

A second head, however, is yet to be considered, with regard to the influence of the Southern church and clergy.

It is well known that the Southern political community have taken their stand upon the position that the institution of slavery shall not be open to discussion. In many of the slave states stringent laws exist, subjecting to fine and imprisonment, and even death, any who speak or publish anything upon the subject, except in its favor. They have not only done this with regard to citizens of slave states, but they have shown the strongest disposition to do it with regard to citizens of free states; and when these discussions could not be repelled by regular law, they have encouraged the use of illegal measures. In the published letters and speeches of Horace Mann the following examples are given (p. 467). In 1831 the Legislature of Georgia offered five thousand dollars to any one who would arrest and bring to trial and conviction, in Georgia, a citizen of Massachusetts, named William Lloyd Garrison. This law was approved by W. Lumpkin, Governor, Dec. 26, 1831. At a meeting of slave-holders held at Sterling, in the same state, September 4, 1835, it was formally recommended to the governor to offer, by proclamation, five thousand dollars reward for the apprehension of any one of ten persons, citizens, with one exception, of New York and Massachusetts, whose names were given. The *Milledgeville* (Ga.) *Federal Union* of February 1st, 1836, contained an offer of ten thousand dollars for the arrest and kidnapping of the Rev. A. A. Phelps, of New York. The committee of vigilance of the parish of East Feliciana offered, in the *Louisville Journal* of Oct. 15, 1835, fifty thousand dollars to any person who would deliver into their hands Arthur Tappan, of New York. At a public meeting at Mount Meigs, Alabama, Aug.

13, 1836, the Hon. Bedford Ginress in the chair, a reward of fifty thousand dollars was offered for the apprehension of the same Arthur Tappan, or of Le Roy Sunderland, a Methodist clergyman of New York. Of course, as none of these persons could be seized except in violation of the laws of the state where they were citizens, this was offering a public reward for an act of felony. Throughout all the Southern States associations were formed, called committees of vigilance, for the taking of measures for suppressing abolition opinions, and for the punishment by Lynch law of suspected persons. At Charleston, South Carolina, a mob of this description forced open the post-office, and made a general inspection, at their pleasure, of its contents ; and whatever publication they found there which they considered to be of a dangerous and anti-slavery tendency, they made a public bonfire of, in the street. A large public meeting was held, a few days afterwards, to complete the preparation for excluding anti-slavery principles from publication, and for ferreting out persons suspected of abolitionism, that they might be subjected to Lynch law. Similar popular meetings were held through the Southern and Western States. At one of these, held in Clinton, Mississippi, in the year 1835, the following resolutions were passed :

Resolved, That slavery through the South and West is not felt as an evil, moral or political, but it is recognized in reference to the *actual*, and not to any Utopian condition of our slaves, as a blessing both to master and slave.

Resolved, That it is our decided opinion that any individual who dares to circulate, with a view to effectuate the designs of the abolitionists, any of the incendiary tracts or newspapers now in a course of transmission to this country, is justly worthy, in the sight of God and man, of immediate death ; and we doubt not that such would be the punishment at any such offender in any part of the State of Mississippi where he may be found.

Resolved, That the clergy of the State of Mississippi be hereby recommended at once to take a stand upon this subject ; and that their further silence in relation thereto, at this crisis, will, in our opinion, be subject to serious censure.

The treatment to which persons were exposed, when taken up by any of these vigilance committees, as suspected of anti-slavery sentiments, may be gathered from the following account. The writer has a distinct recollection of the circumstances at the present time, as the victim of this injustice was a member of the seminary then under the care of her father.

Amos Dresser, now a missionary in Jamaica, was a theological student at Lane Seminary, near

Cincinnati. In the vacation (August 1835) he undertook to sell Bibles in the State of Tennessee, with a view to raise means further to continue his studies. Whilst there, he fell under suspicion of being an abolitionist, was arrested by the vigilance committee whilst attending a religious meeting in the neighborhood of Nashville, the capital of the state, and, after an afternoon and evening's inquisition, condemned to receive twenty lashes on his naked body. The sentence was executed on him, between eleven and twelve o'clock on Saturday night, in the presence of most of the committee, and of an infuriated and blaspheming mob. The vigilance committee (an unlawful association) consisted of sixty persons. Of these, twenty-seven were members of churches; one, a religious teacher; another, the *Elder* who but a few days before, in the Presbyterian church, handed Mr. Dresser the bread and wine at the communion of the Lord's supper.

It will readily be seen that the principle involved in such proceedings as these involves more than the question of slavery. The question was, in fact, this,— whether it is so important to hold African slaves that it is proper to deprive free Americans of the liberty of conscience, and liberty of speech, and liberty of the press, in order to do it. It is easy to see that very serious changes would be made in the government of a country by the admission of this principle; because it is quite plain that, if all these principles of our free government may be given up for one thing, they may for another, and that its ultimate tendency is to destroy entirely that freedom of opinion and thought which is considered to be the distinguishing excellence of American institutions.

The question now is, Did the church join with the world in thinking the institution of slavery so important and desirable as to lead them to look with approbation upon Lynch law, and the sacrifice of the rights of free inquiry? We answer the reader by submitting the following facts and quotations.

At the large meeting which we have described above, in Charleston, South Carolina, the *Charleston Courier* informs us "that the clergy of all denominations attended in a body, lending their sanction to the proceedings, and adding by their presence to the impressive character of the scene." There can be no doubt that the presence of the clergy of all denominations, in a body, at a meeting held for such a purpose, was an *impressive scene*, truly !

At this meeting it was Resolved,

That the thanks of this meeting are due to the reverend gentlemen of the clergy in this city, who have so promptly and so effectually responded to

public sentiment, by suspending their schools in which the *free colored population* were taught; and that this meeting deem it a patriotic action, worthy of all praise, and proper to be imitated by other teachers of similar schools throughout the state.

The question here arises, whether their Lord, at the day of judgment, will comment on their actions in a similar strain.

The alarm of the Virginia slave-holders was not less; nor were the clergy in the city of Richmond, the capital, less prompt than the clergy in Charleston to respond to "public sentiment." Accordingly, on the 29th of July, they assembled together, and Resolved, *unanimously,*

That we earnestly deprecate the unwarrantable and highly improper interference of the people of any other state with the domestic relations of master and slave.

That the example of our Lord Jesus Christ and his apostles, in not interfering with the question of slavery, but uniformly recognizing the relations of master and servant, and giving full and affectionate instruction to both, is worthy of the imitation of all ministers of the gospel.

That we will not patronize nor receive any pamphlet or newspaper of the anti-slavery societies, and that we will discountenance the circulation of all such papers in the community.

The Rev. J. C. Postell, a Methodist minister of South Carolina, concludes a very violent letter to the editor of *Zion's Watchman*, a Methodist anti-slavery paper published in New York, in the following manner. The reader will see that this taunt is an allusion to the offer of fifty thousand dollars for his body at the South which we have given before.

But, if you desire to educate the slaves, I will tell you how to raise the money without editing *Zion's Watchman*. You and old Arthur Tappan come out to the South this winter, and they will raise one hundred thousand dollars for you. New Orleans, itself, will be pledged for it. Desiring no further acquaintance with you, and never expecting to see you but once in time or eternity, that is at the judgment, I subscribe myself the friend of the Bible, and the opposer of abolitionists,
J. C. POSTELL.
Orangeburgh, July 21st, 1836.

The Rev. Thomas S. Witherspoon, a member of the Presbyterian Church, writing to the editor of the *Emancipator*, says :

I draw my warrant from the Scriptures of the Old and New Testament, to hold the slave in bondage. The principle of holding the heathen in bondage is recognized by God. * * * When the tardy process of the law is too long in redressing our grievances, we of the South have adopted the summary remedy of Judge Lynch — and really I think it one of the most wholesome and salutary remedies for the malady of Northern fanaticism that can be applied, and no doubt my worthy friend, the Editor of the *Emancipator and Human Rights*, would feel the better of its enforcement, provided he had a Southern administrator. I go to the Bible for my warrant in all moral matters. * * Let your emissaries dare venture to cross the Potomac, and I cannot promise you that their fate will be less than Haman's. Then beware how you goad an insulted but magnanimous people to deeds of desperation!

The Rev. Robert N. Anderson, also a member of the Presbyterian Church, says, in a letter to the Sessions of the Presbyterian Congregations within the bounds of the West Hanover Presbytery :

At the approaching stated meeting of our Presbytery, I design to offer a preamble and string of resolutions on the subject of the use of wine in the Lord's Supper ; and also a preamble and string of resolutions on the subject of the treasonable and abominably wicked interference of the Northern and Eastern fanatics with our political and civil rights, our property and our domestic concerns. You are aware that our clergy, whether with or without reason, are more suspected by the public than the clergy of other denominations. Now, *dear Christian brethren*, I humbly express it as my earnest wish, that you *quit yourselves like men*. If there be any stray goat of a minister among you, tainted with the blood-hound principles of abolitionism, let him be ferreted out, silenced, excommunicated, and left to the *public to dispose of him in other respects*.

Your affectionate brother in the Lord,
ROBERT N. ANDERSON.

The Rev. William S. Plummer, D.D., of Richmond, a member of the Old-school Presbyterian Church, is another instance of the same sort. He was absent from Richmond at the time the clergy in that city purged themselves, in a body, from the charge of being favorably disposed to abolition. On his return, he lost no time in communicating to the " Chairman of the Committee of Correspondence " his agreement with his clerical brethren. The passages quoted occur in his letter to the chairman :

I have carefully watched this matter from its earliest existence, and everything I have seen or heard of its character, both from its patrons and its enemies, has confirmed me, beyond repentance, in the belief, that, let the character of abolitionists be what it may in the sight of the Judge of all the earth, this is the most meddlesome, impudent, reckless, fierce, and wicked excitement I ever saw.

If abolitionists will set the country in a blaze, it is but fair that they should receive the first warming at the fire.

* * * * * *

Lastly. Abolitionists are like infidels, wholly unaddicted to martyrdom for opinion's sake. Let them understand that *they will be caught* [Lynched] if they come among us, and they will take good heed to keep out of our way. There is not one man among them who has any more idea of shed-ding his blood in this cause than he has of making war on the Grand Turk.

The Rev. Dr. Hill, of Virginia, said, in the New School Assembly :

The abolitionists have made the servitude of the slave harder. If I could tell you some of the dirty tricks which these abolitionists have played, you would not wonder. Some of them have been Lynched, and it served them right.

These things sufficiently show the estimate which the Southern clergy and church have formed and expressed as to the relative value of slavery and the right of free inquiry. It shows, also, that they consider slavery as so important that they can tolerate and encourage acts of lawless violence, and risk all the dangers of encouraging mob law, for its sake. These passages and considerations sufficiently show the stand which the Southern church takes upon this subject.

For many of these opinions, shocking as they may appear, some apology may be found in that blinding power of custom and all those deadly educational influences which always attend the system of slavery, and which must necessarily produce a certain obtuseness of the moral sense in the mind of any man who is educated from childhood under them.

There is also, in the habits of mind formed under a system which is supported by continual resort to force and violence, a necessary deadening of sensibility to the evils of force and violence, as applied to other subjects. The whole style of civilization which is formed under such an institution has been not unaptly denominated by a popular writer " the bowie-knife style ;" and we must not be surprised at its producing a peculiarly martial cast of religious character, and ideas very much at variance with the spirit of the gospel. A religious man, born and educated at the South, has all these difficulties to contend with, in elevating himself to the true spirit of the gospel.

It was said by one that, after the Reformation, the best of men, being educated under a system of despotism and force, and accustomed from childhood to have force, and not argument, made the test of opinion, came to look upon all controversies very much in a Smithfield light,— the question being not as to the propriety of burning heretics, but as to which party ought to be burned.

The system of slavery is a simple retrogression of society to the worst abuses of the middle ages. We must not therefore be surprised to find the opinions and practices of the middle ages, as to civil and religious toleration, prevailing.

However much we may reprobate and deplore those unworthy views of God and religion which are implied in such declarations as are here recorded,—however blasphemous and absurd they may appear,—still, it is apparent that their authors uttered them with sincerity ; and this is the most melancholy feature of the case. They are as sincere as Paul when he breathed out threatenings and slaughter, and when he thought within himself that he *ought* to do many things contrary to the name of Jesus. They are as sincere as the Brahmin or Hindoo, conscientiously supporting a religion of cruelty and blood. They are as sincere as many enlightened, scholarlike and Christian men in modern Europe, who, born and bred under systems of civil and religious despotism, and having them entwined with all their dearest associations of home and country, and having all their habits of thought and feeling biased by them, do most conscientiously defend them.

There is something in conscientious conviction, even in case of the worst kind of opinions, which is not without a certain degree of respectability. That the religion expressed by the declarations which we have quoted is as truly Antichrist as the religion of the Church of Rome, it is presumed no sensible person out of the sphere of American influences will deny. That there may be very sincere Christians under this system of religion, with all its false principles and all its disadvantageous influences, liberality must concede. The Church of Rome has had its Fenelon, its Thomas â Kempis; and the Southern Church, which has adopted these principles, has had men who have risen above the level of their system. At the time of the Reformation, and now, the Church of Rome had in its bosom thousands of praying, devoted, humble Christians, which, like flowers in the clefts of rocks, could be counted by no eye, save God's alone. And so, amid the rifts and glaciers of this horrible spiritual and temporal despotism, we hope are blooming flowers of Paradise, patient, prayerful, and self-denying Christians; and it is the deepest grief, in attacking the dreadful system under which they have been born and brought up, that violence must be done to their cherished feelings and associations. In another and better world, perhaps, they may appreciate the motives of those who do this.

But now another consideration comes to the mind. These Southern Christians have been united in ecclesiastical relations with Christians of the northern and free states, meeting with them, by their representatives, yearly, in their various ecclesiastical assemblies. One might hope, in case of such a union, that those debasing views of Christianity, and that deadness of public sentiment, which were the inevitable result of an education under the slave system, might have been qualified by intercourse with Christians in free states, who, having grown up under free institutions, would naturally be supposed to feel the utmost abhorrence of such sentiments. One would have supposed that the church and clergy of the free states would naturally have used the most strenuous endeavors, by all the means in their power, to convince their brethren of errors so dishonorable to Christianity, and tending to such dreadful practical results. One would have supposed also, that, failing to convince their brethren, they would have felt it due to Christianity to clear themselves from all complicity with these sentiments, by the most solemn, earnest and reiterated protests.

Let us now inquire what has, in fact, been the course of the Northern church on this subject.

Previous to making this inquiry, let us review the declarations that have been made in the Southern church, and see what principles have been established by them.

1. That slavery is an innocent and lawful relation, as much as that of parent and child, husband and wife, or any other lawful relation of society. (Harmony Pres., S. C.)

2. That it is consistent with the most fraternal regard for the good of the slave. (Charleston Union Pres., S. C.)

3. That masters ought not to be disciplined for selling slaves without their consent. (New-school Pres. Church, Petersburg, Va.)

4. That the right to buy, sell, and hold men for purposes of gain, was given by express permission of God. (James Smylie and his Presbyteries.)

5. That the laws which forbid the education of the slave are right, and meet the approbation of the reflecting part of the Christian community. (Ibid.)

6. That the fact of slavery is not a question of morals at all, but is purely one of political economy. (Charleston Baptist Association.)

7. The right of masters to dispose of the time of their slaves has been distinctly recognized by the Creator of all things. (Ibid.)

8. That slavery, as it exists in these United States, is not a moral evil. (Georgia Conference, Methodist.)

9. That, without a new revelation from heaven, no man is entitled to pronounce slavery wrong.

10. That the separation of slaves by sale should be régarded as separation by death, and the parties allowed to marry again. (Shiloh Baptist Ass., and Savannah River Ass.)

11. That the testimony of colored members of the churches shall not be taken against a white person. (Methodist Church.)

In addition, it has been plainly avowed, by the expressed principles and practice of Christians of various denominations, that they regard it right and proper to put down all inquiry upon this subject by Lynch law.

One would have imagined that these principles were sufficiently extraordinary, as coming from the professors of the religion of Christ, to have excited a good deal of attention in their Northern brethren. It also must be seen that, as principles, they are principles of very extensive application, underlying the whole foundations of religion and morality. If not true, they were certainly heresies of no ordinary magnitude, involving no ordinary results. Let us now return to our inquiry as to the course of the Northern church in relation to them.

CHAPTER II.

IN the first place, have any of these opinions ever been treated in the church as heresies, and the teachers of them been subjected to the censures with which it is thought proper to visit heresy?

After a somewhat extended examination upon the subject, the writer has been able to discover but one instance of this sort. It may be possible that such cases have existed in other denominations, which have escaped inquiry.

A clergyman in the Cincinnati N. S. Presbytery maintained the doctrine that slaveholding was justified by the Bible, and for persistence in teaching this sentiment was suspended by that presbytery. He appealed to Synod, and the decision was confirmed by the Cincinnati Synod. The New School General Assembly, however, reversed this decision of the presbytery, and restored the standing of the clergyman. The presbytery,

on its part, refused to receive him back, and he was received into the Old School Church.

The Presbyterian Church has probably exceeded all other churches of the United States in its zeal for doctrinal opinions. This church has been shaken and agitated to its very foundation with questions of heresy; but, except in this individual case, it is not known that any of these principles which have been asserted by Southern Presbyterian bodies and individuals have ever been discussed in its General Assembly as matters of heresy.

About the time that Smylie's pamphlet came out, the Presbyterian Church was convulsed with the trial of the Rev. Albert Barnes for certain alleged heresies. These heresies related to the federal headship of Adam, the propriety of imputing his sin to all his posterity, and the question whether men have any ability of any kind to obey the commandments of God.

For advancing certain sentiments on these topics, Mr. Barnes was silenced by the vote of the synod to which he belonged, and his trial in the General Assembly on these points was the all-engrossing topic in the Presbyterian Church for some time. The Rev. Dr. L. Beecher went through a trial with reference to similar opinions. During all this time, no notice was taken of the heresy, if such it be, that the right to buy, sell, and hold men for purposes of gain, was expressly given by God; although that heresy was publicly promulgated in the same Presbyterian Church, by Mr. Smylie, and the presbyteries with which he was connected.

If it be accounted for by saying that the question of slavery is a question of *practical morals*, and not of dogmatic theology, we are then reminded that questions of morals of far less magnitude have been discussed with absorbing interest.

The Old School Presbyterian Church, in whose communion the greater part of the slave-holding Presbyterians of the South are found, has never felt called upon to discipline its members for upholding a system which denies legal marriage to all slaves. Yet this church was agitated to its very foundation by the discussion of a question of morals which an impartial observer would probably consider of far less magnitude, namely, whether a man might lawfully marry his deceased wife's sister. For the time, all the strength and attention of the church seemed concentrated upon this important subject. The trial went from Presbytery to

Synod, and from Synod to General Assembly; and ended with deposing a very respectable minister for this crime. Rev. Robert P. Breckenridge, D.D., a member of the Old School Assembly, has thus described the state of the slave population as to their marriage relations: "The system of slavery denies to a whole class of human beings the sacredness of marriage and of home, compelling them to live in a state of concubinage; for in the eye of the law no colored slave-man is the husband of any wife in particular, nor any slave-woman the wife of any husband in particular; no slave-man is the father of any children in particular, and no slave-child is the child of any parent in particular."

Now, had this church considered the fact that three million men and women were, by the laws of the land, obliged to live in this manner, as of equally serious consequence, it is evident, from the ingenuity, argument, vehemence, Biblical research, and untiring zeal, which they bestowed on Mr. McQueen's trial, that they could have made a very strong case with regard to this also.

, The history of the united action of denominations which included churches both in the slave and free states is a melancholy exemplification, to a reflecting mind, of that gradual deterioration of the moral sense which results from admitting any compromise, however slight, with an acknowledged sin. The best minds in the world cannot bear such a familiarity without injury to the moral sense. The facts of the slave system and of the slave laws, when presented to disinterested judges in Europe, have excited a universal outburst of horror; yet, in assemblies composed of the wisest and best clergymen of America, these things have been discussed from year to year, and yet brought no results that have, in the slightest degree, lessened the evil. The reason is this. A portion of the members of these bodies had pledged themselves to sustain the system, and peremptorily to refuse and put down all discussion of it; and the other part of the body did not consider this stand so taken as being of sufficiently vital consequence to authorize separation. .

Nobody will doubt that, had the Southern members taken such a stand against the divinity of our Lord, the division would have been immediate and unanimous; but yet the Southern members do maintain the right to buy and sell, lease, hire and mortgage, multitudes of men and women, whom, with the same breath, they declared to be members of their churches and true Christians. The Bible declares of all such that they are temples of the Holy Ghost; that they are members of Christ's body, of his flesh and bones. Is not the doctrine that men may lawfully sell the members of Christ, his body, his flesh and bones, for purposes of gain, as really a heresy as the denial of the divinity of Christ; and is it not a dishonor to Him who is over all, God blessed forever, to tolerate this dreadful opinion, with its more dreadful consequences, while the smallest heresies concerning the imputation of Adam's sin are pursued with eager vehemence? If the history of the action of all the bodies thus united can be traced downwards, we shall find that, by reason of this tolerance of an admitted sin, the anti-slavery testimony has every year grown weaker and weaker. If we look over the history of all denominations, we shall see that at first they used very stringent language with relation to slavery. This is particularly the case with the Methodist and Presbyterian bodies, and for that reason we select these two as examples. The Methodist Society especially, as organized by John Wesley, was an anti-slavery society, and the Book of Discipline contained the most positive statutes against slave-holding. The history of the successive resolutions of the conference of this church is very striking. In 1780, before the church was regularly organized in the United States, they resolved as follows:

The conference acknowledges that slavery is contrary to the laws of God, man and nature, and hurtful to society; contrary to the dictates of conscience and true religion; and doing what we would not others should do unto us.

In 1784, when the church was fully organized, rules were adopted prescribing the times at which members who were already slave-holders should emancipate their slaves. These rules were succeeded by the following:

Every person concerned, who will not comply with these rules, shall have liberty quietly to withdraw from our society within the twelve months following the notice being given him, as aforesaid; otherwise the assistants shall exclude him from the society.

No person holding slaves shall in future be admitted into society, or to the Lord's Supper, till he previously comply with these rules concerning slavery.

Those who buy, sell, or give [slaves] away, unless on purpose to free them, shall be expelled immediately.

In 1801:

We declare that we are more than ever convinced of the great evil of African slavery, which still exists in these United States.

Every member of the society who sells a slave shall, immediately after full proof, be excluded from the society, &c.

The Annual Conferences are directed to draw up addresses, for the gradual emancipation of the slaves, to the legislature. Proper committees shall be appointed by the Annual Conferences, out of the most respectable of our friends, for the conducting of the business; and the presiding elders, deacons, and travelling preachers, shall procure as many proper signatures as possible to the addresses; and give all the assistance in their power, in every respect, to aid the committees, and to further the blessed undertaking. Let this be continued from year to year, till the desired end be accomplished.

In 1836 let us notice the change. The General Conference held its annual session in Cincinnati, and resolved as follows:

Resolved, By the delegates of the Annual Conferences in General Conference assembled, That they are decidedly opposed to modern abolitionism, and *wholly disclaim any right, wish, or intention*, to interfere in the civil and political relation between master and slave, as it exists in the slaveholding states of this Union.

These resolutions were passed by a very large majority. An address was received from the Wesleyan Methodist Conference in England, affectionately remonstrating on the subject of slavery. The Conference refused to publish it. In the pastoral address to the churches are these passages:

It cannot be unknown to you that the question of slavery in the United States, by the constitutional compact which binds us together as a nation, is left to be regulated by the several state legislatures themselves; and thereby is put beyond the control of the general government, as well as that of all ecclesiastical bodies; it being manifest that in the slave-holding states themselves the entire responsibility of its existence, or non-existence, rests with those state legislatures. * * * * These facts, which are only mentioned here as a reason for the friendly admonition which we wish to give you, constrain us, as your pastors, who are called to watch over your souls as they must give account, to exhort you to abstain from all abolition movements and associations, and to refrain from patronizing any of their publications, &c. * *

The subordinate conferences showed the same spirit.

In 1836 the New York Annual Conference resolved that no one should be elected a deacon or elder in the church, unless he would give a pledge to the church that he would refrain from discussing this subject.*

In 1838 the conference resolved:

As the sense of this conference, that any of its members, or probationers, who shall patronize *Zion's Watchman*, either by writing in commend-

ation of its character, by circulating it, recommending it to our people, or procuring subscribers, or by collecting or remitting moneys, shall be deemed guilty of indiscretion, and dealt with accordingly.

It will be recollected that *Zion's Watchman* was edited by Le Roy Sunderland, for whose abduction the State of Alabama had offered fifty thousand dollars.

In 1840, the General Conference at Baltimore passed the resolution that we have already quoted, forbidding preachers to allow colored persons to give testimony in their churches. It has been computed that about eighty thousand people were deprived of the right of testimony by this act. This Methodist Church subsequently broke into a Northern and Southern Conference. The Southern Conference is avowedly all pro-slavery, and the Northern Conference has still in its communion slave-holding conferences and members.

Of the Northern conferences, one of the largest, the Baltimore, passed the following:

Resolved, That this conference disclaims having any fellowship with abolitionism. On the contrary, while it is determined to maintain its well-known and long-established position, by keeping the travelling preachers composing its own body free from slavery, it is also determined not to hold connection with any ecclesiastical body that shall make non-slaveholding a condition of membership in the church; but to stand by and maintain the discipline as it is.

The following extract is made from an address of the Philadelphia Annual Conference to the societies under its care, dated Wilmington Del., April 7, 1847:

If the plan of separation gives us the pastoral care of you, it remains to inquire whether we have done anything, as a conference, or as men, to forfeit your confidence and affection. We are not advised that even in the great excitement which has distressed you for some months past, any one has impeached our moral conduct, or charged us with unsoundness in doctrine, or corruption or tyranny in the administration of discipline. But we learn that the simple cause of the unhappy excitement among you is, that some suspect us, or affect to suspect us, of being abolitionists. Yet no particular act of the conference, or any particular member thereof, is adduced, as the ground of the erroneous and injurious suspicion. We would ask you, brethren, whether the conduct of our ministry among you for sixty years past ought not to be sufficient to protect us from this charge. Whether the question we have been accustomed, for a few years past, to put to candidates for admission among us, namely, *Are you an abolitionist?* and, without each one answered in the negative, he was not received, ought not to protect us from the charge. Whether the action of the last conference on this particular matter ought not to satisfy any fair and candid mind that we are

* This resolution is given in Birney's pamphlet.

not, and do not desire to be, abolitionists. * * *
We cannot see how we can be regarded as abolitionists, without the ministers of the Methodist
Episcopal Church South being considered in the
same light. * * * * *
Wishing you all heavenly benedictions, we are,
dear brethren, yours, in Christ Jesus,

    J. P. Durbin,
    J. Kennaday,
    Ignatius T. Cooper, } Comm.
    William H. Gilder,
    Joseph Castle,

These facts sufficiently define the position
of the Methodist Church. The history is
melancholy, but instructive. The history of
the Presbyterian Church is also of interest.

In 1793, the following note to the eighth
commandment was inserted in the Book of
Discipline, as expressing the doctrine of the
church upon slave-holding:

1 Tim. 1 : 10. The law is made for man-stealers.
This crime among the Jews exposed the perpetrators of it to capital punishment, Exodus 21 : 15 ;
and the apostle here classes them with sinners of
the first rank. The word he uses, in its original
import, comprehends all who are concerned in
bringing any of the human race into slavery, or in
retaining them in it. Hominum fures, qui servos
vel liberos abducunt, retinent, vendunt, vel emunt.
Stealers of men are all those who bring off slaves
or freemen, and keep, sell, or buy them. To steal a
free man, says Grotius, is the highest kind of theft.
In other instances, we only steal human property ;
but when we steal or retain men in slavery, we
seize those who, in common with ourselves, are
constituted by the original grant lords of the earth.

No rules of church discipline were enforced, and members whom this passage declared guilty of this crime remained undisturbed in its communion, as ministers and
elders. This inconsistency was obviated in
1816 by expunging the passage from the
Book of Discipline. In 1818 it adopted an
expression of its views on slavery. This
document is a long one, conceived and written in a very Christian spirit. The Assembly's
Digest says, p. 341, that it was unanimously
adopted. The following is its testimony as
to the nature of slavery :

We consider the voluntary enslaving of one part
of the human race by another as a gross violation
of the most precious and sacred rights of human
nature ; as utterly inconsistent with the law of
God, which requires us to love our neighbor as
ourselves ; and as totally irreconcilable with the
spirit and principles of the gospel of Christ, which
enjoin that "all things whatsoever ye would that
men should do to you, do ye even so to them."
Slavery creates a paradox in the moral system—
it exhibits rational, accountable, and immortal
beings in such circumstances as scarcely to leave
them the power of moral action. It exhibits them
as dependent on the will of others, whether they
shall receive religious instruction ; whether they
shall know and worship the true God ; whether

they shall enjoy the ordinances of the gospel ;
whether they shall perform the duties and cherish
the endearments of husbands and wives, parents
and children, neighbors and friends ; whether they
shall preserve their chastity and purity, or regard
the dictates of justice and humanity. Such are
some of the consequences of slavery, — consequences not imaginary, but which connect themselves with its very existence. The evils to which
the slave is always exposed often take place in
fact, and in their very worst degree and form : and
where all of them do not take place, — as we rejoice
to say that in many instances, through the influence
of the principles of humanity and religion on the
minds of masters, they do not, — still the slave is
deprived of his natural right, degraded as a human
being, and exposed to the danger of passing into
the hands of a master who may inflict upon him
all the hardships and injuries which inhumanity
and avarice may suggest.

This language was surely decided, and it
was unanimously adopted by slave-holders
and non-slaveholders. Certainly one might
think the time of redemption was drawing
nigh. The declaration goes on to say :

It is manifestly the duty of all Christians who
enjoy the light of the present day, when the inconsistency of slavery both with the dictates of humanity and religion has been demonstrated and
is generally seen and acknowledged, to use honest,
earnest, unwearied endeavors to correct the errors
of former times, and as speedily as possible to
efface this blot on our holy religion, and to obtain
the complete abolition of slavery throughout
Christendom and throughout the world.

Here we have the Presbyterian Church,
slave-holding and non-slaveholding, virtually
formed into one great abolition society, as
we have seen the Methodist was.

The assembly then goes on to state that
the slaves are not at present prepared to be
free,— that they tenderly sympathize with
the portion of the church and country that
has had this evil entailed upon them, where
as they say "a great and the most virtuous
part of the community abhor slavery and
wish its extermination." But they exhort them to commence immediately the work
of instructing slaves, with a view to preparing
them for freedom ; and let no greater delay
take place than "a regard to public welfare
indispensably demands." "To be governed
by no other considerations than an honest
and impartial regard to the happiness
of the injured party, uninfluenced by the
expense and inconvenience which such regard may involve." It warns against "un-
duly extending this plea of necessity,"
against making it a cover for the love and
practice of slavery. It ends by recommending that any one who shall sell a fellow-
Christian without his consent be immediately
disciplined and suspended.

If we consider that this was *unanimously* adopted by slave-holders and all, and grant, as we certainly do, that it was adopted in all honesty and good faith, we shall surely expect something from it. We should expect forthwith the organizing of a set of common schools for the slave-children; for an efficient religious ministration; for an entire discontinuance of trading in Christian slaves; for laws which make the family relations sacred. Was any such thing done or attempted? Alas! Two years after this came the ADMISSION OF MISSOURI, and the increase of demand in the southern slave-market and the internal slave-trade. Instead of schoolteachers, they had slave-traders; instead of gathering *schools*, they gathered *slave-coffles;* instead of building school-houses, they built slave-pens and slave-prisons, jails, barracoons, factories, or whatever the trade pleases to term them; and so went the plan of gradual emancipation.

In 1834, sixteen years after, a committee of the Synod of Kentucky, in which state slavery is generally said to exist in its mildest form, appointed to make a report on the condition of the slaves, gave the following picture of their condition. First, as to their spiritual condition, they say:

After making all reasonable allowances, our colored population can be considered, at the most, but semi-heathen. As to their temporal estate —Brutal stripes, and all the various kinds of personal indignities, are not the only species of cruelty which slavery licenses. The law does not recognize the family relations of the slave, and extends to him no protection in the enjoyment of domestic endearments. The members of a slave-family may be forcibly separated, so that they shall never more meet until the final judgment. And cupidity often induces the masters to practise what the law allows. Brothers and sisters, parents and children, husbands and wives, are torn asunder, and permitted to see each other no more. *These acts are daily occurring in the midst of us.* The shrieks and the agony often witnessed on such occasions proclaim with a trumpet-tongue the iniquity and cruelty of our system. The cries of these sufferers go up to the ears of the Lord of Sabaoth. *There is not a neighborhood where these heart-rending scenes are not displayed.* There is not a village or road that does not behold the sad procession of manacled outcasts, whose chains and mournful countenances tell that they are exiled by force from all that their hearts hold dear. Our church, years ago, raised its voice of solemn warning against this flagrant violation of every principle of mercy, justice, and humanity. Yet we blush to announce to you and to the world that this warning has been often disregarded, even by those who hold to our communion. Cases *have occurred, in our own denomination, where professors of the religion of mercy have torn the mother from her children, and sent her into a merciless and returnless exile.* Yet acts of discipline have rarely followed such conduct.

14

Hon. James G. Birney, for years a resident of Kentucky, in his pamphlet, amends the word *rarely* by substituting *never.* What could show more plainly the utter inefficiency of the past act of the Assembly, and the necessity of adopting some measures more efficient? In 1835, therefore, the subject was urged upon the General Assembly, entreating them to carry out the principles and designs they had avowed in 1818.

Mr. Stuart, of Illinois, in a speech he made upon the subject, said:

I hope this assembly are prepared to come out fully and declare their sentiments, that slave-holding is a most flagrant and heinous SIN. Let us not pass it by in this indirect way, while so many thousands and tens of thousands of our fellow-creatures are writhing under the lash, often inflicted, too, by ministers and elders of the Presbyterian Church.

* * * * *

In this church a man may take a free-born child, force it away from its parents, to whom God gave it in charge, saying "Bring it up for me," and sell it as a beast or hold it in perpetual bondage, and not only escape corporeal punishment, but really be esteemed an excellent Christian. Nay, even ministers of the gospel and doctors of divinity may engage in this unholy traffic, and yet sustain their high and holy calling.

* * * * *

Elders, ministers, and doctors of divinity, are, with both hands, engaged in the practice.

One would have thought facts like these, stated in a body of Christians, were enough to wake the dead; but, alas! we can become accustomed to very awful things. No action was taken upon these remonstrances, except to refer them to a committee, to be reported on at the next session, in 1836.

The moderator of the assembly in 1836 was a slave-holder, Dr. T. S. Witherspoon, the same who said to the editor of the *Emancipator,* "I draw my warrant from the Scriptures of the Old and New Testament to hold my slaves in bondage. The principle of holding the heathen in bondage is recognized by God. When the tardy process of the law is too long in redressing our grievances, we at the South have adopted the summary process of Judge Lynch."

The majority of the committee appointed made a report as follows:

Whereas the subject of slavery is inseparably connected with the laws of many of the states in this Union, with which it is by no means proper for an ecclesiastical judicature to interfere, and involves many considerations in regard to which great diversity of opinion and intensity of feeling are known to exist in the churches represented in this Assembly: And whereas there is great reason to believe that any action on the part of this Assembly, in reference to this subject, would tend to distract and divide our churches, and would probably in no wise promote the benefit of those whose welfare is immediately contemplated in the memorials in question.

Therefore, *Resolved*,

1. That it is not expedient for the Assembly to take any further order in relation to this subject.

2. That as the *notes* which have been expunged from our public formularies, and which some of the memorials referred to the committee request to have restored, were introduced irregularly, never had the sanction of the church, and therefore never possessed any authority, the General Assembly has no power, nor would they think it expedient, to assign them a place in the authorized standards of the church.

The minority of the committee, the Rev. Messrs. Dickey and Beman, reported as follows :

Resolved,

1. That the buying, selling, or holding a human being as property, is in the sight of God a heinous sin, and ought to subject the doer of it to the censures of the church.

2. That it is the duty of every one, and especially of every Christian, who may be involved in this sin, to free himself from its entanglement without delay.

3. That it is the duty of every one, especially of every Christian, in the meekness and firmness of the gospel to plead the cause of the poor and needy, by testifying against the principle and practice of slave-holding ; and to use his best endeavors to deliver the church of God from the evil ; and to bring about the emancipation of the slaves in these United States, and throughout the world.

The slave-holding delegates, to the number of forty-eight, met *apart*, and *Resolved,*

That if the General Assembly shall undertake to exercise authority on the subject of slavery, so as to make it an immorality, or shall in any way declare that Christians are criminal in holding slaves, that a declaration shall be presented by the Southern delegation declining their jurisdiction in the case, and our determination not to submit to such decision.

In view of these conflicting reports, the Assembly resolved as follows :

Inasmuch as the constitution of the Presbyterian Church, in its preliminary and fundamental principles, declares that no church judicatories ought to pretend to make laws to bind the conscience *in virtue of their own authority;* and as the urgency of the business of the Assembly, and the shortness of the time during which they can continue in session, render it impossible to deliberate and decide judiciously, on the subject of slavery in its relation to the church ; therefore, *Resolved,* That this whole subject be indefinitely postponed.

The amount of the slave-trade at the time when the General Assembly refused to act upon the subject of slavery at all, may be inferred from the following items.

The *Virginia Times,* in an article published in this very year of 1836, estimated the number of slaves exported for sale from that state alone, during the twelve months preceding, at forty thousand. The *Natchez* (Miss.) *Courier* says that in the same year the States of Alabama, Missouri and Arkansas, received two hundred and fifty thousand slaves from the more northern states. If we deduct from these all who may be supposed to have emigrated with their masters, still what an immense trade is here indicated !

The Rev. James H. Dickey, who moved the resolutions above presented, had seen some sights which would naturally incline him to wish the Assembly to take some action on the subject, as appears from the following account of a slave-coffle, from his pen.

In the summer of 1822, as I returned with my family from a visit to the Barrens of Kentucky, I witnessed a scene such as I never witnessed before, and such as I hope never to witness again. Having passed through Paris, in Bourbon county, Ky., the sound of music (beyond a little rising ground) attracted my attention. I looked forward, and saw the flag of my country waving. Supposing that I was about to meet a military parade, I drove hastily to the side of the road ; and, having gained the ascent, I discovered (I suppose) about forty black men all chained together after the following manner : each of them was handcuffed, and they were arranged in rank and file. A chain perhaps forty feet long, the size of a fifth-horse-chain, was stretched between the two ranks, to which short chains were joined, which connected with the handcuffs. Behind them were, I suppose, about thirty women, in double rank, the couples tied hand to hand. A solemn sadness sat on every countenance, and the dismal silence of this march of despair was interrupted only by the sound of two violins ; yes, as if to add insult to injury, the foremost couple were furnished with a violin a-piece ; the second couple were ornamented with cockades, while near the centre waved the republican flag, carried by a hand *literally in chains.* I could not forbear exclaiming to the lordly driver who rode at his ease along-side, " Heaven will curse that man who engages in such traffic, and the government that protects him in it !" I pursued my journey till evening, and put up for the night, when I mentioned the scene I had witnessed. " Ah !" cried my landlady, " that is my brother !" From her I learned that his name is Stone, of Bourbon county, Kentucky, in partnership with one Kinningham, of Paris ; and that a few days before he had purchased a negro-woman from a man in Nicholas county. She refused to go with him ; he attempted to compel her, but she defended herself. Without further ceremony, he stepped back, and, by a blow on the side of her head with the butt of his whip, brought her to the ground ; he tied her, and drove her off. I learned further, that besides the drove I had seen, there were about thirty shut up in the Paris prison for safe-keeping, to be added to the company, and that they were designed for the Orleans market. And to this they are doomed for no other crime than that of a black skin and curled locks. Shall I not visit for these things? saith the Lord. Shall not my soul be avenged on such a nation as this?

It cannot be possible that these Christian men realized these things, or, at most, they realized them just as we realize the most tremendous truths of religion, dimly and feebly.

Two years after, the General Assembly, by a sudden and very unexpected movement, passed a vote exscinding, without trial, from the communion of the church, four synods, comprising the most active and decided anti-slavery portions of the church. The reasons alleged were, doctrinal differences and ecclesiastical practices inconsistent with Presbyterianism. By this act about five hundred ministers and sixty thousand members were cut off from the Presbyterian Church.

That portion of the Presbyterian Church called New School, considering this act unjust, refused to assent to it, joined the exscinded synods, and formed themselves into the New School General Assembly. In this communion only three slave-holding presbyteries remained. In the old there were between thirty and forty.

The course of the Old School Assembly, after the separation, in relation to the subject of slavery, may be best expressed by quoting one of their resolutions, passed in 1845. Having some decided anti-slavery members in its body, and being, moreover, addressed on the subject of slavery by associated bodies, they presented, on this year, the following deliberate statement of their policy. (Minutes for 1845, p. 18.)

Resolved, 1st. That the General Assembly of the Presbyterian Church in the United States was originally organized, and has since continued the bond of union in the church, upon the *conceded principle that the existence of domestic slavery, under the circumstances in which it is found in the Southern portion of the country, is no bar to Christian communion.*

2. That the petitions that ask the Assembly to make the holding of slaves in itself a matter of discipline do virtually require this judicatory to *dissolve itself*, and *abandon the organization* under which, by the divine blessing, it has so long prospered. The tendency is evidently to separate the Northern from the Southern portion of the church, — a result which every good Christian must deplore, as tending to the dissolution of the Union of our beloved country, and which every enlightened Christian will oppose, as bringing about a ruinous and unnecessary schism between brethren who maintain a common faith.

Yeas, Ministers and Elders, 168.
Nays,   "   "   "   13.

It is scarcely necessary to add a comment to this very explicit declaration. It is the plainest possible disclaimer of any protest against slavery; the plainest possible statement that the existence of the ecclesiastical organization is of more importance than all the moral and social considerations which are involved in a full defence and practice of American slavery.

The next year a large number of petitions and remonstrances were presented, requesting the Assembly to utter additional testimony against slavery.

In reply to the petitions, the General Assembly reaffirmed all their former testimonies on the subject of slavery for sixty years back, and also affirmed that the previous year's declaration must not be understood as a retraction of that testimony; in other words, they expressed it as their opinion, in the words of 1818, that slavery is " WHOLLY OPPOSED TO THE LAW OF GOD," and " TOTALLY IRRECONCILABLE WITH THE PRECEPTS OF THE GOSPEL OF CHRIST;" and yet that they " had formed their church organization upon the *conceded principle* that the existence of it, under the circumstances in which it is found in the Southern States of the Union, is no bar to Christian communion."

Some members protested against this action. (Minutes, 1846. Overture No. 17.)

Great hopes were at first entertained of the New School body. As a body, it was composed mostly of anti-slavery men. It had in it those synods whose anti-slavery opinions and actions had been, to say the least, one very efficient cause for their excision from the church. It had only three slave-holding presbyteries. The power was all in its own hands. Now, if ever, was their time to cut this loathsome incumbrance wholly adrift, and stand up, in this age of concession and conformity to the world, a purely protesting church, free from all complicity with this most dreadful national immorality.

On the first session of the General Assembly, this course was most vehemently urged, by many petitions and memorials. These memorials were referred to a committee of decided anti-slavery men. The argument on one side was, that the time was now come to take decided measures to cut free wholly from all pro-slavery complicity, and avow their principles with decision, even though it should repel all such churches from their communion as were not prepared for immediate emancipation.

On the other hand, the majority of the committee were urged by opposing considerations. The brethren from slave states made to them representations somewhat like these: "Brethren, our hearts are with you. We are with you in faith, in charity, in prayer. We sympathized in the injury that had been done you by excision. We stood by you then, and are ready to stand by you still. We have no sympathy with the party that have expelled you, and we do not wish to go back to them. As to this matter of slavery, we do not differ from you. We consider it an evil. We mourn and lament over it. We are trying, by gradual and peaceable means, to exclude it from our churches. We are going as far in advance of the sentiment of our churches as we consistently can. We cannot come up to more decided action without losing our hold over them, and, as we think, throwing back the cause of emancipation. If you begin in this decided manner, we cannot hold our churches in the union; they will divide, and go to the Old School."

Here was a very strong plea, made by good and sincere men. It was an appeal, too, to the most generous feelings of the heart. It was, in effect, saying, "Brothers, we stood by you, and fought your battles, when everything was going against you; and, now that you have the power in your hands, are you going to use it so as to cast us out?"

These men, strong anti-slavery men as they were, were affected. One member of the committee foresaw and feared the result. He felt and suggested that the course proposed conceded the whole question. The majority thought, on the whole, that it was best to postpone the subject. The committee reported that the applicants, for reasons satisfactory to themselves, had withdrawn their papers.

The next year, in 1839, the subject was resumed; and it was again urged that the Assembly should take high and decided and unmistakable ground; and certainly, if we consider that all this time not a single church had emancipated its slaves, and that the power of the institution was everywhere stretching and growing and increasing, it would certainly seem that something more efficient was necessary than a general understanding that the church agreed with the testimony delivered in 1818. It was strongly represented that it was time something was done. This year the Assembly decided to refer the subject to presbyteries, to do what they deemed advisable. The words employed were these: "Solemnly referring the whole subject to the lower judicatories, to take such action as in their judgment is most judicious, and adapted to remove the evil." This of course deferred, but did not avert, the main question.

This brought, in 1840, a much larger number of memorials and petitions; and very strong attempts were made by the abolitionists to obtain some decided action. The committee this year referred to what had been done last year, and declared it inexpedient to do anything further. The subject was indefinitely postponed. At this time it was resolved that the Assembly should meet only once in three years.* Accordingly, it did not meet till 1843. In 1843, several memorials were again presented, and some resolutions offered to the Assembly, of which this was one (Minutes of the General Assembly for 1843, p. 15):

Resolved, That we affectionately and earnestly urge upon the Ministers, Sessions, Presbyteries and Synods connected with this Assembly, that they treat this as all other sins of great magnitude; and, by a diligent, kind and faithful application of the means which God has given them, by instruction, remonstrance, reproof and effective discipline, seek to purify the church of this great iniquity.

This resolution they declined. They passed the following:

Whereas there is in this Assembly great diversity of opinion as to the proper and best mode of action on the subject of slavery; and whereas, in such circumstances, any expression of sentiment would carry with it but little weight, as it would be passed by a small majority, and must operate to produce alienation and division; and whereas the Assembly of 1839, with great unanimity, referred this whole subject to the lower judicatories, to take such order as in their judgment might be adapted to remove the evil; — *Resolved*, That the Assembly do not think it for the edification of the church for this body to take any action on the subject.

They, however, passed the following:

Resolved, That the fashionable amusement of promiscuous dancing is so entirely unscriptural, and eminently and exclusively that of "the world which lieth in wickedness," and so wholly inconsistent with the spirit of Christ, and with that propriety of Christian deportment and that purity of heart which his followers are bound to maintain, as to render it not only improper and injurious for professing Christians either to partake in it, or to qualify their children for it, by teaching them the *art*, but also to call for the faithful and judicious exercise of discipline on the part of Church Sessions, when any of the members of their churches have been guilty.

Three years after, in 1846, the General

---

* The synods were also made courts of last appeal in judicial cases.

Assembly published the following declaration of sentiment:

1. The system of slavery, as it exists in these United States, viewed either in the laws of the several states which sanction it, or in its actual operation and results in society, is intrinsically unrighteous and oppressive; and is opposed to the prescriptions of the law of God, to the spirit and precepts of the gospel, and to the best interests of humanity.

2. The testimony of the General Assembly, from A. D. 1787 to A. D. 1818, inclusive, has condemned it; and it remains still the recorded testimony of the Presbyterian Church of these United States against it, from which we do not recede.

3. We cannot, therefore, withhold the expression of our deep regret that slavery should be continued and countenanced by any of the members of our churches; and we do earnestly exhort both them and the churches among whom it exists to use all means in their power to put it away from them. Its perpetuation among them cannot fail to be regarded by multitudes, influenced by their example, as sanctioning the system portrayed in it, and maintained by the statutes of the several slave-holding states, wherein they dwell. Nor can any mere mitigation of its severity, prompted by the humanity and Christian feeling of any who continue to hold their fellow-men in bondage, be regarded either as a testimony against the system, or as in the least degree changing its essential character.

4. But, while we believe that many evils incident to the system render it important and obligatory to bear testimony against it, yet would we not undertake to determine the degree of moral turpitude on the part of individuals involved by it. This will doubtless be found to vary, in the sight of God, according to the degree of light and other circumstances pertaining to each. In view of all the embarrassments and obstacles in the way of emancipation interposed by the statutes of the slave-holding states, and by the social influence affecting the views and conduct of those involved in it, we cannot pronounce a judgment of general and promiscuous condemnation, implying that destitution of Christian principle and feeling which should exclude from the table of the Lord all who should stand in the legal relation of masters to slaves, or justify us in withholding our ecclesiastical and Christian fellowship from them. We rather sympathize with, and would seek to succor them in their embarrassments, believing that separation and secession among the churches and their members are not the methods God approves and sanctions for the reformation of his church.

5. While, therefore, we feel bound to bear our testimony against slavery, and to exhort our beloved brethren to remove it from them as speedily as possible, by all appropriate and available means, we do at the same time condemn all divisive and schismatical measures, tending to destroy the unity and disturb the peace of our church, and deprecate the spirit of denunciation and inflicting severities, which would cast from the fold those whom we are rather bound, by the spirit of the gospel, and the obligations of our covenant, to instruct, to counsel, to exhort, and thus to lead in the ways of God; and towards whom, even though they may err, we ought to exercise forbearance and brotherly love.

6. As a court of our Lord Jesus Christ, we possess no legislative authority; and as the General Assembly of the Presbyterian Church, we possess no judiciary authority. We have no right to institute and prescribe a test of Christian character and church membership, not recognized and sanctioned in the sacred Scriptures, and in our standards, by which we have agreed to walk. We must leave, therefore, this matter with the sessions, presbyteries and synods, — the judicatories to whom pertains the right of judgment to act in the administration of discipline, as they may judge it to be their duty, constitutionally subject to the General Assembly only in the way of general review and control.

When a boat is imperceptibly going down stream on a gentle but strong current, we can see its passage only by comparing objects with each other on the shore.

If this declaration of the New-school General Assembly be compared with that of 1818, it will be found to be far less outspoken and decided in its tone, while in the mean time slavery had become four-fold more powerful. In 1818 the Assembly states that the most virtuous portion of the community in slave states abhor slavery, and wish its *extermination.* In 1846 the Assembly states with regret that slavery is still continued and countenanced by any of the members of our churches. The testimony of 1818 has the frank, outspoken air of a unanimous document, where there was but one opinion. That of 1846 has the guarded air of a compromise ground out between the upper and nether millstone of two contending parties, — it is winnowed, guarded, cautious and careful.

Considering the document, however, in itself, it is certainly a very good one; and it would be a very proper expression of Christian feeling, had it related to an evil of any common magnitude, and had it been uttered in any common crisis; but let us consider what was the evil attacked, and what was the crisis. Consider the picture which the Kentucky Synod had drawn of the actual state of things among them :—" The members of slave-families separated, never to meet again until the final judgment; brothers and sisters, parents and children, husbands and wives, daily torn asunder, and permitted to see each other no more; the shrieks and agonies, proclaiming as with trumpet-tongue the iniquity and cruelty of the system; the cries of the sufferers going up to the ears of the Lord of Sabaoth : not a neighborhood where those heart-rending scenes are not displayed; not a village or road without the sad procession of manacled outcasts, whose chains and mournful countenances tell they are exiled by force from all that heart holds dear; Christian professors rending the mother from her child, to sell her into returnless exile."

This was the language of the Kentucky Synod fourteen years before; and those scenes had been going on ever since, and are going on now, as the advertisements of every Southern paper show; and yet the church of Christ since 1818 had done nothing but express regret, and hold grave metaphysical discussions as to whether slavery was an "evil per se," and censure the rash action of men who, in utter despair of stopping the evil any other way, tried to stop it by excluding slave-holders from the church. As if it were not better that one slave-holder in a hundred should stay out of the church, if he be peculiarly circumstanced, than that all this horrible agony and iniquity should continually receive the sanction of the church's example! Should not a generous Christian man say, "If church excision will stop this terrible evil, let it come, though it does bear hardly upon me! Better that I suffer a little injustice than that this horrible injustice be still credited to the account of Christ's church. Shall I embarrass the whole church with my embarrassments? What if I am careful and humane in my treatment of my slaves,—what if, in my heart, I have repudiated the wicked doctrine that they are my property, and am treating them as my brethren,—what am I then doing? All the credit of my example goes to give force to the system. The church ought to reprove this fearful injustice, and reprovers ought to have clean hands; and if I cannot really get clear of this, I had better keep out of the church till I can."

Let us consider, also, the awful intrenchments and strength of the evil against which this very moderate resolution was discharged. "A money power of two thousand millions of dollars, held by a small body of able and desperate men; that body raised into a political aristocracy by special constitutional provisions; cotton, the product of slave-labor, forming the basis of our whole foreign commerce, and the commercial class thus subsidized; the press bought up; the Southern pulpit reduced to vassalage; the heart of the common people chilled by a bitter prejudice against the black race; and our leading men bribed by ambition either

to silence or open hostility."* And now, in this condition of things, the whole weight of these churches goes in support of slavery, from the fact of their containing slave-holders. No matter if they did not participate in the abuses of the system; nobody wants them to do that. The slave-power does not wish professors of religion to separate families, or over-work their slaves, or do any disreputable thing,— that is not their part. The slave power wants pious, tender-hearted, generous and humane masters, and must have them, to hold up the system against the rising moral sense of the world; and the more pious and generous the better. Slavery could not stand an hour without these men. What then? These men uphold the system, and that great anti-slavery body of ministers uphold these men. That is the final upshot of the matter.

Paul says that we must remember those that are in bonds, as bound with them. Suppose that this General Assembly had been made up of men who had been fugitives. Suppose one of them had had his daughters sent to the New Orleans slave-market, like Emily and Mary Edmondson; that another's daughter had died on the overland passage in a slave-coffle, with no nurse but a slave-driver, like poor Emily Russell; another's wife died broken-hearted, when her children were sold out of her bosom; and another had a half-crazed mother, whose hair had been turned prematurely white with agony. Suppose these scenes of agonizing partings, with shrieks and groans, which the Kentucky Synod says have been witnessed so long among the slaves, had been seen in these ministers' families, and that they had come up to this discussion with their hearts as scarred and seared as the heart of poor old Paul Edmondson, when he came to New York to beg for his daughters. Suppose that they saw that the horrid system by which all this had been done was extending every hour; that professed Christians in every denomination at the South declared it to be an appointed institution of God; that all the wealth, and all the rank, and all the fashion, in the country, were committed in its favor; and that they, like Aaron, were sent to stand between the living and the dead, that the plague might be stayed.

Most humbly, most earnestly, let it be

* Speech of W. Phillips, Boston.

submitted to the Christians of this nation, and to Christians of all nations, for such an hour and such a crisis was this action sufficient? Did it *do* anything? Has it had the least effect in stopping the evil? And, in such a horrible time, ought not something to be *done* which will have that effect?

Let us continue the history. It will be observed that the resolution concludes by referring the subject to subordinate judicatories. The New School Presbytery of Cincinnati, in which were the professors of Lane Seminary, suspended Mr. Graham from the ministry for teaching that the Bible justified slavery; thereby establishing the principle that this was a heresy inconsistent with Christian fellowship. The Cincinnati Synod confirmed this decision. The General Assembly reversed this decision, and restored Mr. Graham. The delegate from that presbytery told them that they would *never* retrace their steps, and so it proved. The Cincinnati Presbytery refused to receive him back. All honor be to them for it! Here, at least, was a principle established, as far as the New School Cincinnati Presbytery is concerned,— and a principle as far as the General Assembly is concerned. By this act the General Assembly established the fact that the New School Presbyterian Church *had* not decided the Biblical defence of slavery to be a heresy.

For a man to teach that there are not three persons in the Trinity is heresy.

For a man to teach that all these three Persons authorize a system which even Mahometan princes have abolished from mere natural shame and conscience, is no heresy!

The General Assembly proceeded further to show that it considered this doctrine no heresy, in the year 1846, by inviting the Old School General Assembly to the celebration of the Lord's supper with them. Connected with this Assembly were, not only Dr. Smylie, and all those bodies who, among them, had justified not only slavery in the abstract, but some of its worst abuses, by the word of God; yet the New School body thought these opinions *no heresy* which should be a bar to Christian communion!

In 1849 the General Assembly declared[*] that there had been no information before the Assembly to prove that the members in slave states were not doing all that they could, in the providence of God, to bring about the possession and enjoyment of liberty by the enslaved. This is a remarkable declaration, if we consider that in Kentucky there are

no stringent laws against emancipation, and that, either in Kentucky or Virginia, the slave can be set free by simply giving him a pass to go across the line into the next state.

In 1850 a proposition was presented in the Assembly, by the Rev. H. Curtiss, of Indiana, to the following effect: "That the enslaving of men, or holding them as property, is an offence, as defined in our Book of Discipline, ch. 1, sec. 3; and as such it calls for inquiry, correction and removal, in the manner prescribed by our rules, and should be treated with a due regard to all the aggravating or mitigating circumstances in each case." Another proposition was from an elder in Pennsylvania, affirming "that slaveholding was, *prima facie*, an offence within the meaning of our Book of Discipline, and throwing upon the slave-holder the burden of showing such circumstances as will take away from him the guilt of the offence."[*]

Both these propositions were rejected. The following was adopted: "That slavery is fraught with many and great evils; that they deplore the workings of the whole system of slavery; that the holding of our fellow-men in the condition of slavery, except in those cases where it is unavoidable *from the laws of the state, the obligations of guardianship, or the demands of humanity,* is an offence, in the proper import of that term, as used in the Book of Discipline, and should be regarded and treated in the same manner as other offences: also referring this subject to sessions and presbyteries." The vote stood eighty-four to sixteen, under a written protest of the minority, who were for no action in the present state of the country. Let the reader again compare this action with that of 1818, and he will see that the boat is still drifting,— especially as even this moderate testimony was not unanimous. Again, in this year of 1850, they avow themselves ready to meet, in a spirit of fraternal kindness and Christian love, any overtures for reünion which may be made to them by the Old School body.

In 1850 was passed the cruel fugitive slave law. What deeds were done then! Then to our free states were transported those scenes of fear and agony before acted only on slave soil. Churches were broken up. Trembling Christians fled. Husbands and wives were separated. Then to the poor African was fulfilled the dread doom

* Minutes of the New School Assembly, p. 188.

* These two resolutions are given on the authority of Goodel's History. I do not find them in the Minutes.

denounced on the wandering Jew,— "Thou shalt find no ease, neither shall the sole of thy foot have rest; but thy life shall hang in doubt before thee, and thou shalt fear day and night, and shalt have no assurance of thy life." Then all the world went one way,— all the wealth, all the power, all the fashion. Now, if ever, was a time for Christ's church to stand up and speak for the poor.

The General Assembly met. She was earnestly memorialized to speak out. Never was a more glorious opportunity to show that the kingdom of Christ is not of this world. A protest then, from a body so numerous and respectable, might have saved the American church from the disgrace it now wears in the eyes of all nations. O that she had once spoken! What said the Presbyterian Church? She said *nothing*, and the thanks of political leaders were accorded to her. She had done *all* they desired.

Meanwhile, under this course of things, the number of presbyteries in slave-holding states had increased from *three* to *twenty!* and this church has now under its care from fifteen to twenty thousand members in slave states.

So much for the course of a decided anti-slavery body in union with a few slave-holding churches. So much for a most discreet, judicious, charitable, and brotherly attempt to test by experience the question, What communion hath light with darkness, and what concord hath Christ with Belial? The slave-system is darkness,— the slave-system is Belial! and every attempt to harmonize it with the profession of Christianity will be just like these. Let it be here recorded, however, that a small body of the most determined opponents of slavery in the Presbyterian Church seceded and formed the *Free Presbyterian Church*, whose terms of communion are, an entire withdrawal from slave-holding. Whether this principle be a correct one, or not, it is worthy of remark that it was adopted and carried out by the Quakers,— the only body of Christians involved in this evil who have ever succeeded in freeing themselves from it.

Whether church discipline and censure is an appropriate medium for correcting such immoralities and heresies in individuals, or not, it is enough for the case that this has been the established opinion and practice of the Presbyterian Church.

If the argument of Charles Sumner be contemplated, it will be seen that the history of this Presbyterian Church and the history of our United States have strong points of similarity. In both, at the outset, the strong influence was anti-slavery, even among slave-holders. In both there was no difference of opinion as to the desirableness of abolishing slavery ultimately; both made a concession, the smallest which could possibly be imagined; both made the concession in all good faith, contemplating the speedy removal and extinction of the evil; and the history of both is alike. The little point of concession spread, and absorbed, and acquired, from year to year, till the United States and the Presbyterian Church stand *just where they do.* Worse has been the history of the Methodist Church. The history of the Baptist Church shows the same principle; and, as to the Episcopal Church, it has never done anything *but* comply, either North or South. It differs from all the rest in that it has never had any resisting element, except now and then a protestant, like William Jay, a worthy son of him who signed the Declaration of Independence.

The slave power has been a united, consistent, steady, uncompromising principle. The resisting element has been, for many years, wavering, self-contradictory, compromising. There has been, it is true, a deep, and ever increasing hostility to slavery in a decided majority of ministers and church-members in free states, *taken as individuals*. Nevertheless, the sincere opponents of slavery have been unhappily divided among themselves as to principles and measures, the extreme principles and measures of some causing a hurtful reäction in others. Besides this, other great plans of benevolence have occupied their time and attention; and the result has been that they have formed altogether inadequate conceptions of the extent to which the cause of God on earth is imperilled by American slavery, and of the duty of Christians in such a crisis. They have never had such a conviction as has aroused, and called out, and united their energies, on this, as on other great causes. Meantime, great organic influences in church and state are, much against their wishes, neutralizing their influence against slavery,— sometimes even arraying it in its favor. The perfect inflexibility of the slave-system, and its absolute refusal to allow any discussion of the subject, has reduced all those who wish to have religious action in common with slave-holding churches to the alternative of either giving up the support of the South for that object, or giving up their protest against slavery. This has held out a strong temptation to men who have had benevolent and laudable objects to carry, and who did not realize the full peril of the slave-system, nor appreciate the moral power of Christian protest against it. When, therefore, cases have arisen where the choice lay between sacrificing what they considered the interests of a good object, or giving up their right of protest, they have generally preferred the latter. The decision has always gone in this way: The slave power *will not* concede,— we *must*. The South says, "We will take no religious book that has anti-slavery principles in it." The Sunday School Union drops Mr. Gallaudet's History of Joseph. Why? Because they approve óf slavery? Not at all. They look upon slavery with horror. What then? "The South will not read our books, if we do not do it. They will not give up, and we must. We *can do more good* by introducing gospel truth with this omission than we can by using our protestant power." This, probably, was thought and said honestly. The argument is plausible, but the concession is none the less real. The slave power has got the victory, and got it by the very best of men from the very best of motives; and, so that it has the victory, it cares not how it gets it. And although it may be said that the amount in each case of these concessions is in itself but small, yet, when we come to add together all that have been made from time to time by every different denomination, and by every different benevolent organization, the aggregate is truly appalling; and, in consequence of all these united, what are we now reduced to?

Here we are, in this crisis,— here in this nineteenth century, when all the world is dissolving and reconstructing on principles of universal liberty,— we Americans, who are sending our Bibles and missionaries to Christianize Mahometan lands, are upholding, with all our might and all our influence, a system of worn-out heathenism which even the Bey of Tunis has repudiated!

The Southern church has baptized it in the name of the Father, the Son, and the Holy Ghost. This worn-out, old, effete system of Roman slavery, which Christianity once gradually but certainly abolished, has been dug up out of its dishonored grave, a few laws of extra cruelty, such as Rome never knew, have been added to it, and now, baptized and sanctioned by the whole Southern church, it is going abroad conquering and to conquer! The only power left to the Northern church is the protesting power; and will they use it? Ask the Tract Soci-

ety if they will publish a tract on the sinfulness of slavery, though such tract should be made up *solely* from the writings of Jonathan Edwards or Dr. Hopkins! Ask the Sunday School Union if it will publish the facts about this heathenism, as it has facts about Burmah and Hindostan! Will they? O, that they would answer *Yes!*

Now, it is freely conceded that all these sad results have come in consequence of the motions and deliberations of good men, who meant well; but it has been well said that, in critical times, when one wrong step entails the most disastrous consequences, to *mean* well is not enough.

In the crisis of a disease, to mean well and lose the patient,— in the height of a tempest, to mean well and wreck the ship,— in a great moral conflict, to mean well and lose the battle,— these are things to be lamented. We *are* wrecking the ship,— we *are* losing the battle. There is no mistake about it. A little more sleep, a little more slumber, a little more folding of the hands to sleep, and we shall awake in the whirls of that maëlstrom which has but one passage, and that downward.

There is yet one body of Christians whose influence we have not considered, and that a most important one,— the Congregationalists of New England and of the West. From the very nature of Congregationalism, she cannot give so united a testimony as Presbyterianism; yet Congregationalism has spoken out on slavery. Individual bodies have spoken very strongly, and individual clergymen still stronger. They have remonstrated with the General Assembly, and they have very decided anti-slavery papers. But, considering the whole state of public sentiment, considering the critical nature of the exigency, the mighty sweep and force of all the causes which are going in favor of slavery, has the vehemence and force of the testimony of Congregationalism, *as a body,* been equal to the dreadful emergency? It has testimonies on record, very full and explicit, on the evils of slavery; but testimonies are not all that is wanted. There is abundance of testimonies on record in the Presbyterian Church, for that matter, quite as good and quite as strong as any that have been given by Congregationalism. There have been quite as many anti-slavery men in the New School Presbyterian Church as in the Congregational,— quite as strong anti-slavery newspapers; and the Presbyterian Church has had trial of this matter that the Congregational Church has never been exposed to. It has had slave-holders in its own communion; and from this trial Congregationalism has, as yet, been mostly exempt. Being thus free, ought not the testimony of Congregationalism to have been more than equal? ought it not to have done more than testify? — ought it not to have fought for the question? Like the brave three hundred in Thermopylæ left to defend the liberties of Greece, when all others had fled, should they not have thrown in heart and soul, body and spirit? Have they done it?

Compare the earnestness which Congregationalism has spent upon some other subjects with the earnestness which has been spent upon this. Dr. Taylor taught that all sin consists in sinning, and therefore that there could be no sin till a person had sinned; and Dr. Bushnell teaches some modifications of the doctrine of the Trinity, nobody seeming to know precisely what. The South Carolina presbyteries teach that slavery is approved by God, and sanctioned by the example of patriarchs and prophets. Supposing these, now, to be all heresies, which of them is the worst? — which will bring the worst practical results? And, if Congregationalism had fought this slavery heresy as some of her leaders fought Dr. Bushnell and Dr. Taylor, would not the style of battle have been more earnest? Have not both these men been denounced as dangerous heresiarchs, and as preaching doctrines that tend to infidelity? And pray where does this other doctrine tend? As sure as there is a God in heaven is the certainty that, if the Bible really did defend slavery, fifty years hence would see every honorable and high-minded man an infidel.

Has, then, the past influence of Congregationalism been according to the nature of the exigency and the weight of the subject? But the late convention of Congregationalists at Albany, including ministers both from New England and the Western States, did take a stronger and more decided ground. Here is their resolution:

Resolved, That, in the opinion of this convention, it is the tendency of the gospel, wherever it is preached in its purity, to correct all social evils, and to destroy sin in all its forms; and that it is the duty of Missionary Societies to grant aid to churches in slave-holding states in the support of such ministers only as shall so preach the gospel, and inculcate the principles and application of gospel discipline, that, with the blessing of God, it shall have its full effect in awakening and enlightening the moral sense in regard to slavery, and in bringing to pass the speedy abolition of that stupendous wrong; and that wherever a minister is not permitted so to preach, he should, in accordance with the directions of Christ, "depart out of that city."

This resolution is a matter of hope and gratulation in many respects. It was passed in a very large convention,— the largest ever assembled in this country, fully representing the Congregationalism of the United States,—and the occasion of its meeting was considered, in some sort, as marking a new era in the progress of this denomination.

The resolution was passed unanimously. It is decided in its expression, and looks to practical action, which is what is wanted. It says it will support no ministers in slave states whose preaching does not tend to destroy slavery; and that, if they are not allowed to preach freely on the subject, they must depart.

That the ground thus taken will be efficiently sustained, may be inferred from the fact that the Home Missionary Society, which is the organ of this body, as well as of the New School Presbyterian Church, has uniformly taken decided ground upon this subject in their instructions to missionaries sent into slave states. These instructions are ably set forth in their report of March, 1853. When application was made to them, in 1850, from a slave state, for missionaries who would let slavery alone, they replied to them, in the most decided language, that it could not be done; that, on the contrary, they must understand that one grand object in sending missionaries to slave states is, as far as possible, to redeem society from all forms of sin; and that, "if utter silence respecting slavery is to be maintained, one of the greatest inducements to send or retain missionaries in the slave states is taken away."

The society furthermore instructed their missionaries, if they could not be heard on this subject in one city or village, to go to another; and they express their conviction that their missionaries have made progress in awakening the consciences of the people. They say that they do not suffer the subject to sleep; that they do not let it alone because it is a delicate subject, but they discharge their consciences, whether their message be well received, or whether, as in some instances, it subjects them to opposition, opprobrium, and personal danger; and that where their endeavors to do this have not been tolerated, they have, in repeated cases, at great sacrifice, resigned their position, and departed to other fields. In their report of this year they also quote letters from ministers in slave-holding states, by which it appears that they have actually secured, in the face of much opposition, the right publicly to preach and propagate their sentiments upon this subject.

One of these missionaries says, speaking of slavery, "We are determined to remove this great difficulty in our way, or die in the attempt. As Christians and as freemen, we will suffer this libel on our religion and institutions to exist no longer."

This is noble ground.

And, while we are recording the protesting power, let us not forget the Scotch seceders and covenanters, who, with a pertinacity and decision worthy of the children of the old covenant, have kept themselves clear from the sin of slavery, and have uniformly protested against it. Let us remember, also, that the Quakers did pursue a course which actually freed all their body from the sin of slave-holding, thus showing to all other denominations that what has been done once can be done again. Also, in all denominations, individual ministers and Christians, in hours that have tried men's souls, have stood up to bear their testimony. Albert Barnes, in Philadelphia, standing in the midst of a great, rich church, on the borders of a slave state, and with all those temptations to complicity which have silenced so many, has stood up, in calm fidelity, and declared the whole counsel of God upon this subject. Nay, more: he recorded his solemn protest, that "NO INFLUENCES OUT OF THE CHURCH COULD SUSTAIN SLAVERY AN HOUR, IF IT WERE NOT SUSTAINED IN IT;" and, in the last session of the General Assembly, which met at Washington, disregarding all suggestions of policy, he boldly held the Presbyterian Church up to the strength of her past declarations, and declared it her duty to attempt the entire abolition of slavery throughout the world. So, in darkest hour, Dr. Channing bore a noble testimony in Boston, for which his name shall ever live. So, in Illinois, E. P. Lovejoy and Edward Beecher, with their associates, formed the Illinois Anti-slavery Society, amid mobs and at the hazard of their lives; and, a few hours after, Lovejoy was shot down in attempting to defend the twice-destroyed anti-slavery press. In the Old-school Presbyterian Church, William and Robert Breckenridge, President Young, and others, have preached in favor of emancipation in Kentucky. Le Roy Sunderland, in the Methodist Church, kept up his newspaper under ban of his superiors, and with a bribe on his life of fifty thousand dollars. Torrey, meekly patient, died in a prison,

saying, "If I am a guilty man, I am a very guilty one; for I have helped four hundred slaves to freedom, who but for me would have died slaves." Dr. Nelson was expelled by mobs from Missouri for the courageous declaration of the truth on slave soil. All these were in the ministry. Nor are these all. Jesus Christ has not wholly deserted us yet. There have been those who have learned how joyful it is to suffer shame and brave death in a good cause.

Also there have been private Christians who have counted nothing too dear for this sacred cause. Witness Richard Dillingham, and John Garrett, and a host of others, who took joyfully the spoiling of their goods.

But yet, notwithstanding this, the awful truth remains, that the whole of what has been done by the church has not, as yet, perceptibly abated the evil. The great system is stronger than ever. It is confessedly the dominant power of the nation. The whole power of the government, and the whole power of the wealth, and the whole power of the fashion, and the practical organic workings of the large bodies of the church, are all gone one way. The church is familiarly quoted as being on the side of slavery. Statesmen on both sides of the question have laid that down as a settled fact. Infidels point to it with triumph; and America, too, is beholding another class of infidels,—a class that could have grown up only under such an influence. Men, whose whole life is one study and practice of benevolence, are now ranked as infidels, because the position of church organizations misrepresents Christianity, and they separate themselves from the church. We would offer no excuse for any infidels who take for their religion mere anti-slavery zeal, and, under this guise, gratify a malignant hatred of real Christianity. But such defences of slavery from the Bible as some of the American clergy have made are exactly fitted to make infidels of all honorable and high-minded men. The infidels of olden times were not much to be dreaded, but such infidels as these are not to be despised. Woe to the church when the moral standard of the infidel is higher than the standard of the professed Christian! for the only armor that ever proved invincible to infidelity is the *armor of righteousness.*

Let us see how the church organizations work now, practically. What do Bruin & Hill, Pulliam & Davis, Bolton, Dickins & Co., and Matthews, Branton & Co., depend upon to keep their slave-factories and slave-barracoons full, and their business brisk? Is it to be supposed that they are not men like ourselves? Do they not sometimes tremble at the awful workings of fear, and despair, and agony, which they witness when they are tearing asunder living hearts in the depths of those fearful slave-prisons? What, then, keeps down the consciences of these traders? It is the public sentiment of the community where they live; and that public sentiment is made by ministers and church-members. The trader sees plainly enough a logical sequence between the declarations of the church and the practice of his trade. He sees plainly enough that, if slavery is sanctioned by God, and it is right to set it up in a new territory, it is right to take the means to do this; and, as slaves do not grow on bushes in Texas, it is necessary that there should be traders to gather up coffles and carry them out there; — and, as they cannot always take whole families, it is necessary that they should part them; and, as slaves will not go by moral suasion, it is necessary tHÃt they should be forced; and, as gentle force will not do, they must whip and torture. Hence come gags, thumb-screws, cowhides, blood,— all *necessary* measures of carrying out what Christians say God sanctions.

So goes the argument one way. Let us now trace it back the other. The South Carolina and Mississippi Presbyteries maintain opinions which, in their legitimate results, endorse the slave-trader. The Old School General Assembly maintains fellowship with these Presbyteries, without discipline or protest. The New School Assembly signifies its willingness to reünite with the Old, while, at the same time, it declares the system of slavery an abomination, a gross violation of the most sacred rights, and so on. Well, now the chain is as complete as need be. All parts are in; every one standing in his place, and saying just what is required, and no more. The trader does the repulsive work, the Southern church defends him, the Northern church defends the South. Every one does as much for slavery as would be at all expedient, considering the latitude they live in. This is the practical result of the thing.

The melancholy part of the matter is, that while a large body of New School men, and many Old School, are decided anti-slavery men, this denominational position carries their influence on the other side. As goes the General Assembly, so goes their influence. The following affecting letter on this subject was written by that eminently pious man, Dr. Nelson, whose work on Infidelity

is one of the most efficient popular appeals that has ever appeared:

I have resided in North Carolina more than forty years, and been intimately acquainted with the system, and I can scarcely even think of its operations without shedding tears. It causes me excessive grief to think of my own poor slaves, for whom I have for years been trying to find a free home. It strikes me with equal astonishment and horror to hear Northern people make light of slavery. Had they seen and known as much of it as I, they could not thus treat it, unless callous to the deepest woes and degradation of humanity, and dead both to the religion and philanthropy of the gospel. But many of them are doing just what the hardest-hearted tyrants of the South most desire. Those tyrants would not, on any account, have them advocate or even apologize for slavery in an *unqualified* manner. This would be bad policy with the North. I wonder that Gerrit Smith should understand slavery so much better than most of the Northern people. How true was his remark, on a certain occasion, namely, that the South are laughing in their sleeves, to think what dupes they make of most of the people at the North in regard to the real character of slavery! Well did Mr. Smith remark that the system, carried out on its fundamental principle, would as soon enslave any laboring white man as the African. But, *if it were not for the support of the North, the fabric of blood would fall at once.* And of all the efforts of public bodies at the North to sustain slavery, the Connecticut General Association has made the best one. I have never seen anything so well constructed in that line as their resolutions of June, 1836. The South certainly could not have asked anything more effectual. But, of all Northern periodicals, the *New York Observer* must have the preference, as an efficient support of slavery. I am not sure but it does more than all things combined to keep the dreadful system alive. It is just the succor demanded by the South. Its abuse of the abolitionists is music in Southern ears, which operates as a charm. But nothing is equal to its harping upon the "religious privileges and instruction" of the slaves of the South. And nothing could be so false and injurious (to the cause of freedom and religion) as the impression it gives on that subject. I say what I know when I speak in relation to this matter. I have been intimately acquainted with the religious opportunities of slaves, — in the constant habit of hearing the sermons which are preached to them. And I solemnly affirm, that, during the forty years of my residence and observation in this line, I never heard a single one of these sermons but what was taken up with the obligations and duties of slaves to their masters. Indeed, I never heard a sermon to slaves but what made obedience to masters by the slaves the fundamental and supreme law of religion. Any candid and intelligent man can decide whether such preaching is not, as to religious purposes, worse than none at all.

Again: it is wonderful how the credulity of the North is subjected to imposition in regard to the *kind treatment* of slaves. For myself, I can clear up the apparent contradictions found in writers who have resided at or visited the South. The "majority of slave-holders," say some, "treat their slaves with kindness." Now, this may be true in certain states and districts; setting aside all questions of treatment, except such as refer to the *body*. And yet, while the "majority of slave-holders" in a certain section may be kind, the majority of *slaves* in that section will be treated with cruelty. This is the truth in many such cases, that while there may be thirty men who may have but one slave apiece, and that a house-servant, a *single* man in their neighborhood may have a hundred slaves, — all field-hands, half-fed, worked excessively, and whipped most cruelly. This is what I have often seen. To give a case, to show the awful influence of slavery upon the master, I will mention a Presbyterian elder, who was esteemed one of the best men in the region, — a very kind master. I was called to his death-bed to write his will. He had what was considered a favorite house-servant, a female. After all other things were disposed of, the elder paused, as if in doubt what to do with "Su." I entertained pleasing expectations of hearing the word "liberty" fall from his lips; but who can tell my surprise when I heard the master exclaim, "What shall be done with Su? I am afraid she will never be under a master severe enough for her." Shall I say that both the dying elder and his "Su" were members of the same church, the latter statedly receiving the emblems of á Saviour's dying love from the former!

All this temporizing and concession has been excused on the plea of brotherly love. What a plea for us Northern freemen! Do we think the slave-system such a happy, desirable thing for our brothers and sisters at the South? Can we look at our common schools, our neat, thriving towns and villages, our dignified, intelligent, self-respecting farmers and mechanics, all concomitants of free labor, and think slavery any blessing to our Southern brethren? That system which beggars all the lower class of whites, which curses the very soil, which eats up everything before it, like the palmer-worm, canker and locust, — which makes common schools an impossibility, and the preaching of the gospel almost as much so, — this system a blessing! Does brotherly love require us to help the South preserve it?

Consider the educational influences under which such children as Eva and Henrique must grow up there! We are speaking of what many a Southern mother feels, of what makes many a Southern father's heart sore. Slavery has been spoken of in its influence on the family of the slave. There are those, who never speak, who could tell, if they would, its influence on the family of the master. It makes one's heart ache to see generation after generation of lovely, noble children exposed to such influences. What a country the South might be, could she develop herself without this curse! If the Southern character, even under all these disadvantages, retains so much that is noble,

and is fascinating even in its faults, what might it do with free institutions?

Who is the real, who is the true and noble lover of the South? — they who love her with all these faults and incumbrances, or they who fix their eyes on the bright ideal of what she might be, and say that these faults are no proper part of her? Is it true love to a friend to accept the ravings of insanity as a true specimen of his mind? Is it true love to accept the disfigurement of sickness as a specimen of his best condition? Is it not truer love to say, "This curse is no part of our brother; it dishonors him; it does him injustice; it misrepresents him in the eyes of all nations. We love his better self, and we will have no fellowship with his betrayer. This is the part of true, generous, Christian love."

But will it be said, "The abolition enterprise was begun in a wrong spirit, by reckless, meddling, impudent fanatics"? Well, supposing that this were true, how came it to be so? If the church of Christ had begun it *right*, these so-called fanatics would not have begun it *wrong*. In a deadly pestilence, if the right physicians do not prescribe, everybody will prescribe, — men, women and children, will prescribe, — because something must be done. If the Presbyterian Church in 1818 had pursued the course the Quakers did, there never would have been any fanaticism. The Quakers did all by brotherly love. They melted the chains of Mammon only in the fires of a divine charity. When Christ came into Jerusalem, after all the mighty works that he had done, while all the so-called better classes were non-committal or opposed, the multitude cut down branches of palm-trees and cried Hosanna! There was a most indecorous tumult. The very children caught the enthusiasm, and were crying Hosannas in the temple. This was contradictory to all ecclesiastical rules. It was a highly improper state of things. The Chief Priests and Scribes said unto Jesus, "Master, speak unto these that they hold their peace." That gentle eye flashed as he answered, "I TELL YOU, IF THESE SHOULD HOLD THEIR PEACE, THE VERY STONES WOULD CRY OUT."

Suppose a fire bursts out in the streets of Boston, while the regular conservators of the city, who have the keys of the fire-engines, and the regulation of fire-companies, are sitting together in some distant part of the city, consulting for the public good. The cry of fire reaches them, but they think it a false alarm. The fire is no less real, for all that. It burns, and rages, and roars, till everybody in the neighborhood sees that something must be done. A few stout leaders break open the doors of the engine-houses, drag out the engines, and begin, regularly or irregularly, playing on the fire. But the destroyer still advances. Messengers come in hot haste to the hall of these deliberators, and, in the unselect language of fear and terror, revile them for not coming out.

"Bless me!" says a decorous leader of the body, "what horrible language these men use!"

"They show a very bad spirit," remarks another; "we can't possibly join them in such a state of things."

Here the more energetic members of the body rush out, to see if the thing be really so; and in a few minutes come back, if possible more earnest than the others.

"O! there is a fire!—a horrible, dreadful fire! The city is burning,—men, women, children, all burning, perishing! Come out, come out! As the Lord liveth, there is but a step between us and death!"

"I am not going out; everybody that goes gets crazy," says one.

"I 've noticed," says another, "that as soon as anybody goes out to look, he gets just so excited,—I won't look."

But by this time the angry fire has burned into their very neighborhood. The red demon glares into their windows. And now, fairly aroused, they get up and begin to look out.

"Well, there is a fire, and no mistake!" says one.

"Something ought to be done," says another.

"Yes," says a third; "if it was n't for being mixed up with such a crowd and rabble of folks, I 'd go out."

"Upon my word," says another, "there are women in the ranks, carrying pails of water! There, one woman is going up a ladder to get those children out. What an indecorum! If they 'd manage this matter properly, we would join them."

And now come lumbering over from Charlestown the engines and fire-companies.

"What impudence of Charlestown," say these men, "to be sending over here,—just as if we could not put our own fires out! They have fires over there, as much as we do."

And now the flames roar and burn, and shake hands across the streets. They leap over the steeples, and glare demoniacally out of the church-windows.

"For Heaven's sake, DO SOMETHING!" is the cry. "Pull down the houses! Blow up those blocks of stores with gunpowder! *Anything* to stop it."

"See, now, what ultra, radical measures they are going at," says one of these spectators.

Brave men, who have rushed into the thickest of the fire, come out, and fall dead in the street.

"They are impracticable enthusiasts. They have thrown their lives away in foolhardiness," says another.

So, church of Christ, burns that awful fire! Evermore burning, burning, burning, over church and altar; burning over senate-house and forum; burning up liberty, burning up religion! No *earthly* hands kindled that fire. From its sheeted flame and wreaths of sulphurous smoke glares out upon thee the eye of that ENEMY who was a murderer from the beginning. It is a fire that BURNS TO THE LOWEST HELL!

Church of Christ, there *was* an hour when this fire might have been extinguished by thee. Now, thou standest like a mighty man astonished,— like a mighty man that cannot save. But the Hope of Israel is not dead. The Saviour thereof in time of trouble is yet alive.

If every church in our land were hung with mourning,— if every Christian should put on sack-cloth,— if "the priest should weep between the porch and the altar," and say, "Spare thy people, O Lord, and give not thy heritage to reproach!"— that were not too great a mourning for such a time as this.

O, church of Jesus! consider what hath been said in the midst of thee. What a heresy hast thou tolerated in thy bosom! *Thy* God the defender of slavery!— *thy* God the patron of slave-law! Thou hast suffered the character of thy God to be slandered. Thou hast suffered false witness against thy Redeemer and thy Sanctifier. The Holy Trinity of heaven has been foully traduced in the midst of thee; and that God whose throne is awful in justice has been made the patron and leader of oppression.

This is a sin against every Christian on the globe.

Why do we love and adore, beyond all things, our God? Why do we say to him, from our inmost souls, "Whom have I in heaven but thee, and there is none upon earth I desire beside thee"? Is this a bought-up worship? — is it a cringing and hollow subserviency, because he is great and rich and powerful, and we *dare* not do otherwise? His eyes are a flame of fire; — he reads the inmost soul, and will accept no such service. From our souls we adore and love him, because he is holy and just and good, and will not at all acquit the wicked. We love him because he is the father of the fatherless, the judge of the widow; — because he lifteth all who fall, and raiseth them that are bowed down. We love Jesus Christ, because he is the *Lamb without spot*, the one altogether lovely. We love the Holy Comforter, because he comes to convince the world of sin, and of righteousness, and of judgment. O, holy church universal, throughout all countries and nations! O, ye great cloud of witnesses, of all people and languages and tongues! — differing in many doctrines, but united in crying Worthy is the Lamb that was slain, for he hath redeemed us from all iniquity! — *awake!* — arise up! — be not silent! Testify against this heresy of the latter day, which, if it were possible, is deceiving the very elect. Your God, your glory, is slandered. Answer with the voice of many waters and mighty thunderings! Answer with the innumerable multitude in heaven, who cry, day and night, Holy, holy, holy! *just* and *true* are thy ways, O King of saints!

CHAPTER III.

MARTYRDOM.

AT the time when the Methodist and Presbyterian Churches passed the anti-slavery resolutions which we have recorded, the system of slavery could probably have been extirpated by the church with comparatively little trouble. Such was the experience of the Quakers, who tried the experiment at that time, and succeeded. The course they pursued was the simplest possible. They districted their church, and appointed regular committees, whose business it was to go from house to house, and urge the rules of the church individually on each slave-holder, one by one. This was done in a spirit of such simplicity and brotherly love that very few resisted the appeal. They quietly yielded up, in obedience to their own consciences, and the influence of their brethren. This mode of operation, though gentle, was as efficient as the calm sun of summer, which,

by a few hours of patient shining, dissolves the iceberg on which all the storms of winter have beat in vain. O, that so happy a course had been thought of and pursued by all the other denominations! But the day is past when this monstrous evil would so quietly yield to gentle and persuasive measures.

At the time that the Quakers made their attempt, this Leviathan in the reeds and rushes of America was young and callow, and had not learned his strength. Then he might have been "drawn out with a hook;" then they might have "made a covenant with him, and taken him for a servant forever;" but now Leviathan is full-grown. "Behold, the hope of him is vain. Shall not men be cast down even at the sight of him? None is so fierce that dare stir him up. His scales are his pride, shut up together as with a close seal; one is so near to another that no air can come between them. The flakes of his flesh are joined together. They are firm in themselves, they cannot be moved. His heart is as firm as a stone, yea, as hard as the nether mill-stone. The sword of him that layeth at him cannot hold. He esteemeth iron as straw, and brass as rotten wood. Arrows cannot make him flee; sling-stones are turned with him into stubble. He laugheth at the shaking of a spear. Upon the earth there is not his like: he is king over all the children of pride."

There are those who yet retain the delusion that, somehow or other, without any very particular effort or opposition, by a soft, genteel, rather apologetic style of operation, Leviathan is to be converted, baptized and Christianized. They can try it. Such a style answers admirably as long as it is understood to mean nothing. But just the moment that Leviathan finds they are in earnest, then they will see the consequences. The debates of all the synods in the United States, as to whether he is an evil *per se*, will not wake him. In fact, they are rather a pleasant humdrum. Nor will any resolutions that they "behold him with regret" give him especial concern; neither will he be much annoyed by the expressed expectation that he is to die somewhere about the millennium. Notwithstanding all the recommendations of synods and conferences, Leviathan himself has but an indifferent opinion of his own Christianity, and an impression that he would not be considered quite in keeping with the universal reign of Christ on earth; but he does n't much concern himself about the prospect of giving up the ghost at so very remote a period.

But let any one, either North or South, take the sword of the Spirit and make one pass under his scales that he shall feel, and then he will know what sort of a conflict Christian had with Apollyon. Let no one, either North or South, undertake this warfare, to whom fame, or ease, or wealth, or anything that this world has to give, are too dear to be sacrificed. Let no one undertake it who is not prepared to hate his own good name, and, if need be, his life also. For this reason, we will give here the example of one martyr who died for this cause; for it has been well said that "the blood of the martyr is the seed of the church."

The Rev. Elijah P. Lovejoy was the son of a Maine woman, a native of that state which, barren in all things else, is fruitful in noble sentiments and heroic deeds. Of his early days we say nothing. Probably they were like those of other Maine boys. We take up his history where we find him a clergyman in St. Louis, Mo., editing a religious newspaper. Though professing not to be a technical abolitionist, he took an open and decided stand against slavery. This aroused great indignation, and called forth threats of violence. Soon after, a mob, composed of the most respectable individuals of the place, burned alive a negro-man in the streets of St. Louis, for stabbing the officers who came to arrest him. This scene of protracted torture lasted till the deed was completed, and the shrieks of the victim for a more merciful death were disregarded. In his charge to the grand jury, Judge Lawless decided that no legal redress could be had for this outrage, because, being the act of an infuriated multitude, it was above the law. Elijah Lovejoy expressed, in determined language, his horror of the transaction and of the decision. For these causes, his office was torn down and destroyed by the mob. Happening to be in St. Charles, a mob of such men as only slavery could raise attacked the house to take his life. His distracted wife kept guard at his door, struggling with men armed with bludgeons and bowie-knives, who swore that they would have his heart's blood. A woman's last despair, and the aid of friends, repelled the first assault; but when the mob again returned, he made his escape. Lovejoy came to Alton, Illinois, and there set up his paper. The mob followed him. His press was twice

destroyed, and he was daily threatened with assassination.

Before his press was destroyed the third time, a call was issued in his paper for a convention of the enemies of slavery and friends of free inquiry in Illinois, for the purpose of considering and recommending measures adapted to meet the existing crisis. This call was signed by about two hundred and fifty persons from different parts of the state, among whom was the Rev. E. Beecher, then President of Illinois College. This gathering brought together a large number. When they met for discussion, the mobocrats came also among them, and there was a great ferment. The mob finally out-voted and dissolved the convention. It was then resolved to form an anti-slavery society, and to issue a declaration of sentiments, and an address to the people of the state. Threats were expressed that, if Mr. Lovejoy continued to print his paper, the mob would destroy his expected press. In this state of excitement, Mr. Beecher, at the request of the society, preached two sermons, setting forth the views and course of conduct which were contemplated in the proposed movement. They were subsequently set forth in a published document, an extract from which will give the reader an idea of what they were:

1. We shall endeavor to induce all our fellow-citizens to elevate their minds above all selfish, pecuniary, political, and local interests; and, from a deep sense of the presence of God, to regard solely the eternal and immutable principles of truth, which no human legislature or popular sentiment can alter or remove.
2. We shall endeavor to present the question as one between this community and God, — a subject on which He deeply feels, and on which we owe great and important duties to Him and to our fellow-citizens.
3. We shall endeavor, as far as possible, to allay the violence of party strife, to remove all unholy excitement, and to produce mutual confidence and kindness, and a deep interest in the welfare of all parts of our nation; and a strong desire to preserve its union and promote its highest welfare.

Our entire reliance is upon truth and love, and the influences of the Holy Spirit. We desire to compel no one to act against his judgment or conscience by an oppressive power of public sentiment; but to arouse all men to candid thought, and impartial inquiry in the fear of God, we do desire.

And, to accomplish this end, we shall use the same means that are used to enlighten and elevate the public mind on all other great moral subjects, — personal influence, public address, the pulpit and the press.

4. We shall endeavor to produce a new and radical investigation of the principles of human rights, and of the relations of all just legislation to them, deriving our principles from the nature of the human mind, the relations of man to God, and the revealed will of the Creator.

5. We shall then endeavor to examine the slave-laws of our land in the light of these principles, and to prove that they are essentially sinful, and that they are at war alike with the will of God and all the interests of the master, the slave, and the community at large.

6. We shall then endeavor to show in what manner communities where such laws exist may relieve themselves at once, in perfect safety and peace, both of the guilt and dangers of the system.

7. And, until communities can be aroused to do their duties, we shall endeavor to illustrate and enforce the duties of individual slave-holders in such communities.

To views presented in this spirit and manner one would think there could have been no rational objection. The only difficulty with them was, that, though calm and kind, they were felt to be in earnest; and at once Leviathan was wide awake.

The next practical question was, Shall the third printing-press be defended, or shall it also be destroyed?

There was a tremendous excitement, and a great popular tumult. The timid, prudent, peace-loving majority, who are to be found in every city, who care not what principles prevail, so they promote their own interest, were wavering and pusillanimous, and thus encouraged the mob. Every motive was urged to induce Mr. Beecher and Mr. Love-joy to forego the attempt to reëstablish the press. The former was told that a price had been set on his head in Missouri,—a fashion-able mode of meeting argument in the pro-slavery parts of this country. Mr. Lovejoy had been so long threatened with assassina-tion, day and night, that the argument with him was something musty. Mr. Beecher was also told that the interests of the college of which he was president would be sacrificed, and that, if he chose to risk his own safety, he had no right to risk those interests. But Mr. Beecher and Mr. Lovejoy both felt that the very foundation principle of free insti-tutions had at this time been seriously com-promised, all over the country, by yielding up the right of free discussion at the clamors of the mob; that it was a precedent of very wide and very dangerous application.

In a public meeting, Mr. Beecher ad-dressed the citizens on the right of main-taining free inquiry, and of supporting every man in the right of publishing and speaking his conscientious opinions. He

read to them some of those eloquent pas-sages in which Dr. Channing had maintained the same rights in very similar circumstances in Boston. He read to them extracts from foreign papers, which showed how the American character suffered in foreign lands from the prevalence in America of Lynch law and mob violence. He defended the right of Mr. Lovejoy to print and publish his conscientious opinions; and, finally, he read from some Southern journals extracts in which they had strongly condemned the course of the mob, and vindicated Mr. Lovejoy's right to express his opinions. He then proposed to them that they should pass resolutions to the following effect:

That the free communication of opinion is one of the invaluable rights of man; and that every citizen may freely speak, write or print, on any subject, being responsible for the abuse of the liberty.

That maintenance of these principles should be independent of all regard to persons and senti-ments.

That they should be especially maintained with regard to unpopular sentiments, since no others need the protection of law.

That on these grounds alone, and without re-gard to political and moral differences, we agree to protect the press and property of the editor of the *Alton Observer*, and support him in his right to publish whatever he pleases, holding him re-sponsible only to the laws of the land.

These resolutions, so proposed, were to be taken into consideration at a final meeting of the citizens, which was to be held the next day.

That meeting was held. Their first step was to deprive Mr. Beecher, and all who were not citizens of that county, of the right of debating on the report to be presented. The committee then reported that they deeply regretted the excited state of feeling; that they cherished strong confidence that the citizens would refrain from undue excite-ments; that the exigences of the time re-quired a course of moderation and compro-mise; and that, while there was no disposition to prevent free discussion in general, they deemed it indispensable to the public tran-quillity that Mr. Lovejoy should not publish a paper in that city; not wishing to reflect in the slightest degree upon Mr. Lovejoy's character and motives. All that the meet-ing waited for now was, to hear whether Mr. Lovejoy would comply with their recom-mendation.

One of the committee arose, and expressed his sympathy for Mr. Lovejoy, characterizing him as an unfortunate individual, hoping that they would all consider that he had a wife

15

and family to support, and trusting that they would disgrace him as little as possible; but that he and all his party would see the necessity of making a compromise, and departing from Alton. What followed is related in the words of Mr. Beecher, who was present at the meeting:

As Brother Lovejoy rose to reply to the speech above mentioned, I watched his countenance with deep interest, not to say anxiety. I saw no tokens of disturbance. With a tranquil, self-possessed air, he went up to the bar within which the chairman sat, and, in a tone of deep, tender and subdued feeling, spoke as follows:

"I feel, Mr. Chairman, that this is the most solemn moment of my life. I feel, I trust, in some measure to these, my fellow-citizens, to the church of which I am a minister, to my country, and to God. And let me beg of you, before I proceed further, to construe nothing I shall say as being disrespectful to this assembly. I have no such feeling: far from it. And if I do not act or speak according to their wishes at all times, it is because I cannot conscientiously do it.

"It is proper I should state the whole matter, as I understand it, before this audience. I do not stand here to argue the question as presented by the report of the committee. My only wonder is that the honorable gentleman the chairman of that committee, for whose character I entertain great respect, though I have not the pleasure of his personal acquaintance, — my only wonder is how that gentleman could have brought himself to submit such a report.

"Mr. Chairman, I do not admit that it is the business of this assembly to decide whether I shall or shall not publish a newspaper in this city. The gentlemen have, as the lawyers say, made a wrong issue. I have the right to do it. I know that I have the right freely to speak and publish my sentiments, subject only to the laws of the land for the abuse of that right. This right was given me by my Maker; and is solemnly guaranteed to me by the constitution of these United States, and of this state. What I wish to know of you is, whether you will protect me in the exercise of this right; or whether, as heretofore, I am to be subjected to personal indignity and outrage. These resolutions, and the measures proposed by them, are spoken of as a compromise — a compromise between two parties. Mr. Chairman, this is not so. There is but one party here. It is simply a question whether the law shall be enforced, or whether the mob shall be allowed, as they now do, to continue to trample it under their feet, by violating with impunity the rights of an innocent individual.

"Mr. Chairman, what have I to compromise? If freely to forgive those who have so greatly injured me, if to pray for their temporal and eternal happiness, if still to wish for the prosperity of your city and state, notwithstanding all the indignities I have suffered in it, — if this be the compromise intended, then do I willingly make it. My rights have been shamefully, wickedly outraged; this I know, and feel, and can never forget. But I can and do freely forgive those who have done it.

"But if by a compromise is meant that I should cease from doing that which duty requires of me,

I cannot make it. And the reason is, that I fear God more than I fear man. Think not that I would lightly go contrary to public sentiment around me. The good opinion of my fellow-men is dear to me, and I would sacrifice anything but principle to obtain their good wishes; but when they ask me to surrender this, they ask for more than I can, than I dare give. Reference is made to the fact that I offered a few days since to give up the editorship of the *Observer* into other hands. This is true; I did so because it was thought or said by some that perhaps the paper would be better patronized in other hands. They declined accepting my offer, however, and since then we have heard from the friends and supporters of the paper in all parts of the state. There was but one sentiment among them, and this was that the paper could be sustained in no other hands than mine. It is also a very different question, whether I shall voluntarily, or at the request of friends, yield up my post; or whether I shall forsake it at the demand of a mob. The former I am at all times ready to do, when circumstances occur to require it; as I will never put my personal wishes or interests in competition with the cause of that Master whose minister I am. But the latter, be assured, I NEVER will do. God, in his providence, — so say all my brethren, and so I think, — has devolved upon me the responsibility of maintaining my ground here; and, Mr. Chairman, I am determined to do it. A voice comes to me from Maine, from Massachusetts, from Connecticut, from New-York, from Pennsylvania, — yea, from Kentucky, from Mississippi, from Missouri, — calling upon me, in the name of all that is dear in heaven or earth, to stand fast; and, by the help of God, I WILL STAND. I know I am but one, and you are many. My strength would avail but little against you all. You can crush me, if you will; but I shall die at my post, for I cannot and will not forsake it.

"Why should I flee from Alton? Is not this a free state? When assailed by a mob at St. Louis, I came hither, as to the home of freedom and of the laws. The mob has pursued me here, and why should I retreat again? Where can I be safe, if not here? Have not I a right to claim the protection of the laws? What more can I have in any other place? Sir, the very act of retreating will embolden the mob to follow me wherever I go. No, sir, there is no way to escape the mob, but to abandon the path of duty; and that, God helping me, I will never do.

"It has been said here, that my hand is against every man, and every man's hand against me. The last part of the declaration is too painfully true. I do indeed find almost every hand lifted against me; but against whom in this place has my hand been raised? I appeal to every individual present; whom of you have I injured? Whose character have I traduced? Whose family have I molested? Whose business have I meddled with? If any, let him rise here and testify against me. — No one answers.

"And do not your resolutions say that you find nothing against my private or personal character? And does any one believe that, if there was anything to be found, it would not be found and brought forth? If in anything I have offended against the law, I am not so popular in this community as that it would be difficult to convict me. You have courts and judges and juries; they find nothing against me. And now you come together for the purpose of driving out a confessedly innocent man, for no cause but that he dares to think and speak as his conscience and his God dictate. Will conduct like this stand the scrutiny of your country, of posterity, above all, of the judgment-day? For remember, the Judge of that day is no respecter of persons. Pause, I beseech you, and reflect! The present excitement will soon be over; the voice of conscience will at last be heard. And in some season of honest thought, even in this world, as you review the scenes of this hour, you will be compelled to say, 'He was right; he was right.'

"But you have been exhorted to be lenient and compassionate, and in driving me away to affix no unnecessary disgrace upon me. Sir, I reject all such compassion. You cannot disgrace me. Scandal and falsehood and calumny have already done their worst. My shoulders have borne the burthen till it sits easy upon them. You may hang me up, as the mob hung up the individuals of Vicksburg! You may burn me at the stake, as they did McIntosh at St. Louis; or you may tar and feather me, or throw me into the Mississippi, as you have often threatened to do; but you cannot disgrace me. I, and I alone, can disgrace myself; and the deepest of all disgrace would be, at a time like this, to deny my Master by forsaking his cause. He died for me; and I were most unworthy to bear his name, should I refuse, if need be, to die for him.

"Again, you have been told that I have a family, who are dependent on me; and this has been given as a reason why I should be driven off as gently as possible. It is true, Mr. Chairman, I am a husband and a father; and this it is that adds the bitterest ingredient to the cup of sorrow I am called to drink. I am made to feel the wisdom of the apostle's advice; 'It is better not to marry.' I know, sir, that in this contest I stake not my life only, but that of others also. I do not expect my wife will ever recover the shock received at the awful scenes through which she was called to pass at St. Charles. And how was it the other night, on my return to my house? I found her driven to the garret, through fear of the mob, who were prowling round my house. And scarcely had I entered the house ere my windows were broken in by the brickbats of the mob, and she so alarmed that it was impossible for her to sleep or rest that night. I am hunted as a partridge upon the mountains; I am pursued as a felon through your streets; and to the guardian power of the law I look in vain for that protection against violence which even the vilest criminal may claim.

"Yet think not that I am unhappy. Think not that I regret the choice that I have made. While all around me is violence and tumult, all is peace within. An approving conscience, and the rewarding smile of God, is a full recompense for all that I forego and all that I endure. Yes, sir, I enjoy a peace which nothing can destroy. I sleep sweetly and undisturbed, except when awaked by the brickbats of the mob.

"No, sir, I am not unhappy. I have counted the cost, and stand prepared freely to offer up my all in the service of God. Yes, sir, I am fully aware of all the sacrifice I make, in here pledging myself to continue this contest to the last. — (Forgive these tears — I had not intended to shed them, and they flew not for myself but others.) But I am commanded to forsake father and mother and wife and children for Jesus' sake; and as his professed disciple I stand prepared to do it. The time for fulfilling this pledge in my case, it seems

to me, has come. Sir, I dare not flee away from Alton. Should I attempt it, I should feel that the angel of the Lord, with his flaming sword, was pursuing me wherever I went. It is because I fear God that I am not afraid of all who oppose me in this city. No, sir, the contest has commenced here; and here it must be finished. Before God and you all, I here pledge myself to continue it, if need be, till death. If I fall, my grave shall be made in Alton."

In person Lovejoy was well formed, in voice and manners refined; and the pathos of this last appeal, uttered in entire simplicity, melted every one present, and produced a deep silence. It was one of those moments when the feelings of an audience tremble in the balance, and a grain may incline them to either side. A proposition to support him might have carried, had it been made at that moment. The charm was broken by another minister of the gospel, who rose and delivered a homily on the necessity of compromise, recommending to Mr. Lovejoy especial attention to the example of Paul, who was let down in a basket from a window in Damascus; as if Alton had been a heathen city under a despotic government! The charm once broken, the meeting became tumultuous and excited, and all manner of denunciations were rained down upon abolitionists. The meeting passed the resolutions reported by the committee, and refused to resolve to aid in sustaining the law against illegal violence; and the mob perfectly understood that, do what they might, they should have no disturbance. It being now understood that Mr. Lovejoy would not retreat, it was supposed that the crisis of the matter would develop itself when his printing-press came on shore.

During the following three days there seemed to be something of a reäction. One of the most influential of the mob-leaders was heard to say that it was of no use to go on destroying presses, as there was money enough on East to bring new ones, and that they might as well let the fanatics alone.

This somewhat encouraged the irresolute city authorities, and the friends of the press thought, if they could get it once landed, and safe into the store of Messrs. Godfrey & Gilman, that the crisis would be safely passed. They therefore sent an express to the captain to delay the landing of the boat till three o'clock in the morning, and the leaders of the mob, after watching till they were tired, went home; the press was safely landed and deposited, and all supposed that the trouble was safely passed. Under this impression Mr. Beecher left Alton, and returned home.

We will give a few extracts from Mr. Beecher's narrative, which describe his last interview with Mr. Lovejoy on that night, after they had landed and secured the press :

Shortly after the hour fixed on for the landing of the boat, Mr. Lovejoy arose, and called me to go with him to see what was the result. The moon had set and it was still dark, but day was near ; and here and there a light was glimmering from the window of some sick room, or of some early riser. The streets were empty and silent, and the sounds of our feet echoed from the walls as we passed along. Little did he dream, at that hour, of the contest which the next night would witness ; that these same streets would echo with the shouts of an infuriate mob, and be stained with his own heart's blood.

We found the boat there, and the press in the warehouse ; aided in raising it to the third story. We were all rejoiced that no conflict had ensued, and that the press was safe ; and all felt that the crisis was over. We were sure that the store could not be carried by storm by so few men as had ever yet acted in a mob ; and though the majority of the citizens would not aid to defend the press, we had no fear that they would aid in an attack. So deep was this feeling that it was thought that a small number was sufficient to guard the press afterward ; and it was agreed that the company should be divided into sections of six, and take turns on successive nights. As they had been up all night, Mr. Lovejoy and myself offered to take charge of the press till morning ; and they retired.

The morning soon began to dawn ; and that morning I shall never forget. Who that has stood on the banks of the mighty stream that then rolled before me can forget the emotions of sublimity that filled his heart, as in imagination he has traced those channels of intercourse opened by it and its branches through the illimitable regions of this western world ? I thought of future ages, and of the countless millions that should dwell on this mighty stream ; and that nothing but the truth would make them free. Never did I feel as then the value of the right for which we were contending thoroughly to investigate and fearlessly to proclaim that truth. O, the sublimity of moral power ! By it God sways the universe. By it he will make the nations free.

I passed through the scuttle to the roof, and ascended to the highest point of the wall. The sky and the river were beginning to glow with approaching day, and the busy hum of business to be heard. I looked with exultation on the scenes below. I felt that a bloodless battle had been gained for God and for the truth ; and that Alton was redeemed from eternal shame. And as all around grew brighter with approaching day, I thought of that still brighter sun, even now dawning on the world, and soon to bathe it with floods of glorious light.

Brother Lovejoy, too, was happy. He did not exult ; he was tranquil and composed, but his countenance indicated the state of his mind. It was a calm and tranquil joy, for he trusted in God that the point was gained ; that the banner of an unfettered press would soon wave over that mighty stream.

Vain hopes ! How soon to be buried in a martyr's grave ! Vain, did I say ? No : they are not vain. Though dead he still speaketh ; and a united world can never silence his voice.

The conclusion of the tragedy is briefly told. A volunteer company, of whom Lovejoy was one, was formed to act under the mayor in defence of the law. The next night the mob assailed the building at ten o'clock. The store consisted of two stone buildings in one block, with doors and windows at each end, but no windows at the sides. The roof was of wood. Mr. Gilman, opening the end door of the third story, asked what they wanted. They demanded the press. He refused to give it up, and earnestly entreated them to go away without violence, assuring them that, as the property had been committed to their charge, they should defend it at the risk of their lives. After some ineffectual attempts, the mob shouted to set fire to the roof. Mr. Lovejoy, with some others, went out to defend it from this attack, and was shot down by the deliberate aim of one of the mob. After this wound he had barely strength to return to the store, went up one flight of stairs, fell and expired.

Those within then attempted to capitulate, but were refused with curses by the mob, who threatened to burn the store, and shoot them as they came out. At length the building was actually on fire, and they fled out, fired on as they went by the mob. So terminated the Alton tragedy.

When the noble mother of Lovejoy heard of his death, she said, " It is well. I had rather he would die so than forsake his principles." All is not over with America while such mothers are yet left. Was she not blessed who could give up such a son in such a spirit ? Who was that woman whom God pronounced blessed above all women ? Was it not she who saw her dearest crucified ? So differently does God see from what man sees.

<hr/>

CHAPTER IV.

SERVITUDE IN THE PRIMITIVE CHURCH COMPARED WITH AMERICAN SLAVERY.

> " Look now upon this picture !——and on this."
>   HAMLET.

It is the standing claim of those professors of religion at the South who support slavery that they are pursuing the same course in relation to it that Christ and his apostles did. Let us consider the course of Christ and his apostles, and the nature of the kingdom which they founded, and see if this be the fact.

Napoleon said, "Alexander, Cæsar, Charlemagne and myself, have founded empires; but upon what did we rest the creation of our genius? Upon force. Jesus Christ alone founded his empire upon LOVE."

The desire to be above others in power, rank and station, is one of the deepest in human nature. If there is anything which distinguishes man from other creatures, it is that he is *par excellence* an *oppressive animal.* On this principle, as Napoleon observed, all empires have been founded; and the idea of founding a kingdom in any other way had not even been thought of when Jesus of Nazareth appeared.

When the serene Galilean came up from the waters of Jordan, crowned and glorified by the descending Spirit, and began to preach, saying, "The *kingdom* of God is at hand," what expectations did he excite? Men's heads were full of armies to be marshalled, of provinces to be conquered, of cabinets to be formed, and offices to be distributed. There was no doubt at all that he could get all these things for them, for had he not miraculous power?

Therefore it was that Jesus of Nazareth was very popular, and drew crowds after him.

Of these, he chose, from the very lowest walk of life, twelve men of the best and most honest heart which he could find, that he might make them his inseparable companions, and mould them, by his sympathy and friendship, into some capacity to receive and transmit his ideas to mankind.

But they too, simple-hearted and honest though they were, were bewildered and bewitched by the common vice of mankind; and, though they loved him full well, still had an eye on the offices and ranks which he was to confer, when, as they expected, this miraculous kingdom should blaze forth.

While his heart was struggling and laboring, and nerving itself by nights of prayer to meet desertion, betrayal, denial, rejection, by his beloved people, and ignominious death, *they* were forever wrangling about the offices in the new kingdom. Once and again, in the plainest way, he told them that no such thing was to be looked for; that there was to be no distinction in his kingdom, except the distinction of pain, and suffering, and self-renunciation, voluntarily assumed for the good of mankind.

His words seemed to them as idle tales. In fact, they considered him as a kind of a myth,— a mystery,— a strange, supernatural, inexplicable being, forever talking in parables, and saying things which they could not understand.

One thing only they held fast to: he was a king, he would have a kingdom; and he had told them that they should sit on twelve thrones, judging the twelve tribes of Israel.

And so, when he was going up to Jerusalem to die,— when that anguish long wrestled with in the distance had come almost face to face, and he was walking in front of them, silent, abstracted, speaking occasionally in broken sentences, of which they feared to ask the meaning,— they, behind, beguiled the time with the usual dispute of "who should be greatest."

The mother of James and John came to him, and, breaking the mournful train of revery, desired a certain thing of him,— that her two sons might sit at his right hand and his left, as prime ministers, in the new kingdom. With his sad, far-seeing eye still fixed upon Gethsemane and Calvary, he said, "Ye know not what ye ask. Are ye able to drink of the cup which I shall drink of, and to be baptized with the baptism wherewith I shall be baptized?"

James and John were both quite certain that they were able. They were willing to fight through anything for the kingdom's sake. The ten were very indignant. Were they not as willing as James and John? And so there was a contention among them.

"But Jesus called them to him and said, Ye know that the princes of the Gentiles exercise dominion over them, and their great ones exercise authority upon them; but it shall not be so among you.

"Whosoever will be great among you, let him be your minister; and whosoever will be chief among you, let him be your servant,— yea, the servant of all. For even the Son of Man came not to be ministered unto, but to minister, and to give his life a ransom for many."

Let us now pass on to another week in this history. The disciples have seen their Lord enter triumphantly into Jerusalem, amid the shouts of the multitude. An indescribable something in his air and manner convinces them that a great crisis is at hand. He walks among men as a descended God. Never were his words so thrilling and energetic. Never were words spoken on earth which so breathe and burn as these of the last week of the life of Christ. All the fervor and imagery and fire of the old prophets seemed to be raised from the dead, etherealized and transfigured in the person of this Jesus. They dare not ask him, but they are *certain* that the kingdom must be coming. They feel, in the thrill of that mighty soul, that a great cycle of time is finishing, and a new era in the world's history beginning. Perhaps at this very feast of the Passover is the time when the miraculous banner is to be unfurled, and the new, immortal kingdom proclaimed. Again the ambitious longings arise. This new kingdom shall have ranks and dignities. And who is to sustain them? While therefore their Lord sits lost in thought, revolving in his mind that simple ordinance of love which he is about to constitute the sealing ordinance of his kingdom, it is said again, "There was a strife among them which should be accounted the greatest."

This time Jesus does not remonstrate. He expresses no impatience, no weariness, no disgust. What does he, then? Hear what St. John says:

"Jesus knowing that the Father had given all things into his hands, and that he was come from God and went to God, he riseth from supper, and laid aside his garments, and took a towel and girded himself. After that, he poureth water into a basin, and began to wash the disciples' feet, and to wipe them with the towel wherewith he was girded." "After he had washed their feet and had taken his garments, and was sat down again, he said unto them, Know ye what I have done to you? Ye call me Master and Lord: and ye say well, for so I am. If I, then, your Lord and Master, have washed your feet, ye also ought to wash one another's feet; for I have given you an example that ye should do as I have done to you."

"Verily, verily I say unto you, the servant is not greater than his lord, neither he that is sent greater than he that sent him. If ye know these things, happy are ye if ye do them."

Here, then, we have the king, and the constitution of the kingdom. The king on his knees at the feet of his servants, performing the lowest menial service, with the announcement, "I have given you an example, that ye should do as I have done to you."

And when, after the descent of the Holy Ghost, all these immortal words of Christ, which had lain buried like dead seed in the heart, were quickened and sprang up in celestial verdure, then these twelve became, each one in his place, another Jesus, filled with the spirit of him who had gone heaven-ward. The primitive church, as organized by them, was a brotherhood of strict equality. There was no more contention who should be greatest; the only contention was, who should suffer and serve the most. The Christian church was an *imperium in imperio;* submitting outwardly to the laws of the land, but professing inwardly to be regulated by a higher faith and a higher law. They were dead to the world, and the world to them. Its customs were not their customs; its relations not their relations. All the ordinary relations of life, when they passed into the Christian church, underwent a quick, immortal change; so that the transformed relation resembled the old and heathen one no more than the glorious body which is raised in incorruption resembles the mortal one which was sown in corruption. The relation of marriage was changed, from a tyrannous dominion of the stronger sex over the weaker, to an intimate union, symbolizing the relation of Christ and the church. The relation of parent and child, purified from the harsh features of heathen law, became a just image of the love of the heavenly Father; and the relation of master and servant, in like manner, was refined into a voluntary relation between two equal brethren, in which the servant faithfully performed his duties *as to the Lord,* and the master gave him a full compensation for his services.

No one ever doubted that such a relation as this is an innocent one. It exists in all free states. It is the relation which exists between employer and employed generally, in the various departments of life. It is true, the master was never called upon to perform the legal act of enfranchisement, —and why? Because the very nature of the kingdom into which the master and slave had entered enfranchised him. It is not necessary for a master to write a deed of enfranchisement when he takes his slaves into Canada, or even into New York or Pennsylvania. The moment the master and slave stand together on this soil, their whole relations to each other are changed. The master may remain master, and the servant a servant; but, according to the constitution of the state they have entered, the service must be a voluntary one on the part of the slave, and the master must render a just equivalent. When the water of baptism passed over the master and the slave, both alike 'came under the great constitutional law of Christ's empire, which is this:

"Whosoever will be great among you, let him be your minister; and whosoever will be chief among you, let him be your servant, yea, the servant of all." Under such a law, servitude was dignified and made honorable, but slavery was made an impossibility.

That the church was essentially, and in its own nature, such an institution of equality, brotherhood, love and liberty, as made the existence of a slave, in the character of a slave, in it, a contradiction and an impossibility, is evident from the general scope and tendency of all the apostolic writings, particularly those of Paul.

And this view is obtained, not from a dry analysis of Greek words, and dismal discussions about the meaning of *doulos*, but from a full tide of celestial, irresistible spirit, full of life and love, that breathes in every description of the Christian church.

To all, whether bond or free, the apostle addresses these inspiring words : "There is one body, and one spirit, even as ye are called in one hope of your calling; one Lord, one faith, one baptism, one God and Father of all, who is above all, and through all, and in you all." "For through him we all have access, by one Spirit, unto the Father." "Now, therefore, ye are no more strangers and foreigners, but fellow-citizens with the saints, and of the household of God, and are built upon the foundation of the apostles and prophets, Jesus Christ, himself, being the chief corner-stone." "Ye are all the children of God, by faith in Jesus Christ; there is neither Jew nor Greek, there is neither bond nor free, there is neither male nor female, for ye are all one in Christ Jesus."

"For, as the body is one, and hath many members, and all the members of that one body, being many, are one body, so also is Christ; for by one Spirit are we all baptized into one body, whether we be Jews or Gentiles, whether we be bond or free; and whether one member suffer, all the members suffer with it, or one member be honored, all the members rejoice with it."

It was the theory of this blessed and divine unity, that whatever gift, or superiority, or advantage, was possessed by one member, was possessed by every member. Thus Paul says to them, "All things are yours; whether Paul, or Apollos, or Cephas, or life, or death, all are yours, and ye are Christ's, and Christ is God's."

Having thus represented the church as one living body, inseparably united, the apostle uses a still more awful and impressive simile. The church, he says, is one body, and that body is the fulness of Him who filleth all in all. That is, He who filleth all in all seeks this church to be the associate and complement of himself, even as a wife is of the husband. This body of believers is spoken of as a bright and mystical bride, in the world, but not of it; spotless, divine, immortal, raised from the death of sin to newness of life, redeemed by the blood of her Lord, and to be presented at last unto him, a glorious church, not having spot or wrinkle, or any such thing.

A delicate and mysterious sympathy is supposed to pervade this church, like that delicate and mysterious tracery of nerves that overspreads the human body; the meanest member cannot suffer without the whole body quivering in pain. Thus says Paul, who was himself a perfect realization of this beautiful theory : "Who is weak, and I am not weak ? Who is offended, and I burn not?" "To whom ye forgive anything, I forgive also."

But still further, individual Christians were reminded, in language of awful solemnity, "What! know ye not that your body is the temple of the Holy Ghost, which is in you, which ye have of God, and that ye are not your own?" And again, "Ye are the temple of the living God; as God hath said, I will dwell in them and walk in them." Nor was this sublime language in those days passed over as a mere idle piece of rhetoric, but was the ever-present consciousness of the soul.

Every Christian was made an object of sacred veneration to his brethren, as the temple of the living God. The soul of every Christian was hushed into awful stillness, and inspired to carefulness, watchfulness and sanctity, by the consciousness of an indwelling God. Thus Ignatius, who for his preëminent piety was called, *par excellence*, by his church, "Theophorus, *the* God-bearer," when summoned before the Emperor Trajan, used the following remarkable language: "No one can call Theophorus an evil spirit * *** * for, bearing in my heart Christ the king of heaven, I bring to nothing the arts and devices of the evil spirits."

"Who, then, is 'the God-bearer'?" asked Trajan.

"He who carries Christ in his heart," was the reply. * * * *

"Dost thou mean him whom Pontius Pilate crucified?"

"He is the one I mean," replied Ignatius. * * *

"Dost thou then bear the crucified one in thy heart?" asked Trajan.

"Even so," said Ignatius; "for it is

written, 'I will dwell in them and rest in them.'"

So perfect was the identification of Christ with the individual Christian in the primitive church, that it was a familiar form of expression to speak of an injury done to the meanest Christian as an injury done to Christ. So St. Paul says, "When ye sin so against the weak brethren, and wound their weak consciences, ye sin against Christ." He says of himself, "I live, yet not I, but Christ liveth in me."

See, also, the following extracts from a letter by Cyprian, Bishop of Carthage, to some poor Numidian churches, who had applied to him to redeem some of their members from slavery among bordering savage tribes. (Neander Denkw. I. 340.)

We could view the captivity of our brethren no otherwise than as our own, since we belong to one body, and not only love, but religion, excites us to redeem in our brethren the members of our own body. We must, even if affection were not sufficient to induce us to keep our brethren, — we must reflect that the temples of God are in captivity, and these temples of God ought not, by our neglect, long to remain in bondage. * * * Since the apostle says "as many of you as are baptized have put on Christ," so in our captive brethren we must see before us CHRIST, who hath ransomed us from the danger of captivity, who hath redeemed us from the danger of death; *Him* who hath freed us from the abyss of Satan, and who now remains and dwells in us, to free *Him* from the hands of barbarians! With a small sum of money to ransom *Him* who hath ransomed *us* by his cross and blood; and who hath permitted this to take place that our faith may be proved thereby!

Now, because the Greek word *doulos* may mean a slave, and because it is evident that there were men in the Christian church who were called *douloi*, will anybody say, in the whole face and genius of this beautiful institution, that these men were held actually as slaves in the sense of Roman and American law? Of all dry, dull, hopeless, stupidities, this is the most stupid. Suppose Christian masters did have servants who were called *douloi*, as is plain enough they did, is it not evident that the word *douloi* had become significant of something very different in the Christian church from what it meant in Roman law? It was not the business of the apostles to make new dictionaries; they did not change words,— they changed things. The baptized, regenerated, new-created *doulos*, of one body and one spirit with his master, made one with his master, even as Christ is one with the Father, a member with him of that church which is the fulness of Him who filleth all

in all,— was his relation to his Christian master like that of an American slave to his master? Would he who regarded his weakest brother as being one with Christ hold his brother as a chattel personal? Could he hold Christ as as a chattel personal? Could he sell Christ for money? Could he hold the temple of the Holy Ghost as his property, and gravely defend his right to sell, lease, mortgage or hire the same, at his convenience, as that right has been argued in the slave-holding pulpits of America?

What would have been said at such a doctrine announced in the Christian church? Every member would have stopped his ears, and cried out, "Judas!" If he was pronounced accursed who thought that the gift of the Holy Ghost might be purchased with money, what would have been said of him who held that the very temple of the Holy Ghost might be bought and sold, and Christ the Lord become an article of merchandise? Such an idea never was thought of. It could not have been refuted, for it never existed. It was an unheard-of and unsupposable work of the devil, which Paul never contemplated as even possible, that one Christian could claim a right to hold another Christian as merchandise, and to trade in the "member of the body, flesh and bones" of Christ. Such a horrible doctrine never polluted the innocence of the Christian church even in thought.

The directions which Paul gives to Christian masters and servants sufficiently show what a redeeming change had passed over the institution. In 1st Timothy, St. Paul gives the following directions, first to those who have heathen masters, second, to those who have Christian masters. That concerning heathen masters is thus expressed: "Let as many servants as are under the *yoke* count their own masters worthy of all honor, that the name of God and his doctrine be not blasphemed." In the next verse the direction is given to the servants of Christian masters: "They that have believing masters, let them not despise them because they are brethren, but rather do them service because they are faithful and beloved, partakers of the benefit." Notice, now, the contrast between these directions. The servant of the heathen master is said to be under the yoke, and it is evidently implied that the servant of the Christian master was not under the yoke. The servant of the heathen master was under the severe Roman law; the servant of the Christian master is an equal, and a brother. In these circumstances, the servant of the heathen master is commanded to obey for the sake of recommending the Christian religion. The servant of the Christian master, on the other hand, is commanded not to despise his master because he is his brother; but he is to do him service because his master is faithful and beloved, a partaker of the same glorious hopes with himself. Let us suppose, now, a clergyman, employed as a chaplain on a cotton plantation, where most of the members on the plantation, as we are informed is sometimes the case, are members of the same Christian church as their master, should assemble the hands around him and say, "Now, boys, I would not have you despise your master because he is your brother. It is true you are all one in Christ Jesus; there is no distinction here; there is neither Jew nor Greek, neither negro nor white man, neither bond nor free, but ye are all brethren,— all alike members of Christ, and heirs of the same kingdom; but you must not despise your master on this account. You must love him as a brother, and be willing to do all you can to serve him, because you see he is a partaker of the same benefit with you, and the Lord loves him as much as he does you." Would not such an address create a certain degree of astonishment both with master and servants; and does not the fact that it seems absurd show that the relation of the slave to his master in American law is a very different one from what it was in the Christian church? But again, let us quote another passage, which slave-owners are much more fond of. In Colossians 4: 22 and 5: 1,—"Servants, obey, in all things, your masters, according to the flesh; not with eye-service as men-pleasers, but in singleness of heart as fearing God; and whatsoever ye do, do it heartily as unto the Lord, and not unto men, knowing that of the Lord ye shall receive the reward of the inheritance, for ye serve the Lord Christ." "Masters, give unto servants that which is just and equal, knowing that ye also have a Master in heaven."

Now, there is nothing in these directions to servants which would show that they were chattel servants in the sense of slave-law; for they will apply equally well to every servant in Old England and New England; but there is something in the direction to masters which shows that they were not considered chattel servants by the church, because the master is commanded to give unto them that which is just and equal, as a con-

sideration for their service. Of the words "just and equal," "just" means that which is legally theirs, and "equal" means that which is in itself equitable, irrespective of law.

Now, we have the undoubted testimony of all legal authorities on American slave-law that American slavery does not *pretend* to be founded on what is just or equal either. Thus Judge Ruffin says : "Merely in the abstract it may well be asked which power of the master accords with right. The answer will probably sweep away all of them;" and this principle, so unequivocally asserted by Judge Ruffin, is all along implied and taken for granted, as we have just seen, in all the reasonings upon slavery and the slave-law. It would take very little legal acumen to see that the enacting of these words of Paul into a statute by any state would be a practical abolition of slavery in that state.

But it is said that St. Paul sent Onesimus back to his master. Indeed! but *how?* When, to our eternal shame and disgrace, the horrors of the fugitive slave-law were being enacted in Boston, and the very Cradle of Liberty resounded with the groans of the slave, and men harder-hearted than Saul of Tarsus made havoc of the church, entering into every house, haling men and women, committing them to prison; when whole churches of humble Christians were broken up and scattered like flocks of trembling sheep; when husbands and fathers were torn from their families, and mothers, with poor, helpless children, fled at midnight, with bleeding feet, through snow and ice, towards Canada; — in the midst of these scenes, which have made America a by-word and a hissing and an astonishment among all nations, there were found men, Christian men, ministers of the gospel of Jesus, even,— alas! that this should ever be written,— who, standing in the pulpit, in the name and by the authority of Christ, justified and sanctioned these enormities, and used this most loving and simple-hearted letter of the martyr Paul to justify these unheard-of atrocities!

He who said, "Who is weak and I am not weak? Who is offended and I burn not?"— he who called the converted slave his own body, the son begotten in his bonds, and who sent him to the brother of his soul with the direction, "Receive him as myself, not now as a slave, but above a slave, a brother beloved,"—this beautiful letter, this outgush of tenderness and love passing the love of woman, was held up to be pawed over by the polluted hobgoblin-fingers of slave-dealers and slave-whippers as their *lettre de cachet*, signed and sealed in the name of Christ and his apostles, giving full authority to carry back slaves to be tortured and whipped, and sold into perpetual bondage, as were Henry Long and Thomas Sims! Just as well might a mother's letter, when, with prayers and tears, she commits her first and only child to the cherishing love and sympathy of some trusted friend, be used as an inquisitor's warrant for inflicting imprisonment and torture upon that child. Had not every fragment of the apostle's body long since mouldered to dust, his very bones would have moved in their grave, in protest against such slander on the Christian name and faith. And is it come to this, O Jesus Christ! have such things been done in thy name, and art thou silent yet? Verily, thou art a God that hidest thyself, O God of Israel, the Saviour!

CHAPTER V.

But why did not the apostles preach against the legal relation of slavery, and seek its overthrow in the state? This question is often argued as if the apostles were in the same condition with the clergy of Southern churches, members of republican institutions, law-makers, and possessed of all republican powers to agitate for the repeal of unjust laws.

Contrary to all this, a little reading of the New Testament will show us that the apostles were almost in the condition of outlaws, under a severe and despotic government, whose spirit and laws they reprobated as unchristian, and to which they submitted, just as they exhorted the slave to submit, as to a necessary evil.

Hear the apostle Paul thus enumerating the political privileges incident to the ministry of Christ. Some false teachers had risen in the church at Corinth, and controverted his teachings, asserting that they had greater pretensions to authority in the Christian ministry than he. St. Paul, defending his apostolic position, thus speaks: "Are they ministers of Christ? (I speak as a fool) I am more; in labors more abundant, in stripes above measure, in prisons more frequent, in deaths oft. Of the Jews five times received I forty stripes save one. Thrice was I beaten with rods, once was I stoned, thrice I suffered shipwreck, a night

and a day have I been in the deep: in journeyings often, in perils of waters, in perils of robbers, in perils by mine own country-men, in perils by the heathen, in perils in the city, in perils in the wilderness, in perils in the sea, in perils among false brethren: in weariness and painfulness, in watchings often, in hunger and thirst, in fastings often, in cold and nakedness."

What enumeration of the hardships of an American slave can more than equal the hardships of the great apostle to the Gentiles? He had nothing to do with laws except to suffer their penalties. They were made and kept in operation without asking him, and the slave did not suffer any more from them than he did.

It would appear that the clergymen of the South, when they imitate the example of Paul, in letting entirely alone the civil relation of the slave, have left wholly out of their account how different is the position of an American clergyman, in a republican government, where he himself helps make and sustain the laws, from the condition of the apostle, under a heathen despotism, with whose laws he could have nothing to do.

It is very proper for an outlawed slave to address to other outlawed slaves exhortations to submit to a government which neither he nor they have any power to alter.

We read, in sermons which clergymen at the South have addressed to slaves, exhortations to submission, and patience, and humility, in their enslaved condition, which would be exceedingly proper in the mouth of an apostle, where he and the slaves were alike fellow-sufferers under a despotism whose laws they could not alter, but which assume quite another character when addressed to the slave by the very men who make the laws that enslave them.

If a man has been waylaid and robbed of all his property, it would be very becoming and proper for his clergyman to endeavor to reconcile him to his condition, as, in some sense, a dispensation of Providence; but if the man who robs him should come to him, and address to him the same exhortations, he certainly will think that that is quite another phase of the matter.

A clergyman of high rank in the church, in a sermon to the negroes, thus addresses them:

Almighty God hath been pleased to make you slaves here, and to give you nothing but labor and poverty in this world, which you are obliged to submit to, as it is his will that it should be so. And think within yourselves what a terrible thing it would be, after all your labors and sufferings in this life, to be turned into hell in the next life;

and, after wearing out your bodies in service here, to go into a far worse slavery when this is over, and your poor souls be delivered over into the possession of the devil, to become his slaves forever in hell, without any hope of ever getting free from it. If, therefore, you would be God's freemen in heaven, you must strive to be good and serve him here on earth. Your bodies, you know, are not your own : they are at the disposal of those you belong to ; but your precious souls are still your own, which nothing can take from you, if it be not your own fault. Consider well, then, that if you lose your souls by leading idle, wicked lives here, you have got nothing by it in this world, and you have lost your all in the next. For your idleness and wickedness is generally found out, and your bodies suffer for it here ; and, what is far worse, if you do not repent and amend, your unhappy souls will suffer for it hereafter.

Now, this clergyman was a man of undoubted sincerity. He had read the New Testament, and observed that St. Paul addressed exhortations something like this to slaves in his day.

But he entirely forgot to consider that Paul had not the rights of a republican clergyman; that he was not a maker and sustainer of those laws by which the slaves were reduced to their condition, but only a fellow-sufferer under them. A case may be supposed which would illustrate this principle to the clergyman. Suppose that he were travelling along the highway, with all his worldly property about him, in the shape of bank-bills. An association of highwaymen seize him, bind him to a tree, and take away the whole of his worldly estate. This they would have precisely the same right to do that the clergyman and his brother republicans have to take all the earnings and possessions of their slaves. The property would belong to these highwaymen by exactly the same kind of title,— not because they have earned it, but simply because they have got it and are able to keep it.

The head of this confederation, observing some dissatisfaction upon the face of the clergyman, proceeds to address him a religious exhortation to patience and submission, in much the same terms as he had before addressed to the slaves. "Almighty God has been pleased to take away your entire property, and to give you nothing but labor and poverty in this world, which you are obliged to submit to, as it is his will that it should be so. Now, think within yourself what a terrible thing it would be, if, having lost all your worldly property, you should, by discontent and want of resignation, lose also your soul ; and, having been robbed of all your property here, to have your poor soul delivered over to the possession of the

devil, to become his property forever in hell, without any hope of ever getting free from it. Your property now is no longer your own ; we have taken possession of it ; but your precious soul is still your own, and nothing can take it from you but your own fault. Consider well, then, that if you lose your soul by rebellion and murmuring against this dispensation of Providence, you will get nothing by it in this world, and will lose your all in the next."

Now, should this clergyman say, as he might very properly, to these robbers,— " There is no necessity for my being poor in this world, if you will only give me back my property which you have taken from me," he is only saying precisely what the slaves to whom he has been preaching might say to him and his fellow-republicans.

CHAPTER VI.

BUT it may still be said that the apostles might have commanded Christian masters to perform the act of legal emancipation in all cases. Certainly they might, and it is quite evident that they did not.

The professing primitive Christian regarded and treated his slave as a brother, but in the eye of the law he was still his chattel personal,— a thing, and not a man. Why did not the apostles, then, strike at the legal relation ? Why did they not command every Christian convert to sunder that chain at once ? In answer, we say that every attempt at reform which comes from God has proceeded 'uniformly in this manner,— to destroy the *spirit* of an abuse first, and leave the *form* of it to drop away, of itself, afterwards,— to girdle the poisonous tree, and leave it to take its own time for dying.

This mode of dealing with abuses has this advantage, that it is compendious and universal, and can apply to that particular abuse in all ages, and under all shades and modifications. If the apostle, in that outward and physical age, had merely attacked the legal relation, and had rested the whole burden of obligation on dissolving that, the corrupt and selfish principle might have run into other forms of oppression equally bad, and sheltered itself under the technicality of avoiding legal slavery. God, therefore, dealt a surer blow at the monster, by 'singling out the precise spot where his heart beat, and saying to his apostles, " Strike there ! "

Instead of saying to the slave-holder,

"manumit your slave," it said to him, "treat him as your brother," and left to the slave-holder's conscience to say how much was implied in this command.

In the directions which Paul gave about slavery, it is evident that he considered the legal relation with the same indifference with which a gardener treats a piece of unsightly bark, which he perceives the growing vigor of a young tree is about to throw off by its own vital force. He looked upon it as a part of an old, effete system of heathenism, belonging to a set of laws and usages which were waxing old and ready to vanish away.

There is an argument which has been much employed on this subject, and which is specious. It is this. That the apostles treated slavery as one of the lawful relations of life, like that of parent and child, husband and wife.

The argument is thus stated: The apostles found all the relations of life much corrupted by various abuses.

They did not attack the *relations*, but reformed the *abuses*, and thus restored the relations to a healthy state.

The mistake here lies in assuming that slavery is the lawful relation. Slavery is the corruption of a lawful relation. The lawful relation is *servitude*, and slavery is the *corruption* of servitude.

When the apostles came, all the relations of life in the Roman empire were thoroughly permeated with the principle of slavery. The relation of child to parent was slavery. The relation of wife to husband was slavery. The relation of servant to master was slavery.

The power of the father over his son, by Roman law, was very much the same with the power of the master over his slave.* He could, at his pleasure, scourge, imprison, or put him to death. The son could possess nothing but what was the property of his father; and this unlimited control extended through the whole lifetime of the father, unless the son were formally liberated by an act of manumission three times repeated, while the slave could be manumitted by performing the act only once. Neither was there any law obliging the father to manumit; — he could retain this power, if he chose, during his whole life.

Very similar was the situation of the Roman wife. In case she were accused of crime, her husband assembled a meeting of her relations, and in their presence sat in

judgment upon her, awarding such punishment as he thought proper.

For unfaithfulness to her marriage-vow, or for drinking wine, Romulus allowed her husband to put her to death.* From this slavery, unlike the son, the wife could never be manumitted; no legal forms were provided. It was lasting as her life.

The same spirit of force and slavery pervaded the relation of master and servant, giving rise to that severe code of slave-law, which, with a few features of added cruelty, Christian America, in the nineteenth century, has reënacted.

With regard, now, to all these abuses of proper relations, the gospel pursued one uniform course. It did not command the Christian father to perform the legal act of emancipation to his son; but it infused such a divine spirit into the paternal relation, by assimilating it to the relation of the heavenly Father, that the Christianized Roman would regard any use of his barbarous and oppressive legal powers as entirely inconsistent with his Christian profession. So it ennobled the marriage relation by comparing it to the relation between Christ and his church; commanding the husband to love his wife, even as Christ loved the church, and gave himself for it. It said to him, "No man ever yet hated his own flesh, but nourisheth and cherisheth it, even as the Lord the church;" "so ought every one to love his wife, even as himself." Not an allusion is made to the barbarous, unjust power which the law gave the husband. It was perfectly understood that a Christian husband could not make use of it in conformity with these directions.

In the same manner Christian masters were exhorted to give to their servants that which is just and equitable; and, so far from coercing their services by force, to forbear even threatenings. The Christian master was directed to receive his Christianized slave, " NOT now as a slave, but above a slave, a brother beloved;" and, as in all these other cases, nothing was said to him about the barbarous powers which the Roman law gave him, since it was perfectly understood that he could not at the same time treat him as a brother beloved and as a slave in the sense of Roman law.

When, therefore, the question is asked, why did not the apostles seek the abolition of slavery, we answer, they did seek it. They sought it by the safest, shortest, and most direct course which could possibly have been adopted.

CHAPTER VII.

But did Christianity abolish slavery as a matter of fact? We answer, it did.

Let us look at these acknowledged facts. At the time of the coming of Christ, slavery extended over the whole civilized world. Captives in war were uniformly made slaves, and, as wars were of constant occurrence, the ranks of slavery were continually being reinforced; and, as slavery was hereditary and perpetual, there was every reason to suppose that the number would have gone on increasing indefinitely, had not some influence operated to stop it. This is one fact.

Let us now look at another. At the time of the Reformation, chattel-slavery had entirely ceased throughout all the civilized countries of the world; — by no particular edict, by no special laws of emancipation, but by the steady influence of some gradual, unseen power, this whole vast system had dissolved away, like the snow-banks of winter.

These two facts being conceded, the inquiry arises, What caused this change? If, now, we find that the most powerful organization in the civilized world at that time did pursue a system of measures which had a direct tendency to bring about such a result, we shall very naturally ascribe it to that organization.

The Spanish writer, Balmes, in his work entitled "Protestantism compared with Catholicity," has one chapter devoted to the anti-slavery course of the church, in which he sets forth the whole system of measures which the church pursued in reference to this subject, and quotes, in their order, all the decrees of councils. The decrees themselves are given in an appendix at length, in the original Latin. We cannot but sympathize deeply in the noble and generous spirit in which these chapters are written, and the enlarged and vigorous ideas which they give of the magnanimous and honorable nature of Christianity. They are evidently conceived by a large and noble soul, capable of understanding such views,—a soul grave, earnest, deeply religious, though evidently penetrated and imbued with the most profound conviction of the truth of his own peculiar faith.

We shall give a short abstract, from M. Balmes, of the early course of the church. In contemplating the course which the church took in this period, certain things are to be borne in *mind* respecting the character of the times.

The process was carried on during that stormy and convulsed period of society which succeeded the breaking up of the Roman empire. At this time, all the customs of society were rude and barbarous. Though Christianity, as a system, had been nominally very extensively embraced, yet it had not, as in the case of its first converts, penetrated to the heart, and regenerated the whole nature. Force and violence was the order of the day, and the Christianity of the savage northern tribes, who at this time became masters of Europe, was mingled with the barbarities of their ancient heathenism. To root the institution of slavery out of such a state of society, required, of course, a very different process from what would be necessary under the enlightened organization of modern times.

No power but one of the peculiar kind which the Christian church then possessed could have effected anything in this way. The Christian church at this time, far from being in the outcast and outlawed state in which it existed in the time of the apostles, was now an organization of great power, and of a kind of power peculiarly adapted to that rude and uncultured age. It laid hold of all those elements of fear, and mystery, and superstition, which are strongest in barbarous ages, as with barbarous individuals, and it visited the violations of its commands with penalties the more dreaded that they related to some awful future, dimly perceived and imperfectly comprehended.

In dealing with slavery, the church did not commence by a proclamation of universal emancipation, because, such was the barbarous and unsettled nature of the times, so fierce the grasp of violence, and so many the causes of discord, that she avoided adding to the confusion by infusing into it this element; — nay, a certain council of the church forbade, on pain of ecclesiastical censure, those who preached that slaves ought immediately to leave their masters.

The course was commenced first by restricting the power of the master, and granting protection to the slave. The Council of Orleans, in 549, gave to a slave threatened with punishment the privilege of taking sanctuary in a church, and forbade his master to withdraw him thence, without taking a solemn oath that he would do him no harm; and, if he violated the spirit of this oath, he was to be suspended from the church and the sacraments,— a doom which in those days was viewed with such a degree of superstitious awe, that the most barbarous would scarcely dare to incur it. The custom was afterwards introduced of requiring an oath on such occasions, not only that the slave should be free from corporeal infliction, but that he should not be punished by an extra imposition of labor, or by any badge of disgrace. When this was complained of, as being altogether too great a concession on the side of the slave, the utmost that could be extorted from the church, by way of retraction, was this,— that in cases of very *heinous offence* the master should not be required to make the two latter promises.

There was a certain punishment among the Goths which was more dreaded than death. It was the shaving of the hair. This was considered as inflicting a lasting disgrace. If a Goth once had his hair shaved, it was all over with him. The fifteenth canon of the Council of Merida, in 666, forbade ecclesiastics to inflict this punishment upon their slaves, as also all other kind of violence, and ordained that if a slave committed an offence, he should not be subject to private vengeance, but be delivered up to the secular tribunal, and that the bishops should use their power only to procure a moderation of the sentence. This was substituting public justice for personal vengeance — a most important step. The church further enacted, by two councils, that the master who, of his own authority, should take the life of his slave, should be cut off for two years from the communion of the church, — a condition, in the view of those times, implying the most awful spiritual risk, separating the man in the eye of society from all that was sacred, and teaching him to regard himself, and others to regard him, as a being loaded with the weight of a most tremendous sin.

Besides the protection given to life and limb, the church threw her shield over the family condition of the slave. By old Roman law, the slave could not contract a legal, inviolable marriage. The church of that age availed itself of the catholic idea of the sacramental nature of marriage to conflict with this heathenish doctrine. Pope Adrian I. said, " According to the words of the apostle, as in Jesus Christ we ought not to deprive either slaves or freemen of the sacraments of the church, so it is not allowed in any way to prevent the *marriage* of slaves ; and if their marriages have been contracted *in spite of the opposition and repugnance of their masters*, nevertheless they *ought not to be dissolved.*" St. Thomas was of the same opinion, for he openly maintains that, with respect to contracting marriage, " *slaves are not obliged to obey their masters.*"

It can easily be seen what an effect was produced when the personal safety and family ties of the slaves were thus proclaimed sacred by an authority which no man living dared dispute. It elevated the slave in the eyes of his master, and awoke hope and self-respect in his own bosom, and powerfully tended to fit him for the reception of that liberty to which the church by many avenues was constantly seeking to conduct him.

Another means which the church used to procure emancipation was a jealous care of the freedom of those already free.

Every one knows how in our Southern States the boundaries of slavery are continually increasing, for want of some power there to perform the same kind office. The liberated slave, travelling without his papers, is continually in danger of being taken up, thrown into jail, and sold to pay his jail-fees. He has no bishop to help him out of his troubles. In no church can he take sanctuary. Hundreds and thousands of helpless men and women are every year engulfed in slavery in this manner.

The church, at this time, took all enfranchised slaves under her particular protection. The act of enfranchisement was made a religious service, and was solemnly performed in the church; and then the church received the newly-made freeman to her protecting arms, and guarded his newly-acquired rights by her spiritual power. The first Council of Orange, held in 441, ordained in its seventh canon that the church should check by ecclesiastical censures whoever desired to reduce to any kind of servitude slaves who had been emancipated within the enclosure of the church. A century later, the same prohibition was repeated in the seventh canon of the fifth Council of Orleans, held in 549. The protection given by the church to freed slaves was so manifest and known to all, that the custom was introduced of especially recommending them to her, either in lifetime or by will. The Council of Agde, in Languedoc, passed a resolution commanding the church, in all cases of necessity, to undertake the defence of those to whom their masters had, in a lawful way, given liberty.

Another anti-slavery measure which the church pursued with distinguished zeal had the same end in view, that is, the *prevention of the increase of slavery.* It was the ransoming of captives. As at that time it was customary for captives in war to be made slaves of, unless ransomed, and as, owing to the unsettled state of society, wars were frequent, slavery might have been indefinitely prolonged, had not the church made the greatest efforts in this way. The ransoming of slaves in those days held the same place in the affections of pious and devoted members of the church that the enterprise of converting the heathen now does. Many of the most eminent Christians, in their excess of zeal, even sold themselves into captivity that they might redeem distressed families. Chateaubriand describes a Christian priest in France who voluntarily devoted himself to slavery for the ransom of a Christian soldier, and thus restored a husband to his desolate wife, and a father to three unfortunate children. Such were the deeds which secured to men in those days the honor of saintship. Such was the history of St. Zachary, whose story drew tears from many eyes, and excited many hearts to imitate so sublime a charity. In this they did but imitate the spirit of the early Christians; for the apostolic Clement says, "We know how many among ourselves have given up themselves unto bonds, that thereby they might free others from them." (1st letter to the Corinthians, § 55, or ch. XXI. v. 20.) One of the most distinguished of the Frankish bishops was St. Eloy. He was originally a goldsmith of remarkable skill in his art, and by his integrity and trustworthiness won the particular esteem and confidence of King Clotaire I., and stood high in his court. Of him Neander speaks as follows. "The cause of the gospel was to him the dearest interest, to which everything else was made subservient. While working at his art, he always had a Bible open before him. The abundant income of his labors he devoted to religious objects and deeds of charity. Whenever he heard of captives, who in these days *were often dragged off in troops as slaves that were to be sold at auction*, he hastened to the spot and paid down their price." Alas for our slave-coffles! — there are no such bishops now! "Sometimes, by his means, a hundred at once, men and women, thus obtained their liberty. He then left it to their choice, either to return home, or to remain with him as free Christian brethren, or to become monks. In the first case, he gave them money for their journey; in the last, which pleased him most, he took pains to procure them a handsome reception into some monastery."

So great was the zeal of the church for the ransom of unhappy captives, that even the ornaments and sacred vessels of the church were sold for their ransom. By the fifth canon of the Council of Macon, held in 585, it appears that the priests devoted church property to this purpose. The Council of Rheims, held in 625, orders the punishment of suspension on the bishop who shall destroy the sacred vessels FOR ANY OTHER MOTIVE THAN THE RANSOM OF CAPTIVES; and in the twelfth canon of the Council of Verneuil, held in 844, we find that the property of the church was still used for this benevolent purpose.

When the church had thus redeemed the captive, she still continued him under her special protection, giving him letters of commendation which should render his liberty safe in the eyes of all men. The Council of Lyons, held in 583, enacts that bishops shall state, in the letters of recommendation which they give to redeemed slaves, the date and price of their ransom. The zeal for this work was so ardent that some of the clergy even went so far as to induce captives to run away. A council called that of St. Patrick, held in Ireland, condemns this practice, and says that the clergyman who desires to ransom captives must do so with his own money, for to induce them to run away was to expose the clergy to be considered as robbers, which was a dishonor to the church. The disinterestedness of the church in this work appears from the fact that, when she had employed her funds for the ransom of captives she never exacted from them any recompense, even when they had it in their power to discharge the debt. In the letters of St. Gregory, he reässures some persons who had been freed by the church, and who feared that they should be called upon to refund the money which had been expended on them. The Pope orders that no one, at any time, shall venture to disturb them or their heirs, because the sacred canons allow the employment of the goods of the church for the ransom of captives. (L. 7, Ep. 14.) Still further to guard against the increase of the number of slaves, the Council of Lyons, in 566, excommunicated those who unjustly retained free persons in slavery.

If there were any such laws in the Southern States, and all were excommunicated who are doing this, there would be quite a sensation, as some recent discoveries show.

In 625, the Council of Rheims decreed excommunication to all those who pursue free persons in order to reduce them to slavery. The twenty-seventh canon of the Council of London, held 1102, forbade the barbarous custom of trading in men, like animals; and the seventh canon of the Council of Coblentz, held 922, declares that he who takes away a Christian to sell him is guilty of homicide. A French council, held in Verneuil in 616, established the law that all persons who had been sold into slavery on account of poverty or debt should receive back their liberty by the restoration of the price which had been paid. It will readily be seen that this opened a wide field for restoration to liberty in an age where so great a Christian zeal had been awakened for the redeeming of slaves, since it afforded opportunity for Christians to interest themselves in raising the necessary ransom.

At this time the Jews occupied a very peculiar place among the nations. The spirit of trade and commerce was almost entirely confined to them, and the great proportion of the wealth was in their hands, and, of course, many slaves. The regulations which the church passed relative to the slaves of Jews tended still further to strengthen the principles of liberty. They forbade Jews to compel Christian slaves to do things contrary to the religion of Christ. They allowed Christian slaves, who took refuge in the church, to be ransomed, by paying their masters the proper price.

This produced abundant results in favor of liberty, inasmuch as they gave Christian slaves the opportunity of flying to churches, and there imploring the charity of their brethren. They also enacted that a Jew who should pervert a Christian slave should be condemned to lose all his slaves. This was a new sanction to the slave's conscience, and a new opening for liberty. After that, they proceeded to forbid Jews to have Christian slaves, and it was allowed to ransom those in their possession for twelve sous. As the Jews were among the greatest traders of the time, the forbidding them to keep slaves was a very decided step toward general emancipation.

Another means of lessening the ranks of slavery was a decree passed in a council at Rome, in 595, presided over by Pope Gregory the Great. This decree offered liberty to all who desired to embrace the monastic life. This decree, it is said, led to great scandal, as slaves fled from the houses of their masters in great numbers, and took refuge in monasteries.

The church also ordained that any slave who felt a calling to enter the ministry, and appeared qualified therefor, should be allowed to pursue his vocation; and enjoined it upon his master to liberate him, since the church could not permit her minister to wear the yoke of slavery. It is to be presumed that the phenomenon, on page 176, of a preacher with both toes cut off and branded on the breast, advertised as a runaway in the public papers, was not one which could have occurred consistently with the Christianity of that period.

Under the influence of all these regulations, it is not surprising that there are documents cited by M. Balmes which go to show the following things. First, that the number of slaves thus liberated was very great, as there was universal complaint upon this head.

Second, that the bishops were complained of as being *always in favor of the slaves*, as carrying their protection to very great lengths, laboring in all ways to realize the doctrine of man's equality; and it is affirmed in the documents that complaint is made that there is hardly a bishop who cannot be charged with reprehensible compliances in favor of slaves, and that slaves were aware of this spirit of protection, and were ready to throw off their chains, and cast themselves into the church.

It is not necessary longer to extend this history. It is as perfectly plain whither such a course tends, as it is whither the course pursued by the American clergy at the South tends. We are not surprised that under such a course, on the one hand, the number of slaves decreased, till there were none in modern Europe. We are not surprised by such a course, on the other hand, that they have increased until there are three millions in America.

Alas for the poor slave! What church befriends him? In what house of prayer can he take sanctuary? What holy men stand forward to rebuke the wicked law that denies him legal marriages? What pious bishops visit slave-coffles to redeem men, women and children, to liberty? What holy exhortations in churches to buy the freedom of wretched captives? When have church velvets been sold, and communion-cups melted down, to liberate the slave? Where are the pastors, inflamed with the love of Jesus, who have sold themselves into slavery to restore separated families? Where are those honorable complaints of the world that the church is always on the side of the oppressed? — that the slaves feel the beatings of her generous heart, and long to throw themselves into her arms? Love of brethren, holy charities, love of Jesus,—where are ye?— Are ye fled forever?

CHAPTER VIII.

"Masters, give unto your servants that which is just and equal."

FROM what has been said in the last chapter, it is presumed that it will appear that the Christian church of America by no means occupies that position, with regard to slavery, that the apostles did, or that the church of the earlier ages did.

However they may choose to interpret the language of the apostles, the fact still remains undeniable, that the church organization which grew up immediately after these instructions did intend and did effect the abolition of slavery.

But we wish to give still further consideration to one idea which is often put forward by those who defend American slavery. It is this. That the institution is not of itself a sinful one, and that the only sin consists in the neglect of its relative duties. All that is necessary, they say, is to *regulate* the institution by the precepts of the gospel. They admit that no slavery is defensible which is not so regulated.

If, therefore, it shall appear that American slave-law *cannot* be regulated by the precepts of the gospel, without such alterations as will entirely do away the whole system, then it will appear that it is an unchristian institution, against which every Christian is bound to remonstrate, and from which he should entirely withdraw.

The Roman slave-code was a code made by heathen,— by a race, too, proverbially stern and unfeeling. It was made in the darkest ages of the world, before the light of the gospel had dawned. Christianity gradually but certainly abolished it. Some centuries later, a company of men, from Christian nations, go to the continent of Africa; there they kindle wars, sow strifes, set tribes against tribes with demoniac violence, burn villages, and in the midst of these diabolical scenes kidnap and carry off, from time to time, hundreds and thousands of miserable captives. Such of those as do not die of terror, grief, suffocation, ship-fever, and other horrors, are, from time to time, landed on the shores of America. Here they are. And now a set of Christian legislators meet together to construct a system and laws of servitude, with regard to these unfortunates, which is hereafter to be considered as a Christian institution.

Of course, in order to have any valid title to such a name, the institution must be regu-

16

lated by the principles which Christ and his apostles have laid down for the government of those who assume the relation of masters. The New Testament sums up these principles in a single sentence: "Masters, give unto your servants that which is just and equal."

But, forasmuch as there is always some confusion of mind in regard to what is just and equal in our neighbor's affairs, our Lord has given this direction, by which we may arrive at infallible certainty. "All things whatsoever ye would that men should do to you, do ye even so to them."

It is, therefore, evident that if Christian legislators are about to form a Christian system of servitude, they must base it on these two laws, one of which is a particular specification under the other.

Let us now examine some of the particulars of the code which they have formed, and see if it bear this character.

First, they commence by declaring that their brother shall no longer be considered as a person, but deemed, sold, taken, and reputed, as a chattel personal.—This is "just and equal!"

This being the fundamental principle of the system, the following are specified as its consequences:

1. That he shall have no right to hold property of any kind, under any circumstances.—Just and equal!

2. That he shall have no power to contract a legal marriage, or claim any woman in particular for his wife.— Just and equal!

3. That he shall have no right to his children, either to protect, restrain, guide or educate.—Just and equal!

4. That the power of his master over him shall be ABSOLUTE, without any possibility of appeal or redress in consequence of any injury whatever.

To secure this, they enact that he shall not be able to enter suit in any court for any cause.—Just and equal!

That he shall not be allowed to bear testimony in any court where any white person is concerned.— Just and equal!

That the owner of a servant, for "malicious, cruel, and excessive beating of his slave, cannot be indicted."—Just and equal!

It is further decided, that by no indirect mode of suit, through a guardian, shall a slave obtain redress for ill-treatment. (Dorothea v. Coquillon et al, 9 Martin La. Rep. 350.) — Just and equal!

5. It is decided that the slave shall not only have no legal redress for injuries inflicted by his master, but shall have no re-

dress for those inflicted by any other person, unless the injury impair his property value. —Just and equal!

Under this head it is distinctly asserted as follows:

"There can be no offence against the peace of the state, by the mere breating of a slave, unaccompanied by any circumstances of cruelty, or an intent to kill and murder. The peace of the state is not thereby broken." (State *v*. Maner, 2 Hill's Rep. S. C.)—Just and equal!

If a slave strike a white, he is to be condemned to death; but if a master kill his slave by torture, no white witnesses being present, he may clear himself by his own oath. (Louisiana.)—Just and equal!

The law decrees fine and imprisonment to the person who shall release the servant of another from the torture of the iron collar. (Louisiana.) — Just and equal!

It decrees a much smaller fine, without imprisonment, to the man who shall torture him with red-hot irons, cut out his tongue, put out his eyes, and scald or maim him. (Ibid.) — Just and equal!

It decrees the same punishment to him who teaches him to write as to him who puts out his eyes.—Just and equal!

As it might be expected that only very ignorant and brutal people could be kept in a condition like this, especially in a country where every book and every newspaper are full of dissertations on the rights of man, they therefore enact laws that neither he nor his children, to all generations, shall learn to read and write.—Just and equal!

And as, if allowed to meet for religious worship, they might concert some plan of escape or redress, they enact that "no congregation of negroes, under pretence of divine worship, shall assemble themselves ; and that every slave found at such meetings shall be immediately corrected, *without trial*, by receiving on the bare back twenty-five stripes with a whip, switch or cowskin." (Law of Georgia, Prince's Digest, p. 447.) — Just and equal!

Though the servant is thus kept in ignorance, nevertheless in his ignorance he is punished more severely for the same crimes than freemen.— Just and equal!

By way of protecting him from over-work, they enact that he shall not labor more than five hours longer than convicts at hard labor in a penitentiary!

They also enact that the master or overseer, not the slave, shall decide when he is too sick to work.— Just and equal!

If any master, compassionating this condition of the slave, desires to better it, the law takes it out of his power, by the following decisions:

1. That all his earnings shall belong to his master, notwithstanding his master's promise to the contrary ; thus making them liable for his master's debts.— Just and equal!

2. That if his master allow him to keep cattle for his own use, it shall be lawful for any man to take them away, and enjoy half the profits of the seizure.— Just and equal!

3. If his master sets him free, he shall be taken up and sold again.—Just and equal!

If any man or woman runs away from this state of things, and, after proclamation made, does not return, any two justices of the peace may delare them outlawed, and give permission to any person in the community to kill them by any ways or means they think fit.—Just and equal!

Such are the laws of that system of slavery which has been made up by Christian masters late in the Christian era, and is now defended by Christian ministers as an eminently benign institution.

In this manner Christian legislators have expressed their understanding of the text, "Masters, give unto your servants that which is just and equal." and of the text, "All things whatsoever ye would that men should do to you do ye even so to them."

It certainly presents the most extraordinary views of justice and equity, and is the most remarkable exposition of the principle of doing to others as we would others should do to us, that it has ever been the good fortune of the civilized world to observe. This being the *institution*, let any one conjecture what its abuses must be ; for we are gravely told, by learned clergymen, that they do not feel called upon to interfere with the *system*, but only with its *abuses*. We should like to know what abuse could be specified that is not provided for and expressly protected by slave-law.

And yet, Christian republicans, who, with full power to repeal this law, are daily sustaining it, talk about there being no harm in slavery, if they regulate it according to the apostle's directions, and give unto their servants that which is just and equal. Do they think that, if the Christianized masters of Rome and Corinth had made such a set of rules as this for the government of their slaves, Paul would have accepted it as a proper exposition of what he meant by just and equal?

But the Presbyteries of South Carolina say, and all the other religious bodies at the South say, that the church of our Lord Jesus Christ has no right to interfere with civil institutions. What is this church of our Lord Jesus Christ, that they speak of? Is it not a collection of republican men, who have constitutional power to alter these laws, and whose duty it is to alter them, and who are disobeying the apostle's directions every day till they do alter them? Every minister at the South is a voter as much as he is a minister; every church-member is a voter as much as he is a church-member; and ministers and church-members are among the masters who are keeping up this system of atrocity, when they have full republican power to alter it; and yet they talk about giving their servants that which is just and equal! If they are going to give their servants that which is just and equal, let them give them back their manhood; they are law-makers, and can do it. Let them give to the slave the right to hold property, the right to form legal marriage, the right to read the word of God, and to have such education as will fully develop his intellectual and moral nature; the right of free religious opinion and worship; let them give him the right to bring suit and to bear testimony; give him the right to have some vote in the government by which his interests are controlled. This will be something more like giving him that which is "just and equal."

Mr. Smylie, of Mississippi, says that the planters of Louisiana and Mississippi, when they are giving from twenty to twenty-five dollars a barrel for pork, give their slaves three or four pounds a week; and intimates that, if that will not convince people that they are doing what is just and equal, he does not know what will.

Mr. C. C. Jones, after stating in various places that he has no intention ever to interfere with the civil condition of the slave, teaches the negroes, in his catechism, that the master gives to his servant that which is just and equal, when he provides for them good houses, good clothing, food, nursing, and religious instruction.

This is just like a man who has stolen an estate which belongs to a family of orphans. Out of its munificent revenues, he gives the orphans comfortable food, clothing, &c., while he retains the rest for his own use, declaring that he is thus rendering to them that which is just and equal.

If the laws which regulate slavery were made by a despotic sovereign, over whose movements the masters could have no control, this mode of proceeding might be called just and equal; but, as they are made and kept in operation by these Christian masters, these ministers and church-members, in common with those who are not so, they are every one of them refusing to the slave that which is just and equal, so long as they do not seek the repeal of these laws; and, if they cannot get them repealed, it is their duty to take the slave out from under them, since they are constructed with such fatal ingenuity as utterly to nullify all that the master tries to do for their elevation and permanent benefit.

No man would wish to leave his own family of children as slaves under the care of the kindest master that ever breathed; and what he would not wish to have done to his own children, he ought not to do to other people's children.

But, it will be said that it is not becoming for the Christian church to enter into political matters. Again, we ask, what is the Christian church? Is it not an association of republican citizens, each one of whom has his rights and duties as a legal voter?

Now, suppose a law were passed which depreciated the value of cotton or sugar three cents in the pound, would these men consider the fact that they are church-members as any reason why they should not agitate for the repeal of such law? Certainly not. Such a law would be brittle as the spider's web; it would be swept away before it was well made. Every law to which the majority of the community does not assent is, in this country, immediately torn down.

Why, then, does this monstrous system stand from age to age? Because the community CONSENT TO IT. They re-enact these unjust laws every day, by their silent permission of them.

The kingdom of our Lord Jesus Christ is not of this world, say the South Carolina Presbyteries; therefore, the church has no right to interfere with any civil institution; but yet all the clergy of Charleston could attend in a body to give sanction to the proceedings of the great Vigilance Committee. They could not properly exert the least influence against slavery, because it is a civil institution, but they could give the whole weight of their influence in favor of it.

Is it not making the kingdom of our Lord Jesus Christ quite as much of this world, to patronize the oppressor, as to patronize the slave?

CHAPTER IX.

IS THE SYSTEM OF RELIGION WHICH IS TAUGHT THE SLAVE THE GOSPEL?

THE ladies of England, in their letter to the ladies of America, spoke in particular of the denial of the gospel to the slave. This has been indignantly resented in this country, and it has been claimed that the slaves do have the gospel communicated to them very extensively.

Whoever reads Mr. Charles C. Jones' book on the religious instruction of the negroes will have no doubt of the following facts:

1. That from year to year, since the introduction of the negroes into this country, various pious and benevolent individuals have made efforts for their spiritual welfare.

2. That these efforts have increased, from year to year.

3. That the most extensive and important one came into being about the time that Mr. Jones' book was written, in the year 1842, and extended to some degree through the United States. The fairest development of it was probably in the State of Georgia, the sphere of Mr. Jones' immediate labor, where the most gratifying results were witnessed, and much very amiable and commendable Christian feeling elicited on the part of masters.

4. From time to time, there have been prepared, for the use of the slave, catechisms, hymns, short sermons, &c. &c., designed to be read to them by their masters, or taught them orally.

5. It will appear to any one who reads Mr. Jones' book that, though written by a man who believed the system of slavery sanctioned by God, it manifests a spirit of sincere and earnest benevolence, and of devotedness to the cause he has undertaken, which cannot be too highly appreciated.

It is a very painful and unpleasant task to express any qualification or dissent with regard to efforts which have been undertaken in a good spirit, and which have produced, in many respects, good results; but, in the reading of Mr. Jones' book, in the study of his catechism, and of various other catechisms and sermons which give an idea of the religious instruction of the slaves, the writer has often been painfully impressed with the idea that, however imbued and mingled with good, it is not the *true and pure gospel system* which is given to the slave. As far

as the writer has been able to trace out what is communicated to him, it amounts in substance to this; that his master's authority over him, and property in him, to the full extent of the enactment of slave-law, is recognized and sustained by the tremendous authority of God himself. He is told that his master is God's overseer; that he owes him a blind, unconditional, unlimited submission; that he must not allow himself to grumble, or fret, or murmur, at anything in his conduct; and, in case he does so, that his murmuring is not against his master, but against God. He is taught that it is God's will that he should have nothing but labor and poverty in this world; and that, if he frets and grumbles at this, he will get nothing by it in this life, and be sent to hell forever in the next. Most vivid descriptions of hell, with its torments, its worms ever feeding and never dying, are held up before him; and he is told that this eternity of torture will be the result of insubordination here. It is no wonder that a slave-holder once said to Dr. Brisbane, of Cincinnati, that religion had been worth more to him, on his plantation, than a wagon-load of cowskins.

Furthermore, the slave is taught that to endeavor to evade his master by running away, or to shelter or harbor a slave who has run away, are sins which will expose him to the wrath of that omniscient Being, whose eyes are in every place.

As the slave is a movable and merchantable being, liable, as Mr. Jones calmly remarks, to "all the vicissitudes of property," this system of instruction, one would think, would be in something of a dilemma, when it comes to inculcate the Christian duties of the family state.

When Mr. Jones takes a survey of the field, previous to commencing his system of operations, he tells us, what we suppose every rational person must have foreseen, that he finds among the negroes an utter demoralization upon this subject; that polygamy is commonly practised, and that the marriage-covenant has become a mere temporary union of interest, profit or pleasure, formed without reflection, and dissolved without the slightest idea of guilt.

That this state of things is the necessary and legitimate result of the system of laws which these Christian men have made and are still keeping up over their slaves, any sensible person will perceive; and any one would think it an indispensable step to any system of religious instruction here, that the negro should be placed in a situation where he *can* form a legal marriage, and *can* adhere to it after it is formed.

But Mr. Jones and his coadjutors commenced by declaring that it was not their intention to interfere, in the slightest degree, with the legal position of the slave.

We should have thought, then, that it would not have been possible, if these masters intended to keep their slaves in the condition of chattels personal, liable to a constant disruption of family ties, that they could have the heart to teach them the strict morality of the gospel with regard to the marriage relation.

But so it is, however. If we examine Mr. Jones' catechism, we shall find that the slave is made to repeat orally that one man can be the husband of but one woman, and if, during her lifetime, he marries another, God will punish him forever in hell.

Suppose a conscientious woman, instructed in Mr. Jones' catechism, by the death of her master is thrown into the market for the division of the estate, like many cases we may read of in the Georgia papers every week. She is torn from her husband and children, and sold at the other end of the Union, never to meet them again, and the new master commands her to take another husband; — what, now, is this woman to do? If she take the husband, according to her catechism she commits adultery, and exposes herself to everlasting fire; if she does not take him, she disobeys her master, who, she has been taught, is God's overseer; and she is exposed to everlasting fire on that account, and certainly she is exposed to horrible tortures here.

Now, we ask, if the teaching that has involved this poor soul in such a labyrinth of horrors can be called the gospel?

Is it the gospel, — is it glad tidings in any sense of the words?

In the same manner, this catechism goes on to instruct parents to bring up their children in the nurture and admonition of the Lord, that they should guide, counsel, restrain and govern them.

Again, these teachers tell them that they should search the Scriptures most earnestly, diligently and continually, at the same time declaring that it is not their intention to interfere with the laws which forbid their being taught to read. Searching the Scriptures, slaves are told, means coming to people who are willing to read to them. Yes, but if there be no one willing to do this, what then? Any one whom this catechism has

thus instructed is sold off to a plantation on Red river, like that where Northrop lived; no Bible goes with him; his Christian instructors, in their care not to interfere with his civil condition, have deprived him of the power of reading; and in this land of darkness his oral instruction is but as a faded dream. Let any of us ask for what sum we would be deprived of all power of ever reading the Bible for ourselves, and made entirely dependent on the reading of others, — especially if we were liable to fall into such hands as slaves are, — and then let us determine whether a system of religious instruction, which begins by declaring that it has no intention to interfere with this cruel legal deprivation, is the gospel!

The poor slave, darkened, blinded, perplexed on every hand, by the influences which the legal system has spread under his feet, is, furthermore, strictly instructed in a perfect system of morality. He must not even covet anything that is his master's; he must not murmur or be discontented; he must consider his master's interests as his own, and be ready to sacrifice himself to them; and this he must do, as he is told, not only to the good and gentle, but also to the froward. He must forgive all injuries, and do exactly right under all perplexities; thus is the obligation on his part expounded to him, while his master's reciprocal obligations mean only to give him good houses, clothes, food, &c. &c., leaving every master to determine for himself what is *good* in relation to these matters.

No wonder, when such a system of utter injustice is justified to the negro by all the awful sanctions of religion, that now and then a strong soul rises up against it. We have known under a black skin shrewd minds, unconquerable spirits, whose indignant sense of justice no such representations could blind. That Mr. Jones has met such is evident; for, speaking of the trials of a missionary among them, he says (p. 127):

He discovers Deism, Scepticism, Universalism. As already stated, the various perversions of the gospel, and all the **strong** objections against the truth of God, — objections which he may, perhaps, have considered peculiar only to the cultivated minds, the ripe scholarship and profound intelligence, of *critics* and *philosophers!* — extremes here meet on the natural and common ground of a darkened understanding and a hardened heart.

Again, in the Tenth Annual Report of the "Association for the Religious Instruction of the Negroes in Liberty County, Georgia," he says:

Allow me to relate a fact which occurred in the spring of this year, illustrative of the character and knowledge of the negroes at this time. I was preaching to a large congregation on the *Epistle to Philemon*; and when I insisted upon fidelity and obedience as Christian virtues in servants, and, upon the authority of Paul, condemned the practice of *running away*, one-half of my audience deliberately walked off with themselves, and those that remained looked anything but satisfied, either with the preacher or his doctrine. After dismission, there was no small stir among them: some solemnly declared that there was no such epistle in the Bible; others, " that it was not the gospel;" others, " that I preached to please masters;" others, " that they did not care if they ever heard me preach again."—pp. 24, 25.

Lundy Lane, an intelligent fugitive who has published his memoirs, says that on one occasion they (the slaves) were greatly delighted with a certain preacher, until he told them that God had ordained and created them expressly to make slaves of. He says that after that they all left him, and went away, because they thought, with the Jews, " This is a hard saying; who can hear it?"

In these remarks on the perversion of the gospel as presented to the slave, we do not mean to imply that much that is excellent and valuable is not taught him. We mean simply to assert that, in so far as the system taught justifies the slave-system, so far necessarily it vitiates the fundamental ideas of justice and morality; and, so far as the obligations of the gospel are inculcated on the slave in their purity, they bring him necessarily in conflict with the authority of the system. As we have said before, it is an attempt to harmonize light with darkness, and Christ with Belial. Nor is such an attempt to be justified and tolerated, because undertaken in the most amiable spirit by amiable men. Our admiration of some of the laborers who have conducted this system is very great; so also is our admiration of many of the Jesuit missionaries who have spread the Roman Catholic religion among our aboriginal tribes. Devotion and disinterestedness could be carried no further than some of both these classes of men have carried them.

But, while our respect for these good men must not seduce us as Protestants into an admiration of the system which they taught, so our esteem for our Southern brethren must not lead us to admit that a system which fully justifies the worst kind of spiritual and temporal despotism can properly represent the gospel of him who came to preach deliverance to the captives.

To prove that we have not misrepresented the style of instruction, we will give some extracts from various sermons and discourses.

In the first place, to show how explicitly religious teachers disclaim any intention of interfering in the legal relation (see Mr. Jones' work, p. 157):

By law or custom, they are excluded from the advantages of education; and, by consequence, from the reading of the word of God; and this immense mass of immortal beings is thrown, for religious instruction, upon *oral* communications entirely. And upon whom? Upon their *owners*. And their owners, especially of late years, claim to be the *exclusive guardians* of their religious instruction, and the almoners of divine mercy towards them, thus assuming the responsibility of their *entire* Christianization!
All approaches to them from abroad are rigidly guarded against, and no ministers are allowed to break to them the bread of life, except such as have *commended themselves to the affection and confidence of their owners*. I do not condemn this course of self-preservation on the part of our citizens; I merely mention it to show their *entire dependence* upon ourselves.

In answering objections of masters to allowing the religious instruction of the negroes, he supposes the following objection, and gives the following answer:

If we suffer our negroes to be instructed, the tendency will be to change the civil relations of society as now constituted.
To which let it be replied, that we separate entirely their *religious* and their *civil* condition, and contend that the one may be attended to without interfering with the other. Our *principle* is that laid down by the holy and just One: "Render unto Cæsar the things which are Cæsar's, and unto God the things which are God's." And Christ and his apostles are our *example*. Did they deem it proper and consistent with the good order of society to preach the gospel to the servants? They did. In discharge of this duty, did they interfere with their civil condition? They did not.

With regard to the description of heaven and the torments of hell, the following is from Mr. Jones' catechism, pp. 83, 91, 92:

Q. Are there two places only spoken of in the Bible to which the souls of men go after death?— A. Only two.
Q. Which are they?—A. Heaven and hell.
*   *   *   *
Q. After the Judgment is over, into what place do the righteous go?—A. Into heaven.
Q. What kind of a place is heaven?—A. A most glorious and happy place.
*   *   *   *
Q. Shall the righteous in heaven have any more hunger, or thirst, or nakedness, or heat, or cold? Shall they have any more sin, or sorrow, or crying, or pain, or death?—A. No.
Q. Repeat "And God shall wipe away all tears from their eyes."—A. "And God shall wipe away all tears from their eyes, and there shall be no more death, neither sorrow nor crying;

neither shall there be any more pain ; for the former things are passed away."

Q. Will heaven be their everlasting home ? — A. Yes.

Q. And shall the righteous grow in knowledge and holiness and happiness for ever and ever ? — A. Yes.

Q. To what place should we wish and strive to go, more than to all other places ? — A. Heaven.

*   *   *   *   *

Q. Into what place are the wicked to be cast? — A. Into hell.

Q. Repeat " The wicked shall be turned."— A. " The wicked shall be turned into hell, and all the nations that forget God."

Q. What kind of a place is hell ? — A. A place of dreadful torments.

Q. What does it burn with ? — A. Everlasting fire.

Q. Who are cast into hell besides wicked men ? — A. The devil and his angels.

Q. What will the torments of hell make the wicked do ? — A. Weep and wail and gnash their teeth.

Q. What did the rich man beg for when he was tormented in the flame ? — A. A drop of cold water to cool his tongue.

Q. Will the wicked have any good thing in hell ? the least comfort ? the least relief from torment ? — A. No.

Q. Will they ever come out of hell ? — A. No, never.

Q. Can any go from heaven to hell, or from hell to heaven ? — A. No.

Q. What is fixed between heaven and hell ? — A. A great gulf.

Q. What is the punishment of the wicked in hell called ? — A. Everlasting punishment.

Q. Will this punishment make them better ? — A. No.

Q, Repeat " It is a fearful thing."— A. " It is a fearful thing to fall into the hands of the living God."

Q. What is God said to be to the wicked ? — A. A consuming fire.

Q. What place should we strive to escape from above all others ? — A. Hell.

The Rev. Alex. Glennie, rector of All-saints parish, Waccamaw, South Carolina, has for several years been in the habit of preaching with express reference to slaves. In 1844 he published in Charleston a selection of these sermons, under the title of " Sermons preached on Plantations to Congregations of Negroes." This book contains twenty-six sermons, and in twenty-two of them there is either a more or less extended account, or a reference to eternal misery in hell as a motive to duty. He thus describes the day of judgment (Sermon 15, p. 90) :

When all people shall be gathered before him, " he shall separate them, one from another, as a shepherd divideth his sheep from the goats ; and he shall set the sheep on the right hand, but the goats on the left." That, my brethren, will be an awful time, when this separation shall be going on ; when the holy angels, at the command of the great Judge, shall be gathering together all the obedient followers of Christ, and be setting them

on the right hand of the Judgment-seat, and shall place all the remainder on the left. Remember that each of you must be present ; remember that the Great Judge can make no mistake ; and that you shall be placed on one side or on the other, according as in this world you have believed in and obeyed him or not. How full of joy and thanksgiving will you be, if you shall find yourself placed on the right hand ! but how full of misery and despair, if the left shall be appointed as your portion !

*   *   *   *   *

But what shall he say to the wicked on the left hand ? To them he shall say, " Depart from me, ye cursed, into everlasting fire, prepared for the devil and his angels." He will tell them to depart ; they did not, while here, seek him by repentance and faith ; they did not obey him, and now he will drive them from him. He will call them cursed.

(Sermon 1, p. 42.) The death which is the wages of sin is this everlasting fire prepared for the devil and his angels. It is a fire which shall last forever ; and the devil and his angels, and all people who will not love and serve God, shall there be punished forever. The Bible says, " The smoke of their torment ascendeth up for ever and ever." The fire is not quenched, it never goes out, " their worm dieth not :" their punishment is spoken of as a worm always feeding upon but never consuming them ; it never can stop.

Concerning the absolute authority of the master, take the following extract from Bishop Mead's sermon. (Brooke's Slavery, pp. 30, 31, 32.)

Having thus shown you the chief duties you owe to your great Master in heaven, I now come to lay before you the duties you owe to your masters and mistresses here upon earth ; and for this you have one general rule that you ought always to carry in your minds, and that is, to do all service for them as if you did it for God himself. Poor creatures ! you little consider, when you are idle and neglectful of your masters' business, when you steal and waste and hurt any of their substance, when you are saucy and impudent, when you are telling them lies and deceiving them ; or when you prove stubborn and sullen, and will not do the work you are set about without stripes and vexation ; you do not consider, I say, that *what faults you are guilty of towards your masters and mistresses are faults done against God himself*, who hath set your masters and mistresses over you in his own stead, and expects that you will do for them just as you would do for Him. And, pray, do not think that I want to deceive you when I tell you that *your masters and mistresses are God's overseers ;* and that, if you are faulty towards them, God himself will punish you severely for it in the next world, unless you repent of it, and strive to make amends by your faithfulness and diligence for the time to come ; for God himself hath declared the same.

Now, from this general rule, — namely, that you are to do all service for your masters and mistresses as if you did it for God himself, — there arise several other rules of duty towards your masters and mistresses, which I shall endeavor to lay out in order before you.

And, in the first place, you are to be obedient and subject to your masters in all things. . . . .

And Christian ministers are commanded to "exhort servants to be obedient unto their own masters, and to please them well in all things, not answering them again, or gainsaying." You see how strictly God requires this of you, that whatever your masters and mistresses order you to do, you must set about it immediately, and faithfully perform it, without any disputing or grumbling, and take care to please them well in all things. And for your encouragement he tells you that he will reward you for it in heaven ; because, while you are honestly and faithfully doing your master's business here, you are serving your Lord and Master in heaven. You see also that you are not to take any exceptions to the behavior of your masters and mistresses ; and that you are to be subject and obedient, not only to such as are good, and gentle, and mild, towards you, but also to such as may be froward, peevish, and hard. For you are not at liberty to choose your own masters ; but into whatever hands God hath been pleased to put you, you must do your duty, and God will reward you for it.

*   *   *   *   *

You are to be faithful and honest to your masters and mistresses, not purloining or wasting their goods or substance, but showing all good fidelity in all things. . . . . Do not your masters, under God, provide for you? And how shall they be able to do this, to feed and to clothe you, unless you take honest care of everything that belongs to them? Remember that God requires this of you ; and, if you are not afraid of suffering for it here, you cannot escape the vengeance of Almighty God, who will judge between you and your masters, and make you pay severely in the next world for all the injustice you do them here. And though you could manage so cunningly as to escape the eyes and hands of man, yet think what a dreadful thing it is to fall into the hands of the living God, who is able to cast both soul and body into hell!

You are to serve your masters with cheerfulness, reverence, and humility. You are to do your masters' service with good will, doing it as the will of God from the heart, without any sauciness or answering again. How many of you do things quite otherwise, and, instead of going about your work with a good will and a good heart, dispute and grumble, give saucy answers, and behave in a surly manner! There is something so becoming and engaging in a modest, cheerful, good-natured behavior, that a little work done in that manner seems better done, and gives far more satisfaction, than a great deal more, that must be done with fretting, vexation, and the lash always held over you. It also gains the good will and love of those you belong to, and makes your own life pass with more ease and pleasure. Besides, you are to consider that this grumbling and ill-will do not affect your masters and mistresses only. They have ways and means in their hands of forcing you to do your work, whether you are willing or not. *But your murmuring and grumbling is against God, who hath placed you in that service, who will punish you severely in the next world for despising his commands.*

A very awful query here occurs to the mind. If the poor, ignorant slave, who wastes his master's temporal goods to answer some of his own present purposes, be exposed to this heavy retribution, what will become

of those educated men, who, for their temporal convenience, make and hold in force laws which rob generation after generation of men, not only of their daily earnings, but of all their rights and privileges as immortal beings?

The Rev. Mr. Glennie, in one of his sermons, as quoted by Mr. Bowditch, p. 137, assures his hearers that none of them will be able to say, in the day of judgment, "I had no way of hearing about my God and Saviour."

Bishop Meade, as quoted by Brooke, pp. 34, 35, thus expatiates to slaves on the advantages of their condition. One would really think, from reading this account, that every one ought to make haste and get himself sold into slavery, as the nearest road to heaven.

Take care that you do not fret or murmur, grumble or repine at your condition ; for this will not only make your life uneasy, but will greatly offend Almighty God. Consider that it is not yourselves, it is not the people that you belong to, it is not the men that have brought you to it, but *it is the will of God, who hath by his providence made you servants, because, no doubt, he knew that condition would be best for you in this world, and help you the better towards heaven, if you would but do your duty in it.* So that any discontent at your not being free, or rich, or great, as you see some others, is quarrelling with your heavenly Master, and finding fault with God himself, who hath made you what you are, and hath promised you as large a share in the kingdom of heaven as the greatest man alive, if you will but behave yourself aright, and do the business he hath set you about in this world honestly and cheerfully. Riches and power have proved the ruin of many an unhappy soul, by drawing away the heart and affections from God, and fixing them on mean and sinful enjoyments ; so that, when God, who knows our hearts better than we know them ourselves, sees that they would be hurtful to us, and therefore keeps them from us, it is the greatest mercy and kindness he could show us.

You may perhaps fancy that, if you had riches and freedom, you could do your duty to God and man with greater pleasure than you can now. But, pray, consider that, if you can but save your souls, through the mercy of God, you will have spent your time to the best of purposes in this world ; and he that at last can get to heaven has performed a noble journey, let the road be ever so rugged and difficult. Besides, you really have a great advantage over most white people, who have not only the care of their daily labor upon their hands, but the care of looking forward and providing necessaries for to-morrow and next day, and of clothing and bringing up their children, and of getting food and raiment for as many of you as belong to their families, which often puts them to great difficulties, and distracts their minds so as to break their rest, and take off their thoughts from the affairs of another world. Whereas, you are quite eased from all these cares, and have nothing but your daily labor to look after, and, when that is done, take your needful rest.

Neither is it necessary for you to think of laying up anything against old age, as white people are obliged to do; for the laws of the country have provided that you shall not be turned off when you are past labor, but shall be maintained, while you live, by those you belong to, whether you are able to work or not.

Bishop Meade further consoles slaves thus for certain incidents of their lot, for which they may think they have more reason to find fault than for most others. The reader must admit that he takes a very philosophical view of the subject.

There is only one circumstance which may appear grievous, that I shall now take notice of, and that is correction.

Now, when correction is given you, you either deserve it, or you do not deserve it. But, whether you really deserve it or not, it is your duty, and Almighty God requires, that you bear it patiently You may perhaps think that this is hard doctrine; but if you consider it right, you must needs think otherwise of it. Suppose, then, that you deserve correction; you cannot but say that it is just and right you should meet with it. Suppose you do not, or at least you do not deserve so much, or so severe a correction, for the fault you have committed; you perhaps have escaped a great many more, and at last paid for all. Or, suppose you are quite innocent of what is laid to your charge, and suffer wrongfully in that particular thing; is it not possible you may have done some other bad thing which was never discovered, and that Almighty God, who saw you doing it, would not let you escape without punishment, one time or another? And ought you not, in such a case, to give glory to him, and be thankful that he would rather punish you in this life for your wickedness, than destroy your souls for it in the next life? But, suppose even this was not the case (a case hardly to be imagined), and that you have by no means, known or unknown, deserved the correction you suffered; there is this great comfort in it, that, if you bear it patiently, and leave your cause in the hands of God, he will reward you for it in heaven, and the punishment you suffer unjustly here shall turn to your exceeding great glory hereafter.

That Bishop Meade has no high opinion of the present comforts of a life of slavery, may be fairly inferred from the following remarks which he makes to slaves:

Your own poor circumstances in this life ought to put you particularly upon this, and taking care of your souls; for you cannot have the pleasures and enjoyments of this life like rich free people, who have estates and money to lay out as they think fit. If others will run the hazard of their souls, they have a chance of getting wealth and power, of heaping up riches, and enjoying all the ease, luxury and pleasure, their hearts should long after. But you can have none of these things; so that, if you sell your souls, for the sake of what poor matters you can get in this world, you have made a very foolish bargain indeed.

This information is certainly very explicit and to the point. He continues:

Almighty God hath been pleased to make you slaves here, and to give you nothing but labor and poverty in this world, which you are obliged to submit to, as it is his will that it should be so. And think within yourselves, what a terrible thing it would be, after all your labors and sufferings in this life, to be turned into hell in the next life, and, after wearing out your bodies in service here, to go into a far worse slavery when this is over, and your poor souls be delivered over into the possession of the devil, to become his slaves forever in hell, without any hope of ever getting free from it! If, therefore, you would be God's freemen in heaven, you must strive to be good, and serve him here on earth. Your bodies, you know, are not your own; they are at the disposal of those you belong to; but your precious souls are still your own, which nothing can take from you, if it be not your own fault. Consider well, then, that if you lose your souls by leading idle, wicked lives here, you have got nothing by it in this world, and you have lost your all in the next. For your idleness and wickedness is generally found out, and your bodies suffer for it here; and, what is far worse, if you do not repent and amend, your unhappy souls will suffer for it hereafter.

Mr. Jones, in that part of the work where he is obviating the objections of masters to the Christian instruction of their slaves, supposes the master to object thus:

You teach them that "God is no respecter of persons;" that "He hath made of one blood, all nations of men;" "Thou shalt love thy neighbor as thyself;" "All things whatsoever ye would that men should do to you, do ye even so to them;" what use, let me ask, would they make of these sentences from the gospel?

Mr. Jones says:

Let it be replied, that the effect urged in the objection might result from *imperfect* and *injudicious* religious instruction; indeed, religious instruction may be communicated *with the express design*, on the part of the instructor, to produce the effect referred to, instances of which have occurred.

But who will say that neglect of duty and insubordination are the *legitimate* effects of the gospel, purely and sincerely imparted to servants? Has it not in all ages been viewed as the greatest civilizer of the human race?

How Mr. Jones would interpret the golden rule to the slave, so as to justify the slave-system, we cannot possibly tell. We can, however, give a specimen of the manner in which it has been interpreted in Bishop' Meade's sermons, p. 116. (Brooke's Slavery, &c., pp. 32, 33.)

"All things whatsoever ye would that men should do unto you, do ye even so unto them;" that is, do by all mankind just as you would desire they should do by you, if you were in their place, and they in yours. Now, to suit this rule to your particular circumstances, suppose you were masters and mistresses, and had servants under you; would you not desire that your servants should do their business faithfully and honestly, as well when your back was turned as while you were looking over them? Would you not expect that they should take notice of what you said to them? that they should behave themselves with respect towards you and yours, and be as careful of everything belonging to you as you would be yourselves? You are servants: do, therefore, as you would wish to be done by, and you will be both good servants to your masters, and good servants to God, who requires this of you, and will reward you well for it, if you do it for the sake of conscience, in obedience to his commands.

The reverend teachers of such expositions of scripture do great injustice to the natural sense of their sable catechumens, if they suppose them incapable of detecting such very shallow sophistry, and of proving conclusively that "it is a poor rule that won't work both ways." Some shrewd old patriarch, of the stamp of those who rose up and went out at the exposition of the Epistle to Philemon, and who show such great acuteness in bringing up objections against the truth of God, such as would be thought peculiar to cultivated minds, might perhaps, if he dared, reply to such an exposition of scripture in this way: "Suppose you were a slave,—could not have a cent of your own earnings during your whole life, could have no legal right to your wife and children, could never send your children to school, and had, as you have told us, nothing but labor and poverty in this life,—how would you like it? Would you not wish your Christian master to set you free from this condition?" We submit it to every one who is no respecter of persons, whether this interpretation of Sambo's is not as good as the bishop's. And if not, why not?

To us, with our feelings and associations, such discourses as these of Bishop Meade appear hard-hearted and unfeeling to the last degree. We should, however, do great injustice to the character of the man, if we supposed that they prove him to have been such. They merely go to show how perfectly use may familiarize amiable and estimable men with a system of oppression, till they shall have lost all consciousness of the wrong which it involves.

That Bishop Meade's reasonings did not thoroughly convince himself is evident from the fact that, after all his representations of the superior advantages of slavery as a means of religious improvement, he did, at last, emancipate his own slaves.

But, in addition to what has been said, this whole system of religious instruction is darkened by one hideous shadow,— THE SLAVE-TRADE. What does the Southern church do with her catechumens and communicants? Read the advertisements of Southern newspapers, and see. In every city in the slave-raising states behold the dépôts, kept constantly full of assorted negroes from the ages of ten to thirty! In every slave-consuming state see the receiving-houses, whither these poor wrecks and remnants of families are constantly borne! Who preaches the gospel to the slave-coffles? Who preaches the gospel in the slave-prisons? If we consider the tremendous extent of this internal trade,— if we read papers with columns of auction advertisements of human beings, changing hands as freely as if they were dollar-bills instead of human creatures,— we shall then realize how utterly all those influences of religious instruction must be nullified by leaving the subjects of them exposed "to all the vicissitudes of property."

CHAPTER X.

WHAT IS TO BE DONE?

THE thing to be done, of which I shall chiefly speak, is that the whole American church, of all denominations, should unitedly come up, not *in form*, but *in fact*, to the noble purpose avowed by the Presbyterian Assembly of 1818, to seek the ENTIRE ABOLITION OF SLAVERY THROUGHOUT AMERICA AND THROUGHOUT CHRISTENDOM.

To this noble course the united voice of Christians in all other countries is urgently calling the American church. Expressions of this feeling have come from Christians of all denominations in England, in Scotland, in Ireland, in France, in Switzerland, in Germany, in Persia, in the Sandwich Islands, and in China. All seem to be animated by one spirit. They have loved and honored this American church. They have rejoiced in the brightness of her rising. Her prosperity and success have been to them as their own, and they have had hopes that God meant to confer inestimable blessings through her upon all nations. The American church has been to them like the rising of a glorious sun, shedding healing from his wings, dispersing mists and fogs, and bringing songs of birds and voices of cheerful industry, and sounds of gladness, contentment and peace. But, lo! in this beautiful orb is seen a disastrous spot of dim eclipse, whose gradually widening shadow threatens a total darkness. Can we wonder that the voice of remonstrance comes to us from those who have so much at stake in our prosperity and success? We have sent out our missionaries to all quarters of the globe; but how shall they tell their heathen converts the things that are done in Christianized America? How shall our missionaries in Mahometan countries hold up their heads, and proclaim the superiority of our religion, when we tolerate barbarities which they have repudiated?

A missionary among the Karens, in Asia, writes back that his course is much embarrassed by a suspicion that is afloat among the Karens that the Americans intend to steal and sell them. He says:

I dread the time when these Karens will be able to read our books, and get a full knowledge of all that is going on in our country. Many of them are very inquisitive now, and often ask me questions that I find it very difficult to answer.

No, there is no resource. The church of the United States is shut up, in the providence of God, to one work. She can never fulfil her mission till this is done. So long as she neglects this, it will lie in the way of everything else which she attempts to do.

She must undertake it for another reason, — because she alone can perform the work peaceably. If this fearful problem is left to take its course as a mere political question, to be ground out between the upper and nether millstones of political parties, then what will avert agitation, angry collisions, and the desperate rending the Union? No, there is no safety but in making it a religious enterprise, and pursuing it in a Christian spirit, and by religious means.

If it now be asked what means shall the church employ, we answer, this evil must be abolished by the same means which the apostles first used for the spread of Christianity, and the extermination of all the social evils which then filled a world lying in wickedness. Hear the apostle enumerate them: "BY PURENESS, BY KNOWLEDGE, BY LONG-SUFFERING, BY THE HOLY GHOST, BY LOVE UNFEIGNED, BY THE ARMOR OF RIGHTEOUSNESS ON THE RIGHT HAND AND ON THE LEFT."

We will briefly consider each of these means.

First, "by Pureness." Christians in the Northern free states must endeavor to purify themselves and the country from various malignant results of the system of slavery; and, in particular, they must endeavor to abolish that which is the most sinful,— the unchristian prejudice of caste.

In Hindostan there is a class called the Pariahs, with which no other class will associate, eat or drink. Our missionaries tell the converted Hindoo that this prejudice is unchristian; for God hath made of one blood all who dwell on the face of the earth, and all mankind are brethren in Christ. With what face shall they tell this to the Hindoo, if he is able to reply, "In your own Christian country there is a class of Pariahs who are treated no better than we treat ours. You do not yourselves believe the things you teach us."

Let us look at the treatment of the free negro at the North. In the States of Indiana and Illinois the most oppressive and unrighteous laws have been passed with regard to him. No law of any slave state could be more cruel in its spirit than that recently passed in Illinois, by which every free negro coming into the state is taken up and sold for a certain time, and then, if he do not leave the state, is sold again.

With what face can we exhort our Southern brethren to emancipate their slaves, if we do not set the whole moral power of the church at the North against such abuses as this? Is this course justified by saying that the negro is vicious and idle? This is adding insult to injury.

What is it these Christian states do? To a great extent they exclude the colored population from their schools; they discourage them from attending their churches by invidious distinctions; as a general fact, they exclude them from their shops, where they might learn useful arts and trades; they crowd them out of the better callings where they might earn an honorable livelihood; and, having thus discouraged every elevated aspiration, and reduced them to almost inevitable ignorance, idleness and vice, they fill up the measure of iniquity by making cruel laws to expel them from their states, thus heaping up wrath against the day of wrath.

If we say that every Christian at the South who does not use his utmost influence against their iniquitous slave-laws is guilty, as a republican citizen, of sustaining those laws, it is no less true that every Christian at the North who does not do what in him lies to procure the repeal of such laws in the free states is, so far, guilty for their existence. Of late years we have had abundant quotations from the Old Testament to justify all manner of oppression. A

Hindoo, who knew nothing of this generous and beautiful book, except from such pamphlets as Mr. Smylie's, might possibly think it was a treatise on piracy, and a general justification of robbery. But let us quote from it the directions which God gives for the treatment of the stranger: "If a stranger sojourn with you in your land, ye shall not vex him. But the stranger that dwelleth among you shall be as one born among you; thou shalt love him as thyself." How much more does this apply when the stranger has been brought into our land by the injustice and cruelty of our fathers!

We are happy to say, however, that the number of states in which such oppressive legislation exists is small. It is also matter of encouragement and hope that the unphilosophical and unchristian prejudice of caste is materially giving way, in many parts of our country, before a kinder and more Christian spirit.

Many of our schools and colleges are willing to receive the colored applicant on equal terms with the white. Some of the Northern free states accord to the colored free man full political equality and privileges. Some of the colored people, under this encouragement, have, in many parts of our country, become rich and intelligent. A very fair proportion of educated men is rising among them. There are among them respectable editors, eloquent orators, and laborious and well-instructed clergymen. It gives us pleasure to say that among intelligent and Christian people these men are treated with the consideration they deserve; and, if they meet with insult and ill-treatment, it is commonly from the less-educated class, who, being less enlightened, are always longer under the influence of prejudice. At a recent ordination at one of the largest and most respectable churches in New York, the moderator of the presbytery was a black man, who began life as a slave; and it was undoubtedly a source of gratification to all his Christian brethren to see him presiding in this capacity. He put the questions to the candidate in the German language, the church being in part composed of Germans. Our Christian friends in Europe may, at least, infer from this that, if we have had our faults in times past, we have, some of us, seen and are endeavoring to correct them.

To bring this head at once to a practical conclusion, the writer will say to every individual Christian, who wishes to do something for the abolition of slavery, begin by doing what lies in your power for the colored people in your vicinity. Are there children excluded from schools by unchristian prejudice? Seek to combat that prejudice by fair arguments, presented in a right spirit. If you cannot succeed, then endeavor to provide for the education of these children in some other manner. As far as in you lies, endeavor to secure for them, in every walk of life, the ordinary privileges of American citizens. If they are excluded from the omnibus and railroad-car in the place where you reside, endeavor to persuade those who have the control of these matters to pursue a more just and reasonable course. Those Christians who are heads of mechanical establishments can do much for the cause by receiving colored apprentices. Many masters excuse themselves for excluding colored apprentice by saying that if they receive him all their other hands will desert them. To this it is replied, that if they do the thing in a Christian temper and for a Christian purpose, the probability is that, if their hands desert at first, they will return to them at last,—all of them, at least, whom they would care to retain.

A respectable dressmaker in one of our towns has, as a matter of principle, taken colored girls for apprentices, thus furnishing them with a respectable means of livelihood. Christian mechanics, in all the walks of life, are earnestly requested to consider this subject, and see if, by offering their hand to raise this poor people to respectability and knowledge and competence, they may not be performing a service which the Lord will accept as done unto himself.

Another thing which is earnestly commended to Christians is the raising and comforting of those poor churches of colored people, who have been discouraged, dismembered and disheartened, by the operation of the fugitive slave law.

In the city of Boston is a church, which, even now, is struggling with debt and embarrassment, caused by being obliged to buy its own deacons, to shield them from the terrors of that law.

Lastly, Christians at the North, we need not say, should abstain from all *trading in slaves*, whether direct or indirect, whether by partnership with Southern houses or by receiving immortal beings as security for debt. It is not necessary to expand this point. It speaks for itself.

By all these means the Christian church at the North must secure for itself purity from all complicity with the sin of slavery, and from the unchristian customs and prejudices which have resulted from it.

The second means to be used for the abolition of slavery is "Knowledge."

Every Christian ought thoroughly, carefully and prayerfully, to examine this system of slavery. He should regard it as one upon which he is bound to have right views and right opinions, and to exert a right influence in forming and concentrating a powerful public sentiment, of all others the most efficacious remedy. Many people are deterred from examining the statistics on this subject, because they do not like the men who have collected them. They say they do not like abolitionists, and therefore they will not attend to those facts and figures which they have accumulated. This, certainly, is not wise or reasonable. In all other subjects which deeply affect our interests, we think it best to take information where we can get it, whether we like the persons who give it to us or not.

Every Christian ought seriously to examine the extent to which our national government is pledged and used for the support of slavery. He should thoroughly look into the statistics of slavery in the District of Columbia, and, above all, into the statistics of that awful system of legalized piracy and oppression by which hundreds and thousands are yearly torn from home and friends, and all that heart holds dear, and carried to be sold like beasts in the markets of the South. The smoke from this bottomless abyss of injustice puts out the light of our Sabbath suns in the eyes of all nations. Its awful groans and wailings drown the voice of our psalms and religious melodies. All nations know these things of us, and shall we not know them of ourselves? Shall we not have courage, shall we not have patience, to investigate thoroughly our own bad case, and gain a perfect knowledge of the length and breadth of the evil we seek to remedy?

The third means for the abolition of slavery is "Long-suffering."

Of this quality there has been some lack in the attempts that have hitherto been made. The friends of the cause have not had patience with each other, and have not been able to treat each other's opinions with forbearance. There have been many painful things in the past history of this subject; but is it not time when all the friends of the slave should adopt the motto, "forgetting the things that are behind, and reaching forth unto those which are before"? Let not the believers of immediate abolition call those who believe in gradual emancipation time-servers and traitors; and let not the upholders of gradual emancipation call the advocates of immediate abolition fanatics and incendiaries. Surely some more brotherly way of convincing good men can be found, than by standing afar off on some Ebal and Gerizim, and cursing each other. The truth spoken in love will always go further than the truth spoken in wrath; and, after all, the great object is to persuade our Southern brethren to admit the idea of *any* emancipation at all. When we have succeeded in persuading them that *anything* is necessary to be done, then will be the time for bringing up the question whether the object shall be accomplished by an immediate or a gradual process. Meanwhile, let our motto be, "Whereto we have already attained, let us walk by the same rule, let us mind the same things; and if any man be otherwise minded, God shall reveal even this unto him." "Let us receive even him that is weak in the faith, but not to doubtful disputations." Let us not reject the good there is in any, because of some remaining defects.

We come now to the consideration of a power without which all others must fail, —"the Holy Ghost."

The solemn creed of every Christian church, whether Roman, Greek, Episcopal or Protestant, says, "*I believe in the Holy Ghost.*" But how often do Christians, in all these denominations, live and act, and even conduct their religious affairs, as if they had "never so much as heard whether there be any Holy Ghost." If we trust to our own reasonings, our own misguided passions, and our own blind self-will, to effect the reform of abuses, we shall utterly fail. There is a power, silent, convincing, irresistible, which moves over the dark and troubled heart of man, as of old it moved over the dark and troubled waters of Chaos, bringing light out of darkness, and order out of confusion.

Is it not evident to every one who takes enlarged views of human society that a gentle but irresistible influence is pervading the human race, prompting groanings and longings and dim aspirations for some coming era of good? Worldly men read the signs of the times, and call this power the *Spirit of the Age,*—but should not the church acknowledge it as the spirit of God?

Let it not be forgotten, however, that the gift of his most powerful regenerating influence, at the opening of the Christian dispensation, was conditioned on prayer. The mighty movement that began on the day of Pentecost was preceded by united, fervent, persevering prayer. A similar spirit of prayer must precede the coming of the divine Spirit, to effect a revolution so great as that at which we aim. The most powerful instrumentality which God has delegated to man, and around which cluster all his glorious promises, is prayer. All past prejudices and animosities on this subject must be laid aside, and the whole church unite as one man in earnest, fervent prayer. Have we forgotten the promise of the Holy Ghost? Have we forgotten that He was to abide with us forever? Have we forgotten that it is He who is to convince the world of sin, of righteousness and of judgment? O, divine and Holy Comforter! Thou promise of the Father! Thou only powerful to enlighten, convince and renew! Return, we beseech thee, and visit this vine and this vineyard of thy planting! With thee nothing is impossible; and what we, in our weakness, can scarcely conceive, thou canst accomplish!

Another means for the abolition of slavery is "Love unfeigned."

In all moral conflicts, that party who can preserve, through every degree of opposition and persecution, a divine, unprovokable spirit of love, must finally conquer. Such are the immutable laws of the moral world. Anger, wrath, selfishness and jealousy, have all a certain degree of vitality. They often produce more show, more noise and temporary results, than love. Still, all these passions have, in themselves, the seeds of weakness. Love, and love only, is immortal; and when all the grosser passions of the soul have spent themselves by their own force, love looks forth like the unchanging star, with a light that never dies.

In undertaking this work, we must love both the slave-holder and the slave. We must never forget that both are our brethren. We must expect to be misrepresented, to be slandered, and to be hated. How can we attack so powerful an interest without it? We must be satisfied simply with the pleasure of being true friends, while we are treated as bitter enemies.

This holy controversy must be one of principle, and not of sectional bitterness. We must not suffer it to degenerate, in our hands, into a violent prejudice against the South; and, to this end, we must keep continually before our minds the more amiable features and attractive qualities of those with whose principles we are obliged to conflict. If they say all manner of evil against us, we must reflect that we expose them to great temptation to do so when we assail institutions to which they are bound by a thousand ties of interest and early association, and to whose evils habit has made them in a great degree insensible. The apostle gives us this direction in cases where we are called upon to deal with offending brethren, "Consider thyself, lest thou also be tempted." We may apply this to our own case, and consider that if we had been exposed to the temptations which surround our friends at the South, and received the same education, we might have felt and thought and acted as they do. But, while we cherish all these considerations, we must also remember that it is no love to the South to countenance and defend a pernicious system; a system which is as injurious to the master as to the slave; a system which turns fruitful fields to deserts; a system ruinous to education, to morals, and to religion and social progress; a system of which many of the most intelligent and valuable men at the South are weary, and from which they desire to escape, and by emigration are yearly escaping. Neither must we concede the rights of the slave; for he is also our brother, and there is a reason why we should speak for him which does not exist in the case of his master. He is poor, uneducated and ignorant, and cannot speak for himself. We must, therefore, with greater jealousy, guard his rights. Whatever else we compromise, we must not compromise the rights of the helpless, nor the eternal principles of rectitude and morality.

We must never concede that it is an honorable thing to deprive working men of their wages, though, like many other abuses, it is customary, reputable, and popular, and though amiable men, under the influence of old prejudices, still continue to do it. Never, not even for a moment, should we admit the thought that an heir of God and a joint heir of Jesus Christ may lawfully be sold upon the auction-block, though it be a common custom. We must repudiate, with determined severity, the blasphemous doctrine of property in human beings.

Some have supposed it an absurd refinement to talk about separating principles and persons, or to admit that he who upholds a bad system can be a good man. All experience proves the contrary. Systems most unjust and despotic have been defended by men personally just and humane. It is a melancholy consideration, but no less true, that there is almost no absurdity and no injustice that has not, at some period of the world's history, had the advantage of some good man's virtues in its support.

It is a part of our trial in this imperfect life; — were evil systems only supported by the evil, our moral discipline would be much less severe than it is, and our course in attacking error far plainer.

On the whole, we cannot but think that there was much Christian wisdom in the remark, which we have before quoted, of a poor old slave-woman, whose whole life had been darkened by this system, that we must "hate the sin, but love the sinner."

The last means for the abolition of slavery is the "Armor of Righteousness on the right hand and on the left."

By this we mean an earnest application of all straight-forward, honorable and just measures, for the removal of the system of slavery. Every man, in his place, should remonstrate against it. All its sophistical arguments should be answered, its biblical defences unmasked by correct reasoning and interpretation. Every mother should teach the evil of it to her children. Every clergyman should fully and continually warn his church against any complicity with such a sin. It is said that this would be introducing politics into the pulpit. It is answered, that since people will have to give an account of their political actions in the day of judgment, it seems proper that the minister should instruct them somewhat as to their political responsibilities. In that day Christ will ask no man whether he was of this or that party; but he certainly will ask him whether he gave his vote in the fear of God, and for the advancement of the kingdom of righteousness.

It is often objected that slavery is a distant sin, with which we have nothing to do. If any clergyman wishes to test this fact, let him once plainly and faithfully preach upon it. He will probably then find that the roots of the poison-tree have run under the very hearth-stone of New England families, and that in his very congregation are those in complicity with this sin.

It is no child's play to attack an institution which has absorbed into itself so much of the political power and wealth of this nation, and they who try it will soon find that they wrestle "not with flesh and blood." No armor will do for this warfare but the "armor of righteousness."

To our brethren in the South God has pointed out a more arduous conflict. The very heart shrinks to think what the faithful Christian must endure who assails this institution on its own ground ; but it *must be done.* How was it at the North ? There was a universal effort to put down the discussion of it here by mob law. Printing-presses were broken, houses· torn down, property destroyed.· Brave men, however, stood firm ; martyr blood was shed for the right of free opinion and speech ; and so the right of discussion was established. Nobody tries that sort of argument now,— its day is past. In Kentucky, also, they tried to stop the discussion by similar means. Mob violence destroyed a printing-press, and threatened the lives of individuals. But there were brave men there, who feared not violence or threats of death ; and emancipation is now open for discussion in Kentucky. The fact is, the South *must* discuss the matter of slavery. She *cannot* shut it out, unless she lays an embargo on the literature of the whole civilized world. If it be, indeed, divine and God-appointed, why does she so tremble to have it touched ? If it be of God, all the free inquiry in the world cannot overthrow it. Discussion must and will come. It only requires courageous men to lead the way.

Brethren in the South, there are many of you who are truly convinced that slavery is a sin, a tremendous wrong ; but, if you confess your sentiments, and endeavor to propagate your opinions, you think that persecution, affliction, and even death, await you. How can we ask you, then, to come forward ? *We* do not ask it. Ourselves weak, irresolute and worldly, shall we ask you to do what perhaps we ourselves should not dare ? But we will beseech *Him* to speak to you, who dared and endured more than this for your sake, and who can strengthen you to dare and endure for His. He can raise you above all temporary and worldly considerations. He can inspire you with that love to himself which will make you willing to leave father and mother, and wife and child, yea, to give up life itself, for his sake. And if he ever brings you to that place where you and this world take a final farewell of each other, where you make up your mind solemnly to give all up for his cause, where neither life nor death, nor things present nor things to come, can move you from this purpose,— then will you know a joy which is above all other joy, a peace constant and unchanging as the eternal God from whom it springs.

Dear brethren, is this system to go on forever in your land? Can you think these slave-laws anything but an abomination to a just God? Can you think this internal slave-trade to be anything but an abomination in his sight?

Look, we beseech you, into those awful slave-prisons which are in your cities. Do the groans and prayers which go up from those dreary mansions promise well for the prosperity of our country?

Look, we beseech you, at the mournful march of the slave-coffles; follow the bloody course of the slave-ships on your coast. What, suppose you, does the Lamb of God think of all these things? He whose heart was so tender that he wept, at the grave of Lazarus, over a sorrow that he was so soon to turn into joy,— what does he think of this constant, heart-breaking, yearly-repeated anguish? What does he think of Christian wives forced from their husbands, and husbands from their wives? What does he think of Christian daughters, whom his church first educates, indoctrinates and baptizes, and then leaves to be sold as merchandise?

Think you such prayers as poor Paul Edmondson's, such death-bed scenes as Emily Russell's, are witnessed without emotion by that generous Saviour, who regards what is done to his meanest servant as done to himself?

Did it never seem to you, O Christian! when you have read the sufferings of Jesus, that you would gladly have suffered with him? Does it never seem almost ungenerous to accept eternal life as the price of such anguish on his part, while you bear no cross for him? Have you ever wished you could have watched with him in that bitter conflict at Gethsemane, when even his chosen slept? Have you ever wished that you could have stood by him when all forsook him and fled,— that you could have owned when Peter denied,— that you could have honored him when buffeted and spit upon? Would you think it too much honor, could you, like Mary, have followed him to the cross, and stood a patient sharer of that despised, unpitied agony? *That* you cannot do. That hour is over. Christ, now, is exalted, crowned, glorified,—all men speak well of him; rich churches rise to him, and costly sacrifice goes up to him. What chance have you, among the multitude, to prove your love,— to show that you would stand by him discrowned, dishonored, tempted, betrayed, and suffering? Can you show it in any way but by espousing the cause of his suffering poor? Is there a people among you despised and rejected of men, heavy with oppression, acquainted with grief, with all the power of wealth and fashion, of political and worldly influence, arrayed against their cause,— Christian, you can acknowledge Christ in them!

If you turn away indifferent from this cause,— "if thou forbear to deliver them that are drawn unto death, and those that be ready to be slain; if thou sayest, Behold, we knew it not, doth not he that pondereth the heart consider it, and he that keepeth the soul, doth he not know it, shall he not render to every man according to his works?"

In the last judgment will He not say to you, "I have been in the slave-prison,— in the slave-coffle. I have been sold in your markets; I have toiled for naught in your fields; I have been smitten on the mouth in your courts of justice; I have been denied a hearing in my own church,—and ye cared not for it. Ye went, one to his farm, and another to his merchandise." And if ye shall answer, "When, Lord?" He shall say unto you, "Inasmuch as ye have done it to the least of these, my brethren, ye have done it unto me."

APPENDIX.

FACT *vs.* FIGURES; OR, THE NINE ARAB BROTHERS.

BEING A NEW ARABIAN NIGHT'S ENTERTAINMENT.

It is a favorite maxim that "*figures cannot lie.*" We are loth to assail the time-honored reputation for veracity of this ancient and most respectable race. There may have been days of pastoral innocence and primitive simplicity, when they did not lie. When Abraham sat contemplatively in his tent-door, with nothing to do, all the long day, but compose psalms and pious meditations, it is likely that he had implicit faith in this maxim, and never thought of questioning the statistical tables of Eliezer of Damascus, with regard to the number of camels, asses, sheep, oxen and goats, which illustrated the prairie where he was for the time being encamped. Alas for those good old days! Figures did not lie then, we freely admit; but we are sadly afraid, from their behavior in recent ages, that this arose from no native innocence of disposition, but simply from want of occasion and opportunity. In those days, they were young and green, and had not learned what they could do. The first inventor, who commenced making a numeration table, with the artless play of his toes and fingers, had, like other great inventors, very little idea of what he was doing, and what would be the mighty uses of these very simple characters, when men got to having republican governments, and elections, and discussions of all sorts of unheard-of questions in politics and morals, and to electioneering among these poor simple Arab herdsmen, the nine digits, for their votes on all these complicated subjects. No wonder that figures have had their heads turned! Such unprecedented power and popularity is enough to turn any head. We are sorry to speak ill of them; but really we must say, that, like many of our political men, they have been found on all sides of every subject to an extent that is really very confusing. Of course, there is no doubt of their veracity *somewhere;* the only problem being, on which side, and where. Is any great measure to be carried, now-a-days? Of course, the statistics, cut and dried, in regular columns, on both sides of the question, contradict each other point-blank as two opposite cannons; and each party marshals behind them, firing them off with infinite alacrity, but with no particular effect, except the bewilderment of the few old-fashioned people, who, like Mr. Pickwick at the review, stand on the middle ground.

If that most respectable female person, Mrs. Partington, who, like most unsophisticated old ladies, is a most vehement and uncompromising abolitionist, could only hear the statistics that are to be shown up in favor of slavery, she would take off her spectacles and wipe her eyes in pious joy, and think that the millennium, and nothing less, had come upon earth. Such statistics they are, about the woe, and want, and agony, and heathenish darkness of Africa, which, by that eminent foreign

missionary operation, the slave-trade, have been turned into light and joy and thanksgiving; here she has them, in round figures; she only needs to put on her spectacles and look. "Here, ma'am, you have it," says the illustrator; "look on this side of the column: here are three hundred million of heathen, — don't spare the figures, — down in Africa, sunk in heathenism — never heard the sound of the gospel — actually eating each other alive. Now, turn to this side of the column, and here they all are, over in America, clothed and in their right mind, going to church with their masters, and finding the hymns in their own hymn-books. Now, ma'am, can you doubt the beneficial results of the slave-trade?"

But Mrs. Partington has heard something about that middle passage which she thought was horrid.

"By no means, my dear madam," says the illustrator, whisking over his papers. "I have that all in figures, — average of deaths in the first cargoes, 25 *per cent.*, — large average, certainly; they did n't manage the business exactly right; but then the rate of increase in a Christian country averages twenty-five per cent. over what it would have been in Africa. Now, Mrs. Partington, if these had been left in Africa, they would have been all heathen; by getting them over here, you have just as many, and all Christians to boot. Because, you see, the excess of increase balances the percentage of loss, and we make no deduction for interest in those cases."

Now, as Mrs. Partington does not know with very great clearness what "percentage" and "average" mean, and as mental philosophers have demonstrated that we are always powerfully affected by the unknown, she is all the more impressed with this reasoning, on that account; being one of the simple, old-fashioned people, who have not yet gotten over the impression that "figures cannot lie."

"Well, now, really," says she, "strange what these figures will do! I always thought the slave-trade was monstrous wicked. But it really seems to be quite a missionary work."

The fact is, that these nomadic Arabs, the digits, are making a very unfair use, among us, of the family reputation gotten up during the palmy days of their innocence, when they were a breezy, contemplatively unsophisticated race of shepherds, and, to use an American elegance of expression, had not yet "cut their eye-teeth." All that remains of their Oriental origin in this country seems to be a characteristic turn for romancing. Not an addition of slave territory has been made to the United States, wherein these same Arab brothers have not, with grave faces, been brought in as witnesses, to swear, by the honor of the family, that it was absolutely essential, for the best interest of the African race, that there should be more slavery and more slave territory. To be sure, it was for the pecuniary gain of the *American race,* but that was not the point insisted on. O no! we are always very glad when our inter-

17

est coincides with that of the African race; but the extension of slavery is not to be considered in that light principally; it is entirely a system of Christian education, and evangelization of one race by another. Left to himself, Quashy goes right back into heathenism. His very body deteriorates; he becomes idiotic, insane, deaf, dumb, blind, — everything that can be thought of. "Is this an actual fact?" asks some incredulous Congress man, as innocent as Mrs. Partington. "O yes! for only look; here are the statistics. Just see; here in the town of Kittery, in Maine, are twenty-seven insane and idiotic black people, and down here in the town of Dittery, South Carolina, not a single one. Some simple-minded Kittery man, who overhears this conversation in the lobby, perhaps opens his eyes, and reflects with wonder that he never knew that there were so many black people in the town. But the Congress man shows it to him in the census, and he concludes to look for them when he goes home, as "figures cannot lie."

On the census of 1840 conclusions innumerable as to the capacity of the colored race to subsist in freedom have been based. It has been the very beetle, sledge-hammer and broad-axe; and when all other means fail, the objector, with a triumphant flourish, exclaims, "There, sir, what do you think of the census of 1840? You see, sir, the thing's been tried, and it's *no go.*" We poor common folks cannot tell what to think. Some of us suppose that we know that there were more insane and idiotic and variously dilapidated negroes reported in certain states than their entire negro population. But, of course, as it's down in the census, and as "figures never lie," we must believe our own eyes. We can only say what some people have thought.

That most inconvenient and pertinacious man, John Quincy Adams, made a good deal of trouble in Congress about this same matter. At no less than five different times did this very persistent old gentleman rise in Congress, with the statement that the returns of the census had been notoriously and grossly falsified in this respect; and that he was prepared, if leave were given, to present before the House the most complete, direct, and overwhelming evidence to this effect. The following is an account of Mr. Adams' endeavors on this subject, collected from the *Congressional Globe*, and *Niles's Register:*

TWENTY-EIGHTH CONGRESS OF THE UNITED STATES.

HOUSE OF REPRESENTATIVES. *February* 26, 1844. — Mr. Adams, on leave, offered the following resolution:

Resolved, That the Secretary of State be directed to inform this House whether any gross errors have been discovered in the "Sixth Census, or Enumeration of the Inhabitants of the United States, as corrected at the Department of State in 1841," and, if so, how these errors originated, what they are, and what, if any, measures have been taken to rectify them.

HOUSE OF REPRESENTATIVES. *May* 6, 1844. — The journal having been read, Mr. Adams moved a correction of the same by striking out from the communication of the Secretary of State (in answer to a resolution of this House inquiring whether any gross errors had been discovered in the printing of the Sixth Census), as copied upon the journal, the following words: "That no such errors had been discovered."

Mr. Adams accompanied his motion with some remarks. It could not possibly (Mr. Adams said) be a correct representation, as very gross errors had been

discovered, as he intended and would pledge himself to show. He said they referred to the number of insane, blind, &c., among the colored population. This had been made the subject of a pamphlet on the annexation of Texas, and of a speech by a gentleman from Mississippi (Mr. Hammett), which had been refuted on this floor. The United States were at this time placed in a condition very little short of war with Great Britain, as well as Mexico, on the foundation of these very errors. It was important, therefore, that the true state of facts should be made to appear.

The Speaker remarked that whether errors existed or not would be matter of investigation. In the opinion of the chair, there was no error of the journal, because it contained only a faithful transcript of the communication made by the Secretary of State.

Mr. Adams persisted in his motion. It was (he said) the most extraordinary communication ever made from the State Department. He would pledge himself to produce documents to prove that gross errors did exist. He would produce such proof as no man would be able to contradict.

The House refused to amend the journal.

HOUSE OF REPRESENTATIVES. *May* 16, 1844. — Mr. Adams wished to present a memorial from certain citizens in relation to errors which they say have been committed in compiling and printing the last census of the United States.

Objection being made, he moved to suspend the rules for the purpose of offering the resolution, and moving to refer it to a committee of five members. The yeas and nays were ordered, and, being taken, the rules were not suspended, — ayes 96, nays 49, — less than two-thirds voting in the affirmative.

HOUSE OF REPRESENTATIVES. *Dec.* 10, 1844. — Mr. Adams presented a petition from the American Statistical Society, in relation to certain errors in the last or sixth census.

Mr. Adams said a petition on this subject at the last session was referred to a select committee, and he hoped this petition would take the same direction. He moved the appointment of a select committee of nine members, and that the memorial be printed.

The speaker announced that a majority had decided in favor of a select committee. The motion to print was laid on the table.

HOUSE OF REPRESENTATIVES. *Dec.* 13, 1844. — The following is the Select Committee appointed, on the motion of Mr. Adams, to consider the petition from the American Statistical Society in relation to the errors in the sixth census: Messrs. Adams, Rhett, Rayner, Stiles, Maclay, Brengle, Foster, Sheppard, Cary, and Caleb B. Smith.

This was the end of the affair in Congress. *The false returns stand to this day in the statistical tables of the census*, to convince all cavillers of the unfitness of the negro for freedom. That the reader may know what kind of evidence Mr. Adams had with which to sustain his allegations, we append, as a specimen, an extract from the American Almanac for 1845, p. 156.

The "American Statistical Association," established in Boston, Mass., sent a memorial to Congress during the past winter, drawn up by Messrs. William Brigham, Edward Jarvis, and J. W. Thornton, in which, though they "confined their investigations to the reports respecting education and nosology," they exposed an extraordinary mass of errors in the census. We can find room only for a few extracts from this memorial.

* * * * * * * *

"The most glaring and remarkable errors are found in the statements respecting nosology, the prevalence of insanity, blindness, deafness and dumbness, among the people of this nation.

"The undersigned have compared these statements with information obtained from other more reliable sources, and have found them widely varying from the truth ; and, more than all, they have compared the statements in one part of the census with those in another part, and have found most extraordinary discrepances. They have also examined the original manuscript copy of the census, deposited by the marshal of the District of Massachusetts in the clerk's office in Boston, and have compared this with the printed edition of both Blair and Rives, and Thomas Allen, and found here, too, a variance of statements.

"Your memorialists are aware that some of these errors in respect to Massachusetts, and perhaps also in respect to other states, were committed by the marshals. Mr. William H. Williams, deputy marshal, states that there were one hundred and thirty-three colored pauper lunatics in the family of Samuel B. Woodward, in the town of Worcester ; but on another page he states that there are no colored persons in said Woodward's family.

"Mr. Benali Blood, deputy marshal, states, on one page, that there were fourteen colored pauper lunatics and two colored lunatics, who were supported at private charge, in the family of Charles E. Parker, in the town of Pepperell ; while on another page he states that there are no colored persons in the family of said Parker. Mr. William M. Packson states, on one page, that there are in the family of Jacob Cushman, in the town of Plympton, four pauper colored lunatics, and one colored blind person ; while on another page he states that there are no colored persons in the family of said Cushman.

"But, on comparing the manuscript copy of the census at Boston with the printed edition of Blair and Rives, the undersigned are convinced that a large portion of the errors were made by the printers, and that hardly any of the errors of the original document are left out. The original document finds the colored insane in twenty-nine towns, while the printed edition of Blair and Rives places them in thirty-five towns, and each makes more than ten-fold greater than the state returns in regard to the paupers. And one edition has given twenty, and the other twenty-seven, self-supporting lunatics, in towns in which, according to private inquiry, none are to be found. According to the original and manuscript copy of the census, there were in Massachusetts ten deaf and dumb and eight blind colored persons ; whereas the printed editions of the same document multiply them into seventeen of the former and twenty-two of the latter class of unfortunates.

"The printed copy of the census declares that there were in the towns of Hingham and Scituate nineteen colored persons who were deaf and dumb, blind, or insane. On the other hand, the undersigned are informed, by the overseers of the poor and the assessors, who have cognizance of every pauper and tax-payer in the town, that in the last twelve years no such diseased persons have lived in the town of Scituate ; and they have equally certain proof that none such have lived in Hingham. Moreover, the deputy marshals neither found nor made record of such persons.

"The undersigned have carefully compared the number of colored insane and idiots, and of the deaf and dumb and blind, with the whole number of the colored population, as stated in the printed edition of the census, in every city, town, and county of the United States ; and have found the extraordinary contradictions and improbabilities that are shown in the following tables.

"The errors of the census are as certain, if not as manifest, in regard to the insanity among the whites, as among the colored people. Wherever your memorialists have been able to compare the census with the results of the investigations of the state governments, of individuals, or societies, they have found that the national enumeration has fallen far short of the more probable amount.

"According to the census, there were in Massa-

chusetts six hundred and twenty-seven lunatics and idiots supported at public charge ; according to the returns of the overseers of the poor, there were eight hundred and twenty-seven of this class of paupers.

"The superintendents of the poor of the State of New York report one thousand and fifty-eight pauper lunatics within that state ; the census reports only seven hundred and thirty-nine.

"The government of New Jersey reports seven hundred and one in that state ; the census discovers only four hundred and forty-two.

"The Medical Society of Connecticut discovered twice as many lunatics as the census within that state. A similar discrepancy was found in Eastern Pennsylvania, and also in some counties in Virginia.

"Your memorialists deem it needless to go further into detail in this matter. Suffice it to say, that these are but specimens of the errors that are to be found in the 'sixth census' in regard to nosology and education, and they suspect also in regard to other matters therein reported.

"In view of these facts, the undersigned, in behalf of said Association, conceive that such documents ought not to have the sanction of Congress, nor ought they to be regarded as containing true statements relative to the condition of the people and the resources of the United States. They believe it would have been far better to have had no census at all than such an one as has been published ; and they respectfully request your honorable body to take such order thereon, and to adopt such measures for the correction of the same, — or, if the same cannot be corrected, for discarding and disowning the same,— as the good of the country shall require, and as justice and humanity shall demand.

"We have room for the tables for only three of the states." [We will caution the reader not to skip this statistical table, as he probably never saw one like it before.]

MAINE.

Towns.	Total col'd Inhab'ts.	Col'd Insane.	Towns.	Total col'd Inhab'ts.	Col'd Insane.
Limerick,	0	4	Industry,	0	3
Lymington,	1	2	Dresden,	3	6
Scarboro',	0	6	Hope,	1	2
Poland,	0	2	Hartland,	0	2
Dixfield,	0	4	Newfield,	0	5
Calais,	0	1			

NEW HAMPSHIRE.

Towns.	Total col'd Inhab'ts.	Col'd Insane.	Towns.	Total col'd Inhab'ts.	Col'd Insane.
Coventry,	0	1	Stratham,	0	1
Haverhill,	1	1	Northampton,	0	1
Holderness,	0	2	New Hampton,	0	1
Atkinson,	0	1	Lyman,	0	1
Bath,	0	1	Littleton,	0	1
Lisbon,	0	1	Henniker,	0	1
Compton,	1	1			

MASSACHUSETTS.

Towns.	Total col'd Inhab'ts.	Col'd Insane.	Towns.	Total col'd Inhab'ts.	Col'd Insane.
Freetown,	0	2	Georgetown,	1	2
Plympton,	0	4	Carver,	1	1
Leominster,	0	2	Northbridge,	1	1
Wilmington,	0	2	Ashby,	1	1
Sterling,	0	2	Randolph,	1	1
Danvers,	0	2	Worcester,	151*	133
Hingham,	2	2			

* 36 of these under 10 years of age.

Every fable, allegory and romance, must have its moral. The moral of this ought to be deeply considered by the American people!

In order to gain capital for the extension of slave territory, the most important statistical document of the United States has been boldly, grossly, and perseveringly falsified, and stands falsified to this day.

Query : If state documents are falsified in support of slavery, what confidence can be placed in *any* representations that are made upon the subject?

INDEX.

PART I.

PART II.

ERRATUM.

Page 42, second column, after twenty-fifth line from top, insert :

"At the rolling of sugars, an interval of from two to three months, they (the slaves in Louisiana) work *both night and day.* Abridged of their sleep, they scarcely retire to rest during the whole period."

Printed in Great Britain by
Amazon.co.uk, Ltd.,
Marston Gate.